WEYERHAEUSER ENVIRONMENTAL BOOKS
William Cronon, Editor

Weyerhaeuser Environmental Books explore human relationships with natural environments in all their variety and complexity. They seek to cast new light on the ways that natural systems affect human communities, the ways that people affect the environments of which they are a part, and the ways that different cultural conceptions of nature profoundly shape our sense of the world around us. A complete list of the books in the series appears at the end of this book.

The
REPUBLIC
of
NATURE

AN ENVIRONMENTAL HISTORY OF THE UNITED STATES

Mark Fiege

UNIVERSITY OF WASHINGTON PRESS
Seattle and London

The Republic of Nature: An Environmental History of the United States
is published with the assistance of a grant from the Weyerhaeuser
Environmental Books Endowment, established by the Weyerhaeuser
Company Foundation, members of the Weyerhaeuser family,
and Janet and Jack Creighton.

© 2012 by the University of Washington Press
Printed and bound in the United States of America
Design by Thomas Eykemans
Composed in Sorts Mill Goudy; display type set in League Gothic;
courtesy The League of Moveable Type
16 15 14 13 12   5 4 3 2 1

UNIVERSITY OF WASHINGTON PRESS
PO Box 50096, Seattle, WA 98145, USA
www.washington.edu/uwpress

LIBRARY OF CONGRESS CATALOGING-IN-PUBLICATION DATA
Fiege, Mark.
The republic of nature : an environmental history of the United States / Mark Fiege.
p. cm. — (Weyerhaeuser environmental books)
Includes bibliographical references and index.
ISBN 978-0-295-99167-2 (cloth : alk. paper)
1. Human ecology—United States—History.
2. Nature—Effect of human beings on—United States—History.
3. United States—Environmental conditions.
I. Title.
GF503F54 2012   304.20973—dc23   2011035457

FRONTISPIECE Dedication of the Lincoln Memorial, May 30, 1922.
Library of Congress Prints & Photographs Division, LC-F81-19718

For Alexandra

CONTENTS

ILLUSTRATIONS

FOREWORD

Environmental History Comes of Age

WILLIAM CRONON

Once in a great while, perhaps every decade or two for a given field, a book comes along that changes the way one thinks about an entire subject. Sometimes this happens when a writer of unusual creativity revisits a familiar topic and somehow manages to find in it insights so fresh that it's hard to believe no one noticed them before. Sometimes it happens when a scholar of unusual range wanders across a vast historiography and ties it together in an act of synthesis that discovers unexpected connections among disparate elements that few imagined might be brought together in such a surprising way. And sometimes it happens when an intellectual of unusual generosity takes the questions and findings of a specialized subfield and so compellingly demonstrates their relevance to other fields and disciplines that the subfield suddenly feels far more mainstream than one thought.

It is rare enough for a single book to succeed at one of these tasks; it is rarer still for one book to accomplish them all. And yet that is precisely what Mark Fiege's *The Republic of Nature: An Environmental History of the United States* does. It is surely among the most important works of environmental history published since the field was founded four or more decades ago. No book before it has so compellingly demonstrated the value of applying environmental perspectives to historical events that at first glance may seem to have little to do with "nature" or "the environment." No one who cares about the American past can afford to ignore what Fiege has to say.

Having declared my enthusiasm so unabashedly, I should hasten to make sure that I don't misrepresent the volume you hold in your hands. Despite its subtitle, this is *not* a comprehensive narrative synthesis of American environmental history. Squeezing such a vast subject between the covers of a single book is such a daunting task that few scholars have even attempted it. (The best is Ted Steinberg's *Down to Earth: Nature's Role in American History*, first published in 2002, which can now be supplemented with the superb historiographical essays gathered in Douglas Sackman's *A Companion to American Environmental History*, published in 2010.) Mark Fiege chose for himself quite a different task when he embarked on this project more than a decade ago. Fearing that an encyclopedic account might fall victim to the familiar textbook problem of too much obligatory information trading depth for breadth and thereby undermining storytelling and analysis alike, he chose instead to concentrate on a few carefully chosen but far-flung episodes. Rather than try to synthesize everything that he and his colleagues had learned over the past half century about American environmental history, his goal would be to illustrate by example the kinds of questions and interpretive insights that have become central to the field.

Fiege's real stroke of genius lay in the way he selected episodes to demonstrate the value of an environmental historical perspective for scholars, students, and other readers unfamiliar with the field. As a committed undergraduate teacher, he wanted to write a book that could be used in U.S. history survey courses, where he knew full well that most high school and college teachers must necessarily rely on a standard textbook to guide their students through the vast terrain of the American past. A parallel environmental history textbook with a similar table of contents would have little chance of being adopted in such classrooms, and might even feel repetitious if it were. At the same time, Fiege wanted to write a book that would convey to nonacademic readers the ways environmental history can alter our sense of the past by encouraging us to see familiar events from radically different points of view.

The solution he hit upon was to identify historical episodes that were so utterly familiar that every high school and college teacher was bound to include them in a U.S. history syllabus and every reader would recognize them. Then he applied a more daring and surprising criterion. He decided to seek out classic episodes in American history that are rarely if ever viewed in environmental terms so he could then reinterpret them through the lens of environmental history. Revisiting and rewriting the most familiar of histories to make them seem unexpectedly unfamiliar: this was the high bar Fiege set for himself.

If my own description of the book suddenly feels less abstractly academic and more genuinely intriguing, then you've got a sense of why I was so excited when Mark Fiege first described this project to me. Just let your mind wander a bit: what would be on your own list of classic moments in the American past that are usually discussed as if they had no connection to the natural world? It's a fascinating question, and Fiege ranged far and wide in his efforts to answer it. As he did so, though, he began to realize that writing this book would be a good deal harder than he first thought. Much of the initial excitement that the field of environmental history generated arose from the fact that it studied topics that had been largely ignored by other historians: the impact of epidemic diseases on Amerindian populations; the unrecognized ways that native peoples had used fire to alter landscapes; the consequences of introducing non-native species to North American ecosystems; the effects on soils of cutting down forests and planting agricultural crops in their stead; the harnessing of rivers in the name of progress; the role of national parks in expressing American ideas of nature and nationhood; and so on and on. These and many other subjects were hardly central to American historical scholarship when environmental history began to emerge in the 1960s and 1970s. Few textbooks made more than a passing reference to any of them, so demonstrating their importance was a big part of what made the field feel new.

These early triumphs had helped define what environmental history was... and yet they were precisely the topics that Mark Fiege was choosing to downplay as he selected episodes to explore in his individual chapters. It was not that he would ignore them altogether—*The Republic of Nature* is an environmental history to its core—but by focusing his chapters on topics that had not previously been thought of mainly in environmental terms, he entered historiographical territories that were relatively unexplored by environmental historians. As a result, each new chapter required Fiege not only to read and synthesize the huge secondary scholarship that topics like these necessarily generate, but also to do original primary research to discover environmental aspects that had been previously ignored or downplayed. Each new chapter, in other words, required research and synthesis on a scale that many scholars typically bring to bear on an entire book. Although it wears its scholarship lightly, *The Republic of Nature* has a rigor, literary grace, and depth of interpretive energy that represent historical writing at its very best.

So which classic episodes did Mark Fiege select to show that environmental history has something new to say even about subjects that scholars have been writing about for generations? The Salem witch trials. The Enlightenment invocation of "natural law" in the founding of the American republic. The rise of cotton agriculture in the slave South. The quasi-mythic biography of Abraham Lincoln. The Battle of Gettysburg. The building of the transcontinental railroads. The invention of the atomic bomb. *Brown v. Board of Education*. The oil shortages of 1973–1974.

As I name these, you may be saying to yourself: "Wait, I can think of environmental aspects to each of those events. I thought he was going to pick topics that had *nothing* to do with the environment." But that would be impossible. There is nothing in the world—nothing in place or time or history—that is ever outside of nature or the environment. The point is that few of these topics would be top-of-mind for anyone wanting to illustrate the importance of the environment for understanding the American past. That's what makes *The Republic of Nature* so bold and unusual. Although most readers might guess at a few of the many environmental insights that Mark Fiege shares on the pages of this book, even specialists would fail to think of all of them. That is why the book is such a joy to read, and why it is so worth savoring. Peruse it carefully, and you will make surprisingly intriguing discoveries even about events you already know well. More important, you will learn ways of asking questions and seeking answers that will likely change the way you think about history itself, perhaps even those parts of it that you yourself have lived. And finally, it may change the way you think about nature and its role in the human past. For one book to do all of that is no small achievement. ★

The Republic of Nature

LAND OF LINCOLN

To ENTER THE LINCOLN MEMORIAL is to enter another world. The passage begins on the east side of the building. Behind you stretches the reflecting pool, its glassy, rectangular surface reaching toward the Washington Monument, which towers above the grass and trees in the heart of the nation's city. Farther in the eastern distance rises the Capitol dome. Ahead of you, to the west, ascend broad flights of stairs, the kind that carry citizens into the halls of government or justice—or into heaven. At the top—cool, white, columned, and massive—looms the temple, an American Parthenon. Something timeless and true and powerful dwells there, and it gestures to you, inviting you to cross the boundary that separates your time and place from another realm. The air is hot, heavy, and hazy, typical for a summer day in the District of Columbia, and crowds of sweaty tourists seem to be everywhere. But none of that matters, for you are about to glimpse something unearthly, eternal, infinite.[1]

The initial approach is low and gentle, and you easily climb a series of steps and intervening terraces. Crossing the road that encircles the structure, you climb several more sets of steps and traverse still more terraces. About halfway up, as you near the last and steepest flights, you experience a strange sensation. Each step, repeated again and again, protracts the distance, prolongs the time, and makes you feel small. The effect is even more pronounced if you make the passage at night. Slowly, your disembodied, shrinking self rises toward the luminescent temple floating in the darkness.

At the top stand the enormous fluted columns. Touching one, you sense the solidity and great age of the republic. Looking back, you see an urban park, but you might as well be on a mountaintop, surveying a green and misty valley. You pause for a moment as the enormous compacted weight of the past pushes down on the present. Then you step between the columns—through the portal—and into the temple.

There, huge, silent, and surrounded by shadows, a marble Lincoln presides over a land beyond time. His craggy, uneven face—"so awful ugly it becomes beautiful," the poet Walt Whitman said—is at once stern, weary, tender, and sad.[2] You try to meet his gaze, but you cannot quite make the connection, for his eyes see past you—or through you—to something in the distance, something large and everlasting and more important than you.

"IN THIS TEMPLE AS IN THE HEARTS OF THE PEOPLE FOR WHOM HE SAVED THE UNION," read the words engraved on the wall, "THE MEMORY OF ABRAHAM LINCOLN IS ENSHRINED FOREVER." To the north, behind a row of columns, is a chamber in which appears Lincoln's second inaugural address and its iconic phrase "WITH MALICE TOWARD NONE ... WITH CHARITY FOR ALL." High above the words, so high that you almost miss the scene, a woman with giant wings—an angel or a goddess—seems to be reconciling two groups of white people. Representatives of each group, a man on one side and a woman on the other, reach out and join hands, as if in marriage. The winged woman places her hands on theirs, blessing their bond. To the south, between another set of columns, is a chamber devoted to the Gettysburg Address and its most deeply felt principle, that the United States is "A NEW NATION CONCEIVED IN LIBERTY AND DEDICATED TO THE PROPOSITION THAT ALL MEN ARE CREATED EQUAL." Above the lines carved in marble, the winged woman, reaching in triumph to the heavens, appears to sanctify the emancipation of black people.

Back in the temple's main room, you stand before Lincoln again. It is impossible to be detached, neutral, unmoved. You are in the presence of greatness, of inevitable forces, unspeakable and omnipotent, and suddenly they lift you from yourself and carry you to a reality somewhere beyond your own. For a fleeting moment you are aware of an ultimate purpose and meaning, a higher truth, in the marble.

The wave, however, passes as quickly as it came. Your body, your physical self, now reminds you that you are more of this world than of some other. The heat and humidity are oppressive. You are tired, thirsty, hungry, a little dizzy, and your feet are beginning to ache. The other tourists—their chatter and bustle and relentless picture taking—are starting to annoy you.

Outside, sitting on the steps, you survey the trees, grass, water, and people, and your mind runs free. You think of the dedication and speeches chiseled on the walls. Why did someone choose those words and not others? You picture the newly freed men and women in the mural, their shackles broken. What are they going to do now? Why are they not at the wedding with the white folks? You notice the crystalline grain and varied colors of the marble beneath you, its chips, cracks, and seams, and in the seams, greenish dirt. You look back at the great classical columns and notice their weathered, irregular surfaces. Someone mined, cut, carved, polished, and assembled the marble. Where was the quarry? Who did the work? How and why, you wonder, did this monument come to be? You now realize that you have left behind the sublime otherworld in which the temple hovers. You are back on the ground, in this place, a capital city awash in humid air, perspiration, and imperfection. You are back on this Earth.

The moment when the magic vanishes is powerful because it subverts the temple's unearthly objectives. The temple seeks to magnify transcendent truths by minimizing the importance of the physical body. Its selective presentation of words and pictures attempts to legitimate a racial order that leaves black citizens out of the national reunion. Perhaps above all, by means of its size, beauty, and placement, the building tries to disguise the crass material circumstances of its creation. Yet it cannot completely succeed in any of these purposes. Its symbolic power notwithstanding, it cannot entirely silence a visitor's weary, emotionally spent body. Despite the elegance of its murals and the force of its words, it cannot obscure the reality of black people's experiences. And no matter how magnificent, its marble still weathers, cracks, and crumbles. Rather than culminating in a moment of mystical transcendence, your passage through the temple ends in an unsettling realization that something else—something corporeal, terrestrial, and tangible—is going on here.[3]

That awareness is an essential precondition to a crucially important insight: although the Lincoln Memorial is a monument to a god, it cannot rise, god-like, above its creators, materials, and environment. Even as it expresses the highest of ideals, it objectifies earthbound circumstances. All those circumstances, even conflicts over racial policies and practices, have been, and still are, grounded in a fundament so massive and ubiquitous that people often overlook the multiform ways in which it has shaped, limited, and empowered their lives. That fundament is nature—a nature that takes many forms but includes marble and other minerals; water, trees, grass, algae, and air; and even the body's flesh, blood, and bone. More than anything else, the Lincoln Memorial encapsulates Americans' struggle to capture, use, and find meaning in the matter and energy that swirl around and through them. Like the nation that created it, the Lincoln Memorial is a monument to nature and to the efforts of citizens to shape nature in the image of their ideals.

Between 1914 and 1922, the United States Congress, the Army Corps of Engineers, planners, architects, artists, contractors, and other citizens literally made the Lincoln Memorial from pieces of the national landscape.[4] The transformation began with the construction site and proceeded to the marble that finally capped it. Enormous quantities of earthen fill turned a plot of marshy Potomac River bottomland into solid ground, although not solid enough for the memorial. To provide a stable foundation for ton upon ton of stone, the M. F. Comer Company drove 122 hollow steel cylinders some sixty feet to bedrock, dug out the earth inside them, and refilled them with steel-reinforced concrete. On these sturdy piers, the George A. Fuller Company erected the marble superstructure. Most of the stone came from a quarry situated at an elevation of nearly ten thousand feet in the central Rocky Mountains of Colorado. Milled into architectural components at a nearby village, the brilliant white marble, Colorado Yule, arrived at the construction site on railroad cars.[5] From this downward process—shafts sunk to bedrock and marble rolled from the mountains—the Lincoln Memorial rose toward the sky.

The construction, however, was hardly a simple, instrumental process of transforming nature into a building. It was not just a matter of choosing the best site and the best materials and then shaping them into a stunning piece of architecture. Central to the manipulation of nature—inextricable from it— was a politics of nature. Members of Congress and planners squabbled over the location of the memorial, and the primary designer, Henry Bacon, resisted the meddling of other prominent architects. Most important, the selection of Colorado stone snubbed other marble-producing states, particularly Alabama, Georgia, and Tennessee. Indeed, the politics of marble replicated the sectional politics that had resulted in the Civil War and Lincoln's rise to greatness. Proponents of Colorado Yule pointed to the stone's exceptional brightness; critics claimed it was too expensive and inferior in quality. The Bureau of Standards tested the competing marbles but found only that Colorado Yule absorbed more water and might have a greater propensity to stain. Eventually, Bacon and government officials accepted smaller amounts of stone from the other states, including some in the South—pink Tennessee marble for the interior floor and wall base, for example, and white marble quarried in Georgia for the statue of the man most responsible for the Confederacy's defeat.[6]

Nature itself sometimes obstructed the efforts of the memorial's designers and builders. The building site and materials resisted manipulation. To save money, the approach steps and the upper terrace retaining wall were constructed on spread-slab foundations that rested not on piers rising from bedrock but on soft soil. Eventually the foundations began to sink, damaging the steps, the retaining wall, and the concrete deck underlying the terrace. Contractors removed the foundations, steps, wall, and deck, dug shafts down to bedrock, and then built a massive substructure to support the enormous weight of new architectural components. Organic nature was not fully cooperative, either. To enhance the memorial's timeless look, its site plan called for mature trees and shrubs, species such as yew, boxwood, holly, and magnolia. Yet a search in and around the capital turned up only enough aged specimens to cover the ground on one side of the structure.[7]

The effort and energy necessary to manipulate stone, soil, and plants into art required the labor of people, a human nature that consisted of the minds and bodies of workmen. High in the Colorado Rockies, laborers braved rock falls, bad weather, avalanches, and runaway railroad cars to cut marble blocks from a mountain and then shape them into neoclassical building components. At the construction site, other laborers excavated soil in preparation for the mighty piers that would hold the edifice. The men hand-dug the shafts for the foundation of the steps and terrace, wrote the architectural historian Christopher Thomas, "a job the discomfort of which in Washington's hot, humid summer can be imagined."[8] By such means, human work blended with earthen materials to produce a monument imbued with a powerful, unearthly symbolism that could not admit of sweat and dirt.

In one other way the Lincoln Memorial objectified a struggle over the form, function, and meaning of nature. At the heart of American civilization lay competing assumptions about humankind. Were all people members of the same human family, with the same (natural) propensities, capacities, and potentials? Or were groups of people, identified by their racial characteristics, inherently (that is, naturally) different from one another? The Lincoln Memorial embodied the tension between the two positions. For the most part, the building acknowledged a universal human nature ("ALL MEN ARE CREATED EQUAL") and a unified democracy ("IN THE HEARTS OF THE PEOPLE FOR WHOM HE SAVED THE UNION"). Yet the structure also alluded to division and difference. Jules Guérin's murals contradicted the memorial's universalism and wholeness. *Reunion* (which might have been titled *Reunion of a Race*) left blacks out of the national marriage and confined them, in a kind of aesthetic segregation, to *Emancipation of a Race*. The fracture was more than just symbolic, for the construction force that erected the memorial likely was divided by race and ethnicity, with different groups assigned to particular tasks.

The tension between universal and particular human natures even appeared in the first rituals held at the memorial. At the dedication ceremony in 1922, African American dignitaries sat in a roped-off area apart from other participants, witnesses, and spectators. Robert Russa Moton, president of Tuskegee Institute and the only black speaker at the event, was seated with his white peers, but he addressed the issue of segregation nonetheless. Standing at the top of the steps, he asserted that emancipation was Lincoln's greatest achievement and that it "vindicated the honor of a Nation conceived in liberty and dedicated to the proposition that all men are created equal." Most white Americans ignored Moton and continued to harden the color line across the capital. Racial segregation rested on specious assumptions about the nature of black people—abstract prejudices that had no basis in material reality—yet segregation was a material practice literally grounded in the national landscape. It denied black citizens equal access to the spaces, environments, and resources that offered them the means to a better life. African Americans like Moton, refusing to accept either the assumptions or the practice, continued to assert their equality, often from the Lincoln Memorial's steps. Clustered in front of the portal, their marble patron sitting behind them, they proclaimed their full citizenship in the land of Lincoln.[9]

Surprises, not just transcendent truths, inhere in the temples of American history. The very marble that enables a visitor to intuit an ultimate purpose also manifests the complicated, contested experience of a messy biophysical world. And the environmental surprise within the Lincoln Memorial is but one example of similar surprises latent in the entire American past.[10] Within every famous icon, turning point, movement, or moment is a story of people struggling with the earthy, organic substances that are integral to the human predicament. Focusing on stone, soil, sweat, and other forms of nature makes familiar historical accounts seem strange. That sense of strangeness enables the visitor to see the past with fresh eyes and, in the process, to recover the forgotten and overlooked ground on which so much history has unfolded.

★ ★ ★

My path to the marble temple began in the classroom, where I teach a course on the role and place of nature in American history. Years ago, two young women in the class challenged my choice of subject matter. They appreciated the historical study of diseases, soil, animals, drought, forests, conservation, national parks, irrigation, and industrial pollution, but they wondered if the course was what it purported to be. If it was about American history, they asked, then why weren't we covering the usual American history topics? Why weren't we studying the nature of the American Revolution, for example, or the nature of the Civil War? In retrospect, I see their insightful questions as the beginning of my quest to find the nature embedded in the iconic moments of American history—to begin the steps that led me to the Lincoln Memorial.

My immediate response to the two students was equivocal. A focus on environmental themes, I said, offers an alternative version of the past in which conventional topics matter less. Wars, presidents, elections, economic upheavals, and social movements recede in importance as biological transformations, shifts in climate, and the social and environmental consequences of humankind's manipulation of land and life become more salient. But I had to admit that if the premise of environmental history is correct—that nature is central to the human experience—then the field ought to have something to say about the Revolution, the Civil War, and any other event.

I regret that I do not remember the names of those two young women, but I recall clearly their intelligence and sincerity, and I have been grateful ever since for the questions they pressed on me, which have guided me to better-informed and more thoughtful and complete answers. If I could turn back the clock, here is what I would say to them.

To recover the nature of familiar historical subjects is to come to terms with nature in its fullest sense and with its centrality to the human experience. It is to realize that nature is infinitely large and varied, and as the story of the Lincoln Memorial demonstrates, it has engaged human life in multiple ways, on multiple registers. It is to realize that environmental history broadens the frame of scholarly inquiry and gives people a fresh view of the eternal problem of agency versus determinism, as humanity's freedom to think and act inevitably encounters the limits that nature imposes. It is, finally, to realize that American history, in every way imaginable—from mountains to monuments—is the story of a nation and its nature.[11]

What is nature? Most basically, it is the matter, energy, and forces that constitute the universe and compose all life. It is the marble that crystallizes in the Earth's crust over millions of years, the atmospheric processes that help turn blocks of stone into particles of sand, and the rivers that carry sediments to the sea. It is gravity and sunlight and the electrons that vibrate around the nuclei of atoms. It is the photosynthesizing tissues of trees and other plants and the metabolizing bodies of the creatures that eat them. Nature includes human beings, too, from the carbon and other elements that compose flesh, blood, and bone to the bacteria that assist digestion, the electrical impulses that enliven muscles and enable thought, and the sweat that drips from a weary body on a muggy summer day. Nature is the omnipresent substance of reality, the calloused hands of laborers no less than the materials—marble and all others—with which they alter the world.[12]

Whatever form nature takes, people have arranged their societies, economies, and governments to turn it into food, clothing, warmth, shelter, weapons, art, architecture, and many other things. The complexity of means by which people have sought to realize these ends—and the biophysical and social consequences of their actions—constitutes an enormous part of environmental history. In the United States, the settlement of land, the production of food, the mining and refining of minerals, the harvesting and processing of timber, and other activities generated immense wealth. Much of that wealth enabled the development of modern business corporations, sophisticated technological systems such as railroads, and complex divisions of labor. In the form of tax revenues and proceeds from public land sales, that wealth also funded the bureaucratic organization and physical infrastructure of the federal government. During the early twentieth century, the legislative and executive branches created a special commission that worked with the War Department and one of its subdivisions, the Army Corps of Engineers, to erect a marble monument commemorating the sixteenth president. To accomplish the task, the commission and the Corps of Engineers employed architects, artists, engineers, craftsmen, and construction companies and their workers. In this manner, the United States gathered wealth and materials from the Earth and shaped them into a building that monumentalized the nation and, by its very beauty, masked the circumstances of its creation.[13]

If nature has been intrinsic to social relationships, economics, and government, then it also has been intrinsic to the ideas of the people who create those systems. The capacity of the mind to envision, calculate, and dream is virtually infinite. In their heads, people imagine things that transcend their physical circumstances. They contemplate future and past, perfect forms and supernatural powers, and a reality on the other side of death. Yet their capacity to imagine things beyond nature is rooted in nature, in an organ called the brain, and in the physical body and its experience of its environment.[14] And of all the ideas that cross people's minds, perhaps none is as important as that of nature itself. A providential hand, some Americans believed, guided a sequence of events that culminated in the formal recognition of a universal human nature and the inalienable rights that it conferred—the rights to life, liberty, and happiness. Artists, architects, and engineers later erected a monument to a champion of those universal natural rights, even as their design gestured to the competing notion that nature differentiated people by race. But no matter the message, the monument had to conform to what the architects and engineers knew about the behavior of matter, energy, and forces; the building had to stand. Ideas thus may be abstract, but they are more than just abstractions—they are functions of a natural human capacity and products of people's interactions with the physical environments in which they live.[15]

The difference between what people think and what nature allows them to do is the difference between agency and determinism. People are agents of their histories; they are willful, purposeful, discerning beings who choose among many potential actions. Yet their capacity to act is not boundless; they shape events only within a range of what is possible. The ultimate limit on that range of possibilities, and thus the final determinant of human history, is nature.[16] The citizens who built the marble temple used natural materials to counteract the constraints that nature imposed on them. The greatest of those natural constraints—greater even than gravity or the forces of erosion—was their own mortality. Indeed, the marble temple expressed a profound desire to realize a kind of immortality, to touch an eternal layer of meaning and truth above and beyond the inevitable deaths of people and the republics they create. Yet the temple, which seemed to float above the fray, remained an earthbound structure, altered by the material interests that divided people no less than by the geophysical processes that fracture rock and reduce it to bits. A noble attempt at transcendence could not escape nature's limits.

To recover the nature of American history is to see the story of the Lincoln Memorial writ large. That story is about men and women who struggled, and often failed, to shape themselves and the land according to their faith. It is about a republic made possible by a large expanse of land and premised on the idea that nature and nature's God deposited in every person a capacity for reason, the exercise of which would lead to human betterment. It is about the rapid geographical expansion of the republic and the equally rapid conversion of its biological and geological resources into wealth. And it is about the consequences of those developments: civil war, the oppression of conquered and enslaved peoples, the erosion of soil and the destruction of animals and plants, the creation of terrifying new weapons, and the extension of unsustainable material needs beyond national borders. Although it is an ironic and often tragic story, examples of courage, decency, and profound moral conviction can be found in every chapter.[17] Ultimately, it is a story of people who believed they must align their actions with a natural order intrinsic to their existence; who espoused the inherent—that is, natural—dignity and worth of every human being at the moment he or she came into the world; and who found hope and inspiration not only in machines and the regenerative power of violence but also in organic nature and the rebirth that was—and is—its final purpose.

My path to the Lincoln Memorial required a lengthy sojourn in the library of American history. Over the past century and more, scholars have created an enormous trove of books, articles, and primary documents with which to explain and interpret the nation's past. Some of these materials pertain directly to environmental history, but the bulk of them concern politics and government, armies and war, economics and society, and many other subjects.[18] No one can master this great body of scholarship, but I read as much of it as I could, always keeping before me the basic question posed by my students: What did nature have to do with the major events of American history? While gathering information with which to answer that question, I became aware of how much nature had affected past Americans in virtually all situations, how much it meant to them, and how much they talked about it. I also discovered that some historians before me had written about the importance of nature to mainstream historical events.[19] Yet I realized that over time, scholars and citizens had relegated—segregated, perhaps—the topic of nature to its now conventional haunts: farms, forests, parks, wildernesses, wolf pack territories, and other places "out there" where people had been fewest and their impress least, or sites that people had wasted, polluted, and destroyed.[20] Whatever and wherever nature was, most people no longer recognized it in parchment documents, government buildings, soldiers' bellies, racial oppression, laborers' muscles, bombs, presidents, and marble temples. As I made my way through the library, I decided that my journey would be an act not only of reinterpretation but also of remembering. I wanted to find and restate something that time and circumstances had caused me and my fellow Americans to forget.[21]

In composing my answers, I chose not to write a single synthetic narrative covering all of American history. Such a form would not have allowed me to achieve the level of detail and vividness I desired. Instead, I concentrated my efforts on nine roughly chronological topics, from the colonial period to the twenty-first century, that commonly appear in textbooks. Most readers and citizens know something about them already, and together they suggest the larger trajectory of American history. I am under no illusion that I have gotten each topic exactly right, that I have covered every possible piece of them, or that my interpretations are flawless. Communities of scholars are devoted to each topic, and I make no pretense that my knowledge exceeds theirs. Although necessity required that I select a limited number of topics, my hope is that those who find my method intriguing or compelling will apply it to subjects I left out. I want to open conversation, not end it; I want to suggest possibilities in the past that my fellow historians and citizens might never have considered and that might seem, at first glance, unlikely. At the very least, I hope the stories I have told will help convince readers of something important: that a basic understanding of American history and its major events requires some familiarity with nature's role in them.[22]

The path to the Lincoln Memorial leads, at last, into the heart of American history. Rising from your seat on the steps, you climb to the portal and look out. What you see is the product of a long process in which the republic extracted resources from its landscape and rearranged them in a record of change over time. Everything before you contains an element of the natural, whether marble, trees, or grass, humid air or damp bodies, or the Smokey Bear hats and green uniforms of National Park Service rangers who have guided visitors through capital monuments for almost as long as they have through Yellowstone and Yosemite. In these ways and more, nature tells you something about the republic's birth and development, pain and sorrow, ideals and enduring promise. The marble temple on which you stand is not the culmination of a journey—it is the beginning of one. And so you descend the steps into a land of sunlight and shadow where nature and history meet and merge, and where a once-familiar past seems new. ★

GALLERY NO. 1

Mountains and Monuments

Monuments express the nation's ideals, but spring from earthen origins. Connecting the Lincoln Memorial and other shrines to their material sources reveals the richness, diversity, conflict, and unity at the heart of American nature—and at the heart of American history. Quarrymen hewed enormous blocks of marble from mountains, craftsmen and artists shaped them into architectural components, and workers shipped them to Washington, D.C., for assembly. On one peak, laborers carved the faces of icons, including Lincoln, in granite. "A castle, a fort, a battlefield, a church, all these things bigger than us that we infuse with the reality of past lives, speak of an immensity of which we know little except that we are part of it," wrote Michel-Rolph Trouillot. Monumental marble and granite call on us to explore that immensity, to remove the blinders from our eyes, peel the layers from our icons, fill the silences of the past with sound, and make our way to mountaintops from which to see our history and ourselves whole. The United States of America, the stone declares, is the republic of nature.

1.1   Lincoln Memorial with trees ready for planting.

1.2   Placing of the Lincoln Memorial cornerstone, February 12, 1915.

1.3 Lincoln Memorial near completion. Note the size of the column drums in proportion to the workmen, and the George A. Fuller construction company sign on the shack.

1.4 Lincoln Memorial under construction. Note the scaffolding, derricks, and the resemblance of the site to dam construction projects in the far West.

1.5 Assembling the Lincoln statue, Lincoln Memorial.

1.6   Tate, Georgia, marble quarry. Workers cut the raw marble with steam-powered channeling machines and then removed the blocks from the bed.

1.7   Men and mules, Georgia Marble Company, Tate, Georgia, 1915. The man on the far right is Henry Spikes, the only identity recorded.

1.8   Colorado Yule Marble Company
factory, Marble, Colorado.

1.9   Finish work on the Lincoln Memorial's columns, Colorado Yule Marble
Company factory, Marble, Colorado.
Using machinery, workmen cut and
fluted the columns before shipping them
east by railroad.

1.10   Quarrying marble from the Rocky
Mountains, Marble, Colorado. Note the
derricks and wooden building housing
the steam-powered hoist.

1.11   Lincoln visage, Mount Rushmore National Memorial, Black Hills of South
Dakota. The man in the Lincoln top hat is the artist Gutzon Borglum.

ONE

SATAN IN THE LAND

Nature, the Supernatural, and Disorder

in Colonial New England

T HE AFFLICTION BEGAN WITH A mysterious swelling in his foot. Perhaps he was walking home from the hayfield when he felt the stiffness, or perhaps it was when he stood up from the supper table. Perhaps, too, he noticed it in the morning when he tried to put on his shoe. Much to Benjamin Abbott's dismay, the swollen foot was only a prelude to an agonizing "sickness and misery" that would carry him "almost to death's door." A pain soon developed in his side, followed by a boil that yielded "several gallons of corruption" when Dr. Prescott lanced it. Two more sores then appeared in his groin. Imagine the pustules throbbing, the sting of the physician's razor, and the stink that rose from the drippings. The ordeal went on for weeks, until Benjamin, exhausted, felt himself near the end.[1]

While Benjamin struggled with his sores, his wife, Sarah, noticed "strange and unusual things" in his cattle. Some of the animals wandered out of the forest "with their tongues hanging out of their mouths in a strange and affrighting manner." A few died "strangely and suddenly," for no apparent "natural reason." Most alarming of all was the pregnant cow. Her water broke prematurely, the amniotic fluid draining in anticipation of a birth that did not occur until some two weeks later. The calf came into the world unscathed, as far as Sarah could tell, but the cow expired "strangely."[2]

Benjamin and Sarah Abbott were not alone in their experience of painful and baffling events. Other residents of colonial Andover, Massachusetts, likewise endured odd ailments or looked on helplessly while livestock fell ill and died. Not only did Allen Toothaker's deep, nagging war wound refuse to heal, but several of his cattle fell sick and perished within a matter of days: first a three-year-old heifer, then a yearling, next a mature cow, and finally another yearling. Toothaker was mystified and knew of no "natural causes" that might have brought about their deaths. Samuel Preston suffered peculiar losses of prized livestock, too. A "very lusty" cow died "in a strange manner," on her back, hooves thrust into the air. Later, another fine, healthy cow, "well kept with English hay," abruptly grew ill, lay down as if to sleep, and expired.[3]

Something frightening was happening in Andover, and it threatened the social and agricultural order that the Abbotts, their neighbors, and other English colonists had labored mightily to create and uphold. Some seventy years before, in 1620, the first of them had arrived on New England's rocky shore, intent on remaking the land and themselves. They would transform a savage environment into a stable, wealthy landscape of churches, solid homes, fertile fields, and pastures filled with lowing cattle. In the process, they would purify themselves and create tight-knit communities in which each person knew his or her place and obeyed God's will. It was their special mission, an "errand into the wilderness," as one of their ministers called it, the success of which would ensure their redemption and the world's.[4] But building and maintaining an orderly society and landscape would be more easily imagined than achieved. The very nature of the place, including the nature of the colonists' bodies, would prove too unstable for them to realize the control and security they desired. Striving for God's grace, they and their descendants—the Abbotts and many others—would know sores, pus, pain, strange births, dead cattle, paralyzing fear, and worse.

The Abbotts and their Andover compatriots no doubt struggled to account for their misfortunes. They might have blamed their illnesses on the climate or on imbalances in the bodily substances they called humors. Observing their sick and dying animals, they might have guessed that poisonous plants were responsible. They might have wondered, too, if the hand of God was evident in such events, that the Lord was punishing them for their sins. But in the end, the Abbotts and other community members attributed their problems to no such causes. Instead, they focused their suspicions on a neighbor.

They had never held Martha Carrier in high regard. The daughter of a well-to-do local family, Martha probably lost her good reputation when, as a young woman, she conceived a child out of wedlock with a Welsh servant named Thomas Carrier. After Martha and Thomas married in 1674, they moved to the nearby community of Billerica, but around 1690, they and their children returned, impoverished, to Andover. The community did not welcome them, and the selectmen warned the family out of town. For some reason, perhaps Martha's familial ties, Andover then reconsidered and granted Thomas a small piece of land. But the Carriers' standing, especially Martha's, continued to fall. She and several of her children contracted smallpox, and although officials quarantined the family, the disease spread, eventually killing at least ten people, among them four of Martha's own relatives. Her contentiousness further alienated her from her Andover neighbors, and their anger and resentment deepened.[5]

In this climate, minor differences and petty insults took on sinister implications. Andover had granted to Benjamin Abbott a piece of undeveloped land near the small portion owned by Martha's husband. Benjamin and his wife were a relatively young couple, both about thirty years old, and if they were to remain in the agricultural community, they needed property with which to sustain themselves. It is lost to history precisely why Martha objected to Benjamin's acquisition. Perhaps the parcel had forage, wood, or water that she and her family had used and which would now be closed to them. Perhaps she and Thomas had hoped that they, not Benjamin, would get the land from the town. Perhaps, as Allan Toothaker stated, Martha did not want anyone living so close to the Carrier house. For whatever reason, she evidently felt aggrieved toward Benjamin Abbott and, according to him and Toothaker, directed her malice at him. She would stick to him as the bark stuck to the tree, she said; she would hold his nose to the grindstone.[6] Soon after that, Benjamin's foot began to swell, his side to ache, and his cattle to suffer their strange afflictions.

While Benjamin writhed, events elsewhere in town magnified the sense that Martha, her husband, and their children might be more than just troublesome people. Martha was Toothaker's aunt, and perhaps the very closeness of their relationship exacerbated the hostility between them. Toothaker developed "some difference" with Richard Carrier, Martha's son and Toothaker's cousin, which led to a scuffle between the two men. During the fight, Toothaker went down on his back, unable to move. When he gave up and conceded that Richard was "the best man," he saw Martha rise from his chest, as if she had been sitting on him. By the time he scrambled to his feet, she had disappeared. Later, she taunted him that his war wound would never heal, and during their bickering she sometimes clapped her hands at him and said that he "should get nothing by it." It was after one of these altercations that Toothaker's cattle began to die. And it was after Samuel Preston's own arguments with Martha that his livestock collapsed and expired. You have lost a cow, Martha told Preston one day, and it will not be long before you will lose another.[7]

To the people of Andover, the sequence of events was no mere coincidence. There seemed to be a direct connection between Martha Carrier's reappearance in town, her clashes with extended family and neighbors, and a series of strange illnesses and deaths. Colonial Englishmen and -women knew that invisible forces were at work beneath the surface of things and that malevolent beings could use those forces to hurt, maim, and kill. Sickness, sores, freakish births, faltering cattle, and other disturbances were not events that simply happened. They were the outward, material manifestations of metaphysical troubles within. Benjamin and Sarah Abbott, Allen Toothaker, Samuel Preston, and other Andover inhabitants could draw but one conclusion. Martha Carrier was no mere angry, contentious, spiteful woman. She was a witch.

Martha Carrier's conflict with her Andover neighbors was part of a famous episode of witchcraft that swept Essex County, Massachusetts, during the early 1690s and eventually centered on the community of Salem. The story of Salem witchcraft, like stories of similar incidents in colonial history, has fascinated Americans. Mysterious tales of occult practices and supernatural events, and the high drama of neighbors and families torn apart in a downward spiral of accusations, counteraccusations, and executions, have long appealed to a popular curiosity about the nation's early history. Scholars, too, have sustained a long-term interest in the topic. Studying a colonial community in a moment of crisis has enabled them to gain insights into the social and cultural dynamics of the time.[8] The story of Martha Carrier, however, suggests that there was a side to this iconic American event that scholars and popular audiences alike have largely overlooked: witchcraft was a function of the colonists' experience of bodies, disease, land, and other biophysical things generally known as nature.

Integral to the English settlement of North America was the widespread belief that intangible, invisible, supernatural forces affected the material world. On the grandest scale, New Englanders believed in providence, the idea that God directed the movement of people and things toward a predetermined end. The colonists recognized that they had free will and that they might appeal to God through prayer. They also knew that Satan was engaged in a titanic struggle against God and could shape earthly things. But ultimately God was in charge and knew what the outcome of events would be. Far below that cosmic level, in daily life, colonists believed in the power of magic. Ritual incantations and other practices, they thought, enabled people to influence the future.

Although many ordinary colonists saw magic as a means of curing illness and accomplishing other good deeds, Puritan officials asserted that it was evil, if not satanic.

The colonists shared their belief in a supernatural world with American Indians, Africans, and others. Indeed, all peoples in North America understood in their distinctive ways that a range of immaterial powers and possibilities inhered in the physical reality they co-inhabited. Whether called God, *manitou*, Satan, or some other name, intangible but awesome forces coursed through all natural things. The English typically condemned Indian magic and manitou as savage and diabolical but nonetheless believed in their power. Indians might not have approved of the English God, but they could not dismiss his ability to alter the course of their lives. To speak of natural things was, for all people, to imply—at the very least—the presence and power of the supernatural.

The Puritan colonists recognized that their spiritual purpose was manifested in the order they imposed on their society and the land they inhabited. They had migrated from an island nation wracked by war, demographic upheaval, and environmental change. Their errand into the American wilderness gave them a chance to try again. They organized their lives according to the Order of Creation, the Great Chain of Being, a hierarchy in which authority and power extended from God downward, through men, women, and children, to nonhuman nature on the bottom. They arranged their landscape according to a similar, although horizontal, scale of values. Churches, homes, and towns, their most sacrosanct spaces, formed the spiritual center of their geography; next came barns, fenced fields and pastures, common land, and the environment beyond. Building a controlled, orderly society and landscape—a new England—was deeply satisfying to the Puritan colonists; right living was a manifestation of God's grace and a promise of the great reward that waited on the other side of death.

Yet New Englanders were an exceedingly anxious and fearful people, because the order they tried so hard to impose was difficult, if not impossible, to achieve in a biophysical environment in which nothing was stable. Indian peoples—"savages" in their eyes—and French Catholics competed with them for land and resources. Nature itself challenged them: extreme temperatures, droughts, storms, and insects destroyed their crops, wolves preyed on their livestock, and diseases felled them and their animals. Compounding these external threats were problems internal to their communities. The "natural increase" of livestock and the growth of human numbers placed enormous ecological stress on pastures and fields, provoking conflicts among neighbors and families. Even the nature of their individual bodies, which aged and sometimes unexpectedly died, upset the desired order. Women in particular were a problem for patriarchal Puritans. As bearers and nurturers of children, women were at the center of colonial civilization. Yet women sometimes did things that threatened the Order of Creation. In some cases, the very nature of their bodies disturbed the Puritan quest for control.[9]

Colonial New Englanders understood their insecurity in spiritual, not just material, terms. Disorder might have various causes. Ultimately, God might be testing their faith or punishing them for their lapses. More immediately, colonists often interpreted disorder as evidence that a malign, demonic force was at work in the land. If Indians raided them, strange sicknesses and deaths beleaguered them, or a woman seemed out of place and out of control, then Satan must have infiltrated their defenses. And if Satan had slipped into their midst, then someone must have assisted him. That person must be a witch, and probably a woman like Martha Carrier.

The witchcraft crisis at Andover and nearby communities in the early 1690s marked the culmination of the colonists' decades-long struggle to create an orderly society and landscape in the New England wilderness. That story can be told in a series of episodes, each of which centers on the importance of nature and the supernatural to the people who inhabited New England. In every episode, the story gathers its dark energy from the colonists' troubled relationship to land, animals, diseases, bodies, and other biophysical things. Whether the threat to their control of these things was external or internal to their communities, they blamed the diabolical power of a man in black and the hideous creatures that had surrendered to his will. Eventually, at Andover and other towns, and in the person of Martha Carrier and other members of their communities, the colonists confronted for the last time the fatal consequences of their struggle. Decades of precarious existence on the fringe of empire had conditioned their outlook; their suspicion of Carrier was the direct outcome of their tumultuous past.[10]

GOD HAS CLEARED OUR TITLE TO THIS PLACE

The story of nature, the supernatural, and disorder in colonial New England begins long before Martha Carrier became the object of her neighbors' suspicions and scorn. Although its precise origins are lost in the shadows and silences of the past, perhaps a few places provide opportunities to pick up its strands and follow its course through early American history. One such place is near the mouth of Connecticut's Mystic River. The year is 1637, and although it is springtime, neither the fragrance of blossoms nor the music of birds caresses the senses. The atmosphere is acrid and dissonant. Fire, smoke, and screams warn of the horror unfolding in the village ahead.

Shortly after sunrise, English soldiers and their Narragansett and Mohegan allies surprised the fortified Pequot town. As men, women, and children ran from the burning lodges, the English slaughtered them. One attacker carried a halberd—a wooden shaft topped by a battle-ax, a hook, and a pike. Hefting the weapon, the soldier thrust it into the neck of a Pequot man, driving him to the ground. Despite the crippling, agonizing wound, the man remained alive and tried to withdraw the point from his body. "But this was very remarkable," wrote colonial historian Edward Johnson, "one of [the Pequots] being wounded to death, and thrust through the neck with a halberd; yet after all, lying groaning upon the ground, he caught the halberd's spear in his hand, and wound it quite round."[11] To Indians and English alike, such mettle could not arise solely from ordinary human character and the physical body that contained it. It must have, as well, a supernatural origin.

A man's not dying when he should have was the sort of occurrence that Pequot and other Algonquian Indians attributed to *manitou*, a powerful force that permeated the world. It inhered in plants, stones, animals, and other parts of nature. And it was immanent in people, their bodies, and their artifacts. Any unusual, mysterious, or amazing behavior manifested it: a flash of creative insight, an act of extreme courage, a demonstration of towering rage, a show of phenomenal strength. People endowed with exceptional spiritual abilities— shamans—used ceremonies, incantations, and prayers to evoke and manipulate manitou, ensuring that its positive energy flowed through the community. One type of shaman, the *powwow*, tapped manitou to stimulate abundant crops and game, foretell the future, and heal the sick. Another type, the *pniese*, used it to make warriors strong. Perhaps the Pequot man with the halberd in his neck had acquired his power with the help of a pniese. Or perhaps he had gotten it on his own—perhaps he was one of those gifted people.[12]

Although the Pequot man's grit impressed the Puritans, they had a different explanation of its source. They certainly believed that Indians possessed supernatural abilities and used their powers for beneficial, not malevolent, purposes. The Puritans also recognized that manitou corresponded loosely to their own notion of the divine. But because they considered all magical practices to be diabolical in origin, manitou ultimately was evil. Even before the soldiers marched on the Pequot village, they had heard rumors that some Indians' bodies would resist their weapons. A Pequot man of extraordinary vitality, a man whom they could not slay instantly, evinced the truth. "The Devil was in them," the soldiers believed; Pequot powwows, who could "work strange things with the help of Satan," had drawn him there.[13]

Not only did the Puritans judge such power to be diabolical, but they also understood it to be in conflict with the vastly superior immaterial force that motivated their own actions. God was responsible for their presence in the New World, they believed, and his hand was evident in their attack on the Pequot village. He had led them to the American wilderness, at once a haven from European persecutors and a spiritual testing ground inhabited by savages. There the colonists struggled to overcome the evil that surrounded them and that sometimes crept into their own souls. Although they had faith that God answered their prayers, they were never certain of his favor and continually searched for signs of it.[14] Providence took many forms: safe travel, fair weather, abundant crops—and the fallen bodies of Pequot Indians.

Yet this was not only a spiritual conflict, a war of belief. Inextricable from the religious struggle was a physical contest for the control of nature. The theologian Cotton Mather asserted as much when he wrote that the Puritan purpose was to transform American geography into "Christianography."[15] The colonists needed the New World's bountiful resources—lumber, fur, and fish—to pay the creditors who had financed their transportation and supplies.[16] Most important, they needed land for their burgeoning population. By the late 1620s, the Plymouth colonists totaled about fifteen hundred; a decade later, natural increase and a massive influx called the Great Migration boosted Plymouth and its younger counterpart, the Massachusetts Bay colony, to perhaps twenty-one thousand persons.[17] As the human population rose, so did the number of sheep, goats, horses, pigs, and especially cattle. Soon the settlers filled up the arable land, and livestock crowded pastures and outstripped the natural hay supply. "And no man now thought he could live," wrote Plymouth's William Bradford, "except that he had cattle and a great deal of ground to keep them, all striving to increase their stocks."[18] While colonists dreamed of more and larger farms, their hungry animals wandered onto Indian land. The problem was obvious: the colonists needed more living space.

Their predicament sharpened crucial differences between Native and

English conceptions of land. Indians saw themselves as connected to all things. They told stories of their ancestors' emergence from the Earth or some other part of creation, and they tried to channel the manitou that coursed through the world. Villages claimed sovereignty over territories within which extended families and their members recognized each other's rights to keep plots of corn, beans, and squash, and Indian communities negotiated with one another for access to hunting grounds and gathering sites. Natives typically did not stay in place, but moved through the landscape to take advantage of seasonal abundances of wild plants and animals, finally returning to harvest their crops.[19]

The English colonists, in contrast, asserted a hierarchical relationship to land. God created humans in his image and enjoined them to multiply and to subdue the Earth and make it fruitful. Intensive agriculture, fences, and livestock best fulfilled his wishes and established the basis of property rights, civil society, and political sovereignty. People had a natural right and a civil right to land, John Winthrop of Massachusetts Bay and other colonists believed. "The first right was natural when men held the earth in common, every man sowing and feeding where he pleased." Eventually, "as men and their cattle increased, they appropriated some parcels of ground by enclosing it," cultivating it, and spreading manure on it, "and this in time got them a civil right"—a property right recognized by society. Indians had made no such transition. Some colonists acknowledged Natives' natural right to cultivate crops, but insisted that their impermanent agriculture neither conferred property rights nor legitimized political sovereignty over collective territory. "As for the Natives in New England," Winthrop stated, "they enclose no land, neither have [they] any settled habitation, nor any tame cattle to improve the land by, and so have no other but a natural right to those countries." Unworked, unimproved land was *vacuum domicilium*, land into which the colonists could move. By demography, desire, and belief, the colonists were primed to displace Natives.[20]

In 1633, as the Great Migration rose toward its peak, a smallpox epidemic gave the English an opening. Colonists and Indians both suffered and died, but the disease was harder—in some cases, catastrophically harder—on the tribes. The moment was propitious for the English, because Native deaths opened land onto which colonists could move. Such an opportunity had arisen before. In 1616–1619, a devastating illness, perhaps plague, had emptied Patuxet villages on Cape Cod Bay. The English who arrived in 1620 decided that God had opened the way for them, and they established Plymouth on the site. The area's remaining Algonquians asked the newcomers if they had the ability to summon the disease that had killed so many Indians. No, the English answered, but God, if he chose, could use it to destroy his enemies. Now an epidemic had struck again. "God," John Winthrop wrote in 1634, "has hereby cleared our title to this place."[21]

Smallpox most benefited the English by crippling the Pequots, who lived southwest of the colonies. Through trade, diplomacy, military might, and numerical superiority, the tribe had established its dominance over the Connecticut River valley, a major fur trade route endowed with fertile soil and rich meadows. About thirteen thousand strong by 1633, the Pequots declined to some three thousand under the onslaught of the epidemic. Drastically weakened, they no longer could control tributary tribes and Dutch traders from New Amsterdam (later renamed New York), nor could they counter their major rival, the Narragansetts. In 1634, to compensate for the loss of their power, the Pequots and their sachem, Sassacus, struck up an alliance with the one group that most coveted their land—the English of Massachusetts Bay, who by then numbered about four thousand. To cement the relationship, the Pequots gave the English furs, wampum, and an especially valuable prize: the right to settle along the Connecticut River. Many Massachusetts Bay colonists were pleased to exchange stony soil and cramped confines for the verdant meadows of Connecticut. By 1636, some eight hundred of them had established three settlements in the valley.[22]

Rather than shoring up Pequot power, however, the alliance and the English settlement of Connecticut further destabilized the tribe. To undercut his Pequot overlords, the Mohegan sachem, Uncas, told Governor John Winthrop that the Pequots were preparing for war against Massachusetts Bay. Winthrop responded with stern measures intended to assert English dominance. He demanded that the Pequots pay heavy tribute, give up some of their children as hostages, and turn over the killers of two rogue English traders. Sassacus and the Pequots refused. While Massachusetts organized a military force, the Pequots besieged the colony's trading post at the mouth of the Connecticut River. Violence soon erupted. In April 1637, nervous settlers at Wethersfield, Connecticut, drove off the local Pyquag Indians. In retaliation, the Pyquags— with Pequot assistance—killed nine English people and twenty of their cattle. The colonists perceived a dangerous threat to their precarious hold on the New World. They had to strike back.[23]

They pursued the Pequots with the righteous zeal reserved for foes who were, in the words of Captain John Underhill, "the Devil's instruments."[24]

Underhill and John Mason led ninety colonists, some seventy Mohegans, and approximately five hundred Narragansetts against the Pequots. Sidestepping Sassacus and his warriors, Underhill and Mason struck the fortified village near the Mystic River, the weakest, most lightly defended of the two main Pequot settlements in lower Connecticut. Before the attack, wrote Underhill, the English "yielded" themselves "to God, and entreated his assistance in so weighty an enterprise." So complete and accurate was the soldiers' first volley that they "could not but admire the providence of God in it." It was "as though the finger of God had touched both match and flint." Pequot arrows struck both Underhill and Mason, but God "preserved" them "from any wounds."[25] Indeed, the English lost only two of their soldiers while slaying some five hundred Pequots. The Narragansetts and Mohegans protested the savagery, judging it in excess of Indian custom. The soldiers, conditioned by the extremism of Europe's religious wars, gloried in it. "Thus was God seen in the mount," Mason exulted, "crushing his proud enemies and the enemies of his people," "burning them up in the fire of his wrath, dunging the ground with their flesh. It was the Lord's doings, and it is marvelous in our eyes!"[26]

The war yielded all that the English wanted, and more. In subsequent operations, the soldiers defeated the remaining Pequots, turned over most of the survivors to the Mohegans and Narragansetts, sold others into slavery in the West Indies, and declared the tribe extinct. Sassacus fled west toward the Hudson River, only to die at the hands of Mohawk Indians. But the greatest prize was land. Massachusetts and Connecticut took the Pequots' territory, and the Mohegans and smaller tribes ceded additional terrain to the colonies in acknowledgment of their suzerainty.[27]

John Winthrop interpreted the war's outcome as "Divine Providence" and noted that the "defeat of the Pequots at Mystic happened the day after our general fast." The churches of Massachusetts Bay observed "a day of public thanksgiving" on which ministers proclaimed the Lord's blessings. At Plymouth, William Bradford took satisfaction in the thought of Indians "frying in the fire and the streams of blood quenching the same."[28] Most appreciative, perhaps, were the settlers of Connecticut, the immediate beneficiaries of the conquest. A resolution passed at a Milford town meeting in 1640 illustrated perfectly the colonists' faith in the vital link between God and destiny, the supernatural and the natural: "Voted, that the earth is the Lord's and the fullness thereof; voted, that the earth is given to the Saints; voted, we are the Saints."[29]

Yet the English could not feel secure for long. Even as they rejoiced, Satan pursued them still. In the form of the Pequots, he had challenged them from without. But they also perceived his threat from within. Even in an intimate and seemingly sheltered space, an inner sanctum in which they nurtured some of their most profound hopes and dreams, they felt his presence.

HOLY SPIRITS AND MONSTERS

One day in October 1637, Mary Dyer, a Boston resident and "a very proper and comely young woman" of twenty-six, began to feel the rhythmic muscular contractions that signaled the impending birth of a child. Mary and her husband, William, had arrived in Massachusetts Bay colony almost three years before; shortly thereafter, Boston had granted William forty-two acres on the northeast side of the harbor. The Dyers had become followers and friends of Anne Hutchinson, a midwife and charismatic prophetess in her mid-forties who claimed that a person could attain grace in his or her "immediate witness of the Holy Spirit." Having settled in New England and immersed themselves in its religious life, the Dyers sought to fulfill their divine purpose in another, equally fundamental way. As they and other Puritan colonists believed, procreation was essential to the natural order of things, and women played an especially important role in it. The future inhered in the womb; carrying and birthing a child were the most basic functions a wife could serve. Now, young mistress Dyer would do her part to fulfill the Lord's plan by bringing another soul into the world. After summoning Jane Hawkins, a friend and midwife, she took to her bed.[30]

The Dyers no doubt hoped and prayed that the fruit of their sexual bond would be a healthy daughter or son, a child in God's image and a new member of the pious society that they and their fellow colonists were busily creating. Somewhere along the way, however, maybe at the moment sperm joined egg, Mary's pregnancy had gone terribly wrong. During the intervening months, she might have sensed that the child was not developing properly. When she went into labor a full two months early, it is possible that she and her husband knew the birth would be difficult and unhappy. Overwhelmed by exhaustion and pain, Mary slipped into unconsciousness. Needing help, Jane sent for Anne Hutchinson. With her friends by her side, Mary finally summoned the strength to give birth to a tiny girl. As the infant came into the light, she did not cry, did not suck air into her lungs and wail. She was dead—stillborn. And not only was she stillborn, but her head, spine, and limbs were hideously malformed.

Very likely her spine was cleft, and she probably lacked much if not all of her brain and overlying skull, exaggerating the prominence of her face and causing her eyes to protrude. Rather than giving life to a child, Mary and William had yielded, some would later claim, a monster.[31]

The Dyers wondered what to make of their tragedy. The natural Order of Creation had been subverted and broken. Why? What had they done wrong? Was the birth a sign of God's judgment against them? Should they bury the corpse in private and avoid the shame and scrutiny that a public ritual surely would invite? That night, Anne Hutchinson sought advice from John Cotton, her minister. Cotton, his own wife pregnant for the third time, believed that the Dyers' stillborn child was "a providence of God" intended only for "the instruction of the parents" and others present. If it were his offspring, he said, he would wish to have its existence concealed, and he advised Hutchinson and the Dyers not to register the birth and to conduct a quiet burial.[32]

The child might have lain in her grave forever, a sad memory in the minds of her parents and a few other people, save for an important fact: Mary Dyer, Jane Hawkins, and Anne Hutchinson were not ordinary Puritan women. Hutchinson was a prominent leader of a dissenting theological faction critical of ministers for preaching that virtuous acts and good behavior could be interpreted as signs of salvation. Drawing on the sermons of John Cotton, Hutchinson argued that only the direct experience of God's love offered assurance of grace. Her message proved popular, and men and women crowded into her home to hear her lecture. The ministerial elites of Massachusetts grew alarmed at this challenge to the religious doctrines they sought to harden into orthodoxy. They accused Cotton and Hutchinson of "antinomianism" ("above-the-law-ism"), and they took an especially dim view of the strong and outspoken Hutchinson.[33] She and her staunchest female followers, Mary Dyer and Jane Hawkins included, were precisely the sort of unruly women that the Puritan elites might suspect of witchcraft. The public revelation of a monstrous birth—and more—would give them the opportunity to make just such a claim.

Late in 1637, clerical, political, and legal forces took action against the so-called Antinomians. The Massachusetts Bay General Court convicted Hutchinson of heresy and banished her from the colony. While she was under house arrest, church ministers put her on trial again and, in late March 1638, excommunicated her. In both proceedings, Hutchinson asserted her right as a Christian and a woman to interpret the Bible publicly. She also stated that she received revelations from God. In her defense, she invoked Joel 28–29: "And it shall come to pass afterward, / That I will pour out my Spirit upon all flesh; / And your sons and your daughters shall prophesy, / Your old men shall dream dreams, / Your young men shall see visions."[34]

Hutchinson's behavior aroused suspicions that she had a compact with the devil. She was a proud woman who had challenged the officials and ministers who sat in judgment of her. She had professed powers that, to Puritanism's moral arbiters, might have verged on the magical. The similarity—even the close connection—between prophecy and magic perhaps caused influential people to believe that she resembled the Indian shamans who threatened the New England colonies from without.[35]

What happened after Hutchinson heard her excommunication only heightened her critics' suspicions. As she left the church in the company of Mary Dyer, someone remarked that Dyer was "the woman who had the monster." A church elder overheard the comment and brought it to the attention of his fellows, who then initiated another formal inquiry at which Hutchinson, Hawkins, and Cotton related, in excruciating detail, the story of Dyer's stillborn child. Days after the humiliating ritual, the Dyers, Hutchinson and her family, and some of Hutchinson's followers departed for Rhode Island. Soon after they left, Governor Winthrop sought additional verification of the monster birth and had the "much corrupted" corpse disinterred, which "above a hundred persons" viewed.[36]

Events in Rhode Island would add to Winthrop's stock of evidence that Hutchinson and her friends were instruments of Satan. During her two trials, the forty-six-year-old Hutchinson had been pregnant and had endured debilitating weakness, headaches, and nausea. In May, some six weeks early, she entered the birthing room in hopes of adding one more child to her already great brood of fifteen. An experienced midwife, she must have known the dangers of conceiving and carrying a child at her age, and the outcome was not good. Her labor ended in a miscarriage of tissue that looked like a mass of translucent berries.[37]

Not everyone in seventeenth-century European culture understood monstrous births as signs of supernatural intervention in human affairs. Physicians, natural philosophers, and even some members of the clergy looked for biophysical explanations.[38] But to New England's Puritan leaders, shaken by the Antinomian challenge, the malformed offspring of Dyer and Hutchinson suggested not merely God's disfavor but intercourse with Satan.

Governor Winthrop recorded vivid descriptions of the Dyer and Hutchinson monsters. Dyer's was a combination of "a woman child, a fish, a beast, and a fowl all woven together in one, and without an head." Her ears "were like an ape's," her breast and back were "full of sharp prickles, like a thornback," and "instead of toes," she "had upon each foot three claws, like a young fowl." Protruding from what should have been a forehead were "four horns." Even the circumstances of the birth suggested a satanic influence. Jane Hawkins was "notorious for familiarity with the devil," and when the child expired in the womb just before her delivery, Winthrop reported, the birthing bed shook violently and a terrible odor permeated the room. "The manner of discovery was very strange also," he stated, the public revelation of Hutchinson's miscarriage coinciding with her excommunication for "her monstrous errors, and notorious falsehoods." Hutchinson herself, the governor went on, "brought forth not one (as Mistress Dyer did) but (which was more strange to amazement) thirty monstrous births or thereabouts, at once; some of them bigger, some lesser, some of one shape, some of another; few of any perfect shape, none at all of them (as far as I could ever learn) of human shape."[39]

Winthrop and other Puritan spokesmen never formally charged Dyer, Hutchinson, or Hawkins with witchcraft, but they certainly thought of the three as malign and dangerous people whose very bodies channeled evil into the material world. Massachusetts Bay magistrates restricted Hawkins's use of herbal medicines and later expelled her from the colony.[40] When, in 1643, after Hutchinson had moved to the Dutch colony of New Amsterdam, she died in a raid by Algonquian-speaking Siwanoy Indians, prominent Puritan men rejoiced. Winthrop believed that at last the Lord had relieved the world and "his poor churches" of this "instrument of Satan."[41] Dyer's spiritual transit eventually carried her to the Quakers, radical dissenters who threatened the Puritan hierarchy by asserting a priesthood of all believers, men and women alike. Puritans suspected the Quakers of witchcraft, and the trembling that sometimes accompanied their expressions of religious fervor suggested demonic possession. Such quaking, wrote John Norton in 1659, resembled "the custom of the powwows or Indian wizards, in this wilderness; whose bodies at the time of their diabolical practices, are at this day vexed and agitated in a strange, unwonted, and dreadful manner." Dyer would not tolerate the persecution of her fellow Massachusetts Quakers, and her persistent protests violated her banishment from the colony. Soon the magistrates would no longer tolerate her, and on June 1, 1660, they hanged her from a tree on Boston Common.[42]

Many colonial New Englanders believed that Satan could infiltrate all kinds of things. Much as they detected his traces in the wretched offspring and radical pronouncements of disruptive women, so they recognized his footsteps in the mundane experiences of ordinary females who bore the burdens of New England's material and spiritual ambitions. Indeed, the very nature of those women's world, even the very nature of their bodies, placed them in an inherently hazardous predicament. No woman, perhaps, learned this better than did Katherine Harrison.

HE HAD CARNAL KNOWLEDGE OF HER BODY

Witchcraft must have been on Harrison's mind as she surveyed the damage to her crops and livestock in October 1668. Horses had grazed in her corn and "much damnified" it, and some "30 poles of hops" had been "cut and spoiled." Her own horse had been "wounded in the night." One of her sows came out of the woods with its ears damaged and a hind leg missing, and earmarks had appeared on three young pigs "in the sty." Then there were the cattle: a heifer with Harrison's earmark cut out and new ones put in, a badly bruised ox, a cow with a broken back and ribs, another with a broken jawbone and hoof and with "a hole bored in her side," still another wounded in the udder, and in the meadow, a heifer stabbed to death.[43]

In a terrible irony, it was not Harrison's tormentors—probably some of her own neighbors—who were charged with the crime of witchcraft and faced with the prospect of the noose. It was Harrison herself. You have "familiarity with Satan," read her indictment, "and by his help have acted things beyond and beside the ordinary course of nature, and have thereby hurt the bodies of diverse of the subjects of our sovereign lord, the King, and for which by the law of God and of this corporation you ought to die."[44]

The people of Wethersfield, the town on the Connecticut River in which Harrison lived, believed they had ample evidence of her diabolical arts. Something was strange, they suggested, about the manner in which Harrison and her husband, John, had risen from modest beginnings to accumulate so much property. The "remarkable" improvement of the Harrisons' fortunes seemed, in their eyes, to benefit from Katherine's superhuman feats of strength, dexterity, and skill. Elizabeth Smith witnessed her spin an astonishing quantity of fine linen yarn. According to Richard Montague, Goodwife Harrison had once boasted of fetching a swarm of bees that had flown onto neighboring land. She had gathered stray cattle from the meadow with amazing speed, Joseph Dickinson testified. John Wells claimed that his legs suddenly went immobile when he observed her drawing milk from a cow "that was none of her own."[45]

Worse still, some people reported that Harrison had appeared in frightening spectral form and in some instances had committed *maleficium*, the use of supernatural power to cause bodily harm. Close to midnight one evening, Mary Kercum observed the apparition of Harrison in the company of a black dog, an animal "familiar" that typically suckled from a fleshy appendage or teat somewhere on a witch's body. Terrified, Kercum fled the room.[46] Harrison did more than just scare people, the reports continued; she hurt them. Thomas Bracy watched a cart loaded with hay approach John Harrison's barn. Atop the hay he saw "a red calf's head, the ears standing pert up." Abruptly the calf vanished, and Harrison stood on the cart. Bracy voiced his suspicion that Katherine was involved in witchcraft, and she told him "that she would be even with him." He reported that her apparition later appeared by his bedside, strangling, jerking, and pinching him, making him feel "as if his flesh had been pulled from his bones."[47] Mary Hale claimed to have experienced a similar ordeal. Lying in her bed one night, firelight pushing back the darkness, she had felt a terrible blow on her legs, and suddenly she had seen "an ugly shaped thing like a dog" with Katherine's head on it. For several nights afterward, Hale said, she had endured crushing pressure and bruised fingers while Katherine's voice threatened her with more abuse unless she kept her silence.[48]

Harrison seemed most fiendish in her alleged treatment of Jacob Johnson and the Francis family. Harrison had been a folk healer, and when Johnson became ill, she "did help him with diet, drink, and plasters." But instead of improving his health, her remedies made him worse, and his "nose fell a bleeding in an extraordinary manner." More alarming was the case of Joan Francis, her husband, and their sick child. As the child lay with them one night, the apparition of Harrison appeared. The child remained "strangely ill" for about three weeks, and then, in a fit, died. As the child expired, Francis said that she and her husband "felt a thing run along the sides or side like a whetstone."[49]

Wethersfield's indictment of Katherine Harrison coincided with an intense wave of fear that engulfed Connecticut Valley towns and much of New England during the mid-seventeenth century. From the 1640s through the 1660s, the colonists felt profoundly vulnerable to menacing and potentially wicked forces over which they seemed to have little or no control. Some of those forces were environmental. Epidemics, including smallpox and perhaps influenza, struck the region, as did floods, cold and wet springs, summer droughts, fruit flies, caterpillars, and a fungal blight that devastated wheat fields.[50]

Social conditions also provoked fear, although those, too, were related to the environmental circumstances of colonial life. Ministers noted an alarming decline in church attendance, and they decried wayward congregants who devoted more effort to extracting New England's natural riches—fish, fur, wool, lumber, grain, hay, meat—than to cultivating godliness in the human heart. Religious disagreements divided church members; the splits became final when the disgruntled settled land elsewhere. Colonists who migrated in search of fresh soil to accommodate growing families and burgeoning herds of livestock further weakened the ideal of the tight-knit religious community. The dynamic of fragmentation, dispersal, and expansion threatened the territory of nearby Indians. The colonists had much to dread: a contingent and unstable environment, social disintegration, and potentially hostile tribes.[51]

In the midst of this environmental and social instability, New Englanders saw more witches than ever before. In 1647, Alice Young of Windsor, Connecticut, just upriver from Wethersfield, was the first colonist to be tried and executed for witchcraft. The following year, Mary Johnson of Wethersfield confessed to diabolical activities and swung by the neck for her crimes. Over the next twenty years, magistrates across New England indicted some fifty people, most of them women, and executed thirteen. Allegations of witchcraft were leveled at many others, such as Mary Dyer, the Quaker.[52] Satan and his minions seemed to be everywhere.

The most fearsome episode of witchcraft prosecution took place at Hartford, not far from Wethersfield. On a Sunday night in late March 1661, eight-year-old Elizabeth Kelly awoke in a delirium and cried out that a neighbor, Goodwife Ayres, was choking and pinching her. The girl complained of Ayres's torments into the next day, and she begged her father to find the woman and cut off her head with an ax. On Tuesday night, Elizabeth's sorrowful parents watched their beloved daughter reach an agonizing end. "Goodwife Ayres chokes me" were her final words. A string of indictments and trials followed as townspeople accused one another of diabolical crimes. Ayres fled the community, avoiding prosecution even as her husband, also under suspicion, pointed his finger at someone else. That person, Rebecca Greensmith, soon drew other accusations. One man claimed to have witnessed a satanic rite in a nearby forest during which several local women—Greensmith among them—danced around "two black creatures like two Indians, but taller."[53] At her trial, Greensmith admitted that she had "familiarity" with Satan. He had "carnal knowledge of her body," she testified, and "under a tree in the green," she and other witches had "danced and had a bottle of sack." Although she said she had no covenant with Satan, she had planned to seal her bargain with him come Christmas. Before she finished her confession, she implicated several more people. In the end, she, her husband, and two other people went to the gallows.[54]

Now, a few years after the Hartford cases, Katherine Harrison was under indictment. Harrison was feisty, and she was determined not to depart this world at the end of a rope. But the odds were against her. There were good reasons why a woman—a particular kind of woman—was vulnerable to charges of witchcraft and why her crops had been destroyed and her animals molested. Those reasons bore some relationship to biophysical conditions. And they had everything to do with Puritan notions of what was natural—and what was not.

Like other Puritan women, Harrison was expected to fulfill the natural, God-given, hierarchical Order of Creation. She was supposed to be a subordinate companion to her husband, help him build a household, and bear children and nurture life. But in virtually every respect, Harrison had transcended— or transgressed—those roles. After John Harrison died in 1666, she did not remarry. By then in her forties, she was an aging woman approaching the biological limit of her procreative powers. The £929 estate that John left her and their three daughters put her in an economic position like that of a man—and with no male heir to whom she would bequeath her wealth. To add to her aberrant and undesirable characteristics, she was contentious: she had slandered some of her neighbors, sued others, and opposed at least one—a man—in a dispute over land. In a supremely patriarchal society, Katherine Harrison was a threat, a source of instability and fear.[55]

The accusations against her highlighted her diabolical inversion of woman's essential nature. Rather than healing a sick man, her ministrations worsened his condition. Rather than nurturing children, she tortured and killed them. No less corrupt were her relationships with animals. Livestock and other domestic creatures were economically central to colonial society, and they carried profound symbolic significance. Cattle converted New England greenery into valuable milk, flesh, and hide, but cattle-keeping also differentiated English culture from Indian culture and thus demarcated civilization from savagery. Women often tended cattle, particularly cows, not simply for practicality's sake but because milk and milking were emblematic of women and their primary responsibility for fostering life. Yet again Harrison upended

God's order, reportedly transforming calves into monsters and illicitly diverting the flow of milk to evil ends.[56] No wonder, then, that Harrison's resentful and vindictive neighbors, when they sought to punish her, killed two of her heifers and wounded another in the udder. The attackers struck at the undeserved, milky material gain of a woman out of place, a woman on top—a witch.

Harrison did everything she could to rescue herself. She enlisted the support of the few friends, neighbors, and relatives who would attest to the wrongs done to her. She made contrite apologies—I am "a female, a weaker vessel, subject to passion"—while countering her accusers and petitioning the magistrates for relief. She even proposed a test, "trying whether she could sink or swim in the water." This ancient mode of examination assumed that the truth could be found at the intersection of the natural and the supernatural, the visible and the invisible worlds. The guilty, it was believed, would float when thrown into a lake or pond, while the innocent would sink. Surely Harrison and the Wethersfield magistrates knew that during the recent Hartford cases, authorities had administered the trial by water to two accused witches, probably Rebecca Greensmith and her husband. But the Wethersfield court, perhaps aware that the water test itself bore a dangerous resemblance to magical practice, did not follow through. The final decision would rest on the oral testimony of Harrison's neighbors.[57]

In October 1669, after lengthy delays, the jury rendered its verdict: guilty. It must have been terrifying for Harrison to contemplate her impending doom. Yet just as the end seemed near, the magistrates drew back, apparently because they did not think the evidence was strong enough to execute her. In May 1670, after reviewing the case once more, they issued a sentence. Harrison would live, but in addition to paying fines, she must suffer banishment from the colony.[58]

Katherine Harrison had evaded the gallows. Yet her case did not mark the end of New England's harrowing experience of Satan. Quite the contrary, for the future would be terrifyingly grim, the landscape awash in blood. And witches—many more witches—would swing.

THE IDOL OF NEW ENGLAND

Hellish might be a suitable adjective for the following scenes, the likes of which appeared again and again across New England in 1675–1676:

Outside Falmouth, a settlement on Casco Bay in Maine, the northern frontier of Massachusetts, six dead sprawl amid the charred remains of a house. In the doorway lie the half-burned corpses of Thomas Wakely and his wife. Wakely had been a devout Puritan, but soon after arriving in New England he had moved his family to Falmouth, a small community without an established church. His neighbors had criticized him for settling so far from them. When word arrived of an impending Indian raid, they had urged him to get his family into town, but he had not done so. The ruins of his life now testify to the attachment he felt for his home. Near him are his adult son, his body riddled with musket balls and his head smashed; Wakely's pregnant daughter-in-law, scalped; and two grandchildren, face down, their heads broken apart, an oak plank across their backs. Three other family members are missing. . . .[59]

Strewn along a small, muddy stream lie the bodies of Capt. Thomas Lathrop and some sixty other men, a number of them from Pocumtuck (also known as Deerfield), Massachusetts. The day before, they had collected more than three thousand bushels of stacked corn in Pocumtuck meadow, one of the rich bottomlands astride the Connecticut River. Then they had hauled the crop south toward Hadley, where it would be safer. They had moved slowly and deliberately, Lathrop assuming that the size of his command would deter an attack by Indians. When they arrived at the stream, they stopped to pick some wild grapes. It was, it turned out, their final repast. Many of them now lack scalps and clothing. The next day, Sunday, they will lie together in a mass grave. The stream will become known as Bloody Brook. . . .[60]

At Andover and Chelmsford, Massachusetts, north of Boston in Essex County, people are in a terrible fright. They have garrisoned themselves in a few houses and there await assault by Natives. Outside, a miserable cow wanders across the landscape, one of its horns knocked off and its tongue cut out. Communities around New England witness similar atrocities. Livestock—in some cases entire herds—lie slaughtered on the ground, stumble around without eyes or legs, or, bellies sliced open, trail their guts behind them. Back in Essex County, a hovel containing a horse suddenly goes up in flames. . . .[61]

On the Mount Hope Peninsula in Rhode Island, soldiers from Massachusetts and Plymouth under Major Thomas Savage come across a Bible. It is torn, and its pages are scattered about. Not far back, the troops had passed several houses recently burned. What awaits them farther on, they can only guess. After several miles, they find poles driven into the ground by the side of the road. Stuck on the poles are the heads, scalps, *and hands of Englishmen. Major Savage orders the men to take down the body parts and bury them. . . .*[62]

Inside the burning home, some forty or fifty men, women, and children are stricken with fear. They can hear shouts, screams, and gunshots outside, and they know that the rest of the town—Lancaster, in east-central Massachusetts—is on fire. As the flames shoot up around them, they are near panic. Some beseech the Lord for deliverance. Others act on the overwhelming urge to flee. But when Mary Rowlandson opens the door, musket balls—like a handful of rocks—rattle the house. The colonists' dilemma is excruciating. They can remain inside, certain to perish in the smoke and flames, or they can run for it. Finally, the beleaguered families burst out. Only one person makes it. Twelve die in the bloodbath. The rest find themselves in the clutches of what Mistress Rowlandson likens to a pack of roaring hellhounds. . . .[63]

Breathtaking in its boldness, ferocity, and destructiveness, the Indian uprising of 1675–1676 rocked New England to its core. Wampanoags, Narragansetts, Nipmucks, Abenakis, and other Algonquians attempted to remove virtually all traces of English civilization from their midst. They destroyed some twenty-five towns, more than half of New England's total. They burned houses, barns, fences, crops, and churches and defiled Bibles. They tortured, disfigured, and slaughtered cattle and horses. They peeled skin and scalps from captives, stripped and mutilated the dead, and displayed heads and other body parts as trophies. And they abducted men, women, and children in an effort to restore their own diminished populations. When, after fourteen months, the conflict finally came to an end, perhaps a thousand colonists had perished. Thousands more, now homeless, crowded into settlements along the coast. With its economy severely disrupted and its people in profound turmoil, New England verged on ruin.[64]

The Indians had good reason, in their view, for wreaking such havoc. Many resented English pressure on their land. By 1670, the colonial population had risen to some fifty-two thousand. A new generation had come of age, and now it needed land for families and livestock. To get that land, colonists probed vulnerable Indian neighbors, looking for sachems and villages willing to sell and taking advantage of their dependency on the English economy for firearms and other goods. Intertwined with the Indians' loss of land were disputes over animals. Although the colonists acquired new land through purchase, their wandering livestock still encroached on Indian villages and resources. Cattle and horses devastated Indian crops, and hogs fed on clam beds and raided stores of corn. Indians protested, but colonists proved less interested in paying compensation than in protecting their animals from retaliation.[65]

The problems compounded. To counteract their loss of land and the food it provided, some Indians began keeping and selling hogs. The characteristics of hogs made them a convenient supplement to Indian subsistence practices. The creatures resembled the Indians' dogs, and unlike cows, they did not require milking, special feeding, and other kinds of care. The more that Indians acted like the English, however, the greater the antipathy the English felt. The colonists were not as accepting of Indian swine as they thought the Indians should be of English livestock. The Indians' growing resentment eventually exploded in attacks on colonists and in the destruction and torture of their animals.[66]

Conflict between Wampanoag Indians and Plymouth colonists sparked the war. Metacom, the sachem known to the English as King Philip, purportedly conspired to attack Plymouth, and the colony decided to punish him and enrich itself in the process. For Philip, the price of peace was submission and land loss. In 1671, he conceded to Plymouth the authority to negotiate Wampanoag land sales without his approval. Four years later, Plymouth executed three tribal members for murdering John Sassamon, a Christian Indian who reported that Philip again was preparing for war. In retaliation for these insults, a group of Wampanoag warriors attacked the English settlement at Swansea. Philip then joined his tribesmen in a general uprising against the colonies. As the Indians gained allies and put the English on the run, they grew confident in their power, their manitou.[67]

The English, too, recognized the influence of the supernatural in the course of events, although they viewed it differently from the way the Indians did. Puritan ministers depicted the war as a chapter in the cosmic struggle between good and evil. God, they said, had stirred up the Indians—"those perfect children of the Devil"—in order to punish the colonists for their sins: too much drinking and swearing, too much tolerance of Quakers, too much pride and willingness to pursue material gain at the expense of God's ways.[68] Because of their "inordinate affection of the world," lamented Increase Mather, their covenanted communities had crumbled. "*Land! Land!* has been the idol of many in New England," he fairly shouted. The first colonists, "that they might keep themselves together," were "satisfied with one acre for each person," and "after that with twenty acres for a family." Now they "coveted after the earth," so "that many hundreds, nay thousands, of acres have been engrossed by one man, and they that profess themselves Christians have forsaken churches, and ordinances, and all for land and elbow-room enough in the world." The consequences of such ambitions had fallen hard on everyone, Mather asserted, even on Thomas Wakely, the devout man who had lost his life and family in the attack on Falmouth.[69]

To redeem themselves in God's eyes, Mather and other Puritan leaders told the colonists, they must reverse their path. They must recover the old ways, honor the fathers, and resume the original errand into the wilderness. Above all, they must lay waste to their enemies. Earnest prayers, fasting, days of public humiliation, and stricter ordinances soon followed.[70] So did military reprisals, and with a vengeance: English attacks matched those of Indians in cruelty but far surpassed them in total devastation.

Much as in the Pequot War some forty years before, the colonists retaliated with extreme brutality. In December 1675, for example, an English fighting force some one thousand strong, one of the largest assembled in the New World to that time, traveled deep into Rhode Island's Pocasset Swamp and there attacked the enormous log fort of the ostensibly neutral Narragansetts. After storming the enclosure, the English set fire to its wigwams. As women and children ran from the smoke and flames, the soldiers cut them down. When the screaming stopped, hundreds lay dead.[71] Smaller incidents, no less savage, added to the stain. At Marblehead, a coastal community packed with grieving refugees, a crowd of angry women tore apart and decapitated some captive Indian men, leaving "their flesh in a manner pulled from their bones." Samuel Mosely, a military commander who hated even the Christianized Praying Indians, interrogated a Native woman and then ordered her to be "torn to pieces by dogs." The English, too, took their share of trophies, the most prized being the head of King Philip, which they stuck on a palisade at Plymouth.[72]

Colonial forces did not ravage every New England Indian tribe during the conflict. Old allies, notably Uncas and his Mohegan warriors, took their side. So did some Praying Indians, and so did the few remnant Pequots, who seized the opportunity to exact revenge against their former enemies, the Narragansetts. Still other tribes attempted to remain neutral amid the bloodshed.[73]

For most Indians, however, even those who wanted to avoid conflict, the war proved disastrous. The English attack on the Narragansett fortress destroyed the tribe's neutrality as well as hundreds of its people. When a thousand or more Narragansetts joined in the struggle against the colonists, the Wampanoags rejoiced, but even that infusion of manpower could not help the rebellious tribes in the long run. Weakened by battle, disease, and starvation, desperately short on gunpowder, arms, and ammunition, they eventually gave up the fight. Some three thousand, perhaps one-quarter of New England's Native population, were dead.[74] In a final, devastating blow, the English sold thousands more, many of them women and children, into slavery. The war even took a terrible toll on the passive Praying Indians, who had surrendered their fates to colonial officials. Massachusetts removed an entire community of them to Deer Island in Boston Harbor, where hundreds died of starvation and exposure.[75] Their tragic fate was the price they paid for English antipathy to all Native people. For the Wampanoags, one of the colonists' principal antagonists, the conflict was absolutely ruinous. Besides so many lives, the tribe lost all its land. Despite Puritan concerns about the English lust for land, the colonists were only too happy to take it from their conquered foes.

Although New Englanders congratulated themselves on their victory and found comfort in what they believed was their restoration to God's grace, their troubles were far from over. The war weakened them economically and politically, leaving them deeply in debt and vulnerable to the designs of British imperial administrators. More ominously, the conflict intensified their enemies' thirst for revenge. Indian refugees headed north and west to join other Algonquians and French Catholic allies in future raids against New England settlements. Well into the eighteenth century, in recurring cycles of slaughter and retaliation, the fighting dragged on.[76]

In this insecure environment of land hunger, pestilence, ravaged villages, refugees, war wounds, and nightmares, New England's vaunted wilderness errand stumbled into a dreadful heart of darkness.

IN THE DEVIL'S SNARE

Poised on that unforgiving margin between the visible and invisible worlds, Martha Carrier—the purported agent of Benjamin Abbott's sickness and the bane of Andover—had only a few moments left in which to reflect on her life. Her fate had been sealed two weeks before, on August 5, 1692, when the court had decided against her. Confined to jail, she had waited for the appointed day when a wooden cart would arrive to carry her and four other condemned criminals, all men, through the streets of Salem and to the hill upon which stood the gallows. That day of reckoning had come at last, and now, facing the crowd that had gathered to watch them die, Carrier and her companions prepared to offer their final words.[77]

Martha Carrier's passage to this place had been deeply dispiriting. Poverty, illness, vicious gossip, and fights with neighbors and relatives over land and animals had marked the beginnings of her travail. Then had come the formal complaints—of festering boils, sick cattle, and other strange occurrences—from Benjamin and Sarah Abbott, Allen Toothaker, and Samuel Preston. Those colonists were not alone in their accusations. John Roger, a farmer in the town of Billerica, Carrier's former residence, stepped forward to complain of her malice toward his livestock. His reliable milk cow suddenly had gone dry. Of his "two large lusty sows," he had found one dead, its ears cut off, and the other simply had disappeared. At Andover, Phoebe Chandler, a twelve-year-old neighbor, complained that she had heard Carrier's disembodied voice threaten to poison her. Shortly thereafter, Chandler's face and part of her right hand had swelled, and she had felt such a "great weight" on her chest and legs that she could scarcely move. When Richard Carrier, Martha's son, had looked at her during church services, she said, pain had shot through her hand, her stomach burned, and she became so deaf that she could hear neither prayer nor song.[78]

More demoralizing still were the allegations of fifteen-year-old Mary Lacey, her mother, also named Mary Lacey, and her grandmother, Ann Foster. The younger Lacey claimed that Carrier had enlisted her in the devil's work and that she had accompanied Carrier on errands to afflict people. Carrier, she said, had murdered several of her victims, including children, with "pins, needles, and knitting needles." Lacey's mother and grandmother confirmed the girl's claims; both women said they had traveled with Carrier to a witches' meeting at Salem. According to the Laceys, Satan would reward Martha Carrier's service. He would make her, Carrier supposedly had told them, the "Queen of Hell."[79]

On top of the Lacey and Foster allegations, a group of girls in Salem complained that Carrier, in spectral form, had attacked them. The authorities had arrested Carrier and interrogated her in the presence of her accusers. During the questioning, the girls said that Carrier's apparition had bitten and pinched them, pricked them with a needle, and threatened to cut their throats if they did not sign her book and confirm their allegiance to Satan. Falling "into most intolerable outcries and agonies," they insisted that a "black man"—the devil—had accompanied Carrier, that he was whispering in her ear, and that they could see the ghosts of thirteen people whom she had murdered. Astonished, Carrier defended herself. She knew of no "black man." The girls were liars, "out of their wits." It was "shameful" that the authorities paid attention to them. Their charges were "false," for "the Devil is a liar." Carrier's protestations were useless. When the authorities bound her hands and feet, the girls' apparent torments ceased.[80]

Most disheartening of all were the confessions of Carrier's own children, who, probably out of fear or because of coercion, had turned against their mother. The younger Mary Lacey had implicated Richard Carrier, eighteen, and his brother Andrew, sixteen. During his interrogation, Richard admitted that he was "in the Devil's snare" and that he had "set [his] hand" in a "little red book" belonging to a black man who had promised him new clothing and a horse. He said he had attended meetings in a pasture with dozens of people, and with them had drunk wine and "covenanted with the Devil." Worse, he had hurt people by squeezing likenesses of them, and he had stabbed one man with a spindle. On some occasions, he declared, his mother had been with him. Andrew also confessed to diabolical crimes and, like Richard, claimed to have received the devil's baptism in a nearby river. His mother, moreover, had been present when he had signed the black man's book.[81]

The youngest Carrier children added still more weight to the case against their mother. A yellow bird had spoken to Thomas Jr., and he had attended a meeting at which people rode on poles. Not only that, but his mother had threatened to tear him to pieces if he did not set his hand in her book. His sister Sarah, almost eight years old, declared that she had touched her mother's red book and been baptized in Andrew Foster's pasture, and that her mother, while in jail, had come to her in the shape of a black cat.[82] The Carrier children's testimony was damning, to say the least, and there was little that Martha could do about it.

By the time Martha Carrier's life began to disintegrate, Essex County was in an uproar. Girls in Andover and Salem, including those who later accused Carrier, were at the center of the crisis. Some had experimented with divination and other occult practices and then claimed to be afflicted by witches.[83] Their accusations ramified as confessors accused or implicated others, who in turn confessed and then accused or implicated still more. The pattern ultimately seemed to reveal a satanic conspiracy of frightening proportions. Entire families shattered as its sinister outlines came to light in the complaints and confessions.[84] Martha Emerson, Allen Toothaker's sister and Carrier's niece and namesake, said that her aunt and another woman, Mary Green, had grabbed her by the throat and would not let her confess. Mary Toothaker, Carrier's sister and the mother of Allen and Martha, declared that she had attended spectral meetings with Carrier and her sons Richard and Andrew. In turn, Richard Carrier identified his aunt Mary and cousin Martha as participants in diabolical activities. Even Roger Toothaker, Allen and Martha's father and Mary's husband, soon found himself suspect and under arrest.[85]

Many other families and individuals participated in the nightmare, as accusers, confessors, or deniers. By the time the crisis ended, magistrates had taken legal action against at least 144 people. Some endured long, painful periods in jail, awaiting trial or sentencing. Four-year-old Dorothy Good, for example, was confined in heavy irons for nine months, an experience from which she never recovered. Others, like Roger Toothaker, died before magistrates decided their cases. One man, Giles Corey, expired under the weight of stones that officials stacked on his chest to force him to enter a plea. Nineteen—including Martha Carrier—went to the gallows.[86]

The Essex County witchcraft crisis of 1692 unfolded from colonial society's inherent instability. New Englanders were a hierarchical, patriarchal, and communal people who prized order, consensus, and fidelity to a social and religious code. Security, they believed, depended on the rigorous maintenance of proper social relationships and right beliefs. Such rigidity, however, could be a source of weakness as much as strength. Puritans were convinced of their sinfulness and susceptibility to evil, which predisposed them to believe that Satan could, and probably did, hold them in his thrall. Once allegations of witchcraft began, pressure to conform and admit guilt intensified. This was especially so when people realized that confession, not an assertion of innocence, was the surest way to avoid execution.[87] Essex County colonists might have recovered their equilibrium quickly if the motivations for their accusations had stopped with their doubts about themselves. But the additional sources of instability were too overwhelming.

Among the greatest of these was the colonists' relationship to nature. Puritans tried to establish a rigid social order based on an unvarying set of beliefs, but they did so in a world that shifted beneath their feet. Fixed social objectives were difficult to achieve in a world of unstable physical matter. Human and animal populations rose and fell in relation to a land base that changed according to the economic practices of the people who lived on it. The collapse of Indian populations from war and disease enabled the expansion of fertile colonial families, yet that very demographic increase—and the livestock boom that accompanied it—placed enormous stress on the ideal of the stable, corporate Puritan community. Within agricultural towns and villages, people fought over ever-diminishing slivers of soil. Sometimes the strain was too great, and communities fractured and broke apart, the embittered leaving for new settlements elsewhere. Even as Indian tribes contracted and the survivors searched for alternatives to lost clam beds, deer, plant foods, and other subsistence resources, they disputed—sometimes violently—the colonists' appetite for open space.

The natural sources of social upset extended right down to the organic bodies the colonists inhabited. Everyone knew that people aged, sickened, and died. Yet an inflexible social order often did not—and perhaps could not—accommodate the vagaries of the life course or the practical choices that individual people made in response to them. Robert Prince of Salem died suddenly and left his property to his wife, Sarah, an aging woman who was losing, or had lost, her fertility. Years alone had rendered Sarah suspect, but the doubts only deepened when she married a much younger man with whom she conspired to deprive her own growing sons of their inheritance.[88] In this haphazard, contingent process, rigid social ideals met their limits in individual human choices and the biological transformation of bodily tissues. To the extent that the world shifted and upset social expectations, colonists grew fearful. Nothing so much as fear—of the unknown, the anomalous, the out-of-order, the disruptive—enflamed the diabolical imagination.

The fear that ran through Essex County during its witchcraft crisis was rooted in the colonists' conflicts with Indians over land and its natural resources—its plants, fish, fur, and soil. Strife had continued in the aftermath of the 1675–1676 uprising. Sporadic Indian raids—on the Maine and New Hampshire frontiers and on the periphery of Essex County—intensified during the late 1680s and continued for a decade. In 1688, war erupted when Abenakis attacked the repopulated colonial settlements around Casco Bay in retaliation for their usurpation of Native land. With the help of French forces, the Abenakis conquered Pemaquid in 1689 and, the next year, Salmon Falls and Falmouth. Farther south, Indians attacked Andover in 1689, and Lancaster, Brookfield, and Billerica two years later. In addition to the slaughter and capture of colonists, the movements of refugees and smallpox-infected soldiers destabilized the region and heightened the general feeling of alarm.[89]

Internal pressures in Essex County added to the sense of crisis. Like the stresses that came from without, these inner strains derived from environmental conditions, especially social conflicts over relatively scarce land. Continued population growth exacerbated land and boundary disputes between communities and individuals. Residents of affluent and cosmopolitan Salem Town, a community situated on a fine natural harbor with access to the Atlantic trade, bickered with the people of adjacent Salem Village, a dispersed rural settlement with stonier soil and fewer economic prospects. Within Salem Village, a growing population and shrinking farms fueled bitter rivalries between neighbors over the remaining soil.[90]

Salem was hardly alone in experiencing these kinds of troubles. Andover, which lay immediately northwest of Salem Village, knew them well. By the latter part of the seventeenth century, the town no longer granted relatively large tracts to its inhabitants. Those who owned extensive properties sought to consolidate their control with firmer boundaries and more precise legal records. Everyone else—young people without an inheritance or newcomers to the town—could acquire plots of twenty acres and no more. As the opportunity for land diminished, signs of discontent began to appear.[91]

Connections between environmental pressures and witchcraft fears were evident in the lives of many Andover inhabitants, but perhaps none more so than Martha Carrier. The people of Andover had blamed Martha and her children for bringing smallpox into the town, but the Carriers probably were as much victims as agents of the 1690 epidemic, which the war against the Indians had intensified.[92] Massed and mobile bodies of soldiers and refugees are notorious transmitters of disease, including smallpox, yet the entry of the virus into Andover must have been difficult, if not impossible, to trace with precision. Who was responsible for its sinister infiltration of the town? Was it a refugee or returning soldier? Contentious, spiteful, and poor, Martha Carrier was an obvious culprit. Who better to blame for assisting Satan's dark deed?

War, environmental turmoil, and witchcraft touched Martha Carrier's life in other ways. Allen Toothaker, Carrier's nephew, had served in the military against the Indians, and the jibes of his aunt (she "told me I would never be cured") had done nothing to make his wound less hurtful.[93] Insult heaped upon an injury that mysteriously refused to heal suggested the influence of malicious magic. Mary Toothaker nursed her own war injury, although of a more psychic nature, and this, too, shaped Carrier's fate. The wars and Indian attacks on Andover, Billerica, and other towns had traumatized Mary. When questioned about her involvement in witchcraft, she revealed that her fear of Indians had left her "discontented" and "troubled" and that she often dreamed of fighting her tormentors. As a result, when "the Devil appeared to her in the shape of a tawny man and promised to keep her from the Indians and she should have happy days with her son," she scraped her mark in the white, flakey birch bark that he held before her.[94] Others, like Toothaker, represented Satan as an Indian. The ears sliced from John Roger's fine, lusty sow suggested an attack by a vengeful tribesman, and much as in the Wethersfield man's witness of the satanic rite involving "two black creatures like two Indians," the devil often appeared to colonists around 1692 as a "black man."[95] It was a black man who whispered into Martha Carrier's ear, the Salem girls said. In such terrifying images of Indians and war, Satan haunted the dreams of Essex County colonists, to the detriment of people like Carrier.

The environmental stresses and fears that undid Martha Carrier finally came down to land and animals. The Carriers were a marginal family with limited access to increasingly dear land, and their neighbors evidently resented both their acquisition of a small parcel and their desire for a little more. Livestock conditions, too, seemed to have worked against the family. The narrowing confines of Andover and other Essex County settlements must have imposed as much stress on animals as on the human population that tended them. It is difficult from a remove of some three centuries to know what to make, exactly, of so many reports of sick and dying cattle, but it takes no great leap from the evidence to imagine that Essex County's witchcraft crisis gathered emotional energy from an ecological crisis in its herds.[96] Like people, cattle are susceptible to diseases that are most virulent under congested conditions. Perhaps the human crowding that provoked disputes over land was related to an animal crowding that suddenly sickened and killed cattle and that farmers attributed to the malign influence of witches.

Animals were not just victims of witchcraft; they were, in certain forms, its accomplices as well. When Richard Carrier admitted that he had been "in the Devil's snare," and when his sister Sarah declared that she had received baptism in a pasture, the animal nature of Satan's diabolical landscape came into view. All manner of strange creatures troubled that twilight environment: yellow birds and black cats that whispered in people's ears; a black pig that appeared by the bed at night and blue ones that darted between horses' legs; a monkey with a cock's feet and claws; a talking fly; a shape-shifting cat-dog-turtle that moved with the speed of a horse.[97] Martha Carrier herself reportedly appeared to her daughter and other people in the form of a black cat. Magistrates wondered if they might find on her body a small fleshy protuberance, a "witch's teat," whereat her animal "familiar" suckled. Almost certainly they searched her naked flesh for it, a final humiliation intended to confirm her guilt.[98]

Like Carrier, the four men who accompanied her to the gallows found themselves caught in accusations that arose from the unstable social and environmental bases of colonial society. Firm believers in social hierarchy, all four evidently maintained it by their cruel treatment of their wives and young female servants. Not only did their behavior provoke witchcraft accusations against them, but it did nothing to reassure their neighbors, many of whom had additional reasons to doubt their integrity. John Proctor thrashed Mary Warren, his family's servant, and when she turned against him, so did people who lived on the Village side of Salem. Although Proctor kept a tavern and owned some seven hundred acres of land on the edge of the Village, his social and economic interests connected him to Salem Town. Similar circumstances ensnared John Willard. A land speculator, Willard abused his wife, which probably did not endear him to his in-laws, a family of marginal subsistence farmers on the Village fringe. When the opportunity presented itself, they tore into him with accusations of malefic activities.[99]

Connections to the land wars on the troubled Maine frontier helped to bring down the two other condemned men, George Jacobs Sr. and George Burroughs. Jacobs had a household servant named Sarah Churchwell. The off-spring of a prominent Maine family, Churchwell had arrived in Salem Village as a refugee from the war with the Abenakis. Dislocated and with sadly diminished prospects, she confessed to having fallen in with Satan. Angry about her confession and frustrated with her failure to perform her duties, Jacobs called her a "bitch witch" and very likely beat her. Churchwell assessed the situation somewhat differently. Her master had "afflicted her," she said, and she accused him of witchcraft.[100]

More prominent in the crisis was Burroughs, the former minister to Salem Village. A thrice-married widower, he had moved to Maine and there narrowly escaped the Indian attacks at Falmouth in 1676 and 1689. His miraculous good fortune, his involvement in land and clerical disputes, and his tragic and abusive relationships with his wives probably made him suspect in the eyes of many people. Among his accusers was Mercy Lewis, a young woman who had known Burroughs in Falmouth and whose family—unlike Burroughs—had died at the hands of the Abenakis. Lewis and other young women depicted Burroughs as a "black man" who had conspired with Satan to help the Indians in the war and who had become the ringleader of the monstrous conspiracy to subvert Essex County. For his service, his accusers said, the devil would make him the King of Hell, a fitting counterpart to Martha Carrier.[101]

That Burroughs and the others were men, and relatively affluent, powerful men at that, suggests how extreme the witchcraft crisis had become. But their status as prominent men also gave them greater means to defend themselves. Personal connections were important, and ministers and friends outside Essex County stepped forward to defend them.[102] Literacy, a relatively rare skill in the seventeenth century, helped them as well. On July 23, John Proctor composed a letter to Increase Mather and other leading New England clergymen protesting the legal proceedings that had landed him and the four other people, including Martha Carrier, in jail. Proctor charged that magistrates had tortured Carrier's sons Richard and Andrew as well as his own son William. The magistrates had "tied them neck and heels," he complained, until "the blood was ready to come" from the noses of Richard and Andrew and until the "blood gushed" from William's. "These actions," he asserted, "are very like the Popish cruelties."[103] They also expressed the fears of an insecure society struggling to counter the social and environmental changes that were cracking it apart. If the authorities could not have a voluntary confession, if the world did not fit their conception of reality, then they would win confession by torture, by forcing the world to fit the inflexible design they envisioned for it.

Proctor, Willard, Jacobs, Burroughs, and Carrier might have offered their confessions and thus easily saved their lives. But they did not. Perhaps they all shared a measure of stubborn integrity in the face of the charges leveled against them. Perhaps, too, they had good reason to believe that their protests might clear their names. Already doubts were beginning to arise over the validity of witchcraft trials based on "spectral evidence," on the mere word of the accusers that diabolical apparitions magically pinched, squeezed, choked, stabbed, cut, bit, and threatened them. Those doubts built on a strain of enlightened rationalism that, for some time, had been exerting a subtle but growing influence on English thought and jurisprudence.[104] It had swayed some physicians and clergymen, who believed that a malformed birth was a natural, not a diabolical, event. It had shaped the outlook of the Wethersfield judges, who had refused to dunk Katherine Harrison and who were reluctant to execute her. It had been present, for that matter, in the Essex County proceedings, in the magistrates' zealous desire to find empirical proof in the form of a telling physical mark on a witch's body.

If Carrier and the others grasped the trend, perhaps they imagined that it might pull them into a future in which the law would exonerate them. Shortly after the trials ended and the last executions were carried out, officials and accusers would begin to retract their charges and recant their claims. Even the ministers would reverse themselves. In October 1692, fourteen of them would sign Increase Mather's sermon denouncing the use of spectral evidence, and at last Governor William Phips would suspend the trials.[105] Such actions marked the uneasy transition to a new intellectual world, one far more flexible, pragmatic, and resilient than that of the early Puritans and one in which ghosts, demons, witches, and the devil himself would have no formal standing in a court of law.

As of August 19, 1692, however, that future had yet to arrive. The petitions and protests were of no use. The magistrates and other colonial officials would not be moved. Martha Carrier, John Proctor, John Willard, George Jacobs Sr., and George Burroughs must hang, must accept the fact that their bodies would serve as object lessons to anyone who might be tempted into a pact with the devil. Cut down from the gallows, they would repose not in a cemetery, the resting place of the devout, but in an ignominious rocky crevice under a thin layer of soil that would scarcely conceal their rotting carcasses. Hands, chin, and one foot protruding into the air, Burroughs's corpse would become yet another trophy by which New England declared its conquest of darkness.[106]

Martha Carrier and the others died bravely. Facing the throng, they asserted their innocence and stated their hope that no more blood be shed on false accounts. They forgave their accusers and absolved the juries and judges who had condemned them. They prayed that God would find the real witches and that the Redeemer would pardon the colonists' sins. Burroughs then stepped forward and recited perfectly the Lord's Prayer, an impossible task for a witch, according to popular belief. In spite of the emotion that rippled through the crowd, the executions went forward. While Burroughs swung, the Reverend Cotton Mather, Increase's son, called on the spectators to remember that the devil could appear as "an Angel of Light."[107]

At last Martha Carrier stood on the brink. The tortured errand into the wilderness—an errand that had crossed a considerable stretch of dark and bloody ground by August 1692—had come down to her. And then, the noose her final connection to the living, she dropped away. Her death and the deaths of those who accompanied her would not be in vain, for they freed colonists to find a more harmonious relation among spiritual essence, material condition, and social form. Some of those thinkers proposed to shine the light of reason into the deepest recesses of the universe and by such means discover the laws of nature—or Nature—upon which they might build a new order for the ages. ★

TWO

BY THE LAWS OF NATURE
AND OF NATURE'S GOD

Declaring American Independence

THOMAS JEFFERSON BELIEVED IN AN orderly universe. "The movements of the heavenly bodies, so exactly held in their course by the balance of centrifugal and centripetal forces," impressed him, he explained to John Adams in 1823, in a letter from Monticello, his mountaintop home in Virginia. So did "the structure of our earth itself, with [its] distribution of lands, waters and atmosphere" and "animal and vegetable bodies," and so did the "minutest particles, insects mere atoms of life, yet as perfectly organized as man or mammoth." The harmonious arrangement of all things led Jefferson to an inescapable conclusion. It would be impossible, he declared, "for the human mind not to believe that there is, in all this, design, cause and effect, up to an ultimate cause, a fabricator of all things from matter and motion, their preserver and regulator . . . and their regenerator into new and other forms."[1]

So important was the universe's order to Jefferson that he thought it should serve as the basis of society. Through the exercise of reason and the senses—natural capacities of the mind and body—people should determine the nature of heaven, earth, and humanity, too, and they should arrange their institutions accordingly. Above all, people should construct the form of government that was most reasonable because it most respected the true nature of mankind. Jefferson invoked nature's timeless truths—its natural laws—in all parts of his life, from the house in which he lived to the epochal event to which his name became forever linked: the American Revolution. Because he believed that all things bore some relationship to nature, his life and ideas offer a convenient place to begin exploring the Revolution's environmental history.[2]

The Jeffersonian window into the Revolution opens at Monticello, "little mountain," which he built to express the eternal verities of the universe. He began construction in 1769, when he was in his mid-twenties, but in 1796, having refined his understanding of architecture, he decided to start over. Although the project consumed the rest of his life and stood unfinished at his death in 1826, he completed enough of it to fulfill his purposes. Inspired by Andrea Palladio, the Italian Renaissance architect, he designed it in geometrically perfect proportions that expressed, in his manner of thinking, the universe's natural laws. Among its eye-catching features were the east and west porticoes and a segmented dome. Consisting of smooth Doric columns supporting triangular pediments, the porticoes recalled the classical civilizations' devotion to mathematical symmetry and ratios. Atop Monticello, like a cap symbolizing the authority of nature and reason, sat the dome, its skylight offering a glimpse of heaven, and its circular windows, a panorama of the countryside.[3]

Jefferson made the interior of Monticello a virtual museum of the ordered cosmos, packing it with specimens, artifacts, gadgets, scientific and musical instruments, books, and art. His many clocks—essential to his astronomical observations—stood in corners, sat on mantles, and hung from walls. His parlor featured dozens of portraits, notably of the scientists Francis Bacon and Isaac Newton and the philosopher John Locke, "the three greatest men that have ever lived," Jefferson said, because they "laid the foundation of those superstructures which have been raised in the Physical and Moral sciences." Of Monticello's spaces, the entrance hall most conspicuously situated the building and its maker, in the words of a biographer, "within the history of civilization and human achievement" and "within the context of the universe and the natural world." Maps of the United States and the continents; fossils of a mastodon and a creature Jefferson called *Megalonyx*; heads and horns of elk, moose, and buffalo; robes, moccasins, and arrows of Native tribes; busts of Voltaire, Washington, and Franklin—these and more adorned the room. Above the front door loomed the Great Clock, its mechanism and hands keeping time with the universe.[4]

Jefferson's recognition of nature's order extended from Monticello to revolutionary politics. Toward the end of his life, he displayed in the entrance hall a print based on John Trumble's masterpiece, *The Declaration of Independence* (1787–1820), which depicted the moment when the new nation put the laws of nature into practice. Jefferson early on had recognized and cultivated Trumble's ability. "His natural talents for this art seem almost unparalleled," the sage of

Monticello said in 1786, and he had instructed the young man in details of the meeting at which the republic was born. Jefferson later purchased a copy of the painting for his home. Already it had the makings of an icon; to some people, it literally *was* the event it represented. As sunlight pierces the shadows of Independence Hall, the drafting committee—John Adams, Roger Sherman, Robert Livingston, Benjamin Franklin, and, most prominently, Jefferson—submits the document to the Continental Congress. The moment is both an end and a beginning, darkness retreating as a new age dawns.[5]

Jefferson kept the original draft and several copies of the Declaration of Independence at Monticello, and much as he did with the house, he and his coauthors constructed the text to reflect the universe's truths. Like Monticello, the Declaration was symmetrical in design. Like the building's halves—north and south, or front and back—the Declaration's paragraphs and sentences described two conjoined parts or phases: ending and beginning, or closing and opening. Like the building's central hall and parlor and two extensions, the document also followed a tripartite plan: a preamble and a bill of particulars culminating in a claim to independence. Finally, if the building organized objects and ideas into an explanation of man and the cosmos, then so did the Declaration. The bill of particulars was a Baconian collection—a natural history museum—of the king's violations: "He has erected a Multitude of new Offices, and sent hither Swarms of Officers to harass our People, and eat out their substance"—and so forth. Most important, however, was the text's philosophical core, which appeared in the first lines of its rhetorical entrance hall. The ideas—universal laws evident in the nature of mankind—were at once Newtonian and Lockean.[6] Like the light of reason that shone from the mountaintop, they radiated outward, a beacon to the world:

> When in the Course of human events, it becomes necessary for one people to dissolve the political bands which have connected them with another, and to assume among the Powers of the earth, the separate and equal station to which the Laws of Nature and of Nature's God entitle them, a decent respect to the opinions of mankind requires that they should declare the causes which impel them to the separation.
>
> We hold these truths to be self-evident, that all men are created equal, and that they are endowed by their Creator with certain unalienable Rights, that among these are Life, Liberty and the pursuit of Happiness. That to secure these rights, Governments are instituted

among Men, deriving their just powers from the consent of the governed. That whenever any Form of Government becomes destructive of these ends, it is the Right of the People to alter or to abolish it, and to institute new Government, laying its foundation on such principles and organizing its powers in such form, as to them shall seem most likely to effect their Safety and Happiness.

The Declaration of Independence marked a shift in ideas about nature and was integral to the environmental history of the Revolution. No longer would people such as Jefferson take received wisdom—especially revealed religion—as an article of faith. Instead, they would use their God-given, natural human capacities—reason and the senses—to discover, through experience, empirical observation, and scientific experiment, the natural laws of man and the physical matter of which he was made. Their discoveries told them that men were born with an inherent right to their thoughts, their bodies, and the things their bodies produced—their property. To protect their natural rights, including their right to property, they formed governments. If a government should violate their natural rights by controlling their lives or taking their property without their consent, then they could exercise their natural right to form a new government. The revolutionary ideas of Jefferson and his compatriots were not mere fancy. They offered a compelling description of reality, and they were—and have been ever since—extremely attractive to people the world over.[7]

As important as those ideas of nature were, they alone did not determine the course of the American Revolution, because the New World environment enabled and limited the ability of Jefferson and others to think and act. Demographic changes, an abundance of land relative to population size, climate, soils, and geographical isolation from Europe, among other factors, fostered distinctive colonial cultures and political systems and created the circumstances for an independent American republic. Those environmental conditions, however, did not always favor the Revolution; some contributed to social, economic, and political conflicts that threatened to destroy the new nation. Although Jefferson recognized a clockwork Newtonian universe, he had to acknowledge the volatility and messiness of lived experience. "I hold it," he famously told James Madison in 1787, "that a little rebellion now and then is a good thing, and as necessary in the political world as storms in the physical."[8] Reconciling fixed truths with a world in flux was not easy, as Jefferson and other revolutionaries learned.

Jefferson's Monticello, showing the integration of symmetrical architecture with the rounded, irregular terrain. One of his box-like "porticles," which allowed the flow of air and enabled him to see out while protecting his privacy, is at the right front corner of the main building.

Monticello encapsulated the problem. To build the house according to natural laws expressed in symmetrical forms, Jefferson had to take into account the irregularities of the terrain, the "law of the land," as he called it. He had to tailor the house and the site to fit each other. He had to level the mountaintop for the house and make the house seem as if it rose from the mountain. The result was an orderly structure that modified and absorbed elements of its environment. Set in the ground, it extended its symmetries outward, almost like roots, so that they mingled with curvilinear gardens, pathways, roads, and forest edges. Numerous windows and doors took in sunlight and fresh air; the dome projected the verticality of the mountain.[9]

This apparent harmony of the symmetrical and the irregular masked Jefferson's struggle to achieve it. To get water at such an elevation, he had to dig an unusually deep well. To erect the east portico, he had to correct the mistakes of workmen who misaligned and marred the columns. To insulate the house from fire, he had to replace its wooden shakes with metal roofing. To protect it from lightning—a severe danger on a mountaintop—he had to install one of Benjamin Franklin's lightning rods. Inhabiting Monticello posed challenges, too. Even as Jefferson invested it with universal truths, he invoked the "law of convenience" and installed contrivances to make its geometry more livable. In some cases, the difference between fixed truth and contingent need proved impossible to overcome. Accessible only by a narrow, inconvenient stairway and a dark hall, the dome room, or "sky room," served "miscellaneous purposes" before Jefferson finally relegated it to storage space.[10]

If he could not close the gap between ideal and experience in all parts of his house, neither could Jefferson align the two in all parts of the human community attached to it. He declared the self-evident truth that all men were created equal, but most of the men—and women—who actually leveled his mountaintop, dug his well, erected his house, and attached its lightning rod were laborers whom he enslaved. He favored those with light skin, called them servants and mechanics, and arranged their lives in ways that seemed to uplift them. Drawing on humanitarian ideas of penal reform, for example, he used incentives and rewards to discipline and train the boys who worked in his nail-making shop. He believed he was preparing them to become skilled tradesmen, but as in every other plantation activity, the aspiration did not match the reality. No matter how harmonious Monticello appeared to be, it could not mask Jefferson's violation of nature in its human form.[11]

"The very open nature of the house posed a problem" to Jefferson, the historian Annette Gordon-Reed has written. For such a public figure, he was an intensely private man. One part of his life that he most wanted to keep from view was his relationship with an enslaved woman, Sally Hemings, and the children she bore him. To protect his privacy, Jefferson invoked the law of convenience and ordered John Hemings, Sally's brother, to install louvered structures on the exterior entrances to his chambers. The "porticles," as he called them, gave him a modicum of access to outdoor nature while preventing anyone from seeing his inner world. "Jefferson never explained why he built them," according to Gordon-Reed, and they "destroyed the perfect geometric symmetry of Monticello's Palladian design."[12]

As with Jefferson, so with the nation he helped to found. The American revolutionaries posited a set of ideas about mankind and the universe, but at the core of their experiment a problem persisted. Could they reconcile the contingent nature of the republic—nonhuman and human—with the laws of nature and of nature's God?

The movement for independence that coalesced in 1776 was grounded, literally, in the European settlement of a new environment. The colonists came to a terrain geographically separate from Britain and on it tried to re-create the familiar world they had left behind. They remade the land by occupying it, farming it, and extracting its resources, but as they created a New World, something unexpected and remarkable happened: the colonists transformed themselves, too. They became new people with styles of living and forms of governance that were incompatible with those of the British Empire.[13]

American revolutionaries understood that their geographical isolation from Britain enabled their independence. "Even the distance at which the Almighty hath placed England and America," asserted Thomas Paine in 1776, "is a strong and natural proof, that the authority of the one over the other, was never the design of Heaven. . . . In no instance hath nature made the satellite larger than its primary planet, and as England and America with respect to each other reverse the common order of nature, it is evident they belong to different systems. England to Europe: America to itself." Years later, in 1803, Jefferson praised "the Almighty Being who in gathering together the waters under the heavens in one place, divided the land of [the Old World] hemisphere from the dry land of ours." Paine and Jefferson might have been wrong that geography was proof of providential design, but their claims reflected a certain truth: distance made the colonists different and predisposed them to reject British authority. America did belong to another system. The ocean did matter. Removed from Britain and ensconced in a new environment, the colonists became a different people.[14]

The geographical separation that culminated in political separation began with changes in European resources and population. The explorers who came to the New World returned to the Old with two productive and nutritious plants, potatoes and corn, which increased the food supply and made possible a massive population boom. Europe had roughly 80 million people in 1492; the number rose to 180 million by 1800. Great Britain alone had some 5 million inhabitants in 1492 and 16 million in 1800. Meanwhile, the gold and silver that Spain plundered from the New World sparked a rise in prices. More money allowed increased purchases, which allowed producers and merchants to charge more for their goods. In Britain, mounting profits encouraged landowners to produce more wool and wheat. Aided by the Enclosure Acts, landowners cut off poor villagers' customary access to the fields, forests, and pastures that provided them with food and fuel. Displaced by sheep and grain, rural folk had to find sustenance elsewhere. Some became cottagers, earning meager wages by spinning and weaving wool into textiles inside their small, spare homes. Others became vagrants, wandering the countryside in search of opportunity, stealing if necessary. The problem was too many people and too little land. The solution was migration to the American colonies, where labor was dear and land abundant.[15]

Ecological, economic, and demographic changes also encouraged those who were better off to depart for America. Middling sorts—farmers, artisans, shopkeepers—grew concerned when economic conditions in Britain worsened in the 1620s. The cloth industry went into depression, and crop failures drove up food prices. The number of impoverished people grew, as did the incidence of petty crime. Taxes for poor relief increased, especially as Parliament relieved the wealthiest Britons of that burden. The middling sorts worried about the future. Would conditions eventually push them into the ranks of the poor? What might they do to protect themselves? For thousands, the answer to such questions was immigration to North America.[16]

Deteriorating conditions alone did not compel people to restart their lives in Massachusetts or Virginia; the colonies offered attractive opportunities as well. Here was a new environment in which to gather wealth or refashion society in the image of a spiritual ideal. Not only was land relatively abundant, but it also yielded profitable crops. In the Chesapeake Bay region, British settlers in the early 1600s began raising tobacco, a New World plant that Europeans consumed with zeal, in ever greater quantities. In Pennsylvania, colonists enjoyed the fertile soils of "the best poor man's country." Other colonists came not so much to grow lucrative crops as to cultivate a particular social and religious order. The Puritans, for example, migrated to New England to create "a city upon a hill" that would stand as a model of godly behavior to the entire world.[17]

Once the colonists arrived in America, they benefited from the ecological turmoil into which they pushed Native societies. Disease, starvation, war, and enslavement removed thousands—eventually millions—of American Indians and opened up land for European crops, livestock, homes, and governments. Indians had less immunity than did Europeans to smallpox and other "crowd diseases." As British colonists occupied vacant land and modified it for European agriculture, they destroyed resources on which Indians subsisted. The colonists' livestock proved especially ruinous. Cattle wandered into Indian cornfields; pigs devoured shellfish, nuts, and Indian food caches. Conflict over land and animals generated brutal wars, which more often than not ended with Indian defeat. All these changes diminished Native populations. No one knows for certain, but it is likely that several million Indians inhabited North America in 1500. By 1800, only about six hundred thousand remained. The destruction and dispossession of enormous numbers of the New World's first peoples thus secured the colonists' safe distance from Britain and their eventual independence.[18]

The disappearance of Indians not only made way for British settlers but also contributed to a distinctive labor system that set the colonies apart from their parent country. Tobacco and rice planters in the Chesapeake region needed people to till fields and harvest crops. In short, the wealth derived from sunlight, soil, water, and plants—from nature—required labor. But as Indians died or were forced by colonists into the backcountry, they no longer offered a potential pool of workers. Migrants from Britain met some of the demand, exchanging their labor over a period of years for the cost of ocean passage. This indentured servitude created a class of exploited, poor, often landless people and eventually bred resentment and violent rebellion. During the late 1600s, planters began to draw heavily on a more satisfactory group: African slaves. Two New World plants, corn and cassava, had fueled population growth in Africa; slavers then captured a portion of that burgeoning pool of humanity and diverted it, against its will, to the Americas. As the Indians dwindled, the number of Africans and people of African ancestry increased, until by 1800 about one million inhabited the former North American colonies. American liberty thus came to rest as much on the enslavement of Africans as it did on the elimination of Indians.[19]

As Europeans overwhelmed the Indians and built an economy on slavery, their own numbers shot up, which further differentiated the colonies from Britain. Immigration accounted for a good portion of the growth. So did a healthy environment. New England had swift rivers and a temperate climate, conditions that minimized diseases such as malaria, dysentery, and typhoid. The region also had an adequate food supply and a fairly even ratio of men to women. To the south, conditions were less hospitable. But even there the expansion of settlement from swampy coastal lowlands to higher ground, increasing immunity to disease ("seasoning"), and the migration of women to the region gradually raised the birth rate and life expectancy. By the 1700s, the total number of colonists, boosted by "natural increase," was growing more quickly in North America than anywhere else in the British Empire. In 1770, about 2.1 million persons lived in North America; by the end of the century, the number had risen to 5 million. A measure of the American landscape's healthfulness and fecundity appeared in the terms that male and female colonists used to describe pregnant women: teeming, flourishing, prolific, lusty, fruitful, and big.[20]

The same environmental conditions that attracted immigrants and encouraged natural population growth made American bodies larger and more robust, as Benjamin Franklin demonstrated at a dinner party he hosted in Paris during the Revolutionary era. One can imagine the beautiful china, exquisite food, goblets of fine wine, and erudite, witty guests. The Abbé Guillaume-Thomas Raynal began to hold forth on a question that preoccupied the intellectuals of the day: whether or not "the human race had degenerated by being transplanted to another part of the Globe." Franklin and Jefferson had taken exception to the assertions of Raynal and George-Louis Leclerc, the Comte de Buffon, that New World people and animals were nature's runty offspring—small, decadent, and inferior. Now the clever Franklin saw an opening to counter Raynal. "Come, M. Abbé," he said, adopting the classic empiricist stance of Enlightenment thinkers, "let us try this question by the fact before us. We are here one half Americans, and one half French, and it happens that the Americans have placed themselves on one side of the table, and our French friends are on the other. Let both parties rise, and we will see on which side nature has degenerated."[21]

The result was telling. As William Carmichael explained it: "In fact there was not one American present who could not have tost out of the Windows one or perhaps two of the rest of the Company, if this effort depended merely on muscular force." Jefferson, who was not in attendance, relished the story: "It happened that [Franklin's] American guests were . . . of the finest stature and form; while those of the other side were remarkably diminutive, and the Abbé himself particularly, was a mere shrimp." It was a masculine show, a macho moment in U.S. foreign relations, but Franklin had drawn attention to an important fact: Americans statistically *were* larger than their Old World cousins. Even in the size and strength of their bodies, the colonists' life in the New World environment made them different and helped to distinguish them from Britons and other Europeans.[22]

While the colonists' experience of the New World created a distinctive physique, it also produced a distinctive landscape. This was particularly true of agricultural land. Try as they might, the colonists did not re-create exactly the patterns of land use and ownership they had known in the British Isles. Clover, wheat, hogs, dairy cattle, and fences overspread their fields and pastures, but so did corn, beans, and pumpkins, plants acquired from Indians. Like the Indians, settlers in the backcountry cultivated a piece of ground until it lost its fertility and then cleared a new plot while shrubs and trees grew back on the old. Most important, landownership in America was more widespread than in Britain and the rest of Europe. The deaths and removal of Indians, along with the sheer size of the New World, meant that many male colonists got the soil they had come for.[23]

In combination with the simple physical distance of the colonies from the parent country, population growth, geographical mobility, and an abundance of land undermined social hierarchy and enabled the formation of distinctive republican governments. By the eighteenth century, two-thirds of white colonists owned land, in contrast to one-fifth of the English population. More land and landownership conferred economic independence, weakened the bonds of dependency and the habits of deference that typified monarchical society, and broadened political participation. New England landowners, called freeholders, participated in town governments that sent representatives to colonial assemblies. In the Chesapeake region, property holders elected representatives to colonial legislatures. The institutions were hardly model democracies, but they revealed the extent to which land and material wealth enfranchised colonists.[24]

Those assemblies also jealously guarded important prerogatives: the right to initiate legislation and to levy taxes. Throughout the seventeenth and eighteenth centuries, the assemblies repeatedly resisted the efforts of Britain to weaken their power, especially their power to control the purse. Ultimately, the imperial system was simply too weak and the colonial political system too strong—and too geographically distant from Britain—for governors, parliament, and king to dominate. "The lawes of England are bounded within the fower [four] seas, and does not reach America," the Massachusetts legislature declared in 1678, a telling statement that Paine and Jefferson would echo.[25]

In the process of establishing themselves in a new land and forming new governments, the colonists fashioned what was perhaps their most important characteristic: a unique identity. Puritans likened the dangerous Atlantic voyage to a New Birth, a "literal rite of passage," as the historian Alan Taylor put it, that bonded them and proved that God looked on them with favor. When at last the Plymouth colonists made landfall, wrote William Bradford, they "fell upon their knees and blessed the God of Heaven, who had brought them over the fast and furious ocean, and delivered them from all the perils and miseries thereof, again to set their feet on the firm and stable earth, their proper element." From such travails, the colonists became New Englanders, Virginians, or Carolinians.[26]

During the 1700s, colonial identity moderated and then sharpened. In the middle of the century, the colonists' growing population and wealth and the intensification of trade with the mother country made them feel closer to Britain. The confidence they derived from that feeling, however, encouraged them to see themselves as the equals of anyone else in the empire and to insist on their rights "as Englishmen." Eventually, out of circumstances at once local and imperial, the colonists imagined themselves to be distinctly American. To be American was to have land, wealth, and liberty like no one else in the empire. To be American was to defend that land, wealth, and liberty by joining together in an independent federation. "I am not a Virginian," the orator and political firebrand Patrick Henry declaimed in 1774, "but an American."[27]

What finally drove the colonists to independence was not simply that they had become different people. The New World changed the empire, too, in ways that made its leaders unable to see the growing distinctions between them and the colonies they purported to rule. This final estrangement followed the Seven Years' War, also called, in its North American manifestation, the French and Indian War, which began in 1754 but which officially lasted from 1756 to 1763. The colonists' desire for land in the Ohio Valley, the region west of the Appalachian Mountains drained by the Ohio River, helped bring on the conflict. Britain, France, and the Indian allies of each fought over control of the area, and the contest escalated into a struggle for predominance in North America as a whole. Britain won, and so gained Ohio as well as Quebec and other Canadian lands. But this stunning victory augured poorly for the empire. Exhausted by fighting and bloated by its territorial conquests, Britain needed revenue to pay its enormous war debt and to administer its North American territory. How it attempted to raise that huge sum and govern that vast natural expanse alienated its American subjects.[28]

Several times Britain sought to tax the colonists. George III, his ministers, and a majority in Parliament thought it sensible to levy special duties on the Americans. Since the mid-1600s, the purpose of the empire had been to extract the colonies' natural wealth for the benefit of the parent country. Furs, hides, wool, tobacco, indigo, sugar, pine lumber, and other products were supposed to yield profits for colonists and, in turn, revenue for the treasury. To require the colonists to help pay for the war continued a long-standing policy. That the victory had protected and secured the colonists' place in North America was one more excellent reason why they should contribute their fair share. That some American entrepreneurs had profited handsomely from the parent country's wartime military expenditures only solidified the crown's argument that the colonists should pay for the blessings of empire.[29]

But the distant offspring rejected this imperial logic. No, the colonists concluded, they could not—*would not*—accept taxation imposed from afar. They never had submitted to such authority in the first place. Parliament at times had requisitioned special funds from colonial legislatures but never had imposed an outright tax. During the Seven Years' War, the colonists and their assemblies had resisted British efforts to squeeze revenue from them. Needing their cooperation to win the war, imperial officials had backed off and instead treated the colonies not as subjects but as allies. Rather than requiring them to pay, the British government had asked them for help and reimbursed them for the expense of mobilizing provincial militias. By 1765, the assemblies' power over taxation had evolved into an immutable right. For Britain to violate it now, many colonists believed, would be a monstrous usurpation.[30]

Struggle ensued. British officials responded gently, trying one tax after another—sugar, tea, stamps, and more—to coax revenue from America. At each turn, the colonists dug in their heels. Frustration finally turned to anger as king, ministers, and Parliament vowed to make the colonies pay. But Britain's leaders could not see how their own actions contributed to the problem. As the historian Fred Anderson wrote, the British "did not understand that their efforts had begun to precipitate opposition out of Americans' inchoate, provincial disinclination to be governed from a distance and their widely held belief that taxes should not be levied without consent."[31]

To many colonists, the policies intended to govern western lands were as objectionable as the taxes. The Royal Proclamation of 1763 sought to regulate relations between Britons and Indians in the Ohio Valley. Indians were subjects, too, and to keep colonists away from them and their land and prevent yet another costly war, George III prohibited British settlement west of the Appalachians, from the Great Lakes to Florida. A later elaboration of this policy, the Quebec Act of 1774, safeguarded French law and the Catholic religion among "Canadian subjects" in the Ohio Valley. Such measures frustrated and angered colonists. Speculators and settlers had developed a powerful hunger for trans-Appalachian land. How could the king shut them out? How could he protect Indians while denying the needs of the colonists? How could he put the interests of Catholic subjects ahead of Protestant interests? It was wrong, they said. Nothing should block them from that most cherished of rights: the pursuit of land and wealth.[32]

Taxation and restrictions on settlement weakened rather than strengthened Britain's hold on North America. Rather than bind the colonies to the parent, imperial policies hastened the offspring's alienation. One of the final blows came in 1775 when British forces took up arms against the colonists at Concord, Massachusetts. Younger colonists, with little or no memory of past insults, were especially shocked and outraged.[33] By 1776, Americans of all kinds felt like strangers to the nation that had spawned them. On the periphery of British civilization, on the far frontier of the Anglo world, they sensed the gulf. Paine and Jefferson were right. Distance was the natural basis on which the New World outgrew the Old.

A GOVERNMENT OF OUR OWN IS OUR NATURAL RIGHT

Europeans had moved over the earth and, in an environment different from that which they had left, built a new society. Accompanying this social migration was an intellectual migration in which the colonists imported European notions of natural law and natural rights. But much as society changed under New World conditions, so did ideas. Americans eventually invoked nature not to revive what they saw as the proper relationship between king and subjects but to create a wholly new political arrangement, a new nation. A radical alteration in the order of things needed an equally radical justification, and no source but nature—or Nature, as eighteenth-century people sometimes put it—would suffice. The use of nature to justify liberty then rippled through the country, as people seized on this powerful philosophical tool and modified it to serve their own ends. When African Americans began to claim their natural right to freedom, the Revolution truly had arrived.

Natural law and natural rights had a long history before the colonists brought them to America. The geography of ideas along which they traveled stretched back through the medieval and early Christian periods and into antiquity. For centuries, thinkers pointed to a fundamental, eternal principle, a higher law inherent in humans and the world that set forth a universal standard of justice. According to this natural law, all people, by virtue of their humanity (or by virtue of their status as children of God), had natural rights without which they could not maintain a basic level of dignity. Although divided by race, rank, wealth, or talent, all humans were equal before the law. At times the concept of natural law lay dormant, existing only as a latent potential in the dusty pages of forgotten tracts. But readers rediscovered it again and again, called it back to life, and restated it in terms relevant to their times.[34]

In the 1600s and 1700s, Europeans refashioned natural law to meet the needs of the age. In part, economic changes prompted the revision. In Britain, the intensification of commerce boosted food supplies, uprooted people, and shifted economic activity from the growing of crops and livestock for local communities to the production and exchange of surpluses for imperial markets. Observers—forerunners of modern economists—wondered what motivated the merchants and tradesmen who profited from the new system, which seemed to function with lawlike regularity. These proto-economists suggested that a universal, self-interested human nature impelled individual economic actors. "All men by nature are the same," wrote Josiah Child in 1690. "Trade is in its nature free," stated Charles Davenant in 1695, and "finds its own Channel and best directs its own Course."[35]

Modern economic notions of human nature and natural law derived from and reinforced the "scientific revolution," which emphasized nature as the source of knowledge and truth. Through the observation of physical phenomena and the application of reason, Copernicus, Galileo, Kepler, Leeuwenhoek, Newton, and other "natural philosophers" discovered order in the universe. Peering down through their microscopes, gazing up through their telescopes, or just looking at the world around them, they observed the predictable, mechanistic movement of matter: cells divided, planets orbited, and, as Newton famously discerned, gravity pulled apples down to earth. Nature seemed to have a design, which must, the scientists concluded, be the work of God. Humans were God's creation, too, and other thinkers—economists and political philosophers—saw a correspondence between the laws of physical nature and the laws of human nature. Through the use of reason—a God-given, natural capacity—people could behave and organize their governments properly. When they acted according to reason, people acted naturally, according to natural law.[36]

Europeans placed special value on natural law and the rights it conferred because those principles justified their resistance to the growing power of monarchs and centralized government. During the seventeenth and eighteenth centuries, European kings amassed extraordinary military and political might as they strove to unify their nations and govern them more efficiently. Not everyone was happy with this state of affairs. In Britain, landowners, shopkeepers, and merchants, many of them religious Puritans, struggled against the Stuart monarchs' efforts to raise taxes, circumvent Parliament, and reestablish Catholicism. Twice British subjects deposed their rulers, even going so far as to behead one of them. Such disloyalty angered the kings and their supporters, who contended that authority naturally flowed down through the crown. But many Britons disagreed. In their view, authority naturally originated with the people and served to check the monarchs' aggressive tendencies. Natural law, they said, gave them the right to counter royal arrogance.[37]

By the 1700s, a fully developed theory of natural law that served the needs of the American revolutionaries had evolved. It had no single author, but the English philosopher John Locke was most responsible for elaborating it. Locke was a Puritan who had lived through the political tumult of the 1600s, and late in the century he set down his thoughts on the nature of government.[38]

From the individual person to society as a whole, natural law shaped the human condition. All people were born free and equal, in the sense that no one was born above anyone else and no one should harm the life, health, liberty, or property of another. By exercising reason, people would discover this universal truth, and they would build a society and a government based on it. A crucial stage in the formation of social life was the creation of property. Each person owned his body and the labor it could perform. By cutting trees, plowing soil, hunting animals, or mining gold, a person in effect joined his labor to nature and so made that modified nature his property. This is how Locke put it:

> Though the Earth, and all inferior Creatures be common to all Men, yet every Man has a *Property* in his own *Person*. This no Body has any Right to but himself. The *Labour* of his Body, and the *Work* of his Hands, we may say, are properly his. Whatsoever then he removes out of the State that Nature hath provided, and left it in, he hath mixed his *Labour* with, and joyned to it something that is his own, and thereby makes it his *Property*.

Because people needed to be secure in their individual persons and property, they left the "state of nature" and came together as a society to establish a compact, an agreement, by which they voluntarily turned over to government the power to protect their rights. But if any government or leader violated those rights by acting unnaturally and threatening persons and property—if a tyrant took the people's property or taxed them without their consent—then a change was in order. Under such circumstances, "the People," as Locke said, "have a Right to resume their original Liberty, and, by the Establishment of a new Legislative [government], provide for their own Safety and Security, which is the end for which they are in society."[39]

The Lockean theory of natural law and natural rights appealed to eighteenth-century American colonists. They had come to a part of the world that was in a state of nature, they believed, and by their labor transformed the land into farms, towns, and property. Locke, in fact, had pointed to them as a case study of how humanity created property and built society from the Earth's raw materials. "Thus in the beginning all the World was *America*," he had written. In the process, the colonists had formed colonial legislatures that protected their interests. But the king, his ministers, and Parliament had imposed taxes and restricted westward migration, which threatened the colonists' persons and property. Now it was up to the Americans to establish a new legislative, as Locke would have said, and resume their original liberty.[40]

The concept of natural law traveled through the colonies along several routes. Some people actually read the works of Locke and other political philosophers. A number of books by these scholars appeared on reading lists at Harvard and other colleges. Jean-Jacques Burlamaqui, a professor of natural and civil law at the University of Geneva, authored *The Principles of Natural and Politic Law* (1747, 1751), the English translation of which "became a standard textbook" at American universities. "Natural law," Burlamaqui wrote, "is that which so necessarily agrees with the nature and state of man, that without observing its maxims, the peace and happiness of society can never be preserved. As this law has an essential agreeableness with the constitution of human nature, the knowledge thereof may be attained merely by the light of reason; and hence it is called natural."[41]

Lockean thought also moved along less elite routes. In Philadelphia, the Junto, or Club of the Leather Aprons, served as a forum in which workingmen discussed political and economic ideas, and it eventually evolved into a reading society. "Of the first 375 books the Junto members collected—the foundation of North America's first circulating library—more had come from the pen of John Locke than any other author," the historian Gary Nash has written. Locke and other philosophers were not easy to read, to be sure. As the historian Carl Becker concluded, Locke's theory was "a dreary devil of an argument staggering from assumption posited as premise to conclusion implicit in the assumption." Most people, therefore, learned about natural law indirectly. They listened to sermons at church, read newspapers and pamphlets, and talked to one another.[42]

By such formal and informal means, natural law and natural rights came to pervade the thought and rhetoric of a movement that culminated in the American Revolution. Throughout the colonies, people began to speak and write of "natural law," the "first law of nature," "natural rights," and the "rights of human nature" and how neither the king's dictates nor parliamentary statutes could overrule them. James Otis, in *The Rights of the British Colonists Asserted and Proved*, a pamphlet published in 1764, said so. "There can be no prescription old enough," he stated, "to supersede the law of nature and the grant of God Almighty, who has given to all men a natural right to be *free*, and they have it ordinarily in their power to make themselves so if they please."[43]

Similar assertions continued up to the Revolution and beyond. "What are all the Riches, the Luxuries, and even the Conveniences of Life compared with that Liberty where with God and Nature have set us free?" asked the artisan Alexander McDougal in 1770 in an open letter to the people of New York. "Among the natural Rights of the Colonists," wrote Samuel Adams in 1772, "are these: First, a Right to *Life*; Secondly to *Liberty*; thirdly to *Property*; together with the right to support and defend them in the best manner they can." If the colonists had natural rights, then surely a king who disregarded those rights was an "unnatural parent," as the satirist and playwright Mercy Otis Warren explained to an acquaintance in 1774. That year, Jefferson wrote *A Summary View of the Rights of British America*, in which he claimed that the colonists "possessed a right which nature has given to all men" to migrate to new lands and there establish new societies with laws and regulations suited to the changed circumstances. Numerous local and state declarations of independence employed the language of natural law and natural rights. Pennsylvania severed its ties to Britain in 1776 "in obedience to the first principles of nature . . . as the only measure left to us to preserve and establish our liberties, and to transmit them inviolate to posterity."[44]

Perhaps the strongest voice for the colonists' natural rights, and the one that finally pushed the Continental Congress toward its declaration, was that of Thomas Paine. A corset maker who only recently had emigrated from Britain to America, Paine was among the first to call openly for separation. In *Common*

Sense, published in January 1776, he attacked the monarchy as unnatural and asserted that "a government of our own is our natural right." The time had come for independence, he claimed: "The blood of the slain, the weeping voice of nature cries, 'TIS TIME TO PART."[45]

When Congress met in Philadelphia in June 1776, it assigned the task of drafting a declaration of independence to Jefferson, Adams, Franklin, Livingston, and Sherman. The committee asked Adams and Jefferson to write the text; Adams then turned the responsibility over to Jefferson, who retired to his portable writing desk and quickly scratched out a statement containing the philosophical proposition that nature was the source of American liberty. As he later explained, the point was not to advance new ideas, "but to place before mankind the common sense of the subject," to put forth a document that would "be an expression of the American mind." Jefferson then brought the document to the committee, which made a few alterations before presenting it to the entire assembly. More deliberation and revisions ensued. Finally, on July 4, in the now-famous meeting hall topped by a steeple, Congress adopted the Declaration of Independence.[46]

TRUE PRINCIPLES OF LIBERTY AND NATURAL RIGHT

So far, so good—in theory. The question stood: would the new nation be able to square the self-evident, timeless truths in the Declaration with the contingencies of environment and history? One obstacle to the survival of the natural rights republic was the nature of the Revolutionary War. To secure the Revolution, the Continental Army had to remain intact in the face of considerable odds. Not only did it have to endure the onslaught of British military forces, but it also had to cope with smallpox, the ravages of winter, the pangs of hunger, and the seedtime and harvest that lured soldiers back to their farms. General Washington and his officers had to contend with a transformation in the composition of the army as landless men replaced the ranks of the landed. No less important, the new United States had to transform its timber, grain, and animals—its natural bounty—into resources for its troops and convert the lay of its land—its topography—into strategic and tactical advantages. To protect the revolutionary social compact and its recognition of man's true nature, the nation and its army had to negotiate a biophysical world in flux.[47]

The greatest problem for the new republic, however, emerged from its founding idea. Once the concept of natural rights spread, no one could control it. Many elite revolutionaries struggled with its unsettling implications, which went far beyond the purpose they had envisioned for it. For Americans lower in the social hierarchy, natural rights were not a disturbing concept but a golden opportunity. These people made it speak on behalf of a liberty more universal than some of their elite countrymen wanted to allow. The groups of Americans that seized the Revolution's promise of natural rights included backcountry settlers, women, and African Americans. Could they live the dream? Could they square ideal and reality? Would powerful men stand for it?[48]

So much of the American experience has been wrapped up in the settling of land—in coveting, conquering, controlling, using, and profiting from it. The historian Gary Nash has noted the centrality of land and its resources to the Revolution. Some colonists, he has written, aspired to create a society akin to that of Indians, in which "traits of morality, generosity, bravery, and the spirit of mutual caring" prevailed. More often than not, the colonists "were pulled in the opposite direction by the natural abundance around them—toward individualism, disputatiousness, aggrandizement of wealth, and the exploitation of other humans." As the Revolution unfolded, settlers across the emerging nation struggled against wealthy proprietors and speculators who sought to deny them the land they coveted. In their world, Lockean natural rights had special meaning.[49]

From 1764 to 1779, settlers and large landholders vied for control of the forested slopes and fertile valleys of the Green Mountains, which formed a rough border between western New Hampshire and eastern New York. Both colonies asserted ownership of the area, called the Hampshire Grants or the Grants. New York and its elite families had the superior legal claim, but New Hampshire and its wealthy governor and council moved first to sell the land—fraudulently—to speculators and settlers. Many of those settlers came from Massachusetts and other New England colonies where booming populations were running out of arable soil. By the mid-1770s, some twelve thousand people had settled in the Grants, and another four thousand had been born there. Their lives were difficult. The first arrivals cultivated meadows or the sites of Indian villages wiped out by disease and war, but most hacked their farms from the forest. Game, free-roaming hogs, and corn sustained them, but the growing season was short and the fare was poor. One feature of the settlers' lives made their deprivation worthwhile: they owned their farms. Or so they believed, for even as they struggled to open the land, New York ordered sheriffs, justices of the peace, and surveyors to take control of it. The grandees of that powerful colony wanted not landed yeomen but tenants from whom they could squeeze rents.[50]

The settlers resisted. Eventually, they united under the leadership of a charismatic, profane freethinker named Ethan Allen. Early in his adulthood, Allen had formed a friendship with Thomas Young, a failed land speculator and itinerant physician with an abiding interest in political philosophy. Together they studied the work of John Locke, and along with other inhabitants of the region, they articulated a philosophy of natural rights that trumped the legal claims of New York. Land title, Allen declared, was "sealed and confirmed with the Sweat and Toil of the Farmer." Others agreed; one community resolved "that Every Mans Estate Honestly Acquired is his own and no person on Earth has A Right to take it Away without Proprietor Consent." Allen and his compatriots opposed New York in court and on the ground, where, organized in a militia called the Green Mountain Boys, they harassed sheriffs, threatened justices, and thrashed surveyors with branches—"the twigs of the wilderness." The radical enthusiasm of Allen and the Green Mountain Boys impelled them beyond their immediate concerns; when the Revolution engulfed the colonies, they transferred their antipathy from New York to Britain as a whole.[51]

The contest between New York and the people of the Grants intensified when the Continental Congress met. After asking Congress to recognize their independence, the Green Mountain inhabitants held a series of conventions between 1775 and 1777 in which they produced a constitution for the new state of Vermont. A radical democratic document, it provided for unrestricted manhood suffrage, stated "that private property ought to be subservient to public uses," freed the few African American bondpeople who resided in the state, and denounced slavery as a violation of "natural, inherent, and unalienable rights." Jailed by the British but released in a prisoner exchange, Ethan Allen returned to the Green Mountains in 1778 to become the state attorney. "They were a people between the heavens and the earth," he said of his fellow Vermonters, "as free as is possible to conceive any people to be; and in this condition they formed a government upon the true principles of liberty and natural right."[52]

From Georgia to the Carolinas, from Pennsylvania and Massachusetts to Maine, many settlers shared Allen's beliefs, but already the wealthy and the powerful were moving to suppress them. New York tried to convince the Continental Congress to recognize its claim to the Hampshire Grants, and in 1777 it promulgated a constitution as conservative as Vermont's was radical. It had no bill of rights, vested extraordinary power in the executive and judicial branches, retained a substantial property qualification for voting, made most public offices appointive, and recognized colonial land grants.[53] Soon enough, the political reaction that appeared in New York gathered force throughout the nation. Would the republic honor the sweat and toil of farmers whose exertions turned raw nature into property? Or would it constrain those small producers from exercising their natural rights?

GOD AND NATURE DESIGNED IT SO

Similar questions pertained to women. Some Americans believed that natural law might apply to them as well as to men, and the Revolution provoked them to question women's subordinate status in the patriarchal society of colonial America. "Are not women born as free as men?" asked James Otis, one of the Revolution's great pamphlet writers. "Would it not be infamous to assert that the ladies are all slaves by nature? . . . If upon abdication all were reduced to a state of nature, had not apple women and orange girls as good a right to give their respectable suffrages for a new King as the philosopher, courtier . . . and politician? Were these and ten millions of others . . . consulted?"[54] Few people uttered such words in eighteenth-century America, but Otis was hardly alone in wondering about the meaning of natural rights for women. Would the Revolution make them full citizens of the new republic?

When the ties to Britain finally dissolved, women performed tasks and made sacrifices that demonstrated their commitment to the patriot cause and established the grounds for their claim to natural rights. One of their most important contributions was labor, that all-important Lockean category of property. Women played crucial roles as transformers of raw materials—natural resources—into useful things. The "daughters of liberty," as they sometimes called themselves, spun, wove, and sewed so that they would not have to buy British textiles and clothing; saved rags to make paper and bandages; gathered lead weights from windows to make bullets; collected urine from family pisspots for its natural nitrate, an essential ingredient of gunpowder; organized boycotts of cloth, tea, and other British manufactures; and managed shops and farms in the absence of husbands. In classic Lockean fashion, women derived a sense of ownership from their labor. "Your" farm, as one woman called it when dutifully reporting to her soldiering husband, soon became "ours," and by the end of the war, it was "my" farm.[55]

Thousands of women labored directly for the Continental Army. They cooked and delivered food, hauled water (the soldiers called the female water carriers Molly Pitcher), nursed the wounded, raised money and gathered supplies, washed and mended clothing, conveyed messages, transported ammunition, and served as wives and companions to the men. A few shouldered arms, but most performed conventional kinds of service labor. Trudging behind the marching soldiers, their belongings hoisted on their backs, thousands followed the Continental Army across the landscape of the newborn republic. Their presence caused Washington and other generals no end of frustration, but their participation in military campaigns was vital.[56]

Women experienced physical stress and were agents and victims of violence during the Revolution. Price increases and food shortages led to hunger that provoked them to riot. "The marketplace," in the words of Gary Nash, "was women's terrain," and when necessary, mobs of women forced greedy shopkeepers and merchants to sell food at prices they believed were just and moral. Disease epidemics also hurt women and their families, and more than a few of Liberty's daughters suffered the pain and degradation of rape as invaders conquered them along with enemy land. "Women's bodies," the historian Joan Gunderson noted, "were literally territory claimed by victorious soldiers."[57]

Having placed—or sacrificed—their bodily natures in the service of the revolutionary cause, some American women developed a corresponding political consciousness. Intellectuals such as Abigail Adams and Mercy Otis Warren, James Otis's sister, denounced the British in terms of natural rights. "I fear the Tragic part of the Drama will hastily ensue," Warren wrote to Adams in 1774, "and that Nothing but the Blood of Virtuous Citizens Can repurchase the Rights of Nature, unjustly torn from us by the united arms of treachery and Violence." As the Revolution progressed, some women claimed the rights of nature for themselves. "Yes, you lordly, you haughty sex," Judith Sargent Murray wrote in *Massachusetts Magazine* in 1790, "our souls are by nature *equal* to yours."[58]

Mary Wollstonecraft's *A Vindication of the Rights of Woman* drew widespread attention in the United States after its publication in 1792. Denouncing social conventions that kept women weak and subservient, the English radical declared her sisters to be "human creatures, who, in common with men, are placed on this earth to unfold their faculties." With proper education, she said, a woman could fulfill an innate potential that was equal to that of a man's. In fact, she asserted in Newtonian-inflected rhetoric, some women had "more sense than their male relatives; and, as nothing preponderates where there is a constant struggle for an equilibrium, without [which] it has naturally more gravity, some women govern their husbands without degrading themselves, because intellect will always govern."[59]

The country had changed, observed Elias Boudinot of New Jersey in 1793. "The Rights of women are no longer strange sounds to an American ear," he wrote. "They are now heard as familiar terms in every part of the United States." Attention to those rights had striking consequences, one of which was a decline in the birthrate. The Revolution disrupted childbearing and enabled women to begin abandoning conventional notions of pregnancy as an organic, natural cycle over which they had little control, if any. Susanna Hopkins, for example, asked a friend whether she thought someone was "very contracted in his notions" if he "would have us to be nothing more than domesticated animals." Some women stopped referring to childbearers in terms of organic abundance, as teeming, fruitful, prolific, and the like. Some limited their fertility by delaying marriage, restricting sexual relations with their husbands, or, as a means of birth control, ingesting herbal medicines or resorting to vigorous physical activity or douches.[60] In effect, women began to do what revolutionary ideas of nature said they would do, which was to use their innate powers of reason to plan and improve their lives. Jefferson tried to create a harmonious, rational order in designing his house, Monticello; women tried to do the same in their families.

The Revolution engendered other changes as well. Literacy increased among females and began to approach the same proportion as among males. More girls attended school, female academies flourished, and in the aftermath of Wollstonecraft's manifesto, some Americans called for the creation of a college for women. Some went so far as to advocate suffrage. In 1776, New Jersey extended the vote to unmarried and widowed women with personal property worth at least £50. New Jersey was exceptional, but its experiment with limited woman suffrage was a logical outcome of the natural rights revolution.[61]

The gap between self-evident truth and lived experience did not close completely for women, however. At nearly every point, scholars, politicians, activists, and almost everyone else either stopped short of or retreated from acknowledging women's full equality as rooted in natural law. John Locke had imagined greater rights for women, positing, for example, that they ought to control their own property, but he never fully or clearly articulated what the political role of women might be. When he used the terms *man* or *men*, he tended to mean them literally, not as generic references to people or humankind.[62]

Even more than Locke, Americans backed away from the implications of their revolutionary creed. James Otis gradually lapsed into mental illness and never could answer his own question about women and natural rights. More important, people ignored or dismissed the equalitarian potential of natural law and resorted to a conventional hierarchical conception of nature to justify the continued subordination of sisters, mothers, wives, and daughters. Natural equality extended only to white men, especially white propertied men, went this line of thought; all other beings, women included, were arrayed below in a natural ranked order of superiority and inferiority, dominance and submission. Women were inherently weaker, more emotional, and less capable of reason than were men. They had admirable qualities—they could think, nurture men and children, and assist their husbands—but ultimately they could not be fully independent because they were inferior to and dependent on men. Jefferson knew women were intelligent and, in the case of those he enslaved, capable of intense physical exertion, yet he believed that a properly ordered society should maintain clear gender distinctions. Women "are formed by nature for attentions and not for hard labour," he wrote. Women themselves often accepted their subordinate place, at times referring to the "natural timidity of our sex."[63]

If a natural hierarchy defined a woman's place in society, then any woman who presumed to be equal to men—intellectually, politically, or economically—behaved unnaturally. The critics of assertive women used vivid analogies, metaphors, and fables to emphasize the point. A "mild, dove-like temper is so necessary to Female beauty, is so natural a part of the sex," wrote Mason Locke Weems, George Washington's biographer. "A masculine air in a woman frightens us." *Lady's Magazine* agreed, although it established its position somewhat differently. If a natural woman was like a dove, as Weems suggested, then an unnatural woman was a strange kind of bird indeed. An educated woman, the journal proclaimed, would be like the "jackdaw"—a noisy, sassy, imitative crow or jay—in one of Aesop's fables. In that story, the jackdaw steps out of nature's order and bedecks itself (herself, in some versions) in peacock plumes. But the peacocks tear off the feathers and peck the interloper, who then returns, hurt and ashamed, to its kind. There it receives a stern admonition: "It would be better if you had contented yourself with what nature gave you."[64]

This conservative side of the Revolution was perhaps most evident in the laws that governed relations between husbands and wives. The Revolution provided numerous instances in which women asserted their roles as producers and as owners of property, but legally they remained subordinate to men. In this sense, natural law had little influence, if any, on statutes and court decisions. Long after the Revolution, the law of coverture continued to subordinate wives to their husbands. A husband controlled, or "covered," nearly all aspects of his wife's physical nature. He governed her sexually, at least in theory, and when her labor yielded a child, that offspring belonged not to her, as a Lockean analysis might suggest, but to him. Any property that she brought to the marriage or accrued during the union became his. In effect, the wife herself was the husband's property. The persistence of coverture underscored a crucially important feature of early American society: men refused to allow natural rights to challenge the fundamental authority they exercised over women.[65]

Ultimately, the Revolution was less for the daughters of liberty than for the sons. Thomas Paine made this clear in *Common Sense*. Paine, who believed in the natural basis of American independence, portrayed the Revolution in masculine terms, analogizing it to the natural outcome of men's biological and social life-course. Men had outgrown a patriarchal system that subjected them to the arbitrary dictates of a king; now was the time for them to break free. Paine asked, "Is it in the interest of a man to be a boy all his life?" Implicit in the question and in its answer was the idea that women had not outgrown the patriarchal social, economic, and political order but remained fixed in a weak, dependent, girlish condition. Such sexism had consequences. In 1807, an amendment to New Jersey's constitution disfranchised female citizens.[66]

Some women resisted the gender conservatism of the Revolution. Abigail Adams challenged her husband to think of women's place. "Remember the Ladies," she said to John Adams in a famous letter in 1776. "Remember all Men would be tyrants if they could. . . . That your Sex are Naturally Tyrannical is a Truth so thoroughly established as to admit of no dispute." In 1782, Eliza Wilkinson complained that although women might not be physically as strong as men, intellectually they were as capable of forming "conceptions of things of higher nature; and have as just a sense of honor, glory, and great actions, as these 'Lords of Creation.'" In comparison with representations of women as beasts of burden, doves, or jackdaws, Wilkinson railed, men viewed women as something even lower—as "contemptible *earth worms*." All she wanted, she said, was "the liberty of thought." As the years passed, Abigail Adams continued to assert her natural rights. "I will never consent to have our sex considered in an inferior point of light," she wrote to her husband in 1799. "Let each planet shine in [its] own orbit. God and nature designed it so—if man is Lord, woman is Lordess—that is what I contend for."[67]

Because of the Revolution's radical implications and the unsettling questions that women raised, Americans did create a place for women in the new order, but that position reflected the conservative view that women were naturally suited to maternal and domestic tasks. The "Republican Mother," as the historian Linda Kerber called her, inculcated in her children, especially sons, the virtues necessary for republican citizenship, encouraged her husband to uphold those virtues, and ran the household in ways that would serve the needs of the republic. A woman's revolutionary place thus derived not from her inherent individuality and natural rights but from her role as the natural nurturer of her children and spouse.[68]

Ironically, female revolutionaries participated in keeping themselves and their sisters in this honored but unequal place, and their rhetoric at times undermined equality rooted in natural law. When Abigail Adams wrote of men's natural propensity for tyranny, for example, she reinforced notions of difference—men inherently more aggressive, women inherently more passive—even as she strove to break down political inequalities based on such distinctions. It would be left to later generations to move beyond the Republican Mother to achieve a fuller, more equal place in American society.[69]

An indication of the demands that those restive cohorts would make appeared in 1839 at Litchfield, Connecticut, at Sara Pierce's school for girls. The impassioned students redirected the nation's revolutionary heritage by composing, in celebration of the Fourth of July, a "Ladies Declaration of Independence":

> When in the Course of Human Events it becomes necessary for the Ladies to dissolve those bonds by which they have been subjected to others, and to assume among the self styled Lords of Creation that separate and equal station to which the laws of nature and their *own talents* entitle them, a decent respect to the opinions of mankind requires, that they should declare the causes which impel them to the separation. We hold these truths to be self evident. That all *mankind* are created equal.[70]

The schoolgirls' rephrasing of the Declaration of Independence anticipated a much more famous statement, the Declaration of Sentiments, authored by

Elizabeth Cady Stanton and Lucretia Mott for a national convention on women's rights held at Seneca Falls, New York, in 1848. "We hold these truths to be self-evident: that all men and women are created equal," Stanton and Mott proclaimed before listing the grievances and making the claim to equal rights. Such broadened conceptions of the Declaration of Independence were telling examples of how some Americans imagined a better fit between timeless truths and the nation's political order. But the key idea in the Litchfield and Seneca Falls statements—that equality applied to mankind, not just to men—had important implications for more than just white women. In natural law's challenge to slavery and racial inequality, the American Revolution struggled with its equalitarian potential.

WE HAVE A NATURAL RIGHT TO OUR FREEDOMS

Americans could hardly miss what natural rights meant for humans held in bondage. Locke had something to say about the matter. "The *Natural Liberty of Man*," he wrote, "is to be free of any Superior Power on Earth, and not be under the Will or Legislative Authority of Man, but to have only the Law of Nature for his rule." Furthermore, no man or men could voluntarily suppress their natural impulse to protect themselves and resist enslavement: "whenever any one shall go about to bring them into such a Slavish Condition, they will always have the right to preserve what they have not a Power to part with; and to rid themselves of those who invade this Fundamental, Sacred, and unalterable Law of *Self-Preservation*, for which they enter'd into Society."[71] Self-preservation is the first law of nature, eighteenth-century proponents of natural rights often said. Would the American revolutionaries construct a republican architecture that honored the truth?

Circumstances forced the issue. After the Seven Years' War, economic development and trade intensified the importation of enslaved people to the colonies. At the same time, Atlantic commerce increased the publication and sale of books, pamphlets, almanacs, and newspapers. Merchants extracted human nature from Africa and forced it to labor in the colonies; tradesmen extracted cotton, flax, and other materials from the Earth and turned them into paper on which writers conveyed ideas of natural rights. The expanding commercial economy fostered both slavery and liberty and magnified the contradiction between them. Writer, publisher, scientist, and self-made man Benjamin Franklin owned five slaves but founded the Locke-filled library of the Philadelphia Junto, helped draft the Declaration of Independence, and publicly opposed slavery. A few years before Jefferson penned the Declaration, the slaveholder represented in a legal case a mixed-race man, Samuel Howell, who had run away from his master and sued for his freedom. "Under the law of nature," Jefferson wrote in 1771 on Howell's behalf, "all men are born free, [and] every one comes into the world with a right to his own person, which includes the liberty of moving and using it at his own will. This is what is called personal liberty, and is given him by the author of nature."[72] Neither Franklin nor Jefferson was exceptional in his ownership of slaves and defense of natural rights. They typified the fundamental problem of the republic's founding, which the citizens of the United States had to confront.

In part, white Americans initiated the revolutionary reappraisal of slavery by representing themselves as the victims of an arbitrary and capricious power that, in effect, turned them into slaves. A slave was someone who, being subject to the will of another, had no power of self-determination, no power to maintain property or to exercise basic rights. In taxing the colonists without their consent, shutting down their legislatures, and restricting their settlement, king and Parliament had reduced them to a slavelike condition. John Dickinson said it forcefully in one of his famous pamphlets: "*Those* who are *taxed* without their own consent expressed by themselves or their representatives are *slaves*. We are *taxed* without our consent or our representatives. We are therefore—SLAVES." Some drew parallels between their predicament and the enslavement of blacks. The difference between the two forms of servitude, concluded another colonist, was that slaves deserved pity while whites under the rule of an arbitrary governor deserved "to be held in the utmost contempt."[73]

Some white Americans felt compelled to confront directly the contradiction that liberty and chattel slavery posed. They argued that natural law and natural rights must apply not just to whites but to all men regardless of color. In his zeal to expose and question colonial society's basic premises, James Otis boldly propounded this position. "The Colonists are by the law of nature free born, as indeed all men are, white or black," he wrote in 1764. "Does it follow that 'tis right to enslave a man because he is black? Will short curled hair like wool rather than Christian hair . . . help the argument? Can any logical inference in favor of slavery be drawn from a flat nose, a long or short face?" Ultimately, Otis asserted, slavery corrupted the enslavers as much as it degraded the enslaved. A "trade that is the most shocking violation of the law of nature," he thundered, "has a direct tendency to diminish the idea of the inestimable value of liberty, and makes every dealer in it a tyrant." Others pursued the same line of thought, pointing out the hypocrisy of claiming rights for oneself while denying them to blacks. As Thomas Paine asked in 1775, how could Americans "complain so loudly of attempts to enslave them while they hold so many hundreds of thousands in slavery?"[74]

What white people said and did, however, mattered less than the words and actions of the blacks who had been brought from Africa or whose ancestors had arrived from that place. In America, the trade routes along which ships had carried thousands of heartbroken souls intersected with an ideological geography along which had migrated the idea of natural rights. At the point where they crossed paths, at the place where the pain of oppression met the inspiration of an ideal, a revolutionary partnership resulted. In their efforts to claim their rights and win their freedom, the historian Ira Berlin noted, African Americans "extended the egalitarian legacy of the Declaration of Independence and became its greatest champion."[75]

When Africans first landed on North American shores, they had no antislavery philosophy. They had come from societies in which hierarchy and slavery were common. Those societies, however, also had traditions of resistance, and their members did not willingly accept their bondage. From the moment the manacled people crawled from the sour holds of slave ships—dark prisons that reeked of excrement, vomit, sweat, and death—they pondered ways in which they might alleviate or escape their predicament. Over the years they devised an array of techniques by which to counter their masters' power, win degrees of autonomy, make life easier, and so preserve themselves. They slowed the pace of work, sabotaged tools, and feigned illness, injury, or ignorance. They manipulated emotions, appealing to a master's paternalistic self-importance or fears. Some went further—by the radical acts of flight or rebellion, they tried to break away altogether.[76]

The Revolution provided slaves with new opportunities to physically resist their masters and reclaim control over their lives. Some took advantage of the war's turmoil and fled. Joining the many refugees trying to escape the fighting, these fugitives sought British protection or tried to pass as free people. Perhaps three dozen of Thomas Jefferson's slaves left him when the British neared his plantations. Other enslaved laborers used threats of malingering, sabotage, flight, or rebellion to soften their masters' domination. That they might disrupt production at a crucial moment, that they might run away or revolt, made their owners more cautious in assigning a brutal work regimen or meting out punishment. Still other slaves not only fled but also volunteered their services to either the British or the Americans. As draymen, wood gatherers, foragers, cooks, road builders, trench diggers, pilots, scouts, and soldiers, they used their physical natures—their bodies and "embodied knowledge"—to prove their loyalty, demonstrate their power, and leverage their freedom.[77]

The Revolution did something more than just broaden the opportunities for physically counteracting slavery. It gave blacks a philosophy of liberation. It was one thing to act; it was quite another to act in the context of ideas. As the historian Peter Wood has suggested, African Americans before 1776 may have "thought longer and harder than any other sector of the colonial population about the concept of liberty, both as an abstract ideal and a tangible reality." What made African American participation in the independence movement so powerful was the combination of physical resistance with the idea of natural rights. This potent union reinvigorated the Revolution and pushed it toward its ultimate potential.[78]

Free blacks, some of them intellectuals, played an important role in drawing attention to natural law. Reading books, official documents, and letters, poring over newspapers and pamphlets, and listening to sermons, they learned the language of natural rights and doggedly reminded whites of its implications. In 1774, Phillis Wheatley, a poet and former slave, wrote to the Rev. Samson Occom: "I . . . am greatly satisfied with your Reasons" for African American freedom "and think highly reasonable what you offer in Vindication of their natural Rights . . . for in every human Breast, God has implanted a Principle, which we call Love of Freedom." The African as well as the Englishman, wrote Lemuel Haynes, who fought at Lexington and Concord in April 1775, "has an undeniable right to his Liberty. . . . Those privileges that are granted to us by the Divine Being, no one has the least right to take from us without our consent." Paul Cuffe, a ship captain and merchant, led several other African Americans in protesting to the Massachusetts legislature that they could not vote even though they paid taxes and had taken up arms against Britain. "We are not allowed the Privilage of freemen of the State[,] having no vote or Influence in the Election of those that Tax us," they stated in 1780, "yet many of our Colour . . . have cheerfully Entered the field of Battle in the defence of the Common Cause and . . . against a similar Exertion of Power (in Regard to taxation) too well Known to need a recital in this place."[79]

When the scientist and surveyor Benjamin Banneker wrote to Thomas Jefferson in 1791, he did nothing less than quote the Declaration of Independence back to its original author, arguing that "it is the . . . duty of those who maintain for themselves the rights of human nature, and who profess the obligations of Christianity, to extend their power and influence to the relief of every part of the human race from whatever burthen or oppression they may unjustly labour under." Thanking Banneker for the letter and the scientific almanac that accompanied it, Jefferson responded: "No body wishes more than I do to see such proofs as you exhibit, that nature has given to our black brethren, talents equal to those of other colors of men, and that the appearance of a want of them is owing merely to the degraded condition of their existence, both in Africa and America."[80]

But it was slaves who truly united physical with ideological resistance and so had the greatest influence on the Revolution. They had little access to print, and few of them had read Locke, but they had no problem grasping the meaning of revolutionary rhetoric. As Ira Berlin observed, "The language of tyranny was one blacks well understood." In the southern colonies, slaves overheard— and appropriated—the revolutionary conversations of the whites whom they served. Thousands of enslaved laborers who packed Charleston, South Carolina, in 1765 repeatedly heard the word liberty, and its meaning "was not lost" on them, according to Gary Nash. When slaves joined street protesters and shouted "Liberty! Liberty and stamp'd paper!" or just "Liberty!" they subtly transformed opposition to the Stamp Act into a demonstration against human bondage.[81]

In the northern colonies, slaves learned their revolutionary lessons equally well. Massachusetts slaves asserted in 1774 that "we have in common with all other men a naturel right to our freedoms without Being depriv'd of them by our follow men[,] as we are a freeborn Pepel and have never forfeited this Blessing by aney compact or agreement whatever." In 1777, another group claimed to "have in Common with all other men a Natural and Unaliable Right to that freedom which the Grat Parent of the Unavers hath Bestowed equalley on all menkind." Connecticut petitioners stated in 1779 that because they were "endowed with the same Faculties" as their owners, "we are [no] more obliged to serve them, than they us." The "more we Consider this matter," they concluded, "the more we are Convinced of our Right (by the Laws of Nature and by the whole Tenor of the Christian Religion, so far as we have been taught) to be free."[82]

As the Revolution advanced and African Americans pressed their cause, many whites believed they had no choice but to end the practice that mocked their ideals. For some it was a matter of conscience, of honestly facing the glaring contradiction and acting accordingly. For others, it was a practical matter. Maintaining slaves was costly, Benjamin Franklin had pointed out in 1751. Slaves needed food, clothing, shelter, and supervision, and they might fall ill and die. It was "natural," furthermore, for slaves to "neglect" work from which they derived no benefit; in fact, slaveholders could expect to lose property to pilfering, "every Slave being *by Nature* a thief." Many slave owners could no longer ignore their laborers' continual hectoring and petitioning and their impulse to commit the greatest theft of all, which was to steal themselves and run away. Enslaved people were especially problematic during the war, because the patriot cause needed their loyalty.[83]

First came an assault on the slave trade. From the late 1760s through the early 1770s, Massachusetts, Rhode Island, Connecticut, Delaware, and Pennsylvania passed laws that weakened or banned the trade. In April 1776, Congress took the lead and honored an earlier pledge to prohibit the importation of slaves into the thirteen colonies. And when Thomas Jefferson penned his draft declaration of American independence, he attacked slavery and the royal governor's veto of the Massachusetts legislation. The king, Jefferson wrote, "has waged a cruel war against human nature itself, violating [its] most sacred rights of life and liberty in the persons of a distant people who never offended him. . . . Determined to keep open a market where *Men* should be bought & sold, he has prostituted his negative [veto] for suppressing every legislative attempt to prohibit or restrain this execrable commerce."[84]

Next came a wave of emancipations and manumissions. In the 1770s, Vermont, Massachusetts, and New Hampshire took the first legal steps to end slavery. Pennsylvania, Connecticut, and Rhode Island followed in the 1780s. Meanwhile, New York, Maryland, and Virginia liberalized or enacted manumission laws, allowing individual whites voluntarily to free their slaves. As one Marylander acknowledged, slavery violated "the inalienable Rights of Mankind," and she liberated the people who had served her. Enslaved people were not merely passive recipients of freedom; many purchased themselves and their families.[85]

The growing momentum for emancipation seemed to be lifting the nation toward a monumental achievement in human history that henceforth would demarcate old from new, a harsher time from a world made better. The wheel of revolution had turned and turned again, until the least powerful of all Americans seemed poised to claim their place in a republican architecture that embodied timeless, universal truths. But even as African Americans shook off their bonds and took surnames like Freeman, Freeland, and Liberty, the forces of reaction halted the construction and revised the plans. Freedom would meet its limits.[86]

For some powerful Americans, slavery was an economic necessity, and they would not accept its abolition. This was especially so in southern states, where large numbers of blacks were engaged in the plantation production of rice, tobacco, and cotton; it was the case as well in northern states with relatively large slave populations. It might have been easy for yeomen dairy farmers and small shopkeepers in Vermont or New Hampshire to do away with slavery, and Virginians converting their fields to wheat might give it up without too much distress. But for Carolinians or Georgians involved in the mass production of agricultural staples and for a substantial number of New York and New Jersey residents deeply involved the commerce of the Atlantic world, the dismantling of slavery was virtually unthinkable.[87]

Ideological and economic justifications for slavery appeared in combination, as slave owners appealed to nature to defend the practice against ideas of natural rights. If all men were created equal, went their logic, then slaves could not be men—at least not in the same sense as white men. Something in the African Americans' essence, something in their biological nature, made them lesser. Building on this line of thought, the apologists argued that if slaves were not men and thus were legitimate property, and if natural law protected property, then compulsory abolition violated natural law. They could point to none other than John Locke in support of their position. Locke's major writings had addressed the abstract concept of slavery but not its real-world, racial variant. And in 1669, before he penned those great political treatises, he had composed colonial Carolina's *Fundamental Constitution*, which gave a master "absolute power and authority over his negro slaves."[88]

Despite his comments to Benjamin Banneker, Thomas Jefferson in other contexts was ambivalent about the nature of African Americans. In *Notes on the State of Virginia* (1785), he opposed slavery but wondered if enslaved people were equally capable as whites. Were African Americans inferior, he asked, and was their inferiority because of a fixed nature or because of a degraded condition? He was not yet intimately involved with Sally Hemings, but he pointed to the perceived consequences of racial intermixture as evidence of innate black inferiority. "The improvement of the blacks in body and mind," he wrote, "in the first instance of their mixture with whites, has been observed by every one, and proves that their inferiority is not merely the effect of their condition in life." He noted African Americans' equality in physical fortitude, bravery, adventurousness, and memory but believed them to be inferior in reason and imagination. He disparaged Phillis Wheatley and other black intellectuals, writers, and artists, and he conjectured "that the blacks, whether originally a distinct race, or made distinct by time and circumstances, are inferior to the whites in the endowments both of body and mind."[89]

More observation of blacks was necessary, Jefferson said, but their apparent inferiority had an important consequence: "Will not a lover of natural history then, one who views the gradations in all the races of animals with the eye of philosophy, excuse an effort to keep those in the department of man as distinct as nature has formed them? This unfortunate difference of colour, and perhaps of faculty, is a powerful obstacle to the emancipation of these people." Jefferson was reluctant to recognize a single human nature that cut across superficial physical differences. In the sense that blacks had a right to life, liberty, and happiness, they may have been equal to whites, but their inferiority in other regards justified, to some Americans, their subjugation.[90]

Contingent nature, finally, undercut African Americans' efforts to exercise their rights according to a timeless natural law. During the war, thousands of blacks flocked to the British and American armies for protection or for the opportunity to win their freedom through military service. In Virginia, perhaps ten thousand absconded to British forces; members of Lord Dunmore's Ethiopian Regiment wore sashes that proclaimed "liberty to slaves." Their enlistment was a death trap. Compared with British forces, black American soldiers were less experienced in the diseases that ravaged massed populations. They had neither served in large units, as had the British, nor, at the start of the war, been inoculated in the same proportion. Because they were less resistant to smallpox and other crowd diseases, epidemics devastated them. At the same time, British soldiers had comparatively little experience with, and resistance to, the mosquito-borne malaria that was endemic to the New World. Their commanders procured too little of its antidote, quinine from cinchona bark, and too few fresh soldiers to replenish the ranks. The combined deficiencies of African American and British bodies contributed to the British army's weakness and final surrender. For African Americans who sought freedom in British service, the Revolution ended in misery and despair.[91]

In the face of so many obstacles, the Revolution's antislavery momentum slowed and finally stopped. In the end, state laws amounted to halfway measures that paid as much attention to property rights in slaves as to the rights of the enslaved people. No southern state abolished slavery, and in the North, where the Revolution did the most to end the practice, human chattel existed well into the nineteenth century. In 1806, Virginia began to restrict the rights of slave owners to emancipate enslaved laborers. A similar trend played out on the national level. The Northwest Ordinance of 1787 prohibited slavery north of the Ohio River, but the federal Constitution of that year tacitly condoned its prolongation in other states. In the Naturalization Act of 1790, Congress established race as a condition of citizenship by limiting immigration to "any alien, being a free white person . . . of good character." In 1798, Congress forbade the foreign importation of slaves into Mississippi Territory, but not their transfer from other parts of the United States. Among the Revolution's slave owners, voluntary manumission achieved only partial success. George Washington's will contained provisions for liberating his slaves after his death. James Madison freed one man, a personal servant. Benjamin Franklin never freed any of his slaves, even as he opposed slavery. Thomas Jefferson continued to denounce slavery and predicted its gradual demise, but he never summoned the moral strength necessary to let his own people go. The institution was too convenient and too important to the accumulation of the material resources that made possible his intellectual life.[92]

Most telling was the reaction embedded in the document that most defined the Revolution: the Declaration of Independence. When the committee charged with drafting it finally brought it before Congress, certain delegates objected to the clause that denounced the king's alleged perpetuation of the slave trade. Jefferson's angry statement went too far, they said—it was too dangerous. Other delegates no doubt recognized that the denunciation raised a host of troubling issues, not the least of which was the colonists' own responsibility for perpetuating the dreadful market in human property. In the end, to preserve political unity and to avoid any moral dilemmas that might undermine the Revolution's force, Congress eliminated the offending language. Even as it voiced a language of liberation, the Declaration restrained the radical momentum to which those very words contributed.[93]

The sons and daughters of the Revolution never forgot their forebears' original ambition to design a house that would harmonize all people. Their call to natural rights resounded in the words of a president who, surveying the aftermath of a Civil War battle, urged Americans to rededicate themselves "to the proposition that all men are created equal." A century later, it echoed in the words of a leader who, from the steps of a marble temple, inspired a crowd with his dream of a promised land in which children would be judged not by the color of their skin but by the content of their character.[94]

But for the time being, as the Revolution's egalitarian potential lost its initial force, as expedience and reality stood in the way of the ideal, the message was clear: the United States of America was a white man's republic.

WHAT NATURE DESIGNS WE SHOULD HAVE

The Revolution was far from over, however. From the moment in 1776 when they declared their independence, white Americans sought to make the republic as large as possible—north, south, and west, into the trans-Appalachian country and beyond. They needed territory to insulate themselves from future British threats. More important, they needed land on which their growing population could settle and prosper. By right and by destiny, with the sanction of both nature and nature's God, the United States would expand.[95]

To justify their imperial desires, Americans appealed to that ultimate source of authority: natural law. They believed that the first law of nature, self-preservation, applied to republics as well as to individuals. To save themselves from tyranny, the former colonies had joined together and declared independence. To ensure their survival, the newly united states then sought to absorb territory from which Britain otherwise might launch attacks. As Samuel Adams, one of the great revolutionary agitators, explained in 1778, "We shall never be upon a solid Footing till Britain cedes to us what Nature designs we should have, or till we wrest it from her." But Americans also grasped territory for commercial, not just military, security; the right of self-preservation included the right to flourish economically. The Convention of Kentucky in 1788, for example, called attention to "the natural right of the inhabitants of this country to navigate the Mississippi."[96]

Americans augmented their rationale for empire by smoothly merging their belief in natural law with their faith that the nation's expansion realized God's will. "The Citizens of America," George Washington triumphantly wrote in 1783, "placed in the most enviable condition, as the sole Lords and Proprietors of a vast Tract of Continent . . . are . . . to be considered as Actors on a most conspicuous Theatre, which seems to be peculiarly designated by Providence for the display of human greatness and felicity." Jedediah Morse, in *American Geography* (1789), voiced a similar message: "The God of nature never intended that some of the best part of his earth should be inhabited by the subjects of a monarch." Such statements appeared again and again in the coming decades, a robust rhetoric as unstoppable as the nation's burgeoning population. "It belongs *of right* to the United States to regulate the future destiny of *North America*," proclaimed a writer in the *New York Evening Post* in 1803. "The country is *ours*; ours is the right to its rivers and to all the sources of future opulence, power and happiness, which lay scattered at our feet."[97]

Of all the justifications for empire, perhaps the most compelling derived from a naturalistic theory of republics expounded by Franklin, Madison, Jefferson, and other founders. Here they departed from their triumphal imaginings of the Revolution. In this somber view, a republic resembled an organism with a natural life cycle of birth, growth, maturation, decay, and death. America was young and vigorous, they believed, but inevitably its maturation would bring conditions ruinous to liberty: population growth that exceeded the land base, extreme wealth and poverty, class conflict, political and moral corruption. In time, a decadent United States would succumb to its sicknesses, and the great experiment in republican government would come to an end. It was a tragic view of history, one consistent with the world's harsh realities.[98]

But, these influential founders claimed, the nation had at its disposal an antidote that might delay the inevitable. By expanding westward through space, the republic might forestall its decay through time. A western "empire of liberty" would allow the nation to retain, at least for a while, its youthful vitality. Such an empire would provide land for America's ambitious multitudes. Attached to a commercial policy of open markets, it would encourage the people to be industrious. Moreover, it would spread wealth, ensuring equality and perpetuating republican institutions. Jefferson even believed that this magical West would "diffuse" slavery until it experienced its natural demise. How this would happen was not entirely clear, but proceeds from land sales might compensate slave owners for emancipation and pay for the colonization of freed people outside the United States.[99]

To secure the West, the proponents of empire believed that the republic must reconstruct itself so that it would harmonize its national needs with the competing interests of its geographically disparate states and citizens. Britain had lost most of its North American colonies. Would the states—could the states—remain united? Their conflicting claims to the West threatened to tear them apart. Alexander Hamilton wondered if they would become "the wretched nurseries of unceasing discord," fighting one another and seeking advantage by entering into corrupt and dangerous alliances with European empires.[100]

Political restiveness within the states posed another problem. To pay their Revolutionary War debts, the states had levied heavy taxes on their citizens. Distance from coastal and urban markets, scarcity of gold and silver specie, and restrictions on paper currency prevented backcountry farmers from paying not only their taxes but also their personal debts. The angry farmers' political rebellions—some of which turned into armed rebellions—were the "storms" that Jefferson imagined would cleanse and refresh the republic. Reactionary republicans disagreed, and their concern intensified when investors, fearful of state instability, withheld capital for speculation in western land. The nation suffered from too much democracy and decentralization, the reactionaries believed; its central government was too weak to ensure the republic's security. Hamilton used an architectural metaphor to convey the magnitude of the danger. The government's "principal defects," he wrote, "do not proceed from minute or partial imperfections, but from fundamental errors in the structure of the building, which cannot be amended [except] by an alteration in the very elements and main pillars of the fabric. . . . Each state, yielding to the persuasive voice of immediate interest or convenience, has withdrawn its support, till the frail and tottering edifice seems ready to fall upon our heads, and crush us beneath its ruins."[101]

To stabilize the republic and its hold on the West, Americans—led by Hamilton and other influential founders—undertook to rebuild it. Between 1781 and 1802, the states ceded their western land claims to the federal government. The federal Land Ordinance of 1785 prepared the region for settlement. Beginning at the spot where the Pennsylvania-Ohio boundary intersected the north bank of the Ohio River, surveyors used compasses, transits, and measuring chains to delineate 640-acre, square-mile sections of land. As the surveyors moved westward, their geometric section lines created a symmetrical "grid" that incorporated the republic's natural topography into its Newtonian design. The section and its derivations—half sections (320 acres), quarter sections (160 acres), quarter-quarter sections (80 acres), and so forth—established a clear record of property ownership, which facilitated land sales and settlement. The 1787 Northwest Ordinance provided a system for creating territories and admitting them as new states in the federal union. The sale of gridded public land generated revenue that paid the war debts, which the states turned over to the federal government in 1790.[102]

Most important to Hamilton and like-minded Americans was the Constitution promulgated in 1787 and ratified by the states in 1788. Hamilton, James Madison, and the delegates to the constitutional convention framed the document and its ideas symmetrically, much as Jefferson had composed the Declaration of Independence and Monticello. The new architecture of government attempted to reconcile the needs of the nation with the rights of the states and people. It gave the federal government extraordinary powers, which it separated according to a tripartite plan: legislative, executive, and judicial. Among other legislative powers, the Congress—divided into two houses—could "lay and collect taxes" and "provide for calling forth the militia to execute the laws of the Union, suppress insurrections, and repel invasions." Overall, the document constrained democracy, which reflected the framers' belief that human nature—and thus the nature of the citizenry—was flawed. Yet the framers, in particular Madison and Hamilton, also believed that human flaws could be turned into strength. In a large, geographically extensive republic, the people's innate differences and narrow self-interests would counteract each other, such that no faction would become strong enough to form a tyranny. The framers believed that the people needed no special protections, but to satisfy critics such as Jefferson, they added a fourth component to their symmetrical plan: ten amendments constituting a "bill of rights."[103]

Although the Constitution presented a fixed political architecture, it also was like a machine that enabled citizens to convert a vast landscape into property and wealth. Madison wrote of the extensive republic under the Constitution as a "great mechanical power in government" because it combined in one secure, enlightened unit the productive capacities of diverse regional environments. Article 1, Section 8, authorized Congress "to establish Post Offices and post Roads," the beginnings of a national infrastructure of highways, canals, and railroads that would integrate and reinforce commercial activities. Madison enthused about "new improvements" in transportation that would unite the states, in particular "those numerous canals, with which the beneficence of nature has intersected our country . . . and which art finds it so little difficult to connect and complete." The prospects seemed unlimited. Nature had laid out the basic plan, Madison suggested; now it was up to the citizens "to improve and perpetuate . . . the structure of the union" by fulfilling nature's potential.[104]

After the states ratified the Constitution, only one obstacle to the Madisonian dream remained: American Indians. Even as the framers were fashioning the theories and instruments of a republican empire, they and their compatriots were busily sweeping aside thousands of people—Shawnees, Delawares, Cherokees, Creeks, and others—who stood in the way. To Indians, the Revolution and the empire for liberty had presented a choice. They could give up their distinctive ways of life and blend into the oncoming American mass, or they could join together, announce their opposition to the encroaching empire, and fight. Most chose the latter course.[105]

This radical Indian resistance to the American Revolution was the consequence of deteriorating Indian-European relations. By the early 1700s, Indians in the trans-Appalachian West had created a world in which they coexisted with Britain and France. By playing off one power against the other—by forming or threatening alliances with one or both—the Indians gained political leverage and a measure of autonomy. Within this reasonably (although not completely) secure world, they created villages, even entire tribes, out of the shattered remnants of families and bands devastated by disease and war. For a time, their economies and cultures flourished. They exchanged furs and hides for goods brought by European traders. They adopted an eclectic mixture of European and Indian food, clothing, technology, and religion, and they intermarried with Europeans, producing children with complex, blended identities. But by around the mid-1700s, this relative stability began to collapse. The growing population of the British colonies intruded as settlers and still more Indian refugees pushed across the Appalachians. The Seven Years' War resulted, and many Indians, hoping to stop the British invasion of their land, took the French side. The fighting was brutal, as Indians and British slaughtered one another with increasing ferocity.[106]

The British victory and the Proclamation of 1763 promised but failed to restore Indian country to its former stability. British settlers continued to move in, and the pressure for land sparked a powerful reaction. In the culturally fluid world of the villages, religious leaders appeared who preached a doctrine that amounted to nothing less than an Indian declaration of independence. They did not base their doctrine in natural law, but they did frame it in relation to their sense of the right, proper, inherent, and thus natural order of the universe. The Delaware Neolin and prophets like him called on Indians to obey the Master of Life, who said that they must reject all things European. They must give up alcohol, guns, Bibles, fiddles, livestock, and mixed-gender dancing. They must give up exchanging animal skins for trade goods. They must recognize their cultural and racial commonality as Indians—as red people, they said. And they must cleanse the whites from their land.[107]

As the Indian revolution gathered force, so did that of the Americans. In its own way, the Declaration of Independence was as anti-Indian as the words of the prophets were anti-European. The document exhibited an intense racial hatred crystallized through years of bitter fighting. Among the many grievances against George III, it noted that the king had "endeavoured to bring on the inhabitants of our frontiers, the merciless Indian Savages, whose known rule of warfare, is an undistinguished destruction of all ages, sexes, and conditions." The Declaration left open the possibility that African Americans or women could claim it as their own. It did not, perhaps could not, offer the same to Indians.[108]

After Britain's defeat, the struggle between Indians and Americans built to a climax. For a time, the Indians rallied and formed a confederacy that kept the Americans out of the area north of the Ohio River. But in 1794, at the battle of Fallen Timbers, the tribes suffered a stunning defeat that foretold their military demise. There would be future prophets and future battles as they struggled to hold on, and contrary to popular myth, these people would never disappear. But for all practical purposes, their ability to physically resist was coming to an end.[109]

With the Indians nearly out of the way, the door to the empire of liberty swung wide. Destiny beckoned, and the United States stood poised to claim fully what nature designed it should have.

★ ★ ★

The year 1803 was an auspicious one for the United States and the empire of liberty. America's third president, Thomas Jefferson, had arranged for the purchase of Louisiana, a vast territory west of the Mississippi River. In one fell swoop, he nearly doubled the republic's size and redefined the country that he and other Americans called the West.

From the vantage of Monticello, Jefferson looked across a spacious vista toward the Blue Ridge Mountains and imagined this western empire, a land he would never see. Beyond the Blue Ridge lay the Shenandoah Valley, and on the other side of that rose the Appalachians. From their far shoulders, shrouded in mist, the land sloped to the Cumberland Plateau, and from there dropped to the bluegrass of Kentucky and the forests and prairie openings of Indiana and Illinois. Through it all flowed the Ohio, which gathered water from the heights and fed it to the Mississippi. Beyond the great river stretched Louisiana, an enormous grassland drained by the Missouri, whose waters emerged from a stony mountain range somewhere deep in the continent's interior. Already people were moving over the Appalachians, settling, raising crops and families, founding governments, writing constitutions. The scenario captivated Jefferson, held him in its thrall, played endlessly in his head: an untroubled land of virtuous yeoman farmers, generation after generation of chosen people laboring quietly in the Earth's fertile soil.

Jefferson ignored the dark underside of his bright dream, and he did not envision that the fair land stretching before him might be riven with fratricidal violence and haunted by the Declaration's omissions and unfulfilled promises. Even as he assisted in the subjugation of Indians, even as he enjoyed the benefits of the slaves who toiled at Monticello, he, like other white Americans, looked forward to a classless, monochromatic, tranquil republic, the realization of nature's great laws. Like his countrymen, Jefferson did not imagine that although destiny beckoned, it would bring war as much as peace, sorrow as much as joy, great tragedy as much as profound triumph.

Jefferson looked west from Monticello, and the mountains, the forests, the prairies, the rivers, and the distant horizon called to him. Out there lay the happy, democratic dream that he and the other fathers had enshrined in the Declaration. Now it was for their many children—all of them—to pursue it. ★

THREE

KING COTTON

The Cotton Plant and Southern Slavery

EVERYONE IN AVOYELLES PARISH, Louisiana, agreed that Platt Epps had no peer when it came to playing the fiddle. No one else could make the instrument sing as well as the "Ole Bull of Bayou Boeuf." At balls, feasts, and festivals, his fleet bow and nimble fingers called forth tunes that moved people to dance. Whether "Jump Jim Crow," "Katy Hill," "Pumpkin Pie," "Old Joe Clark," or the "Virginia Reel," his hands worked magic on wood and horsehair and gut. Always people clamored for more, and in gratitude they filled his pockets with coin. Platt Epps had no more appreciative an audience than the children of Holmesville. Whenever he passed through town, they surrounded him and begged him to play. Sitting on his mule, he sent the notes into the humid southern air and across the eardrums of his delighted little listeners.[1]

But if Platt Epps's gifted hands and their agile digits made the sweetest music, those same appendages failed him when he took up an equally important although dreadfully onerous task. Try as he might, he could not pick cotton as dexterously as he could play the fiddle. The hands that flew over the strings turned clumsy and leaden when they reached for the bolls. The fastest pickers walked between the rows and plucked with both hands, demonstrating a "natural knack" for the job. In one motion, each hand grabbed a boll, or pod, extracted its fluffy white fiber, and put it in a sack. But Platt could not keep pace. Not only did he need both hands for each boll, but the sack that hung from his neck swung clumsily from side to side, breaking branches and killing green bolls not yet ripe enough to pick. As often as not, Platt dropped the precious fiber into the dirt before he got it into the sack. Something in his bones, muscles, sinews, and nerves prevented him from picking with greater speed and coordination. As Platt concluded, "I was evidently not designed for that kind of labor."[2]

The consequences of his inept body materialized when he toted his basket of cotton to the gin house and dropped it on the scale. Each time the load was drastically underweight, often by more than half. Rather than the standard two hundred pounds, it might total ninety-five. Edwin Epps, the master, at first forgave Platt because he was an inexperienced "raw hand." But when practice yielded no improvement, curses and the crack of a whip followed. Stripped, lying face down on the ground, Platt absorbed the master's rage, lash after lash striping his buttocks, shoulders, and back. *Platt*, the master bellowed, *you are a damned disgrace—you are not fit to associate with a cotton-picking nigger!*[3]

Still Platt did not improve, and the disgusted master finally gave up and ordered him to work on other tasks. Eventually, he went back to the cotton field, but for now he hauled baskets to the gin house, cut and hauled wood, and, at the insistence of Edwin Epps, played his fiddle. Perhaps once a week the master returned, drunk and devilish, from a day's spree in Holmesville. Assembling his exhausted laborers "in the large room of the great house," he ordered them to dance. "Dance, you damned niggers, dance," he shouted, whip in hand, as Platt struck up a tune. And then Epps joined in, "his portly form mingling with those of his dusky slaves, moving rapidly through all the mazes of the dance." *Dance, niggers, dance!* On some occasions they did not stop until late at night.[4]

Platt dreamed of escaping his nightmare. He prayed that God would deliver him from the tyrannical master, and he waited for an opportunity to escape. Often his hopes crumbled in the face of circumstances that he could not control, and he feared that he would live out his days in his Louisiana prison. When despair settled in, he took solace in his fiddle. At night in his rude cabin or on the bayou bank on a Sunday afternoon, its gentle "song of peace" carried him back to a place where his hands did not pick cotton, where loving arms encircled him, and where he was not the slave Platt Epps but someone else entirely: the husband, father, farmer, carpenter, fiddler, and free man Solomon Northup.[5]

The story of Platt Epps–Solomon Northup reveals in intimate detail the horrors of a slave economy that consumed the lives of so many African Americans during the nineteenth century—even a few, such as Northup, who were born free and later forced into bondage. Northup's story also illuminates a crucially important but insufficiently examined feature of that shattering experience: the centrality of nature.[6] Because Solomon Northup worked the cotton fields and keenly observed those landscapes, his experiences and observations provide a window into the problem of nature and slavery in American history.

Nineteenth-century southern slavery unfolded from a symbiotic relationship between cotton and people. Synthesizing water, soil nutrients, atmospheric gases, and sunlight, cotton produced seedpods filled with a fiber that humans found enormously useful and profitable. To supply a growing trans-Atlantic market of textile manufacturers and consumers, southern cotton producers cultivated more of the plant, expanding its geographical range and furthering its existence. Human labor was integral to the plant-people symbiosis. Because farmers and planters in the South chose to cultivate cotton using African American slaves, the growth of cotton production there necessarily involved the enlargement of slavery.[7]

Between about 1790 and 1860, a conjunction of interdependent developments enabled growers to spread cotton plants throughout the South. The perfection of the saw gin, a muscle-powered machine distinguished by its fine-toothed blades, gave farmers and planters the means to separate extraordinary quantities of cotton fiber from cottonseed. At virtually the same time, the adoption of short staple (short fiber) cotton varieties suited to upland soils allowed growers to move their cultivation of the plant beyond the South Carolina and Georgia coasts. Meanwhile, the territorial enlargement of the United States—resulting from conquests, treaties, and settlement policies—opened up vast areas into which growers could expand. The movement of cotton followed two primary routes: from New Orleans up the Mississippi River and from the Sea Islands of South Carolina and Georgia onto the Piedmont. By the 1850s, as growers clustered in areas with the best soils, most timely rainfall, greatest number of frost-free days, and readiest access to transportation, they formed a broad "cotton belt" that extended from North Carolina to Texas and along the Mississippi River from Louisiana to lower Missouri. The volume of fiber increased in proportion to the expanding range of the plant. In 1814–1815, the South put out some 363,000 cotton bales; by 1859–1860, the total had risen to 4.8 million, roughly two-thirds of the world's supply.[8]

As the number of acres and bales escalated, the demand for slaves shot up. When the United States banned the importation of slaves in 1808, the states of the upper South, most notably Virginia, became the major source of cotton

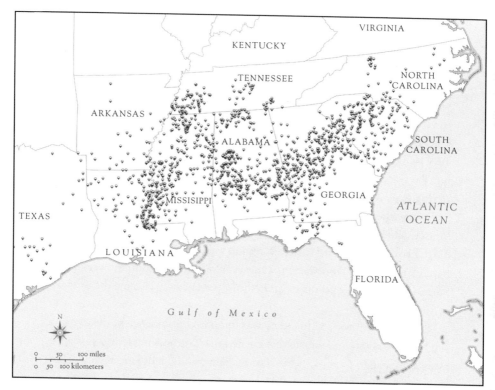

Distribution of cotton production across the South, 1850, showing a broad belt arcing across the upland South and a concentration of fields along the lower Mississippi River.

labor. A "naturally growing" slave population, as one historian has observed, ensured upper South slaveholders a perennial, and profitable, surplus. The southward movement of human property was astonishing. Between 1790 and 1860, slaveholders transported about 1.1 million people from the upper to the lower South, some 875,000 of them in the years 1820–1860. The demand caused the price of bondmen to soar. The average value of a slave rose from about $300 in 1810 to some $800 in 1860, and the price for a prime male field hand in New Orleans reached $1,800. That same year, the worth of all slaves may have risen to $4 billion, making them the most important form of property in the South, more valuable than livestock and land, and the second most valuable form of property in the United States as a whole.[9]

The demand for slaves was so great that it enticed some traders to kidnap free people and sell them into bondage. In 1841, two strangers lured Solomon

Northup from his hometown of Saratoga Springs, New York, with promises that they would employ him as a fiddler. In Washington, D.C., the men evidently drugged Northup and sold him to a Washington slave trader, who beat the unfortunate man into silence and transported him to the South. Northup's wife, Anne, soon learned of his abduction, and Northup secretly mailed a letter to a friend in Saratoga Springs asking for help, but neither Anne nor the friend knew of the enslaved man's precise location. It might have made little difference anyway, because by then Northup's captors had erased his identity, renamed him Platt, and put him up for sale at the New Orleans slave market. It was a horrifying experience. Northup witnessed the mental breakdown of Eliza, a fellow slave, when she lost her two small children on the auction block. Northup himself sold for $1,000 to a planter named William Ford. A "kind, noble, candid, Christian man," Ford treated Northup well, and the enslaved man worked hard for the master. Ford's decency, however, did not keep him from selling his human chattel to pay off debts, and Northup eventually became the property of Edwin Epps.[10]

Solomon Northup's kidnapping was but one consequence of the dynamic symbiosis of plants and people that created the Cotton Kingdom, a vast apparatus composed of crops, fields, farms, plantations, laborers, technologies, laws, political institutions, ideologies, and economic arrangements. At the top of the kingdom were the slaveholders, people such as Edwin Epps but also far wealthier planters. At the bottom of the kingdom, straining under its enormous weight, were laborers such as Solomon Northup.

Given the kingdom's size and power, it might seem logical to presume that masters such as Edwin Epps ruled it with the ease and grace of the authoritarians they were proud to be. Yet this was not the case, for the slaveholders perpetually stood in danger of losing control. Their problems began with the cotton plant itself. The long rows that Solomon Northup and other slaves tended did not automatically yield the quantity or quality of fiber that growers desired. For various biological and environmental reasons, cotton resisted complete systematization and thus weakened the farmers' and planters' power over their kingdom. It is reasonable to speculate that southerners' use of a related term, King Cotton, subtly acknowledged that the plant had mastered them at least as much as they had mastered it.[11]

Slaves compounded the farmers' and planters' problems. Any environmental condition or biological process that the masters could not control or that disrupted steady production provided laborers with an opportunity to resist enslavement. Among the sources of conflict were the slaves' very bodies. Much as cotton resisted absolute agricultural discipline, so did the human organism. Solomon Northup's otherwise capable hands and fingers failed him when he tried to pick cotton, and no amount of whipping could make his body conform to the physical requirements of the job. Numerous other natural bodily conditions—disease, childbearing, exhaustion—prevented farmers and planters from forcing enslaved people to work longer and harder than they were physically able. The masters' dominance grew even weaker when Northup and other slaves consciously used their bodies as tools of resistance. Northup was a talented fiddler, and eventually that talent helped him to do more than just make music. Historians have said much about slave resistance, but they have said little about the ways in which it flowed from the organic nature of agricultural production—from both cotton plants and human bodies. Forms of resistant nature enabled slave resistance.

The environmental history of King Cotton can be told in two parts. The first describes the agricultural life cycle of cotton as it played out each year across the expanse of the American South. The second details the life cycle of the slaves who did the work of cultivation. The crop cycle of cotton was the point of struggle between masters and slaves, as masters tried to discipline slaves for agricultural work and as slaves resisted that domination. The botanical characteristics of cotton, along with environmental conditions that stressed or ruptured the crop cycle, intensified the master-slave struggle and opened opportunities for slave resistance. One of the greatest sources of stress in the crop cycle was the life cycle of enslaved people. From conception to death, human bodies had physical characteristics and needs that conflicted with the cultivation of cotton. Meeting those bodily needs detracted from the masters' ability to accumulate wealth and retain control of their human chattel.[12]

As we follow the organic cycles of cotton and bodies, the full story of Solomon Northup will come clear. The grand movements of nature and history coursed through him as they coursed through the lives of so many other seemingly insignificant people who inhabited the Cotton Kingdom before the Civil War. To examine his life is to witness on a local scale the forces that shaped an entire society. Northup, in sum, provides answers to questions about large themes lived small. How did it feel to lose your life to a plant? Despite the pain, was there beauty? What was it like to be chased by bloodhounds, to feel their bite? What was the taste of hoecake and hog fat on a humid day in July? Did hope have a sound? Did the notes of a fiddle set you free?

Of all the great cycles that shaped the history of the early United States, few were more powerful than the seasonal development of staple crops such as cotton. Inherent in germinating seeds, budding leaves, bursting blossoms, and ripening bolls was an organic process of such vitality that it could deflect the course of history. First and foremost, the dynamic crop cycle of the cotton plant was the medium of perpetual struggle between masters and slaves. Southern agriculturalists sought to discipline the bodies of slaves for the purpose of disciplining the growth of the cotton plant. Although the masters were successful in making both slaves and plants produce phenomenal quantities of cotton fiber, they failed to achieve the total dominance they desired. The inherent instability of the crop cycle, the environmental conditions that shaped it, and the very nature of enslaved people's bodies disrupted production and provided slaves with opportunities to resist the masters' designs. This process—the master-slave struggle with nature as its dynamic core—animated southern society and drove it toward a crisis that eventually threatened to undermine it.

Deforestation opened up the land for the crop cycle of cotton. Cotton production required the removal of the trees, vines, and brush that covered much of the South. On many farms and plantations, enslaved laborers cleared land during all seasons of the year, gradually bringing more land into cultivation. One summer activity was tree girdling, in which slaves cut through the bark of a tree, severing the tender cambium layer through which flowed the life-giving sap and killing the tree so that it eventually collapsed. Most forest clearing took place from January to early March, after the yearly harvest and before the warmth and sunlight of spring caused plants to begin growing again. During this late-winter interval, masters and overseers ordered field hands into the forest. Men wielded axes, felling trees and cutting logs into sizes that they could pile. Meanwhile, women and children grubbed brush and vines and added the woody debris to the piles. When nightfall precluded further clearing, masters and overseers assigned the slaves a task suited to darkness: igniting the piles and tending them while they burned.[13]

Soil preparation and planting followed the removal of wild vegetation. Newly cleared land had roots and stumps that interfered with the growth of tender cotton roots, so laborers first planted new ground in corn. The following year, after the remaining wood had decomposed and cultivation had loosened the soil, the land was turned over to cotton. On ground already devoted to cotton, the slaves' first late-winter task was to break down old stalks and pile them for nighttime burning. Then, in March, the slaves began plowing. A heavy share pulled by a team of oxen or mules carved deep furrows four to six feet apart, heaping soil between them to form a ridge. Around April 1, the laborers ran a lighter plow down the middle of the ridge, opening a space called the drill. As the plow proceeded, a sower followed, broadcasting cottonseed into the drill. Then a work animal dragged a toothed rake, called a harrow, over the drill, covering the seed with soil.[14]

With the cottonseed lodged in its soil medium, both the pace of work and the struggle between slaves and masters intensified. In seeking to discipline cotton to make it produce, the masters submitted to a kind of biological discipline. In effect, they subordinated their lives and fortunes to the dictates of a botanical clock—germination, maturation, and fruition—that marked the passage of time and determined all agricultural tasks. To meet the discipline of that clock—to raise the crop and protect it from weather, insects, and fungi— the masters increased their regimentation of their enslaved laborers.[15] As the crop matured, the tempo and discipline of work increased. Anxious masters and overseers drove slaves to their physical limits, working them faster and for longer hours, demanding precision, and beating them if they showed any signs of slowing down or making mistakes. At such moments, hungry, tired, pained, miserable, and rebellious slaves were more likely to resist domination, and at such moments, nature often provided them with opportunities to carry out that resistance. Most important, slaves seized the opportunity presented by ripening cotton to wrest a margin of power from their oppressors. As cotton cells divided and the plant reached toward the sun, the bolls began to open, revealing their precious white fiber along with tiny pieces of a powerful thing called liberty.

Developments in the ground influenced the onset of the cyclical master-slave struggle. Masters hoping for a prolonged and thus especially lucrative harvest ordered their slaves to plant early. But if the seeds went into the soil too early and the weather turned cool and wet, the seeds remained dormant. Soil bacteria and fungi then preyed on them, and they rotted.[16] If that happened, the master who wanted to get ahead ended up behind, and he drove his slaves all the harder to replant and make up for lost growth and lost time. Planting too early thus might cause the tempo of the work to begin accelerating sooner than normal.

Regardless, the tempo increased within five to ten days of successful germination. About mid-April, cotton sprouts poked from the soil. It was an anxious moment, for the shape of the future rested on the survival of those tender shoots. To nurture them, the slaves began a process of thinning and cultivation called scraping. Although the methods varied, scraping required great dexterity and skill. Using fingers, hoes, and a light "bull-tongue" plow, the slaves deftly thinned excess cotton shoots, creating rows of single plants spaced at roughly two-foot intervals. They also removed the sprouts of weeds and grass that, if left unchecked, might crowd if not overwhelm the cotton. Yet no matter how carefully executed, scraping could not compensate for uncontrollable and unanticipated natural occurrences such as late frosts and cutworms (caterpillars) that might destroy the crop.[17] Returning to the fields early in the morning, the slaves might discover that a cold snap or an insect infestation had ruined their work. Then the crop cycle would begin again, but at a considerably more rapid and emotionally edgy pace.

In early May, some two weeks after scraping, and continuing through July, cultivation reached a fever pitch. During this time, masters and overseers found themselves locked in struggle with the unwanted vegetation that continued to sprout and thrive in open soil alongside the cotton. T. B. Thorpe, who reported on cotton production for *Harper's Magazine*, wrote that "grasses and weeds of every variety, with vines and wild flowers, luxuriate in the newly-turned sod, and seem . . . determined to choke out of existence the useful and still delicately-grown cotton." The competing vegetation grew especially rank in wet years. Under such conditions, rain not only nourished the weeds and grass but also protected them from plows and hoes. Plows did not work well in muddy soil, and masters concerned about their financial investment in healthy slaves ordered them to take shelter when rain fell. "That was the devil of a rainy season," observed the landscape architect Frederick Law Olmsted, who traveled widely throughout the antebellum South. "Cotton could stand drouth better than it could grass." To Thorpe, the struggle was a "race" that cotton growers must win at all costs: "Woe to the planter who is outstripped in his labors, and finds himself 'overtaken by the grass.'"[18]

To prevail over the grass, the masters and overseers increased the pressure on slaves. On small farms with a handful of slaves, some masters ordered their entire force—house servants, coachmen, the very old, and the very young— into the fields alongside the regular hands. During the early 1800s, the slave Charles Ball passed through South Carolina in the company of his new master and a group of fellow bondmen. While the party rested at a farm along the way, Ball heard the owner remark that "the planters were so hurried by their crops, and found so much difficulty in keeping down the grass" that they had to put all nine of their slaves in the field, including his "coachman . . . and even the waiting maids of his daughters."[19]

On large plantations with dozens or perhaps hundreds of slaves, overseers ran hoe gangs along military lines. Charles Ball experienced such regimentation on a South Carolina plantation worked by some 170 field hands. The laborers woke well before dawn to the call of the overseer's horn. After assembling in front of their quarters, they walked to the cotton fields. At the edge of a field, the "captains"—themselves slaves—called the names of the slaves whom they commanded and assigned each a row of cotton plants. Captains and companies then went to work, each subordinate member being required to keep pace with the captain. Around 7:00 a.m., they stopped briefly for a breakfast of water and rough cornbread. At noon, they stopped again for the same fare, plus salt and one radish for each hand. Then they toiled through the remainder of the day and into the darkness, until they could no longer see well enough to continue. Once more the overseer sounded his horn, and the hoe gang returned to its quarters.[20]

Frederick Law Olmsted witnessed a similar spectacle decades later while traveling through Mississippi. A "heavy thunder shower" had just passed, and "from the gin-house to which they had retreated" appeared an impressive phalanx of sturdy field hands. At the front were some forty women, "the largest and strongest women I ever saw together," wearing blue checked cloth around their bodies and colorful handkerchiefs, turban fashion, on their heads. Hoes over their shoulders, they walked "with a free, powerful swing." Next "came the cavalry, thirty strong," mostly men, along with a few plow mules. "A lean and vigilant white overseer" astride a pony "brought up the rear."[21]

Violence kept the hoe gangs in line. Winning the struggle against unwanted vegetation required masters and overseers, in their judgment, to subject the enslaved laborers to rigorous discipline. Speed was of the essence; thus the slightest indication of tardiness, loafing, lagging, malingering, error, or incompetence required physical correction, even harsh punishment. The whip was the favored instrument, a tool arguably as important to southern cotton production as the ax, plow, or hoe. "Everything was in a bustle," recalled Louis Hughes of the Mississippi plantation where he worked during the 1840s, and "always there was slashing and whipping." Often slaves were required to keep up with the fastest hoer; if they fell behind, the lash came down. On the small Louisiana plantation where Solomon Northup toiled, the master required slaves to stay even with the pacesetter. If anyone fell behind or moved ahead, he or she felt the whip's sting. Northup and the other workers seldom satisfied the master. "In fact," he said, the lash flew "from morning until night, the whole day long." The intensity of the punishment sometimes depended on the nature of the ground the slaves worked. "Some fields are easy," reported the former slave James Brown, and "some hard; some have more grass; others more roots; and it very often happens that the hands are hardest pressed where the land is most difficult to clean."[22]

On some plantations, the master or overseer tried to break the slaves' solidarity and maximize their productivity by ordering one of them to mete out field discipline. If the driver proved insufficiently harsh, he or she received a whipping. This whip-or-be-whipped tactic inspired clever responses. When Edwin Epps handed Solomon Northup a whip, the enslaved man used a ploy to deceive the master. If Epps was nearby, Northup cracked the whip within a hair's breadth of his fellows, who "squirm[ed] and screech[ed] as if in agony." When Epps was within earshot of the slaves' conversation, they made a point of grumbling about Northup's punishments. On some occasions, Northup and other drivers genuinely whipped other slaves when the master ordered; in other instances, they chose to absorb punishment rather than administer it. Assigned the role of driver on a frontier plantation in Alabama, James Williams agonized about punishing female slaves. "I used to tell the poor creatures," he later said, "that I would much rather take their places and endure the stripes than inflict them." Soon enough, he made good on his word.[23]

The violence that pervaded the struggle against weeds and grass often forced slaves into awful predicaments other than the one Northup and Williams experienced. One dilemma was that overseers compelled slaves to work quickly, which might come at the expense of working carefully. And care was often essential to their chores. If slaves did not perform tasks correctly, those tasks might not get done at all; performed imprecisely or recklessly, they might actually damage the precious cotton plants. Sometimes slaves had to choose between speed and care, and a wrong choice or hasty mistake would incur the wrath of a master or overseer.[24]

John Brown well knew the terrors. One morning on the Georgia plantation where he regularly endured brutal punishment, a mare in Brown's plow team became overheated in the sun. Intent on accomplishing his work, Brown failed to notice that the animal was ill. When he took her into the barn at noon to feed her, he saw that she failed to eat, but evidently he did not take this as a sign that something was wrong. About an hour after he returned to work, he finally recognized that the mare was in trouble. By then it was too late, and the animal "dropped down and died in the plough." Before he told Thomas Stevens, the master, Brown tried to protect himself from punishment. Returning to the barn, he removed the corn from the mare's feed bin and replaced it with gnawed cobs from another bin. The ruse was successful, in that Stevens did not blame Brown for returning the mare to work without food. Stevens still blamed Brown for the death, however, and gave him a "very severe flogging."[25]

On another occasion, Brown experienced the dilemma of having to choose between speed and care. While running a buzzard plow along the cotton to remove grass and weeds, the metal share came loose in the wooden helve that gripped it. A conscientious laborer might have stopped and repaired the device, since cultivation had to be done precisely so as not to injure the roots of the cotton plants, but Brown evidently did not believe he had that latitude. Nearly paralyzed, he tried to split the difference—he kept plowing, periodically stopping to push the loose share back into place. The tactic failed. Observing Brown's erratic progress, Stevens confronted him. When Brown bent over to show Stevens the share, the master kicked the slave "right between the eyes, breaking the bone of my nose, and cutting the leaders of the right eye, so that it turned quite round in its socket." Another slave wiped away the blood, gently pushed Brown's eye into the proper position, and applied a bandage. The wound healed, but the eye was never the same.[26]

In some instances, the imperative of controlling grass and weeds intensified the master-slave struggle to the point that it became lethal. On the far western edge of the booming cotton frontier, the landscape was rough and the exploitation of labor especially harsh. Slaves who had performed household or specialized work in the upper South lacked the physical stamina necessary to endure the rigors of this rugged plantation environment and its overseers, who had few social or institutional restraints on their behavior. On a remote Alabama cotton plantation, an overseer named Huckstep terrorized James Williams and other slaves. "Very well!" roared the tyrant, whip in hand, as he stood before Sarah, one of the soft "Virginia ladies" whom he despised. The daughter of a white planter and a slave, Sarah was pregnant, sick, and unable to keep up with the pace of hoeing. Having absorbed one hundred lashes for her failure, she was now completely spent. "Nature," Williams observed, "could do no more." Yet Huckstep had no room in his heart for forgiveness. As she hung by her wrists from the tree, her body limp, the overseer prepared to escalate the punishment:

"I shall bleed you then, and take out some of your Virginia blood. You are too fine a miss for Alabama." After slicing off her flimsy garment, he stepped back and proceeded to apply the lash. When the second blow "cut open her side and abdomen with a frightful gash," Williams could stand it no longer, and he cried out to the overseer to stop. Startled, Huckstep dropped his whip and told Williams to untie her. Williams and the other slaves carried the unconscious woman into the house, but they could not revive her. Within three days she was dead.[27]

Such violence in the service of rescuing cotton plants from weeds and grass provoked slaves to resist their oppressors, using techniques that ranged from verbal defense to physical defiance. James Williams's outburst momentarily disarmed Huckstep; in other instances, verbal defense was subtler. "You have a good deal of grass in your crop," a southern "gentleman" told a "negro manager" as they surveyed the field for which the enslaved laborer was responsible. Much more than the slave's honor and pride was at stake; negligence could have dreadful consequences. The man deflected that potentially disastrous outcome with a cool, calculated response: "It is poor ground, master, that won't bring grass." Slaves used equally subtle work techniques to resist their oppressors. Many laborers, for example, adjusted the pace according to the presence or absence of authority. If the overseer left for a moment, they slowed their toil; when he returned, they picked up the pace.[28]

When the labor of plowing and hoeing grass became too onerous, or when the violence that accompanied the work became intolerable, some enslaved people took drastic steps to protect themselves. Slaves fled bondage for many reasons, but among them was the deteriorating quality of life that accompanied the advance of the cotton crop cycle. Such was the case on the Alabama plantation where James Williams labored. "Soon after we commenced weeding our cotton," he recalled, "some of the hands, who were threatened with a whipping for not finishing their tasks, ran away." Such flight usually was temporary and created a kind of cooling off period in which masters and runaways renegotiated their expectations of work. While in hiding, the runaways often communicated with the masters through friends who served as intermediaries.[29] In other cases, the resistance of enslaved people escalated the struggle as masters and overseers retaliated with still greater violence.

When that happened, resisters paid dearly for their transgressions. While traveling across a plantation in the lower South, Frederick Law Olmsted witnessed an overseer brutally beat Sam's Sall (probably short for Sally), a teenage girl who had fled her hoe gang and whom he caught hiding in a nearby forest. "Oh, don't sir!" she begged, lying face down on the ground as the overseer savaged her naked body with a rawhide whip. "Oh, please stop, master! Please sir! Please, sir! Oh, that's enough, master! Oh, Lord! Oh, master, master! Oh, God, master, do stop! Oh, God, master! Oh, God, master!" Outright insolence cost some slaves their lives. Big Harry, recalled James Williams, was a proud, physically powerful, diligent laborer who vowed never to submit to a whipping from Huckstep, the plantation overseer. After Harry threatened to kill him, Huckstep—fortified with peach brandy—pointed a gun at the enslaved man and ordered him to drop his hoe and "come forward" for punishment. Raising the tool above his head, Harry warned the overseer to "stand back." As the other field hands watched in horror, Huckstep fired, and Harry fell across a row of cotton. "Oh Lord!" he groaned, and within minutes he was dead.[30]

Like the destruction of Sarah, the shooting of Big Harry was an unusual event, for masters and overseers—Huckstep included—could ill afford to take the lives of valuable laborers. Yet these incidents exemplify the extreme violence that could occur during a phase of the production cycle when cotton growers struggled to protect their crop from grass and weeds. Unwanted vegetation did not automatically incite murder, but it did make physical demands that escalated the master-slave struggle to the point that an enraged, drunken overseer could kill a weak or rebellious field hand. Creeping plants and brutality were linked in clusters of causal connections that could result in whippings or, in rare cases, deaths.

Rescued from grass and weeds, the cotton continued to mature. By July it had grown above the competing vegetation, its development foretelling the abundant harvest to come. "The cotton leaf is of a delicate green, large and luxuriant," wrote T. B. Thorpe, and "the stalk indicates rapid growth, yet it has a healthy and firm look." The height of the plant depended on soil type and other factors; cotton grown in the rich soil of river bottoms might grow above a man's head, while that raised in the leaner soil of upland pine forests would be smaller and shrubbier. Whether the plant was tall or short, a blooming cotton field was impressive. "There are few sights more pleasant to the eye," stated Solomon Northup, "than a wide cotton field when it is in bloom. It presents an appearance of purity, like an immaculate expanse of light, new-fallen snow." The colorful blossoms, which ranged from a rich cream to light purple or pink, lasted only a couple of days. As their petals faded and dropped to the ground, they left behind the ripening bolls, which in a matter of weeks would expand and split, a botanical transformation of profound social significance.[31]

Even now the plants were not safe, the cotton fiber not secure, the race not won. As the crop cycle neared its climax, a host of problems might still disrupt it, even wreck it. Although a powerful organic process drove the cotton plant to maturity, the equally powerful life cycles of other organisms intersected with, and fed upon, the life cycle of cotton. Unusually wet weather fostered the growth of fungal rust, which might destroy the cotton plant's leaves, and fungal rot, which might invade the boll, corrupting and consuming it from within. A moth species laid eggs that, when hatched, became the cotton worm, a caterpillar that fed on leaves and the tender boll. Whenever "these worms put in an appearance," recalled Louis Hughes, they "raised a great excitement among the planters."[32]

Of all the natural threats to cotton, perhaps none was potentially more disastrous than the army worm. T. B. Thorpe noted that the mature form of the insect, a seemingly innocuous brown moth, "would never be taken for the destroyer of vast fields of luxuriant and useful vegetation." Yet those vast fields presented an ideal habitat for the moth and its voracious caterpillar progeny. In 1804, 1827, and 1839, army worms stripped foliage from "entire districts" of cotton. By the 1840s, conditions for the species had become even better. By then, cotton culture extended in unbroken swaths across the South, in a broad belt running from South Carolina west through central Georgia, Alabama, and Mississippi, and in another centered on the lower Mississippi River. In 1846, army worms "spread throughout the entire Cotton Belt, and such destruction was never before witnessed." The caterpillars struck again in 1853, this time in conjunction with a fungal rot.[33]

Thorpe observed firsthand the army worm's impressive power, probably during the 1853 infestation, when a horde "attempted to pass from a desolated cotton field to one untouched." Enslaved laborers had deepened a ditch between the fields, creating a barrier that might obstruct and contain the worms' advance. Through this "trench the caterpillars rolled in untold millions, until its bottom, for nearly a mile in extent, was a foot or two deep in [a] living mass of animal life." The slaves then hitched an enormous log to a yoke of oxen, "and as this heavy log was drawn through the ditch, it seemed absolutely to float on a crushed mass of vegetable corruption." To Thorpe, the brute organic magnitude of the event was not fully evident until the next day, when "the heat of a tropical sun" stimulated the decomposition of the caterpillars' remains. "The stench arising from this acidulated decay was perceptible the country round," he wrote, "giving a strange and incomprehensible notion of the power and abundance of this destroyer of the cotton crop."[34]

The army worm and other pests posed serious threats to the disciplined production of cotton, yet the disruption they caused did not necessarily ruin farmers and planters or intensify the master-slave struggle. In some cases, the wreckage caused by pest infestations stalled the escalating master-slave dialectic and provided enslaved people with fleeting opportunities to better their lives, even to escape bondage altogether. By destroying the crop cycle of cotton, the pests momentarily altered the terms of an oppressive social relationship.

So Solomon Northup found in 1845, after caterpillars nearly destroyed the entire cotton crop along the Red River. Northup's master decided to recoup some of his losses by renting his slaves to sugar planters on the Gulf Coast, who would pay him up to a dollar per day for each hand. The cane crop was ready to be harvested, and the planters needed help. Master Epps and the other cotton growers of Avoyelles Parish, their slaves idled by caterpillars, were happy to oblige. In September, Northup joined a drove of 147 Red River slaves on the march southward some 140 miles to St. Mary's Parish. There he was hired out to a Judge Turner, a wealthy planter whose land adjoined the Bayou Salle, which emptied into Atchafalaya Bay. In contrast to his poor aptitude for picking cotton, Northup had an innate talent for cutting cane. The work "came to me naturally and intuitively," he recalled, "and in a short time I was able to keep up with the fastest knife." Soon he was promoted to driver, whip replacing sharp instrument. Although cane labor was strenuous, it offered side benefits. Not only did Judge Turner pay him for working on Sundays, but the other planters rewarded him for the services of his fiddle. An evening performance in the town of Centerville once earned him seventeen dollars, a sum that made him nearly "a millionaire" in the eyes of the other slaves.[35]

Most important, a fiddling job in Centerville opened an opportunity for Northup to contemplate escape. A steamboat captain had brought his vessel up the Rio Teche to dock at the town. Northup overheard the captain say that he was a northerner, and this emboldened the enslaved man to ask the captain for help in getting away. Although the captain expressed sympathy, he would not allow Northup to hide on his boat. The risk was too great; if authorities discovered Northup on board, they would punish the captain and confiscate his vessel. The captain's refusal plunged the slave into despair, and he soon returned to the Bayou Boeuf. The incident had raised his hopes, however, and he began planning for the day when he would make good his escape. The agricultural ruin caused by caterpillars oriented Northup in the direction of freedom.[36]

When and where the army worm and other pests did not devastate the fields, the organic power of cotton drove the crop cycle to its climax. From late July to late August, the bolls on the bottom branches began to split open, and the wooly fiber was ready for picking. The pods on the middle branches ripened next. Finally, until autumn frost killed the plant, its uppermost layers continued to blossom and yield ripe bolls. Tensions ran high during picking time. An ample, high-quality crop promised great profits, and masters were eager to gather the harvest at its peak, before rain, dew, dust, or frost discolored it and before the shell of the pod grew brittle and cracked into woody fragments that stuck in the fiber. "I often saw Boss so excited and nervous during the season," Louis Hughes recalled of his owner, "that he scarcely ate."[37]

Under such conditions, masters and overseers ordered all available hands into the fields, including house servants, again whipping them onward. "The season of picking was exciting to all planters," said Hughes, and "every one was zealous in pushing his slaves in order that he might reap the greatest possible harvest." The work could be brutal. Hour after hour, the hands dragged their sacks down the rows, their backs and arms aching, the tender skin around their fingernails scraped, pricked, and lacerated by the sharp ends of the brittle pod, their blood threatening to stain the cotton and render it worthless. Each laborer was required to pick a minimum weight, and if he or she fell short, the master or overseer administered punishment, in some cases one lash for every pound below the standard. "With the fear of this punishment ever before us," recalled John Brown, "it was no wonder we did our utmost to make up our daily weight of cotton in the hamper."[38]

A combination of physical ability and experience enabled some laborers, called top hands or crack pickers, to gather the crop with extraordinary speed. Charles Ball believed that "the art of picking cotton depend[ed] not upon superior strength, but upon the power of giving quick and accelerated motion to the fingers, arms, and legs." John Brown's gendered assessment essentially agreed with Ball's; although men's superior strength enabled them to carry heavy baskets of cotton more easily, women were faster pickers, because their more delicate, tapered fingers made them "more naturally nimble." Perhaps a combination of controlled, forceful, agile movement impelled the splendid Patsey, an athletic young woman who drew Solomon Northup's admiration. No man or woman on the Epps plantation jumped higher or ran faster or chopped wood, drove a team, turned a furrow, or rode a horse more expertly. And no one, Northup asserted, matched her skill in picking cotton. When the production standard was two hundred pounds, Northup claimed that Patsey on occasion gathered five hundred. Because of the "lightning-like motion . . . in her fingers," at "cotton picking time, Patsey was queen of the field."[39]

Like no other phase of the crop cycle, the harvest magnified all the biological and cultural pressures inherent in cotton production. It was the masters' moment of truth, the yearly event in which they most conclusively demonstrated their dominance over their world. While driving their slaves onward, they gazed in satisfaction at the mounds of white fluff piling up inside their gin houses.

Paradoxically, the harvest also demarcated the limits of the masters' power. For all their efforts to control land and life, the masters never controlled the cotton plant exactly as they desired. They struggled to make it produce fiber more quickly and in greater, more easily harvestable quantities, but they were never completely successful. Cotton always imposed physical limits on their ambitions. To counter that botanical power, the masters responded in three ways. They tried to invent machines that speeded the harvest. Then they altered the nature of the cotton boll in an effort to make it meet their production goals; in effect, using natural hybridization and selective breeding, they tried to turn cotton's botanical power to their own ends. When these strategies were not completely successful, they tried to manipulate the size or efficiency of their labor force.

None of these options was simple or easy to accomplish. The first two were extraordinarily difficult. For various reasons, pre–Civil War cotton growers never created satisfactory picking machines.[40] Southerners also experimented with cotton plants, but finding, cultivating, and disseminating new varieties required years of effort. Thus the most immediate, day-to-day means by which masters could counter the botanical power of cotton was to squeeze more work from their slaves. Yet this, too, had physical limits; slave bodies and the persons who inhabited them imposed restrictions on the amount of labor slaves could, and would, perform. To induce slaves to extract cotton fiber from the boll more quickly, masters found it expedient to concede to the slaves an additional slice of power.

This is how the process unfolded. As late as the 1830s, most southern cotton growers raised two varieties, Georgia green seed, introduced from the West Indies, and Siamese (or Creole) black seed, introduced from Siam, the southeast Asian country now called Thailand. Because the ripe bolls of these plants did not open wide, slaves, no matter how dexterous, could not easily extract their fiber. Besides the physical structure of the bolls, a range of natural conditions—the length of daylight, the speed and agility of human hands, the capacity of the human body to withstand fatigue—imposed absolute limits on picking. Fatigue also had a cultural component: the Sabbath. Six days you shall labor, the Bible said, and on the seventh, like God, you shall rest. Many slaves, moreover, devoted evenings and Sundays to gardens that supplemented their diets. The human body, in sum, needed rest and rejuvenation to pick cotton.[41]

Thus the dilemma for the masters was to increase production up to the absolute physical limits imposed by daylight, handwork, and fatigue. The masters tried physical force, but this, too, had natural limits. When they pushed the hours of work into the evening and Sunday, the slaves grew malnourished, weary, and slow. If they whipped the slaves, the physical pain they inflicted inspired resistance, perhaps flight. And eventually, violence broke down the human body, which contradicted the whip's instrumental purpose.[42] The masters tried another tactic, premised not on force and punishment but on incentive—they began to pay premiums to slaves, often a penny per pound, for picking above a targeted daily minimum, and they began to pay the slaves to work on Sundays. Thus, in the midst of a brutal slave regime, something remarkable happened: the difficult, resistant natures of the cotton boll and the human body contributed to the formation of an incipient wage system characteristic of a "free labor" economy. In many places in the South during the early 1800s, a market developed for the Sunday labor of people who were slaves during the remainder of the week. Some masters, in fact, found themselves engaged in competition with each other for the services of their own laborers.[43]

Even as slaves profited from this economy, some growers were busy introducing, discovering, and breeding new cotton varieties that gradually altered the nature of the master-slave struggle. One of the greatest developments in the history of the Cotton Kingdom was the combination of accident and design that caused the spread of new cotton varieties across the South. In 1811, a fungal rot afflicted Mississippi Valley cotton fields, reducing yields of the Creole black seed variety by as much as 50 percent. The bolls on cotton plants grown from seed recently introduced from Mexico resisted the fungus. In subsequent years, pollinating insects cross-fertilized the Mexican, Creole, and Georgia varieties. These plants then generated new seeds that grew into a hybrid variety of impressive vigor and productivity. Not only did the hybrid

"Mexican cotton" resist rot and produce more bolls per plant, but its bolls matured earlier and often simultaneously and, when ripe, opened much wider, enabling a laborer to pluck their fiber more easily. Over the years, systematic selection elaborated these traits into monster plants. An observer in Mississippi during the 1850s, for example, recorded 54 bolls growing on a bush two and one-half feet tall, and 134 bolls bursting from a plant of three feet. Such fecundity changed the nature of harvest labor. Whereas a top hand picked thirty to fifty pounds per day of Creole or Georgia cotton, he or she now picked two hundred or more pounds of the Mexicanized hybrid. By serendipity and selectivity, the masters had harnessed the botanical power of cotton to their agricultural ambitions.[44]

Mexican cotton's phenomenal organic productivity, however, did not necessarily give the masters greater power over their slaves. Although the plant required slaves to pick more pounds, those pounds offered the laborers important opportunities to retain or win autonomy from the masters. In South Carolina, for example, the productivity of Mexican cotton invited slaves to tend their own patches at night and on Sundays and to sell the small harvest for cash.[45] More important, the abundant nature of the Mexican hybrid motivated masters to continue to pay premiums for pounds of cotton harvested above the prevailing standard. As fiber flooded the market and drove down prices, the masters tried to uphold their profits by growing and harvesting even more cotton.[46] Just as they had offered incentives to slaves to pluck small quantities of Creole or Georgia cotton faster, so they now offered similar incentives to entice their laborers into collecting as much as possible of the massive surplus generated by the Mexicanized hybrid.

Here was a startling botanical paradox: a fixed number of field hands could cultivate more acres of Mexican cotton than it could harvest. The laborers could plow, sow, scrape, and hoe as many acres as they were physically able, but they could never work long or hard enough to pick all the fiber from those acres before spring arrived and they had to begin plowing and planting again. Thus, at picking time, masters still found themselves in the predicament of having to mobilize additional labor in order to maximize the harvest and their economic gain. They had three alternatives. They might pay a hefty fee to another master for the temporary use of additional hands. They might create their own labor reserve by purchasing more slaves, in which case they had to find work for those extra hands before and after the harvest. Or they might try to boost the efficiency and productivity of their existing slave force by paying premiums.[47]

Whenever they paid premiums, they revealed the power of the Mexicanized hybrid to alter the terms of the master-slave struggle.

The masters tried to win back a measure of the power they ceded. In particular, a national depression during the 1830s compelled some cotton growers to intensify their regimentation and control of their laborers. While some masters began marketing their slaves' Sunday cotton production, often for less than the highest price, others prohibited such production altogether. On some plantations, masters introduced credit and other forms of noncash incentives. Louis Hughes recalled that his owner organized field laborers into two teams for a cotton-picking competition. The winning team received a cup of sugar for each hand. "The slaves were just as interested in the races as if they were going to get a five dollar bill," Hughes remarked. John Brown recalled that his master organized competitions "for an old hat, or something of the sort."[48] Still, the superabundance of Mexican cotton continued to encourage some masters to pay cash premiums. In 1849, one Alabama planter used the technique to entice his labor force to harvest an average of 350 pounds per hand every day for three weeks straight. Other planters retained the practice of cash wages for Sunday labor. "It is usual," Solomon Northup said, "in the most hurrying time of cotton-picking, to require the same extra service."[49]

Premiums or not, as fall turned to winter, the picking continued. Although the stalks had turned brown and brittle and the fiber inside the bolls dusty and yellow, the slaves still pulled their rough sacks down the rows. On Christmas day, rather than resting according to custom, some laborers—now momentarily, conditionally free—chose to pick cotton in exchange for cash. January arrived and then came February, and the pursuit of botanical wealth persisted. Across the lifeless landscape of the South, the thinly clad laborers toiled on.[50]

Soon, nature brought cotton production full circle. Lengthening days, moisture, and the promise of warmth signaled a new beginning to the cotton cycle, the awesome driver of southern history. Late one winter, while traveling through Louisiana, Frederick Law Olmsted paused at the edge of a Red River cotton field, perhaps in the vicinity of the Epps plantation and the sad little prison of Solomon Northup. As Olmsted looked on, the laborers "[broke] down, in preparation for re-ploughing the ground for the next crop, acres of cotton plants" on which "a tolerable crop of wool still hung, because it had been impossible to pick it."[51]

A magnificent botanical pulse of birth, growth, fruition, death, and decay, the crop cycle of cotton marked the passage of time across a good portion of the American South. There was another organic cycle that shaped the southern agricultural landscape as well, a cycle on which cotton depended but against which it also competed: the life cycle of enslaved people. Although cotton progressed from seed to fiber by means of cell division, respiration, photosynthesis, and other physiological processes, the plant still required human labor to survive. Without people to sow and till the crop, it would weaken and diminish and possibly perish. At the same time, the human body had physical needs that were not necessarily consistent with those of cotton. The human body required food, water, rest, nurture, and reproduction. Fulfilling those needs—bearing children, procuring food, recovering from fatigue, recuperating from illness, caring for the aged—took labor away from the cultivation of cotton. In short, the production and reproduction of the human body both supported and conflicted with the production and reproduction of the plant. The tension between the needs of the plant and the needs of the body shaped cotton culture in profound ways.

Solomon Northup's life and experience encapsulated the tension between cotton and the body. To get the wealth and power that cotton conferred, Edwin Epps needed Northup's body and its labor, but Northup could be included among the many organic obstacles that stood between Epps and his objective. Northup had no natural knack for picking cotton, nor had society disciplined his body from childhood to perform the task. His need for food and sleep absorbed energy and time, and microbial illnesses occasionally laid him low. His eating, sleeping body, moreover, supported an intelligent brain and a mysterious life force that people then and since have called the soul. Body, mind, and soul, one and inseparable, were the font of slave resistance, a perpetual challenge to the masters' power.[52] Fiddling, a bodily activity for which Northup had great natural aptitude, focused his mind, soothed and inspired his soul, and opened opportunities for him to experience moments of liberty—moments at which he might even contemplate escape. Epps used physical force to counter the organic obstacle that Northup's body posed, but force undercut the slave's instrumental and economic value. Ultimately, in sustaining Northup, Epps sustained an obstacle to the accumulation of wealth in botanical form.

The tension between bodies and plants that shaped southern cotton culture began with the formation of children. Masters recognized early in the history of North American slavery that human fertility and "natural increase," not just crop commodities, promised to enrich them. More slaves meant more hands to do more work, and more slaves meant more chattels that could be sold or rented to others. Yet the reproduction of slaves and cotton often conflicted.[53]

Some enslaved women resisted the masters' efforts to control and profit from their reproductive powers. Abstinence enabled them to postpone or prevent pregnancy. So did the prolongation of breastfeeding, which stimulated the release of hormones that delayed ovulation. Enslaved women also drew on African and New World pharmacological knowledge and ingested contraceptives or abortifacients such as calomel, turpentine, indigo, calamus root, and the root of the plant to which they yielded so much labor: cotton. One of the plant's evolutionary adaptations was gossypol, a toxic chemical compound that reduced the fertility of the herbivores that consumed it. The irony was as rich as river bottom soil: cotton's resistant nature enabled enslaved women to resist the reproduction of more children who would cultivate more cotton. "Maser [master] was going to raise him a lot more slaves," Mary Gaffney later explained, "but still I cheated Maser[.] I never did have any slaves to grow and Maser he wondered what was the matter. . . . I kept cotton roots and chewed them all the time but I was careful not to let Maser know or catch me."[54]

The nature of field labor intensified the rivalry between human and botanical reproduction. Slave owners needed women's labor and the labor (and commodity value) of the children the women bore. Long workdays, exhaustion, and poor nutrition, however, reduced the female laborers' ability to conceive, and once pregnant, the women experienced working conditions that threatened the security of their unborn children. Jepsey James demanded hard labor from the pregnant women on his Mississippi cotton farm. When one of them failed his expectations or resisted him, he confronted a problem: how to punish her—how to hurt her—while leaving untouched the valuable property in her womb. His solution was to order the woman to lie face down over a hole in the ground, her distended belly projecting into the cavity. With her unborn child thus shielded, James freely applied the lash.[55]

Even if the unborn escaped such violence unscathed, the contrary pulls of cotton cultivation and childbearing shaped children's prenatal and neonatal development. Pregnant field hands who received insufficient nourishment produced small, unhealthy babies; the average birth weight of an enslaved child in the American South may have been as low as five and one-half pounds, and many entered the world stillborn. Should an infant survive birth, his or her mother enjoyed momentary freedom from the most exhausting forms of work. Masters assigned nursing women, called sucklers, light tasks such as repairing fences and shucking corn or allowed them to hoe or pick less than the other hands. Easier duties allowed sucklers to breastfeed their infants several times a day. On some plantations, the master regimented even this limited freedom; each day at the appointed times, the overseer sounded his horn, calling the mothers to breastfeed their offspring. Regular breastfeeding strengthened the newborns. Kept in a nursery under the care of aged women or older children, placed at the side of a field, or slung across a mother's back, the infants held their own.[56]

Within a few months of delivery, the masters decided that cotton needed more attention and babies less, and they pressured nursing mothers to return to full-time field labor. Infants that breastfed less often lost the nutritional and immunological protections that mothers' milk provided. Antibodies in the milk no longer flowed regularly into their stomachs, but disease organisms did, from contaminated water, tainted cow's milk, and unsanitary utensils. The children were most vulnerable when the needs of cotton were most urgent—at the beginning of the crop cycle, when all hands were needed to sow, thin, and weed, and at the end, when the cotton needed to be picked. Mortality increased dramatically at those times, as cotton accumulated at the cost of children's lives. Infancy and early childhood were a grim struggle for many enslaved children. Fewer than half survived to age five, a mortality rate roughly double that of America's free population.[57]

After enslaved children reached the age of eight, their diet improved, their mortality declined, and their bodies began to grow normally. Not only were older children better able to fend for themselves and get the nourishment they needed, but their participation in fieldwork earned them more food, including meat.[58] The maturation of children, however, did not completely reconcile the competing needs of bodies and plants.

To produce cotton, the masters and their slaves had to raise food crops and food animals. Corn was the most important source of plant food, and by the 1860s, the South devoted more acres to corn than to cotton. Corn offered important ecological, agricultural, and economic advantages to cotton producers. The plant grew well in the South's climate and soils and, when dried, stored well. Corn's crop cycle, moreover, was different enough from the crop cycle of cotton that the two did not always conflict. Corn was planted around March 1, "about a month earlier than the cotton," recalled Louis Hughes. "It was, therefore, up and partially worked before the cotton was planted and fully tilled before the cotton was ready for cultivation." Corn cultivation, moreover, had the potential to absorb surplus labor kept in reserve for the cotton harvest.[59] Corn also made excellent feed for livestock, especially hogs, the South's greatest source of meat and fat. Hogs foraged for acorns and other nuts on unused land that southerners called the open range; masters and slaves later fattened the animals on corn.[60]

Despite their advantages, corn and hogs posed obstacles to cotton and its kingdom. One obstacle was agricultural. The crop cycles of corn and cotton were still close enough that slaves had to coordinate their cultivation of both plants carefully, maneuvering from one to the other in an effort to meet the needs of each. The diary of Levin Covington, a Mississippi planter, suggests the complexity and difficulty of the work. "All hands transplanting corn in No. 4 till breakfast," wrote Covington in spring 1829, "then started 4 Ploughs throwing off from corn in old Sheep pasture, finished that & broke up middles in cotton part of same—Hoes finished transplanting and commenced after the ploughs to scrape corn at 12 o'clock, finished and scraped small piece of cotton the second time & stopped an hour by sun."[61]

The other obstacle that corn and hogs posed was physiological: corn and pork—especially pork fat—were insufficient sources of human nourishment. Slaves normally received a weekly ration of corn and bacon. Each day they ground the corn into meal, mixed it with a little water, and formed it into cakes or fritters, often called hoecake or Johnnycake. Then they baked the cakes and dipped them in grease from the bacon or fried the fritters directly in the melted fat. On the Epps plantation, Solomon Northup consumed such fare. Sundays at the corncrib and smokehouse, he took possession of the coming week's food: enough corn to make a peck of meal (eight quarts, or two gallons) plus three and one-half pounds of bacon.[62] Corn and bacon certainly could provide the calories that Northup and other enslaved people needed for strenuous labor, but they could not provide the nutrients necessary for a healthy diet. Many slaves thus suffered from diseases such as pellagra, caused by a deficiency of niacin, an essential B vitamin. Corn contained niacin in a chemical form that required the amino acid tryptophan to release it. Lean meat furnished the necessary tryptophan, but fat pork did not. Symptoms of the disease included body pains, scaly skin, reddish eyes, a coated tongue, headaches, dizziness, and, in its worst stages, diarrhea, hallucinations, stupor, and death.[63]

Charles Ball observed signs of malnutrition, perhaps pellagra, among slaves during the many years he labored in South Carolina and Georgia. "A half starved negro is a miserable looking creature," he recalled. "His skin becomes dry, and appears to be sprinkled over with whitish husks, or scales; the glossiness of his face vanishes, his hair loses its colour, becomes dry, and when stricken with a rod, the dust flies from it." John Brown remembered the symptoms of malnutrition in his own body. "In truth I was not much to look at," he recalled of his humiliating sale on the auction block. "I was worn down by fatigue and poor living till my bones stuck up almost through my skin, and my hair was burnt to a brown red from exposure to the sun."[64]

Slave masters strove to overcome the obstacles that corn and pork imposed, directly or indirectly, on cotton production. Depending on the season, some gave their slaves additional food, such as potatoes, cabbage, rice, peas, fish, molasses, and a little salt.[65] John Brown told about the soup made of corn and potatoes—called loblolly, mush, or "stirt-about" (stirabout)—that the cooks dished out to the field hands, one pint per hand, for their noon meal. One day Brown's master added something else to the mix: cottonseed. Sheep and cattle consumed "oil cake" made from crushed surplus cottonseed, and perhaps a little of the same might suit the slaves. It was a logical idea, at least in the abstract, because feeding cottonseed to slaves would help reconcile the opposing pulls of cotton production and food procurement. In effect, it would allow the master to have his cotton and eat it, too. Brown ate the cottonseed as ordered, but the experiment backfired. The swill was "unwholesome," he remembered, and "I broke out in great ulcers, from my ankle-bone upwards."[66]

Unless they were willing to devote more time, labor, or money to the sustenance of slaves, the masters had but one solution to the deficiencies of corn and pork: allowing enslaved people the time, space, and resources to procure additional food. By tending their own gardens and livestock and by hunting, fishing, trapping, and gathering, slaves could supplement their cracked corn and greasy bacon. The alternatives, smaller quantities of cotton or run-down slaves, were unacceptable.[67] But by allowing enslaved people to tend gardens, keep chickens, pursue wild game, and gather berries and nuts, the masters relinquished a measure of power and liberty to them. Slaves who engaged in their own provisioning enjoyed greater personal autonomy, accumulated small amounts of cash, strengthened their bodies, perfected survival skills, and gained access to spaces that enabled their attempts to escape.[68]

Gardens tended by enslaved people were some of the most important resources in the Cotton Kingdom. Near the slave quarters, on small plots of unused farmland or in the forests that surrounded the plantations and farms, the slaves tilled small patches, one per family or cabin, of onions, potatoes, cabbages, cucumbers, pumpkins, melons, peas, turnips, and other fare. The size, number, and location of the patches depended on the farm or plantation and the number of slaves who lived there. On the South Carolina cotton plantation where Charles Ball toiled, some 250 slaves tended about thirty gardens, most of them located "in some remote part of the estate, generally in the woods." Bondmen such as Ball worked their gardens in the evening, at night (on some occasions to the light of torches held by children), and on Sundays. Not only did gardens provide nutritious food, but they also allowed the slaves to produce small surpluses, which they sold to masters and other free people. The cash permitted the slaves to purchase basic clothing, additional food, and small luxuries such as tobacco, candy, and alcohol.[69]

Livestock enabled enslaved people to put additional protein on their tables. Slaves kept chickens, ducks, geese, and turkeys around their own quarters, as well as hogs, horses, mules, and cattle, which foraged on the uncultivated land that stretched away from farms and plantations into unsettled areas—a vast open range encompassing more than 90 percent of the South's total acreage. The keeping of livestock connected enslaved southerners to a great regional herding tradition, and although they were not legally free, they nevertheless claimed their right to a common landscape.[70]

The open range also provided a diverse array of wild foods, which slaves collected at night and on Sundays. Uncultivated areas on and off the farms and plantations supplied nuts, berries, and greens. George Ball recalled eating a simple meal with his adopted slave family: cold cornbread and boiled leaves from lamb's-quarters, a plant common to North America and an excellent source of vitamin C, which was necessary for preventing scurvy. The South's immense commons teemed with animal life—deer, rabbits, opossums, raccoons, groundhogs (marmots), wild pigs, squirrels, turtles, fish, and other creatures—that provided extra protein. Some of the animals thrived in ecological relationship to food crops. Solomon Northup, for example, explained that the masters encouraged slaves to hunt raccoons, "because every marauding coon that is killed is so much saved from the standing corn." Although meat from all the animals was nutritious and tasty, the slaves preferred some to others. "The flesh of the coon is palatable," Northup pronounced, "but verily there is nothing in all butcherdom so delicious as a roasted 'possum."[71]

Enslaved southerners employed an impressive array of techniques and skills to capture their prey, some probably inherited from their African forebears. Masters generally prohibited the use of firearms, so slaves resorted to traps, snares, weirs, sticks, clubs, stones, bows and arrows, and, when necessary, their bare hands. Some methods required great cunning, inventiveness, and patience. Frederick Law Olmsted met a slave who had attached a scythe blade or butcher's knife to a wood staff, making a kind of lance. He positioned the lance "near a fence or fallen tree which obstructed a path in which the deer habitually ran, and the deer in leaping over the obstacle would leap directly on the knife. In this manner he had killed two deer the week before my visit." Solomon Northup, skilled in carpentry as well as fiddling, fashioned an ingenious fish trap from short pieces of wooden board and sticks. Wet cornmeal and pieces of cotton rolled together and dried into hard lumps served as bait.[72]

Other hunting methods required extraordinary stealth. Charles Ball stepped softly along the edge of the South Carolina swamp. Spotting his prey, he stopped; slowly, carefully, he reached down—and snatched the turtle. Tying a strip of hickory bark around a flailing rear leg, he hung the animal from a nearby tree branch. After catching several turtles, he carried them back to his quarters and put them in a hole surrounded by a low fence made of split wood. Now and then he poured water into the hole to sustain his captives. When he was hungry, he pulled one out, butchered and cooked it, and enjoyed its meat.[73]

Perhaps the most important hunting method involved the use of dogs. Widespread throughout the South, dogs played crucial roles in the agroecology of the region. Masters used them for hunting foxes, deer, bears, game birds, and other wild creatures and for herding livestock, guarding family and property, catching rats, and, in the form of bloodhounds, pursuing runaway slaves. In "a world teeming with dogs," as one historian has described the canine South, slaves easily acquired the animals and trained them to hunt. Masters had reason to tolerate if not encourage the practice, because it checked varmint populations and helped slaves augment meager rations. Charles Ball, one of the rare bondmen whose master allowed him to hunt with a gun, did so in the company of Trueman, his dog. Most slaves used dogs alone. Dogs flushed the prey, chased it, and treed it. Slaves then shook the tree and dislodged the prey or climbed up and knocked the animal from its perch. When it fell to the ground, the dogs clenched it in their jaws and shook it to death.[74]

The slaves' procurement of food nourished their bodies, enabled the production of cotton, and, in effect, strengthened the institution of slavery. Yet such self-sufficiency also posed problems for the masters. One problem was physiological and instrumental: slaves devoted so much effort at night and on Sundays to gardening, hunting, and other subsistence activities that they were too exhausted to be efficient field hands. Masters wanted slaves to feed themselves, but they did not want any reduction in the labor and energy expended on cotton.[75] Even more problematic for the masters, slave self-sufficiency encouraged slave independence. Hunting with dogs allowed enslaved men to be manly producers who provided important sustenance for their families.[76] Subsistence practices such as hunting also opened opportunities for slaves to resist the regime that dominated them, by helping them to steal from the masters and by allowing them to acquire knowledge and learn skills that enabled their attempts to escape.

A dog trained to hunt raccoons could also be used to hunt one of the master's hogs. The more forests, fields, thickets, ravines, wetlands, streams, and other subsistence environments a plantation encompassed, the harder it was for a master or overseer to detect such pilfering. A trained dog, moreover, could stand sentinel while a slave raided a smokehouse or other storage building.[77] Similar circumstances abetted the slaves' theft of garden produce. If a hog belonging to a slave ate some of the master's corn or potatoes, how would the master know the damage had not been done by one of his own animals? If slaves kept gardens, how would the master know whether the slaves' reserves of corn, potatoes, or other fare came entirely from their own patches or partly from the master's fields and storehouses?[78]

Charles Ball's experience with fishing demonstrates the process by which self-provisioning and theft overlapped. Early one year, at the conclusion of the cotton harvest, Ball embarked on a scheme to use his knowledge of fishing to improve his standing with the master and escape the drudgery of field labor. When Ball caught some fish in his weir, he gave them to the master. Pleased and impressed, the master summoned Ball to the great house and discovered that the slave had learned to use a seine on the Patuxent River in Maryland. The master then ordered Ball to lead an expedition to the nearby Congaree River to catch fish for the entire plantation. With the assistance of a few other hands, Ball made some canoes, knit a seine with ropes and twine furnished by the master, and began hauling in fish from the slow, tepid, swampy stream. The master allowed Ball and his crew to eat all the catfish, pike, perch, mullet, and suckers they desired, but he forbade them to consume shad, the fattest and most flavorful of the fish. Shad, the master made clear, were to be reserved for him alone.

To ensure the success of the project and to ensure that Ball and his fellow slaves turned over all the shad, the master appointed a white supervisor.[79]

Ball was disappointed at having to put up with the oversight of a "fish-master," but he soon contrived a means to elude the man's gaze and steal some of the shad. Not only was the fish master ignorant of seine fishing, but he was also uninterested in working at night, the best time for taking shad. In Ball's view, the fish master "had not been trained to habits of industry, and could not bear the restraints of uniform labour." By working hard and dutifully surrendering the shad, Ball and the other slaves convinced the man that he could trust them to work at night without supervision. Once alone, Ball and his co-workers ate some of the forbidden fish. Not only that, but they exchanged shad for bacon with traders who boated the Congaree by night. Ball's scheme almost fell apart when one of his co-workers, Nero, decided to use the cover of fishing and darkness to sell stolen cotton to a trader. When the plantation overseer arrived at the fish camp to investigate, he was startled by the plumpness—indeed, the very smell—of the slaves, the result of their rich diet. He could only scratch his head, curse, and wonder about the fatness of the fishermen while "the hands on the plantation were as lean as sand-hill cranes."[80]

Slaves did not trouble themselves over the means by which they procured their food. They needed nourishment sufficient to perform the hard labor of bringing in the cotton, and whether they grew food for the masters to dole out to them, produced it by their own private efforts, or stole it mattered little to them. "If we did not steal," explained John Brown, "we could scarcely live."[81] Slaves were eclectic producers and foragers, and the Cotton Kingdom in its totality constituted a vast environment of multiple possibilities for subsistence, including thievery.

Much as subsistence opened opportunities for slaves to steal, so it opened opportunities for them to learn skills and acquire knowledge that helped them to escape. Roaming the fringes of the plantations and farms, they learned to use forests, hills, ridges, ravines, swamps, thickets, cane brakes, and other landscape features for concealment and escape. Hunting, fishing, foraging, and thievery also proved to be essential preparation for running away. Charles Ball made excellent use of his skills during his flight from Georgia to Maryland in 1812–1813. Whether traveling by night, hiding in swamps and thickets, kindling a fire, fording swift streams, eluding alligators, evading slave patrols and killing their dogs, stealing corn and potatoes, or taking opossums and wild pigs, Ball proved himself to be a consummate outdoorsman and survivalist.[82]

For some enslaved people contemplating or attempting escape, dog handling skills were invaluable. Solomon Northup well knew the savagery of hounds whose teeth ripped and slashed fleeing bondmen. Edwin Epps evidently loaned his dogs to Northup for hunting, and whenever the slave was alone with the animals, he whipped and dominated them until they "obey[ed] my voice at once when others had no control over them whatever." Thus, should Northup run and Epps sic the hounds on him, he was prepared to preempt their attack. James Williams would have appreciated Northup's cunning. He grew close to the bloodhounds on the Alabama plantation where he toiled under the watchful eye of the brutal Huckstep. When the enslaved man finally fled, Huckstep sent the dogs after him. The animals did not bite Williams when they caught up with him, but greeted him eagerly and responded to his commands. Eventually he "started them in pursuit of a deer." As the dogs bounded away, Williams continued his escape to Pennsylvania. James Smith relied on his personal hunting dog for protection. After he fled the Georgia cotton plantation on which he had been enslaved, the loyal canine helped him fight off a pack of bloodhounds. The animal then accompanied him all the way to Ohio and freedom.[83]

The subsistence needs of enslaved people opened opportunities for James Smith and others to weaken the hold of the masters but also imposed sharp limits on their lives. Natural vagaries such as insects and inclement weather affected gardens no less than cotton fields, and the annual round of the seasons brought periods of want as well as plenty. Eventually, the shad runs tapered off, the garden patches quit yielding, and the fat on opossums and raccoons dissolved. Even when nature cooperated, not all slaves could take advantage of its bounty. The very young and the very old, people burdened by dependents, and field hands on the most regimented plantations often lacked the ability to glean more from the world.[84]

Most important, the masters still had the upper hand. Some allowed slaves to tend gardens—but only as a reward for meeting production goals. During the 1850s, masters across the South placed greater restrictions on their slaves' subsistence practices, sometimes prohibiting such activities or claiming a portion of their fruits. And beginning in South Carolina, southern states took steps to reduce their dog populations in order to reduce the autonomy of enslaved people. Slaves with dogs faced a choice: pay a tax or kill the trusty friend. Cash poor but dog rich, many chose the second option.[85] Across the South, the bloodhounds still bayed, but for untold numbers of slaves, hunting with dogs took place only in the landscape of their dreams.

Yet the struggle continued—the overseer still called the field hands to the cotton, and natural forces still resisted his summons. At night, in the fatigue that overtook all people, in moments of illness, in advancing age, and eventually in death, the life cycle of human bodies ran counter to the crop cycle of cotton.

Nature's omnipresence often dulls our awareness of its significance. Such has been the case with nightfall, that moment when the world turns and darkness descends. The diurnal cycle of light and dark was important to the Cotton Kingdom, because night invariably made possible a shift in the power relations of crop production. Nightfall not only weakened the visual sense but also stimulated the release of hormones in fatigued bodies, inducing sleep. Bodies no longer worked as well—and eventually they stopped working at all. At such moments, the masters' authority lessened while the slaves' autonomy increased. Like nothing else, night cracked open the slave regime and allowed its people to be more fully human. Some succumbed to weariness and found release in dreams. Others delayed sleep to participate in a vibrant nocturnal culture. Night was for companionship, conversation, prayers, lullabies, and love; for tending a garden, perhaps by moon glow; for running with dogs in pursuit of a 'coon; for folktales, foraging, and fiddling. Night, too, was for evading the slave patrol, for pilfering shad and prowling around, for sighting the North Star and following it to freedom.[86]

The masters recognized night and fatigue as obstacles to accumulation. The most domineering among them tried to make the dark hours as productive and as brief as possible. They extended all kinds of work into the evening: tending bonfires of woody debris, caring for animals, pressing cotton into bales, spinning yarn, weaving cloth, and cracking, grinding, and cooking corn. By encouraging procreation, the masters even tried to align an intimate nocturnal activity with the agricultural objectives of farm and plantation. And by rousing the slaves before sunup, they hastened the work of a new day. The predawn routine was familiar: an overseer raised the conch shell to his lips and blew, and the weary laborers rose from their pallets for another round of toil.[87]

Fatigue, too, some of the masters believed, must be minimized. Compelled to eat cottonseed mush, John Brown found himself subjected to yet another experiment: making laborers resistant to heatstroke. Thomas Stevens, Brown's master, loaned the enslaved man to a Dr. Hamilton, who ordered Brown to sit in a hole that had been heated by a fire so that only his head protruded above ground level. After Brown consumed a dose of experimental "medicine,"

Hamilton swathed the slave's body in wet blankets and laid small boards so that they trapped the heat and humidity in the hole. Brown tried to maintain his composure but fainted within half an hour. Hamilton repeated the experiment again and again during the next several weeks, each time with a new concoction. "I used to be put in [the hole] between daylight and dark, after I had done my day's work," Brown recalled, "for Stevens was not a man to lose more of the labour of his slaves than he could help." At last Hamilton isolated the optimal potion: cayenne pepper tea.[88]

John Brown's experience as a human subject no doubt was exceptional, but no matter how unusual or extreme, it was the logical outcome of a social institution that defined people as property and that construed fatigue as an obstacle to be overcome by manipulation and force. Bodies must be made—or, rather, remade—to meet the rigors of agricultural production.

There were limits, of course, to how far the masters could drive the slaves. Even if Dr. Hamilton's antidote to heatstroke had actually worked, nature still restricted the potential of the human body to withstand exertion. And much as fatigue constrained the amount of labor a body could perform, so, too, did the body's susceptibility to disease. The life cycles of viruses, bacteria, protozoa, hookworms, and mosquitoes intersected with and disrupted the life cycle of slaves, which in turn interfered with the crop cycle of cotton.

Although people in all regions of the United States experienced debilitating diseases during the eighteenth and nineteenth centuries, major portions of the South, including the Cotton Kingdom, were especially unhealthy. Living communally in the cramped confines of the slave quarters, black people shared viral "crowd diseases" such as diphtheria, measles, mumps, scarlet fever, smallpox, and whooping cough. Unsanitary conditions, including outhouses situated close to wells from which the slaves drew their drinking water, contributed to the spread of cholera, a bacterium that caused severe diarrhea, dehydration, and death. Some of the worst disease organisms thrived in relationship to nearby wetlands. *Aedes* and *Anopheles* mosquitoes, the life cycles of which included aquatic larval stages, spread yellow fever and malaria. When an *Aedes* sucked blood from a human, it transferred the yellow fever virus, causing severe headache, backache, fever, nausea, and vomiting. An *Anopheles* that drew blood either picked up or passed on the *Plasmodium* protozoan. Inside the bloodstream, the one-celled parasites underwent a life cycle stage in which they inhabited and consumed red blood cells. Chills, fever, and anemia resulted.[89]

As Solomon Northup learned, disease reduced an enslaved person's ability to work. Frederick Law Olmsted noted that the Red River valley, the location of the Epps plantation, was a low environment "subject to floods and fevers." One of those fevers—malarial, yellow, or some other—struck Northup down the summer he began to labor for Epps. The chills, high temperature, weakness, emaciation, and dizziness came on suddenly. Worst of all was the dizziness, which caused Northup "to reel and stagger like a drunken man." Northup's illness was extremely debilitating; not even the brutal lash of a driver could force him to keep up with his fellow slaves as they scraped their assigned rows of cotton. Eventually, Northup grew so ill that he could not rise from his bed in the morning. For the time being, he was worthless as a field hand.[90]

Disease was a painful, often lethal experience for thousands upon thousands of slaves, but it also opened opportunities for a few of them to increase their autonomy. Americans knew little about the causes of disease in the eighteenth and nineteenth centuries. Masters often attributed illness to bad air or "miasmas"; slaves often attributed it to witchcraft or other supernatural forces. No matter the attribution, both white and black had remedies. When a slave fell ill, a master might summon a white physician, as Edwin Epps did for Solomon Northup. A master also might call for the services of an enslaved folk doctor to administer herbal remedies made from plants gathered on the commons. By caring for slave and nonslave patients, the folk doctors enhanced their reputations and cemented their positions as specialized laborers. Disease did something else as well: it opened an unexpected opportunity for slaves to feign illness and win a momentary exemption from toil.[91]

The masters had no choice but to let valuable slaves recuperate from illness, and they often had no choice but to spend money on the services of a physician. Ultimately, though, the masters needed labor, and they were reluctant to let slaves linger on their sickbeds. The condition of the crop, not the health of the slave, was paramount. Thus Edwin Epps cut short Solomon Northup's sick leave. Picking time had arrived, and the master needed help. "One morning, long before I was in a proper condition to labor," Northup remembered, "Epps appeared at the cabin door, and, presenting me a sack, ordered me to the cotton field." Some slaveholders and overseers suspected that illnesses were illusory and their apparent victims only good actors. "I have heard of your tricks," a Mississippi plantation manager admonished a woman named Carline as she lay on her bed, groaning. "You had a chill when I came to see you yesterday morning; you had a chill when the mistress came here, and you had a chill when the master came. I never knew a chill to last the whole day. So you'll just get up now and go to the field, and if you don't work smart, you'll get a dressing; do you hear?" Ill or not, Carline's brief respite was over.[92]

No master or overseer, however, would have the final say. Like other organisms, the human body aged, weakened, slowed, and eventually died. A master might prolong the usefulness of an old hand by assigning him or her lighter tasks, such as caring for the youngest children, or a slaveholder might try to sell his aging property before it became a liability or collapsed altogether. But no maneuver could mitigate indefinitely the advancing decay. As time passed, the slave's value declined in conjunction with the body and in the end amounted, in dollars, to nothing.

The final years could be difficult. Edwin Epps might have been an exceptionally violent man, but his actions followed directly from the principle that masters had total power over their property. One of Epps's chattels was the elderly Uncle Abram, the kindly patriarch of the small black community that labored on the Epps plantation. Solomon Northup and the other slaves cherished Uncle Abram's warmth and wisdom, but that mattered little to Epps, especially when he had consumed too much liquor. One day a drunken Epps returned to the plantation to find Uncle Abram spreading cotton on a scaffold. The master's bitter criticism and contrary orders befuddled the old man, who then "committed some blunder of no particular consequence." Enraged, Epps drew his knife and stabbed Uncle Abram in the back, disabling him and preventing him from doing the very thing that Epps wanted him to do: work. The elderly slave staggered back to his cabin, where Northup found him on the floor, his clothing soaked in blood. Mistress Epps sewed up the "long, ugly" wound, and she denounced her husband, not simply for his inhumanity but because his violent behavior threatened the economic security of the Epps family.[93]

It was no wonder that across the Cotton Kingdom, many enslaved people did not fear death. By the 1850s, the vast majority looked forward to their eventual resurrection—rebirth—in a place without toil, pain, and sorrow. Solomon Northup never forgot Eliza, driven to mental illness and physical decrepitude by the forced sale of her children. Rendered "useless in the cotton field" and "bartered for a trifle" to a man who whipped her unmercifully, she came to a lonely, heartbreaking end on the floor of a dilapidated cabin. In death, however, she transcended her enslavement. Her soul gathered up by "the Angel of the Lord," she departed for a better world. Exclaimed Northup, "She was *free* at last!"[94]

No matter how discouraged, Solomon Northup never abandoned his dream of returning to his family. His desire to leave no doubt grew more powerful one terrible Sunday when Epps savaged Patsey for leaving the plantation to ask a neighbor for a piece of soap. Epps first ordered Northup to administer the punishment, but after laying on dozens of stripes, the enslaved man threw down the whip and declared that he would not continue. Epps finished the job. As the lash "bit out small pieces of her flesh," Patsey stopped screaming and slipped into bloody unconsciousness. She was never the same afterwards, Northup later recalled, never the same lively, hopeful young woman.[95]

As the years passed, Northup waited for his opportunity. Then, in the summer of 1852, Epps began construction of a fine new house. The very nature of the structure ruptured the crop cycle and opened a small space in which the enslaved man finally could make his bid for freedom.[96]

Epps's house was a product not only of his ambition but also of the environment in which he built it. Like other planters, he chose to erect a comfortable shelter that symbolized his wealth and power. Constructing his abode on the level, wet land of the Red River valley required an extraordinary commitment of materials and labor. "Such is the low and swampy nature of the ground," observed Northup, that "the great houses are usually built upon spiles." Driven into the ground, the numerous spiles (or piles) provided a foundation that elevated the houses well above the damp earth. The same flat terrain influenced the manner in which planters procured lumber. The valley's gentle gradient, noted Northup, precluded "waterpower [sites] upon which [saw]mills might be built," thus requiring intensive labor, usually in the form of slaves, to cut lumber by hand.[97]

Epps certainly could afford the materials and labor that his house required. For more than a decade he had exploited nature—land, plants, and human bodies—for the purpose of accumulating wealth and, presumably, gaining access to credit. Hiring a carpenter and a crew, driving spiles, whipsawing planks and boards, and assigning slaves to the project posed no insurmountable financial obstacles.

That Edwin Epps could afford his house, however, in no way obviated the rupture that its construction caused in his plantation's routine. Not only did the ambitious project draw outside laborers onto his property, but it also diverted slaves from cotton production and from his direct oversight. One of the white carpenters who came to work on the house was a Canadian named Bass. The white people of the area, Epps included, liked and respected the genial, hardworking bachelor, despite his antislavery views. Evidently, Epps did not imagine what might happen if Bass came into contact with Solomon Northup, whom Epps had ordered to work on the house. At a moment when Epps "was absent in the field," the enslaved man discretely asked the carpenter for help. Bass welcomed Northup's plea, and the two men decided to meet at a naturally advantageous time and place: late at night "among the high weeds on the bank of the bayou, some distance from [the] master's dwelling." At the start of their consultation, Bass reassured Northup that because "he was growing old, and must soon reach the end of his earthly journey," he had decided to risk his remaining time in support of Northup's freedom. He agreed to write letters to prominent citizens of Saratoga Springs, alerting them to the enslaved man's predicament and general location. Rescue would follow.[98]

As the months passed and no rescue materialized, Northup grew down-hearted. When Bass visited Epps at Christmas, he quietly told Northup that he had mailed the letters and that the enslaved man should be patient. If neces-sary, Bass said, he would go to Saratoga Springs himself. Northup threw him-self into the usual round of holiday fiddling—and still nothing. Deliverance came on a bleak January day. He was in the cotton field with Uncle Abram, Patsey, Bob, and Wiley, picking the remains of the year's growth. Their fin-gers were numb and moved slowly—no doubt in Northup's case, extra slowly. Evidently not a master inclined to pay his laborers for such work, Epps cursed them and declared that he was going to retrieve his rawhide whip and warm them up a little. While Epps was inside, a carriage pulled up to the house. Two men strode across the cotton field.[99]

The letters had arrived at their destinations. One had been passed to Anne Northup and the children, now grown, and they had gone straight to the lawyer Henry B. Northup, a descendant of the Rhode Island family that had owned Solomon's grandfather. Henry Northup had received Solomon's first letter, mailed twelve years before from New Orleans; the lawyer had taken it to Gover-nor William Seward, who was obligated by state law to secure the release of citi-zens kidnapped into slavery. Seward had advised Henry to wait until Solomon's exact location was known, but by then, the Cotton Kingdom had swallowed the unfortunate man and obliterated his identity. This time, Henry Northup moved more aggressively. After procuring the official papers, he traveled to Pittsburgh and boarded a downriver steamboat. Above New Orleans, he transferred to a vessel going up the Red River. At the parish seat he engaged the services of a local attorney, contacted a judge, and met Bass. Now, sheriff by his side, he stood before a shabby field hand around whose neck hung a dirty sack. The sheriff asked Solomon if he knew the stranger. After studying the face for a moment, the enslaved man's emotions erupted. "*Henry B. Northup!* Thank God—thank God!" The sheriff asked a few more questions, and then Solomon reached across the chasm of twelve lost years. "Sol," Henry said, taking his hands. "I'm glad to see you. Throw down that sack; your cotton picking days are over."[100]

The farewells were quick. The mistress said goodbye; the master cursed him one last time. ("Ah! You damned nigger.") Patsey clung to him, tears streaming down her face. "Oh! Platt, you're goin' to be free—you're goin' way off yonder where we'll neber see ye any more," she said. "You've saved me a good many whippins, Platt; I'm glad you're goin' to be free—but, oh! de Lord, de Lord! what'll become of me?" Northup finally climbed into the carriage. As it drove away, he looked back. Uncle Abram, Bob, Wiley, Aunt Phebe, and Patsey gazed after him. He lifted his hand to wave—but the carriage turned a bend, and they disappeared from sight.[101]

Northup returned home to his family. On the way, he and Henry stopped in Washington, D.C., where Solomon pressed charges against the slave trader William Birch for kidnapping and selling him. The trial was a farce. Among other injustices, the law prevented Northup, a citizen of New York, from testifying because of his color. His oppressor went free.[102]

Northup's legal effort, nevertheless, was an indication of mounting resistance to the Cotton Kingdom. As cotton production gained momentum, it generated its own internal opposition. With each new acre, crop, and enslaved laborer—and with them, each new stripe, cut, rape, broken bone, abduction, betrayal, premature death, drop of sweat, pool of blood, and pound of flesh—the collective outrage increased. The masters tried to contain and destroy the resistance, but their repression only fed its growth and forestalled the day when it would burst forth. Until then, enslaved laborers always had alternatives short of organized rebellion. The vast southern commons, the open range, the upcountry, the night, and the North—these were environments, refuges, spaces that perennially supported the enslaved workers of the Cotton Kingdom in their struggles against their masters and to which they could always try to flee. One day a civil war ruptured the crop cycle, however, and the combined resistance of generations swept away the Cotton Kingdom—as it had been, at least—in an instant.

Solomon Northup evidently did not live to witness that moment. He spent his final years as a carpenter and small landowner in his native New York, surrounded by family and friends. No doubt he could not quiet the memories, which must have been as painful as they were vivid. Perhaps in moments of reflection he sat on his porch with his fiddle and called forth the notes that carried him back to a place where the conjoined cycles of plants and bodies drove the movement of history. What was it like? How can something so soft have felt so bad? Did the whip enlarge or diminish your humanity? Did bitterness have a sound? In our imaginations, the bow dances and the fingers fly, and the answers issue forth on the breeze. ★

GALLERY NO. 2

Animal Familiars

Animals were integral to American history, participants in the creation of the United States and sources of food, power, and meaning. In colonial North America, people believed that familiars—devilish imps, cats and other small animals, and weird composites of various creatures—did the bidding of the witches, almost always women, on whom they suckled. Conversely, to call a man a bull or a maverick paid him a compliment, and spouses used a term of endearment when they referred to each other as yokemates. Affections ran in the opposite direction, too, in cattle named Brindle, Spark, or Velvet, or in mules identified as Tom. More often, the human-animal association was negative, as revealed in the satirical political cartoon that likened Thomas Jefferson to a strutting rooster and Sally Hemings to a hen. The language and imagery of animal familiarity continued, unabated, into the future. When the gonzo journalist Hunter Thompson likened a motorcycle gang to packs of wild boar, he engaged in an ancient rhetoric that associated marginal, unstable, alien, politically objectionable, or dangerous people with animals.

2.1 Illustration from Nathaniel Crouch, *The Kingdom of Darkness: or The History of Daemons, Specters, Witches, Apparitions, Possessions, Disturbances, and Other Wonderful and Supernatural Delusions, Mischievous Feats, and Malicious Impostures of the Devil*, 1688.

2.2 Frontispiece from Matthew Hopkins, *The Discovery of Witches*, 1647. The witches depicted are Rebecca West and Elizabeth Clarke.

2.3   James Akin, political cartoon of Thomas Jefferson and Sally Hemings, 1804:
"T'is not a set of features or complexion or tincture of skin that I admire."

Political Ecology

American revolutionaries aspired to incorporate the nation's physical substance—land, human constructions, and people—into a rational, republican
architecture that expressed timeless natural laws. In flags, political tracts, government halls, survey lines, houses, schools, books, bodies, and brains, they
combined symmetrical, unchanging forms with the irregular, organic, changing nature of everyday life. Mary Wollstonecraft's admirers coded the architecture of the revolutionary republic as female. An eighteenth-century engraving
depicted Lady Liberty in a classical temple below a soaring mountain, and
women—her daughters—as heralds, muses, and petitioners. But how well
could Americans assimilate the diversity and contingency of everyday nature,
human and nonhuman, into the republic's symmetries?

2.4 Revolutionary flags. Animals, trees, and heavenly bodies gave Americans powerful symbols with which to assert their causes.

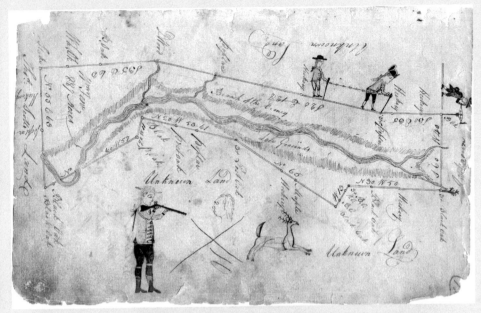

2.5   Early metes and bounds survey, irregular parcel surrounded by unmapped, "unknown land," with oak trees and other landscape features serving as corners.

2.6   The abstract, timeless symmetry of the rectangular survey in relation to the ecological and cultural textures of the landscape. California Township, Starke County, Indiana, 1876.

2.7 Republican nature. Pierre-Charles L'Enfant's design of Washington, D.C., 1791, as revised by Andrew Ellicott, 1792.

2.8 Mary Wollstone-craft petitioning Lady Liberty with *A Vindication of the Rights of Woman*, 1792.

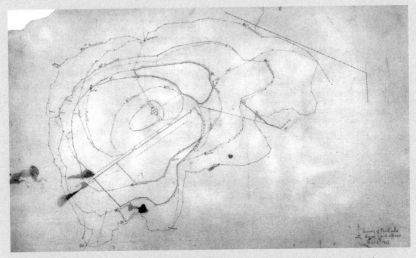

2.9   Thomas Jefferson, survey of Monticello, 1803. Note the integration of the house and the topography, the combination of Newtonian natural law and the "law of the land." Note, too, the ancillary buildings on Mulberry Row, the workspaces of enslaved laborers and the heart of economic activity on the plantation.

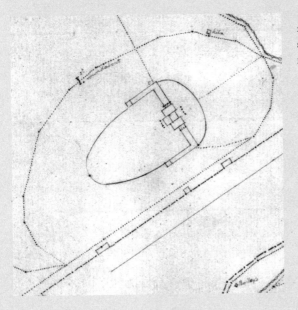

2.10   Thomas Jefferson, survey of Monticello, 1803, detail.

2.11 Improving matter and mind. Lincoln's student sums book, c. 1824–1836.

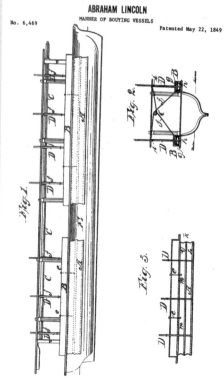

2.12 Lincoln's plan for a pneumatic device using "expansible buoyant chambers" to lift vessels over sand bars. U.S. patent 6469, issued May 22, 1849.

Hard Labor

Most Americans knew nature through the labor they performed, the historian Richard White observed. Among the most important but underappreciated sites in the American past are the millions of places where human hands worked nature into useful, meaningful things. Where fingers plucked cotton from a boll or gripped the handles of a plow, identities formed, dreams died, anger smoldered, liberty blossomed, and history moved. Work in nature reduced differences among people, especially when the fruits of labor went to others. A young Abraham Lincoln resented turning over his earnings to the family patriarch, an act that made him feel like a slave. No wonder Frederick Douglass, who also knew something about stolen labor, recognized him as "a son of toil" who "was linked in brotherly sympathy with the sons of toil in every loyal part of the Republic." To understand the history of slavery, we might begin by examining the nature of labor—of arms cradling babies, of aching hands wielding hoes and axes, of scarred fingers extracting soft fiber from hard, prickly shells.

HARD LABOR   149

OLD ABEWATHA.

Where was he born—in a bed or in a manzer?
Who had the first glimpse of the wonderful stranger?

Who were at his birth—were they but few or many?
And who was his granny—or did he have any?

Did he have a father—or only a mother?
Did he have a sister—or only a brother?

Or had he neither—ne'ther one nor the other?
Or was he *sui generis*—just to pother?

Where was he first seen—at the North or at the South?
Was his nativity known by the shape of his mouth?

Were his lips very thick—or were they very thin?
Did they pout out—or were they drawn up and tuck'd in?

Or did they both stand out like the bill of a cock?
And could they be mum-sealed with some sort of a lock?

Were his arms very stout and his legs very strong?
Were his eyes very large and his nose very long?

How old was he called when he split his first rail?
And did he take good aim with intent not to fail?

Did he go to the woods to see what he could see?
And to get him a log did he cut down a tree?

Was the tree very large, or was the tree very small?
Or was it of medium size and not very tall?

Which way did it lean, or did it not lean at all?
Did he take a good look to see how it would fail?

Did he look for a tree that was solid and sound?
Or did he find a log ready out on the ground?

How heavy was his maul and how big was his wedge?
Was his maul made of wood or was it a big sledge?

When he struck with his maul did he take a bold stand?
And which did he put foremost—his left or right hand?

Of what kind of wood was the log that he split?
On which end of the log did he make his first hit?

Was the log knarly and tough, or decayed with disease?
Or was it straight grained, did it open with ease?

What number of hard blows with his maul did he strike
Had he one wedge, or had he two, exactly alike?

What number of sound rails from the log did he make?
In length how many feet, for each rail, did he take?

If put to the test could fond memory recall
Whether he split his rails in the winter or fall?

Or *vice versa*—were they all split in the spring?
When the early song birds their sweet melodies sing?

How many young and old coons first sat on his rails?
Had they very long noses or very long tails?

Were they all "Wide-Awakes" with a lamp in each hand?
Did they make tracks in the mud, or tracks in the sand?

When they cheered Old Abewatha where were their tails?
Standing up very steep, or hanging down on the rails?

When he fought "Little Giant" out in Illinois?
Did he fight like a man or get whipt like a boy?

And did that same old coon from the old Empire State
Come early in the ring, or came he rather late?

Was he "sittin' on a rail and sleepin'" very sound,
When this Old Abewatha flung him to the ground?

Did he fling him *a la* Heenan or *a la* Sayers—
Did he take him fair holt or take him unawares?

When he "riz" from the ground and track it through the west,
Did he say, of all the coons, Abewatha was the best?

Will the time ever come when the people will say,
Let Old Abewatha now have his full sway?

When "no half way to freedom" shall any one see,
And "when all shall be slaves or when all shall be free?"

2.13　The nature of cotton production—enslaved laborers in front of gin house, 1862, Smith's plantation, Port Royal Island, South Carolina.

2.14　Cotton press and gin. Note the combination of human and mule power integral to the mechanism.

2.15　Slaveholders harnessed various powers of nature to the production of cotton. Note the steamboat stacks in the background.

2.16　The Rail Splitter, 1860, cleaving the Union with a "nigger wedge." Lincoln's labor in nature symbolized the free labor ideal but also, as in this satirical cartoon, served the purposes of his critics.

Butcher's Bill

No other conflict was as costly to the United States as the Civil War, and no other conflict demonstrated so fundamentally that the nation was an organic republic, a republic of muscles and meat. Agricultural production was central to the war, as cause, military means, and—as a political cartoon of Lincoln cultivating a crop of soldiers showed—metaphor. Although the conflict coincided with industrialization and the beginnings of a national railroad network, Union and Confederate armies were powered by muscle more than they were mechanized. Untold numbers of horses, mules, and other animals perished in service to the opposing sides. The round figure often given for the human toll—some 620,000 dead—suggests the magnitude of the struggle. Disease took the preponderance. The rest fell to iron and lead. In camp, on the march, and in battle, slaughter equalized man and beast. The republic of muscles and meat required a trans-species democracy of death.

VANITY FAIR.

OLD ABE.—Aint there a nice crop? There's the hardy Bunker Hill flower, the Seventh Regiment Pink, the Fireboy Tulip—That tricolored flower grows near Independence Hall—the Western Blossoms and Prairie Flowers will soon begin to shoot.

COLUMBIA.—What charming plant is this?

OLD ABE.—That is rare in this country—it will bloom shortly and bear the Jeffersonia Davisiana.

2.17   Lincoln watering improved varieties of soldier seeds in the garden of Columbia, 1861.

2.18 "Symptoms of Spring—Uncle Abraham's Crop Begins to Shoot," 1864.

2.19 Confederate fortifications reinforced with cotton bales at Yorktown, 1862.

2.20   A stampede of army horses. Alfred R. Waud sketch, 1864.

BEEF DEPOT MONUMENT

2.21   Union army beef cattle depot at the foot of the unfinished
Washington Monument, 1862.

2.22   Union army soldiers butchering cattle, February 7, 1863.

2.23   Dead meat—the aftermath of Gettysburg. Edwin Forbes field sketch, July 4, 1863.

FOUR

NATURE'S NOBLEMAN

Abraham Lincoln and the Improvement of America

AT SOME MOMENT DURING THE mid- to late 1850s, Abraham Lincoln sat down to compose one of his least remembered and least appreciated speeches. The exact location of the chair, desk, or table where he reposed his lanky frame is unknown. Perhaps it was in his house, a two-story wooden structure on the northeast corner of Eighth and Jackson Streets in Springfield, Illinois. A domestic Parthenon recently renovated in the Greek Revival style, its parlor contained a small desk where he sometimes wrote. Or perhaps he prepared the speech in his law office, on the second floor of a commercial building that faced Fifth Street and a public square from which rose the columns and dome of the Illinois state capitol. Although the office was so cluttered and filthy that seeds once sprouted in the residue on its floor, it provided him with a convenient place at which to work.[1] No matter where Lincoln sat, his arrangement of words on a page repeated the same process that had made the architecture and landscape around him. Whether he and his fellow citizens used paper and ink or stone, brick, and wood, they believed that their creations fulfilled nature's potential and thereby improved the world.

Poised above the blank sheet, Lincoln focused his mind on his theme: mankind and nature, or more precisely, the nature and destiny of man. It was a subject of profound importance to him and his contemporaries. Virtually every discipline or practice—science, law, geography, history, politics, economics, and others—in some way addressed it. The books that William Herndon, Lincoln's law partner, placed on the shelves of their office conveyed the range of thought devoted to it. As Lincoln's eyes moved down the pages of John Stuart Mill's *Principles of Political Economy* (1848), for example, he read that labor redirected natural processes to human ends. By guiding the muscular action of cattle or channeling the flow of water and wind, people turned the wheels of economic production. As Mill stated, labor "in the physical world is always and solely employed in putting physical objects in motion; the properties of matter, the laws of nature, do the rest." Whether making production more efficient or distributing wealth more justly, society's goal should be "improvement."[2]

Books alone did not speak to the importance of the human place on Earth and its prospects for betterment; so, too, did the environment that Lincoln observed and experienced every day. In Illinois and across the nation, people were transforming the raw materials of nature into finished forms at once useful, valuable, even beautiful: a gridded, rectilinear landscape of farmsteads, city blocks, and public squares; houses, churches, commercial buildings, factories, and government halls; sidewalks, planked streets, canals, railroads, and bridges; horses, wagons, locomotives, steamboats, and farm implements; sacks of grain, stacks of lumber, piles of brick and coal, bundles of wool, reams of paper, shelves of books; and much, much more.[3] First as a laborer and later as a lawyer, Lincoln had built and benefited from this endlessly dynamic and productive landscape. Now it inspired some of the words that flowed from his pen.

"All creation is a mine, and every man, a miner," he began. "The whole earth, and all *within* it, *upon* it, and *round* about it, including *himself*, in his physical, moral, and intellectual nature, and his susceptibilities, are the infinitely varied 'leads' from which, man, from the first, was to dig out his destiny." Lincoln drew on the story of Genesis to explain his point. Man had come into the world without skill and with little means, almost like a child: "In the beginning, the mine was unopened, and the miner stood *naked*, and *knowledgeless*, upon it." Yet man's discovery of his primal condition—his nakedness—prompted his first great invention: clothing, specifically a "fig-leaf-apron." Such inventiveness distinguished man from the other animals. Fish, birds, beavers, ants, honeybees, and other "beasts" and "creeping things" gathered food and even built houses for themselves. But only man had the capacity to advance his skills and transform natural substances into instruments of progress: "Man is not the only animal who labors; but he is the only one who *improves* his workmanship."[4]

A summary of major "discoveries" and "inventions" followed: spinning and weaving, iron and iron tools, wheeled carriages and watercraft, food production and draft animals, waterwheels and steam engines. Yet the story of improvement remained incomplete, Lincoln thought. "Of all the forces of nature" available to man, "the *wind*" still defied his ingenuity. "Take any given space of the earth's surface—for instance, Illinois—and all the power exerted by all the men, and beasts, and running-water, and steam, over and upon it, shall not equal the one hundredth part of what is exerted by the blowing of the wind over and upon the same space." Sailing ships, windmills, and wind-powered pumps were important improvements in world history, but the wind remained "an *untamed* and *unharnessed* force; and quite possibly one of the greatest discoveries to be made, will be the taming, and harnessing of the wind."[5]

If Lincoln anticipated a marvelous future of wind-powered inventions, he also believed that humanity already had made its most important advancement. "The inclination to exchange thoughts with one another," he mused, "is probably an original impulse of our nature" and had led to the "*instrumentality*" of language: first speech, then writing, and finally—most revolutionary of all—printing. Most people, Lincoln asserted, remained ignorant of the written word's power, because "the capacity to read" far outstripped the availability of printed matter. Consequently, "the great mass of men" for years were "utterly unconscious, that their *conditions*, or their *minds*, were capable of improvement," and thus they "supposed themselves to be naturally incapable of rising to equality." Americans only with difficulty could imagine "how strong this slavery of the mind was; and how long it did, of necessity, take, to break its shackles, and to get a habit of freedom of thought, established." But eventually, the printed word had begun to realize its promise in a "new country," the United States, where conditions were "most favorable—almost necessary—to the immancipation of thought."[6]

Lincoln delivered his speech on discoveries and inventions six times to paying audiences hungry for ideas that would help them to make sense of their world. Soon, however, he set it aside as he became deeply involved in the national political struggles that eventually carried him into the White House. After his death, his son Robert, his personal secretaries John Hay and John Nicolay, and a string of biographers agreed that the speech was mediocre and anomalous in comparison with the Gettysburg Address and his other political writings and pronouncements.[7] Their judgment probably reflected, and helped to shape, the views of their countrymen. Although many Americans admired Lincoln as a common man who rose from earthy roots, they worshipped him as a kind of god who hovered in a timeless realm above the material concerns of ordinary human beings. By emphasizing his outsized qualities and enshrining their memory of him in a marble temple in the nation's capital, they sometimes overlooked crucial features of his life: his hard labor in difficult landscapes, his abiding interest in discoveries and inventions, and most of all, how much he thought and talked about nature and improvement.[8]

When Lincoln wrote that all creation is a mine, and every man, a miner, he did more than make a simple metaphorical point; he expressed an idea that informed his entire worldview. In his way of thinking, the basic problem of humankind was its need to turn its material circumstances into its sustenance. To live, people had to feed, clothe, shelter, and protect themselves. To do these things, they had to manipulate nature—to mine, tame, and harness it. Lincoln made a crucial distinction regarding nature: it consisted of the physical world external to man, and it consisted of man, too. In mining out his destiny, man thus transformed both his environment and himself. The result of his labor was improvement, which meant the fulfillment of nature's potential to nurture and sustain human life.

Lincoln's ideas of nature inevitably shaped his politics. He frequently used the word *nature* and its synonyms in his speeches and writings, and he rooted some of his grandest statements in organic metaphors. And if improvement meant the fulfillment of nature's potential to nurture and sustain human life, then by extension it also meant the fulfillment of nature's potential to nurture and sustain a democracy and the republican form of government built upon it. The improvement of the United States, the realization of its great promise, thus required citizens to "break the shackles" of ignorance and backwardness. Most important, it required them to break the shackles of slavery, a system that violated the natural rights of human beings and threatened the survival of the republic. In Lincoln's view, improvement was the key to the fulfillment—and preservation—of the world.

Lincoln's speech on discoveries and inventions was an important marker in the trajectory of his life. His passage to and from that document—the process by which he dug out his destiny—gathered momentum from a series of roughly chronological experiences and events: his origins and upbringing, the hard physical labor he performed as a boy and young man, his involvement in politics, his participation in war and his witnessing of death, and, in the end, his expression of faith in the republic's enormous capacity for rebirth.[9] Ultimately, Lincoln's struggles, defeats, and triumphs reveal much more than just the nature of the man; they speak volumes about the very nature of the United States.

Generations of Americans have known Lincoln as the rail-splitter, the rustic backwoodsman whose life of hard, honest toil prepared him to lead a great democracy. Created for the presidential campaign of 1860, the rail-splitter image stood for the free white American man whose labor enabled him to accumulate property and establish his economic independence.[10] But the rail-splitter also symbolized mankind's relationship to nature, and in that sense it was especially important to Lincoln because it acknowledged the difficult, physically taxing work that defined his relationship to the land. Upon that bodily experience, Lincoln began to fashion his ideas of improvement.[11]

The work from which Lincoln derived so much meaning began when he was very young. In 1811, at about the age of two, he moved with his family to a thirty-acre farm on Knob Creek in central Kentucky. A beautiful area of steep, cedar-topped hills, gorges, clear-running streams, and verdant bottoms, Knob Creek delighted Lincoln and the other children who romped through it. Knob Creek also was a landscape of agricultural production, and Lincoln's earliest memory of the place centered not on play but on food and work. One Saturday afternoon in springtime, he joined his family in sowing corn and pumpkins. No doubt all seemed well that evening; the growth and increase that anticipated the harvest was about to begin. Dark clouds above the hills on Sunday morning, however, signaled disaster. A heavy rain delivered a flood to the farm below, washing away soil, seeds, and the labor that the Lincolns had devoted to the crop.[12]

Lincoln continued to work the soil at a succession of family farms, but the labor that most preoccupied him involved the ax, not the plow. By means of the ax and the splitting maul, he experienced arboreal nature in many varieties, but almost certainly elm, beech, black cherry, oak, maple, hickory, and ash, each with its own natural properties of hardness, density, and grain. He began the work early in life. In December 1816, when he was seven years old, his family abandoned its Knob Creek farm and moved across the Ohio River to Little Pigeon Creek in southern Indiana. From that time forward, Lincoln had responsibility for felling trees and turning them into firewood, cabins, flatboats, and, of course, fence rails. "He settled in an unbroken forest," he later recalled of himself, "and the clearing away of surplus wood was the great task [ahead]. A[braham] though very young, was large of his age, and had an axe put into his hands at once; and from that till within his twentythird year, he was almost constantly handling that most useful instrument—less, of course, in plowing and harvesting seasons." Neighbors eventually hired his services, extending his apprenticeship of the ax beyond his father's eighty acres. In 1830, shortly after he turned twenty-one, he and his family moved to central Illinois, and once again he went to work with his ax. On the north bank of the Sangamon River, he and his father cleared and enclosed fifteen acres. He also split thousands of rails for nearby settlers.[13]

Lincoln's experience of nature made him what he was. As one of his early biographers observed, he "hewed out his path to manhood" with the sharp-edged tool.[14] Partly the process was physical. As he cleared the forest, he grew stronger, more muscular, and more skilled; his modification of nonhuman nature altered the very nature of his body.[15] The process also was intellectual. Cutting and splitting trees gave Lincoln an identity; at the point of contact between calloused hands and ax handle, he began to develop a mature sense of himself and his relationship to the world.[16]

Although his legal and political career distanced him from the forest, Lincoln's supporters never forgot his origins, and Lincoln himself never completely let go of the ax that first defined his place and identity. After an important political victory in 1837, his fellow Whig Party members hailed him as "one of Nature's Noblemen." His speech on discoveries and inventions drew on his experience. How, he wondered, could the Ark or almost anything else have been built without iron and iron tools? His answer was unequivocal: "It seems to me an axe, or a miracle, was indispensable." Even though he had been out of the forest for many years by 1860, he evidently never objected to the rail-splitter image invented for his presidential run, and he maintained symbolic and literal connections to it until the end of his life.[17] In spring 1865, he visited a field hospital and for several hours shook the hands of wounded soldiers. When a surgeon remarked that his arm must be tired, he smiled, said that he had "strong muscles," and picked up an ax. After energetically chopping on a log for several minutes, he held the ax in his right hand, straight out, level, and completely steady.[18]

For all Lincoln's pride in his ax work, perhaps the greatest lesson he learned from it was that he disliked it. He never judged physical labor to be dishonorable; to the contrary, he celebrated it as the basis of the republic. But he did not like the endless drudgery of chopping wood, grubbing out stumps, plowing soil, hoeing weeds, splitting rails, and other menial tasks that defined the world of nineteenth-century agriculture. The historical record does not indicate that he ever intended to remain on the land, nor does it show that he ever expressed admiration for, or the desire to emulate, his father, Thomas, an illiterate backcountry farmer and builder of rough furniture. Lincoln knew all too well the harsh reality of the older man's struggle: the perspiration, the aching muscles, the vulnerability to nature's freaks—as when an unexpected rainfall washed away your seeds and soil and the labor you had invested in them. Lincoln's speech on discoveries and inventions included one reference to the fall from grace: farming, he wrote, was "a *penalty*—a *curse*—we find the first born man— the first heir of the curse—was a 'tiller of the soil.'"[19]

Lincoln's physical drudgery in nature also taught him to appreciate its products, whether food, clothing, or shelter. Their value was especially important to him because he experienced firsthand the loss of it. He did not pocket the money he received for splitting thousands of rails for fellow pioneers. Instead, he turned the proceeds over to his father, who had hired him out and who then used his earnings to support the family farm. Until he was twenty-one, Lincoln continued to turn over at least some of his wages to his father, as required by law. When, around the age of seventeen or eighteen, he finally began to savor some of his labor's fruits, he was transformed. While working for a ferry operator at the confluence of the Anderson and Ohio rivers, he built a small rowboat in his spare time. One day he transported two men to a steamboat that was heading downstream. As the men clambered aboard the steamer, each tossed a silver half-dollar coin into Lincoln's boat. "I could scarcely believe my eyes as I picked up the money," he recalled. "I could scarcely believe that I, a poor boy, had earned a dollar in less than a day; that by honest work I had earned a dollar. The world seemed wider and fairer before me; I was a more hopeful and thoughtful boy from that time."[20]

If he was a more hopeful, thoughtful boy, he was, in all likelihood, a more empathetic one as well. Historians have long wondered where Lincoln acquired his antislavery convictions. Certainly his parents opposed slavery, and he might have heard sermons against it in the backcountry Baptist church that his family sometimes attended. On more than one occasion, he witnessed the sad, disheartening spectacle of people in chains. The most persuasive argument about the source of Lincoln's antislavery views, however, encourages us to go deeper, right down to muscle and bone and the painful natural fundament that was the common lot of all toilers. Whether mauling apart logs to make rails or rowing against the current, Lincoln experienced not only drudgery but also exploitation and deprivation. He had empathy for slaves precisely because he felt that his father treated him like one, by physically dominating him, hiring him out, and then taking the fruits of his labor. Lincoln might have objected to slavery for any number of reasons, but stolen labor most aroused his opposition. "We were all slaves one time or another," he later said of himself and some friends, but "white men could make themselves free and the negroes could not. . . . I used to be a slave, and now I am so free that they let me practice law."[21]

At bottom, slavery violated Lincoln's understanding of nature, which he formed from his experience and observation of the world as much as from the information he gathered from books, newspapers, and conversations. Once, during a private moment, he struggled to express his thoughts. A vivid image occurred to him that might have come from the pages of Aesop's *Fables* or Dilworth's *Speller*—or from the experience of a rail-splitter and ploughboy observing the natural world at the edge of a field. "The ant who has toiled and dragged a crumb to his nest," he wrote, "will furiously defend the fruit of his labor, against whatever robber assails him. So plain, that the most dumb and stupid slave that ever toiled for a master, does constantly *know* that he has been wronged." Some ten years later, in 1864, he summarized the same idea. "I am naturally anti-slavery," he stated. "If slavery is not wrong, nothing is wrong. I can not remember when I did not think so, and feel."[22]

NEITHER A SLAVE NOR A DRUNKARD ON EARTH

Lincoln's dislike of physical toil likely reinforced its importance to him; precisely because it was so wretched, the worth of its products was so great. Yet in spite of the esteem in which he held it, he still sought to break free from it and from the rail-splitter's landscape to which he felt chained. His escape route— the "lead" that he followed as he dug out his destiny—was marked *improvement*.

Improvement took various forms and had various meanings during the early years of the United States. Its broadest sense was biblical. The original improver, God, created the heavens and the earth, brought light to the world, and established a garden over which the first two humans had dominion. Cast from the garden for violating God's law, the pair then set about redeeming— and thus improving—their fallen world. The biblical concept of improvement informed a meaning that was popular among American colonists and pioneers: to clear land and convert it to agriculture was to improve it. The modern intellectual and cultural shift known as the Enlightenment extended the definition of improvement by claiming that the exercise of reason enabled mankind to better, and perhaps even to perfect, its circumstances. In this way of thinking, the American Revolution, the Declaration of Independence, the Land Ordinance of 1785, and the Constitution were physical and legal instruments that improved people's relationships to one another and to their environment. The Constitution and its separation of powers, for example, would structure politics and governance so that regrettable human proclivities—among them self-interest and unreason—would counteract and even negate each other, thereby contributing to the stability of the republic.[23]

By Lincoln's time, Americans had added new variations to the theme. Discoveries and inventions associated with industrialization improved humanity's lot. Many farmers adopted methods of soil improvement in which they used fertilizers and crop rotation to check erosion and restore—and even increase—the land's fertility. Horticulturalists embarked on a systematic program of plant improvement, developing more productive and tastier varieties of fruit trees and other crops. Ordinary men and women attempted self-improvement. Through discipline, education, or training, they sought moral, intellectual, and physical betterment. Most important, the proponents of improvement advocated that all citizens apply a God-given, natural capacity—reason—to the resolution of economic, social, and political problems.[24]

Finally, "internal improvement," a political program most often associated with the Whig Party, proposed government-sponsored environmental modifications that would help citizens achieve their individual and public ambitions. The United States was a sprawling, naturally variegated country that presented enormous obstacles to anyone who tried to move commodities to market. Vast distances, dense forests, muddy tracks, waterways clogged with driftwood, snags, gravel bars, and ice—these and other biophysical conditions frustrated the most determined of producers. To this problem, the Whigs and other citizens said, there was an answer: improvement. Tax monies or proceeds from the sale of public land could be used to clear rivers, dredge harbors, and build roads, canals, railways, and bridges, liberating producers from the mud and detritus that choked them. Steamboats would reach backcountry towns once isolated by shallow channels. Canals would link waterways and connect far-flung communities to metropolitan centers and seaports. Where water would not flow or when ice blocked the way, trains would run. A vast, intricate network of commercial exchange would unite the nation. Harmonizing geographical differences and making regionally distinctive commodities available to all, internal improvement would put "the whole country," as Lincoln later said, "on that career of prosperity, which shall correspond with its extent of territory, its natural resources, and the intelligence and enterprise of its people."[25]

No matter what form improvement took, its ultimate purpose was largely the same: the fulfillment of nature's potential to nurture and sustain human life and a republican form of government.[26] Clearing land and systematically surveying it, adopting constitutions, amending the soil with fertilizers, harvesting better fruit, developing new technologies, removing obstacles from rivers, building new systems of transportation, and educating children would enable the nation to sustain a level of economic production that would enrich and strengthen its citizens.

Lincoln exemplified the national project of improvement. His desire to better himself and increase his chances in life directly followed from his experience of hard labor in a rough and frustrating landscape. As he matured and began to participate in politics, he aligned his personal quest for self-improvement with the improvement program of the Whig Party. For Lincoln, improvement became a twofold process that simultaneously modified and upgraded both human and nonhuman nature. The bettering of one was a function of bettering the other. To improve the land was to improve body and mind—and vice versa.[27]

Lincoln's path to improvement began with reading. Opening and deciphering books was not simply an exercise in abstraction; it was a material act grounded in the experience of nature. When, as a child, Lincoln took his first reading lessons, he began to develop his innate capacity to understand the physical world and to judge and act upon that knowledge. He could not have known it, of course, but reading books and practicing mathematics induced minute but crucially important changes in the structure of his brain. His lifelong habit of reading aloud intensified the physicality of the act; he believed that the sound of words, in addition to the sight of them, improved his memory. Lincoln's alienating experience of physical labor, furthermore, conditioned—perhaps provoked—his early reading efforts. While working in the fields, he often took breaks in the company of a book; on other occasions, he walked long distances along muddy routes to attend school or to borrow books found only in private libraries.[28]

The volumes that enabled Lincoln's improvement were the products of the same wrenching environmental transformations from which he sought escape. During the early nineteenth century, the mechanization and industrialization of paper production required increasing quantities of natural resources drawn from America's forests, soils, and streams. Raw materials flowed into the mills; rolls of finished paper and gallon upon gallon of liquid effluent poured out. Delivered to printers, the paper became books. Steamboats, railroads, and canals—each requiring intensive environmental modifications for wood, coal, iron, roadbed, and channel—then conveyed the books into the American interior. Although those books consisted of nonhuman physical matter, prodigious quantities of labor also made them possible. Sunlight, soil, water, and plant tissues converged in the stream of pulp that culminated in the tomes that readers held. So did the exertions of thousands of laborers, ordinary men and women like Lincoln, all of them straining, perspiring, striving, hurting, hoping, and dying. Lincoln could not have imagined the many human destinies packed into the books he read. In turning their pages, he probably touched a few fibers plucked from cotton bolls by the calloused and scarred fingers of enslaved people.[29] Books literally encapsulated American nature. In them and through them, the nation advanced toward a future that Lincoln and many others hoped would be better than the past.

For Lincoln, the desire for improvement and a future without physical drudgery took him, in 1831, to New Salem, Illinois. A village on the Sangamon River, it consisted of about one hundred people, some log buildings, and an economy centered on a water-powered sawmill and gristmill. Despite its small size, New Salem offered plenty of opportunities for the uprooted young man, who called himself "a piece of floating driftwood."[30] By the time he left in 1837, the driftwood had found its purpose and had embarked on a legal and political career aimed at improvement.

Lincoln's efforts to better himself took different forms. He worked his way up from laborer to store clerk, store owner, postmaster, surveyor, lawyer, and legislator. Along the way, he followed a disciplined program of bodily improvement. While working at the store, one New Salem resident remembered, he practiced "athletic sports, such as wrestling, jumping, pitching quoits or heavy weights and similar exercises." He became a "scientific wrestler," the biographer Douglas Wilson has said, meaning that he eschewed the free-form style of backcountry brawlers in favor of "prescribed rules," according to which he "succeeded as much by skill, agility, and mastery of the standard holds and techniques as by main strength."[31]

Most important to Lincoln's personal improvement, though, was reading. In newspapers, political tracts, mathematics texts, survey manuals, and legal treatises, he immersed himself in a philosophical language of nature. In

Volney's *The Ruins, or, Meditation on the Revolutions of Empires* (1791), he read that "self love, the desire of happiness, [and] aversion to pain, are the essential and primary laws imposed on man by NATURE herself." In Paine's *The Age of Reason* (1794), he met the idea that "science, whether connected with the geometry of the universe, with the systems of animal and vegetable life, or with the properties of inanimate matter, is a text as well for devotion as for philosophy—for gratitude as for human improvement." Blackstone's *Commentaries on the Laws of England* (1765–69) told him that God had formed all matter in the universe and put it into motion according to certain principles, called the "laws of nature." In the process, the Almighty had given humanity "the faculty of reason," a "natural liberty" that enabled it to discover and obey his laws.[32]

Lincoln undoubtedly learned something about nature from books, but those many volumes added to the knowledge he gained firsthand from his bodily struggles in the biophysical world. Although words printed on leaves of paper increasingly absorbed his attention, the nature that lay beyond them—the nature of water, earth, plants, and flesh—continued to shape him. Of all the forms of nature in and around New Salem, the Sangamon River perhaps did the most to make him who he was and to goad him toward improvement.

Lincoln's struggle with the Sangamon—or "Sangamo," as he and others called it—began upon his arrival in New Salem. Denton Offutt, a backcountry entrepreneur from nearby Sangamo Town, hired Lincoln and some other men to build a flatboat on which to convey a load of agricultural commodities—barrels of bacon, wheat, and corn—down the Sangamon, Illinois, and Mississippi rivers to New Orleans. No rails or finished roads existed in those days; anyone who wanted to move products to market had to use rivers. Like other American waterways in the early nineteenth century, the Sangamon physically challenged those who traveled it. Steering their flatboat downstream from Sangamo Town, Lincoln and his co-workers soon came to New Salem and its mill-dam, a low structure made of heavy timber cribs filled with rock and earth. The boatmen intended to float across the dam, but their heavily laden vessel stuck on the crest and began to take on water. To free the craft, the sweating, straining men first carried its cargo to dry land. Lincoln then bored a hole in the bow, allowing the water to drain out. After plugging the opening, he and the crew maneuvered the boat clear.[33]

While the men labored, something happened that would have important consequences for Lincoln's quest for improvement. The residents of New Salem came down from the bluff on which the town sat, gathered on the riverbank, and enjoyed the drama, especially the energetic actions of the tall, lean, raw-boned young man. When the crew poled the vessel to shore, the townspeople offered their congratulations, and Denton Offutt bragged about his employee's strength and intelligence. Lincoln was not yet a politician, but he got what politicians crave: attention. It was significant, moreover, that his first sizable public audience had witnessed not his oratorical talents but his physical prowess in horsing a boat over a dam.[34]

As Lincoln and the other laborers descended the Sangamon, steering their craft through the river's meanders, they encountered "drifted timber"—piles of trunks and branches that posed a "formidable barrier" to their progress. Navigating the slow-moving, snarled stream and its "zig zag course," they made their way into the Illinois and at last the Mississippi, the current of which they followed to New Orleans. While on the Mississippi, Lincoln probably heard about and observed federal government efforts to remove snags and bars from the river's channel. After selling their cargo, Offutt and his crew boarded a steamboat to St. Louis. From there, Lincoln walked about one hundred miles to Sangamon County. The flatboat journey to New Orleans and back was not the first such trip he made, but the experience reinforced a deepening conviction: something had to be done to improve the condition of the Sangamon and other Illinois streams.[35]

It might be said that Lincoln's physical exertions in the cool waters of the Sangamon gave birth to his political career. In March 1832, not quite a year after returning from New Orleans, he announced his candidacy for the state legislature. Drawing on his knowledge of river improvement techniques and his reputation as a river man, he reminded voters of the New Salem milldam incident, told them that he had been observing the Sangamon's seasonal flows, and outlined his plan for improving the stream. His "calculations with regard to the navigation of the Sangamo," he stated, were founded "in reason" and indicated that the river's "natural advantages" could be "greatly improved by art." Clearing away the drifted timber would be simple enough, he asserted, but conditions called for a more sweeping innovation. By cutting the narrow necks of land that separated the river's loopy meanders and by digging a new channel straight to Beardstown on the Illinois, the lower thirty-five miles of the Sangamon could be reduced to as few as twelve. The river itself could be used to excavate the new channel. If the prairie sod were stripped away and the Sangamon diverted into the cleared path, the water would "wash its way through."[36] Shorter, faster, without drifted timber, the new river would enable transportation and bring prosperity to the small towns that dotted its banks.

At the same time, Lincoln seized another opportunity to demonstrate his physical skills and his commitment to the river's improvement. Vincent Bogue, a Springfield businessman, believed that large vessels could navigate the Sangamon, and he chartered the steamboat *Talisman* to prove it. From Cincinnati, the *Talisman* traveled down the Ohio and then up the Mississippi and Illinois to Beardstown. There the steamer waited while Bogue hired citizens to remove obstructions from the Sangamon. While one group chopped ice that clogged the river's mouth, another came downstream in a boat, clearing trees, snags, and overhanging vegetation along the way. In that boat, armed with an ax, was Lincoln. Once again, his strength and skill helped cut a path through the fibrous plant tissues that he knew so well.[37]

At Beardstown, Lincoln joined the *Talisman*. His expert knowledge of the Sangamon helped pilot the craft up the river, past New Salem to its final destination at Portland Landing, a few miles from Springfield. Within days, the river volume fell, forcing the *Talisman*, Lincoln again on board, to depart for Beardstown. At New Salem, the vessel became stuck on the milldam, but Lincoln helped guide it over the impasse. After backing off the structure, the crew used the anchor to tear away part of it. Then, under full steam, the *Talisman* shot across to the downstream side. From there, the boat descended to the relatively open waters of the Illinois.[38]

The voyage showed that the Sangamon, with improvement, was navigable. It also established Lincoln's reputation as a rough-cut but impressive young politician eager to alter nature and better the fortunes of Sangamon County. That he finished eighth among thirteen candidates in the August election did not diminish his political prospects. Many people had learned about him and now associated him with an improvement program that they believed would help them. Two years later, in 1834, he won a seat in the Illinois House of Representatives, where he promoted state-supported railroad and canal projects that would benefit his Sangamon constituents.[39] He soon moved from New Salem to Springfield, the new state capital. His experience of the river had launched him on a political career centered on the physical modification of the Illinois landscape.

While navigating his way into politics on the Sangamon, Lincoln participated in improvement projects off the river that furthered his program of self-betterment. Appointed deputy surveyor of Sangamon County in 1833, he involved himself in the ordering—and thus the improvement—of land. After Congress passed the Land Ordinance of 1785, surveyors had divided major portions of western America into giant rectangles, called sections, each one square mile—640 acres—in size. In turn, each section could be subdivided (theoretically, at least) into half sections, quarter sections, acres, and so forth. By providing a systematic, standardized method of measuring and mapping property boundaries, the rectangular survey fostered a dependable market in land. Thomas Lincoln, in fact, had taken his family to Indiana in late 1816 precisely because he wanted to escape the erratic, irregular survey boundaries that prevented him from establishing clear title to his Kentucky property. Years later, when Abraham Lincoln struggled and sweated through the Illinois underbrush with a compass and measuring chain, the process of improving land—of ordering it and making it more economically valuable—continued.[40]

To order and improve the land, Lincoln recognized that he also had to order and improve his mind. To change one kind of nature, he first had to change the other; the structuring of land and the structuring of knowledge were related parts of the same improvement program. Once more he reached for books that would help him, in this case Flint's *System of Geometry and Trigonometry with a Treatise on Surveying* (1825) and Gibson's *Treatise on Practical Surveying* (first American edition, 1785). Through study, he trained his brain to calculate the angles and areas of particular parcels of land.[41]

During Lincoln's years in New Salem and Springfield, his interest in improvement broadened to include human nature beyond himself. Although rivers, canals, and railroads remained the focus of his advocacy, the same document that outlined his ambitions for the Sangamon committed him to public education. His thoughts about human nature and its prospects for improvement also took a philosophical turn when he pondered the destructive propensities of his fellow man.

In particular, Lincoln expressed concern about the ability of people to control their passions—"the basest principles of our nature"—by which he meant emotions such as hate and the desire for revenge. Properly channeled, the passions could be used for constructive purposes, as in the passion that motivated the American Revolution. Unchecked, the passions fostered a "mobocratic spirit" among the people that emboldened them to take their grievances into the streets, lynching, robbing, burning, and destroying.[42] Lincoln evidently never observed such actions personally, but he read about them in newspapers. And he certainly knew from experience that the passions could sway unchecked groups of men.[43]

Lincoln was no less concerned about another form of unreason that similarly threatened the stability of the republic: overindulgence in alcoholic drink. Whiskey and other liquors were widespread during his time. Rather than trying to ship their bulky, low-value grain to market, many backcountry farmers distilled it into alcohol and shipped it in compact, economical kegs and barrels. Water-borne diseases also predisposed people to prefer the relative safety of whiskey, cider, wine, or beer. Alcohol thus pervaded virtually all aspects of life and was especially popular at events that combined laboring and socializing. In Lincoln's observation, "to have a rolling or a raising, a husking or a hoe-down, any where without it, was *positively insufferable.*" Lincoln himself briefly found employment in a New Salem distillery; and when the *Talisman* headed up the Sangamon with the rail-splitter aboard, it carried 121 barrels of whiskey, beer, brandy, and cider.[44] Whether he recognized the contradiction—an instrument of improvement that enabled the alcoholic degradation of citizens—is unclear. Nonetheless, Lincoln understood that strong drink enflamed the passions, crippled the capacity for reason, and enslaved its victims, thus damaging the political, economic, and moral potential of the American republic.[45]

In his estimation, the solution to the problem of the passions and their close cousin, drunkenness, was improvement. Lincoln's ideas in this regard were analogous to his plans for controlling and channeling the Sangamon; body and river were both forms of nature that needed discipline and development. Reason—"cold, calculating, unimpassioned reason"—would provide "all the materials" that Americans needed to better themselves. They would mold reasoned thought "into *general intelligence, sound morality* and, in particular, *a reverence for the constitution and laws.*"[46] Lincoln's reason instructed him to eat moderately, avoid tobacco, and abstain from alcohol, although of these behaviors, avoiding alcohol was most important. Reason also told him that empathy and compassion, not harsh moral judgment, would encourage drunks to change their ways.[47] Although Lincoln never called for a radical public intervention in human nature along the same lines he envisioned for rivers, he did advocate a mild form of internal improvement for people. Education, he suggested, would curtail alcohol consumption by cultivating appropriate thought and behavior. As he had told the people of Sangamon County, education would promote "morality, sobriety, enterprise and industry."[48]

Improved by reason, Americans would channel their passions, control their urge to imbibe, exercise ever more reason, and further the ends of the Revolution. For newly sober Americans and their fellow citizens, the experience would be liberating. The day would come, Lincoln imagined, when the enslavement of both laborers and drinkers would be no more. "And when the victory shall be complete," he proclaimed in a speech to the Washington Temperance Society, "when there shall be neither a slave nor a drunkard on the earth—how proud the title of that *Land*, which may truly claim to be the birthplace and cradle of both those revolutions, that shall have ended in that victory. How nobly distinguished that People, who shall have planted, and nurtured to maturity, both the political and moral freedom of their species."[49]

Lincoln thus proposed bodily improvement as the answer to the emotional and alcoholic excesses that constrained, if not threatened, the promise of the American republic. To curb anger and hatred and the substance that fueled them, he called for the exercise of reason, the most important of humanity's natural capacities. To counter the physical ruin and death that alcohol brought down on its victims, he offered the alternative of birth, nurturance, and growth, the vital organic processes that animated the backcountry agricultural landscapes of his youth and from which, he believed, the republic had sprung. To all problems, alcohol included, there was an answer: improvement.

Lincoln's personal and public commitment to improvement persisted as he matured into middle age. In 1849, the man who had horsed a flatboat over a dam registered a patent for "an Improved Method of Lifting Vessels over Shoals." The document and plan proposed "a new and improved manner of combining adjustable buoyant air chambers with a steam boat or other vessel," enabling those craft "to pass over bars, or through shallow water, without discharging their cargoes."[50] The human potential for improvement was integral to the technological. Long after he left New Salem, he continued to expand and sharpen his brain power by reading and by learning mathematics. During the early 1850s, he studied the six volumes of *Geometry* by Euclid, the classical Greek mathematician. What worked for him would work for others. Universal education was the "natural companion" of free labor, he said to the Wisconsin State Agricultural Society in 1859, and "every head should be cultivated...and improved."[51]

The possibilities were virtually limitless. By drawing out the God-given, natural potential of all things, Lincoln and his fellow Americans would better themselves and the nation. By learning to read and calculate and by applying reason to the problems of human and nonhuman nature, they would lift themselves from poverty and backwardness and realize the promise of their landscape. Nothing stood in their way—nothing, that is, save for the destructive tendencies that lurked in the human heart.

A GROSS OUTRAGE ON THE LAW OF NATURE

The great turning point in Lincoln's life was the period from 1854 to 1860. During that time, events endangered the nation's prospects for improvement and summoned him to refine his thoughts about mankind and nature. He recommitted himself to the principle of universal natural rights, which he believed lay at the heart of the Declaration of Independence: the inherent right of all people to control their bodies and immediate material circumstances. Like many other Americans, he argued that western territories should be opened to the enterprising energies of free citizens but closed to slavery. His ideas amounted to a story that described a progression, in space and time, of human development. The Revolution had liberated characteristics of thought and behavior intrinsic to human beings. Properly cultivated, those qualities might enable the republic to achieve unprecedented affluence and moral growth. Yet the conclusion to the story was undecided. The arc of history might end, not in happiness, light, and the fulfillment of humankind's vast potential, but in chaos, destruction, and darkness.

The two events that alarmed Lincoln and prompted him to action were the Kansas-Nebraska Act of 1854 and the decision of the United States Supreme Court in *Dred Scott v. Sanford* three years later. Both Kansas-Nebraska and *Dred Scott* enabled the extension of slavery into western territories. Both intensified a national debate about nature: the nature of human beings and the nature of the American West. Both provoked a vigorous reaction from Lincoln and other Americans who saw in the spread of slavery a mortal danger to the nation's revolutionary promise.

At issue in the Kansas-Nebraska Act was its repeal of the Missouri Compromise of 1820, the congressional act that admitted Missouri as a slave state but prohibited slavery anywhere else in the Louisiana Purchase north of latitude 36°30'. The Missouri Compromise stood for more than three decades, but events gradually destabilized it. As a result of its victory in the Mexican-American War of 1846–1848, the United States had acquired a huge tract of southwestern land. The Mexican Cession, so called, offered a vast new field of settlement for American citizens but also raised once more the troubling and potentially divisive question: would the West be open to slavery? Congress decided the issue in the Compromise of 1850, according to which California would be a free state while the residents of New Mexico and Utah territories, operating under the concept of "popular sovereignty," would determine the status of labor, free or slave, for themselves.[52]

If popular sovereignty seemed appropriate for the Southwest, it was poisonous when applied to other areas. Senator Stephen Douglas of Illinois, a Democrat, proposed to organize Kansas and Nebraska territories on that basis. He was eager to benefit his state by promoting the settlement and economic development of the prairies to the west. To gain southern support in Congress for his program, he fashioned a bill that would repeal the Missouri Compromise and potentially open the new territories to slavery. A skillful, powerful politician, he steered the Kansas-Nebraska Act to its passage in 1854. In achieving what was perhaps his greatest political victory, he aroused a fervent opposition, at the center of which was Abraham Lincoln.[53]

In *Dred Scott v. Sanford*, the Supreme Court did even more to pry open the West, and perhaps the entire nation, to slavery. The case involved an enslaved family from Missouri, Dred and Harriet Scott and their children, whose owner, a U.S. Army surgeon, had taken them, individually and collectively, to Illinois, Minnesota, and Wisconsin Territory during the 1830s. After the owner's death in 1846, Dred and Harriet Scott sued the heirs on the grounds that their residence on free soil—two free states and a territory in which the Missouri Compromise prohibited slavery—made them free. The case made its way through state and federal courts until 1857, when the Supreme Court ruled against them. Black people, according to the most famous opinion among the majority justices, were not citizens under the Constitution, and the United States could not restrict the movement of private property, human beings included, across territorial lines. Lincoln and like-minded Americans were shocked. The West was wide open to a deeply objectionable institution. Not only that, but the decision seemed to suggest that slavery could be carried into states outside the South as well, subjecting the entire nation to slaveholder tyranny.[54]

Lincoln had served one term in the U.S. House of Representatives, where he had cast his final votes in favor of bills that would have excluded slavery from the western territories and banned the slave trade in the District of Columbia. After his return to Illinois in 1849, he continued to participate in politics, even though his declining political fortunes persuaded him that he would not hold elective office again. But Kansas-Nebraska roused him from the mundane routine of his law practice, fired his outrage and ambition, and compelled him to reenter the political fray. He gave a series of stirring, combative speeches around the state, denouncing the measure and its architect, Stephen Douglas. As the Whigs broke apart along sectional lines, he became a stalwart of the new Republican Party, which united various northern antislavery factions. In 1858, he campaigned for the Senate against Douglas, and although he lost, his skill and tenacity in debating his opponent vaulted him to national prominence and positioned him as a presidential contender. Wherever he spoke, he hammered his message: slavery was an egregious wrong, and its extension into the western territories would destroy the republic and the great hope it held out to humankind.[55]

Lincoln's objection to slavery and is extension into the West arose primarily from his reading of the Declaration of Independence. Many Americans construed the words at the heart of the preamble—"all men are created equal"—to mean propertied white men. But as expressed in the Declaration, "all men" was an inherently expansive concept. Other Americans, Lincoln among them, interpreted the words to mean all mankind, all humans.[56] Poor white men, black men, American Indian men, women—were they not human, too, and therefore born with the same fundamental right to life, liberty, and the pursuit of happiness? White propertied men might have manipulated the American Revolution to serve their particular ends, but by adopting the term "all men," they could not confine the Declaration's promise to themselves alone. As Lincoln recognized, the difference between limited and universal constructions of those words was impelling the nation toward a crisis.

Lincoln recognized something else as well. At its foundation, the debate in which he was embroiled was about the very nature of things, about the supposed immutable qualities of people. Were all people born with characteristics of mind and behavior that entitled them to citizenship and the enjoyment of rights? Or were some groups, such as blacks and women, different, inferior, and naturally subordinate? The answer to those questions was crucially important, because it determined which Americans had the greatest freedom to claim parts of nature essential to survival, the accumulation of wealth, and the exercise of power. It determined who had the most control over material property, generally land, but more precisely soil, minerals, plants, and animals; who had the right to dominate other human bodies and the products of their labor; and who governed, perhaps the most important means by which citizens sorted out who had access to the biophysical world.

The argument for a hierarchy of human nature had been gaining force for decades. White people generally believed in equality, but not necessarily for black Americans (and not necessarily for white women, either). This was especially so in the South, where slavery had become the dominant form of labor in the production of cotton and other crops. The rhetoric of "all men" carried great moral weight in the South, as elsewhere in the nation, but white southerners argued that its ambit was limited, that black Americans were persons of a different, and lesser, order. Many slavery apologists said that all men might be created equal, but blacks could not be counted as members of the group. Some slaveholders, moreover, resisted charges that slavery necessarily was a backward practice contrary to improvement. Slavery not only improved the lives of the enslaved, they said, but agriculturalists could use slave labor to improve soil conditions and thereby strengthen the institution of slavery. Inequality was inherent in nature and was a source of improvement.[57]

Southerners' commitment to a natural inequality intensified as they projected their ambitions for slavery onto the West. Since the Revolution, white citizens of all sorts had imagined that the region would secure the republic's future. The slaveholders certainly saw it this way, and they tailored the dream so that it was consistent with their particular economic circumstances and fit their particular view of the world. Some—Thomas Jefferson and Henry Clay, for example—believed that slavery would weaken and die in the West, enabling the republic to serve as a beacon of liberty to the world.[58] Other slaveholders, more realistically, recognized that the West promised to revitalize slavery, not kill it. Those people sought to extend southern agricultural production into the region's fertile soils. The westward movement of southern agriculture would expand the market for enslaved people and their labor. The growth and persistence of slavery, finally, would justify the slaveholders' place atop the social hierarchy and affirm the legitimacy of a republic based on human bondage.[59]

Among the outstanding proponents of slavery and its extension was South Carolina statesman John C. Calhoun, a graduate of Yale University (class of 1804) and, at various times, U.S. congressman and senator, secretary of war, secretary of state, and vice president. Like many other slaveholders, Calhoun looked on African Americans as naturally inferior beings whose enslavement was a "positive good." Slavery, he and others argued, precluded the antagonism typical of employer-wageworker relationships in a free labor system. Slaves and their masters mutually benefited one another, and the masters showed more genuine concern for their charges than capitalists did for wage laborers. By stabilizing society, slavery stabilized the political system and in the process promoted white equality and elevated the enslaved above savagery. It was a "dangerous error" to assume that "all men are born free and equal," to believe in an "unbounded and individual liberty supposed to belong to man in the hypothetical and misnamed state of nature." The United States thus had no alternative but to open the West to slavery. Freedom and the right to property—which included the natural right to own members of an inferior race—demanded it.[60]

Like Calhoun, who died in 1850, Chief Justice Roger Taney was a reactionary who argued for a racially exclusive interpretation of the Declaration of Independence. A Marylander, Taney had manumitted eleven of his slaves and in 1819 had referred to slavery as "a blot on our national character" that was inconsistent with the Declaration of Independence. Over the next forty years, he reversed and hardened his views. As he expressed in his *Dred Scott v. Sanford* opinion, black people had no inherent natural rights. Although the Declaration "would seem to embrace the whole human family," he wrote, its authors had intended otherwise. They understood that "negroes of the African race" were "beings of an inferior order" with whom intermarriage was "unnatural and immoral." Dred Scott, "a member of that unfortunate race," had no standing as a citizen and thus could not be "naturalized."[61]

During the 1850s, Lincoln himself was hardly an unqualified civil libertarian or humanitarian on racial matters. His personal circumstances shaped his politics. He was among a white majority that tended to assert its interests over those of African Americans and other people of color. His wife's family owned slaves, as did some of his friends. On one occasion he legally represented a Kentuckian seeking to reclaim human property in Illinois. Short of a constitutional amendment, he did not think that the federal government could prohibit slavery in the states where it existed. He often asserted that the republic was for white people, and he made his strongest political appeals to European Americans who opposed the extension of slavery because it deprived them of economic opportunity, not necessarily because it degraded blacks. Throughout the 1850s and well into the Civil War, he advocated that African Americans be emancipated and then colonized somewhere close to the equator, in a climate to which they were racially adapted. Although historians continue to debate his attitudes on race, political expedience impelled him to speak to the interests and prejudices of whites.[62]

If Lincoln did not advocate outright abolition of slavery and social equality for black people, he did take a principled stand against something he believed was deeply wrong. Again and again, drawing on the sum of his experiences—all that he had read, heard, witnessed, and felt—he countered the likes of Calhoun and Taney and argued that slavery contradicted the Declaration of Independence, violated natural rights, and, if allowed to expand, mortally endangered the republic.

To deliver his message, Lincoln refined his story of nature, nation, and improvement, making it more complex and sophisticated. The human body, by his account, occupied the physical and moral center of nature. The body's innate need to satisfy its hunger and protect itself from harm was the source of each person's desire, "planted" there by God, to benefit from and enjoy the products of his or her own work. Whatever a person grew or made—through the application of energy, ingenuity, dexterity, strength, or skill—belonged to that person and no one else. As Lincoln put it, "each individual is naturally entitled to do as he pleases with himself and the fruit of his labor." Food procurement—mankind's "first necessity"—was especially important; nothing was more basic and essential to the human body than the two hands that fed its mouth. But no matter the activity, the individual who engaged in it owned its product. Protecting the body was the most fundamental of all "natural rights," he asserted, and it was common to all people.[63]

Lincoln expanded his understanding of human nature and natural rights into a broad conception of national nature and how the republic ought to function, develop, and improve. Collectively, the people of the United States— "the great body of the people," "the body politic"—composed an indissoluble organic unity, like a human body. The health and future prosperity of that body depended on its access to land and other "natural resources." Americans would apply their labor and ingenuity to transforming "the physical world" into wealth and property, the basis of their economic self-sufficiency and independence.[64] To Lincoln, people fashioned liberty from the application of their productive energies to the raw materials of nature. Plowing prairie sod, cutting trees, splitting rails, building fences, planting and harvesting wheat, mining ore, and beating iron into horseshoes: by these and many other means, they made a living for themselves independent of anyone else. This was not "*mudsill*" labor, in which a hired man was "fatally fixed in that condition for life." This was "*free* labor—the just and generous, and prosperous system, which opens the way for all—gives hope to all, and energy, and progress, and improvement of condition to all." Joined in a body politic, an indissoluble national whole, free laborers would continue to benefit from—and improve on—their individual productive activities.[65]

Lincoln's story of American nature ultimately projected a nation of hard-working, independent producers busily shaping a beautiful, wondrous, steadily growing, always improving landscape that would embody the republic's ideals. His speech on discoveries and inventions, which he wrote and delivered during this time, was not a deviation or departure from his political message, as some people later thought; his views of nature were integral to his politics. Furthermore, if machines, mining, and other technological innovations fascinated him, he did not imagine they would turn the republic into a giant mechanism. Modern devices enabled citizens to improve the organic republic and the agricultural environment that was its basis. The United States constituted an enormous "field," he proposed; if properly tended and improved, it could become a "garden."[66]

Although Lincoln sketched a rosy picture of America, he acknowledged that troubling issues, foremost among them slavery, threatened its future. He charged that slavery was "founded in the selfishness of man's nature"—greed—rather than in "the abundance of his heart"—generosity. It not only enflamed the "eternal antagonism" between those two human propensities, but also brutalized the enslaved.[67] The slave trade was "no more than bringing wild negroes from Africa, to sell as such would buy them."[68] At the slave market in Washington, D.C., "in view from the windows of the capitol," a citizen could observe "a sort of negro-livery stable, where droves of negroes were collected, temporarily kept, and finally taken to Southern markets, precisely like droves of horses." Slavery prevented its victims from being anything "but as the beasts of the field."[69] Douglas and his ilk, moreover, were "blowing out the moral lights around us; teaching that the negro is no longer a man but a brute; that the Declaration has nothing to do with him; that he ranks with the crocodile and the reptile; that man, with body and soul, is a matter of dollars and cents."[70]

By "dehumanizing" black people, Lincoln said, slavery undercut the nation's mission of upholding liberty in a world dominated by monarchies and authoritarian regimes. Human bondage was "a gross outrage on the law of nature," and it "deprives our republican example of its just influence in the world—enables the enemies of free institutions, with plausibility, to taunt us as hypocrites—causes the real friends of freedom to doubt our sincerity, and especially because it forces so many really good men amongst ourselves into an open war with the very fundamental principles of civil liberty—criticizing the Declaration of Independence, and insisting that there is no right principle of action but self-interest."[71]

Ultimately, slavery and its extension into the West, Lincoln believed, would destroy the republic. Slavery depressed wages and enabled slaveholders to monopolize land, cutting off other white people's access to the resources that made them independent and able to improve their lives. Lincoln described slavery's threat in terms consistent with his naturalistic sense of the body, its labor, and the nation. If slavery were confined to the South, it would not threaten the republic as a whole. It would be a "wen"—a cyst—that would die "a natural death" of its own accord, without harming the great body of the people. In his estimation, however, slavery was not likely to remain in place. Southern slaveholders recognized that the need for fresh soil and a profitable market for slave labor required its expansion into Kansas, Nebraska, and other western territories.[72] Lincoln rejected the claim, which Calhoun, Douglas, and other Democrats had made, that soil and climate would establish a natural boundary between slave and free areas. "Climate will not" limit slavery, he charged. "No peculiarity of the country will—nothing in *nature* will."[73] And if slavery entered the West, he said, it would ruin the chances of the nonslaveholding white Americans who migrated there. Under those circumstances, slavery would be a "cancer," a "sore," a "venomous snake" that induced "shocks, and throes, and convulsions" in the body politic.[74] Once "planted" in the West, it would resemble "the Canada thistle, or some other of those pests of the soil" that "cannot be dug out by the millions of men who will come thereafter."[75] Eventually, slavery would invade the free states, too. The consequences would be dire.

In the face of slavery's expansive tendencies, Lincoln asserted the positive elements in his story of human and national development. Enslaved people were not "property in the same sense" as "hogs and horses" but were possessed of "mind, feeling, souls, family affections, hopes, joys, sorrows—something that made them more than hogs or horses." Thousands of free blacks lived without owners and tenders; they were not livestock but human beings.[76] And as human beings, they had the right to sustain themselves much as did anyone else. "I hold," Lincoln said, "that if there is any one thing that can be proved to be the will of God by external nature around us, without any reference to revelation, it is the proposition that whatever any one man earns with his hands and by the sweat of his brow, he shall enjoy in peace."[77] More succinctly, in words that he put to the Kentucky abolitionist Cassius Clay: "I always thought that the man who made the corn should eat the corn." Lincoln never relented on this point. "In their right to 'life, liberty, and the pursuit of happiness,'" all people, regardless of color or condition, were equal.[78]

Lincoln defended a universal interpretation of the Declaration of Independence on many occasions, but perhaps never more forcefully than on June 26, 1857, at Springfield, Illinois, in response to the *Dred Scott* decision. Speaking to a white audience, he conceded that the authors of the Declaration of Independence did not believe that all human beings were equal "*in all respects*," in "color, size, intellect, moral development, or social capacity." And he acknowledged "a natural disgust in the minds of nearly all white people, to the idea of an indiscriminate amalgamation of the white and black races." Yet he took issue with Justice Taney, Senator Douglas, and other proponents of a racially narrow reading of the Declaration. The document in fact did apply to "the whole human family." All people shared an irreducible, natural quality: the need for personal survival and bodily integrity. The Declaration's authors, he argued, recognized this universal human condition and envisioned that popular recognition of it would grow and flower. They "meant to set up a standard maxim for free society, which should be familiar to all, and revered by all; constantly looked to, constantly labored for, and even though never perfectly attained, constantly approximated, and thereby constantly spreading and deepening its influence, and augmenting the happiness and value of life to all people of all colors everywhere."[79]

Lincoln emphasized his point by answering Douglas's charge that the Republicans—"black Republicans," in the senator's words—propounded not just complete equality but also total social and biological integration. Citizens who asserted that the Declaration applied to "ALL men," Lincoln exclaimed, did not necessarily "want to vote, and eat, and sleep, and marry with negroes!" That "I do not want a black woman for a *slave* does not mean that I must necessarily want her for a *wife*. I need not have her for either, I can just leave her alone. In some respects she is not my equal; but in her natural right to eat the bread she earns with her own hands without asking leave of anyone else, she is my equal, and the equal of all others."[80]

If the federal government did not have the constitutional authority to end slavery in the South, Lincoln argued, it did have the power to prevent the extension of the practice into Kansas and other federal territories. He and his Republican allies pointed to a string of precedents: the Declaration of Independence, the Northwest Ordinance and its prohibition of slavery north of the Ohio River, the Constitution's restriction of the slave trade, and other measures that authorized the federal government to regulate or prohibit slavery short of abolishing it in the states where it already existed. Slavery was rooted in the South, Lincoln said, but there it must remain.[81]

Lincoln recognized that the controversy over the extension of slavery would determine the nation's future. In digging out its destiny, the nation had followed two divergent leads. One culminated in the republic "that Jefferson foresaw and intended—the happy home of teeming millions of free, white, prosperous people, and not a slave among them."[82] The other ended in a corrupted landscape "in which you have planted the seeds of despotism around your own doors," where bestialized human beings, their hopes crushed, labored "in darkness like that which broods over the damned" and where tyrants ruled. The nation no longer could follow both leads. A body could not come apart and still live; the house that it inhabited could not stand against itself. The United States must be one thing or the other.[83]

THE BETTER ANGELS OF OUR NATURE

Lincoln admitted that he never completely understood the reasons for the catastrophe that followed. He recognized that the extension of slavery into the western territories had started it. Other than that, it baffled him, weakened his belief in mankind's ability to shape a rational future, and reinforced his intuition that some immanent force—ominous, irresistible, inscrutable—was sweeping the country toward an unknown destiny. As the disaster worsened, he wondered if it was a form of punishment for the great moral wrong of slavery. Yet he never lost hope that the Almighty again might grace the poor matter of humankind, might call forth "the better angels of our nature" and inspire the nation to cease the slaughter and reunite.[84]

Lincoln did all he could to turn the conflict to a higher end. An event so horrible and so destructive of human life might yet achieve a progressive outcome. Improvement in its various forms became the means by which he prosecuted the war and preserved the Union, the improved geopolitical combination that ensured all future improvement. By 1863, the conflict was nothing less than a revolution in the name of improvement. Yet even by then, he was beginning to believe that only God could know the ultimate purpose of the struggle. He had no choice but to do what he thought was right, but in a war so terrible, what was truly right was beyond human comprehension.

The essential feature of Lincoln's program was the Union, the indivisible, irreducible (although mortal) body of states that composed the republic. Although he often spoke of the Union in near-mystical terms, it was as real as the land on which he walked. Few Americans have appreciated his geopolitical and geostrategic vision, which was grounded in his understanding of how agricultural, technological, topographical, hydrological, and biological things were distributed across the Earth.

Lincoln's direct experience of the American landscape informed his view. As a settler, boatman, militiaman, surveyor, lawyer, congressman, and presidential aspirant, he had traveled extensively. His political opponents and detractors had tried to depict him as a crude backcountry hick, but for a man of his time, he was unusually cosmopolitan. He had seen more of the United States than any previous president, and his firsthand knowledge helped him grasp the importance of a geographically far-reaching republic.[85] Echoing James Madison and other founders, he believed that a large number of integrated states—the Union in its broadest sense—was the key to a productive economy and a federal government powerful enough to maintain political stability and to guarantee natural rights and their attendant liberties.[86]

As war approached and then broke out in spring 1861, Lincoln's first and foremost challenge was to maintain the Union and restore the seceded states to it. In his famous "House Divided" speech of 1858, he had said that the United States would become free or slave—all one thing or all the other: "Either the *opponents* of slavery, will arrest the further spread of it, and place it where the public mind shall rest in the belief that it is in course of ultimate extinction; or its *advocates* will push it forward, till it shall become alike lawful in *all* the States, *old* as well as *new*—*North* as well as *South*."[87] His reference to the "ultimate extinction" of slavery outraged southerners, and as president he tried to reassure them that the Constitution did not give the executive and legislative branches the political power to end slavery where it already existed. In particular, he did not want to alienate Missouri, Kentucky, Maryland, and Delaware, slave states that had not seceded but might.

While he tried to maintain the Union, Lincoln equipped himself to oversee military operations against Confederate armies. He had almost no experience or knowledge on which to draw. He once joked that during the 1832 Black Hawk war, in which the United States suppressed Indian resistance in the area north of the Ohio and east of the Mississippi, he "had a good many bloody struggles with the musquetoes" but had done little else that would qualify him as a wartime leader.[88] To make up for his deficiency, he fell back on a tried and true practice: self-improvement. Much as he had mastered survey manuals, legal treatises, and the geometry of Euclid, so he undertook a systematic study of military strategy. "He gave himself, night and day, to the study of the military situation," wrote his personal secretary, John Hay. "He read a large number of strategical works. He pored over the reports from the various departments and districts of the field of war. He held long conferences with eminent generals and admirals, and astonished them by the extent of his special knowledge and the keen intelligence of his questions."[89]

Lincoln's study helped him understand, and act upon, the geostrategic requirements and geopolitical implications of the conflict. He soon realized that he must abandon a war of limited means and ends for an all-out war that would destroy his opponent's armies. More than reestablishing federal authority over rebellious locales in the South, the Union forces must control large areas of Confederate territory. They must sweep down the Mississippi River, over the Cumberland Plateau, into Virginia, and across the South's coastal lowlands and Piedmont, and they must blockade southern ports. By controlling geographical space, they must deprive Confederate forces of the material resources—horses, corn, salt, lead, and many other things drawn from nature—necessary for military campaigns. Lincoln also understood that geography was not the final military goal; the Union armies must not merely capture and hold territory, they must also move quickly and flexibly to deliver relentless, crushing blows against Confederate forces. Slow-moving generals reluctant to commit their armies frustrated the president and drew his ire; Ulysses Grant, William Sherman, Philip Sheridan, and George Thomas, fast-moving generals who ruthlessly hammered the enemy, earned his praise and rewards.[90]

While the battles unfolded, Lincoln supported measures that improved and perpetuated the Union. Between late spring and early summer 1862, he signed legislation that many southern congressmen had opposed and that used the republic's enormous natural strength—its land base—for democratization and development. The Homestead Act enabled citizens to settle 160 acres, a quarter section of the public domain, essentially for free. The Pacific Railway Act provided land grants to railroads that would connect California to the Union. The Morrill Act used proceeds from the sale of public land to support a college in each state that would teach "scientific and classical studies," "military tactics," and "agriculture and the mechanic arts . . . in order to promote the liberal and practical education of the industrial classes in the several pursuits and professions of life."[91]

More important to the direct conduct of the war, Lincoln fostered the development and use of new military technologies, including weaponry. He ordered the army, for example, to adopt seven-shot repeating rifles and carbines manufactured by the Connecticut inventor Christopher Spencer. Lincoln personally tested the weapons in Treasury Park, south of the White House, and on one occasion tried a prototype gun sight of his own design and fabrication. "I believe I can make this gun shoot better," he said late one afternoon, and he fitted his whittled wooden sight to his carbine. Raising the weapon, he fired at the target, and bullet after bullet tore through the sheet of stationery affixed to the woodpile. "He emptied the magazine, reloaded and emptied it again," the historian Robert Bruce later wrote. "Of the fourteen shots, nearly a dozen hit the paper." Although Spencer never used Lincoln's improved sight, the repeaters transformed Union cavalrymen into a formidable fighting force.[92]

Nothing that Lincoln did in the war, however, mattered more than his efforts to achieve the ultimate form of improvement: the destruction of slavery. While he always had opposed slavery, and never more vociferously than after 1854, he also believed that getting the nation to live up to the eternal principle of natural rights required careful, prudent maneuvering in the unstable, compromised world of politics. He did not believe that the Constitution gave the president the unilateral right to abolish slavery. He was leery of any measure, furthermore, that might fracture the Republican Party or alienate Missouri, Kentucky, Maryland, and Delaware and drive them into the Confederacy. If he moved too precipitously, he reasoned, he might undermine the Union—the preservation of which was his first priority—and with it any chance of ending bondage. When military officers announced the liberation of slaves in Confederate-held areas, he countermanded them.[93]

Gradually, political circumstances gave Lincoln the opportunity to act. Soon after the conflict began, enslaved laborers sought refuge behind the lines of Union armies. Lincoln offered no immediate response, but he told a confidant that "the government neither should nor would send back to bondage such as come to our armies." When Congress passed the Confiscation Act, which authorized the seizure of all property, including slaves, used for military purposes against the United States, he signed it into law. Soon thereafter, he affixed his signature to a measure that banned slavery in the District of Columbia.[94]

As the war intensified and as increasing numbers of enslaved people escaped to the Union side, Lincoln advanced a plan to stop the fighting and end slavery in the Confederacy altogether. He tried to persuade the border states—the slave states still in the Union—to accept compensated emancipation, paid for by the United States. If they did this, he reasoned, it might weaken the

Confederacy by convincing some of the seceded states that the momentum of the war was against them and that they should return to the Union.[95]

The border states rebuffed his proposal, and as the conflict intensified and casualties mounted, he decided to take stronger measures. In August, he allowed the army to begin organizing black regiments on the South Carolina coast. In the meantime, he formulated an emancipation plan using the commander-in-chief's war powers. Although the Constitution constrained the federal government from summarily abolishing slavery, it did give the president wartime authority to implement policies designed to weaken an enemy. In Lincoln's view, nothing could do more to weaken the Confederacy than to turn its enslaved laborers against it. He feared, however, that a sudden effort to emancipate slaves in the Confederacy might seem to his enemies a sign of weakness. Lonely and frustrated, he waited for a victory that he would take to be evidence of the Divine will and a measure of Union strength. A battlefield triumph would give him the chance to act.[96]

In late September, following a qualified Union victory at Antietam in Maryland, he issued the Preliminary Emancipation Proclamation, which directed that on January 1, 1863, enslaved people in areas still in rebellion against the United States would be "forever free." Delaying the implementation of the proclamation for a few months was prudent, in his view. The intervening time would allow the Confederate states to consider the choice he presented them: end the bloodshed and keep the slaves, or remain in rebellion and lose them. The lag also would give Unionist slaveholders an opportunity to consider his offer to them: manumission in exchange for gradual, compensated emancipation and the colonization of "persons of African descent" in areas apart from the nation's white majority, with the consent of the colonists.[97]

In support of his plan, Lincoln delivered an annual message to Congress in December 1862 that was the fullest expression of his geopolitical—*earth*-political—vision. He believed that in spite of the war and the possible breakup of the Union, geography ultimately would hold the free and slave states together. The land, he stated, "is well adapted to be the home of one national family; and it is not well adapted for two, or more. Its vast extent, and its variety of climate and productions, are of advantage, in this age, for one people, whatever they might have been in former ages. Steam, telegraphs, and intelligence, have brought these, to be an advantageous combination, for one people." Disunion will never work, he argued. Escaping slaves would cross from South to North with ease; the rivers and abstract surveyors' lines that formed the political boundary would pose little obstacle, if any, to their movement. Furthermore, dividing the "great interior region" of the United States—"the great body of the republic"—into separate nations would lead to burdensome trade regulations that would deny northern and southern producers access to each other's seaports. Sooner or later, the land and the economic imperatives of living on it would force the disunited states back together: "In all its adaptations and aptitudes, [the land] demands union, and abhors separation. In fact, it would, ere long, force reunion, however much blood and treasure the separation might have cost."[98]

This enormously productive national landscape offered a solution to the problems of slavery and war, Lincoln argued. "Our abundant room—our broad national homestead—is our ample resource," he said, and it had a "natural capacity for sustaining a dense population" capable of paying slaveholders for emancipating their human property and covering the cost of colonizing freed people outside the country. The rate of population growth from births and immigration, he pointed out, would outstrip the rate of interest, thereby reducing the proportional amount that each citizen would pay. Although Lincoln did not specify how the funds would come into the national treasury, presumably taxation—income, excise, and tariff—and the sale of public land would be the instruments.[99]

No matter the channels along which the wealth flowed, Lincoln believed that the consequences would be democratic and just and would improve the nation. Because all white Americans bore some responsibility for slavery, all would share the cost, and all Americans, black and white, would benefit. Slaves would be liberated, and his plan would not require "free colored persons"—he also called them "free Americans of African descent"—to leave the country. They would not, as some white people feared, "swarm forth, and cover the whole land"; the nation and its land base were too capacious for that. They already were "in the land," Lincoln said, and their proportion of the nation's population—one for every seven whites—would not change. He pointed out that "many communities" already had "more than one free colored person" for every seven white citizens, "and this, without any apparent consciousness of evil from it." Nor would the freed people overrun the northern states. Freedom would unfold over several decades, he predicted, and those former slaves who remained in the United States likely would continue to live and work in the South. Emancipation posed no threat to white people, and its benefits were incalculable. It would remove a major obstacle—slavery—that blocked the nation's path to improvement, and it was far less expensive than war. Most important, it "will cost no blood, no precious life."[100]

Lincoln recognized that the United States was on the verge of revolutionary change. "The dogmas of the quiet past, are inadequate to the stormy present," he stated in the conclusion to his message. "The occasion is piled high with difficulties, and we must rise with the occasion. As our case is new, so we must think anew, and act anew. We must disenthrall ourselves, and we shall save our country." The way was clear: "We—even we *here*—hold the power, and bear the responsibility. In *giving* freedom to the *slave*, we *assure* freedom to the *free*—honorable alike in what we give, and what we preserve. We shall nobly save, or meanly lose, the last best, hope of earth."[101]

Although Lincoln intended his plan to restore the Union and stanch the flow of blood on the battlefield, nothing came of it. No southern state agreed to the plan, and Congress never considered the constitutional amendments that would have put it into action. To his regret, keeping the nation from fragmenting and settling the meaning of the Declaration of Independence exacted an ever more fearsome toll. In battle after battle, the bodies piled high.

Yet in the midst of the bloodshed, Lincoln and the nation moved closer to realizing the Declaration's promise. On January 1, 1863, the president signed the final Emancipation Proclamation. "I do order and declare," he stated, "that all persons held as slaves" in those areas still under Confederate control "henceforward shall be free. . . . And upon this act, sincerely believed to be an act of justice, warranted by the Constitution, upon military necessity, I invoke the considerate judgment of mankind, and the gracious favor of Almighty God."[102]

It was a revolutionary moment in American history. Slavery was crumbling, and for the first time, by order of the president and commander-in-chief, the nation restricted the commercialization of a major portion of nature—human nature. Capitalism was crucial to American society, but Lincoln and his supporters believed that citizens could not allow it to turn human beings into commodities.[103] In reversing one of society's most egregious abuses of nature, the Emancipation Proclamation instantly transformed Union forces into an army of liberation. The freedmen and free black citizens who soon enlisted in it, some 180,000 strong, magnified its revolutionary power and created opportunities for their countrymen to think anew and act anew, as Lincoln had said.[104]

More than ever before, the president began to imagine the outlines of a society that must include both whites and blacks. He never again spoke of his colonization plan, which had been unrealistic, unfair, and motivated more by politics than by his convictions. In a public letter widely published in northern newspapers, he chastised the critics of emancipation. "You say you will not fight to free negroes," he wrote. "Some of them seem willing to fight for you." Black soldiers weakened the Confederacy, he said, which eased the burdens of white soldiers. Yet why should black soldiers "do any thing for us, if we will do nothing for them? If they stake their lives for us, they must be prompted by the strongest motive—even the promise of freedom. And the promise being made, must be kept."[105]

Keep the promise he did. Confederate commanders, their ranks thinning, wished to exchange prisoners with their Union foes; the Confederate military would release captive Union soldiers for an equivalent number of Confederate men. The Confederate side had one condition, however: under no circumstances would it give up U.S. Army soldiers who had been slaves. Lincoln and his administration came under intense pressure from civilians and imprisoned white soldiers, many of them suffering under abysmal conditions, to accept the terms. At Andersonville, Georgia, where the Confederacy packed some thirty-three thousand prisoners into a stockade intended to accommodate ten thousand, the men desperately wanted their commander-in-chief to redeem them, and they could not understand why he would sacrifice them. "It appears that the federal government thinks more of a few hundred niggers than of the thirty thousand whites here in bondage," one man wrote in his diary. The Confederacy allowed delegations of prisoners to carry petitions to Washington, D.C., pleading with Lincoln to relent. Some Republicans warned the president that he was in danger of losing political support because of his stubbornness. But Lincoln and his administration refused to abandon the commitment. Why, he replied, should black soldiers "give their lives for us, with full notice of our purpose to betray them?"[106]

Lincoln's personal circumstances also manifested the social changes reshaping the nation. When he first left Springfield, Illinois, for Washington, D.C., he brought with him a black valet named William Johnson. Johnson performed various menial tasks for the president, but the young man also took on more important responsibilities, such as serving as the president's bodyguard and friend. Lincoln liked Johnson and depended on him. When Lincoln came down with smallpox, Johnson nursed him back to health. In late December 1863, Johnson contracted the same disease, and the following January, after lying ill for weeks, he died. His body might have come to rest in an obscure segregated cemetery somewhere around the capital, but Lincoln paid for his burial at Arlington National Cemetery in ground reserved for African Americans whose gravestones carried one descriptive word: "CITIZEN."[107]

The war had a remarkable effect on Lincoln: it created conditions in which he personally experienced, more than ever, the consequences of his natural rights principles. Perhaps this was most evident in his relationship with Frederick Douglass, the great African American abolitionist. Lincoln's politically motivated favoritism toward white Americans and his careful approach to emancipation outraged Douglass, who bitterly criticized the president for not taking aggressive action to end slavery and achieve civil and social equality for blacks. Twice Lincoln heard Douglass's concerns in meetings at the White House. In those encounters, Lincoln learned to appreciate Douglass's intelligence and honesty. In their second meeting, Lincoln prolonged his conversation with the abolitionist while the governor of Connecticut, the next person with an appointment to see the chief executive, waited. At the White House reception following Lincoln's second inauguration, the president enthusiastically and publicly greeted "my friend Douglass." For his part, Douglass grew to understand Lincoln's political motivations and appreciate the president's moral commitment to antislavery. Douglass continued to criticize the president but recognized him as a kindred soul in the struggle for improvement and a crucial ally in the cause of black freedom. "A son of toil himself," Douglass remembered later, "he was linked in brotherly sympathy with the sons of toil in every loyal part of the Republic."[108]

As the war neared its conclusion, the nation's revolutionary momentum swept Lincoln along, and he helped to accelerate its pace. In late 1864, Congress was on the verge of a momentous achievement: passage of a thirteenth amendment to the Constitution, which would abolish slavery. Lincoln recognized that the measure would complete the process the Emancipation Proclamation had begun, and he also believed it would solidify the Republican Party and perhaps end the war. He threw his political weight behind it, using all his persuasive powers to sway the votes of wavering Democrats and former Whigs. He told one House member whose brother had perished in the conflict, "Your brother died to save the Republic from death by the slaveholders' rebellion. I wish you could see to it to vote for the Constitutional amendment ending slavery." Final passage of the measure thrilled Lincoln and many other Americans. To perfect "the reunion of all the States" and "to remove all causes of disturbance in the future," he said, "it was necessary that the original disturbing cause should be rooted out," like a vile weed, thereby achieving for all Americans and for "the whole world" a "great moral victory."[109]

Although Lincoln continued to take cautious stands on civil rights and social equality, he was demonstrating his openness to a radical fulfillment of the republic's potential. It is impossible to know how he would have responded to later constitutional amendments granting full citizenship to all persons "born or naturalized in the United States" and voting rights to all adult males without regard to "race, color, or previous condition of servitude."[110] Perhaps some indication might be derived from guarded comments he made while discussing his ideas for "reconstruction," the political process by which the Confederate states would be restored to their proper relationship to the Union. His own preference, he said, was that "the elective franchise" be extended to "very intelligent" black people and to "those who serve our cause as soldiers."[111]

Black suffrage certainly was consistent with his view of the republic. "Advancement—improvement in condition," he had written in 1859, "is the order of things in a society of equals." He was referring to improvement in economic terms, but he did not always construe the concept so narrowly. "Let us hope," he had told the Wisconsin State Agricultural Society in September 1859, "that by the best cultivation of the physical world, beneath and around us; and the intellectual and moral world within us, we shall secure an individual, social, and *political* prosperity and happiness, whose course shall be onward and upward, and which, while the earth endures, shall not pass away." The consequences of the war—the destruction of slavery and the incipient extension of voting rights—could count, within Lincoln's view of the world, as improvement.[112]

ROUGH HEW THEM HOW WE WILL

Still, it was a terribly destructive war, and if it yielded improvement, it also exacted an enormous physical, psychological, and spiritual cost on the nation's citizens, not least on Lincoln himself. The war and his responsibility for it haunted him. As the battles took ever more lives and victory seemed remote, he grew weary, frustrated, angry, and at times mistrustful. He appeared "exhausted, care-worn, spiritless, extinct," observed a State Department translator who saw him regularly. "The old clear laugh never came back," wrote Noah Brooks; "the even temper was sometimes disturbed and his natural charity for all was often turned into an unwanted suspicion of the motives of men."

To his wife, Mary Todd Lincoln, he was "worn down," and he "spoke crabbedly to men, harshly so."[113]

The Civil War brought Lincoln closer to an organic condition familiar to all human beings but which had special meaning for him during a time of national crisis and disorder: death. Among all Lincoln's close companions in life, death was among the most important, and it had taught him that improvement was never guaranteed. The man who struggled to lift himself above squalor, ignorance, and degradation was fully aware that unpredictable physical events could shatter the finest of plans and the grandest of dreams. Death, Lincoln's experience taught him, always lurked on the edges of reason, hope, and happiness. Death gave him a tragic view of life and made him acutely aware of the power that kept tomorrow unknowable from today.

Death had come to Lincoln early and often. When he was about four, he lost his younger brother, Thomas. When he was nine, shortly after the family relocated to Indiana, death again called. White snakeroot grew in the thickets around Pigeon Creek. Cows that grazed on the plant's slender stalks, brilliant white blossoms, and toothed leaves absorbed a toxic compound, trematol, which people ingested when they drank the animals' milk. Dizziness, nausea, stomach pains, irregular breathing, and erratic heartbeat ensued, followed by coma and death. Nancy Hanks Lincoln, Abraham's mother, contracted the "milk sickness." In her death throes, she called for her children and "told them to be good and kind to their father—to one an other and to the world." Lincoln's father went to Kentucky to court a new wife, leaving him and his sister Sarah to fend for themselves. Hungry, ill clothed, and grieving, they clung to each other for consolation and sustenance. Lincoln seldom mentioned the pain that his mother's death caused him. His words to a child whose father had fallen in Civil War combat, however, perhaps expressed his feelings. "In this sad world of ours," he wrote, "sorrow comes to all; and, to the young, it comes with bitterest agony, because it takes them unawares. . . . I have had experience enough to know what I say."[114]

Death's bitterness followed Lincoln throughout his life. When he was a few weeks shy of nineteen, his beloved sister Sarah died in childbirth. Upon receiving the news, he sat down on a log and buried his face in his hands "while the tears rolled down through his long bony fingers."[115] During his years in New Salem, he grew fond of a young woman named Ann Rutledge. One wet summer, a Sangamon Valley flood carried typhoid into her family's well, and fever and diarrhea struck her down. Within a week, she was gone. Lincoln eventually married and fathered four sons, but no amount of devotion could shield his boys from the microorganisms that swirled through air and water on their way from one body to the next. Somewhere in his young life, Edward Baker Lincoln—Eddie—contracted tuberculosis, a bacterium that ravaged the lungs. After fifty-two days of struggle, not quite four years old, he breathed his last.[116]

Death and its counterpart, grief, stalked Lincoln into the White House. Battlefield fatalities hurt him deeply. The combat death of his beloved friend Edward Baker, after whom he had named Eddie, crushed him. The demise of anonymous thousands of soldiers wounded him no less. "My God! Stanton, our cause is lost!" he exclaimed to his secretary of war following the Union defeat at Chancellorsville. "We are ruined—we are ruined; and such a fearful loss of life! My God! This is more than I can endure! . . . Defeated again, and so many of our noble countrymen killed! What *will* the people say?"[117]

But of all the casualties of the Civil War, none devastated Lincoln more than that of his favorite son, Willie. It is impossible to know exactly when or how *Salmonella typhosa* crossed the eleven-year-old's lips and traveled into his stomach and intestines. The organism's source may have been the Union and Confederate armies camped on the banks of the Potomac River, where the diarrheic bowel movements of infected soldiers passed the bacterium into the environment. From the river, it entered the White House water supply, and then into Willie and his brother Tad. No matter its origin, typhoid destroyed Willie as it had destroyed Ann Rutledge years before. The boy's parents were inconsolable. "He was too good for this earth," a tearful Lincoln said, "but then we loved him so."[118]

Death's contingent nature predisposed Lincoln to a tragic sensibility and the feeling that a mysterious higher power controlled human destiny. Shakespeare's *Hamlet* furnished one of his favorite quotations, and it was appropriate for a rail-splitting American who had fashioned a critical understanding of the world by means of the ax: "There's a divinity that shapes our ends, / Rough-hew them how we will."[119] Shakespeare, the Bible, and other texts did not cause Lincoln to believe in providence. Rather, they spoke to his physical experience of life and the environment that contained it. Words were significant only in relation to his painful, tear-streaked, flesh-and-blood encounter with the hard reality—the nature—of all things.

The man so often touched by death anticipated his own. Living in a world of pain and loss, he imagined that soon his time must come. Standing at the train depot in Springfield before departing for Washington, D.C., in 1861, he gave an emotional farewell to his friends and neighbors. "Here my children have been born," he said, "and one is buried. I now leave, not knowing when, or whether ever, I may return."[120] His awareness of his mortality grew more intense as the war progressed. In the summer of 1862, after the border states rejected his plan for compensated emancipation and when prospects for victory appeared bleak, Senator Orville Hickman Browning of Illinois visited him in the White House and found him "weary, care-worn, and troubled." Browning told the president that his fate and the republic's fate were "bound up" in one another, and urged him to "preserve" his "life and health." Lincoln replied that he felt well enough, but he held his friend's "hand, pressed it, and said in a very tender and touching tone, 'Browning I must die some time.'"[121]

In his second inaugural address, delivered in March 1865, Lincoln tried to come to terms with the pain and death that slavery and the Civil War had visited on the nation. Thousands of people clustered around the wooden platform that extended over the capitol's east portico; never before had so many black citizens attended such an event. "It may seem strange," the president said, "that any men should dare to ask a just God's assistance in wringing their bread from the sweat of other men's faces; but let us judge not that we be not judged." Slavery was not just a southern offense, but a national offense that "the Almighty" intended to remove by means of "this mighty scourge of war." North and South might hope and pray for favor or deliverance, but neither could control the outcome. For "if God wills" the conflict to "continue, until all the wealth piled by the bond-man's two hundred and fifty years of unrequited toil shall be sunk, and until every drop of blood drawn with the lash, shall be paid by another drawn by the sword, as was said three thousand years ago, so still it must be said 'the judgments of the Lord, are true and righteous altogether.'" All that remained was to renew the promise declared decades before: "With malice toward none, with charity for all; with firmness in the right, as God gives us to see the right, let us strive on to finish the work we are in; to bind up the nation's wounds; to care for him who shall have borne the battle, and for his widow, and his orphan—to do all which may achieve a just and lasting peace, among ourselves, and with all nations."[122]

Lincoln, of course, did not live to continue that monumentally important work. In his speech on discoveries and inventions, he had said that every man was a miner who dug out his destiny from creation's infinite leads. In the 1850s and 1860s, laborers across the United States extracted lead, iron, wood, and coal from the Earth, and in the factories of the industrial Northeast, other workers transformed them into useful things. In Philadelphia, craftsmen fabricated single-shot .41 caliber pocket pistols according to Henry Deringer's design. A Confederate named John Wilkes Booth acquired one of the guns, took it to Ford's Theater on an April evening in 1865, and pointed it at the president's head. Lincoln had intuited a mysterious providential purpose in the conjunction of destinies that caused the Civil War; perhaps a divine power guided the bullet that tore into his brain.[123] The environmental historian can only conclude that in death as in life, the rail-splitter was inseparable from the earthly substances that were the origin, object, and end of his great struggle for improvement.

A NEW BIRTH OF FREEDOM

As much as death shaped Lincoln, it did not define him. Some of his most deeply felt beliefs concerned birth, growth, and fruition, the vital natural processes that he believed had given rise to the republic. At no moment was this more evident than in November 1863, when he traveled to the Civil War battlefield at Gettysburg, Pennsylvania, and there delivered a 272-word oration that throbbed with a revolutionary message of life not so much restored as remade.[124] In a series of sweeping declarative sentences, he invited the throng to imagine the arc of progress that the nation, and the world, might follow.

> *Four score and seven years ago our fathers brought forth on this continent, a new nation, conceived in Liberty, and dedicated to the proposition that all men are created equal.*

Although the words issued from Lincoln's mouth in a succinct, telegraphic style, they spoke to the cycles, rhythms, and impulses of living things. An organic act had brought the nation to life, pulled it to its feet, and pushed it toward the promise posited in the Declaration of Independence. The Declaration had dissolved an organic whole—the "political bands" that connected Britain and America, the ties that joined their "common kindred"—and announced the colonies' assumption of a "separate and equal station" in the world. But more important than dissolution, the Declaration created life anew. The founding fathers had brought forth a new nation—not a group of states, but a singular entity, a unity, a *Union*—devoted to the idea that all men were born with the same natural rights. Like its youthful citizens, the nation was alive, sentient, and growing, its potential arising from the anticipated trajectory of its life course.[125]

> *Now we are engaged in a great civil war, testing whether that nation, or any nation so conceived and so dedicated, can long endure. We are met on a great battle-field of that war. We have come to dedicate a portion of that field, as a final resting place for those who here gave their lives that that nation might live. It is altogether fitting and proper that we should do this.*

In the organic republic, death, pain, and destruction powerfully shaped popular consciousness. Slavery was not a venomous snake or cancer, but it often had deathly consequences for its victims, and it could overwhelm and destroy a republic composed of free citizens who made their living from the land. One instrument of death might be a Supreme Court decision that transplanted an oppressive social institution to the open soil of a federal territory. Other instruments might include whips, diseases, bullets, or shell fragments. The epitome of death—the antithesis of improvement—was the battlefield, where flies swarmed over putrefying bodies. For mourners, the only solace, the only hope, was life and the irrepressible regenerative power of birth. The fallen, Lincoln said, had given their lives so that the republic might live.

> *But, in a larger sense, we can not dedicate—we can not consecrate—we can not hallow—this ground. The brave men, living and dead, who struggled here, have consecrated it, far above our poor power to add or detract. The world will little note, nor long remember what we say here, but it can never forget what they did here.*

The ceremony at Gettysburg was an act of consecration. To consecrate means to set aside—to conserve—a burial ground or other physical thing for a sacred purpose. At the Soldiers' National Cemetery, mourners might remember the fallen and take comfort in signs that death is but a prelude to life. In trees, grass, flowers, sky, and the seasonal turn from winter to spring, they might detect an impending renaissance. There, too, they might find renewed purpose in symbols of the nation's fundamental values. William Saunders, the cemetery's architect, honored the republic by arranging the graves according to the states, such that each state's section and each grave were of "relatively equal importance." When Lincoln spoke of "a new nation . . . dedicated to the proposition that all men are created equal," his words aligned with the principle embodied in the ground and acknowledged that in this place a tremendous sacrifice had advanced the American Revolution and reinvigorated the promise of a new order for the ages.[126]

It is for us the living, rather, to be dedicated here to the unfinished work which they who fought here have thus far so nobly advanced. It is rather for us to be here dedicated to the great task remaining before us—that from these honored dead we take increased devotion to that cause for which they gave the last full measure of devotion—that we here highly resolve that these dead shall not have died in vain—that this nation, under God, shall have a new birth of freedom—and that government of the people, by the people, for the people, shall not perish from the earth.

The most famous passage in American oratory called on citizens to turn the destruction of war into the fulfillment of the republic's promise. A new birth of freedom would reopen the way to improvement.

After the ceremony, Lincoln made his way through the town to the depot and the train that transported him back to the capital. Leaving Gettysburg, he passed through an autumnal landscape, the vast productive powers of which were slowing and soon would rest. Rolling through the countryside, he went back to Washington and a future that might be as cold, hard, and bleak as winter. Yet it was, he knew, a future that always would hold out the potential of springtime, an awakening from which the richest and loveliest of the republic's many hues might burst forth.

In that favored land, citizens valued natural rights above all else, and they rejected the disorder of an uncontrolled capitalist market that would make private property of their fellow men. They were disciplined thinkers and doers who realized that the fulfillment of nature's republican possibility required coordinated action to remove obstacles—whether sand bars in rivers or ignorance in human minds—so that all might have an equal chance to make something of themselves. They were creative, inventive, hardworking, hopeful people who drew inspiration from the bustle of economic production. They were the kind of people who might imagine the past as a series of progressive discoveries and inventions—language, law, mechanical arts, clothing, more and better food—that unshackled humanity's innate talents and so improved the world.

En route to Gettysburg the day before, Lincoln's train had made several stops at small towns where local people had turned out to greet him. Some of them bore gifts, the products of a landscape in which citizens, through the application of intelligence and labor, had enriched and diversified the Earth and revitalized the republic. A boy handed him an apple. A group of women approached with flowers. One admirer in particular enabled Lincoln to see the radiant promise latent in the troubled present. "Flowerth for the Prethident!" a little girl lisped, holding up a bouquet of roses. Could it have been true, such blossoms in November? "You're a sweet little rose-bud yourself," he said as he stooped to kiss the child. "I hope your life will open into perpetual beauty and goodness."[127] ★

FIVE

THE NATURE OF GETTYSBURG

Environmental History and the Civil War

I

N LATE SPRING 1863, IN THE MIDST
of the Civil War, Confederate General Robert E. Lee led his Army of Northern Virginia on a bold expedition out of the South and onto northern terrain. Somewhere in the Pennsylvania countryside, Lee hoped to defeat the Army of the Potomac in battle, thereby convincing the Union that it should abandon its objective of keeping the nation, North and South, whole. He had great confidence in his force of some seventy thousand men. Their morale—their fighting spirit—was high; for two years, they had bested their more numerous, better-equipped opponents in nearly every contest of arms. They adamantly believed in their cause: to preserve both slavery and liberty and to defend self-government and the Confederate nation. Their resolve was remarkable given their circumstances. Food shortage had shriveled the fat from their bodies, making them lean and gaunt. Diseases had swept through their ranks. Many had no shoes. For a sizable number, joining the army required them to neglect farms and families, and some believed that military service had become undemocratic, a "rich man's war and a poor man's fight." No wonder, then, that a few became discouraged and deserted their comrades. But most did not. Tough, resilient men, they pressed on despite the hardships and the bitterness, following their officers along rough roads, across swift rivers, and through mountain passes.[1]

Pursuing them, searching for them, was the Army of the Potomac, under the generalship first of Joseph Hooker and then of George Gordon Meade. Their objective was to blunt Lee's offensive, turn him and his men back, and thus weaken if not destroy the Confederacy's dream of independence. They had a capable if as yet unsuccessful army. Despite its defeats in Virginia, it was a numerically superior force of about ninety thousand battle-hardened soldiers, and it had ample food, shoes, and other supplies. Like the Rebels, the men who filled its ranks had powerful motivations for fighting, including the desire to destroy slavery, protect liberty, and ensure the survival of a single American republic. They had problems, to be sure. The setbacks in Virginia had been disheartening. Hooker's inept pursuit of Lee frustrated Abraham Lincoln, leading the president to place Meade in charge. The "blood money" that men could pay to defer a draft call or hire a substitute to take their place in the army sparked class resentment. Diseases, too, had taken their toll. But through it all the Army of the Potomac remained undaunted, and as its men passed from Virginia and Maryland into Pennsylvania, their spirits rose and their resolve deepened.

On July 1, west and north of Gettysburg, the two armies confronted each other. The initial fighting drove the Army of the Potomac into a defensive position along a series of hills and gentle ridges south of the town. There, crouching below rock walls that separated farm fields, hunkered behind breastworks of log, rock, and soil, it endured a massive Confederate assault that went on for two days. The fighting was a reversal of what had happened earlier in Virginia. At Fredericksburg in 1862, the Army of the Potomac had attacked a well-protected enemy occupying high ground. At Gettysburg the tables turned—now it was the Army of Northern Virginia that advanced uphill, exposed, in the face of terrible fire from a foe that had the advantage of elevation and cover. Lee's men went forward bravely, their eerie, distinctive battle cry, the Rebel yell, rising from their ranks. Several times they tried to divide, flank, encircle, and disperse the enemy. On July 3, Lee mobilized his forces in a final all-out charge against the center of the Union line. From then on, people remembered Gettysburg as the "high tide of the Confederacy," the greatest and most important battle in the Civil War and perhaps in American history.[2]

A stunning moment when the clash of titanic forces decided the shape of the future, Gettysburg had all the makings of a national epic. The Army of Northern Virginia's long march out of the South, its fateful meeting with the Army of the Potomac in the beautiful Pennsylvania countryside, the awesome power and destructiveness of the fighting, the climactic Rebel charge, and the shifting momentum of the war gave the battle enormous historic and emotional significance. Gettysburg's epic quality, however, did not derive from the collision of Union and Confederate armies alone. Implicit in the massive struggle was an equally epic encounter between Americans and nature, between two armies, two societies, and the American land.[3]

Every part of this drama turned on the inescapable ties between people and the material world in which they lived. North and South had evolved in separate environments, and those unique experiences fostered economic, social, political, and cultural differences that eventually impelled the two sections into conflict. The ability—or inability—of each side to procure resources from nature, furthermore, powerfully shaped the course of the war; thin Rebel bodies and bare Rebel feet had everything to do with the bold Rebel presence in Pennsylvania in spring 1863. Then there were the problems of weather and disease, which both armies had to endure and overcome in the course of the fighting. Finally, the campaign, the battle, and ultimately the war centered on the use and control of terrain, especially the highest ground; it was no accident that the fighting on July 3 culminated in an uphill charge. In these and so many other ways, the connections between humans and their physical environment gave rise to and drove the battle of Gettysburg. Nature was at once a cause of conflict, an object and instrument of conquest, and a powerful antagonist against which both North and South struggled.

SOIL—SLAVE OR FREE?

North and South had taken up arms because they disagreed over the meaning of liberty and the definition of a proper republic. They also fought because the physical basis of each society—the manner in which each made a living from nature, from the land—had helped to cause those disagreements. Thomas Jefferson, the primary author of the Declaration of Independence and America's third president, had envisioned a single, harmonious and prosperous republic expanding westward across the Mississippi River. North and South, however, developed along separate lines. The South's climate proved ideal for growing tobacco, rice, sugar cane, and especially cotton, and farmers based the region's economy on those plants. Cultivating cotton and other staple crops required intensive labor, and the South chose a system, African slavery, to supply it. A booming market for cotton in turn invited the planters to grow more of the crop, and they began to look to the West for land into which they could expand. No less important, the West seemed to offer the fresh ground needed to replace the older farm soils that cotton and tobacco had depleted of nutrients, as well as an expanding market for the buying and selling of enslaved laborers. In time, the South's prosperity, power, and even survival seemed to depend on its ability to move slave agriculture westward.[4]

Northern society had followed a different course. The North's temperate environment was unsuited to staples such as cotton, and its farmers had chosen to raise wheat, corn, potatoes, hay, dairy cows, and many other kinds of crops and livestock. If northern farmers needed help, they hired it. This system of wage labor, or "free labor," was also a basic feature of the mines, factories, and railroads with which the North extracted wealth from the Earth. Wageworkers dug coal, cut timber, refined iron from ore, and then fashioned those materials into factory buildings, waterwheels, looms, locomotives, steel rails, cloth, rifled muskets, and thousands of other things. The South, too, developed its "natural resources," but it preferred the quiet virtues of its agriculture to the tumultuous prosperity of industrialization. North and South grew up at the same time and needed each other—Georgia cotton plantations and Massachusetts textile mills served each region's economic purposes—but as the two matured they became estranged, and their estrangement led them into war.[5]

The North had its own plan for the West. It should be the home not of plantations and slaves but of small farmers and free laborers, especially white ones. Western soil, "free soil," should perpetuate a free society as northerners imagined it. If slavery should take root, independent farmers and wageworkers could not thrive, because there would be little economic need for them. How could a family farm compete against a plantation? Who would need hired hands if he had slaves? With western opportunity cut off, the North would wither and die. And so many northerners came to believe just as fervently as did southerners that their way of life, their future, depended on the realization of their dream for the western landscape.

Eventually, each side feared that the other would try to impose its will not just on the West but on the entire nation. Northerners alleged that the South sought to pervert the laws of the country to allow slavery everywhere. Southerners charged that the North would not merely stop slavery from spreading to the West but seek to abolish it entirely. Extremists on both sides began to dominate the debate. When these absolutists asserted that only violence could resolve the issue, the moment of disunion had arrived. Two parts of the United States had evolved under separate physical conditions, and their different environmental histories and competing land ideologies had produced distinct societies that no longer could compromise or coexist.

The war that broke out in 1861 was a test of each side's ability to use its culture, society, economy, and government to mobilize natural resources in the service of maintaining control over its geographical territory. The challenge to the Union was to keep the South in the United States; the challenge to the Confederacy was to establish its independence. Nature in its broadest sense—the location and condition of soil, water, minerals, plants, animals, topography and other bio- and geophysical things—limited and enabled each side's ability to achieve its objectives. By design and by accident, the side that best coped with nature's constraints and exploited its opportunities was the side that would win.[6]

At the start of the conflict, the environment conferred important strategic advantages on the Confederacy. The size of the would-be nation, some 750,000 square miles, daunted Union forces. The Appalachian Mountains posed a formidable barrier to their east-west movement, and the rivers that ran eastward from the Appalachians blocked them. Virginia's Shenandoah Valley, which trended northeast to southwest, steered them away from Richmond, the Confederate capital; conversely, it guided Confederate forces in the direction of Washington, D.C. Irregular, unmapped roads confused northern armies and dissipated their energy; the problem worsened when heavy rain and snow on the South's red clay soils turned roads into slippery, gooey tracks. The Union's transportation problems, furthermore, increased in proportion to the distance its forces traveled from their supply sources.[7]

The Confederacy also had advantageous biophysical resources, as a few examples illustrate. In the many caves in states such as Arkansas, Alabama, Georgia, Tennessee, and Virginia, bats and other animals, over millennia, had deposited ton upon ton of guano, a source of the nitrate that was an essential ingredient in gunpowder. The southern landscape also was rich in swine. Even though the animals were not as plump as their northern cousins, they were relatively numerous: the ratio of hogs to humans in the South was double that in the North. Perhaps the most valuable and useful resource in the southern landscape was cotton. The harvest of 1861 yielded some 4.5 million bales, a reserve of natural wealth that the Confederacy could convert into the cash necessary to buy war materiel and pay its soldiers.[8]

In spite of such advantages, the Confederacy was less effective than the Union in turning nature into the instruments of victory. In the North, sunlight, soil, and iron readily became wheat, animal flesh, and weaponry, and the Union military directed those and other materiel toward the defeat of Confederate forces at key geographical points in the western and eastern theaters of the conflict. The Confederacy, in contrast, was unable to furnish enough food, materiel, horses, and even men to sustain its military. At first, it experienced physical difficulties in delivering food and other resources in sufficient amounts, at the most propitious times, and in the right places. By 1863, changing environmental circumstances had exacerbated its basic problem. The geographical area from which it drew its food and materials was contracting, as was the size of its enslaved labor force. No less important, environmental deterioration from war, drought, and other causes diminished Confederate resources and their availability. The incipient nation's urgent need to reverse this contraction and deterioration influenced Lee's decision to invade Pennsylvania.[9]

The Confederacy's use of its "strategic environment," in the words of military historian Donald Stoker, put it at a disadvantage. For the nation to win foreign recognition and protect its resource base, President Jefferson Davis believed it had to hold onto its entire territory. It could ill afford to evacuate portions of its geography in order to gain time in which to mobilize counterattacks or concentrate its force elsewhere. The Confederacy needed to prove to itself, the Union, and the world that it could defend and control its national landscape. A subsidiary problem derived from the slave labor system, which Davis feared the Union would destroy in the areas it occupied. The desire to control geographical space, including the space of enslaved labor, therefore committed him to a perimeter or cordon defense that "created an unnecessary and inefficient compartmentalization of forces" by dispersing Confederate armies across a broad front.[10]

Compounding these environmental problems, the Confederacy was weak in the technologies, skills, and administrative capacities with which to achieve more efficient resource use. It lacked an integrated transportation infrastructure, primarily railroads, that would have enabled it to procure and distribute its resources more quickly, more cheaply, and with less waste. Southern railroad systems were much less developed than those in the North, and most were relatively short lines that connected seaports with interior towns and cities. All told, the Union had some 22,000 miles of rail, and the South, about 8,500. In 1860, the North manufactured 451 locomotives, and the South, 19. The South's dispersed, predominantly rural and agricultural economy, moreover, meant that its economic and governmental leaders were relatively inexperienced in the mass mobilization that the Civil War required.[11]

One set of problems created others. Without better railroads, the Confederacy had to rely more heavily on rivers, roads, and animal power. In the western theater of the war, rivers worked against the Confederacy. "The Cumberland and Tennessee Rivers were highways of invasion into Tennessee, northern Mississippi, and northern Alabama," the historian James McPherson has written, "while the Mississippi River was an arrow thrust into the heart of the lower South." The roads that mired Union men also mired those of the Confederacy.[12]

Greater reliance on roads imposed greater reliance on the muscle power of horses, mules, and men, which magnified the Confederacy's organic vulnerability. The dispersed nature of Confederate forces required them to be more mobile so that their commanders could divide, shift, and then concentrate them against a numerically superior foe. General Robert E. Lee and his officers in the Army of Northern Virginia proved especially adept at quick, nimble movement. Yet Lee's mobility was not without biophysical costs. "Armies that maneuver and thus expend high levels of physical energy demand even greater logistical resources," the military historian Brian Holden Reid has observed. "There was a tension latent in Lee's chosen mode of warfare. In order to keep his army mobile, he needed large logistical stocks."[13] As long as Lee had access to those stocks, his army was battle ready; should something threaten the availability of food, forage, and flesh, his men were in trouble.

Those threats were precisely what Lee encountered. A propensity for logistical problems was latent in the South's environment, landscape, economy, and culture, and it worsened as the war progressed. For decades the trend in the South had been to produce less food in favor of the money-making but inedible staples. In the 1850s, booming demand, especially for cotton, made the region less self-sufficient in food than ever. When the war came, the Confederacy abruptly reversed the trend and converted millions of cotton acres to corn and other food crops, but this rapid transformation still did not allow the fledgling nation to provision itself adequately.[14]

The Confederacy might have sold the 1861 cotton harvest as soon as possible in order to feed, clothe, and arm itself, but many producers advocated an embargo on cotton exports, which they believed would hurt British textile manufacturers and force Britain to recognize the South's independence. Although some Confederate leaders opposed the embargo, the central government never fashioned a coherent, workable cotton policy with which to buy the crop from farmers and planters, sell it abroad, and use the profit for military purposes. Southerners had counted on the global demand for cotton to help leverage their independence. But withholding their environmental bounty from the market simply prompted the extraction of an alternate bounty from landscapes in other parts of the world. By 1863, Britain was importing supplies from Egypt, Brazil, India, and the West Indies.[15]

The North's blockade of the Mississippi River and southern seaports and its capture of southern territory deprived the Confederacy of food and productive land and drove it deeper into poverty. Even as the Gettysburg campaign began, Union forces had besieged the town of Vicksburg, the last major Confederate stronghold on the Mississippi. The gradual closure of the river, along with the capture of New Orleans and other southern ports, cut off Confederate access to outside food sources. At the same time, Union armies invaded and conquered major portions of southern terrain. Each acre of farmland behind northern army lines deprived Rebel stomachs of more corn or pork. If a nation's environment includes that part of the Earth from which it draws food, then the Confederacy's environment was undergoing rapid contraction by 1863.[16]

The geographical noose that Union forces placed on the Confederacy was not the only source of deprivation and hunger. Across the South, armies from both sides stripped and ruined agricultural landscapes. Union forces took food and horses for their own use and systematically destroyed crops and livestock along with farm machinery, barns, granaries, and other agricultural facilities. Confederate foragers, too, took what they needed from southern farms. This vast consumption and destruction of resources had side effects that further hurt the South's ability to provide for itself. The enormous Union and Confederate armies that crisscrossed the region regularly knocked down wood fences to build shelters and campfires and to allow for the passage of men and animals, leaving corn and other crops vulnerable to wandering livestock. The Civil War's voracious appetite for men, animals, and labor may have done the most to hurt southern agriculture. The movement of men and horses from farm to army, the impressment of slave labor for military purposes, and the loss of slaves to the Union side made it difficult to keep land in production, even as white women, girls, boys, and older men tried to compensate. But the problem went even deeper. The removal of labor had serious environmental consequences: on poorly tended or fallow land, weeds moved in, making it even harder for those who remained to raise crops and produce food.[17]

A conjunction of environmental disasters in 1862 also ravaged the South. By spring, the war was consuming horses and mules faster than the South could resupply them. As the year unfolded, drought in Virginia and other southern states drastically reduced corn, wheat, and hay harvests. Cattle were abundant in Texas, but grass shortage stopped the eastward-moving drives in their tracks. Other livestock starved, exacerbating the shortages of animal power and meat. According to historian Richard Goff, the drought "nullified any potential increased food production that might have come about by agricultural conversion . . . from cotton to foodstuffs and provender." A massive flood devastated the Delta, a fertile, food-producing area along the lower Mississippi. Bacterial afflictions, including glanders, anthrax, and hoof and mouth disease, killed or weakened thousands of horses and mules. A viral epidemic, hog cholera, swept the South. In Mississippi during 1862, disasters compounded as drought killed corn and cholera killed hogs.[18]

Salt shortage worsened the Confederacy's livestock problems. The South could not produce enough salt to compensate for imports lost because of the war. It certainly tried—an effort to increase the regional output of salt accompanied the boost in food production—but in turn, Union forces strove to destroy Confederate saltworks. The resulting "salt famine" had serious environmental consequences. Without salt, horses and mules were less robust and more prone to hoof and mouth disease and other maladies. Without salt, the South could not preserve pork, beef, and butter from bacteria. Without salt, the South could not properly tan leather.[19]

As the conflict wore on, agriculture deteriorated across the Confederacy, and people grew hungry, malnourished, and increasingly desperate. Not only did the total acreage in production fall, but so did yields per acre: land already exhausted by cotton could not sustain the intensive cropping of corn. Rebels complained of short or spoiled rations, and the Union soldiers who captured them looked in amazement at their lean bodies. With so many animals dying and leather in short supply, Confederates often went into battle without shoes. Desertion increased as conditions degenerated. For some men, especially the poorest, the desire to return home to care for land and families became irresistible.[20]

Conditions for the Confederacy and for Lee's Army of Northern Virginia continued to decline through the winter of 1862–1863 and into the following spring. Freezing temperatures, snow, rain, and muddy roads paralyzed the army, which settled into winter camp along the south bank of the Rappahannock River. Lingering around their campfires, huddled in tents or in crude log, rail, and canvas huts, the shivering soldiers waited for the weather to change and for orders to begin moving again. The ravaged, depleted landscape supplied them with almost no food, and other parts of the Confederacy contributed little of the flour, corn, rice, peas, dried fruit, sugar, and bacon on which the soldiers subsisted. Lee wondered whether hunger itself might not be a more formidable foe than the Army of the Potomac, bivouacked on the opposite bank.[21]

In early spring, disease appeared among the famished troops. First came scurvy, a vitamin deficiency caused by a lack of fresh fruits and vegetables. In a sensible but ultimately inadequate response, soldiers fanned out across the countryside to gather sassafras buds, wild onions and garlic, lamb's-quarters, and poke sprouts. Then came typhoid, one among many diseases of the gut that afflict people living close together under unsanitary conditions. A Civil War army was a "city without sewerage," the Massachusetts cavalry veteran Charles Francis Adams Jr. later wrote, and it takes little effort to envision the passage of microbes from oozing bowels into water sources, onto hands and food, and into human mouths. Typhoid did not overwhelm the Army of Northern Virginia, nor was the Army of the Potomac immune to such diseases, but the outbreak was one more indication of the deteriorating conditions that Rebel soldiers suffered in 1862–1863.[22]

Another sign of trouble was the degradation of the army's horses and mules, the animals upon which all fighting forces utterly depended. Under the best of circumstances, the life of a Civil War cavalry horse or draft animal was hard, but during the winter of 1862–1863 it was especially bad for those creatures in the Army of Northern Virginia. The surrounding farms, disturbed and exhausted, furnished little fodder. Hungry, malnourished, emaciated, the horses and mules became more vulnerable to harsh weather and diseases. Troops had a difficult time finding replacements when the animals died. When spring came, Lee worried that the survivors might be so weak that his army would be unable to move. Without healthy mounts, cavalrymen could not ride. Without fit horses and mules, supply wagons and artillery would stand idle.[23]

To make matters worse, the desperate hunger of starving civilians threatened the Confederate government and the war effort. In spring 1863, women in cities from Richmond to Mobile joined in "bread riots," marching to shops and granaries and robbing them of food. In late March, a storm deposited as much as a foot of heavy, wet snow on roads leading to Richmond, turning them into quagmires and stalling food transport into the city. After merchants raised prices on the remaining provisions, a mob of mostly working-class women rampaged through stores, shouting for bread and decrying the wealthy. No less than Jefferson Davis, the Confederate president, confronted the angry women and ordered them to disperse. Only the threat of gunfire from militia convinced them that they should return to their homes.[24]

Environmental contraction, deterioration, and impoverishment and the desperation and social disorder that followed at last set into motion a series of events that culminated in the Gettysburg campaign. The Army of Northern Virginia sent out detachments on forage sweeps for flour, hay, and animals—anything the Confederates might need. One force went into West Virginia, and Lee and his staff contemplated another raid into Kentucky. A contingent under General James Longstreet advanced into North Carolina. These efforts yielded little, for the rest of the South was in much the same condition as Virginia. Ruined fences, fields overrun with weeds, looted or destroyed farm buildings, and empty pastures were everywhere.[25]

The situation called for something more. Lee's imagination shifted away from Virginia, from the South. Perhaps the answer lay in the North. A strike against the Army of the Potomac on northern soil promised to break the Union's geographic stranglehold on the South. By boldly carrying the war into Pennsylvania, the Army of Northern Virginia would draw Union forces away from Vicksburg, the besieged Confederate bastion on the Mississippi. By crossing the Potomac River and threatening the enemy capital, the Confederacy might win the loyalty of foreign governments and strengthen northern politicians who wished to end the war and give the South its independence. By moving the Army of Northern Virginia out of the South and forcing the Union side to follow, an offensive would allow the land to rest and farmers to bring in a harvest. Perhaps most important, such an aggressive strategy would permit Lee's army to replenish itself. Rebel soldiers would feed on the Pennsylvania landscape in proportion to their starvation in Virginia. In sum, a daring push into the North would dramatically alter military geography, reshape the political landscape, and shore up, if not outright restore, the environmental basis of Confederate power.[26]

THE TERRAIN IS NEVER NEUTRAL

A stunning victory over the Army of the Potomac in early May at Chancellorsville, a tiny Virginia crossroads, filled Lee and his army with confidence and provided them the opportunity to head north. General Joseph Hooker, certain that he could destroy the Rebels and open the way south to Richmond, initiated the fighting. First, he ordered a part of his army across the Rappahannock to attack the Confederates and hold them in place. Then he sent the bulk of his soldiers upstream, west and north, where they crossed the river and then turned east and south in anticipation of smashing into the Rebels from behind. The odds against the Army of Northern Virginia were overwhelming. Not only did it suffer from a dearth of food, equipment, and horsepower, but it also was vastly outnumbered. With a substantial portion of his army foraging for supplies, Lee could muster only about 60,000 men to face the Yankee onslaught of some 110,000. What the "gray fox" lacked in manpower, however, he made up for in nimble maneuvering. In direct violation of the military doctrine that a massed force was strongest, Lee and his commanders twice divided their army and deftly flanked and routed the Union attack. After first clashing with the enemy in a thicket of trees and brush called the Wilderness, the Rebels pushed the Yankees back across the Rappahannock. The way was now clear. The war's momentum would shift north as Lee wanted, not south as Hooker had planned.[27]

The battle of Chancellorsville and the Gettysburg campaign that followed demonstrated the importance of terrain to Civil War combat. Engaging the enemy was nothing if not the art and science of moving thousands of men and animals across the land in a way that maximized power at the expense of the enemy. At Chancellorsville, roads, river, bluffs, hills, forests, fields, and fences served as tactical objectives and as instruments of war. Perhaps the most outstanding example was the Rappahannock, which protected the Confederates and hid the Union attack. In the weeks to come, more features of the terrain would be added to this list: mountains, valleys, orchards, railroad cuts, towns, buildings. The Gettysburg campaign might be characterized as a massive duel in which each army struggled to use the land to its advantage. As weapon, shield, and prize, the terrain was never neutral.[28]

Lee and his generals formulated a plan in which the Confederates would make extensive use of landforms and waterways in their northern push. Shielded from the Yankees by the Rappahannock, the Army of Northern Virginia first would march northwest, through the Blue Ridge Mountains. Hidden by that range, the Rebels then would head north, down the Shenandoah Valley toward the Potomac River. After crossing the Potomac, they would continue north through the Cumberland Valley of Maryland and Pennsylvania, all the while using another north-south range, South Mountain, to obscure their whereabouts. Somewhere, perhaps around Chambersburg, York, or Gettysburg, the Army of Northern Virginia would turn and face the Army of the Potomac, which Lee knew would be searching for him and his men.[29]

Although Lee was personally familiar with the geography of his native Virginia, as well as of Maryland and Pennsylvania, his knowledge of the terrain owed much to a map prepared by Jed Hotchkiss, a civilian topographer and mapmaker working in the service of the Confederacy. In his youth and early adulthood, Hotchkiss studied nature because it fascinated him and because he loved it. His obsession resembled that of John Muir, the famous scientist, conservationist, and founder of the Sierra Club. Unlike Muir, who avoided the Civil War, Hotchkiss turned his knowledge of the Earth to military ends. Figuring distances, calculating grades, and plotting landscape features were standard cartographic and engineering tasks and were crucial to military movement. An army best outfoxed its enemy if it knew how far it must travel, the locations of forests and river crossings, and how hard its horses would have to work pulling their loads uphill against gravity. The army that best knew nature, in other words, had the best chance of defeating the other side. Lee was an engineer, trained, like many other officers, at the United States Military Academy, and he appreciated Hotchkiss's map. It was a model of the cartographer's craft, depicting in fine detail a broad swath of land from Virginia to Pennsylvania. It showed watercourses, major landforms, cities, villages, roads, even individual farmhouses. It would guide Lee and his forces to Gettysburg.[30]

In early June, the Army of Northern Virginia escaped the Army of the Potomac and headed north. Along the way, Lee masterfully deployed his army across the terrain. Prior to Gettysburg, he had divided his infantry force into two large groups, called corps, each numbering about thirty thousand soldiers and each under the command of a general subordinate to him. But Lee decided that a corps of this size was too large for the officer in charge. Spread out over fields, forests, hills, or mountains, it was "always beyond the range of his vision, and frequently beyond his reach." So Lee divided the two large corps into three smaller, more manageable groups. To prevent them from getting in each other's way, he sent them north on separate roads at different times. To hasten their progress still more, he ordered them to wade across the Potomac River at two fords rather than one. Such adroit manipulation of men, horses, and wagons in relation to land helped the Confederates enormously. They clashed with Union troops in skirmishes and minor battles at several places on the route north, but they eluded and outpaced the Army of the Potomac's main body. By the time they arrived in Maryland, they had gained two days, two revolutions of the Earth, on their opponent. Ahead lay Pennsylvania.[31]

Once there, the soldiers in the Army of Northern Virginia marveled at the pastoral terrain, so rich in comparison with the impoverished farmland in the South, and now their prize. "The country . . . is beautiful, and everything in the greatest abundance," wrote William Christian to his wife. "You never saw such a land of plenty." John West reported that wheat, corn, clover, and other crops, orchards, beehives, neat fences, and impressive barns "met the eye at every turn," making the landscape "one bright panorama for miles." Although a few Confederates wondered about the possible virtues of the free-soil, free-labor agricultural system that had produced such wealth, most simply regarded Pennsylvania's resources as a necessity and a payback for their own victimization at Yankee hands.[32]

In keeping with Confederate strategic objectives, the Army of Northern Virginia systematically stripped the terrain. Rebel soldiers diligently rounded up all horses, mules, cattle, and sheep, even searching out animals that farmers had hidden in remote corners of their properties or in nearby mountains. Exactly how many head the Confederates took is impossible to know, but the total surely was in the tens of thousands. Historian Kent Brown's estimates are staggering: 45,000 to 50,000 cattle, 35,000 sheep, 20,000 horses and mules, and thousands of hogs. The Confederate requisition extended to hay and corn for livestock and much else as well. They captured a number of free African Americans. A white woman recalled seeing black people being "driven by just like we would drive cattle." Confederates also seized immense quantities of food and other supplies. In each town, they summoned the citizenry and demanded not only flour and other foodstuffs but also saddles, harness, horseshoes and horseshoe nails, rope, firearms, lead, salt, clothing, hats, socks, shoes, leather, and cash—all the resources that the South's impoverished environment could no longer furnish in sufficient quantities.[33]

The Army of Northern Virginia consumed the terrain over which it moved; as men and animals passed through the land, the land passed through them. Consider the food they took in. Soldiers feasted on bread, eggs, butter, milk, cheese, beef, pork, chicken, cherries, sauerkraut, molasses, fresh vegetables, beer, and whiskey. Horses and mules grazed in pastures and munched on oats and hay. Both men and animals drank enormous quantities of water. This gigantic appetite for moisture, nutrients, protein, and fat in turn had environmental consequences, for the act of eating on such a scale impoverished the land. Wherever the army went, it knocked down fences, emptied barns and granaries, ransacked larders and stores, trampled crops, and literally drank wells dry. General Lee, always the proponent of civilized warfare, ordered his soldiers to pay for what they took. Confederate money and promissory notes, however, had no value in the North, and often the troops paid nothing at all. In their view, plundering Pennyslvania's terrain, consuming its riches, was retribution for the ruin the Yankees had visited on the South. Lee evidently tolerated their violation of his orders.[34]

By the end of June, the Yankees were drawing near. They had started slowly; the Army of the Potomac's commander, General Hooker, was much less adept than Lee in negotiating terrain. When Hooker learned that the Confederates had departed for the North, he tarried, thinking that perhaps he and his men should strike south toward Richmond, which was now vulnerable to attack. President Lincoln would not have it—Hooker must find the Army of Northern Virginia. Hooker had lost the initiative, however, and geographical and topographical obstacles on the way north compounded his army's disadvantage. Crossing the Potomac at a bottleneck of roads and bridges, infantry and supply trains became snarled, and rainfall turned the roads into morasses of mud. Once in Maryland, the Union soldiers gained speed. After pausing briefly and regrouping at the town of Frederick, they headed for the Pennsylvania line. The final round of the great duel for terrain was about to begin.[35]

HIGH TIDE

Lee had centered his foraging operations on the Cumberland Valley and Chambersburg, a town on the west side of South Mountain, a range that extended roughly northeast-southwest and spanned the Pennsylvania-Maryland line. From there, he began to shift the bulk of his army east-southeast on the Chambersburg Pike to Cashtown on the other side of South Mountain. From Cashtown, he planned to protect his foragers in the Cumberland Valley on his rear and in south-central Pennsylvania on his front. Should the Army of the Potomac approach, he would be in an excellent defensive position at the entrance to the mountains.[36]

A growing problem for Lee was the enormous size and complexity of his Pennsylvania campaign, which loosened the tight control he had exerted over his army. His foraging and supply operations had grown to immense proportions and extended throughout the countryside. Kent Brown estimated that some 6,000 to 10,000 black laborers, mostly slaves, drove approximately 5,000 to 6,000 quartermaster, subsistence, ambulance, and ordnance wagons that were organized in trains up to 20 miles long. Combat troops protected the quartermaster and subsistence foraging units, a necessary precaution that also dispersed the army's fighting power. J. E. B. (Jeb) Stuart's cavalry had lost contact with Lee and was unable to give him information about the enemy's location. Under these circumstances, Lee lost much of his ability to determine when, where, and how his army would fight.[37]

Neither Lee nor his opponent had anticipated fully that the battle would occur at Gettysburg, a town of some twenty-four hundred people located amid farms and forests and at the hub of several roads. Each knew that the other was near, but where exactly neither could say—space and time precluded precise information. The two armies felt their way toward each another, at last making contact almost by accident. On June 30, a brigade of North Carolinians left Cashtown and traveled down the pike toward Gettysburg in search of shoes and other supplies. As they neared the town, they encountered Union cavalry that General Meade, now in charge of the Army of the Potomac, had sent out on reconnaissance. On July 1, along a series of low ridges northwest of the town, the two sides skirmished. The fighting quickly escalated as Confederate General A. P. Hill, unbeknownst to Lee, ordered in reinforcements to protect the foraging operations. Meanwhile, Unionists hurried in along roads from the south.[38]

At first the battle went in favor of the Army of Northern Virginia as the Rebels drove Union forces back through Gettysburg. As it retreated, however, the Army of the Potomac seized that all-important feature of the terrain—the high ground. General Oliver Howard, a corps commander, had earlier recognized the potential importance of Cemetery Hill, just south of the town. The site of Evergreen Cemetery, it offered panoramic views and fields of fire to the north and west, the directions from which the Confederates were advancing. Howard and other Union generals now concentrated their forces among the gravestones and from there deployed them south along Cemetery Ridge and east toward a much higher, wooded eminence, Culp's Hill. The Confederates might have attacked these positions right away, before the enemy consolidated its hold on them, but the general at the scene, Richard Ewell, decided against it—his men were too few, too dispersed, and too tired. An assault on the Union line would have to wait until Rebel forces had rested and massed in sufficient numbers.[39]

As the battle developed, Lee proceeded to Gettysburg and there pondered how to respond to a situation that he had not devised and that had lured his army from the safety of Cashtown. On the morning of July 2, his trusted subordinate, General James Longstreet, argued against an attack on the Union line. Thousands more men had reinforced it during the night, and Longstreet thought it was too strong. He proposed that the Army of Northern Virginia instead shift to its right, south of Cemetery Ridge, and take a defensible position that would force the Union side to attack it. Lee, however, was inclined to continue the offensive against the Army of the Potomac. His forces had prevailed the day before and had taken some four thousand prisoners, which gave him physical and psychological momentum. Topographically, his army was not in the best position, but the high ground and Union forces were vulnerable. The Army of the Potomac had not fought well in previous encounters, and he believed he could deliver a decisive blow before the rest of it was in place.[40]

More important, the environmental constraints on the Pennsylvania campaign convinced Lee that going forward was the best option. A turning movement of the sort that Longstreet advocated would have been difficult and might have enabled the enemy to cut off the Army of Northern Virginia's safe route back through Cashtown Gap and into Maryland and Virginia. In addition, delaying the battle might not have been possible in light of the army's need to replenish itself from the countryside. The Confederates could not afford to sit and wait while Union forces threatened their foraging. As Lee later explained, "We were unable to await an attack, as the country was unfavorable for collecting supplies in the presence of the enemy, who could restrain our foraging parties by holding the mountain passes with local and other troops. A battle had, therefore, become in a measure unavoidable." Lee's mind was made up. "The enemy is there," he said to Longstreet, pointing to Cemetery Hill, "and I am going to attack him there."[41]

This is how it was supposed to happen: Longstreet would lead a flanking maneuver to the south, around the Union left, and as Meade shifted his forces to meet this threat, Ewell and his men would hit the weakened Union right. The Army of the Potomac would then collapse, its units broken up, its soldiers fleeing in demoralized, disorderly retreat. Civilian morale and support for the war would dissolve, the North would ask for peace, and the South would have its independence.

It didn't turn out that way, of course. The Union side was too strong, and its hold on the high ground too skillful and tenacious. Lee and his forces were at a disadvantage topographically and in the distances they had to cover. From above, the battle line was like a fishhook curving eastward around Cemetery Hill. Rebel soldiers were on the exterior of the fishhook, and they covered

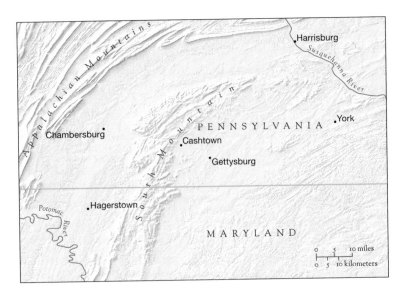

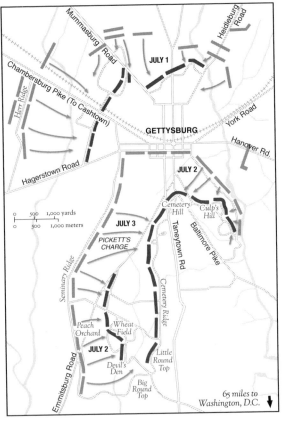

Valleys and mountain ranges channeled and constrained military movements leading to Gettysburg. The fishhook shape of the Union battle line resulted from tactical maneuvering in relationship to geographic space and topography, particularly elevated ground.

some five miles of battle line in contrast to the three miles of their enemy. The problems of topography and distance hurt the Confederates from the start. Union forces detected Longstreet's flanking maneuver—imagine the difficulty of keeping the movement of fifteen thousand men concealed in the terrain. Longstreet then ordered a countermarch, a reversal of direction that did less to deceive the enemy than to delay the attack until late afternoon. During this crucial interval, Union forces on the southern extension of Cemetery Ridge, the lowest and most vulnerable part of the line, advanced west onto elevated ground, including a knoll on which grew a peach orchard. There they might better defend against the impending onslaught.[42]

While these men absorbed the brunt of Longstreet's attack, soldiers at the far end of the line fought off the Rebels' effort to turn the Union army's left flank. Meade had sent his chief engineer, General G. K. Warren, to assess the strength of this vulnerable position. Accompanied by Lieutenant Washington Roebling (who later built the Brooklyn Bridge), Warren scrambled up a hill that would come to be known as Little Round Top. The engineer recognized the importance of this landmark—its deforested western face would give whoever held it the ability to deliver a devastating fire into the enemy below. Instantly, he ordered in reinforcements. Led by Colonel Joshua Lawrence Chamberlain, the "fighting professor" from Bowdoin College, they arrived just in time to protect the hill and stop Longstreet's men cold. The Confederates recognized what they were up against in attempting to storm this choice piece of elevated ground. One of them, Captain George Hillyer, called Little Round Top "the strongest natural position I ever saw."[43]

As the Confederate challenge at Little Round Top withered, so, too, did it die at Culp's Hill. There the Yankees did more than hold onto terrain—they actually remade it to serve their purposes. Union commanders, among them General George Greene, yet another West Point engineer, ordered their men to build defensive breastworks out of logs, rocks, and soil. Literally turning nature into a shield, they withstood a fire of lead and iron so ferocious that it splintered and toppled entire trees. General Edward Johnson of the Army of Northern Virginia acknowledged the tactical significance of Culp's Hill. It was, he wrote, "a rugged and rocky mountain, heavily timbered and difficult of ascent; a natural fortification, rendered more formidable by deep intrenchments and thick abatis [log defenses]."[44]

As Lee saw it, the Army of Northern Virginia had one option left: to concentrate as many men as possible and send them straight into the Union line on Cemetery Ridge. Fearing a Fredericksburg in reverse, Longstreet again objected—and again Lee insisted. And so Gettysburg concluded with the legendary attack named for one of the three generals who led it. In Pickett's Charge, the Rebels reached their high-water mark.

On July 3, from the wooded fringe of Seminary Ridge, some three-quarters of a mile away, the Confederates opened with an intense artillery barrage. The Yankees did what they could to find cover. "Every man in our lines," one of them later recalled, "protected himself the best he could behind such protection as nature afforded and his own genius and labor could devise." As they crouched behind walls, fences, and boulders and in shallow trenches they had scraped from the thin, rocky soil, their own batteries thundered out a response. Then the Yankee artillerists stopped, saving ammunition for what was to come. Some fourteen thousand Rebel infantrymen—the precise number will never be known—assembled in neat ranks in front of Seminary Ridge. Holding their battle flags high and their rifles at the ready, they felt enormous pride but also a deep sense of foreboding.[45]

At the command they marched forward, shoulder to shoulder, across farm fields and up the long, gentle, undulating, heartbreaking slope. Their precise movement inspired awe on both sides. "What a sublime sight!" one Confederate private exclaimed. "Beautiful, gloriously beautiful, did that vast array appear in the lovely little valley," wrote a Union officer a few days afterward. "It was the most beautiful thing I ever saw," recalled another. To Lieutenant Frank Haskell, it was "an overwhelming restless tide of an ocean of armed men sweeping upon us! . . . Right on they move, as with one soul, in perfect order, without impediment of ditch, or wall or stream, over ridge and slope, through orchard and meadow, and cornfield, magnificent, grim, irresistible."[46]

The Yankees on Cemetery Ridge were ready for them, and as the Confederates approached, the bluecoats blasted out a terrible fire that tore into the oncoming mass. The Rebel advance slowed, but the ranks retained their discipline, returned fire, and continued. Rallying his troops, one Confederate officer waved his sword and shouted, "Home, home, boys! Remember, home is over beyond those hills!" At a few hundred feet they charged, their high-pitched battle cry erupting from their throats. For a brief time, all the strength that each side could muster, all the lead, iron, and muscle that each could wring from nature, smashed against the other, raw power against raw power. Cannons barked; muskets roared; men and horses screamed in fury, terror, and pain. This, too, was a sublime moment, although one derived not from order and beauty but from the intensity of the violence that exploded across the landscape. Then came the end, as the distance closed and the bullets and shells gave way to saber strokes, rifle butts, and finally fists and even rocks. In the midst of this desperate hand-to-hand combat, a few Rebels breached the Union line. Blasting, clubbing, and slashing their way through, they almost attained their objective, almost made their way home.[47]

That was as far as they got. Meade's legions stood firm and then, sensing weakness, pressed forward. The long Confederate wave crested and fell back, its once-solid ranks in disarray, its remaining able-bodied men fleeing to the safety of Seminary Ridge. As the last Rebels trickled in, the high cost of the assault became painfully clear: of those who had gone forward, only half returned. The outcome of the battle was now obvious to all. With so many men dead, wounded, captured, or simply worn out, the Army of Northern Virginia could not continue. The life, energy, and resolve necessary to sustain the fight were no longer there. Lee and his men, who had deftly outmaneuvered the enemy in previous engagements, had lost the duel for terrain.

The war was turning against the Confederacy. Lee's foray into Pennsylvania gained food, animals, materiel, and time, but his losses were severe. His army nearly ran out of artillery ammunition, 17 of 52 generals died or sustained wounds, and all told, perhaps one-third of his entire force—between 25,000 and 28,000 men—were dead, wounded, or missing.[48] And while Lee was failing to wrest the high ground from the Yankees at Gettysburg, another Rebel force was losing its hold on a prominent piece of land somewhere else. On July 4, as rain fell on the retreating Army of Northern Virginia, the Confederacy surrendered the heights at the strategically important Mississippi town of Vicksburg. The war would continue, but in a sense all land now tilted against the South, all power now flowed downhill with the advancing Union armies.

ONE VAST HIDEOUS CHARNEL HOUSE

As the Army of Northern Virginia headed south and the Army of the Potomac pursued it, civilians emerged from their hiding places and walked onto the battlefield. What they found, what they experienced, horrified them and brought tears to their eyes. No longer militarily important, these few square miles of green Pennsylvania countryside had become a nightmare of destruction and death, a macabre landscape that seemed, as one man put it, like "one vast hideous charnel house." There, in all its terrible finality, was the physical aftermath of the two armies' cataclysmic struggle to harness nature in the service of military gain.[49]

Virtually every spot, it seemed, contained some evidence of profound turmoil. Shattered and fallen trees, torn earth, trampled crops, bullet-riddled buildings, collapsed and burnt fences, and blasted wagons testified to the ferocity and destructiveness of the conflict. So, too, did the abandoned equipment that lay all about: rifles, cartridge boxes, sabers, hats, coats, blankets, haversacks, canteens. Some of the remains offered powerful evidence of the resource scarcity that had driven the Army of Northern Virginia into Pennsylvania. The feet of some Confederate dead, if not bare, wore shoes made of canvas. Rebel haversacks contained mutton, veal, lard, crocks of butter, preserves and other delicacies, bonnets, baby shoes, socks, shirts, gaiters, writing paper and envelopes—an incredible array of Pennsylvania loot. Perhaps the sorriest of the remnants were the letters from home and the pictures of loved ones, evidence of the human anguish that Gettysburg would yield.[50]

What most horrified the civilians who toured the battlefield were the thousands of bodies of men and animals that littered the ground. At least seven thousand Union and Confederate soldiers (and probably more) rested behind breastworks, rock walls, boulders, and trees or lay in fields, in orchards, and on hillsides. Some of them bore no discernible mark of the flying metal or concussion that had killed them, but most were slashed, torn, mangled, crushed, dismembered, disemboweled, or decapitated. Among the fallen men were the carcasses of some three thousand horses. Lying for days in the warm, moist air, the remains—an estimated six million pounds, or three thousand tons—fed a disgusting orgy of decomposition. Bacteria proliferated inside the bodies, bloating them with gases so foul that Union army burial details and civilian onlookers gagged, retched, and covered their faces with scarves. Millions of fat, loathsome flies swarmed over the entire rotting mass, their squirming maggot offspring taking their fill. Worst of all, perhaps, were the loose hogs that roamed among the piles of carrion, gorging on tender, putrefying bellies.[51]

For a time, a few downed soldiers remained alive on the field. Moaning in pain, calling for help, fighting off the gruesome hogs with what little of their strength remained, they sustained themselves on hope and prayer. Rescue came to a few, in some cases from local people who happened upon them. The rest lay unconscious and unnoticed for days, their final hours slipping away.

Nearby, in homes and barns transformed into makeshift field hospitals, surgeons labored amid pools of blood, piles of amputated limbs, and heartrending cries, trying to save the astonishing numbers of wounded, more than thirty-three thousand of them. It was indeed a ghastly sight. A surgeon wiped his bloody hands on his apron and—"Next!"—called for a patient. Knife clenched in his teeth, he helped lift the shrieking, writhing man onto the operating table. While an assistant silenced the screams with an ether-soaked rag, the surgeon examined the wound and determined where to make the cut. Snatching the knife from his teeth, quickly wiping it on his apron, he went to work. Down he cut, down through the torn flesh and tendons, straight down to the bone. Then came the saw, and in a moment the damaged member dropped off. After tossing it on the growing heap, the surgeon made ready to perform the hideous task all over again.[52]

Given such grossly unsanitary conditions—physicians of the time knew virtually nothing about germs and the need to keep hands and instruments clean—it is no wonder that many of the amputees never recovered. These sad, broken men lay on the floor or ground awaiting the end, the final earthly victory going to the bacteria that multiplied in their bloodstreams and tissues. Their hearts continued to beat, but their glassy eyes already saw through the twilight to a distant shore where their souls at last would find relief from their wretched bodies.[53]

Although profound destruction marked the Gettysburg battlefield, in time it would heal. For years afterward, visitors claimed to find evidence of new life springing from the blood-soaked soil. In the summer of 1865, a Gettysburg man stopped at a farm where a girl displayed a basket of red berries for sale, "all the redder, no doubt, for the blood of the brave that had drenched the sod. So calm and impassive is Nature, silently turning all things to use! The carcass of a mule, or the godlike shape of a warrior cut down in the hour of glory—she knows no difference between them, but . . . convert[s] both alike into new forms of life and beauty."[54]

AN ORGANIC WAR

The image of nature transforming the fleshly remains of men and beasts into new growth hints at a key feature of Gettysburg and the Civil War: just how *organic* the conflict really was. Ultimately, Gettysburg—and by implication, the Civil War as whole—was a biological struggle. The distinctive interactions of two societies with the natural world powerfully motivated it. The failure of one of those societies, the South, to procure what it needed to thrive ultimately compelled Lee's decision to go north. To defeat the enemy, men and animals had to be mobilized, not just against the enemy but against the vagaries of weather, bacteria, and terrain. The "symbolic center of American history," Gettysburg and the Civil War were all about biology, all about organisms in relation to their environment.[55]

The organic nature of Gettysburg highlights some of the ways in which the Civil War combined ancient and modern military ecologies. It is a truism, a cliché almost, to say that the Civil War was the last of the old wars and the first of the new. It was the last in which honor, chivalry, the humane treatment of civilians, and the use of cavalry still mattered; it was the first based on industrial power, the destruction of civilian property, and the remorseless consumption of thousands upon thousands of men. This theme has enduring value, but the Civil War was ecological as much as cultural, social, political, economic, and technological. The conflict had much in common with past wars because its armies lived so intimately with disease organisms and because those armies relied on human and animal power for much of their movement. In addition, the Civil War was one of the last in which soldiers (mostly Confederate) drew much of their sustenance—food, water, energy, clothing—from household production and from the landscapes on which they fought. In other respects, the war had a modern cast. It was one of the first in which soldiers (mostly Union) drew much of their livelihood from agricultural and industrial production systems located in distant landscapes. In these environmental ways and more, the Civil War was the last of the old and the first of the new.

The experience of the Confederate and Union armies with microorganisms was consistent with the past. Spoiled food, sick animals, loose bowels, and wounds that refused to heal showed the influence of bacteria, viruses, and amoebas, some of the eternal foes—or partners—in humanity's travails. Like enormous fighting forces in previous centuries, Civil War armies were easy prey for an astonishing array of microbes. However effectively the Army of Northern Virginia and the Army of the Potomac maneuvered, neither evaded their most persistent and debilitating antagonists.[56]

If the microorganisms that afflicted Civil War armies harked back to an older military ecology, so, too, did the means by which Union and Confederate forces moved across the landscape. Historians have made much of the use of railroads in the Civil War, but what is so striking about Gettysburg is how little this modern technology mattered and how much both armies still moved by their legs and feet. This was a conflict in which men marched much as armies had done for centuries. Indeed, the power of Civil War armies often flowed from the ability of their soldiers to walk under conditions of extreme heat, cold, damp, exhaustion, or hunger. After the battle at Gettysburg, President Lincoln criticized General Meade for not pursuing the retreating Army of Northern Virginia with greater speed and vigor. Lincoln's desire for victory overwhelmed his ability to understand the situation—that after a hard march from Virginia and then three days of hot, bitter fighting followed by a drenching rain, his soldiers were simply worn out and physically unable to move more quickly. Lincoln exhibited the modern machine-age mentality, but his army was not a machine—it was a collection of organisms, of biological bodies, that quite simply got tired.[57]

Not only did men have to walk and continually confront their physical limits, but the armies in the Gettysburg campaign also relied heavily on the legs and feet of their animals. This was especially so for the Army of Northern Virginia. General Lee's letters and dispatches from the winter of 1862–1863 reveal a deep concern not just for the condition of his troops but also with the quantity and quality of his army's livestock. To have ample horses and mules was to be able to move artillery, carry supplies, and send the cavalry out to find the enemy. To have too few animals meant potential paralysis and defeat. In stripping so many horses and mules from the Pennsylvania countryside, the Army of Northern Virginia showed just how much more in common it had with ancient armies than with modern ones.

Lee's army also was ancient in the simplicity and directness of its ecological connections to the land. The virtual hand-to-mouth existence of the Army of Northern Virginia is startling in retrospect. As Lee lamented in the spring of 1863, nothing was as important as the simple act of getting food. "The question of food for this army," he wrote, "gives me more trouble than everything else combined." Nowhere else was the physical condition of an army so dependent on, so tied to, the physical condition of the land around it. The fat on the Rebel soldiers literally waxed and waned in relation to the richness or poverty of the surrounding farms. Bodies, food, and environment were linked in an immediate and compelling way.[58]

In contrast to the Army of Northern Virginia, the Army of the Potomac exhibited more of the characteristics of a modern fighting force. Unlike the Rebels' simple, direct ecological ties to the land, the Union soldiers' links more often were long and complex and connected them to distant and powerful systems of mass production. Unlike the Rebels, who often went into battle wearing homemade clothing dyed a gray color that faded to butternut, the Union men's blue pants, coats, and hats came in standardized industrial lots. Unlike their adversaries, Union soldiers did not have to scrounge their sustenance from the land around them. Unlike Lee, Meade did not have to concern himself with a massive foraging operation to ensure his army's fighting capacity, nor did he have to worry about executing a tactical maneuver for fear that he had too little food to sustain it. The productivity of thousands of distant northern farms, from New England to the Great Plains, yielded barrels of preserved meat, the dry crackers called hardtack, and other foods in such volumes that Union soldiers always had the calories necessary to do whatever their commanders ordered. Sometimes the fare was of dubious quality, but the quantity was never in doubt.[59]

A seemingly trivial organic artifact, the shoe, underscores the disparity between Confederate forces and the modern power of the Union side. The humble shoe tells a profound and moving story of blockades, drought, and disease, of the South's failure to provide itself with leather and other necessities, of the war's voracious consumption of animals, and of the growing impoverishment and ultimate defeat of the Confederate army. The march of those North Carolina soldiers toward Gettysburg on that day in late June was anything but trivial; their hope of finding shoes in the town spoke volumes about the material deprivation that underlay the South's desperate quest for independence. That so many Confederate men came into Pennsylvania barefoot, and that northerners found dead Rebels wearing shoes made of cotton canvas, was powerful testimony to the collapse of the South's economy and ecology.

The northern shoe traces a different story, a tale of the vast material power of a society whose productivity increased as the war progressed. Despite the Union's consumption of millions of horses, mules, and cattle, and even though the glanders epizootic also killed many northern animals, the conflict hardly dented the size of the North's herds and thus its leather supply. This is not to say that Union soldiers never lacked shoes. At the conclusion of Gettysburg, many of Meade's forces no longer had them—the hard march from Virginia and then the battle had worn them out. But the problem was not that the North had trouble producing the shoes; it was that the Army of Northern Virginia had cut the railroad line to Gettysburg, temporarily disabling resupply. Soon enough, soldiers in the Army of the Potomac put on new shoes, the products of the North's overwhelming economic and ecological might.[60]

The Army of the Potomac's wastefulness perhaps offers the surest sign of its power and its modernity. The Army of Northern Virginia traveled light, each man carrying only the bare essentials. Soldiers in the Army of the Potomac, in contrast, often carried a burden of clothing, blankets, and other equipment. If, during a campaign, the weather became too warm and the load too heavy, the men simply discarded it by the side of the road. When the Union army marched in Virginia, poor civilians, whom the soldiers called "ready finders," followed behind, eager to scavenge the droppings. This juxtaposition of wealth and poverty, of well-endowed Yankees and destitute Virginians, paints a stark and telling picture of the North's fabulous command of resources and the South's relative environmental collapse. The South was ill, hungry, and dying; the North had become an awesome superorganism with the capacity to produce—and consume—virtually unlimited quantities of wool, meat, leather, flour, lead, iron, horses, and, ultimately, human life.[61]

The Army of the Potomac anticipated future American military forces, which, by the late twentieth century, projected their power around the planet without the need to rely on local ecologies, even for water. The same abundance that sustained the Army of the Potomac later supported forces in Europe, the Pacific, Korea, Vietnam, Afghanistan, Iraq, and other places. Ultimately, the global reach of the United States arose from its ability to harness an abundant nature in the service of its military objectives. The Army of the Potomac, of course, did not travel as freely as its descendents, but to the extent that it could move independently of local resources and draw on reserves from far away, it had much more in common with the future than with the past.

GHOSTS

Almost from the moment the armies withdrew from Gettysburg, Americans sought to commemorate what had happened there. This was the final and perhaps most enduring product of the battle: a landscape in which citizens used the fields, rocks, trees, and terrain to help them remember events and reflect on their meaning. The Gettysburg Battlefield Memorial Association, formed in 1863, only a short time after the shooting stopped, purchased and preserved important parcels of ground. In 1895, the War Department took control of the battlefield, renamed Gettysburg National Military Park. In 1933, the National Park Service assumed oversight.[62]

When Americans visited Gettysburg, they did more than simply remember. Pilgrimages to this national shrine also provided opportunities to confront an array of controversial issues. In his Gettysburg Address, Abraham Lincoln recommitted the United States to the cause of union and the rebirth of liberty. Beginning in the 1880s, ceremonies held on the battle's anniversary brought together veterans from both armies who reached out to one another in a spirit of sectional reconciliation that ignored the Civil War's racial underpinnings and affirmed a national code of white supremacy. In the twentieth century, all sorts of Americans used Gettysburg to express their political viewpoints: state's rights politicians gave angry speeches; peace activists demonstrated against war; patriots celebrated military valor.

For still others, Gettysburg served not just as a site of commemoration but also as a place for recreation, for family outings and picnics in a beautiful, pastoral park. A landscape that was the product of incredible suffering and bloodshed became a place for fun. Most notable were the "reenactors" in replica uniforms who restaged dramatic moments in the battle. The visitors alone were not responsible for this softening of the past; the National Park Service also unwittingly participated. Gradually the agency smoothed the landscape's ragged edges. Pavement covered rough roads; neat fences superseded crooked, tumbledown posts and rails; carefully tended lawns replaced uneven pastures and fields. Nature, too, erased some of the harsher legacies of combat. Tourists had once flocked to Culp's Hill to see the shattered trees, the trenches, and the breastworks, which of all the physical remnants most imparted a sense of the sublime power at the heart of the battle. In time, however, the damaged and fallen timbers rotted, erosion filled in the excavations, new trees sprouted, and a tranquil forest grew where once had raged a hellish maelstrom of ordnance and anger. As the years passed, as the Park Service "maintained" the site, as grass grew and saplings matured, the rough landscape of a wounded republic faded away. With it went the nightmares. A pretty landscape was left to produce only pretty memories.[63]

A few thoughtful Americans came to believe that the nation had lost sight of Gettysburg's true meaning. Bruce Catton, one of the great popular historians of the Civil War, fretted during the 1950s about the battlefield's superficiality. The manicured, pastoral landscape had become, he wrote, a place of "romantic memories which are in themselves a kind of forgetting." Some thirty years later, National Park Service historian Richard Sellars arrived at much the same conclusion. Gettysburg, he asserted, was now more about commemoration than about the past. "Today," he stated, "amid green, pastoral beauty, I find it difficult to comprehend the battle that took place here."[64]

There was another point of view, however, one at odds with those of the celebrants, protesters, recreationists, and critics. For some, Gettysburg still was a place in which to make an "imaginative entry into the past," as the historian Edward Linenthal put it, a place to touch material things—rocks and trees and earth—and so come into direct contact with history. The landscape had changed, to be sure, but it still could evoke powerful feelings. To the perceptive visitor who walked up the slope of Cemetery Ridge, traipsed through the shadows on Culp's Hill, climbed Little Round Top, or sat among the boulders at the Devil's Den, the battle and the combatants could seem suddenly real and startlingly close. For brief electric moments, the barrier that separates present and past, living and dead, could seem to disappear.[65]

Each person experienced such epiphanies in his or her own way. A man peered over a stone fence and imagined the Texans who, barefoot and so far from home, fought on that spot. An off-duty Marine Corps officer gazed across a field and heard men and horses and saw sunlight glint on metal; this place, he said, somehow seemed right for a battle. Two friends drove into the park and instantly felt an overwhelming spiritual presence. Stopping at the side of the road, they got out and said prayers for the dead and their families.[66]

A few visitors sensed something early in the morning or late in the evening, those fleeting, transitional periods between light and dark when the mind is most open to alternate realities. "The battleground at Gettysburg offers the bright face of a vacation destination at warm noontime," the historian Russell Weigley wrote, "but there is always a chill in the air nevertheless, and at dawn or dusk the emanations from too much violence, suffering, and killing become palpable. I have been surprised alone by an abrupt November nightfall at the Devil's Den; I know the ghosts."[67]

The virtue of a landscape such as Gettysburg is that it helps us comprehend the lives and souls that rest beyond it. To touch the things that past people touched is to touch those people. We cannot see them or talk to them, but we sense their presence nonetheless. They remind us of the animate in the inanimate, that the republic is a composite of flesh as well as of ideas, of beating hearts as much as of rocks, trees, lead, soil, or steel. Haunting us, they do not let us forget the mass of human and animal life that energized the nation and created the world that we call our own. ★

SIX

IRON HORSES

Nature and the Building of the First

U.S. Transcontinental Railroad

O
N A MAY MORNING IN 1869, 690 miles east of Sacramento and 1,086 miles west of Omaha, a small crowd gathered to witness the driving of the final spike in an ambitious project: a single railroad line that spanned the remote western interior of North America. For six years, laborers for the Central Pacific had laid tracks eastward over the Sierra Nevada and across the Great Basin desert. At last they had pushed the construction into the Promontory Mountains, a dry, windswept range that jutted south into the Great Salt Lake. There, in a high, sun-drenched valley encircled by ridges still covered with patches of snow, they met the crews of the Union Pacific, which since 1864 had been toiling west across the Great Plains, through the Rockies and the Wasatch Range, and up the last grade to Promontory Summit. Now, in the cool, clear air, some five thousand feet above sea level, amid the sagebrush, bunchgrass, and juniper, several hundred people came together at the spot where the rails would converge.[1]

The members of the group hailed not just from the United States but also from countries as distant as Ireland and China. There were Central Pacific Railroad and Union Pacific Railroad Company officials, state and territorial governors, Mormon dignitaries from Ogden and Salt Lake City, journalists and photographers, a smattering of women and children, and a band. To one side, the troops and musicians of the 21st U.S. Infantry stood at parade rest. Mostly there were the railroad laborers, lean, weathered, and roughly clothed. "Grouped in picturesque confusion," wrote one observer, "were men of every color, creed, and nationality—the Indian, the Mongolian, the Saxon, the Celt, and the half-caste Mexican, some arrayed in gorgeous costumes, and some innocent of any, mingling freely with American citizens and soldiers." Although the description no doubt exaggerated the scene, it surely revealed a general awareness that the people in attendance—in particular, the laborers whose brains and brawn had built the railroad—were not of one racial type or ethnic identity. The world had come to America, and America had become, in effect, the world.[2]

If the Promontory Mountains and the valley landscape provided the backdrop for the diverse gathering, things of another nature—the railroad and its components—formed the immediate frame. Locomotives loomed on either side. The Central Pacific's *Jupiter*, a wood-burning engine with a distinctive funnel-shaped bonnet smokestack designed to arrest sparks and prevent fires, pointed due east. The Union Pacific's *No. 119*, a coal-burner with a tall, straight stack, faced due west. Each machine sat atop its own distinctive tracks. The Central Pacific's wood crossties were standardized and clean-cut with squared edges, while the Union Pacific's were rough-hewn and irregular. Telegraph lines ran parallel to the rails; atop one pole an American flag snapped in the breeze. Horses, some hitched to wagons and others carrying riders, stood on the edges of the crowd, highlighting the transition from animal to machine power that the railroad represented.[3]

The organizers of the ceremony intended it to celebrate the transcendent purpose they perceived in the land. Just before noon, to the cheers of the crowd and the shrieks of locomotive whistles, a Chinese crew from the Central Pacific and an Irish gang representing the Union Pacific each brought forward a final rail. The Rev. Dr. John Todd offered a prayer, thanking God for his blessings and asking that he acknowledge the railroad as "a monument of our faith and our good works." With his help, Todd intoned, "this mighty enterprise may be unto us as the Atlantic of thy strength, and the Pacific of thy love, through Jesus, the Redeemer."[4]

Leland Stanford, the Central Pacific president and former California governor, then received an array of ceremonial spikes to be fitted into pre-drilled holes in a polished laurel tie. Arizona presented a spike plated with silver and gold; Nevada's was made of silver. The California spike, destined to become the most famous of all, contained eighteen ounces of pure gold. "The Last Spike" was engraved on its head, and on its side appeared these words: "May God continue the unity of our Country as this railroad unites the two great Oceans of the world." Stanford accepted the spikes and spoke of the railroad's great commercial promise. Grenville Dodge of the Union Pacific addressed the crowd, invoking the memory of Sen. Thomas Hart Benton of Missouri, an enthusiastic proponent of the transcontinental railroad: "The great Benton prophesied that some day a granite statue of Columbus would be erected on the highest peak of the Rocky Mountains, pointing westward, denoting the great route across the continent. You have made the prophecy today a fact. This is the way to India."[5]

Then the ceremony reached its high point, a symbolic culmination of the labor that had transformed earthen materials into an instrument of extraordinary mechanical power. Samuel Reed of the Union Pacific and James Strobridge of the Central Pacific positioned the laurel tie. The Chinese and Irish tracklayers put the last two rails in place, and various officials and dignitaries drove the penultimate spikes. Standing over the final iron spike, Stanford and Thomas Durant, the Union Pacific's vice president, looked at each other. They raised their hammers, and in turn—first Stanford, then Durant—brought them down. That the moguls and their soft, untrained muscles missed the spike detracted nothing from the significance of their swings.[6]

The news—"DONE"—shot down the telegraph lines. In cities around the nation, cannons boomed, gongs sounded, steam whistles screamed, alarms pealed, bands played, fireworks exploded, and thousands upon thousands of people cheered. In San Francisco, artillery thundered over the ocean. Locomotive crews in Omaha yanked their whistles while a crowd exulted. At Independence Hall in Philadelphia, where more than ninety years earlier the Continental Congress had promulgated the Declaration of Independence, the bells rang with the sound of an expanding nation.[7]

Back at Promontory Summit, Union Pacific photographer Andrew Russell recorded an image that would become an icon of the American experience. The *Jupiter* and the *No. 119* moved so close that their cowcatchers almost touched. The crowd parted, giving Russell a clear shot. Workmen leaned forward from the locomotive pilots, extending champagne bottles. Below them, chief engineers Samuel Montague and Grenville Dodge clasped hands. To people then and since, Russell's picture symbolized the marriage of the rails, the joining of East and West, and the fulfillment of national destiny, human purpose, and natural potential.[8]

Like every icon of American history, the surface features of the last spike and the joining of the rails provide clues to a deeper ecological story. Embodied in every feature of the scene in Russell's photograph were the close connections between an expanding nation and the biophysical conditions that have shaped and reshaped life on Earth. Basic to those connections was the land itself. Laying the tracks across hundreds of miles of space involved a fundamental encounter with rock, soil, water, and topography. The railroads passed over deserts and prairies, moved through canyons and across rivers, and climbed mountains. In part, the Earth determined the route and the pace of construction, as high elevations blocked, gaps and canyons invited, and gentle gradients offered paths of least resistance. In part, the Central Pacific and Union Pacific Railroad companies decided the way, by excavating cuts, filling ravines, erecting bridges, drilling wells, and boring tunnels. If the geometric ideal of the straight line was the railroads' goal, they still had to consider the steepness of the grade, the widths of the canyons, the hardness of the rocks, the relative merits of potential mountain passes, and—crucially important for steam power—the locations of streams, springs, and underground bodies of water. When the locomotives finally met in Utah, behind them stretched a tremendous story of the way earthen resources and human manipulations made possible a continuous mechanized path across the American West.

The railroads' vital connection to nature included their material composition and thermodynamic function. To lay tracks and run trains, the two lines incorporated enormous quantities of resources, some of them from extreme distances. Laborers extracted iron from the Earth, purified it in blast furnaces, and, in foundries, mills, and machine shops, turned it into rails, spikes, and locomotives such as the *Jupiter* and the *No. 119*. In each engine, the iron components redirected two fundamental physical processes—steam pressure and atmospheric pressure—to create mechanical power. Boiling water produced steam that rushed into horizontal cylinders located at the front of the engine. As the steam entered each cylinder, it pushed a piston forward. As the steam escaped through a vent, it left a vacuum in the cylinder, and the pressure of the Earth's atmosphere shoved the piston back into the void. Each stroke—first from steam, then from atmospheric pressure—made a distinctive chuffing sound, as the reciprocating piston alternately pushed and pulled a drive rod that turned the large locomotive drive wheels and propelled the train along the track.[9]

The railroad's connection to nature went deeper still. As metallic and mechanical as it was, the movement of a locomotive required the miracle of organic life. The timbers and boards that composed bridges and poles, the crossties that held rails, and the chunks of wood in the *Jupiter's* firebox—how many trees, how many forests, succumbed to the ax? Looking at Russell's picture, it is easy to miss a remarkable paradox: that a technology epitomized by iron and steel relied so heavily on plants. Not all those plants were cut live. Excavated from underground deposits, ton upon ton of coal burned in furnaces, foundries, and the fireboxes of locomotives such as *No. 119*. And whether of coal or cordwood, combustion—a chemical reaction essential to life on Earth—powered the engines to Promontory.[10]

Of all the material paradoxes at the heart of the last-spike ceremony, the greatest was nearly absent from Russell's iconic portrait. Creating the mechanical power of the locomotives—the burning of fuel and the boiling of water that drove the movement of metal on metal—necessitated incalculable expenditures of muscular energy. Moving earth, rails, ties, wood, and other materials required draft animals, especially horses. Although those animals stood on the periphery of the last-spike ceremony, it could not have taken place without their grass-eating, water-slurping, metabolizing, sweating, farting, defecating bodies. Nor, for that matter, could the locomotives have chuffed their way up the grades to Promontory without the muscle power of humans. In the days before steam shovels and bulldozers, it took men and horses to move mountains. Much as the railroad drew iron or wood from far away, so, too, did it draw muscles from distant environments: pastures in California, villages in China, farms in Ireland. More than anything else, muscle power—animal power—showed that the railroad, which could seem so artificial, so antithetical to living, breathing nature, was at its heart a profoundly organic creature. For good reason was a steam engine called an "iron horse" and its capacity to move and pull calculated in units of horse power.[11]

When officials and dignitaries made their pronouncements—when they spoke of the railroad as uniting the two great oceans of the world, as opening the fabled passage to India, or as the divinely inspired realization of national destiny—they attached high purpose to a moment in history when nations like the United States built industrial systems out of the natural substances of the planet. Fully understanding that great transformation and what it meant to the people who lived it requires more than an analysis of the last spike or a perusal of Russell's famous image. It requires an excursion down the rails into the earthy history of the nineteenth-century American republic.

Long before the meeting of the rails in that high mountain valley, Americans dreamed of a transcontinental railroad that would bring them wealth and power and fulfill the promise of what Thomas Jefferson called the "empire of liberty." Through the mid-nineteenth century, visionaries put forth ideas for a line of tracks that would stimulate commerce, carry civilization to savage and heathen peoples, unite America's disparate parts, and extend the nation's control across prairies, mountains, and deserts to the Pacific. "Are we chimerical in this opinion?" asked the *New Orleans Bee* in 1836. "If we live for 10 years more, we may then exclaim with the poet—Westward the star of empire takes its way." The journalist William Gaylord Clark added in 1838: "Let the prediction be marked. This great chain of communication will yet be made, with links of iron. . . . The granite mountain will melt before the hand of enterprise; valleys will be raised, and the unwearying fire-steed will spout his hot, white breath where silence has reigned since the morning hymn of young creation was pealed over mountain, flood, and field." Clark issued his forecast at a time when the United States did not yet have three thousand miles of track, but already the locomotive—"the unwearying fire-steed"—had begun to capture the imagination of people who believed that the nation's future would unfold in the far West.[12]

Events in the 1840s inspired a flurry of calls for a Pacific railroad. In 1846, the United States acquired the Oregon country through diplomatic negotiations with Britain. In 1848, following war, the nation took control of the northern provinces of Mexico. That same year, thousands of freebooters began rushing into California in search of gold. With the far West open for business, a chorus of voices sang the praises of a railroad that would enable the full exploitation of the region's natural resources and that would boost America to global prominence. New York businessman Asa Whitney declared that the line "would open the wilderness to the husbandman, and take the products of the soil to all the markets of the world." The railroad would "be the avenue of all the trade between Western Europe and all China and India," the *Philadelphia Public Ledger* predicted. And promoter William Gilpin asserted that it would be "a great artificial monument, an iron path, a NATIONAL railway to the *Western* Sea."[13]

No railroad proponent exceeded Senator Thomas Hart Benton of Missouri in sheer grandiosity of vision. Exemplifying a point of view that the art historian Albert Boime called the "magisterial gaze," Benton pictured an enormous stone monument at the continental crest, facing the setting sun and proclaiming the American triumph: "And let [the railroad] be adorned with its crowning honor, the colossal statue of the great Columbus . . . hewn from the granite mass of a peak of the Rocky Mountains overlooking the road, the mountain itself the pedestal, and the statue a part of the mountain, pointing with outstretched arm to the western horizon, and saying to the flying passenger, 'There is the East! There is India!'"[14]

In order for such fantasies to materialize, the United States first had to settle important questions. Would the federal government sponsor the project, or would private interests take responsibility for it? More important, what route would the railroad take? Would it follow a northern path across the continent or a central or a southern one? Where would the line begin? Chicago? St. Louis? New Orleans? Into the 1850s, cities, states, and their representatives in Congress competed with one another to claim the eastern terminus. Tensions increased when the railroad's location became a political issue between northern and southern states. Each section, North and South, sought a route that would favor it economically and help it dominate the West.[15]

Some Americans believed nature could break the deadlock. Finding the most optimal route—the easiest and least expensive to build, the most efficient on which to run trains, the one, in short, along which nature posed the fewest obstacles—would decide the issue. As the historian William Goetzmann concluded, resorting to the "disinterested judgement of science . . . was a way of letting nature . . . decide, not only because it placed the decision beyond the control of mere mortals but also because the decision seemed to depend on the overarching justice of the natural law."[16]

In 1853, Congress authorized a comprehensive final search for the one best route to carry the star of empire westward. The U.S. Army's Corps of Topographical Engineers, an agency dedicated to the scientific study of nature, surveyed three potential transcontinental locations, north, central, and south. Traversing prairies, mountains, rivers, and deserts, the army explorers gathered detailed information about the land and its resources. But when the officers finally reported their findings, they did not speak in one voice. Each way had advantages and disadvantages, and the information about each was so varied and complex as to defy easy comparison. Rather than resolve the issue of the one best route, the railroad surveys further confused it, adding to the political paralysis that hindered the progress of empire.[17]

The outbreak of the Civil War in 1861 at last removed the impasse. With southerners absent from Congress, the remaining senators and representatives turned their attention to the railroad. All the nationalist and imperial reasons for the line still held, but the war added one more crucially important motivation: the project was imperative if the Union wanted to avoid further fragmentation. A railroad would connect the West to the rest of the nation, "linking by a great federative bond," Senator Milton Latham of California said, "the whole political fabric from ocean to ocean."[18]

Accordingly, Congress passed and Abraham Lincoln signed into law the Pacific Railway Act of 1862.[19] The measure authorized an existing California corporation, the Central Pacific Railroad, to build east across the Sierra Nevada. It chartered a new business, the Union Pacific Railroad, to forge west from Nebraska. The act allowed each line to lay its tracks across public land, and it permitted each to gather earth, stone, and timber from that land for construction materials. For every mile of track put down, the federal government would reward each railroad with money. A mile of track over relatively level terrain would earn the Central Pacific or Union Pacific a loan of government bonds worth $16,000. In the Sierra Nevada and Rockies, where the challenges of steep terrain, rock, and bad weather would require more laborers, draft animals, food, fuel, and explosives, along with larger engines and heavier rails, each mile would accrue bonds valued at $48,000. Across the Great Basin, which posed additional environmental obstacles, the amount would be $32,000 for every mile. A revision of the act in 1864 also enabled the railroads to sell bonds to private investors, which was necessary because the federal government's support was insufficient to pay for the initial construction.[20]

Just as important as payment in money, the Pacific Railway Act and the 1864 revision stipulated that each mile of track constructed would earn from the government a form of natural capital: land. For every mile of bed, ties, and rails, the Central Pacific or Union Pacific could claim ten alternating square miles, five on either side of the line. The 1864 law increased this amount to twenty alternating square miles, ten on each side of the line, for a total of 12,800 acres of land for every mile of track. The railroads could, if they chose, harvest timber and, by the later amendment, mine coal from these enormous terrestrial checkerboards. Or the corporations could sell the land for cash.

By such means were the Central Pacific and Union Pacific to proceed toward their final meeting. Now the star of empire could make its way over the grasses, arid spaces, forests, and mountain ridges of the West.

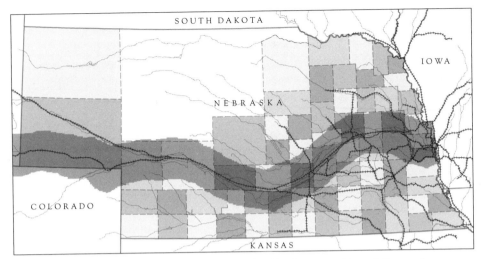

Union Pacific Railroad, the accompanying federal land grant, and branch lines and counties in Nebraska, 1880. The tracks generally follow watercourses and other natural contours, while the county boundaries reflect the rectangular pattern of the federal survey grid.

THE LORD HAD SO CONSTRUCTED THE COUNTRY

The extension of the railroads across that vastness began with teams of engineers who tried to pinpoint the location of the lines. These men were students of nature, of geology, materials, and fundamental physical forces. Trained in the sciences of land survey and structural design, they mapped and diagrammed the curves, grades, cuts, fills, tunnels, and bridges that would carry the tracks. Some imagined a higher purpose in their work. It was a heroic struggle to overcome a wild land; a masculine encounter with elemental nature; an intelligent use of valleys, ridges, passes, and other natural formations that manifested God's design. "The Lord had so constructed the country," wrote Grenville Dodge, "that any engineer who failed to take advantage of the great open road . . . would not have been fit to belong to the profession." Mostly, though, it was tedious, physically taxing, bewildering work in lonely and fearsome landscapes where finding the way was more a matter of luck or politics than of providence—and where the route chosen might leave much to be desired.[21]

Theodore Judah found an avenue through the Sierra Nevada. A New Yorker, he had earned a reputation as a skilled, resourceful, energetic engineer while working on several eastern railroad construction projects. In 1854, he went to California to survey some of the state's first railways. Driven by professional ambition and dreams of glory, he became such a passionate advocate of a transcontinental line that acquaintances referred to him as "Crazy Judah." In 1856, with the support of California boosters, he traveled to Washington, D.C., to lobby Congress for federal sponsorship of the project. Frustrated by the sectional split that stymied legislation, he determined to begin the work himself. Returning to California in 1860, he searched for a route across the Sierra Nevada. While exploring the western foothills, he met "Doc" Strong, a druggist in the town of Dutch Flat. Strong guided Judah many miles up a long, steadily rising ridge flanked by rivers—the American on the south, the Bear on the north. The ridge ended at Donner Pass, and from there Judah looked down on crystalline Donner Lake, its outlet into the Truckee River canyon, and the route into Nevada, which would pass relatively close to the Comstock mining district. Perhaps he wasn't so crazy after all. Back at Dutch Flat, he and Strong drafted the articles of incorporation for a railroad. By 1861 they had lined up investors, and the Central Pacific became a reality.[22]

Early that year, Judah began a series of intensive surveys that brought him into intimate contact with the nature of the Sierra Nevada and yielded the final plans for the Central Pacific's transmountain path. Beginning at Sacramento, aided by a team of ten to fifteen assistants, he examined environmental conditions and fixed the railroad's route. To decide the general direction, he noted "water-courses, ravines, the elevations to be overcome, the undulations of the ground, the most feasible points for crossing rivers, and the character of the soil." Then, with a measuring chain and a transit for recording angles, he and his survey party established and mapped the precise line that the tracks would follow, including distances and curves. Next, using a barometer and a level, Judah and his men noted elevations along the line. Plotted on a chart was the route's profile, a "vertical representation of the surface of the ground and its undulations." Finally, on the basis of the line and the profile, Judah calculated the railroad's grade, its degree of inclination, or slope, of which the lowest possible was the objective. For the sake of efficiency, "excavations and embankments," the cuts and fills of the grade, would "balance each other as nearly as possible." Physical conditions compounded the intellectual challenge of surveying. Judah and his team had to contend with inclement weather, balky horses, and steep, dangerous terrain. Evidently this was not, as in Grenville Dodge's conceptualization, the great open road of God; rather, as Judah said at one point, it was "the most difficult country ever conceived of for a Rail Road."[23]

The work had its rewards. At times the party enjoyed the beauty of the mountains. When Judah's wife, Anna, joined him, she brought a sketchpad, and her drawings later illustrated the Central Pacific's original stock certificates. More important, Judah learned essential facts about the mountain environment. He noted the many kinds of trees—pine, fir, cedar, and tamarack—that would be useful in building the railroad. He recorded the hardness of the Sierra Nevada granite, anticipating "quite heavy rock-cutting" during construction. And he collected evidence of snow. Hard winters made some people doubt that a railroad across the mountains was possible. Indeed, the pass took its name from the Donner party, overland migrants who, trapped while attempting a crossing in 1846, resorted to cannibalism to survive. But no official record of the snow's average accumulation existed. To find out, Judah looked closely at the trees. Thirteen feet seemed to be an important marker: he saw broken branches and ax marks above that height, and below it, a lack of moss. Thirteen feet—extraordinarily heavy snow—but surely it didn't come down all at once. With the application of Yankee ingenuity, Judah thought, the railroad would make it through.[24]

In 1862, Judah completed the final maps and plans for a railroad over the Sierra Nevada. Beginning at the foot of K Street in Sacramento, the line would run about one hundred miles to the summit, for a total elevation gain of some seven thousand feet. Rising a maximum of 105 feet per mile, it would follow the long ridge between the American and Bear rivers, moving "from gap to gap"— from low point to low point—along the rocky spine. Judah foresaw no major river or canyon crossings, so the line would have no unusually high or long trestles. It would, however, have many cuts and fills and would require eighteen tunnels through the dense granite. From Donner Pass the railroad would drop down into Nevada, finally meeting the oncoming tracks of the Union Pacific somewhere in the hazy distance.[25]

Although Judah prepared his plans carefully, they contained one especially controversial feature—his determination of the western base of the Sierra Nevada. Identifying that point was crucial, because there the Central Pacific would begin to receive government bonds valued at $48,000 per mile, well above the $16,000 rate for relatively flat land. Judah believed the base was near Newcastle, some thirty miles east of Sacramento. Leland Stanford, Charles Crocker, and other members of the board of directors were hungry for capital, and they decided that his calculation was not advantageous enough to the railroad. Stanford asked the California state geologist, Josiah Whitney, for an opinion. Whitney's decision reflected corporate needs and ambitions more than objective geological conditions. About seven miles east of Sacramento, where the survey line crossed Arcade Creek near its confluence with the American River, the professor detected a slight rise in the terrain which, he thought, might reasonably be called the beginning of the mountains. Whitney's selection of the site was fraudulent, Judah charged, but Stanford and the other directors paid no heed to the engineer, whose financial power and influence they were already taking steps to minimize. They transmitted Whitney's report to President Abraham Lincoln, who named Arcade Creek the beginning of the corporation's mountain miles. Thus the politics of nature, not simply nature, shaped the Central Pacific's progress.[26]

Judah would not live to see the tracks pass Arcade Creek. In 1863, crossing Panama on his way to New York to raise capital that would help him regain control of the Central Pacific, he contracted yellow fever from a mosquito. By then, the corporation no longer needed him. Using his plans and guided by the expertise of a new chief engineer, Samuel Montague, the corporation was poised to transform what had been fantasy into hard, material reality.[27]

Meanwhile, hundreds of miles to the east, the Union Pacific Railroad Company prepared to send its own engineers and survey crews across the Great Plains and into the Rockies. Chartered by the Pacific Railway Act, the Union Pacific came into existence in 1862 and 1863 when investors purchased stock in the corporation and appointed its first officers. These businessmen, including vice president Thomas Durant, hired Peter Dey as chief engineer and ordered him to complete a survey. Dey had a longer distance to cover than did Judah, his Central Pacific counterpart, and he had to consider a wider range of potential routes. He couldn't do the work himself, as Judah had done; he needed teams of men to complete the job.[28]

In 1864–1865, Dey sent no fewer than four parties across the prairies, through the Rocky Mountains, and into the Great Basin in search of a way that would combine minimum grades, curves, and crossings with the shortest possible distance. One team followed the geographically easy Platte River route, well trod by overland migrants in covered wagons. Another roamed Colorado's formidable Front Range, probing for a potential route through the mountain wall. A third headed into the mountains, deserts, and prairies that later would be incorporated into Wyoming. The fourth group went straight to the Wasatch Range in Utah, the last of the Rocky Mountains before the Great Basin and the eventual meeting with the Central Pacific. Moving across the landscape, the surveyors slowly established a line, profile, and grade, and they noted useful timber and mineral resources, especially timber and coal.[29]

It was arduous work, for nature presented many challenges: the Black Hills (now the Laramie Mountains) of southeastern Wyoming, a seemingly impenetrable barrier of steep slopes, rock outcrops, and deep gulches; farther west the Red Desert, an enclosed basin some two hundred miles wide with almost no fresh water; and finally Echo and Weber canyons, rugged slashes in Utah's Wasatch Range. Harsh conditions punished the bodies of the surveyors and their horses. Crossing the Red Desert, their tongues swelled from lack of water; drinking from a brackish alkali lake, they fell desperately ill. To the west, in the sagebrush and greasewood country beyond the Green River, one party member thought the tepid water tasted like lye.[30]

Despite such hardships, some of the men reveled in a strenuous masculine experience that brought them close to wild nature. Among others, Samuel B. Reed—in charge of the Wasatch survey and later the Union Pacific construction—enjoyed the striking geological formations, the meals of trout and venison, the crystalline air, the challenge of advancing a line through the wilderness. "The scenery is magnificent," he exulted, writing of Weber Canyon, with "mountains composed of granite and gneiss towering four to five thousand feet above us. The deep narrow gorge in which the river runs is only about 300 feet wide and is the wildest place you can imagine." As Union Pacific historian Maury Klein has observed, Reed and the other engineers experienced "the pilgrimage from civilization back to nature," a central theme in nineteenth-century European American history. Reed and his compatriots, of course, missed the irony of their journey: a return to wildness for the purpose of building a technology that would help to sweep that wildness aside.[31]

By 1867, the surveyors, now under the supervision of a new chief engineer, Grenville Dodge, had completed the basic work. There would be additional tasks—marking the cuts and fills for the road builders, staking the location of ties and rails for the tracklayers, designing tunnels and trestles—but otherwise the draftsmen were hard at work inking the maps. From Omaha, the railroad would follow the Platte River over the seemingly interminable Nebraska prairie. In the far southwestern corner of the state, after briefly crossing into Colorado to the town of Julesburg, the line would curve along Lodgepole Creek into Wyoming. Then came "the natural pass over the Rocky mountains," as Dodge called it. Traversing a ridge between Crow and Lone Tree creeks, as significant—and as problematic—a choice as the route that Doc Strong had revealed to Theodore Judah, the tracks would head into the rugged Black Hills and across Sherman Summit, at 8,236 feet the highest point on the entire transcontinental route, higher even than Donner Pass in the Sierra Nevada. After a sudden elevation drop, the railroad would make its way over the expanse of southern Wyoming. It would travel along creeks and rivers, skirt mountains, and slice through the Red Desert. Leaving Bitter Creek, it would cross the Green River. A series of streams—Blacks Fork, Muddy Creek, and Bear River—would guide the line into Utah, where it would angle west through Echo and Weber canyons on its way toward its ultimate link with the eastward-moving Central Pacific tracks.[32]

The Lord had so constructed the country, Dodge said, and the engineers certainly had done their best to take advantage of the route that the Almighty— or nature's contingency—had laid down for them. But now their task changed. Now it was time to supervise the construction of roadbed, tunnels, bridges, and track. The brainwork already was under way. Now muscles would move; now earth would shift.

INSATIABLE APPETITE

In February 1863, from K Street in Sacramento, the Central Pacific's contractors began shoveling and scraping rock and soil into a linear bed that soon left the city and headed northeast into the countryside. Passing irrigated fields and orchards, moving through rangeland grazed by cattle and horses, the graders built the bed across the gentle terrain, which rose only 129 feet over 18 miles to a town called Roseville. Tracklayers followed the graders, placing ties and spiking down rails. Beyond Roseville, the workmen gradually pushed into the high country, up through oak and manzanita in the foothills and then, farther on, into pines, tamarack, and fir, fragrant in the warm air. Up the railroad went, through cuts, across fills and bridges, and toward the summit. In November, the Central Pacific fired up its first locomotive. By December, the engine could roll a mile beyond the American River bridge on the outskirts of Sacramento. In the summer of 1864, the tracks reached the town of Newcastle, 31 miles out. By June 1865, trains ran 43 miles to Clipper Gap, and by October, the tracks made it to Colfax, a mountain settlement 54 miles from the point of beginning.[33]

The Union Pacific started more slowly, but like a locomotive building a head of steam, it gathered momentum as it moved along the line. In March 1864, while the Central Pacific crews were preparing to advance into the Sierra

Nevada, a small Union Pacific workforce on a muddy street in Omaha began throwing up earth into a roadbed. Not until July 1865 did the first rails go down, and by the end of that year only forty miles of track could carry a Union Pacific train. But in 1866 the prairie miles began rapidly to fall away. By June, tracklayers had completed one hundred miles of road. In October, 247 miles out, they crossed the hundredth meridian, the rough dividing line between the tallgrass prairie of the humid East and the dry prairie of the West, with its wiry short-grasses, spiky yuccas, and dusty sagebrush. By late December they had reached 305 miles, far up the Platte Valley.[34]

In these opening phases of construction, the transcontinental railroad manifested some of its deepest connections to nature. Building bed, laying track, and running trains not only required the railroad to follow what seemed to be the most natural route across the West; the project also required industrialists to extract, modify, and use vast quantities of natural substances. From its earthen bed to its iron locomotives and its ties and fuel wood, the railroad was a powerful system—a massive force—that sucked up raw materials, some of them from environments far away.[35]

In effect, the construction of the Central Pacific and Union Pacific railroads began not at Sacramento and Omaha but at the places where workmen procured the materials necessary for manufacturing spikes, rails, car wheels, and locomotives. In New Jersey, New York, and Pennsylvania, iron miners pierced the bedrock with drills, blasting powder, picks, and shovels. First digging pits, then excavating underground, they removed the ore and transported it by wagon to mills where other workers crushed and washed it, separating as much of the iron as possible from the rock that contained it. Then, by wagon, canal boat, and railroad, the ore went to Pennsylvania bloomeries and blast furnaces. There laborers heated it with fuels drawn from subsidiary environments. Charcoal made from trees fired the bloomeries; coal and its refined form, coke, burned in the furnaces. Ore, fuel, and heat, whether in bloomeries or furnaces, yielded a bright orange stream of purified iron.[36]

After it cooled, the iron went to factories that turned it into railroad components. At Johnstown, Danville, Allentown, Scranton, and other Pennsylvania industrial centers, mills rolled the iron into rails. The Cambria Rolling Mills at Johnstown and the Lackawanna Iron Company at Scranton, among other operations, manufactured rails for both the Central Pacific and the Union Pacific. Some iron went to foundries and forges, where workmen and machines squeezed, cast, and hammered it into car and locomotive parts. Danforth,

Cooke, and Company of Paterson, New Jersey, Norris and Company of Philadelphia, and William Mason and Company of Taunton, Massachusetts, fabricated the first locomotives for the Pacific railroad. The Schenectady Locomotive Works in New York state built the Central Pacific Railroad's *Jupiter*. The Rogers Locomotive Works of Paterson, New Jersey, constructed the Union Pacific Railroad's No. 119.[37]

Finally, rails, locomotives, and other iron materials made their way to the American West and to the construction sites of the Central Pacific and Union Pacific. Some went by wood-fired steamboat to Omaha; some shipped out from Philadelphia and other eastern seaports and traveled by sail around Cape Horn or by sail to Panama and across the isthmus by railroad before reaching Sacramento.[38]

The railroads' intense demand for iron was matched by their enormous consumption of wood. The farther they built into the West, the greater their need for fuel, crossties, and bridges and other structures. The two corporations extracted some of the material from the environments through which they built their lines and some of it from distant places. The hunger for trees that typified the Central Pacific, the Union Pacific, and other lines moved one commentator to call the nineteenth-century American railroad "the insatiable juggernaut of the vegetable world."[39]

The Central Pacific easily exploited the forest wealth of California and the far West. Schooners arrived at the Sacramento wharf laden with timber from the state's coast range and from Puget Sound and other points in the Pacific Northwest. By October 1865, the corporation had laid some 135,000 redwood ties, around 2,500 per mile of track. When the line pushed into the mountains, the railroad no longer had to import wood. Workmen cut a swath roughly sixty to two hundred feet wide through the trees, yielding an abundance of pine, tamarack, cedar, and fir, much of which became ties or went into locomotive fireboxes. Much of the rest fueled a lumber boom. By 1867, twenty-four sawmills on the Truckee River spewed some twenty-five thousand board feet of lumber per day, providing the Central Pacific with material for bridges and other structures.[40]

As it built toward the Rocky Mountains, the Union Pacific similarly took in wood from near and far. Axmen and sawyers harvested cedar, oak, and cottonwood from along the Missouri River, one hundred miles upstream and sixty miles downstream from Omaha. Meanwhile, woodchoppers labored far up the Platte River, cutting cedar from nearby draws and stripping cottonwood from groves next to the stream. Along both the Missouri and the Platte, wood came from land that the Union Pacific had purchased or acquired in its grant, from unclaimed public domain, and from private land under contract. In a few instances, cutters invaded the homesteads of squatters. Because these settlers did not yet have legal claim to their land, the woodchoppers felt free to move in and take what they wanted. One helpless victim stood by while workmen raided his cottonwoods. Another squatter resisted, holding off his adversaries with a pistol and a shotgun. But there was little stopping the "hordes," as historian Robert Athearn called them, from sending all available trees to the many sawmills and locomotives of the Union Pacific.[41]

A major problem for the Union Pacific was that the local and regional supply of wood suitable for crossties failed to meet its needs. Cottonwood offered some compensation for the deficiency, but it was moist and soft and when used as crossties held spikes poorly and soon disintegrated. Until the corporation reached the Medicine Bow Range and other parts of the Rocky Mountains, it had to find alternative sources. Soon it purchased ties from Chicago, Pennsylvania, and New York, paying $3.50 or more for each. Bridge timbers, too, traveled some distance. Lumberjacks reduced the white pine forests of Minnesota, Michigan, and Wisconsin to logs. Sawmills trimmed and shaped the logs into timbers and sent them to lumberyards in Chicago, "nature's metropolis." From there, brokers shipped the timbers into the far West.[42]

As workmen stacked rails in Omaha or ties in Sacramento, as they unloaded locomotives, as mechanics set up the machines and got them running, as the graders and tracklayers built bridges into the mountains and laid ties across the prairies, few people thought about the amazing journey the iron and wood had made. Fewer still likely gave much thought to the amazing places left behind: deep pits and denuded hillsides, fouled streams and smoke-congested valleys, cutover forests and piles of sawdust. But every rail, every timber, every spike, nut, bolt, beam, tie, and wheel embodied a powerful truth. Only in relation to distant environments did the Central Pacific and Union Pacific lay down their track; only through a massive alteration of nature in far-flung places could they push their rails through the American West.

MUSCLES AND MINERALS

The transcontinental railroad's consumption of resources revealed a crucial connection between industry and nature, but that intense hunger was remarkable for another reason as well. The railroad's use of fuel and materials centered it in an epochal ecological and economic transformation distinguished by humanity's adoption of a new major energy source. On one side of that nineteenth-century transition was an advanced organic economy almost entirely reliant on solar energy as radiated daily through wind, current, and the tissues of living things. On the other side was a modern, mineral-based economy defined by its intensive use of fossilized energy embedded in coal and converted to movement in metal machines.[43]

The advanced organic economy gave rise to the transcontinental railroad. For thousands of years, people had made their living from natural processes closely connected to the sun's energy flows. The sun stimulated plants on which people and other animals depended, and it helped drive the hydrologic cycle, the flow of rivers, the movement of air and ocean water, and thus the currents that conveyed vessels to market. In the late eighteenth century, people began to transform the organic economy. Improvements in agriculture and transportation—roads, wagons, ships, canals—enabled them to amass surplus wealth with which to build new technologies such as railroads. People also used organic economy technologies, processes, materials, and fuels to build the new. Iron locomotives and rails arrived in Sacramento on ships with canvas sails that caught the wind. Trees that became logs, ties, and timbers floated downstream to sawmills. The first locomotives of the Central Pacific and Union Pacific burned wood.[44]

The plant production at the heart of the organic economy also fueled the muscle power and "embodied knowledge" necessary to construct the Central Pacific and Union Pacific railroads. Horses, mules, and oxen metabolized the energy in hay and grain into the kinetic energy of muscle power. In much the same way, men transformed the energy inherent in their food into muscular force. The Central Pacific and Union Pacific required massed mammalian effort, and they employed it in bovine, equine, and human forms.[45]

Although rooted in an organic world, the transcontinental railroad also took shape from the materials, processes, technologies, and fuels of the mineral-based economy. The mining and milling of iron, its industrial transformation into railroad technology, and the operation of locomotives consumed copious amounts of coal. Not only was coal more abundant than wood in parts of the American West such as Wyoming's Red Desert, but it contained more energetic potential per unit of weight. The Union Pacific oriented its operations to coal virtually from the start. The locations of deposits influenced

Grenville Dodge's location of the line, and by 1867, the company was extracting coal from mines at Carbon, Wyoming, for use in the No. 119 and other engines. The Union Pacific's relatively direct access to the fossil fuel—Carbon was about four miles from its main tracks—gave the company an advantage over its eastward-moving counterpart. The Central Pacific did not have ready access to coal in adequate amounts, and until it acquired the fuel from sources near Evanston, Wyoming, and in the Puget Sound region, it had to rely on wood.[46]

The meeting of the wood-fired *Jupiter* and the coal-burning No. 119 at Promontory Summit was a striking demonstration of the shift from the advanced organic to the mineral-based economy, but the railroads, like most other industrial operations, did not experience the transition in a simple linear progression. If the organic economy made possible industries such as railroads, then the railroads and other industrial operations intensified, well into the twentieth century, the production and exploitation of muscle power and other organic energy sources. It is a little-known fact that the horse population in the United States and worldwide peaked around 1920. It is a better-known but still underappreciated fact that the use of human labor for muscular force climaxed at almost the same time.[47]

MEN AND MULES

Like iron and wood, the muscles and brains that moved earth and laid track originated in environments near and far. The pastures and ranges of California, Utah, and the Midwest supplied horses and oxen. Homelands around the planet, many of them in ecological turmoil, yielded workmen. The majority of the Central Pacific's employees, for example, came from Guangdong in southeastern China, where population growth and land shortage in the Pearl River delta during the eighteenth and nineteenth centuries compelled people to leave. Many who went to California in search of gold ended up working on the Central Pacific. Irish laborers took jobs on both railroads in the aftermath of a fungal disease that, in the mid-1840s, wreaked havoc on their nation. The fungus destroyed the potato crop, causing a famine that killed a million people and scattered refugees across North America. Portuguese from the Azores and other islands in the eastern Atlantic Ocean experienced some of the same kinds of pressures and disasters as did the Chinese and the Irish. From the 1830s to the 1860s, many islanders escaped by taking jobs on American ships that hunted whales for their blubber and spermaceti oils, which were among the most valuable of the advanced organic economy's energy sources. The whalers eventually took the Portuguese to California, where the immigrants made their way to the Central Pacific line. A number of Union Pacific workers were veterans of the American Civil War, which uprooted men from local communities and transformed them into a mobile labor force that later headed west. These were just a few of the sources from which the railroads gathered laborers, a massive buildup of muscle and embodied intelligence necessary for construction.[48]

A subsidiary but essential flow of resources from across North America fed the railroads' mammalian workforce. Where grass was unavailable locally, especially in mountains and deserts, supply trains and horse-drawn wagons brought in hay and grain. To feed the survey parties and construction crews, the railroads employed hunters. Bison, among other wildlife, disappeared into the stream of energy that laid iron rails across the West. The railroads also consumed cattle herds that they trailed beside the advancing workmen. Fresh meat was not enough, so contractors shipped in flour, cornmeal, potatoes, dried meat, beans, and sugar. The Chinese preferred a more varied diet, and businessmen supplied them with rice, fish, mushrooms, dried seaweed, bamboo shoots, cabbage, and other fare. And laborers of all sorts consumed large quantities of psychoactive and narcotic substances. Coffee, tea, and tobacco stimulated greater energy in the men, and at the end of the day, alcohol and opium numbed them and diverted their minds from their troubles.[49]

The muscular exertions of the working men would have been much more difficult, if not impossible, without the working women who followed the construction. Prostitutes satisfied one of the most basic of human urges, and housekeepers set up tents, erected crude buildings, and took in boarders. "From four in the morning until midnight this slave of the camp is on her feet," wrote the journalist Cy Warman of the housekeeper. Feeding the workers, nursing their wounds and applying horse liniment to their bruises, making them feel at home, "she is at once a mother to the beardless and a sister of charity to the bearded men." Almost no employees of the Central Pacific or Union Pacific brought their wives. One exception was James Strobridge, the Central Pacific's construction superintendent. Strobridge turned a boxcar into a comfortable home complete with a front porch, and for a part of each day he took refuge there in the company of his wife, their three children, and a caged canary—a bit of genteel, domesticated nature.[50]

From such varied environments, bodies, resources, and social circumstances, the railroads mobilized considerable muscular power and skill. Between 1866 and 1868, the peak of construction, the Central Pacific at any given time employed from twelve thousand to fourteen thousand workmen, most of them Chinese, and many thousands of horses and oxen. During the same period, the Union Pacific fielded a labor force of comparable size and strength. "At one time we were using at least 10,000 animals," recalled Grenville Dodge, "and most of the time from 8,000 to 10,000 laborers." Massing men, horses, and oxen created a reserve of organic energy that the corporations then unleashed on a sequence of heavy construction tasks. The immediate precedent for such mobilization was the Civil War, in which generals and other officers had commanded thousands of men and draft animals in coordinated movements. Some of the construction supervisors, such as the Union Pacific's Grenville Dodge and Jack Casement, had served in the war, and they adapted their military techniques to the management of horses and men, some of them also war veterans, for the building of the railroad.[51]

Most of the railroads' muscle flexed during the movement of rock and soil. Under the direction of bosses, men and horses rearranged ton upon ton of earth. In gangs of several hundred each, laborers with picks and shovels excavated the material and mounded it into road bed, sometimes in a vivid coordinated movement that caught the attention of observers. "The place is black with laborers; they stand as near together as they can shovel," wrote U.S. Army Captain John Currier upon witnessing construction work on the Union Pacific. It was odd, he observed, "to see five hundred shovels going into the air at one time." In conjunction with the pick and shovel crews, hundreds of horse teams and their drivers pulled plows and scrapers, gouging and pushing the ground into shape. The work went on with great regularity, men and draft animals working in unison. At noon, wrote one journalist, the boss called time: "Every man hears him. The mules hear, and if the scraper is ready to dump, the team will stop instantly and let it fall back. Five minutes later the animals are cooling their feet and quenching their thirst in a running brook."[52]

Muscular and mental effort continued and blood flowed more profusely at cuts and tunnels. Workmen with sledgehammers and hand-held drills bored holes into rock. Then they filled the holes with black powder, lit fuses, and took cover from the explosion and the spray of sharp projectiles. For a time, the Central Pacific and Union Pacific tried a new, fearsome chemical compound, nitroglycerine, but its instability made it prone to accidental explosions and so the railroads limited its use. No matter the compound, blasting took its toll on life and limb. "A deplorable accident occurred on the Pacific Railroad, near Gold Run, on Monday last," reported the *Auburn Placer Herald*, a California newspaper, on April 24, 1866. Smoldering embers from a previous detonation had ignited the fresh powder that the workmen poured into place. Six died; the "foreman . . . was blown to pieces, and one man was blown fifty feet in the air and one hundred feet from the blast." By such means, the railroad consumed the muscles that built it.[53]

After loosening the rock and soil, men and horses carried it to the many fills that extended across gullies and ravines. At cuts and tunnels, workmen piled soil and rubble into hundreds of small, one-horse dumpcarts, each guided by a man. One after another, the carts then trundled to the advancing fill, where a grade boss directed the placement of the earthen material. Cartload upon cartload cascaded down, creating an embankment across which the tracks would run. Men and horses labored in a coordinated, orderly fashion. "The mules are well trained," wrote Capt. Currier; "they climb up and down the bank, stop at the right place and wait till their load is dumped; then take their place in line and go back to get another." And as co-laborers of men, the four-legged mammals were just as vulnerable to workplace hazards. Too much exertion in hot weather, for example, could kill mules. "Six nice fat ones died in less than an hour today," reported a Union Pacific construction boss one summer. Such losses were an essential feature of the relentless resource consumption that fueled the railroad's drive across the West.[54]

At rivers and at ravines too deep to fill with earth, muscle power, intelligence, and skill erected bridges. Supply trains delivered the timbers, often prefabricated for quick assembly, to the advancing railhead. Draft animals hauled the timbers to the construction site and, in conjunction with human laborers, hoisted them into position. The railroads also used animal power to drive wooden bridge piles. Horses lifted a heavy weight, called a hammer, by means of a cable attached to a tall gin pole. Released, the cable dropped the hammer onto the pile, driving it into the ground. At some places, the railroads used small steam engines connected to winches to raise the hammer. But even these machines required organic energy. Men and horses muscled the steam engine into position, and heat from burning wood boiled the contraption's water into steam.[55]

At last came the laying of track. Supply trains delivered ties, rails, spikes, and other iron hardware close to the end of the line. In rapid, coordinated movements, workmen transferred the material to horse-drawn wagons or to a horse-drawn flatcar, which lurched forward a short distance to the waiting roadbed and the advancing track. A team of men lifted and bedded the cross-ties. Another group hoisted and placed the thirty-foot rails, bolters clamped the rails together at their joints, and spikers armed with mauls followed, play-ing "the anvil chorus." Then several hundred tampers equipped with shovels and crowbars leveled the track by raising or lowering the ends of ties and pack-ing earthen ballast around them. Laying track was an elaborate dance, a grand rhythmic movement of muscles and materials. "It is in triple time, three strokes to the spike," wrote one journalist. "There are 10 spikes to a rail, 400 rails to a mile, 1800 miles to San Francisco—21,000,000 times are those sledges to be swung; 21,000,000 times are they to come down with their sharp punctuation before the great work of modern America is complete."[56]

Construction bosses knew their task to be the command of massed mam-mals, and at times they treated and understood human laborers and draft animals similarly. The Union Pacific's Jack Casement, barely five feet tall but stocky, carried a bullwhip with which to intimidate tracklayers. Similar prac-tices and attitudes prevailed on the Central Pacific, where foremen were known as "China herders." Perhaps the railroad's construction superintendent, James Strobridge, provided the most telling example of the bestialization of human labor. Large, loud, profane, and violent, he dominated workmen, cursing them and hitting them with a pick handle, much as the railroad's mule skin-ners beat out of their teams every possible ounce of muscular effort. Charles Crocker, one of the Central Pacific's "Big Four" business magnates and a hard man himself, objected to Strobridge's methods. Also known as Bull Crocker, he no doubt believed that men, much like horses, had to be mastered; he just wanted "Stro" to be humane about it. (A popular term for the railroad's Chi-nese workers, "Crocker's pets," perhaps reflected his sentiments.) Crocker thus implored his construction superintendent: "Don't talk so to the men. They are human creatures. Don't talk so roughly to them." Strobridge—who sometimes referred to himself as a bull—would not have it. "You have got to do it, and you will come to it," he retorted. "You cannot talk to them as though you were talking to gentlemen, because they are not gentlemen. They are about as near brutes as they can get."[57]

In such organic circumstances—and often, in such bestialized terms—the construction of the transcontinental railroad went on, each increment mea-sured not just in inches, feet, yards, and miles but also in the steady accumula-tion of calloused skin, in metallic vibrations that stung hands, arms, and legs, and in crushing burdens that swayed backs and that made knees wobble. With iron and the application of muscle and mind, the corporations pounded raw nature into an industrial empire.

By December 1867, the Union Pacific reached Granite Canyon in Wyoming's Black Hills; in April 1868 the tracks crossed the cold, windswept expanse of Sherman Summit, 549 miles from Omaha. The tracklayers then followed the roadbed across Dale Creek Bridge, a breathtakingly tall and flimsy structure that swayed in strong winds and threatened to collapse if trains went too fast. By June they had reached Laramie, at mile 573, one among several stations at which the Union Pacific pumped water from wells by means of enormous windmills. In October, after spending the summer crossing the Red Desert, they arrived in Green River, 845 miles from the starting point. "Every mile of the Union Pacific," the historian Maury Klein wrote, relied "less on machines than on the sweat, stamina, and muscles of the men who built it."[58]

The Central Pacific, meanwhile, continued its ascent toward Donner Pass. In July 1866 the road lay open to Alta, 69 miles from Sacramento. By December the trains had passed through Emigrant Gap and steamed toward Cisco, 92 miles out, 5,911 feet up, and but a short, steep ascent away from the summit. Along the way, laborers excavated through and around a series of forbidding geological formations. At the Bloomer Cut, 63 feet deep and some 800 feet long, they chipped and blasted through conglomerate rock, a kind of natural concrete. The walls of the cut were sheer and clean, almost as if the workmen and their teams had sliced a wedge from a cake or a cheese. Barely wide enough for a train to pass through, the opening reflected the labor that produced it. Because animal power could remove only so much earth in a given period, the narrowest cut was the most economical.[59]

Much farther up in the mountains, the Central Pacific laborers came to Cape Horn, a granite outcrop that jutted some thirty-eight hundred feet above the American River. Rounding Cape Horn, much like rounding its namesake at the tip of South America, was a perilous enterprise. But gradually men and horses excavated a ledge along which they could extend the tracks. The sight of thousands of laborers removing the rock impressed observers. "They are laying siege to Nature in her strongest citadel," wrote one. "Swarms" of Chinese, he added, invoking an insect metaphor popularly applied to massed laborers, especially Asians, "made the rugged mountains look like stupendous anthills."[60]

At last the Central Pacific concentrated the power of muscles and brains on the most daunting phase of the construction—a series of tunnels underneath

Donner Pass. Located 105.5 miles from Sacramento, 1,659 feet long when completed, Summit Tunnel was the most difficult of the bores. In August 1866, well before the arrival of tracks, workmen began excavating at both ends of its planned route. They also began sinking a shaft to the tunnel's projected center point, from which they would then dig outward toward the two openings already under way. To assist the removal of rock, Central Pacific officials decided to position a steam-powered hoist above the shaft. They purchased a small locomotive at Sacramento, hauled it to the end of the track, dismantled it, and then loaded its essentials—firebox, boiler, cylinders, pistons—onto a logging wagon pulled by ten yoke of oxen and driven by a teamster known as Missouri Bill. Straining under Missouri Bill's lashes and curses, the oxen freighted the engine—which the colorful teamster dubbed the *Black Goose*—across the rugged mountain terrain. After six arduous weeks, the engine arrived at the shaft. Mechanics then attached it to a drum and cable and put it to work.[61]

Central Pacific officials probably knew even before Missouri Bill and his ox team reached their destination that the *Black Goose* would be useful not just for hoisting rock but also for powering an air compressor that would drive a drill. By such means, the excavations would go faster. But when a mechanic unpacked the newly arrived drill and prepared to assemble it, he ran into trouble. Under no circumstances would Strobridge allow the workman to divert steam to the pneumatic device. Strobridge objected in part because it would interfere with the hoist's capacity to remove rock, but the old bull had another reason for prohibiting the drill. As the writer David Bain noted, Strobridge had spent virtually his entire construction career "supervising human muscle over rock." When it came to drilling, he preferred hand labor to a form of mechanical power that was unproven and perhaps unreliable. In the question of man or machine, Strobridge would not give up the means that was most familiar to him. Crocker and others of the Big Four pleaded with him to reconsider, but Strobridge would have his way. Strong muscles and skilled hands it would be.[62]

BREAKING ROCK, BREAKING BODIES

Humans, however, posed their own problems to construction. As Strobridge certainly knew, they could be as stubborn as mules and as obstinate as granite. Surmounting the rock and snow of Donner Pass required thousands of workmen, but those workmen could thwart progress just as surely as any jagged peak. Keeping them on the job was not easy: laborers might collect their pay and head off to the next gold strike or land rush. If they stayed, they might object to working conditions or agitate for higher wages. To overcome the mountains, the Central Pacific had to manipulate and control—conquer if necessary—the bodies of workmen.[63]

The Central Pacific reached a turning point in its relations with wageworkers in 1865, when it began to recruit Chinese. Ever the conservative, Strobridge at first had refused to hire Chinese, saying that he would not accept employees who by nature were unsuited to construction tasks. Could little yellow men in pigtails swing mauls, heft stone, guide mules? But after Irishmen approached him to ask for higher wages, he agreed with Crocker that Chinese might be useful after all. By expanding the labor pool with low-paid Chinese, Strobridge could undercut the wage demands of the Irish. The Chinese, for their part, had good reason to take the work. Legally discriminated against, denied entry into the most lucrative gold fields, and indebted for their transportation to California, they might well have seen the $30 per month that the railroad promised them as the best of a limited set of options. By the time Strobridge had some twelve thousand Chinese workers on the payroll, whites were already learning the price of the new dual labor system. Asked about his wages—$35 a month plus board—one Irishman summarized his group's situation. "But if it wasn't for them damned nagurs," he said, "we could get $50 and not do half the work."[64]

Environmental conditions soon upset the stability that the Central Pacific gained from its predominantly Chinese workforce. In 1866–1867, a combination of harsh weather and stubborn rock pushed the railroad and its laborers to the limits of their endurance. Some forty-four winter storms inundated the tracks with foot upon foot of snow. Avalanches buried men. Ox teams hauling supplies floundered. To rouse the exhausted beasts, drivers twisted their tails, sometimes so hard and so often that the tails broke off. Snowplows, some backed by multiple locomotives, penetrated only a foot into compacted drifts. When machines failed, thousands of men armed with shovels removed the white stuff, sending it down mountainsides or pitching it into train cars that carried it away. In places, laborers had to excavate passages under the snow so they could get to construction sites. Many feet below, other tunnelers "lived like moles," according to one report, and they removed rock in eerie twilight during brutal twelve-hour shifts.[65]

When spring came, the arduous work of snow and rock removal continued. Hoping to attract additional labor, Crocker increased the wages of the Chinese to $35 a month, but this raise came nowhere near the fewer hours, greater pay, and board that the remaining white workers, by now most of them foremen, received. Even the horses did better; according to one calculation, monthly feed for one animal in the mountains cost $50. As the toll on their bodies mounted, as the energy they expended seemed less equal to the gold and silver coin they received as pay, the Chinese grew less willing to endure their exploitation. By the end of June they could take it no longer, and one morning thousands of them refused to work. To get them back, their leaders told Strobridge, they must have a $40 per month pay standard, a ten-hour day for work above ground, an eight-hour day for tunneling, an end to whipping, and the right to leave the job without harassment.[66]

The demands were unacceptable to the railroad, which the costly mountain environment had driven to the verge of bankruptcy. An outraged Crocker first tried to find an alternative labor force that would undercut the Chinese, and he proposed hiring ten thousand former slaves. (Cotton planters at virtually the same time considered importing Chinese laborers into the South to compete with the freedmen.) But Crocker and Strobridge quickly turned to a far more cunning and effective strategy: they simply stopped the supply trains that carried food to the laborers. By denying the Chinese the organic energy they needed not just to work but to live, the Central Pacific destroyed their collective will. After a week, the hungry, isolated, demoralized strikers gave up and returned to their jobs. Much as the Central Pacific broke the Sierra Nevada granite, so it broke the bodies and spirits of the men it needed to accumulate wealth. Once more did nature give way, once more did capital flow, once more did the line progress.[67]

MACHINES AS THE MEASURE OF MEN

But progress required more than just breaking rock and strikers. It also required the railroads to make their way through the territories of American Indians. When the Central Pacific and Union Pacific advanced across the West, they and their proponents viewed Indians as savages against whom to record the triumph of an industrializing civilization. As the historian Michael Adas has pointed out, European colonizers around the planet pointed to railroads and other technologies as a sign of their superiority over the native peoples they met. They had locomotives, they reasoned, and so they were destined to prevail over the outmoded darker races. Machines, in sum, were the measure of men.[68]

Profound environmental and social turmoil shaped the Indians' responses to the Pacific railroad. By the 1860s, many Indians across the West, especially some Great Plains peoples, were struggling with a range of problems. Decades of war and epidemics had ravaged their populations. The plants, animals, and landscapes that had sustained them were disappearing as European Americans spread across the continent. The bison herds already were in a downward spiral, victims of anthrax and tuberculosis, competition from horses and other livestock for grass, habitat destruction, drought, and hunting. These ecological disturbances contributed to the outbreak of wars. Indian peoples fought one another for the dwindling buffalo herds and for the diminishing grass that their horses needed, and they struck back at whites. While most tribes lost power in these conflicts, one—the Lakotas—evolved into an imperial nation that conquered neighboring peoples and briefly challenged the U.S. Army on the high plains.

Ecological disturbance and war in turn focused many Indians' attention on the railroad. Members of some Plains Indian tribes raided the Union Pacific for its freight and livestock. In carrying out the attacks, Indian groups asserted power over the United States, and warriors brought honor to themselves. But the raids also had a practical economic purpose. As the historian Pekka Hämäläinen pointed out, Indian raids were "act[s] of resource extraction." For some tribes, raiding the railroad was less a sign of strength than a sign of waning power and incipient dependence on the wealth of European Americans. Not all Indians attacked; for the weakest and most vulnerable, raiding was not an option. These people believed they had no choice but to work for the railroads in exchange for wages.[69]

Arapahos, Cheyennes, and Lakotas frequently raided the Union Pacific as it moved up the Platte Valley into Wyoming. Although the Indians killed and scalped surveyors and members of grading crews, they usually seemed less interested in stopping the railroad and murdering its men than in taking livestock. In May 1867, approximately one hundred Indians surprised a grading camp in western Nebraska, but by the time the graders picked up their rifles, the Indians had fled with "several horses and mules." That same month, Indians killed three men and took thirty-one animals. In July, some three hundred Lakotas besieged eight surveyors in the Red Desert. The Indians killed one man and probably could have wiped out the rest of the party, but they left when they captured the terrified group's stampeding horses. Virtually every attack on the Union Pacific yielded more animals than deaths and sometimes no deaths at all. "Horses, mules, and livestock were run off by the hundreds, perhaps by the thousands," one business historian concluded, which suggests what the Indians most wanted: animals that brought them wealth, power, and prestige and that could be used as trade items and gifts.[70]

One of the most famous raids took place in August 1867 near Plum Creek, far up the Platte Valley. To avenge a defeat at the hands of the U.S. Army—and to replenish their shrinking resources—a group of Cheyennes decided to plunder a train. "Now the white people have taken all we had and have made us poor and we ought to do something," a man known as Porcupine later recalled his compatriots saying. "In these big wagons that go on this metal road, there must be things that are valuable—perhaps clothing. If we could throw these wagons off the iron they run on and break them open, we should find out what was in them and could take whatever might be useful to us." Under cover of darkness, the raiders loosened a rail, bent it up, and waited. When a locomotive finally came to the twisted rail, the machine "jumped into the air," wrecking the train behind it. The Cheyennes killed and scalped some of the surviving crew, the rest of whom fled into the night. After taking flour, sugar, coffee, tobacco, and clothing, the Indians set fire to the broken cars. The Plum Creek raid brought honor to the men who carried it out, but the raid also occurred just as the bison herds were about to disappear from the central Great Plains and just as the Cheyennes were beginning to suffer from resource deprivation. The Indians' act of counting coup also represented the inception of their dependency on the United States for survival.[71]

Not all Natives resorted to force to get something from the railroad. Indian dependency on European Americans became clearest when people chose not to attack the railroad but to scavenge its waste and work on its behalf. Hungry and desperate, some Indians clung to the fringes of European American settlements, looking for scraps. From such a plight it was but a small step for a few Omaha women to join the crew that graded the roadbed westward from the hardscrabble town that bore their tribal name. Farther up the Platte Valley, recalled Hezekiah Bissell, a civil engineer for the Union Pacific, "Pawnees followed the track-laying camps, living on the kitchen refuse and what they could pick up after the beeves had been dressed." In the face of such poverty, it probably seemed practical to small groups of Pawnee women to pick up shovels for the railroad, and no doubt it made sense to Pawnee men to begin scouting for the army units that guarded the construction crews. The Pawnee scouts were, after all, famished. Bissell watched one group bolt down three days' rations in a single sitting. Moreover, Lakotas and Cheyennes had been their competitors for land and buffalo—their enemies and victimizers—well before the railroad had made its appearance.[72]

European Americans sometimes recognized Indian dependency as the consequence of hunger rooted in an impoverished landscape, but mostly they interpreted it as yet another sign that their machine-driven civilization was about to overwhelm people who, they believed, still lived a primitive existence. On the basis of that belief, the railroaders and their advocates began to perform rituals and tell tales that for decades shaped a popular mythology of Native people's encounter with the iron horse. Virtually all these dramas centered on a contest between modern machines and Indians. Sometimes the dramas played with the fear that Indians actually might threaten a train, even derail it. But in every case, they concluded with white men and their locomotives triumphant.[73]

In some incidents, European American and American Indian rituals blended in struggles for power and resources. Spotted Tail and seventeen other Lakota Indians appeared one day in 1866 at the Union Pacific construction site as it moved up the Platte Valley. They said they had come to learn how the crews laid track. After showing them the routine and taking them on a tour of the railroad cars, the hosts asked the Lakotas to demonstrate their skill in archery. All but one sent arrows through the hole in a shovel handle at a distance of some sixty feet. When the Lakotas expressed interest in the engines, the crews proposed a race. The Indians lined up on horseback, and at the signal they and the locomotive took off. At first, the horsemen outdistanced the machine, but it soon passed them. As the engineer sped by, he startled the Indians with a blast of the steam whistle, a shrill reminder that machines were the measure of men. The contest over, the Lakotas asked for a meal, and their hosts obliged. Spotted Tail then asked for sacks of flour and quarters of beef, perhaps as tribute, perhaps because his people needed it. When refused, he threatened to return with more warriors and take the food by force. The railroaders responded with curses and counterthreats, and the Lakotas leaped on their horses and rode away.[74]

A central feature of this event—Indians defeated and turned aside by a locomotive—also found expression in popular European American ceremonies, art, and stories. The passage of the 1862 Pacific Railway Act prompted a parade in San Francisco, in which a float bore the legend "Little Indian Boy, Step Out of the Way For the Big Engine." In 1868, a similar motif appeared in a soon-to-be famous Currier and Ives print, *Across the Continent: "Westward the*

Course of Empire Takes Its Way," by the artist Fanny Frances Palmer. Both float and picture depict a locomotive pulling a train out of a frontier settlement and down perfectly straight tracks that pierce the vast wilderness of the American West. Nearby, two mounted Indians recoil from the stream of smoke pouring from the locomotive's stack. The next year, during a private dinner at Promontory that followed the public ceremony, James Campbell, a Central Pacific executive, evoked virtually the same imagery. "Where we now stand," Campbell said in a speech to other railroad officials, "but a few months since could be seen nothing but the path of the red man or the track of the wild deer. Now a thousand wheels revolve and will bear on their axles the wealth of half the world, drawn by the Iron Horse, darkening the landscape with his smoky breath and startling the wild Indian with his piercing scream."[75]

The coming of the Pacific railroad was a hard moment in the lives of many Plains peoples. It is incumbent on students of history to peer into that difficult time and glimpse a reality more complicated than the myth that machines measured the value of men. By wrapping life in a simple story, the myth has hidden the manner in which European Americans, American Indians, and many other kinds of people together experienced the Pacific railroad. It has masked the way the builders assessed their own lives, in relation not to machines but to animals. It has obscured any commonality that might have existed between one man named Porcupine and another with the moniker of Bull. It has veiled the fact that the locomotives of which the railroaders were so proud depended utterly on animals and energy that were central to the Indians' existence. Most of all, it has removed from plain view the ways in which Indians, once rooted in an organic economy, attempted to squeeze the means of life from a modern industrial machine.

TEN MILES IN ONE DAY

The final leg of the journey to Promontory turned into a race. Because the Pacific Railway Act did not specify where, precisely, the tracks would meet, each corporation sought to outdo the other in putting down as many miles as possible. Each mile brought land and loans from the federal government, increased the area from which to generate customers and revenue, hastened the repayment of debts, and minimized the interest on those obligations. The railroads eventually decided on a meeting point, thus ending the race, but until that moment and almost until the tracks joined at Promontory, the westering star of empire shone down on an intense competition to overcome nature, win land and markets, and accrue wealth.[76]

With the hard winter and spring of 1866–1867 over and with the Chinese workmen's strike broken, the Central Pacific forged ahead. From 1867 to 1868, the corporation removed the last rock from Summit Tunnel and other bores and laid the final rails over Donner Pass. It covered the tracks with some thirty-seven miles of sheds and galleries, embodiments of the Yankee ingenuity that Theodore Judah believed would be necessary to overcome the Sierra Nevada snowfall. Sheds were free-standing structures made of wood beams and topped with slanting, gabled roofs. Galleries abutted the mountainsides and had roofs with one pitch that carried avalanches across the tracks. In spite of their utility and solid construction, the sheds and galleries were not perfect. They reduced the problem of heavy snowfall, but they increased the danger from locomotive fireboxes; the mitigation of one kind of nature exacerbated the hazards of another. The Central Pacific had to install vents on sheds and galleries to rid them of locomotive smoke, but the greater threat was from sparks that escaped the fireboxes and ignited the wooden structures. "For several years the loss from fires was considerable," reported the historian George Kraus, "and several miles of sheds were burned down and had to be rebuilt. In 1870 water trains were installed to fight fires and for sprinkling down the sheds twice a week, thus helping to protect them from fire." Sheds and galleries were important technologies to the Central Pacific, but the railroad had to use them with care.[77]

Even before it completed its summit work, the Central Pacific moved down the east slope. Horses and oxen hauled rails, flatcars, locomotives, and other equipment to the town of Truckee, from which the track advanced along the Truckee River into Nevada. In mid-June 1868, the Central Pacific united the pieces of its transmountain project when the *Antelope* pulled the first passenger train from Sacramento to the new settlement of Reno, Nevada. By then the construction had advanced to the town of Wadsworth, where the tracks soon would head across the Great Basin desert.[78]

In comparison with the Sierra Nevada, that arid landscape offered one important advantage to the Central Pacific—it was a basin-and-range environment, much of it relatively flat and dry, which allowed grading and tracklaying to move at a faster pace. Aside from topography, the desert bestowed no favors. Whereas the Sierra Nevada had timber, building stone, and clean water, the Great Basin offered little more than a grim array of deficits. "There was not a tree that would make a board on over 500 miles of the route, no satisfactory quality of building stone," and virtually no coal, recalled Lewis Clement, a Central Pacific civil engineer. Precious little forage grew there, especially away from river bottoms. The water that could be found was often salty and mineral laden, and it corroded locomotives and foamed so much that the machines could not use it. The alkaline mixture was just as hard on the mammals unfortunate enough to ingest it. Coffee made from it, wrote Mark Twain, "was the meanest compound man has yet invented." All told, the Great Basin was a poor environment for building a railroad and developing a modern capitalist economy—so poor that in the future the Central Pacific would be unable to sell most of its Nevada land grant. "The country offered nothing," said Clement, summing up its bleakness.[79]

The Chinese laborers' response to the Great Basin intensified the railroad's potential problems in getting across it. The vast salt flats, lunar mountainsides, prickly vegetation, unrelenting sunlight, and bad water were enough to repel anyone not native to the place, including the hardened Chinese. Rumors of murderous Indians and enormous, lethal snakes intensified their anxiety. Hundreds of laborers decided to turn back while they still had a chance, and they grabbed their belongings and fled. Crocker and Strobridge, always in need of a stable workforce, sent men on horseback to round them up. The horsemen "handled these Chinamen like a cowboy would cattle and herded most of them back again," recalled the civil engineer J. M. Graham.[80]

The Central Pacific stubbornly pressed forward, extracting what it could from the land. Cutters transformed the gnarled trunks of juniper trees into stacks of fuel wood. When wells turned up useless alkali water, drillers went to nearby mountain ranges, tapped aquifers, and piped the fresh water across the desert to the tracks.[81]

The Central Pacific also drew Great Basin Indians—Paiute and Shoshone men and women—into its labor force. Corporate officials offered the Indians free passage on the railroad in the hope that this would pacify them. But disease, environmental destruction, and diminishing resources already had knocked out much of their fight. In weakening them, those calamities drove them deeper into the cash economy and closer to the primary agent of its extension into the Great Basin: the Central Pacific Railroad. More important than the free rides on the cars were the railroad's grading jobs. Exchanging muscular effort for pay no doubt represented an opportunity for Indians to reverse their impoverishment and retain a degree of cultural autonomy. But wage work also marked their more direct involvement in a modern economic system from which few colonized people, once ensnared, ever escaped. Hoping to preserve themselves, Paiutes and Shoshones thus deepened their economic dependence on the railroad as they helped propel it across the desert.[82]

As the Central Pacific sucked in what it could from the Great Basin, it simultaneously mobilized enormous quantities of resources from the Central Valley and Sierra Nevada in California. Then the corporation concentrated all its material power on the advancing railhead. Trains and wagons brought in food, hay, grain, fuel wood, crossties, spikes, rails, tools, and other supplies. Special tank cars—which were flatcars on which the railroad mounted large wooden tanks—delivered water to men, horses, and locomotives.[83]

The railroad made rapid progress. In July 1868, the tracks arrived at Wadsworth, 189 miles from Sacramento. In August the crews reached mile 232 at Humboldt Sink, a stagnant, salty pool in which the Humboldt River abruptly died. Following the Humboldt, the advancing tracks left behind a succession of newly created small towns and supply points: Cold Springs and Rye Patch, Raspberry and Rose Creek, and, on October 1, Winnemucca, 325 miles out. Next came Tule and Golconda, Iron Point and Stone House, Shoshone and Beow-awe; then Cluro, Elko, and Peko. Early in 1869, the tracks reached mile 526 and Humboldt Wells, the headwaters of the river. Despite the fast pace—perhaps in part because of it—the work took its toll. Heat exhaustion felled men and horses. Outbreaks of smallpox and cholera compounded the miseries. Yet the laborers pushed on, and in spring 1869 they entered Utah and the Great Salt Lake Desert, some six hundred miles from Sacramento. Curving along the lakeshore, the railhead advanced toward Promontory, ninety miles away.[84]

While the Central Pacific built across the Great Basin, the Union Pacific tracks passed into Utah and moved through Echo and Weber canyons in the Wasatch Range. Along the route, the railroad overcame bad weather, difficult terrain, striking workers, and shortages of water, crossties, and rails—a full complement of problems that matched or exceeded any that the Central Pacific faced.[85]

In Utah, both Union Pacific and Central Pacific turned to the Mormons— members of the Church of Jesus Christ of Latter-day Saints—for assistance in grading. Mormons participated in the Pacific railroad for much the same reasons other people did: to reverse their ecological misfortunes. Brigham Young, the president of the church, hoped that the railroad would open an avenue of commerce that would bring wealth to Utah, a largely arid landscape of limited biological production, organic energy sources, and economic means. In 1862,

Young purchased shares in the Union Pacific, and in 1865 he joined its board of directors. Three years later, when he contracted with both the Central Pacific and the Union Pacific to grade the Utah portion of the roadbed, he hoped to hasten, and profit from, the railroad's advance into the land that Mormons called Zion. Equally important, he sought much-needed jobs and income for church members. After twenty years of settlement, the Mormon population was growing, arable land was becoming scarce, and drought, along with insects, had destroyed crops. The railroad, Young and other Mormons realized, would remedy their predicament. But by embracing the iron horse, they solved one set of problems only to invite another—the partial loss of their economic autonomy and with it their cherished isolation. For the Mormons, dependency was but a variation on the eternal dilemma of religious idealism: how to live in the world but not be of it.[86]

With the assistance of hundreds of Mormon laborers and horse teams, the two competitors raced through Utah. In December 1868, the Union Pacific tracks arrived at the head of Echo Canyon, 969 miles from Omaha. Weeks later, on January 20, 1869, tracklayers reached an important marker, a solitary evergreen—the 1,000 Mile Tree—at the top of Weber Canyon. From there the crews worked down the rocky gorge toward Ogden, and by March they extended the tracks northwest along the Great Salt Lake. The Central Pacific, meanwhile, followed the lake's north shore, through Kelton and then Monument Point at mile 674. The Promontory Mountains now loomed before both lines.[87]

Besides excavating cuts, raising trestles, and laying track, the Central Pacific and Union Pacific companies had one last obstacle to overcome: deciding on the final meeting place. Where the rails would come together was still an open question. In fact, Mormon graders working in opposite directions had long since passed each other as they prepared lengthy sections of parallel roadbed. Then, in early April, a federal government commission in conjunction with the two corporations settled on Promontory Summit.[88]

The agreement did not stop the competition. Rather, the momentum of the rivalry propelled the two corporations through the remaining miles. Like the final blow on a spike—hit it once more, for good measure—this concluding burst of energy drove home the significance of the first transcontinental railroad.

Charles Crocker wanted to claim the record for miles of track laid in one day. The Union Pacific had set the standard—eight miles—in October 1868, and afterward its vice president, Thomas Durant, wagered Crocker $10,000 that the Central Pacific could not do better. Now, as the tracklayers neared Promontory, Crocker sensed his opportunity. He devised a tightly coordinated, continuously moving system of machines, muscles, and materials that would roll across the desert. He and Strobridge stockpiled a sufficient quantity of rails, ties, spikes, and other components. They offered quadruple wages if the workmen beat the record, and they waited until the Union Pacific tracks were less than ten miles from the summit, depriving their rival of the opportunity to win back the honor.[89]

Early in the morning of April 28, with Crocker, Strobridge, Durant, Dodge, and other officials looking on, men and horses went to work. All told, some five thousand employees were involved in the operation. Of these, around 850 directly participated in tracklaying. Tie setters, ironmen, levelers, spikers, bolters, and tampers—all worked with precision, each crew, man, and horse performing a specialized task in concert with others.[90]

Some people glimpsed the future in that bustle of activity. "I never saw such organization as that," said a military officer present that day; "it was just like an army marching over the ground and leaving a track built behind them." "These tracklayers are a splendid force," recorded a journalist, "and have been settled and drilled until they move like machinery." The idea of workmen as "human machines," as parts in a mechanism, has appealed to modern scholars predisposed to see the railroad in a progression of technological and industrial development that began with smoking locomotives and ended with robots and rockets. Each laborer involved in the tracklaying, wrote one historian a century later, "was an important cog in the smooth-working machinery."[91]

Yet to describe that moment in terms of subsequent events obscures the organic nature of the first transcontinental railroad. The Central Pacific on April 28, 1869, did push its tracks forward into the blue sky and bright sunshine of a dynamic American republic. But tracks run in two directions, and the same rails that ascended the grade toward Promontory and an industrial future also led backward to a vital organic past. That older world—pungent with the smell of manure, sweat, and wood smoke, resonant with curses, grunts, and the sound of hooves—relied on the strength of mammals more than on the mechanical productions of engineers. It was a brute force world in which muscles still mattered, a world not of human machines but of iron horses.[92]

By one-thirty that afternoon, when the whistle blew for a one-hour dinner break, the Central Pacific had made six miles. After eating and resting, the horses went back to their positions, the men picked up tools and materials, and again they all moved, yard after yard, a relentless metabolizing collectivity. Water wagons and workmen with buckets of lukewarm tea followed, ready to slake a thirst that only straining bodies could generate. Because the rhythm of daylight and darkness structured the workday, at dusk the whistle sounded for the last time. Cheers from the exhausted laborers confirmed the victory: 10 miles and 56 feet. Together, the men and teams had placed approximately 21,100 ties, laid 3,520 rails—1,056 tons total—and hammered some 84,500 spikes. Ten miles and a thousand tons—muscles, not machines, registered the achievement.[93]

Only three days and but a few miles separated the meeting of the Central Pacific and the Union Pacific at Promontory Summit and the future beyond that. The changes that followed the joining of the rails—and the joining of countless other rails across the West—ramified into the twentieth century. The railroads integrated the nation, furthered industrialization, produced enormous amounts of wealth, and brought far-reaching changes to land and life. Among the ecological transformations that the railroads engendered, one of the greatest was the spread of cattle, sheep, and horses into the mountains, deserts, and prairies of the West. Wherever the railroads penetrated, they connected remote pastures to feedlots and slaughterhouses in distant cities, demonstrating again the vital connection between the iron horse and animal flesh.[94] And much as the old organic economy made possible a system centered on coal, so the railroads enabled transitions to new energy forms even more radical in their possibilities. Seven decades after Promontory, scientists comprehended the nature of something too small to see but with an energetic potential of cataclysmic proportions. ★

GALLERY NO. 3

Iron Horses

Historian Richard Orsi said that the railroad "was nailed to the Earth," so closely was it connected to mineral and organic resources. The builders transformed rock, ore, water, trees, wind, and flesh into envirotechnical systems powered by combustion, steam and atmospheric pressures, gravity, and the metabolisms of mammalian bodies. Hasty, muscle-powered construction limited the size of cuts, fills, and tunnels that both modified and conformed to topography. The proximity of cutover forests and wooden snowsheds, beef carcasses and sweating workmen, giant windmills and steaming boilers, charred timbers and glowing fireboxes, horseflesh and iron horses demonstrated how much the railroad was integral to the Earth. A composite of materials, energies, and forces, an agent of geomorphological and ecological change, the railroad—socially, culturally, politically, economically, technologically—was embedded in nature.

3.1   Joining of the rails, Promontory Summit, Utah, May 10, 1869. Note the different smokestack designs of the *Jupiter* (*left*) and *No. 119* (*right*) an indication of the wood-to-coal energy transition under way.

3.2   Horseflesh and iron horses, Promontory Summit, Utah.

3.3   Wind, water, and steam, Union Pacific Railroad, Wyoming.

3.4   Water tank car, Central Pacific Railroad, Winnemucca, Nevada.

3.5 Central Pacific Railroad snow sheds at Summit Station in the Sierra Nevada. Note the forests, stumps, logs, wooden structures, and smoke vents.

3.6 Chinese workmen and fuel wood in the Bloomer Cut, Central Pacific Railroad, California.

3.7 Wood chutes, Central Pacific Railroad, Sierra Nevada.

3.8 Mules, men, and dump carts, Central Pacific Railroad, Sierra Nevada.

3.9   Remains of slaughtered beef cattle, Union Pacific Railroad, Wyoming. Note the tents in the background and the trestle on the horizon.

Nature Study

It is axiomatic among many Americans that the experience of nature is essential to the development of well-rounded human beings and citizens. Although no doubt true, the axiom belies the ways that the experience of nature—including childhood nature study—also prepared some people to invent horrifically destructive weapons. The Manhattan Project scientists experienced feelings of awe and wonder when, in the course of their study and research, they confronted the sublime beauty of submicroscopic particles in a cosmos immeasurably large. They took joy in horseback riding, mountain climbing, skiing, and hiking, and in communing with nature on rocky peaks, along streams, in meadows, forests, and deserts, and under the setting sun. As they labored on the bomb, the mountains inspired and consoled them. An aerial view of Trinity Site suggests the physical and moral ambiguity of their work. The blast pattern that radiates from ground zero—like a meteor crater, a sunburst, or a flower—contradicts the linear, instrumental rationality of their military-technological imperatives.

3.10 Albert Einstein in the desert at Palm Springs, California, c. 1930. The physicist Freeman Dyson remarked that the "the chief reward for being a scientist is not the power and the money but the chance of catching a fleeting glimpse of the transcendent beauty of nature."

3.11 Robert Oppenheimer relished grueling horseback rides across undeveloped terrain, one of which he memorialized in the poem "Crossing."

3.12   Manhattan Project
scientists in the mountains.
Standing, left to right, Emilio
Segrè, Enrico Fermi, Hans
Bethe, Hans Staub, Victor
Weisskopf; *seated*, Erika Staub,
Elfriede Segrè.

3.13   Niels Bohr, Sawyer's
Hill ski run, Los Alamos, New
Mexico.

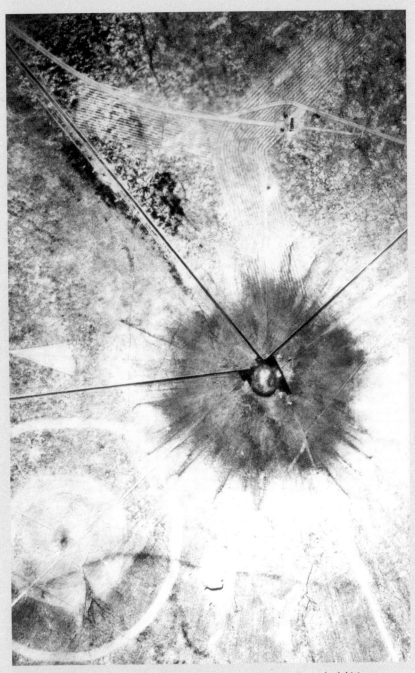

3.14   Trinity Site, July 16, 1945, Alamogordo Bombing Range, Jornada del Muerto, New Mexico.

Natural Hazards

The arrangement of social relationships involved the arrangement of ecologies and landscapes—and vice versa. Nowhere was this truer than in places defined by the creation, maintenance, and evolution of the color line. The color line structured the relationship of racial groups to one another and to the land. Membership in a group influenced if not determined access to resources and spaces derived from the nonhuman natural fundament—sunlight, soil, minerals, water, topography, plants, and animals. Membership in the group also influenced if not determined the hazards to which the color line exposed individual human bodies—human nature, most vulnerably the bodies of children. A tool of social and biophysical containment and control, the color line was the foundational instrument of environmental racism.

3.15   Sandtown, Topeka, Kansas, in the aftermath of the 1903 flood.

3.16   House and outbuildings, urban renewal area, the Bottoms, Topeka, Kansas, 1961.

3.17   Nature study. Kindergarten teacher, students, and cotton, Tennesseetown, Topeka, Kansas.

3.18   Linda and Terry Lynn Brown walking to school bus stop, Topeka, Kansas, 1953.

Lipids and Liberty

A fundamental problem for any society is the need to capture a modicum of the energy that streams through the universe. For the republic of nature, the problem is to capture energy sufficient for citizens to realize and conserve their core values of freedom and democracy. The picture of a prostrate Lady Liberty mainlining oil raises troubling questions about the ability of the nation to achieve its purposes. To what extent was the age of democratic revolutions, an age that gave rise to the United States, underwritten by surpluses of food, wood, coal, petroleum, and other energy sources? Is a republic possible without such surpluses? What is the proper equation of energy and liberty? The questions call on scholars, students, and citizens to do the work of environmental history, to look into the nature of the past to find optimal routes into the future.

3.19 Dave Berg, "The Lighter Side of the Energy Crisis," *MAD Magazine*, 1974.

3.20 Roadmaster Finer Bicycles, wartime bicycle advertisement, 1941.

3.21 Renting bicycles at a service station in East Potomac Park, Washington, D.C., 1942.

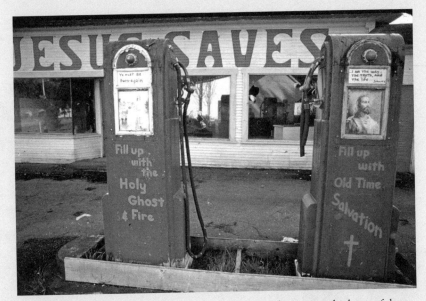

3.22　"All nature is full of God." Matter meets spirit on the entropic highway of the universe, Potlatch, Washington, 1974.

3.23　Addicted to oil, Iraq War. Frank Boyle cartoon.

SEVEN

ATOMIC SUBLIME

Toward a Natural History of the Bomb

M OSTLY PONDEROSA PINE TREES, the forest spread for miles across a high, dry, sun-splashed plateau in the mountains of northern New Mexico. For centuries it had provided material and spiritual sustenance to Natives and newcomers alike. Now, on a spring day in 1943, it was under assault. A United States Army soldier revved his bulldozer and drove the clanking machine, blade raised, toward a stand of pines. He was only following orders, and he was doing only what citizens expected of the Army Corps of Engineers, which was to rearrange nature for military purposes.

His work was important. The Corps had to clear the plateau quickly to make way for the roads, parking lots, offices, laboratories, residences, and landscaping of Los Alamos, the secret city where scientists would build the atomic bomb. As the bulldozer crunched into a tree, its diesel engine roared, its stack blew exhaust, and its tracks dug into the gritty soil. Brute force technology pushed against a nature that could bend only so far, resist only so long. As the pine crashed to the ground, the soldier stopped, backed up, stopped again, and once more clanked forward to topple yet another tree.[1]

The forest, however, had defenders. Near the charging bulldozer stood a block of flimsy-looking wooden apartments, some of the first buildings erected to house the atomic scientists and their families. As another pine went down, a slight, pretty woman with short dark hair emerged from one of the apartments and headed toward the machine. Mici Teller was the wife of physicist Edward Teller, a theoretician and dreamer who gazed at the world from beneath a pair of dark, bushy, brooding eyebrows. As Mici Teller strode out of her apartment that day, her husband was probably at one of the labs, absorbed in the creation of the atomic bomb. Edward Teller's greatest contribution, however, would not be to that weapon. Before it was complete, he would imagine the vastly more powerful hydrogen bomb, "the Super." He also would make his mark as a proponent of Project Plowshare, an effort to use atomic bombs to excavate canals, tunnels, harbors, and mines. "If your mountain is not in the right place, just drop us a card," he would say. Mici loved Edward and was his confidante and staunchest ally, yet as she approached the bulldozer, she was not thinking about her husband's dream of making a better world.[2] She was focused on the soldier who was knocking down pine trees.

Although their exact words are lost to history, the evidence suggests a likely scenario. Standing next to the bulldozer, her voice raised against the rattle of its idling diesel engine, Mici pleaded in Hungarian-accented English: *Leave me please the trees here so my baby boy can have some shade.* The soldier, louder: *Sorry, lady, but I got orders to level off everything so we can plant it.* Mici, voice straining: *But why? It was planted by wild nature and suits me better than dust.* Soldier, resignedly: *Okay, lady, take it easy, you win.* With that, he left, but to Mici's displeasure, he was back the next day: *Calm down, lady, I got orders to finish this neck of the woods.* Then, as Mici looked on helplessly, he returned to his work, and again an aromatic pine tree hit the ground.[3]

A strong, resourceful woman, Mici Teller would not relent, and she rallied the other wives and mothers of her apartment block against "the danger," as she called it. Carrying chairs, the women walked to a nearby grove of pine trees, set the chairs down, and sat in them. Edward Teller remembered the moment somewhat differently. In his imagination, Mici spread a blanket under the pines and sat on it with their infant son, Paul (also known as Piggily), his bottles and rattles, and a picnic lunch. Either way, when the bulldozer approached, Mici and her neighbors politely refused the soldier's entreaties to step aside. Shaking his head, he was at a loss over what to do. Contemplating the scene, calculating the odds, he finally made his decision. He raised the blade, shifted into gear, revved the engine . . . and backed up and drove away, this time for good.[4] The soldier had learned an important lesson: sometimes it is easier to move a pile of granite than to budge a group of determined women. Although Mici Teller did not gloat, her act of civil disobedience had yielded a small but impressive victory. Using a technique that would become popular among environmentalists, she had stopped the Army Corps of Engineers and saved some pine trees.

To most people, the bomb probably has no obvious connection to women, babies, pine trees, or saving nature. It might appear to be the very antithesis of all that is human, natural, and good.[5] According to the popular story, cold, calculating scientists manipulated—or perverted—nature in the service of creating a terrifyingly unnatural death machine. Those ruthless instrumentalists lived in their heads and comprehended the world through abstract mathematical equations that construed nature as a set of inanimate, malleable materials. Nature, they believed, was not warm and alive, a source of spiritual insight or morality, or something to be saved. Rather, it was merely physical matter subject to human control. Concretely, it was substances in a laboratory; abstractly, it was the periodic table of the elements or numbers calculated on a slide rule.[6]

Of all the people at Los Alamos, Mici and Edward Teller should have fit the stereotype. The incident at the pine grove, however, shows they were more complex than that. No innocent bystander to the atomic bomb project, Mici was a mathematician who worked in its computations division, yet she also had strong feelings about the Los Alamos environment. Nor did Edward quite fit the caricature. A zealous proponent of atomic power, he actually loved mountains and found great joy in them. How, then, to explain the Tellers? How could the devoted wife of an atomic scientist—a dangerous, mad scientist, in the view of his later critics—want to save some pine trees? How could that mad scientist take pride in the actions of his wife, whom he called a "free spirit"?[7] How could either of them express a preference for wild nature over manmade settings?

Answering those questions requires us to set aside some assumptions: that the Tellers and other atomic scientists had no affinity for the wonder and power of nature, and that only ruthless, insensitive people can create awful weapons. If we abandon these assumptions, then the significance of Mici's defiance of the bulldozer becomes clearer, and a richer and more troubling story of the atomic bomb begins to take shape.

Let us start, then, with an entirely different assumption: that the atomic scientists and their families felt a deep affinity for all that was human, natural, and good. A new question now presents itself: How could nature-loving humanitarians create the bomb? One possible answer is that they compartmentalized their lives so that they enjoyed nature in one compartment while manipulating it in the other.[8] Maybe Mici Teller drew no connection between the pine grove where she cuddled Piggily and the desk where she performed calculations that would help to annihilate women and babies in another part of the world. Perhaps Edward Teller separated his love of the Rocky Mountains, the Cascades, the Alps, and the Carpathians from the mountains that he later dreamed of removing with bombs.

Perhaps, however—and this is a more compelling possibility—the compartments weren't so separate after all, and the physicists' embrace of nature in one compartment made possible their work in the other. Perhaps a powerful attraction to nature in all its guises, whether pine trees or submicroscopic particles, encouraged intellectual processes that enabled the scientists to imagine and design the bomb. Perhaps—and here is a truly unsettling thought—the bomb was the fulfillment of all that was human, natural, and good. Numerous interdependent variables came together to produce the bomb, of course: the Second World War, the Army Corps of Engineers, bulldozers knocking down pine trees. But without the scientists' deep human urge to understand the universe, without the awe and wonder they felt in the presence of sublime natural forces, and without the solace that mountains, plateaus, pine trees, and babies provided them, that most destructive of weapons would have been impossible. The story of Mici Teller is precisely the place to begin a discussion of the bomb. Standing in her pine grove, taking in the fragrant air, we sense the mystery and the tragedy of America's atomic quest.[9]

The natural history of the atomic bomb can be told through the lives of the scientists who attempted to comprehend the universe by exploring particles so small that they were virtually invisible. At Los Alamos, they merged their desire to understand nature with the imperative of building military might. High on the pine-covered Pajarito Plateau, in the shadow of the Jemez Mountains, they and their families withdrew to an isolated community surrounded by stunning vistas and miles of open country and there oriented their lives to the technological, bureaucratic, and military objectives of the United States government. The uneasy partnership of science and war that developed under the pines had ambiguous moral consequences. As the bomb came to fruition, the scientists began to discuss and debate the rightness of their actions. Some developed an even stronger faith in the course they had chosen. Others were not so certain.

WE TOUCHED THE NERVE OF THE UNIVERSE

The events that brought the atomic scientists to Los Alamos began in the late nineteenth and early twentieth centuries with the investigation of submicroscopic nature. Exercising their imaginations, perhaps their most important analytical skill, scientists gradually formed a picture of a minute atomic realm that they could not see directly but that their laboratory experiments and mathematical calculations told them must exist. Their picture was not an exact, literal representation of reality, but it was close enough.

As of the mid-1930s, the atom seemed to consist of a dense core, or nucleus, around which moved lighter electrons. The nucleus included two kinds of particles: protons, which carried a positive electrical charge, and neutrons, which carried none. A mysterious, powerful force held the protons and neutrons together. The negatively charged electrons, meanwhile, seemed to vibrate or oscillate in stable positions called ground states. When heat or other energy excited the electrons, they made discontinuous, quantum leaps to fixed higher positions. Removal of the energy returned them to their original ground states.[10] Physicists could not explain why the atom functioned as it did, but their willingness to accept such indeterminacy allowed them to think with extraordinary clarity and creativity. "It is wrong to think that the task of physics is to find out how nature *is*," asserted Niels Bohr, one of the greatest scientists of the twentieth century. "Physics concerns what we can *say* about nature."[11]

Until the late 1930s, physicists doubted that their investigation of the atom would teach them how to release the enormous energy it contained. "If it could be tapped and controlled, what an agent it would be in shaping the world's destiny!" exclaimed Frederick Soddy, a physicist at Cambridge University's Cavendish Laboratory, in 1904. "The man who put his hand on the lever by which a parsimonious nature regulates so jealously the output of this store of energy would possess a weapon by which he could destroy the earth if he chose." Soddy believed that the inscrutable physical properties of atoms would prevent mankind from laying its hand on that lever. "We may trust Nature," he concluded, "to guard her secret."[12] For the next several decades, in spite of much science fiction and popular speculation, atomic scientists diverged little from Soddy's position. They might have dreamed of pushing levers to exploit nature's powers, but nature limited their ability to do so.

What, then, impelled them forward? In their desire to reveal a kind of hidden terrain, the atomic scientists perhaps resembled the great explorers of their time.[13] Much as Himalayan peaks, polar ice caps, and the dark interiors of continents called to explorers, so the recesses of atoms called to physicists. Atomic research, however, did not involve the strenuous muscular challenge that made geographical exploration such an appealing masculine adventure, nor did it invite the same kind of imperial rivalry. The atom had a geography, but it was a submicroscopic geography that lacked the utilitarian and symbolic value of terrestrial-scale environments and landmarks. Probing the nucleus, in short, was not the same as colonizing a region or planting a flag at the North Pole. Moreover, atomic physics created a remarkably open, transnational community of scholars as American, Austrian, British, Canadian, Danish, Dutch, French, German, Hungarian, Italian, Japanese, Polish, Russian, Swiss, and New Zealand men and women found common cause in science.[14] Although international rivalries at times enflamed them, they worked peacefully together in laboratories and think tanks, even through the First World War, which strained but did not break their community. Only during the Second World War did powerful nations seek to colonize the atom by excluding other countries from its military applications.

In the absence of overt utilitarian, instrumental, or imperial rationales, we must take seriously the claims of Ernest Rutherford, Niels Bohr, and other physicists that curiosity alone motivated their inquiries. In Rutherford's words, atomic research was "bound up with the urge and fascination of a search into one of the deepest secrets of nature."[15] The atomic scientists' desire to know nature flowed from sources deep within them and had profound religious and philosophical implications. In part, their impulse might be interpreted as the adult expression of what the conservationist Rachel Carson called "the sense of wonder." In Carson's observation, "a child's world is fresh and new and beautiful, full of wonder and excitement." She lamented that by adulthood most people lost "that clear-eyed vision, that true instinct for what is beautiful and awe-inspiring." She noted, however, that some people were able to retain it.[16]

As a child, Isidor Rabi, the 1944 Nobel laureate in physics, looked down a New York street one evening and saw the rising moon staring down at him. "It scared the hell out of me!" he recalled of that profound moment, and its magic remained with him for the rest of his life. When Robert Oppenheimer, the scientific director of the atomic bomb project, was a boy, the crystals in his mineral collection mesmerized him. His curiosity led him first to chemistry, then to physics. "As far as I can see," Leo Szilard wrote near the end of his life, "I was born a scientist. I believe that many children are born with an inquisitive mind, the mind of a scientist, and I assume that I became a scientist because in some ways I remained a child." Edward Teller believed that his father's enjoyment of the mountains inspired his own love of them, but he recalled that his "interest in mathematics was self-generated. From earliest childhood, in a barely remembered way, I have had an unrelenting desire to understand. Soon after our summer vacation [to the mountains], when I was about four and a half years old, I began consistently spending time thinking about numbers."[17]

Richard Feynman's father, Melville, was a salesman with frustrated scientific aspirations who carefully nurtured his son's interest in natural phenomena. According to Feynman's biographer, when the two took walks near their home in Far Rockaway, New York, the father "would turn over stones and tell [his son] about the ants and the worms or the stars and the waves." Robert Wilson enjoyed the practical tinkering, repairing, and fabricating that took place in the blacksmith shop of his uncle's Wyoming ranch, and he and a friend built an early version of a hang glider, which they flew over the prairie. Yet the practitioner of cowboy physics also was a romantic who later recalled having "a very strong feeling about nature." In particular, the Wyoming landscape sparked his sense of wonder: "A sunset or looking at a mountain . . . I remember being strongly affected by that and wanting to know more about it. A kind of reverence for nature, and desire to identify with it." He believed that such feelings were a hidden part of the cowboy tradition, "a 'sissy' part," he said, "which doesn't normally . . . show through."[18]

The sense of wonder that the atomic scientists brought to their work can be interpreted as part of a widespread emotional, intellectual, and spiritual response among modern people to nature's awe-inspiring features.[19] Bohr, Oppenheimer, Rabi, Szilard, Teller, and many others knew well the deep feelings experienced while traversing a remote mountain pass or wandering along a lonely, windswept shore. But mountains, canyons, and oceans alone did not inspire such sentiments; so did the quantum nature of atoms. If anything, the downward shift in scale only intensified the feeling. Here was the power and paradox of the atomic sublime: the smaller the physicists went, the more they could understand. "We touched the nerve of the universe," said Victor Weisskopf. "It was a great revolution that allowed us for the first time in history to get at the root of the matter—why are leaves green, why are metals hard, why are the mountains so high and not higher." Physics, Rabi concluded in middle age, was "infinite," and it had led him to perceive "the mystery of it: how very different it is from what you can see, and how profound nature is." When a graduate student brought a scientific finding to him, he would ask: "Does it bring you near to God?"[20]

One scientist came so close to the divine that it may have diverted his attention from his scientific objectives. Robert Oppenheimer loved the poetry of John Donne and read the *Bhagavad Gita* in the original Sanskrit, and his spiritual emotions extended to his physics. "It was as if he were aiming at initiating his audience into Nature's divine mysteries," Abraham Pais recalled of an Oppenheimer lecture. Rabi, ironically, believed that Oppenheimer's reverence posed a problem: "His interest in religion . . . resulted in a feeling for the mystery of the universe that surrounded him almost like a fog. He saw physics clearly . . . but at the border he tended to feel that there was much more to the mysterious and the novel than there actually was."[21]

Nonetheless, for Oppenheimer as for others, the sense of wonder was crucial to the study of quantum physics. For some scientists, the experience of sublime landscapes helped them to imagine the sublime geography of atoms. During the 1920s and 1930s, Niels Bohr often retreated to his summer home at Tisvilde, a dispersed rural community about thirty miles north of Copenhagen. Through forests of birch, spruce, and pine, across moorland of heather and along the seashore, Bohr took long walks in the company of family, friends, and colleagues. The landscape, he believed, stimulated his intellectual creativity. He "felt . . . that here he received inspiration," wrote his biographer, that "here his mind was in tune with nature."[22] Robert Oppenheimer had somewhat the same experience at Perro Caliente, his log cabin and 154-acre ranch in the mountains of northern New Mexico. Oppenheimer first saw the rustic dwelling in 1928, while on a horseback ride. Perched in a meadow at an elevation of some ninety-five hundred feet in the Sangre de Cristo range, the cabin offered a view, framed by ponderosa pines, of the mountains and the Pecos Valley. Oppenheimer often visited Perro Caliente during summer breaks from his academic duties at the University of California at Berkeley, and hikes and horseback rides into the nearby wilderness nourished him spiritually and intellectually. "My two great loves are physics and New Mexico," he wrote to a friend in 1929. "It's a pity that they can't be combined."[23]

In the aesthetic sensibility that informed their engagement of both terrestrial and atomic nature, the scientists who created the bomb had much in common with artists. The sublime is not just an objective natural condition; it is also an aesthetic, culturally influenced way of seeing, analyzing, and depicting things of great magnitude. In their own way, the physicists—especially those inclined toward the theoretical end of the work—were as able as any poet or painter in reflecting on the beauty and wonder that surrounded them. Niels Bohr is a good example. Tisvilde appealed not only to him but also to painters, sculptors, and writers. Bohr admired these artists and patronized their work; in return, they visited him frequently and were among his closest friends. Bohr was a kindred spirit whose shimmering schematic depiction of the atom was his contribution to the modern movement.[24]

Bohr was not alone among physicists in his aesthetic impulses. Edward Teller loved poetry and classical music and often contemplated the atom while playing his piano late into the night.[25] But of all the physicists who helped create the bomb, Richard Feynman perhaps most resembled an artist. Eccentric and irreverent, he thought intuitively, in rhythms, sounds, textures, and images. When he worked on a problem, he sometimes rolled on the floor, murmuring and drumming his fingers, imagining himself inside an atom. He generally did not care for poetry, but a line from Nabokov caught his attention: "Space is a swarming in the eyes; and time a singing in the ears." A crucial component of Feynman's method was drumming. Long after midnight, he could be found in his room, beating his bongo drums. At times his ability bordered on the mystical; although he wasn't certain how he did it, he could judge the accuracy of a complex mathematical calculation simply by the numbers' relationships or by their "smoothness." Eventually, he perfected schematic "Feynman diagrams" that expressed his unique perspective on the behavior of subatomic particles. "He had a physical picture of the way things happen," wrote his friend and fellow physicist Freeman Dyson, "and the picture gave him the solutions directly with a minimum of calculation." Dyson's summation of Feynman might just as well have described abstract expressionist art: "He had this wonderful vision of the world as a woven texture of world lines in space and time with everything moving freely, and the various possible histories all added together at the end to describe what happened."[26]

Finally, there was Oppenheimer. "It was evening when we came to the river / with a low moon over the desert / that we had lost in the mountains, forgotten, / what with the cold and the sweating / and the ranges barring the sky," he wrote in "Crossing," published in 1928. Oppenheimer carried a poet's sensibility into all parts of his life—art, film, literature, music, women, food, drink, and of course, his work. As two of his biographers have noted, he "loved quantum mechanics for the sheer beauty of its abstractions."[27]

By the late 1930s, the world of Oppenheimer and other atomic scientists was about to change. The adventure of pure research, the horseback rides through pine-covered mountains and the long walks on the beach, the brilliant desert sunsets and the sense of wonder, the tickling of ivory and the beating of drums, all were about to combine with the instrumentalist imperatives of the twentieth century's most devastating war.

On a snowy November afternoon in 1942, Robert Oppenheimer and General Leslie Groves of the Army Corps of Engineers arrived at the Los Alamos Boys' School, situated on a narrow eastern extension of the Pajarito Plateau. They believed that the school and its collection of rustic log buildings might be just the place for a secret facility at which to build an atomic bomb. As they surveyed the site, the pair presented a study in contrasts. Oppenheimer was in his late thirties, thin—around 130 pounds—and possessed of luminous blue eyes. Only slightly older—in his mid-forties—and about the same height, Groves packed up to 250 pounds on a massive torso that bulged above and below his belt. His short, neatly cropped mustache was consistent with a severe, nonsense military demeanor. Egotistical, harsh, and judgmental, Groves was loathed by his subordinates. "The biggest S.O.B. I have ever worked for," one said. Yet they respected him for his discipline, intelligence, and ability to get things done. Nothing in either man's background suggested that the two would ever be able to cooperate. Oppenheimer was the romantic, mystical aesthete, the lover of sublime natural beauty; Groves was the quintessential utilitarian, a commander of bulldozers in an agency devoted to moving earth and harnessing rivers.[28] Yet there they were, in the falling snow, working together.

A series of dramatic events had delivered them to this place. In December 1938 and January 1939, a team of German researchers—Otto Hahn, Fritz Strassmann, Lise Meitner, and Otto Frisch—discovered that a neutron particle could split an atom in two, releasing light, heat, radioactive gamma rays, and two or more neutrons. Borrowing a term from biology, they called the process fission. It was a stunning, unexpected revelation. Here was evidence that mankind at last might have access to the atom's vast power. In theory, the neutrons would strike other atomic nuclei, creating an exponential chain reaction that, if uncontrolled, would escalate until it yielded an explosion of phenomenal proportions.

The outbreak of the Second World War in September 1939 motivated the atomic scientists to turn that theory into a reality. Physicists working for Britain made the first practical calculations. Across the Atlantic, the United States government moved slowly, but in 1941 it began aggressively assisting the scientific effort to build the bomb. In September 1942, the army took control of the work, assigned it to the Manhattan Engineer District, headquartered in New York City but "without territorial limits," and placed General Groves in charge. Groves then selected Oppenheimer to be the director of the project's Los Alamos laboratory.[29]

Despite their differences, Groves and Oppenheimer agreed on certain matters. Both believed in the absolute necessity of building the bomb and that, for purposes of efficiency, the work should be centralized. As they surveyed the area, both acknowledged that Los Alamos was the place to accomplish the task. Oppenheimer liked it because there, at last, he could combine his two great loves, physics and New Mexico. Groves liked it because of its isolation, which he insisted was essential to the secrecy and security of the project. As the two men drove back down the winding gravel road to the Rio Grande Valley, the future was set. Within days, the army took steps to purchase Los Alamos and have additional land transferred from the U.S. Forest Service.[30] Soon, the bulldozers and the construction crews arrived on the school grounds. Beauty and utility, science and construction, began to blend. It would not be a smooth mixture. Warily, uneasily, the scientists found a way to adapt their culture and values to the needs of the military emergency. The war drew out their latent utilitarian, even violent, proclivities, but they struggled to hold on to their belief that science—including their work on the Manhattan Project—was an expression of hope and optimism, a means to a better world.

As humanitarians who had reservations about the military application of scientific knowledge, the scientists might have resisted Oppenheimer's impassioned plea to come to Los Alamos in spring 1943. But mostly they did not. They had various reasons for wanting to participate, but most important was the fear that Nazi Germany would build the bomb first. Many of the Jewish refugee scientists had lost family and friends to the fascists, and they in particular had reason to fear a German victory in a race for the bomb.[31] For some, support for the project grew from experiences peculiar to their childhoods. In his youth, Edward Teller had taken delight in music, mountains, and numbers, but the terror of war, revolution, anti-Semitism, darkness, and nightmares also shaped his young psyche. In fact, the numbers that Teller loved had given him a sense of security in an insecure world.[32] Those numbers and the anxieties they calmed but could not dispel brought him to Los Alamos.

A vision of a higher purpose for the bomb gave some atomic scientists additional incentive to heed Oppenheimer's call. Like Oppenheimer, the other Americans felt a patriotic obligation to defend the country they loved, and many, refugee or American, believed their work could become part of a larger struggle of freedom against oppression. In this frame of mind, a number of them began to imagine the bomb as a humanitarian force. Some believed the bomb might actually save lives and shorten the conflict, and a few even began to invest the bomb with a high moral purpose. Its ferocious power, they contended, might make future wars so destructive as to be unwinnable—and therefore unthinkable. More than anyone else, Niels Bohr advanced this seemingly contradictory position, which he subsumed in a philosophy that he called "complementarity." Not only would the bomb establish peace, Bohr believed, but controlling it would require the nations of the Earth to create an "open world" in which they must share scientific knowledge for the betterment of all. The only question was whether the bomb had enough sheer might to produce this outcome. When Bohr arrived at Los Alamos on December 30, 1943, he immediately asked Oppenheimer, "Is it really big enough?"[33]

Making it big enough, however, required resources and expertise that scientists alone could not provide. Here was another atomic paradox. The big (meaning powerful) bomb would require a relatively small amount—perhaps a matter of pounds—of uranium 235 or plutonium 239. In size, the weapon's core would approximate a melon, or perhaps an orange. Yet extracting just a few pounds of rare isotope from nature and putting the material in a bomb was extraordinarily difficult and would require a production complex of staggering proportions. Among U.S. government agencies, the Army Corps of Engineers was best suited to the task. The Corps already had supervised several massive constructions, including Bonneville Dam on the Columbia River and the Pentagon building just outside Washington, D.C. In scale, the Manhattan Project topped even these. By 1945, the Corps oversaw a bomb-making operation that included some 870 square miles in New Mexico, Tennessee, and Washington state; hundreds of buildings, some of them the largest on the planet; dozens of giant corporate contractors; and some six hundred thousand workers.[34]

Such extensive facilities required a strong, skilled leader, and the army had one in Leslie Groves. A graduate of the U.S. Military Academy at West Point, one of the nation's finest engineering schools, the hard-driving Groves was a master manager—a manipulator—of people and material resources. He was thoroughly imbued with the Corps's instrumentalist, control-of-nature ethos. That rigid, disciplined approach had guided him through many engineering exploits, including his supervision of the construction of the Pentagon. He even had carried it into his personal life. A vacation in the American West during the summer of 1931, for example, followed a "well orchestrated plan devised by the patriarch" and enabled the Groves family to "experience the vastness and diversity of America" at historic sites, Indian reservations, national parks, and Hoover Dam, then under construction and soon the nation's premier example of brute-force technology.[35] Groves carried his domineering mentality into the Manhattan Project, which to him continued America's conquest of the frontier. As an army brat raised on western military posts, he had been "dismayed, wondering what was left for me to do now that the West was won," but the "Atomic Age" gave him the opening he thought he had missed. "We know now that when man is willing to make the effort," he wrote, "he is capable of accomplishing virtually anything."[36]

The atomic scientists were ambivalent about the militarized environment that Groves prepared for them at Los Alamos. Oppenheimer, Teller, and others respected and trusted the general, but some had their doubts. Even Groves's supporters recognized that the culture of science clashed with the culture of the military. Science required free inquiry, open communication, and unhindered debate, and Groves's plan to commission the scientists as officers, his zeal for secrecy, and the army's unceasing surveillance were antithetical to those values. Richard Feynman delighted in picking locks, evading security, writing encoded love letters to his wife, and other pranks that mocked the rigid military discipline. Leo Szilard despised Groves. After one difficult encounter with the general, he asked his fellow scientists: "How can you work with people like that?"[37]

The ambivalence that the scientists felt about the military extended to Los Alamos itself and was often shared by their families. "It is set in the pines at 7,300 feet in very fine country," Oppenheimer had written to the scientists and their families. "The country is a mixture of mountain country such as you have met in other parts of the Rockies, and the adobe-housed, picturesque, southwest desert that you have seen in Western Movies."[38] Yet their initial reaction was far different from what Oppenheimer might have intended with his romantic portrayal. The remoteness of the site unsettled them. "Nobody could think straight in a place like that," said the urbane Szilard to his colleagues at the University of Chicago. "Everybody who goes there will go crazy."[39]

Although few other inhabitants of Los Alamos shared Szilard's extreme assessment, many were less than completely happy with the place. "Not Quite Eden," Jane Wilson, Robert Wilson's wife, titled her reminiscence of the time she spent there. Among the many inconveniences of life behind the town's barbed wire fence, problems with the water supply were arguably the most irritating. In winter, the pipes froze; in summer, the inconsistent trickle flowing from the tap carried sediment and tiny red worms. Compounding such hardships were rationing and resource shortages. The milk supply was unreliable, at least until the families persuaded the army to buy milk from local producers instead of shipping it from Texas. And there was the incessant construction as the town's population soared to more than six thousand. Ramshackle buildings, all painted green, rose on expanses of bare soil. "I am responsible for ruining a beautiful place," Oppenheimer concluded.[40]

For their part, Groves and the army were just as ambivalent about the scientific community. Groves respected and trusted Oppenheimer, Teller, Rabi, Ernest Lawrence, and some others, but mostly he viewed the scientists as a bunch of impractical eccentrics. "At great expense," he told a group of army officers, "we have gathered on this mesa the largest collection of crackpots ever seen." He later acknowledged a culture clash between "scientists with little experience outside the academic field; and uniformed members of the armed services, nearly all nonprofessionals, who had little experience in, or liking for, the academic life."[41] Groves's assessment was, in part, a stereotype. Szilard, whom Groves despised as much as Szilard despised him, had served in the Austro-Hungarian army during the First World War. Colonel Kenneth Nichols, Groves's aide, had a Ph.D. from the University of Iowa, and Norris Bradbury had a Ph.D. from the University of California, had been a professor, and was a lieutenant commander in the U.S. Navy.[42] In a general sense, though, Groves was correct about the differences, which could yield bitter consequences. Before the war, for example, Oppenheimer had associated with communists. Convinced that he must be a Soviet agent, army intelligence officers investigated him with such zeal that they overlooked the spies who actually had infiltrated Los Alamos.[43]

In spite of their differences, the atomic scientists and the army engineers shared the desire to build the bomb and win the war. Equally important, the disciplinary—and cultural—boundary between them could be indistinct. Some scientists, it turned out, were not so different from engineers, especially those experimentalists who were adept with tools and laboratory apparatus and were most interested in practical results. The Manhattan Project highlighted an important characteristic of the physics profession—the distinctions between the experimental physicists and the theoreticians, the artistic dreamers and aesthetes like Oppenheimer, Teller, and Bohr, who used their powers of imagination and mathematical reasoning to discern the atom's features.[44]

Perhaps the best example of an experimental physicist was Ernest O.

Lawrence, the director of the Radiation Laboratory at Berkeley and a key participant in the Manhattan Project. A clean-cut man with wire-rimmed glasses, Lawrence had an entrepreneurial, can-do approach to life. As a boy, he had been less interested in the beauties of nature than in radio and the practical applications of electronics. To earn money for college, he sold aluminum kitchenware door-to-door. As a young assistant professor at the University of California, Lawrence invented the cyclotron, an achievement for which he won the 1939 Nobel Prize.[45] The massive instrument used an electrical field to accelerate particles along a circular path and into a target, shattering the particles and allowing scientists to examine the fundamental nature of matter. Tellingly, the popular term for such a device was *atom smasher*. The Calutron, another cyclotron device that Lawrence developed, used "raw brute force," as the physicist Robert Wilson said, to separate uranium 235 for the bomb. Oppenheimer appreciated the contrast between himself and his friend, whom he admired: "His interest was so primarily active [and] instrumental," while "mine [was] just the opposite." Their differences extended through all aspects of their lives, right down to their aesthetic tastes. Whereas Oppenheimer liked unusual foods and fine restaurants, Lawrence preferred barbequed spareribs, fried rice, and Mai Tais at Trader Vic's.[46]

Even the theoreticians, however, Oppenheimer included, had a practical side. Edward Teller's boyhood enthusiasms encompassed mountains, music, and numbers but also structures and machines. Leo Szilard was a practical tinkerer interested in electronics who studied engineering before switching to physics. Richard Feynman had built radios as a boy, and as an MIT graduate, he knew his way around a machine shop.[47] Before the Manhattan Project, nothing about Oppenheimer would have suggested that he could think and work like an engineer. One of his closest friends had said that he could not even run a hamburger stand. Always the dreamer and the poet, his laboratory skills were notoriously bad, and his Berkeley office was a mess. The largest number of people he had supervised at one time was fifteen graduate students. Groves had wanted Lawrence to become the scientific director at Los Alamos, but the experimentalist couldn't be spared from his work at the Berkeley Radiation Laboratory. Despite Oppenheimer's weaknesses, Groves believed his brilliance and ambition would make him an excellent alternative, as would a charismatic but plastic personality capable of adapting to the army and persuading other scientists to cooperate with it. The call to duty and the war's higher purpose roused Oppenheimer and summoned his hidden talents, surprising colleagues who had doubted his ability to meet the demands of the position. He proved to be an energetic administrator, a superb troubleshooter, and, as his biographers have observed, capable of "seemingly instantaneous comprehension of any facet of engineering."[48]

Ultimately, Los Alamos became a site of collaboration and compromise between the atomic scientists and the Army Corps of Engineers. The scientists got much of what they wanted. They remained civilian employees of the Manhattan Project, and they carried on a vigorous, uncensored dialogue among themselves. They and their families got the army to try, at least, to make Los Alamos more livable, to bring them milk, start a school, site new buildings along natural contours, and leave a few pine trees standing. General Groves got some things he wanted, too. The surveillance and censorship remained, as did the security. The scientists could talk among themselves, but that talk would go no further than their elite circle, and much of it would take place behind the inner barbed-wire perimeter that surrounded the Tech Area, where they worked with the engineers to make calculations, conduct experiments, and fabricate bomb components.[49]

The natural beauty of the Los Alamos area helped reconcile the atomic scientists and their families to their predicament, consoling and inspiring them, relaxing them so that they could focus on their work, and allowing them to believe that their ultimate purpose was to build civilization, not destroy it. "After the first shock" of the isolated, ramshackle settlement, wrote Kay Mark, "we got used to it, and when we went outdoors we were conscious instead of the exuberant pervasive sunshine, the clear air, and the serene mountains in the distance." Hans Bethe, the project's chief theoretician, recalled that although the conditions at first made him uneasy, the environment was "absolutely beautiful." The physicist in charge of radioactivity studies, Emilio Segrè, soon came to appreciate the charms of Los Alamos. It was "a beautiful and savage country," he wrote, and he grew fond of his secluded laboratory, located in a log cabin that had once served as a ranger station. Segrè rhapsodized about the "purple and yellow asters" and Indian rock carvings that lined the route to the site, the "large rattlesnake" that he and other scientists encountered one day on their way to work, and the site itself: "The cabin-laboratory, in a grove shaded by huge broadleaf trees, occupied one of the most picturesque settings one could dream of."[50]

Outdoor activities were popular among the inhabitants of Los Alamos. The chemist George Kistiakowsky, the Manhattan Project's explosives expert, felled trees with plastic explosive to make "a nice little ski slope," which went into operation in late 1944. Some 150 people joined the Sawyer's Hill Ski Tow Association, including Enrico Fermi, Hans Bethe, Robert Bacher, and Niels Bohr.[51] There were other activities, too, such as horseback riding, fly-fishing, baseball, and golf. "There was a feeling of mountain resort, in addition to army camp," said Françoise Ulam, the French wife of the Polish mathematician Stanislaus Ulam.[52]

Of all the outdoor pursuits at Los Alamos, hiking and mountain climbing best combined the atomic scientists' love of nature with their intellectual work. These mountaineering activities cleared their minds and assisted their thought processes. "The ability to hike in the mountains on Sundays was one of the things that kept one sane," recalled Cyril Smith, a member of the British delegation, whose favorite hiking partner was none other than Edward Teller. For a number of scientists who were accomplished technical climbers, the ascent of tall peaks yielded deep insights. "Very often on a Sunday," wrote Joseph Hirschfelder, Hans Bethe "would climb to the top of Lake Peak" in the Sangre de Cristo range "with Enrico Fermi and some of his other friends and sit there in the sunshine discussing physics problems. This is how many discoveries were made."[53]

Some Los Alamos residents liked to hike in the canyons that cut into the Pajarito Plateau. On the day he arrived, T. A. Welton joined Richard Feynman on a hike into the newly named Omega Canyon. As Welton gasped for breath, Feynman told him the secrets of the atomic bomb. In the fall of 1944, Laura Fermi led Niels Bohr on a hike into nearby Frijoles Canyon, "where his mind could focus on the marvels of nature that surrounded us." Bohr, some sixty years old, took great delight in a skunk, his first view of the North American mammal. As he jumped across a stream, "his eyes glowed with pleasure." When Fermi and Bohr arrived at the mouth of the canyon, they "stopped in silence" to gaze at the Rio Grande, the cacti, the canyon wall, and a puffy cloud against the blue sky. "There is a sense of reverence in the perception of some landscapes," Fermi recalled of that enchanted moment.[54]

The scientists fashioned a community that embodied their life-affirming values. Oppenheimer, who would be known as the "father of the atomic bomb," did more than anyone to foster that community. "We shall all be one large family doing work inside the wire," he told his fellow scientists in 1943. Then, by coaxing, cajoling, sympathizing, encouraging, chastising, troubleshooting, and inspiring, Oppie, as everyone called him, pulled them into a cohesive group.

Evidently he relished his paternalistic role. One scientist recalled Oppenheimer's Sunday custom of riding his chestnut horse, Chico, through town, "greeting each of the people he passed with a wave of his pork-pie hat and a friendly remark. He knew everyone who lived in Los Alamos, from the top scientists to the children of the Spanish-American janitors—they were all Oppenheimer's family."[55]

The Los Alamos community was not limited to the scientists and their dependents but expanded to meet the requirements of the army and the exigencies of building the bomb. Civilian maintenance workers moved from nearby Hispano villages and Indian pueblos and from around the United States and took up residence at Los Alamos. On most weekday mornings, women from San Ildefonso Pueblo arrived by bus to provide maid service. The maids enabled the scientists' wives to serve as secretaries, laboratory assistants, and calculators in the computations division, which minimized the town's resident population and limited the number of people who might jeopardize security.

Los Alamos was hardly a democratic, multiethnic utopia; a hierarchy differentiated the scientists and their families from the military personnel, technicians, maintenance staff, and their dependents.[56] Nevertheless, the town was unusually integrated for the 1940s and provided numerous opportunities for creative cross-cultural exchanges. Bernice Brode, wife of the physicist Robert Brode, remembered Pop Chalee, a Taos Pueblo artist "who wore artistic clothes and long blue-black braids that reached below the waist," lecturing at Fuller Lodge on Indian customs. Brode and others also fondly recalled the multicultural event at San Ildefonso in December 1945, which combined square dancing with Indian styles of dancing. As the evening wore on, the dancing and drumming intensified until Montoya, Brode's friend and the pueblo's governor, climbed atop "a chair and shouted above the din, 'This is the Atomic Age—this is the Atomic Age!'"[57]

At the heart of Los Alamos's family were children. Husbands and wives brought their offspring to Los Alamos, but many wives also gave birth while there, a biological increase that anticipated the nation's postwar baby boom. In June 1944, the Los Alamos medical director observed that "approximately one-fifth of the married women are now in some stage of pregnancy." Eighty babies arrived during the first year; all told, some two hundred were born between 1943 and 1945. In nearby Santa Fe, a rumor circulated that the secret facility on the mesa was a camp for pregnant members of the Women's Army Corps (WAC). Robert and Kitty Oppenheimer, who already had a three-year-old son,

Peter, exemplified the fertility trend. In December 1944, Kitty gave birth to a daughter, nicknamed Tyke (and later called Toni).[58]

The arrival of the new children heightened the tensions between the army and the scientific community. Groves responded with alarm to the added stress on the town's limited resources and physical space. A popular Los Alamos limerick captured his reaction: "The General's in a stew / He trusted you and you / He thought you'd be scientific / Instead you're just prolific / And what is he to do?"[59] A model officer, Groves had disciplined and compartmentalized the most intimate parts of his own life. As a young bachelor, he had refrained from casual relationships with women, shunned prostitutes, abstained from alcohol, and despised French culture (his sole sensual outlet appears to have been sweets, especially chocolate). On the first day of his marriage, he told his wife, Grace, never to ask him about his work. Grace had borne children in 1923 and 1928, apparently according to plan, and by the 1940s, husband and wife slept in separate bedrooms.[60] It appears that the general was temperamentally unsuited to handling a situation in which biology and sentiment intruded on military structure. He could supervise the construction of a bomb, but coping with the messiness of a baby boom was an entirely different matter.

Frustrated, Groves complained to Oppenheimer, but the general received no help from the physicist, whose own disorderly life was a monument to sensual indulgence and romantic passions and whose wife already was pregnant. Oppenheimer liked women, including expectant ones, and he welcomed their children. "He really was a man of women," recalled his secretary, Anne Wilson. "Women at Los Alamos who were pregnant would say, 'The only one who would understand was Robert.'" Although Oppenheimer could empathize with women, in this instance he could not extend the same kind of feeling to Groves. In the words of his biographers, the father of the atomic bomb replied to the general "that the duties of a scientific director did not include birth control."[61]

Like their parents, the children of Los Alamos grew to appreciate the undeveloped landscape around them. Joan Bainbridge, daughter of Kenneth Bainbridge, the physicist who directed the first atomic bomb test, was nearly seven when she and her family arrived in 1943. Joan, her brother, and their friends loved the woods near her family's apartment, and they "became for us a wonderful thing." They were "different from New Hampshire, the only woods I was familiar with. There were these tall pines. We immediately took to the woods ... and created our own kinds of imaginary world there. . . . It gave us a great freedom." Teenagers, too, valued the natural environment. Johnnie Martinez, who came to Los Alamos from Santa Fe in 1943 when his father took a job as a janitor, liked its open landscape and its social inclusiveness. "You could hike in the canyons," he recalled. "You could go fishing. You didn't have to worry about 'These people don't like you and these people do like you.'"[62]

Of all the Los Alamos children, those born and raised in the town perhaps loved it the most and best exemplified its complicated convergence of science, nature, and military necessity. David Bradbury, born in 1944, son of the physicist Norris Bradbury, recognized that his interest in natural history and his "reverence for the natural world" grew out of his childhood experience of the New Mexico landscape. Later in his life, after earning a Ph.D. in biogeography and returning to Los Alamos, he reflected on the values he had derived from the place. He believed that weapons might be necessary to reduce the planet's unsustainably large human population, but "I am not pro-war," he said. "I'm mostly strongly pro-nature, pro-earth, pro-tree."[63]

BABY BOOM

While children gestated in the wombs of Los Alamos women, the bomb took shape in the laboratories of the Tech Area. Day after day, hour after hour, the scientists pushed to bring the weapon into the world, to advance it from conception to fruition. This part of their work most resembled engineering, and they focused so intently on the process that they did not have the time and energy to concentrate just as hard on its consequences. Furthermore, it was difficult for them to separate scientific research from its application. At what point, at what moment, was a scientist no longer a scientist but a bomb builder? Eventually, however, circumstances compelled some of them to reconsider what they were doing. Should they continue? Should they bring into existence such a weapon? Did humanity need it? Virtually all decided that they should press on, and they held fast to their belief that the bomb, however objectionable, must affirm life, must stop the war and make the world a better place. This final decision was crucial. As the moment to use the bomb approached, the atomic scientists fully transmuted the pursuit of atomic beauty into the production of atomic terror.

The scientists faced two important tasks in building the weapon. They needed enough of the right kind of fissionable material to create the critical mass necessary for a chain reaction and a spontaneous explosion, and they had to incorporate this material into a device of such size, shape, and weight that an airplane could deliver it to a target.

Of these two tasks, the first was by far the most difficult. Either uranium 235 or plutonium 239, each of which fissioned more easily and emitted more neutrons than did other isotopes (or forms) of the same elements, was necessary for the bomb. Isolating even a few pounds of U-235 or Pu-239 posed a formidable challenge. Uranium ore for the Manhattan Project came from Shinkolobwe Mine in the Belgian Congo, where indentured laborers dug it out of the Earth. The Shinkolobwe ore was about 65 percent uranium oxide, which General Groves judged to be unusually rich. Of the pure uranium in the uranium oxide, about 99.3 percent consisted of the most common, and stable, uranium isotope, U-238. The rest, about 0.7 percent, was the prized U-235. At Berkeley, Ernest Lawrence began using his giant cyclotron to isolate U-235. Compounding the uranium with other elements to form a gas, he passed it through the cyclotron's magnetic fields, separating it into beams according to isotope. Directed into a collector, the atoms in the U-235 beam lost their electrical charge and deposited as silvery-white metal flakes. Lawrence's process, however, was glacially slow. In one month of continuous operation, it yielded only one microgram of U-235: one-millionth of a gram, or one-millionth of roughly one-third of an ounce, or, to put it another way, the equivalent of about one-millionth of one-sixth of a candy bar. To build a bomb, Oppenheimer wanted approximately one billion times that amount: one hundred kilograms, around twenty-two pounds.[64]

To meet Oppenheimer's seemingly impossible demand, the army built the Clinton Engineer Works at Oak Ridge, Tennessee, a vast complex that encompassed hundreds of buildings and soon employed some one hundred thousand people. Gargantuan cyclotrons with electromagnets weighing up to ten thousand tons—so powerful that they tugged at boot nails and hair pins and pulled fourteen-ton water tanks inches out of alignment—operated day and night. Even that wasn't enough, so Groves added a parallel gaseous diffusion plant. In this process, uranium hexafluoride gas passed through microscopic holes in porous nickel membranes. Lighter molecules containing U-235 diffused through the barrier before the heavier U-238 molecules did so. Repeated again and again, gaseous diffusion yielded minute quantities of enriched uranium that contained 70 percent or more U-235. It was a lengthy, tedious process, and the entire apparatus required a breathtakingly huge building that enclosed forty-five acres.[65] All this for one bomb.

As contractors erected the Oak Ridge facility and engineers began collecting

U-235, Manhattan Project employees at the Hanford Engineer Works in the desert of central Washington state busied themselves collecting Pu-239. Hanford was another immense facility, the centerpiece of which was a set of chain-reacting atomic piles—stacks of processed U-238—which Du Pont corporation engineers called reactors. Inside the reactor piles, neutrons released by controlled fission transmuted the U-238 into Pu-239. Du Pont then subjected the Pu-239 to a chemical purification process in enormous concrete buildings that workers called Queen Marys, in reference to the ocean liner launched in 1934. The end product of Hanford's atomic alchemy was mere pounds of a silvery metal—plutonium—that tarnished yellow, blue, and plum in the open air.[66]

It was a strange but useful substance. Although an element—one of the fundamental forms of matter—it was, as the *Encyclopaedia Britannica* explains, "not primeval," meaning it was not present at the creation of the universe. Humans first encountered it early in 1941 when the chemist Glenn Seaborg and a team of researchers caused it to form inside Lawrence's Berkeley cyclotron. Scientists later discovered minute traces of it in uranium ore, where it had been "naturally produced by neutron irradiation." Whatever its origins, the Pu-239 isotope was exceptionally lethal. Because of its spontaneous emission of alpha particles, a low-level, relatively benign form of radiation stopped by human skin, it was warm to the touch, "like a live rabbit," according to one observer. Ingested in the body, it became one of the most toxic substances known to humankind. Most important for the bomb designers, Pu-239 fissioned readily—almost too readily—and thus was excellent for a bomb.[67]

As America's two great atomic complexes slowly plucked minute quantities of fissile material from the Earth's ancient fundament, the atomic scientists at Los Alamos worked feverishly to transform that material into a weapon, the second of their major tasks. Oppenheimer organized the researchers—most of them ensconced inside the flimsy wood buildings of the Tech Area—into several main divisions, notably experimental physics, theoretical physics, chemistry and metallurgy, and ordnance. Group leaders in each division reported to division heads, who then reported to Oppenheimer.[68]

Beyond this basic structure, Oppenheimer and his scientists insisted on informality, egalitarianism, and intellectual freedom. Junior scientists regularly challenged their superiors. Richard Feynman, for example, often told Hans Bethe that he was "crazy" or "mad" or that his ideas were "nuts." Bethe welcomed Feynman's irreverence, believing that his ideas, to be valid, must withstand the younger scientist's rigorous skepticism.[69] Oppenheimer further encouraged the intellectual openness of the laboratories by resisting the demands of army efficiency experts that he run the place according to the dictates of a time clock.[70] Such informality was conducive not only to wide-open thought and experimentation but also to free-ranging observation. Wondering about the potential physical effects of the bomb, a group of scientists decided to take a lesson from natural history and traveled into the desert near Flagstaff, Arizona, to examine Meteor Crater, 4,100 feet across, 570 feet deep, and thousands of years old. An absence of structure also carried risks. A family cat wandered into a laboratory and absorbed a lethal dose of radiation. Army veterinarians observed it closely as its hair fell out, its tongue swelled, and ulcers appeared on its skin. Then they euthanized it.[71]

Although they were absorbed in the technical problem of building the bomb, most of the scientists were never in so deep that they ignored completely the potential political and moral consequences of their actions. As the bomb designs progressed and then as the bomb itself took physical shape, many of the scientists expressed doubts. From the beginning of the project, some had struggled to reconcile the bomb with their scruples. Isidor Rabi, a devout Jew convinced that science was a holy endeavor, never went on the Manhattan Project payroll, never lived at Los Alamos, and served only as a special adviser to Oppenheimer. Robert Wilson agonized about his participation in the project. He wanted to be persuaded that he was doing the right thing, but the earnest, square-jawed young man could never completely overcome his feelings to the contrary.[72] Now, as the moment to use the bomb loomed, others began to share his doubts, and a crisis developed.

The atomic scientists reached a turning point late in 1944, when they realized that Nazi Germany, their major reason for enlisting in the Manhattan Project, was going to lose the European war. Unable to justify his participation any longer, Joseph Rotblat, another future Nobel laureate—in peace, not physics—quit.[73] Suddenly the scientists felt the need to confront directly the bomb's ethical implications. Must the United States drop the bomb on Japan? Must civilians suffer? What might be the bomb's long-term effect? Early in 1945, Wilson organized a forum, "The Impact of the Gadget on Civilization," and more discussions, formal and informal, soon followed. Doubts deepened with Germany's surrender in April and the discovery that the Nazis' own atomic bomb project had been woefully inadequate and had stalled much earlier. Some of the scientists produced petitions opposing the bomb on moral grounds, asserting that it would spark a new arms race with the Soviet Union, or asking the

United States government for a nonlethal demonstration before emissaries from the nations of the world. In July, an army poll of 150 atomic scientists revealed that 72 percent preferred that the United States openly demonstrate the bomb's power before dropping it on Japan.[74]

For some of the scientists, the future seemed to hang in the balance. Oppenheimer listened to the discussions and read the petitions, but he did not leave the growing doubts unchallenged. What right did they have, he countered, to decide before anyone else the course of events? What did scientists know about politics? Where should a demonstration take place? And what if it failed? Then, speaking softly but passionately, summoning the full measure of his persuasive powers, he appealed to their idealism, to their hope that the bomb would become a force for peace and the basis of an open world. Before nations abandoned war, he declared, people must first know the bomb's terrible devastation. Forever after, they would live in fear—gnawing, agonizing, omnipresent fear—but a fear that would ensure a world without war. That was the bomb's great promise. To realize that promise, the bomb must fall.[75]

Oppenheimer's charisma, the force of his atomic logic, and his depiction of a peaceful world won over some of the doubters and provided a moral guidepost for those who shared his certainty. Some, like Wilson, could not resist Oppenheimer's appeal, and they continued to follow his lead, although with trepidation. Rabi and Szilard, despite deep reservations, hung on. Others, including Bethe, Bohr, Fermi, Lawrence, Teller, and many more, stood firm with Oppenheimer.[76] But no matter what the scientists thought, there was no doubt among military and civil authorities about whether or not to use the weapon. General Groves, Secretary of War Henry Stimson, Secretary of State James Byrnes, and President Harry Truman never contemplated an alternative.[77] When the scientists joined the Manhattan Project, they had subjected themselves to political decision-makers over whom they exerted little control. The bomb was theirs, but they did not control its final disposition.

By the summer of 1945, the Manhattan Project scientists had brought into existence two types of the bomb. Little Boy, so named, measured 10 feet in length and 28 inches in diameter, weighed nearly 5 tons (of which about 140 pounds was enriched uranium, roughly the size of a football), and had a blunt nose and boxed tail fins. This was a gun-type bomb in which conventional explosives propelled a subcritical U-235 slug into a subcritical target of additional U-235. When the U-235 masses came together, their fissioning neutrons reached criticality, and a chain reaction yielded an explosion. The atomic scientists had tested Little Boy's potential by dropping ever-greater weights of U-235 through a hole in a subcritical mass of the same substance, until for a fraction of a second, as weight zipped through hole, they could detect the fission frenzy that preceded an atomic explosion. Richard Feynman, irreverent as always, called the dangerous experiment "tickling the dragon."[78]

The other bomb was Fat Man: egg-shaped, about 5 feet in diameter at its widest point, roughly 10.5 tons in weight (of which its softball-sized plutonium core totaled about 13.5 pounds), nearly 11 feet long, and also with tail fins. Fat Man was an implosion bomb suited to the unique characteristics of plutonium. The scientists had discovered that they could not propel subcritical masses of Pu-239 together fast enough to produce a full-scale detonation; neutrons fissioned faster than the moving slug and so produced only a premature, subcritical detonation—basically a dud. Thus the implosion design. When detonated, precisely shaped and fitted conventional explosives, called lenses, squeezed— or imploded—a subcritical ball of Pu-239 into a dense critical mass, thereby initiating the chain reaction. The advantage of Little Boy was its simplicity; its disadvantage was the extreme difficulty with which the Corps of Engineers gathered U-235. The advantage of Fat Man was the relative ease with which the Corps collected Pu-239; its disadvantage was its complex design. Almost until the very end, Oppenheimer and his scientists were not completely sure it would work.[79]

There are at least two ways to interpret the deep meaning of these technological fraternal twins and the scientific labor that birthed them. In one interpretation, fearful, aggressive men sought to dominate and exploit Mother Nature in the service of creating a weapon of terrifying power and malignity. This explanation is plausible, and much evidence supports it. Almost all the people directly responsible for creating the bomb were men. During the 1940s, patriarchal control and gender equality were hardly popular issues. Most men probably still thought about humanity and nature in terms of the male domination of a female nature. Not coincidentally, the atomic scientists gave the bombs masculine names, and they spoke of technical competence as masculine: a successful detonation was a "boy," while a dud was a "girl."[80] And certainly those manly bombs carried powerful charges of the dark emotions: anger, aggression, malice, and, especially, fear.

Another way to interpret the bomb's meaning requires a more complex, subtle sense of history and its possibilities. In this account, the men who created the bomb loved nature, did not in every instance categorize it as female, and did not necessarily want to dominate it. Feelings of awe and wonder motivated many of them to become scientists. Above all, they sought to understand nature, and they found great intellectual and emotional satisfaction in their study of it. When they worked on the bomb, fear and other dark impulses did drive them, but those emotions were deeply intertwined with profound—one might say sublime—feelings of hope and love.[81] The atomic scientists loved life, humanity, and nature, and they desperately wanted to see beyond the bomb to a better world. They experienced those feelings, moreover, in the company of women and children. Although women held few positions of official power and authority at Los Alamos, they participated in the project as physicists and mathematicians in a few cases and in larger numbers as technicians, secretaries, clerks, teachers, wives, and mothers. The male atomic scientists could not have built the bomb without them.[82] And without those women, there would have been no children. While Oppenheimer and his men fathered Fat Man and Little Boy, they also fathered Piggily, Tyke, David, and many more. In these familial relationships, perhaps, lies the bomb's greatest significance. Rather than the exclusive product of male scientists, the bomb was the offspring of an entire atomic community—men, women, and children—at the heart of which throbbed a powerful emotion that gave life its very purpose.[83] Fat Man and Little Boy indeed carried a considerable burden of darkness, but without love, they would have remained unborn.

Still, the bomb must drop, as Oppenheimer had argued, and so in July 1945 the atomic scientists readied it for use. They completed their final experiments and prepared their creation for delivery to the army. Their last great act was to test Fat Man. Tickling the dragon had convinced them beyond a shadow of a doubt that Little Boy would work. They were not so certain about Fat Man. If the lenses contained the slightest imperfection, the uneven implosion that resulted would fail to squeeze the plutonium ball into a critical mass. A test, therefore, was necessary. General Groves had already approved an 18-by-24-square-mile plot of desert in a remote corner of the Alamogordo Bombing Range, along an old route through central New Mexico that the Spaniards had called the Jornada del Muerto, the Journey of Death. Mountain ranges at the site promised to maintain the secrecy that had shrouded the bomb from the beginning.[84]

Manhattan Project personnel called the site Trinity. Although the name's precise origin is in doubt, it had obvious religious connotations. To some, it probably called to mind the Father, Son, and Holy Ghost of Christian belief.

To Oppenheimer, it may have evoked the Hindu trinity of Brahma, Vishnu, and Shiva. For Hindus as for physicists, matter and energy are never destroyed; they are only transformed. What Brahma creates, Vishnu preserves and Shiva reduces to primordial nature; and what Shiva destroys, Brahma refashions and Vishnu again sustains—an endless cycle of transfigurations that is the fundamental dynamic of the universe.[85]

By July 15, a handful of atomic scientists was putting into place the final pieces necessary for the test, which would take place early the next morning. At ground zero stood a 100-foot-high steel tower on top of which sat the bomb, its plutonium core enclosed in layers of explosive lenses and steel plates, the entire giant ball covered with detonator knobs and swathed in seemingly endless strands of electrical wire. That night, buses would bring the rest of the scientists from Los Alamos. At safe distances, in bunkers and trenches and from a nearby mountain, they would peer into the darkness and wait. When the countdown reached zero, an electrical charge would zap all the detonators at once, and a fierce unearthly light would signal the arrival of the world's atomic moment.[86]

Afternoon turned to evening, and the last of the day's heat waves shimmered from the desert floor. While Groves fretted over weather reports, others tried to find some way to preoccupy their minds and calm their nerves. George Kistiakowsky, the chemist who led the team that designed and fabricated the crucially important lenses, borrowed a jeep and drove into the desert "to look for rare cacti."[87] Alone atop the tower, Oppenheimer made sure Fat Man was set to go. "The bomb was Robert's baby," recalled Kenneth Bainbridge, the test site director, "and he follow[ed] every detail of its development until the very end."[88]

Having done as much as he could, Oppenheimer climbed down and returned to base camp several miles away, where he chatted with Cyril Smith about "family, home, and life on the mesa." Pausing from the conversation for a moment, the slender physicist gazed east toward the sheer wall of the darkening Sierra Oscura range. "Funny," he mused, "how the mountains always inspire our work."[89]

DEATH—AND RESURRECTION

Ten! Samuel Allison's amplified voice rang through the early morning air of the New Mexico desert, the first countdown in history. It was Monday, July 16, 1945, 5:29:35 a.m., Mountain War Time.[90]

Nine!

As the clock ran down, the atomic scientists and other personnel assumed their positions around ground zero. At South 10,000 yards (5.68 miles) stood the control center, a bunker made of reinforced concrete, massive oak beams, and earth. Inside were Oppenheimer, Bainbridge, Fermi, and Kistiakowsky; General Thomas Farrell, Groves's deputy; and others. About five miles beyond the control center, at the base camp, Groves waited with a group that included Rabi and James Conant, Nobel laureate and chief architect of the nation's early atomic policy. Some twenty miles to the northwest of zero, Bethe, Feynman, Lawrence, Teller, and many more looked down from Compania Hill. Ten miles or so beyond Bethe's group, the physicists May and Al Argos gazed through binoculars from their campsite atop Chupadera Peak. At Carrizozo, thirty miles to the east of Trinity, another scientific team, Elizabeth "Diz" Graves and her husband, Al, stood by with monitoring equipment at Harry Miller's Tourist Camp. Diz was seven months pregnant and didn't want to get too close.[91]

Eight!

And there were more. Joan Hinton, a graduate student who had worked on the experimental reactor at Los Alamos, stood on a low hill twenty-five miles from ground zero. Hinton and a friend had arrived at the site at sundown, on a motorcycle.[92] Dorothy McKibben, a close friend of Oppenheimer's and the office manager of 109 East Palace Avenue in Santa Fe, the disguised public face of the Manhattan Project, waited in her car atop Sandia Peak outside of Albuquerque.[93] From Sawyer's Hill ski run near Los Alamos, a group of women gazed southward.[94]

Seven!

"The air seemed empty and bitter cold, although it was July," recalled Jane Wilson, one of the Sawyer's Hill observers. "It was very dark and only when one's eyes became accustomed to the night could one make out the silhouettes of the pine trees against the starless sky. . . . It hardly seemed worthwhile to stand here, scanning the sky, cold and afraid."[95]

Six!

Closer to ground zero, scientists and soldiers shared some of her anxiety. For several nights running, Robert Wilson's nightmare had been the same: a misstep as he reached the top of the tower, an agonizing, slow-motion fall, and a jolting, sweat-soaked awakening just before he hit the ground. There was reason for Wilson and the other scientists to feel as they did: the relentless pace, the pressure to succeed, and, for Wilson and others, the moral burden.

Technical problems also had begun to intrude. That last night, thunderstorms had threatened to disrupt the test, although toward dawn the weather had cleared. Now, fears of malfunctions played through their heads. What if the bomb misfired, Groves worried, or its firing was delayed?[96]

And what if, many wondered, their elaborate preparations were simply wrong, and the bomb proved to be a complete dud? "Human calculation indicates that the experiment must succeed," said Bethe, the project's chief theoretician, in a speech to his colleagues before they boarded the buses. "But will nature act in conformity with our calculations?"[97]

Five!

And what if the bomb went to the opposite extreme and proved too powerful? Bethe and Teller already had determined that it would not exceed its predicted bounds—well before that, the chain reaction would diffuse and expend itself. Lawrence had added that "we're winning greater, not less, control over nature."[98]

Yet as the remaining time disappeared, no one could be certain. To underscore the point, Fermi had "suddenly offered to take wagers from his fellow scientists on whether the bomb would ignite the atmosphere, and if so, whether it would merely destroy New Mexico or destroy the world."[99]

Groves was annoyed with Fermi, but his own uncertainty was such that he had made sure that he would be separated from Oppenheimer and Farrell at the moment of detonation, "in case of trouble." At T-minus-twenty-minutes, Groves had departed the control center for the base camp.[100] Not only that, but he had instructed William Laurence of the *New York Times*, the only reporter present, to compose an article describing an accident in the New Mexico desert that claimed the lives of scientists, soldiers, and a single journalist.[101]

Four!

During the final seconds, some did as Groves had ordered: lie face down, eyes covered, feet toward ground zero. Others donned welder's glasses and looked squarely in the direction of the tower, now illuminated with floodlights. On Compania Hill, Bethe and Teller offered suntan lotion to their colleagues, and Teller put on dark glasses and a pair of heavy gloves.[102]

Three!

At the control center, Oppenheimer steadied himself against a post. "Lord," he muttered, "these affairs are hard on the heart."[103]

Two!

Those final seconds, Rabi recalled, were the longest he had ever experienced.[104]

One!

Had they done it? Were their breaths the last of what would soon be a pre-atomic past? Or had they failed?

Now!

The light, they agreed, was extraordinary. Its suddenness and warmth startled them, "like opening the heavy curtains of a darkened room to a flood of sunlight," recalled Teller; "like opening a hot oven with the sun coming out at sunrise," in the words of Philip Morrison; a "blinding light," wrote Jane Wilson, "like no other light one had ever seen." It was brilliant "beyond any comparison," Groves reported. "It blasted; it pounced; it bored its way right through you," remembered Rabi.[105]

Shock and sound waves followed instantly. Frank Oppenheimer, Robert's brother and also a Los Alamos physicist, later remembered "the thunder from the blast. It bounced on the rocks . . . and it never seemed to stop. . . . It just kept echoing back and forth in that Jornada del Muerto."[106]

Then a fireball arose, and above that a cloud shot skyward. The "huge ball of fire," Groves reported, was "equal to several suns in midday." Frank Oppenheimer remembered it as "brilliant purple, with all that radioactive glowing. And it just seemed to hang there forever." General Farrell described it as "golden, purple, violet, gray and blue." The "ball mushroomed and rose to a height of over ten thousand feet before it dimmed," Groves stated, and above that a "massive cloud . . . surged and billowed upward with tremendous power, reaching the substratosphere at an elevation of 41,000 feet."[107]

Emotions overwhelming reason, those present struggled to comprehend the spectacle that unfolded before them. Their words described nothing less than a transmutation of the atomic sublime. Submicroscopic particles so small that scientists could only imagine them had yielded a holocaust of stupefying power and size; the infinitely small had become the infinitely large. "I thought the explosion might set fire to the atmosphere and thus finish the earth," recalled Emilio Segrè, "even though I knew that this was not possible." Kistiakowsky was certain that this was how "the last millisecond of the earth's existence" would appear to people at some future end-time. A line from the *Bhagavad Gita* flashed through Robert Oppenheimer's brain: "Now I am become Death, the destroyer of worlds."[108]

Yet if the blast was terrifying, it also was beautiful. It was, General Farrell stated, the kind of "beauty the great poets dream about but describe most poorly and inadequately." Robert Serber concurred. "The grandeur and magnitude of the phenomenon," he exclaimed, "were completely breathtaking." Everyone, Groves reported, experienced "profound awe." Some alternated between terror and exaltation. "My God, it's beautiful," blurted an assistant to Julian Mack, one of the British scientists. "No," said Mack, "it's terrible." Something had happened, Jane Wilson thought, "for good or for ill. Something wonderful. Something terrible. The women waiting in the cold are a part of it. The atomic bomb has been born." Victor Weisskopf recalled that the fireball reminded him of a medieval painting of Jesus ascending to heaven in a bright yellow sphere surrounded by a blue halo: "The explosion of an atomic bomb and the resurrection of Christ—what a paradoxical and disturbing association!" Perhaps Kenneth Bainbridge's comment best summarized such feelings: "No one who saw it could forget it, a foul and awesome display."[109]

Relief and elation swept through them, inspiring hearty congratulations, handshakes, and swigs of whiskey. Weariness soon followed.[110] And not long after that, other feelings began to settle in—feelings of worry and dread and awareness that the world, as Dorothy McKibbin said, would never be the same. The morning air carried a chill, recalled Rabi, "a chill that came . . . when I thought of my wooden house in Cambridge, and my laboratory in New York, and all of the millions of people living around there, and this power of nature which we had first understood it to be—well, there it was." Even the tough-minded Groves recognized the experiment's fearsome implications. "I no longer consider the Pentagon safe shelter from such a bomb," he wrote to Secretary Stimson.[111]

Norris Bradbury rejected such afterthoughts. "Some people claim to have wondered at the time about the future of mankind," he recalled. "I didn't. We were at war and the damned thing worked." Yet the historical record suggests that among the scientists, Bradbury was the exception who proved the rule. Back at Los Alamos, the mathematician Stanislaus Ulam watched as the buses rolled up and disgorged the weary scientists. "You could tell at once they had [undergone] a strange experience," he said. "You could see it on their faces. I saw that something very grave and strong had happened to their whole outlook on the future."[112]

For now, that future did not belong to them, or to places such as Cambridge, Los Alamos, New York, and the Pentagon. The future now belonged to cities far across the Pacific Ocean. There, people truly would experience the awful magnitude of the atomic sublime.

At Hiroshima and Nagasaki, the bombs accomplished all that their fathers intended. At both cities, Little Boy and Fat Man utterly demolished everything within a radius of about one and one-half miles and severely damaged what remained out to three miles. The heat—5,400 degrees Fahrenheit at ground zero—incinerated all nearby combustible material, including thousands of buildings made of pine and other wood. Three-quarters of a mile away, tile roofs bubbled; beyond two miles, wood charred. What the heat did not destroy, the blast reduced to rubble. Nothing could withstand such power, equivalent to 12,500 tons of TNT at Hiroshima and 20,000 tons at Nagasaki. Even modern, reinforced concrete buildings stood gutted and in danger of collapse. Along with structures, institutions and people crumbled. Government offices, transportation facilities, Mitsubishi corporation shipyards, military headquarters and installations, all disappeared or were seriously disabled. Thousands of soldiers, workers, and ordinary citizens—most of whom had supported or acquiesced to Japan's military conquests, slaughter of civilians, and suicidal resistance—lay dead or dying, their bodies burned, crushed, dismembered, irradiated, their skin and hair sloughing off in huge ghastly patches.[113]

Yet the bomb's greatest toll was not its annihilation of strategic sites and their personnel. The bomb's mightiest effect, the purest expression of its power, was its destruction of people who bore no responsibility for the war at all. The bomb forever marked thousands of surviving children, in the scars that would cover their wounds, in the cancers that would grow inside them, in what would remain of their shattered souls. "Too much sorrow makes me like a stranger to myself," wrote one, recalling the moment his mother died, "and yet despite my grief I cannot cry."[114] Other children had precious little time, if any, for emotion. Of the two hundred thousand people who died in Hiroshima and Nagasaki by the end of 1945, an unknown number—probably tens of thousands—were the very youngest. Perhaps the most fortunate of these were the ones who went quickly. Days after the bombings, traces of their lives remained among the ruins: a schoolgirl's blackened lunch box containing charred peas and rice; a little boy, his body burned to a crisp, reaching to the sky; a woman sitting on some steps, breathing hard, her empty arms still curved as if holding her baby.[115]

Like the children of Los Alamos, the children of Hiroshima and Nagasaki were made mostly of carbon, hydrogen, and oxygen, with a pinch of iron and a dash of salt. And like the children of Los Alamos, the children of Hiroshima and Nagasaki amounted to far more than the sum of a few common elements. Near ground zero of each city, only a fraction of a second passed before the ferocious heat drove the temperature of their hearts and other watery organs beyond 212 degrees Fahrenheit. Boiling, vaporizing, and then igniting, their disintegrating tissues yielded to a vast convection that pulled them skyward, 10,000 feet, 20,000 feet, 40,000 feet and rising, as near to heaven as possible without leaving the Earth.

SUDDENLY THIS HORROR

When news of Hiroshima reached Los Alamos, the atomic community celebrated. The revelry was spontaneous and intense. "We jumped up and down, we screamed, we ran around slapping each other on the backs, shaking hands, congratulating each other," Richard Feynman wrote. "People came out into the hallways of the building and milled around like a Times Square New Year's crowd," Ed Doty, a soldier, remembered. "We had a parade," Kim Manley recalled of the children's response. "All of the kids in the neighborhood got together and marched around . . . banging on pots and pans and spoons and anything else we could find."[116]

That evening, having received Groves's congratulations, Oppenheimer addressed the Los Alamos community at the town auditorium. As the crowd cheered, he clasped his hands and "pumped them over his head like a prize fighter." He told them that he was proud of them, that whatever the damage to Hiroshima, he was certain the Japanese didn't like it, and that he wished they had been able to use the bomb against Germany. The last comment, recalled Sam Cohen, one of the younger physicists, "practically raised the roof." Then came round upon round of parties, a wild release of pent-up emotion. Feynman sat on the end of a jeep and beat his drums. Kistiakowsky detonated twenty cases of TNT.[117]

But already the misgivings were beginning to filter through the euphoria. At one point, Feynman encountered Robert Wilson "sitting there moping." What's the matter? Feynman asked. "It's a terrible thing that we've made," Wilson replied. Feynman, who had stopped thinking about the consequences, began thinking again. Otto Frisch, an expatriate German physicist, recalled his "feeling of unease, indeed nausea, when I saw how many of my friends were rushing to the telephone to book tables at the La Fonda Hotel in Santa Fe, in order to celebrate." Frank Oppenheimer had a similar reaction. "One suddenly got this horror," he said, "of all the people that had been killed." Philip Morrison, who had helped ready the bomb for the first drop, sat on an army cot "wondering what it was like on the other side, what was going on in Hiroshima that night."[118]

Such feelings worsened when news of the Nagasaki bombing arrived. Another round of parties and drinking began, but this time the spirit just wasn't there. A wave of nausea engulfed Wilson, who felt "betrayed." Bernard Feld, another scientist, hesitated before entering the La Fonda bar, knowing that the other patrons would recognize him and buy him drinks but feeling guilt over what he later called "the Nagasaki binge." Teller claimed to have experienced a like reaction, and there is no reason necessarily to doubt him. "If this goes on," he remembered telling Laura Fermi, "I want to leave."[119]

The atomic scientists and their families hit bottom when, weeks later, Robert Serber and Philip Morrison returned from an inspection of Hiroshima and Nagasaki. Serber and Morrison were the first of the atomic scientists to view the destruction. The stories they told—of weird, grotesque burns and mass carnage, of the manner in which "one bomber and one bomb turned a city of three hundred thousand into a burning pyre"—rattled the Los Alamos community. Jean Bacher, wife of the physicist Robert Bacher, remembered that Morrison in particular had "a wizard tongue and descriptive power. I was just absolutely undone. I went home and couldn't go to sleep; I just shook all night, it was such a shock."[120]

But of all the Los Alamos community, none took the bomb harder than Oppenheimer. The horror that he had wanted the world to witness affected him most of all, and he plunged into a dark depression. When Serber described a severely burned horse "happily grazing" amid the ruins of Nagasaki, the horse-loving Oppenheimer "scolded" him "for giving the impression that the bomb was a benevolent weapon." Kitty Oppenheimer told Jean Bacher that her husband "was just definitely beside himself" and that she didn't know what might happen in the aftermath of his "terrible reaction." Oppenheimer began to air his misgivings—"a profound grief, and a profound perplexity over the course we should be following"—before close friends. One, Ernest Lawrence, reminded him of his own logic, that the bomb was necessary to end not only this war, but all wars.[121] In spite of his guilt and remorse, Oppenheimer clung to that justification. His life, however, like the lives of Robert Wilson and so many other atomic scientists, would never be the same.

At the heart of every war lies deep moral ambiguity, an inherently tragic condition that permanently alters the lives of the people ensnared in it. The atomic scientists' tragedy is clearest when viewed from the perspective of natural history, from the pine grove where Mici Teller and her friends, babies cradled in their arms, stopped the bulldozer. The men and women of Los Alamos were good, not evil, and they built the bomb not *in spite* of their goodness but *because* of it. Precisely because they were good—precisely because they loved life, loved each other, loved children, loved mountains and atoms and pine trees—they found the means to create the esoteric knowledge without which the bomb could not have been born. The greatest killing machine in history was the product of all that was good, beautiful, and true, including the innocent curiosity that Rachel Carson called the sense of wonder.

It was no mere accident, furthermore, that Germany failed to produce the bomb while Britain and the United States succeeded. Authoritarianism and racism crippled German science and stopped its bomb project cold.[122] In contrast, the relative openness, toleration, and democracy of British and American science favored the Allied cause. Eccentrics, immigrants, Jews, and the unorthodox flourished at Los Alamos. General Groves might not have liked most of those people, but he put up with them, and some of them he actually admired. There can be no doubt, then, that the liberal conventions of Anglo American science, including a love of nature, made the bomb likely. That Little Boy and Fat Man were so horribly destructive in no way detracted from this great truth. The ultimate atomic paradox—and the ultimate atomic tragedy—was that good and bad, delight and terror, required and produced one another.

Oppenheimer wrestled with this atomic dilemma before his resignation from Los Alamos and his return to the University of California at Berkeley. On a November evening in 1945, he addressed some five hundred members of the newly formed Association of Los Alamos Scientists, an organization intended to educate the public and influence the politics of the atomic age. They had built the bomb, he told his colleagues, "because it was an organic necessity," because no clear line separated the pursuit of knowledge from its application. His use of the word *organic* all but stated his conviction that the quest to know and the quest to create were, quite *naturally*, intrinsic to one another. A scientist, he said, believes that "it is good to learn," "good to find out how the world works," "good to find out what the realities are," and "good to turn over to mankind at large the greatest possible power to control the world and to deal with it according to its lights and values." His analysis was not an evasion, not an attempt to naturalize the scientific method as a way of exempting its practitioners from moral responsibility. To be a scientist, he told them, means that you must bring knowledge to the world "and the power which this gives," and you must be "willing to take the consequences." Ultimately, he asserted, echoing Niels Bohr, the bomb posed "a great peril" but also "a great hope," a means for humanity to come together in the interest of peace.[123]

Perhaps the strongest proponent of this viewpoint, the one who faced it most squarely and unflinchingly, was Hans Bethe, whose wife, Rose, called him a "tough dove." In Bethe's calculation, the bomb had been necessary and had saved far more lives than it had taken. Blockade and starvation, invasion, a demonstration of the bomb—every alternative to Hiroshima and Nagasaki would have been costlier, and the first alternative might have permitted the resurgence of a vengeful postwar Japanese military. As it turned out, the bomb allowed Japan to surrender quickly and completely to a seemingly "supernatural" power, thereby saving the lives of both Allied forces and Japanese people. The bomb was "good," Bethe concluded toward the end of his life. And yet he admitted that it was "evil" as well, and he would concede to the historian Mary Palevsky that the innocents of Hiroshima and Nagasaki were "martyrs" to the wars that their horrible deaths had forestalled.[124]

No matter how convincing such a moral calculus seemed, Bethe and many of his colleagues could not escape the fact that they had blood on their hands, as Oppenheimer later would lament. They could not hide from the reality of the force they had released upon the world, could not always keep their vivid imaginations from drifting into nightmares. The postwar years would not be easy for them. Oppenheimer would wrestle with his demons while hounded by officials for his past communist associations. Wilson would carry hurts that his wife's consolation could not heal. Feynman would *look* at buildings and bridges under construction but *see* them smashed and destroyed and think to himself, "They're *crazy*, they just don't understand, they don't *understand*. Why are they making new things? It's so useless." Before he plunged into the production of the Super, Edward Teller would retreat into research and the security of his beloved Mici, who bore another child. Yet even he could not avoid the bomb's awful reality. "One is struck," he would write in 1947, "by the fires raging unopposed, wounds remaining unattended, sick men killing themselves with the exertions of helping their fellows."[125]

But all this lay in the future. While the dust still settled on a ruined city in Japan, the natural history of the bomb continued to unfold under the pine trees at Los Alamos. Upon leaving a celebration of Hiroshima, Oppenheimer observed a physicist—it appeared to be Robert Wilson—spewing the contents of his stomach in some bushes.[126] The spasms that shook the young man's body were the unavoidable natural reaction to his feeling of revulsion, and the acid bile that poured through his mouth and splatted on the ground was the purest, most noble of substances: drop by bitter drop, it took the measure of his humanity. ★

EIGHT

THE ROAD TO BROWN V. BOARD

An Environmental History of the Color Line

HER ROUTINE COULDN'T HAVE BEEN
more ordinary. Every weekday morning at 7:40, Linda Carol Brown, age eight, left her
home at 511 West First Street in Topeka, Kansas, for school. A happy child, she was
the picture of all-American girlhood: dark hair in pigtails, soft brown eyes and chubby
cheeks, long wool coat over sweater and skirt, ankle socks and scruffy shoes. Bidding
goodbye to her mother and younger sisters, she passed through the front door, slowed
momentarily to check for traffic, and headed into the street. To the east, six blocks away
at Quincy, was the school bus stop.

There were no sidewalks, so Linda followed a path between the railroad tracks that
ran along the southern half of the wide thoroughfare. The Rock Island line operated a
small switching yard there, with five tracks. From the yard, spurs curved toward factories and warehouses that fronted both sides of the street. Switch engines shuttled over
the rails, delivering cars of lumber and eggs, beer and potatoes, oil and ice, electrical
wire and plumbing fixtures—all the food, fuel, material, and manufactures that kept
Topeka moving.

It was a long way to the bus stop through the busy railroad zone. Underfoot lay
the residue of industrial America: gravel ballast and greasy mud, metal fragments
and glass shards, wood splinters and cardboard scraps, grass and weeds. The trains
seemed especially enormous to a little girl. Kansas Avenue, a major street that cut
through the east end of the yard, added to the danger. On winter mornings, freezing
or wet weather made the trip downright uncomfortable, and sometimes Linda was
so cold that she cried all the way to the bus stop. On a few occasions, she turned back
and went home.

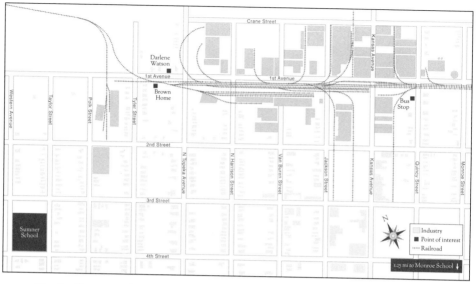

Topeka, Kansas, in the early 1950s, showing Linda Brown's home, a white neighbor's residence, the white Sumner School, and Linda's route through the railroad yard to the bus stop.

Most of the time, the journey wasn't so bad. Still, Linda wondered why her morning walk was necessary when a neighborhood school stood a comparable distance southwest of her home. In less time than it took her to reach Quincy, she could have been safe, dry, and warm. Some of her friends attended that nearby school; why couldn't she? Why did she have to walk six blocks through the railroad yard? Why did she have to wait in the cold for a bus ride that would take twenty minutes to get to a school that did not open until 9:00?

Lunch sack clutched in dimpled fist, her questions notwithstanding, Linda made her way toward Quincy, the bus stop, and school.[1]

Despite her youth and innocence, Linda Brown already was learning an important lesson about life in the twentieth-century United States. Like the paths of many other Americans, the route she followed down First Street skirted a troubled boundary called the color line. Consisting of laws, institutional practices, customs, and the landscape, the color line served two related functions. It excluded blacks from physical resources with which they might improve their lives and participate more fully in society, and it confined them to marginal, unsafe, unhealthy, or demeaning environments. In Linda's case, it kept her from attending the school closest to her home and exposed her to harsh weather in a hazardous industrial space on her way to a segregated school some two miles away. Her experience was mild compared with what African Americans in other parts of the nation endured, but nonetheless it demonstrated in a small way that the color line in any guise was inherently environmental.[2]

Linda Brown's brush with the color line revealed other features of it as well. As oppressive as it was, it was not an all-powerful construct that left blacks defenseless. In their hands, a tool of *segregation* also became an instrument of *separation*. Excluded from some environments, the blacks of Topeka used others—homes, churches, businesses, neighborhoods, parks, and schools—to build a separate existence over which they exerted greater control. That Linda Brown wished she could enroll in her neighborhood school did not mean that she and her family disliked Monroe Elementary, which she attended; to the contrary, the Browns and other people had fond feelings for Monroe and its teachers. In this and many other ways, blacks transformed their exclusion and confinement into a means of their empowerment.

Perhaps the color line's greatest weakness, as Linda Brown's life demonstrated, was its inherent instability. Outside of the schools, segregation in Topeka was an informal practice that concentrated blacks and whites but did not keep them completely apart. People of various ethnicities often lived together on the fringes of predominantly black or white neighborhoods. Linda Brown and her family inhabited a fringe, itself a kind of neighborhood, in which she and white children befriended each other. The mixed populations of Topeka's fringe neighborhoods increased over time and gave families such as the Browns a sense of what life might be like in a racially integrated society. By the 1940s and 1950s, the Browns and other African Americans in Topeka no longer wanted to tolerate the color line, which was absurd, demeaning, inconvenient, and oppressive, especially to their children during cold, inclement weather. Joining forces in a lawsuit, they attempted to alter the racial landscape of their city.

Ironically, the legal argument that would change the course of American history did not refer to the environmental features of the color line to which the Browns and other families objected. At the inception of *Brown v. Board of Education*, national civil rights leaders took over the case and advanced it to the U.S. Supreme Court using an abstract argument premised not on the importance of local geography but on its irrelevance. The court found the argument compelling, and its final decision struck down the color line in every school in America.

In the end, however, efforts to implement the ruling reproduced some of the conditions that its architects intended for it to overcome. Rather than killing the color line, *Brown* provoked its revival in new forms. Nowhere was its revival more evident, more tangible and real, than in local places such as Topeka.

EXODUS

First Street, the heart of Linda Brown's world, sat in an urban environment that extended north and south of the Kansas River. North Topeka encompassed residences, shops, warehouses, and railroad yards while the bulk of the city sprawled to the south. Between the Kansas River and First Street stood some ten square blocks of warehouses, small factories, storage yards, grain elevators, meat-packing plants, and other industrial operations. At the east end of First loomed the massive repair shops of the Santa Fe, the most prominent of Topeka's railroads. South of First, the land sloped upward some sixty-five feet, through the city's main business district, toward Ninth and the state capitol. East, west, and south of this commercial and governmental core spread the tree-lined streets of residential neighborhoods, mostly white but some black and some mixed. On the city's south end sat the fairgrounds and Washburn University (formerly Washburn College). A little farther on, the land sloped down toward Shunganunga Creek, which flowed northeast toward the Kansas River. Beyond the city limits, beyond where the streets ended and the railroads thinned to single tracks, stretched the gentle hills and open space of the Kansas countryside.[3]

Topeka counted some one hundred thousand residents in the early 1950s, of whom about seventy-four hundred were black.[4] *Most blacks resided in enclaves that stood apart from adjacent white neighborhoods and that tended to be in topographically low places near the Kansas River and Shunganunga Creek. The color line, which took shape from the interaction of Topeka's residents with one another and with their physical environment, influenced the locations of the black neighborhoods and thus of their elementary schools. Blacks such as Linda Brown and her family, however, did not live squarely within ethnic enclaves but in mixed neighborhoods on their fringes. The Browns lived with other working-class people close to the Kansas River, between industrial and white residential areas, but Linda had to attend an elementary school in a black neighborhood.*

The events that brought Linda Brown's family and other blacks to Topeka and divided the city on racial lines were both social and environmental. They began in the nineteenth century, following the Civil War.

By the late 1870s, some seven hundred of Topeka's roughly seven thousand residents were African American, and most of them lived in a racially mixed area at the east end of First Street, near the railroads and industries that employed them.[5] Within a short time, however, the size and geographical location of the city's black population began to change.

The source of that change was the South. Before the Civil War ended in 1865, the United States government instituted a policy of "reconstruction" that was intended to restore the former Confederate states to the Union and ensure the civil rights of freed people. The Thirteenth, Fourteenth, and Fifteenth amendments to the U.S. Constitution abolished slavery, guaranteed that all citizens would enjoy the equal protection of the laws, and extended the franchise to black men. From the start, southern white supremacists worked to defeat interracial democracy and institute a violent, repressive system of racial segregation that confined blacks to menial labor in the region's agricultural and extractive economies. In 1877, when the federal government ended Reconstruction and withdrew the U.S. Army from the former Confederacy, white supremacists intensified their efforts to undercut the freed people. Deprived of sufficient land, education, and jobs, their access to fish, game, and other subsistence resources reduced, and unable to advance politically, many black families began to leave, first on foot, then by steamboat, and finally on the railroad. Decade after decade, hundreds of thousands followed the steel rails out, north to New York, Pennsylvania, Ohio, and Illinois and west to Oklahoma, Kansas, and beyond.[6] Wherever the emigrants went, they did not so much escape the color line as experience its rebirth in new forms.

Such was the case with African Americans whose one-way tickets brought them to Topeka.[7] Estimates vary, but in 1879–1880, perhaps forty thousand emigrants made their way to Kansas in a mass exodus from Tennessee, Mississippi, and other southern states. Most of them headed for the prairie, intent on acquiring the land that white southerners had denied them. Some three thousand ended their journey in the state capital. Stepping off the train at the Kansas Pacific depot on the city's north side, the Exodusters, as they called themselves in reference to the biblical exodus, no doubt hoped that they had left their troubles behind.[8]

Topeka gave the Exodusters a chilly reception. Homeless and hungry, the first emigrants in spring 1879 congregated in tents, dugouts, and makeshift shelters along the river just south of the Kansas Pacific depot. Public officials might have helped them. Kansas law required counties and cities to aid indigent people, and in 1874, federal and state governments had assisted white farm families driven from the prairie by swarming grasshoppers. But the Exodusters received virtually no public assistance. In Congress, southern Democrats blocked efforts to appropriate money for relief, and the state provided nothing more than jobs for ten Exodusters who worked on the construction and repair of the Kansas capitol. Shawnee County and Topeka rendered no aid, and the mayor of Topeka declared that city funds would be better spent returning the emigrants to the South.[9] The Exodusters were simply too poor, black, and alien to warrant much official help.

They did attract a small amount of private support. A group of black and white citizens, including Governor John St. John, organized the nongovernmental State Central Relief Committee, which obtained permission from the Shawnee County commissioners to shelter about seventy Exodusters at the fairgrounds just south of Topeka. In May 1879, the privately funded Kansas Freedmen's Relief Association (KFRA) took over the work and began caring for the emigrants' physical needs while helping them find jobs and homes. When the county commissioners asked the KFRA to move the group at the fairgrounds to north Topeka, where other emigrants had gathered, the organization decided to build a shelter. By June, the KFRA had erected a temporary wood structure, called the Barracks, several blocks east of the Kansas Pacific depot, between the railroad tracks and the Kansas River. As new emigrants arrived in the city, KFRA representatives greeted them and escorted them to the facility.[10]

For some north Topeka residents, the Barracks was too close for comfort. They declared that the emigrants would flood the labor pool and drive down wages. More ominously, they feared that the newcomers carried contagious diseases. It was true that some of the Exodusters were in poor health—according to various reports, one boy had measles, other children had whooping cough, and some adults had tuberculosis. They were, after all, malnourished former slaves and sharecroppers living in close quarters. It also was true that Tennessee, where some of the Exodusters originated, was experiencing a yellow fever epidemic. Topeka was no more biologically vulnerable to the Exodusters than to any other travelers who arrived in the city, but the presence of blacks in poor health was enough to inspire aggression. In June 1879, white vigilantes descended on the Barracks, tore it down, and threw its lumber into the Kansas River.[11]

Although the residents of north Topeka proclaimed themselves innocent of racial animosity, they effectively stigmatized and isolated a group of people already shunned for its skin color. In response to the vigilante attack, the KFRA built a permanent Barracks complex three-quarters of a mile north of the city limits.[12] Topeka had begun to draw its color line.

THE PLACES WE ARE WANTED

As Linda made her way down First Street, she passed the Rock Island freight depot, an ice company, a packing company, and other shipping facilities and factories. After carefully crossing Kansas Avenue, she left the tracks and made a beeline for the vacant lot at the southeast corner of East First Street and Quincy. There she waited for the school bus, which arrived at ten past eight. Mr. Grimes, the driver, opened the door, and Linda climbed on board.[13]

Then began the trip southward, generally following Quincy but with a few detours to pick up students. All told, Grimes would have some thirty-five students on his bus, most of them headed for Monroe School but some for Washington, another of Topeka's four black elementary schools. The bus was full and the children were lively, but Grimes, who had been driving the route for decades, kept them in line. "Boy, he was something," Linda's mother remembered. "If [you] didn't act right he'd put you off. Stop—off!—and make you walk home. So you had to act right if you were going to ride that bus."[14]

Linda's route passed through two of Topeka's most prominent black neighborhoods. First and Quincy, where she caught the bus, was located in the northwest corner of the Bottoms; beyond Tenth Street, the bus entered Mudtown. The Bottoms was named for its proximity to the Kansas River and for its location on Shunganunga Creek, which ran through its heart. Mudtown straddled Shunganunga Creek, too, but took its name from the condition of its unpaved streets after a rainfall.

When the Exodusters finally left the Barracks, they clustered in residential enclaves on Topeka's periphery. The locations of these neighborhoods resulted, in part, from the white majority's racial exclusivity, which pushed the black newcomers to the social and geographical margins. Even the names of neighborhoods suggested black people's social inferiority and environmental subordination. "Mudtown" and "the Bottoms" connoted dirty, unpaved, poorly drained, unstable environments and subtly associated the conditions of the places with the character of the people who lived there. Stigmatized as dark, earthy, and low (that is, unclean, unhealthy, illicit, and dangerous), black people were often trapped in both landscape and language. Yet the power of the color line was not straightforward. As much as racial exclusion, racial solidarity built Topeka's black neighborhoods. In reaction to white people's indifference and hostility, and on the foundation of shared culture and history, the Exodusters and their descendants came together for self-help, self-defense, and self-determination.

The first Exodusters who found permanent homes in Topeka did not move far, if at all, from the hovels that some had erected near the Kansas Pacific depot. Along the north Topeka riverfront, a short distance from the tracks, they inhabited a neighborhood that at first carried the name of Redmonsville but eventually came to be known by the alluvial earth on which it sat—Sandtown. By renting property or buying lots and building houses, and by working at menial jobs or founding businesses, the people of Sandtown established a small component of Topeka's black community.[15]

Most of the Exodusters who came to Topeka lived south of the Kansas River. Hundreds relocated to an isolated, undeveloped site in the countryside southwest of the city's developed core, where the KFRA purchased house lots and sold them at cost to approximately five hundred black emigrants from Tennessee, Mississippi, and other southern states. Centered approximately west of Topeka Avenue, south of Eighth Street, and north of Huntoon, the area became known as Tennesseetown. Emma Crabb, who grew up in the neighborhood and became one of its historians, recalled that the Exodusters "were at the edge of town when they came and formed a colony—like people from another country."[16]

The first residents of Tennesseetown immediately began building the economic basis of a new life. A few men practiced skilled trades such as carpentry and masonry, but most had to take jobs as low-paid menial laborers. Many women found employment as maids and cooks in the homes and establishments of Topeka's white citizens. Other Tennesseetown residents established their own businesses such as dressmaking and barbering. Some ran illicit enterprises in violation of Topeka's ordinances against alcohol, gambling, and prostitution. In conjunction with this cash economy, the people of Tennesseetown established an informal economy based on small-scale subsistence practices adapted from the South. By tending vegetable gardens, raising fruit trees, and keeping chickens, cows, and hogs, they put food on their tables beyond that which money alone could buy.[17]

By genteel standards, the Tennesseetown landscape was disordered and dirty. The first houses were ramshackle wooden structures lacking paint or plaster. Chickens foraged in the yards and gardens while hogs roamed past outhouses, tumbledown fences, dance halls, and churches. All around lay the open soil of the neighborhood's streets. Mud—"bottomless Kansas mud"— was a major problem, "for there were no sidewalks or paved streets then and following every rainy spell or spring thaw streets and footpaths were almost impassable."[18]

Other Exodusters made their way to Mudtown, on the southeast edge of Topeka. Like Tennesseetown, Mudtown had an earthy texture, only more so. Roughly bounded by Tenth Street on the north, Indiana Avenue on the east, and Kansas on the west, the neighborhood sloped inward to Shunganunga Creek. Rising south and west of Topeka, Shunganunga Creek meandered northeast for more than ten miles, through the middle of Mudtown and toward its confluence with the Kansas River. As Mudtown's name implied, water turned its unpaved thoroughfares into quagmires. Even "the streets that were paved didn't have sidewalks," recalled Joe Douglas, a Topeka native, "so you [still] got your feet muddy when it rained." Mudtown's many outhouses enhanced its organic reputation. Few of its homes had indoor toilets until after the Second World War. "I've been outside for forty years," one older resident remarked, "and I've been inside for forty years."[19]

Despite the condition of their landscape, the residents of Mudtown began to create new lives for themselves. Like the people of Tennesseetown, they kept gardens and chickens, worked for wages, established businesses, and erected homes and churches. And like the people of Tennesseetown, they built their lives in a place apart, an enclave of color in a landscape that was predominantly white. "It was all but totally black," recalled Jack Alexander, who grew up in Mudtown's northeast corner, "and it was sort of an isolated area."[20]

North of Mudtown, east of Kansas Avenue, and south of the Kansas River sprawled the Bottoms, the lowest in elevation of Topeka's major African American neighborhoods and the final destination for many Exoduster families. The newcomers to the Bottoms fashioned lives from a patchwork of economic activities, and their rough dwellings, which spread south and east from First Street and the Santa Fe Railway shops, embodied their new circumstances and harked back to their southern roots. They built shotgun houses, a distinctive African American vernacular form—long, slender, one room wide and usually three rooms deep. Suited to narrow lots and simple to build, their low cost and flexible interior spaces made them ideal for black families with little money and few possessions. Yet it was not so much houses that physically defined the

Bottoms and set the neighborhood apart from white Topeka; it was the proximity of those dwellings and their inhabitants to lower Shunganunga Creek and the Kansas River. The Bottoms was both black and low.[21]

That lowness was an important feature of the color line. Except for the inhabitants of Tennesseetown, Topeka's black residents—in Sandtown and Mudtown as well as the Bottoms—tended to live in relatively low areas. And lowness had consequences. Repeatedly, floods scoured low-down Topeka from the nineteenth century onward, and although they hurt white people and their businesses, blacks suffered the most. The 1903 deluge was the worst in the city's history, and it hit Sandtown hardest. Fourteen of the twenty-four people who died were black—that is, blacks made up 58 percent of the flood's fatalities, even though they constituted only about 12 percent of the local population. One elderly black woman recognized an unearthly force at work in the roiling waters that carried away her possessions. "No, honey," she said when asked if the flood had destroyed her faith. "I don't go so much now on His mercy, but I have a higher 'preciation of his powerfulness."[22] Yet it was human relationships that made the color line intrinsic to Topeka's geography and contributed to Sandtown's vulnerability. The flood was not simply an act of God; the color line bore some responsibility for the disproportionate harm it visited on blacks.

Despite floods and other problems, the residents of Topeka's black neighborhoods continued to fashion relationships and institutions apart from white society. The decades from the 1890s to the 1930s were pivotal to the solidification of black Topeka. Black businesses catered to a black clientele. Black fraternities facilitated black fellowship and enabled black self-help. Black political organizations empowered black politics. Black elementary schools taught black children. And black churches ministered to the black spirit and served as an indispensable social support for the entire black community. By the twentieth century, these institutions served nearly five thousand people, including Linda Brown's father, Oliver, born in 1918 on the far northwest edge of Tennesseetown.[23]

Topeka's African Americans were hardly alone in their quest to determine their futures apart from white people. Insular black communities appeared across the United States during the late nineteenth and early twentieth centuries. In 1912, for example, the historian W. E. B. Du Bois described the efforts of blacks in Durham, North Carolina, to fashion an independent economic and institutional infrastructure—a "closed circle of social intercourse"—beyond the reach of whites. At all times, Du Bois asserted, Durham's African

Americans needed to interact with no one but themselves. At work or at home, in school, church, or business, theirs was a totally black world.[24]

Du Bois himself propounded a form of separatism that is relevant to an understanding of Topeka's black neighborhoods. He grounded his advocacy in a program he called "the conservation of races." Today, *conservation* almost exclusively refers to the protection or maintenance of forests, endangered species, coal, and other nonhuman natural resources, but in the late nineteenth and early twentieth centuries, the term had a broader, more flexible meaning that allowed Du Bois to argue that people were in need of protection and maintenance, too. People must be shielded from the worst effects of industrial capitalism, he said. Their bodies must have food, warmth, and protection from disease, and their intellects must be nurtured. Only then could they offer humankind their unique skills, talents, and accumulated wisdom. Although Du Bois believed that all people, regardless of race, were brothers and sisters, he recognized that some used skin color as the pretext for exploiting others. Among America's racial groups, his fellow black people, he believed, most urgently needed help. It was the "duty" of African Americans, he wrote in 1897, "to conserve" their "physical powers," "intellectual endowments," and "spiritual ideals" and, through "race organization" and "race solidarity," separate themselves from whites to ensure their own physical, moral, and cultural survival.[25]

Although the black people of Topeka did not call themselves race conservationists, their actions in certain respects conformed to the program that Du Bois laid out. Their geographical separation expressed their desire to maintain the material and cultural ties that had sustained them during slavery and the transition to freedom, and their many organizations embodied their ambition to institutionalize those solidarities. If not explicitly conservationist in design, their actions at least expressed the intent to nurture and protect themselves and their interests.

A key feature of Topeka's black neighborhoods was their economic vitality. Although white people, corporations, unions, and government agencies excluded blacks and forced them into poorly paid, menial labor in the late nineteenth and early twentieth centuries, two developments countered this trend. One was the opening of railroad jobs. After the Exodusters arrived in Topeka, most railroad work, especially the better-paying, skilled positions with the Santa Fe, remained off-limits to blacks. But in 1894, in the midst of a devastating depression, railroad workers across the nation went on strike. In retaliation, the Santa Fe fired thousands of employees and placed their names on an industry blacklist. In need of labor, the railroad began to hire substantial numbers of African Americans, a strategy the Santa Fe continued into the twentieth century; in 1922 and 1936, strikes by white laborers resulted in more jobs for blacks.[26] The positions were not unqualified victories—the railroad tended to hire blacks as cooks, porters, and physical laborers, and it paid them less than it did whites—but the work gave Topeka's black people and their neighborhoods an important economic boost.

The second economic development important to Topeka's black community was the maturation of black businesses and with them a class of black entrepreneurs and professionals. By the twentieth century, African Americans operated some thirty enterprises in Topeka, including newspapers, restaurants, catering businesses, mortuaries, construction companies, grocery stores, coal dealerships, barbershops, and a theater. In 1900, following a visit by Booker T. Washington, the nation's leading advocate of black self-help, the city's black entrepreneurs organized a chapter of the National Negro Business League. Meanwhile, professionals—some of whom had degrees from Washburn College—flourished. Elisha Scott, for example, upon graduation in 1916 established a law practice that eventually attracted clients from as far away as Oklahoma and Texas. The prosperity of Topeka's black entrepreneurs and professionals gave them the means to pursue outdoor and other leisure activities characteristic of middle-class Americans. Martin Oglesvie, for example, a Tennesseetown vegetable and fruit producer, hunted pheasants in western Kansas, and Nathaniel Sawyer, a teacher and writer, toured the Colorado Rockies, which he described "in romantic detail" in local newspapers.[27]

Social institutions and relationships solidified Topeka's black community and its geography in ways that economic activities alone could not. Beginning in the late nineteenth century, the city's African Americans created dozens of clubs, fraternities, leagues, lodges, organizations, societies, and churches. These included the Shawnee County Colored Horse Fair Association, a chapter of the International Industrial Association (which provided insurance), the Mascots baseball club, the Shawnee Cornet Band, Lodge No. 3 of the Women's Benevolent Society, and St. John's African Methodist Episcopal Church.[28] Black people sustained most of these associational activities in buildings and other geographical spaces within their neighborhoods; they grounded others in pastoral environments around the city. Topeka's blacks interred their dead in their own cemetery, Mount Auburn, founded in 1881 on the east side. They held concerts, games, meetings, reunions, picnics, and other recreational activities at City Park, on the riverfront one block north of First Street. In 1903, black community leaders moved the Kansas Industrial and Educational Institute, a trade school modeled on Booker T. Washington's famous Tuskegee Institute, to a 105-acre hilltop site about one and one-half miles east of Topeka. Later in the twentieth century, a group of black sportsmen laid out the Twin Lakes Golf Club, an all-black club, southeast of the city.[29]

Perhaps most important to the solidarity and success of Topeka's black people, however, were the daily, face-to-face interactions enabled by neighborhood geography. Regular contacts on the streets and in shops, churches, and schools built trust and encouraged right behavior, especially among children. Jack Alexander, for example, developed a healthy respect for the neighborhood women who monitored him and other Mudtown youths during the 1930s: "I remember all those old sisters in that neighborhood who would take care of you. You didn't do the things kids do running wild because they would come out and get you."[30]

Children embodied black Topeka's hope for the future, and the four segregated elementary schools were crucial to the neighborhoods they served. Those schools had originated and evolved in relation to the environmental conditions of the color line. In 1874, the Kansas legislature had passed a civil rights act that prohibited discrimination in public transportation, public accommodations, places of entertainment licensed by municipalities, and public institutions such as schools. Five years later, when thousands of Exodusters rolled into Topeka, the state retreated from its commitment to racial equality and enacted a law that permitted, but did not require, cities of more than fifteen thousand people to segregate their elementary schools. Topeka opted for segregation. The color line that isolated the Exodusters in the Barracks and then in their neighborhood enclaves also placed their youngest children in separate elementary schools: McKinley in Sandtown, Buchanan in Tennesseetown, Washington in the Bottoms, and Monroe in Mudtown.[31]

Few of the city's black residents objected to segregated schools, and they identified the institutions with their ethos of separatism, self-sufficiency, and pride. In the early 1890s, black newspapers and community leaders pressured the Topeka Board of Education to hire only black teachers for the city's black children. "We should not attempt to be in places that we are not wanted," wrote James Guy, a prominent attorney. "We should recognize our differences and need to establish race pride and confidence." Topeka's blacks reached a turning point in 1894, when the board yielded to their demands.[32] Thereafter, the ties between the segregated elementary schools and their neighborhoods grew tight and emotionally intense. Only the black churches rivaled the schools as institutional foundations of black identity and cultural cohesion.

Inside those educational spaces, deep devotion, affection, and respect bonded the teachers and their students. Believing that they were preparing the children for the challenges of life in a largely white world, the teachers set high standards for academic excellence and personal behavior. Yet they delivered their stern discipline with doses of kindness and love. Joe Douglas, whose mother died when he was five, had "very warm feelings" for his teachers at Monroe School during the 1930s, because "they related to us in most instances as though we were their own children rather than like we were charges or wards." If you fell and hurt yourself, he said, a teacher would "hug you or pick you up or hold you to her bosom" even though "[your] nose was snotty and your hair was full of sand." In other instances, teachers delivered children to medical appointments or, in the case of kindergarten students, drove them home in their own vehicles.[33] In such circumstances, a child could feel as if the neighborhood school was an extension of his or her own family.

The teachers' commitment to nurturing their students included intensive exposure to black history and culture. When Christina Jackson attended Washington School during the 1930s, the principal, Mr. Ridley, drilled the children in African American history. He patrolled the hallways, stopping students to ask them, for example, if they knew of Marcus Garvey, the prominent black nationalist and founder of the Universal Negro Improvement Association. If they did not, Ridley made them sit in his office and read a history book. Jackson especially loved Ridley's enthusiasm for music. Every morning, he asked the children to rise for "Lift Every Voice and Sing," the Negro National Anthem. On special occasions, he assembled the entire school around the flagpole, where students and staff recited the Pledge of Allegiance and sang "America" before joining together in "Lift Every Voice."[34] Composed in 1900 by the poet James Weldon Johnson and his brother, J. Rosamond Johnson, the song, like the other American anthems, invoked the universal theme of struggle, liberation, and redemption in an awesome providential landscape. Yet it expressed that theme in a distinctively black form—in a story uniquely black and in the sweeping cadences of black gospel music. James Weldon Johnson wrote in 1935 that "Life Every Voice and Sing" inspired in him feelings of "elation, almost of exquisite anguish," whenever he heard children perform it:

Lift every voice and sing
Till earth and heaven ring,
Ring with the harmonies of Liberty;
Let our rejoicing rise
High as the listening skies,
Let it resound loud as the rolling sea.
Sing a song full of the faith that the dark past has taught us,
Sing a song full of hope that the present has brought us.
Face the rising sun of our new day begun
Let us march on till victory is won.

Stony the road we trod,
Bitter the chastening rod,
Felt in the days when hope unborn had died;
Yet with a steady beat, have not our weary feet
Come to the place for which our fathers sighed? . . .

Shadowed beneath Thy hand,
May we forever stand.
True to our God,
True to our native land.[35]

A nation within a nation, a people within a people, but no less American: the lyrics proclaimed a black version of triumph over adversity, of progress toward liberty and light, of arriving, finally, in God's sheltering grace. Although Topeka, Kansas, was a small town, one among thousands, its black citizens could imagine that divine favor also extended to them and their neighborhoods, houses, streets, parks, and institutions: to Sandtown, Mudtown, Tennesseetown, and the Bottoms; to St. Mark's African Methodist Episcopal, Shiloh Baptist, and other churches; to businesses such as Doc Washington's pharmacy in Mudtown and the Apex Theater in lower downtown; to City Park by the river or Mount Auburn Cemetery on the east side; to Buchanan, McKinley, Monroe, and Washington elementary schools; and to the flagpole around which sang Mr. Ridley, his teachers, and their students. Such was the faith that defied the racism of the color line and shaped the black geography of Topeka.

Around 8:25, Mr. Grimes stopped the bus at Tenth and Washington streets, roughly where Mudtown and the Bottoms merged. A few of the children got off and walked about one-half block to Washington School, situated on low ground a stone's throw from Shunganunga Creek. There they joined other students who had walked the entire distance or who had arrived on another bus from the Bottoms. Seeing his charges safely off, Grimes then headed west on Tenth, across the concrete bridge that spanned the creek, and south on Quincy toward Fifteenth Street and Monroe School.[36]

Despite common experiences, family connections, and shared identity, black Topeka did have divisions, although they were subtle and not easily detected by outsiders. Some people disputed that color distinctions had any social significance; others recognized a racial hierarchy that privileged lighter skin. Gender differentiated community members; female teachers in the elementary schools, for example, tended to receive lower salaries than their male colleagues.[37] Of all the divisions, perhaps the greatest was social class. While some blacks gained wealth and status, others fell behind.

A person's position in the social hierarchy usually bore some relationship to the physical environment in which he or she lived, an association that was the product of historical changes and geographical conditions. The city's black enclaves and their inhabitants may have started out much the same economically and socially, but they developed differently, in part because of the environments in which the neighborhoods were situated. Most important were the circumstances that shaped Tennesseetown, which had the advantage of sitting above the flood zone. Beginning in the 1890s and accelerating through the early twentieth century, Tennesseetown and the Bottoms grew even less alike—environmentally, economically, socially, and culturally. Tennessee-town acquired a cleaner, more genteel ambience and reputation, and the Bottoms, just the opposite. This polarization would have important consequences for black identity in Topeka and for the evolution of the city's color line.

The Exodusters who first inhabited Tennesseetown received help from a white Congregationalist minister named Charles Sheldon, who tried to help them overcome problems of race prejudice, crime, alcoholism, poverty, and the negative reputation that those conditions invited. In one sense, Sheldon's humanitarian efforts exemplified the principles of the Social Gospel, a reform movement popular among Protestant ministers. In another sense, his plans aligned with the call of W. E. B. Du Bois for race conservation. Among other projects, Sheldon was instrumental in founding a kindergarten, a literary society and library, and a training program in the manual arts, all in the interest of helping black people maintain their physical, economic, and moral integrity in the face of debilitating forces.[38]

Sheldon also did something that combined the conventional definition of conservation with the concept as put forward by Du Bois. In 1898, in a project that linked environmental and social reform, he organized the Village Improvement Society to clean up the Tennesseetown landscape. Like other reformers of his time, Sheldon believed that environment shaped behavior. In his words, "a man who lives in an unpainted, squalid, gardenless place will naturally get from his surroundings a shiftless disposition," but "as his surroundings and his body and house become clean, his daily work begins to conform to it." Some residents of Tennesseetown protested that they did not need white do-gooders to tell them how to live and that Sheldon's plan threatened their hogs, an important food source. Others, including local black ministers, welcomed his proposal and moved to implement it. Using cash prizes as incentives, and aided by a new city ordinance that banned livestock, the Village Improvement Society and its supporters went to work. They removed trash, repaired fences, painted houses, planted lawns and flowers, and raised vegetables. By 1901, when a slate of black officers took over the society's administration, Tennesseetown had a refurbished look and a more respectable reputation.[39]

As Tennesseetown's star rose, the standing of the Bottoms fell. Through the twentieth century, the Bottoms retained—and perhaps gained—some of the social and environmental characteristics that Tennesseetown tried to shed. Although the neighborhood encompassed prosperous citizens and fine buildings, it also harbored impoverished people who lived adjacent to railroad yards or in the shadow of industrial plants. Whereas Tennesseetown seemed to benefit from its elevated position and the conservationist impulse that shaped it, the Bottoms increasingly drew much of its economic and cultural energy from unseemly if not illicit enterprises concentrated along East Fourth Street: taverns, billiard parlors, dance halls, skating rinks, cheap restaurants, gambling joints, bootlegging operations, prostitution. William Mitchell played many crap games in the Bottoms and eventually became the protégé of a gambler named "Black Sam" Coleman. "Naturally coming around in that environment I was skilled at [crap]," Mitchell said, perhaps confirming Rev. Sheldon's theory that surroundings indeed make the man.[40]

Topeka's blacks felt apprehensive about the Bottoms and its violent under-world. If you weren't careful, said Clementine Martin, whose husband walked a police beat through the neighborhood, "somebody would flim-flam you or do something to you down there." Recalled one Mudtown resident: "I was never down there after dark." Joe Thompson, raised in a tiny black enclave on the far southeast edge of Topeka, remembered: "We were almost scared to go down in there because of the cutting and the shooting and the gambling." Even William Mitchell, who reveled in the action of the Bottoms, understood its dangers. "You don't get drunk and go down there with a pocket full of money," he said, "and think you ain't going to be cleaned, because you would be, just like a white fish—cleaned." Recalled Berdyne Scott, whose husband was a prominent African American attorney: "It was a lawyer's delight."[41]

The fear and anxiety that some Topeka blacks felt about life "down there" eventually hardened into a stereotype: the Bottoms was a place of filth, poverty, and squalor. Here was an important feature of Topeka's color line. Although race prejudice had called the color line into existence, black people sometimes transformed it into a marker of environmental degradation and inferior social class. The Bottoms was black, but it was also geographically, economically, and socially low, an unstable, dangerous place of gamblers and prostitutes and poor people. To Ida Norman, the divisions were clear. "You want to know the truth?" she asked. "There was a lot of scared people. Negroes stayed by them-selves. The better class stayed by themselves. The lower class stayed down on Fourth Street. It was groups."[42]

Geography and class constrained many of those "lower-class" residents of the Bottoms, but especially the impoverished and destitute children. Berdyne Scott had direct experience with one such youngster. She often accompanied her husband when he visited the neighborhood on legal business, and during one trip in the mid-1950s she had an opportunity to adopt the baby of a prosti-tute. Although Scott felt drawn to the child—"he had the most gorgeous dimple in his chin that you ever saw"—she decided not to take him, "because it would have gone out all over town that I had adopted a whore's baby." Children such as Wilmer Henderson may have had greater freedom than did this unfortunate infant, but he, too, struggled against geographic and class prejudice. Henderson grew up near the Santa Fe tracks at the east end of First Street, and he remem-bered coal cars parked in his front yard and "running errands for prostitutes and gamblers for fifty cents." He also remembered that other children called him a "Bottom rat," a taunt that signified his environmental and social degradation.[43]

Not all black people feared the Bottoms or believed that its residents were inferior. "Everyone would say, 'Oh the Bottoms, the Bottoms!'" said Zelma Henderson, but she explained that the place wasn't as fearsome as most people perceived. "We all would walk to the show and walk home at night," she remembered. "No one bothered you."[44] Others recognized that "good people" lived in the neighborhood along with the gamblers, dealers, and sex workers. "There were good families also in the Bottoms," recalled Berdyne Scott. "Everybody in the Bottoms did not sell liquor and prostitute [themselves]." William Mitchell's memories agreed with Scott's, and he listed some of the names of "the good people who lived down there."[45]

One of Clementine Martin's memories expressed the ambivalence that some Topeka blacks felt about the Bottoms and the mixture of pleasure and degradation they found there. The neighborhood had many places to eat, Martin told an interviewer, "and they had good food." Her favorite was Robbie's Chili. "The chili was so hot," she recalled. "It was something else." But "Robbie's Chili was just as dirty as Robbie's Chili was hot. It was one of those [places] that you would go in and sit down and see the bugs and the what not, anything crawling." When asked if the chili was famous, she replied: "Yes, it was."[46]

START OUR CHILDREN TOGETHER

Around 8:30, Linda's bus pulled up to the curb in front of Monroe School, and she and the other children filed off. Monroe was a simple but attractive structure. Two stories tall and rectangular in plan, it featured brick walls and a red tile roof enclosing thirteen classrooms and a gymnasium, enough space for 420 students. Along the east and west sides of the building were rows of multipaned windows, designed to allow abundant fresh air and sunlight into the classrooms. Built in 1926, Monroe was the most modern and best equipped of Topeka's black elementary schools. In spite of its quality, however, Monroe was not quite the physical equal of comparable white schools. Monroe had less playground space, for example, and its landscaping was less appealing. The differences were part of a subtle but important distinction between the city's white and black schools. Overall, the Topeka School Board devoted somewhat more resources to the white institutions. The average insured value of classrooms, to cite one measure, amounted to about $6,300 for black schools and $10,500 for white ones. Although in terms of class size and quality of instruction the schools were roughly the same, the color line did demarcate a certain inequality of condition.[47]

Linda and her schoolmates did not dwell on such details. With free time before class, they played in the schoolyard. A few minutes before 9:00, the doors opened. Pausing for a moment at the mud scraper next to the arched limestone entry, they cleaned the soles of their shoes—this was, after all, Mudtown.[48] *Then they went inside.*

Not all of Topeka's black citizens favored segregated education, nor did they necessarily want to live entirely apart from white people. Despite their pride in Monroe and the other elementary schools, their love and respect for their teachers, and their attachments to other blacks, they wanted to live, work, play, and learn wherever they chose. Thus, while the black people of Topeka created neighborhoods, institutions, and human relationships that sustained them apart from whites, at least some of them desired a world in which race mattered less than individual freedom, a world that was, of necessity, racially mixed or integrated. The members of this group included the parents of Linda Brown.

A combination of circumstances motivated the proponents of integration. On the one hand, the Great Depression of the 1930s reduced economic disparities between some blacks and whites and focused their attention on survival, not racial difference. On the other hand, although periods of general economic prosperity strengthened Topeka's black community and its neighborhoods, they gave some blacks the means to pursue ambitions apart from their racial group. Of particular significance were jobs with the Santa Fe Railway, especially during World War Two, when the movement of men into the armed forces created a labor shortage and compelled the railroad to hire more people of color. The color line still existed—it still determined the kind of work a Santa Fe employee performed—but nonetheless the company flexed enough to admit more blacks and other minorities to its workforce. For men such as Oliver Brown, the Santa Fe was a boon. Once a boxer and a porter at the Elks Club, Brown now had another option. Soon after returning from military service, he became a car welder at the Santa Fe shops, a job that came with union membership and reasonably good pay.[49]

Demographic changes, environmental factors, and ideology also impelled the integrationists. In conjunction with extreme drought, the Great Depression had driven some African American farmers off the Kansas prairie and into cities such as Topeka. Because they were accustomed to living among whites, and because their children had attended integrated schools, they objected to the urban color line. For these and other black people, a democratic ethos sometimes surpassed racial identity in importance. During the 1920s, Zelma Henderson's father moved his family from their western Kansas farm into

Oakley, so that Zelma and her siblings could attend a better school and associate with other blacks. When Zelma asked him about the family's nationality, he told her that she was "American." "That's the way I grew up," Zelma said. "We didn't have no black, white, or this type of thing."[50] When she moved to Topeka in 1940 to find work, she brought that color-blind egalitarianism with her.

Of all the factors that turned black people toward integration, perhaps none was more important than local geography. Economic changes in conjunction with population growth, especially by the 1920s and 1930s, placed some African Americans in areas of unusual cultural dynamism: the vaguely defined outer edges of the black neighborhoods. There, spatial conditions—the distribution of people in relation to one another and their environment—weakened the color line and fostered a movement for integration. No single race dominated this fringe zone; people of different backgrounds and identities—especially children—intermingled, adjusted to each other, and, in exceptional cases, learned to appreciate and desire interracial fellowship. Blacks asked an important question: if black children were good enough to play with white children, why couldn't they attend the white children's school?

Just as black people's proximity to whites weakened the color line, so did their distance from the black elementary schools. Blacks on the neighborhood fringe resented sending their children to school on long trips over dangerous streets, especially in winter. Some parents simply objected to their children's morning commute through the cold; as much as anything else, the sheer distance in frigid weather encouraged parents to challenge segregated education.

During the first half of the twentieth century, the pressure for integration focused on key places around Topeka: businesses, public facilities, real estate, the fringes of black neighborhoods, and especially schools. Despite their growing strength, the proponents of integration met stiff resistance. Many black people opposed them out of a desire to protect the black elementary schools, their teachers, and their students. More important, white business owners and public officials not only defended segregation but also attempted to strengthen it. By the 1940s, the movement to demolish the color line was colliding with the reactionary effort to sustain it. The result was a legal struggle with implications that extended far beyond the boundaries of Topeka.

Public spaces constituted one of the primary pressure points. Because Kansas prohibited discrimination in municipally licensed businesses and most public facilities, Topeka blacks did not have to endure segregated water fountains, restrooms, buses, railroad passenger cars, depots, high schools, or courtroom bibles. They did, however, have to suffer the indignities of informal, illegal forms of segregation. These racist practices reflected whites' fear of bodily intimacy with people of color. In general, anywhere that whites ate, slept, sat in dimmed light, or exposed their skin was off-limits to blacks. Many restaurants west of Kansas Avenue would not seat blacks and other minorities; signs read "Negroes and Mexicans Served in Sacks Only" (prompting an east-side eatery to post its policy: "Negroes and Mexicans Served Inside"). Certain hotels would not accommodate black guests. The Grand Theater at Sixth and Jackson admitted blacks only on one side of a balcony, called "peanut heaven," which whites also called "nigger heaven." Another theater, the Jayhawk, confined blacks to the "crow's nest." Clothing stores would not allow black customers to try on garments in dressing rooms. Swimming pools at Gage Park on the west side and Ripley Park on the east were closed to blacks, except for one day a year at Gage.[51]

Topeka's African Americans resented these "customary" forms of the color line, although some accepted their predicament. "During those days," William Mitchell recalled in a revealing use of spatial language, "you knew where your place was" and you "did not try to break the structure of it." But blacks also continually tested the racial boundaries. Eugene Johnson fondly remembered Freddy Rogers, who used his ambiguous complexion—evidence of past interracial intimacy—to mock the color line and its presumptions. "I ain't white," Rogers would insist, but his light skin, freckles, and red hair allowed him to pretend otherwise. One day while Johnson, Rogers, and several other young men walked to City Park, Rogers entered a restaurant, took a seat at the bar, and passed for white. As Rogers carried on his deception, his friends peeked through the windows and laughed.[52]

By the 1940s, some blacks openly challenged the color line that ran through the city's downtown business district. In 1944, Lucinda Todd, a former teacher at Buchanan Elementary, purchased a ticket at the Grand Theater and headed upstairs to peanut heaven only to find the black section full. After she took a seat in the white area across the aisle, a policeman appeared and told her she must move to the black side or leave. She left. Three years later, Phillip Burton, a Washburn University law student, tried to purchase a ticket at Dickinson Theater, another downtown Topeka establishment. Denied admission, he sued, claiming that the theater had violated a local ordinance against discrimination in municipally licensed businesses. Burton won the case, and the theater paid the minimum $10 fine. Then the city commission, much to the outrage of black citizens, hardened the color line by repealing the licensing requirement for theaters.[53]

This pattern—pressure for integration conflicting with pressure to strengthen the color line—also affected real estate. Beginning in the 1920s, as Topeka's black population grew and its members accrued earnings from the Santa Fe Railway and other employers, some tried to purchase homes in white neighborhoods, mostly on the west side. There, a building boom was pushing into the only undeveloped, elevated, flood-free land available to the city. Topeka homebuilders and real estate agents recognized that white people would pay premium prices to live in racially exclusive neighborhoods, and they sought to maintain the racial whiteness of the far west side and other residential pockets. They inserted clauses, or covenants, into property deeds, restricting ownership to whites, or they simply refused to sell certain properties to blacks.[54] Residential segregation fueled black anger and bitterness. Berdyne Scott recalled her childhood in Sandtown during the 1920s and 1930s. "My family could have afforded to live some place other than next to the railroad tracks on Jefferson Street," she said. She had envied the "pretty little houses" belonging to the Germans from Russia whom the Santa Fe had "brought here and sponsored." Those people "were the reason why my father and grandfather couldn't work except in certain places in the Santa Fe shops. I was sensitive about those things even as a youngster; I could see the differences."[55]

Even as the racist practices of homebuilders and real estate companies bolstered the residential color line in places such as the far west side, African Americans began to interact with white people in the racially mixed zones on the edges of the black enclaves. In these areas, especially during the Great Depression, bodily proximity and the common denominator of class began to transcend the divisive condition of race. As events transpired, the color line shifted, weakened, fragmented, and even began to disappear.

At times the color line depended on complex, sometimes fleeting racial encounters. In east Topeka, where Christina Jackson grew up in the 1930s, the white "lady across the street . . . wouldn't allow her kids to come on [the black] side of the street," but white and black children "would holler at each other" anyway, the sound of their voices carrying across the barrier that separated them. If the woman heard her children talking to Jackson, she "would make them come in the house."[56] During the late 1920s and early 1930s, Frederick Temple often played with the white children who lived around him in an area called Quinton Heights on Topeka's south side, but whenever Temple's friends from Monroe School showed up, his white friends left. The white children told Temple that they would associate with him, but that he shouldn't bring his "nigger friends out here because we aren't going to play with them."[57]

At other moments, the Great Depression's leveling effect diminished or nearly eliminated racial differences. Joe Douglas's family lived in east Topeka near Ripley Park in a "mixed neighborhood" of blacks, "Mexicans," and whites, including a fair number of "old German" people. "Everybody got along pretty well," Douglas recalled. "There was not a lot of racial problems because people were more concerned about survival then."[58] William Mitchell remembered the "mixed neighborhood in Mudtown," where black and white parents disciplined each other's errant children. "Them white women would grab your butt and whip it just like they would theirs," he said. "And the black would whip their kid's butts just like that. That's how close it was back in that Depression." As swats rained down on the bottoms of squirming youngsters, the color line virtually disappeared.[59]

For some black people, the interracial fringe eventually provided a normative standard by which they judged the quality of their lives and to which they aspired. Leola Williams, whose father and uncles worked for the Santa Fe, grew up during the 1920s and 1930s on the west end of First Street, in a neighborhood of black, white, Hispanic, and American Indian families. "You know I liked that," she told an interviewer as she recalled the white friends with whom she had played and who had visited her home. When Williams married, she and her husband moved back to West First Street and started a family of their own. As Leola Brown, wife of Oliver Brown, she was pleased that her daughters could play with children of varied racial backgrounds, as she had done.[60] What displeased her was that her eldest child, Linda, could not attend the neighborhood school with her playmates. Leola Brown was not alone. By the early 1940s, an increasing number of blacks wanted the city to integrate its schools. But the color line was still powerful, even in those parts of the educational system that were supposed to be free of discrimination.

Within nominally integrated Topeka High School, for example, a range of informal practices upheld the color line. Located three blocks west of the capitol in an impressive collegiate Gothic building, Topeka High was the city's only school for the advanced grades. Students of both races attended class together, but otherwise the administration tried to keep them apart. Although the school permitted African American boys to compete for spots on the Trojans football team, the informal color line shut them out. In reality, black males who wanted to participate in athletics could not play for any school team except the Ramblers, a separate basketball team that the black community organized in 1935 and that participated in the black Kansas and Missouri High School League. Cheerleading squads, too, remained distinct, as did extracurricular clubs and student councils. The swimming pool, always a troublesome environment for segregationists, went unused. Black and white students attended separate parties and proms. Before class, black students congregated on the school's second floor, where they had their lockers. One bell directed white students to assemble in the auditorium, while a different bell, the "nigger bell," called black students to their own assembly in another room.[61]

But in spite of its stubborn persistence, the educational color line already was showing signs of breakdown. Evidence appeared in the informal, daily interactions of students. The color line certainly separated them, but not like an impenetrable wall. Berdyne Scott, who graduated from Topeka High in 1935, recalled the heterosexual attraction that some black and white students felt for one another and that led to covert interracial dating. These young people did not engage in open courtship, she stated, but "slipped around" instead. Most such meetings involved black boys and white girls, although some black girls and white boys also yearned for each other. "We always knew when the white guys liked us," Scott remembered. "I can think of different guys I liked, despite their color, but we didn't go out with them."[62] Romantic urges mattered to race relations; to feel the stirrings of desire was to sense the color line's weakness. To act on that desire, to "slip around," was to circumvent it.

Legal efforts to break the educational color line accompanied its covert decay. A key event was the desegregation of Topeka's junior high schools. Black students attended elementary school through the eighth grade, went to segregated Roosevelt Junior High for grade nine, and then completed their studies at Topeka High. White students, in contrast, attended junior high for three straight years before entering high school. In 1940, Oaland Graham, a Tennesseetown resident who had attended Buchanan School through the sixth grade, tried to enroll for seventh grade at Boswell Junior High, where his family believed he would receive a superior education. When Boswell refused to admit him, he and his uncle successfully sued the Topeka Board of Education. In 1941, the city's junior high schools opened their doors to all students.[63]

Although junior high integration weakened the color line, its full effect was not instantaneous, as Jack Alexander's experience revealed. Because he was leaving a black school, Alexander's departure from Washington Elementary was "traumatic," but at East Topeka Junior High he formed friendships with children "of other races." The relatively "homogenous . . . social and economic level" of the students, he believed, softened their differences and encouraged their interaction in the classroom, in extracurricular activities, and in sports. Simple bodily proximity was important; at least for boys, sports contests and locker room nakedness—what might be called the interpersonal geography of athletic competition—broke down the color line like nothing else. "We all played on all of the athletic teams together," said Alexander. "We all showered [together] and wore each other's clothes." When Alexander and his classmates arrived at Topeka High, however, the color line eventually separated them. He gravitated toward his black friends on the second floor, and his aspiration to play for the Ramblers basketball team prevented him from questioning—to his later regret—the school's segregated athletics.[64]

In contrast, Joe Douglas developed resentments at East Topeka Junior High that he carried into high school. Although Douglas had white friends, he recalled that white teachers were reluctant to make eye contact with him, that white coaches refused to acknowledge his athletic abilities, and that he received lower grades for work superior to that of white students. He also remembered his frustration with a white instructor whose willful ignorance of history prevented her from confirming that black soldiers had served in Cuba during the Spanish-American War. His bitterness continued at Topeka High. A small but rugged boy who held his own on the mean streets of the Bottoms, he was angry that he could not turn out for wrestling, his best sport. The inequities violated a democratic principle that his father had instilled in him: "You are better than no man, and no man is better than you."[65]

For Douglas and other black students, junior high may have been less a seedbed of interracial harmony than an incubator of grievances against the color line. Beginning in 1943, black high school students, including Douglas, began to protest inequities in extracurricular activities and athletics. Some students, for example, believed that the Ramblers did not receive the financial support that the Board of Education had promised. Others, such as Douglas, harbored personal resentments.[66]

Conservatives did not stand by and watch the color line deteriorate. In 1942, after Oaland Graham's lawsuit, the Board of Education fired Superintendent A. J. Stout and replaced him with Kenneth McFarland, a native Kansan and staunch segregationist. McFarland appointed a black teacher and old friend, Harrison Caldwell, to oversee the district's black students, teachers, and elementary schools. A segregationist Kansan like his patron, Caldwell reinforced the high school's color line and quelled unrest among the black students. He monitored the cafeteria for interracial tables and summoned black students to assemblies ("good nigger assemblies," some disgruntled students called them) at which he ridiculed them for questioning their treatment. Caldwell also upbraided the district's black teachers and engineered their segregation within the Topeka Teachers Association.[67]

Although many African American teachers despised Caldwell—in their view, a "bigot," "con man," and "Uncle Tom"—a good number of them shared his commitment to segregating black and white students.[68] Some, including Mamie Williams, a Columbia University graduate and Topeka's most respected African American teacher, opposed junior high integration. Black teachers best understood black children and their needs, Williams and her colleagues said, and integration would result in the elimination of crucially important mentors. Events seemed to confirm their fears. After the opening of the junior high schools, the Topeka school district spared Williams but fired eight other black teachers, including the sister of a district employee who had testified on behalf of Oaland Graham.[69]

No one, though, could arrest the momentum for change. In 1948, the Topeka High School football team fielded its first black player. The next year, the Board of Education ordered the complete integration of Topeka High, including its assemblies, clubs, student government, and athletics. Although the record does not reveal the reasons for these decisions, high school coaches and the board may have acted on the realization, as Jack Alexander suggested, that a pool of integrated athletic talent would produce "bigger trophy rooms at Topeka High School."[70]

As the educational color line receded, parents and community activists prepared to destroy it in the one place where official policy still sanctioned it: the elementary schools. The grassroots experience and emotional energy that motivated this final push for integration came from the families, especially the mothers, who lived on the interracial fringes of the black neighborhoods. They were not the first fringe dwellers to resist the racial geography that conscribed them. During the early twentieth century, Topeka's demographic and economic growth prompted the city to annex outlying communities, including the elementary schools that served them. Because those schools—prior to annexation—lacked the legal option to segregate, they often enrolled small numbers of African American students. Once the Topeka school district took over the schools, principals and district officials allowed black children to continue to attend them, but the color line shifted when new blacks—the leading edge of Topeka's expanding black enclaves—moved in. Then the Board of Education invoked its segregationist policy and required the newcomers to send their children to distant black schools. The newcomers resisted, and in 1902, 1928, and 1929, parents sued the Topeka school district. But the Board of Education had committed itself to the black elementary schools, and sometime around 1920, perhaps even earlier, the district had instituted bus transportation for black pupils, a service that white children never received. The black neighborhoods, centered on separatism and self-help, provided little support. All the lawsuits failed.[71]

By the late 1940s, Topeka had changed. Increasing numbers of parents in the fringe places such as First Street rejected the spatial status quo. They did not want to send their children to black schools if other schools were closer, and they disagreed that busing compensated for the geographical inconveniences of long distances. The parents' objections were especially vehement during winter, when temperatures on the Great Plains plunged below zero. Leola Brown loved Monroe and its teachers, but she disliked "the distance the kids had to go to school. Standing, waiting on the school bus in all kinds of weather: freezing cold, sleet, snow, rain." Other mothers echoed her concerns. Christina Jackson respected the teachers at Washington, but she grew tired, she later said, of having "to bundle my kids up when it was 2 below zero and walk them down to catch the bus."[72] And there were the parents, Leola Brown and others, who no longer believed in segregation or separatism. Silas Hardrick Fleming, who lived down in the Bottoms, objected to black and white schools. "The entire colored race is craving light," he would later proclaim, "and the only way to reach the light is to start our children together in their infancy and they come up together."[73] The meaning of Fleming's vivid scenario was clear. Equal treatment required bodily proximity; children of all races must learn together in the same classrooms, with the same teachers, books, curricula, activities, and ideas.

The entire racial landscape was about to shift. Whether the color line could withstand such a sudden movement was an open question.

HAZARDS TO THEIR PHYSICAL BODIES

On a September morning in 1950, on the day Linda Brown was to begin third grade, her father took her by the hand and they started off to school. Rather than taking their usual route to the east, toward the bus stop at Quincy, they walked west a short distance before turning south on Western Avenue, a tree-lined street that sloped up from the river. Three blocks farther on Western, they arrived at Sumner Elementary. Built in 1936, Sumner was a two-story brick structure with two wings, an auditorium, and ten classrooms, enough to accommodate 240 students. Perhaps the building's most striking feature was the main entry tower and its bas-relief wall sculpture, which depicted children playing under a beaming sun. Hand in hand, father and daughter mounted the short flight of steps and went into the school.[74]

Linda's father had told her that Sumner officials probably would refuse to enroll her, and as he entered the principal's office, she took a seat outside the door. She could not make out the words that passed between the two men, but she later remembered that "they spoke very sharply." After a few minutes, her father emerged and they walked home "very briskly." Holding his hand, she "could just feel the tension in him." When they got home, Leola could tell what had happened. "Naturally," she recalled, "the principal gave the expected excuse: there wasn't anything he could do about it—Negro children couldn't attend Sumner because of the school board's policies."[75]

Twenty Topeka black families attempted to enroll children in white elementary schools that day. Of these, thirteen, including the Browns, became plaintiffs in a lawsuit claiming that the Topeka Board of Education, by maintaining segregated schools, denied them equal protection under the law and thus violated the Fourteenth Amendment to the United States Constitution. All the plaintiffs objected to segregation and its geographical constraints. They disliked sending children into cold air on long trips to school, they resented the policy that their offspring could not attend schools closest to their homes, and they disapproved of physically separating black and white students.

The plaintiffs acted with assistance from the National Association for the Advancement of Colored People (NAACP). Established in 1909, the NAACP was devoted to attacking segregation with lawsuits and legislation. African American citizens had founded the Topeka chapter of the NAACP in 1914, but the organization had never enjoyed the unequivocal support of the black community. Still, by the late 1940s, the Topeka NAACP had retained energetic leaders committed to the cause: its president, McKinley Burnett, who lived across the alley from Monroe Elementary and worked as a stock clerk at the Veterans Administration Hospital; its secretary, Lucinda Todd, the former schoolteacher who dared sit in the whites-only section at the Grand Theater; and Charles Bledsoe, a Washburn University law school graduate who headed the chapter's Legal

Redress Committee. In 1948, the chapter had petitioned the Topeka Board of Education to end its policy of segregated elementary schools. When the board angrily rebuffed the group, Bledsoe began to prepare a lawsuit. He invited the attorneys Charles and John Scott, fellow Washburn alumni and sons of pioneer lawyer Elisha Scott, to work with him. And he took a fateful step: he wrote to the Legal Defense Fund (LDF), the litigation arm of the national NAACP, and asked for help.[76]

The LDF expressed keen interest in the Topeka situation and offered its expertise. Under Thurgood Marshall (later a U.S. Supreme Court justice), Robert Carter, Jack Greenberg, and other lawyers, the LDF sought opportunities for an all-out legal initiative against segregation. The timing seemed right. Recent U.S. Supreme Court decisions had chipped away at segregation in Oklahoma and Missouri universities, and now, lawsuits against local boards of education—in Topeka and other communities—would allow the NAACP to broaden its campaign.[77]

The LDF's involvement marked a crucially important geographical shift in the challenge to the color line. The Brown family and other African Americans were absorbed in the local conditions that had provoked their grievances, but the LDF operated on a national scale.[78] The strategy of Marshall, Carter, and Greenberg was not to win local cases but to find exemplary cases that would help them to argue before the United States Supreme Court that the fundamental "separate but equal" legal premise of the color line was false and therefore unconstitutional. The LDF attorneys probably expected to lose the local lawsuits, which would allow them to build their national strategy through the appeals process. When they finally appeared before the Supreme Court—the supreme national stage—they planned to present an argument that would convince the justices to strike down school segregation across the nation.[79]

In accordance with LDF instructions, Bledsoe and his colleagues identified potential plaintiffs whose reliability, community standing, employment, and involvement in school segregation suited them to participation. Among them was Oliver Brown, a friend of attorney Charles Scott. The NAACP needed Oliver. Leola Brown could not take on the responsibility; although she was a chapter member and an integrationist, she was pregnant, which diminished her energy and constrained her ability to get around. Oliver's union job at the Santa Fe Railway, the NAACP lawyers reasoned, shielded him from white people who might retaliate by having him fired. There also was the simple fact of geography. It was a long way from the Brown home at 511 West First Street to Monroe Elementary School. A reserved man anxious about his railroad job and his part-time position as an assistant minister in the African Methodist Episcopal Church, Oliver was reluctant to join the case. Eventually, after some arm-twisting from Scott, he agreed to participate.[80]

In a coordinated action, the participants attempted to have their children admitted to white schools. When officials turned them away, they reported back to Bledsoe and the Scotts, who finalized the lawsuit. The attorneys did not arrange the list of plaintiffs alphabetically. Perhaps because Oliver Brown was the only adult male in the group, Bledsoe put his name first. A geographical calculation, not gender, also might have led the attorney to place Oliver's name at the top, for no other plaintiff experienced a more inconvenient spatial ratio of distance from a black school to distance from a white school. No other plaintiff, to be precise, lived as far from a black school yet as close to a white one.[81] It was clear that Bledsoe was focused on geography and the environmental conditions intrinsic to it. In violation of the Fourteenth Amendment, Bledsoe wrote in the complaint, the Topeka Board of Education, by requiring black children to attend segregated schools "far removed" from the neighborhoods in which they resided, "exposed" the children "to extreme hazards to their physical bodies" and thus deprived them of the educational advantages that white children received.[82] The complaint directly challenged the "separate but equal" doctrine that, for more than a half century, had institutionalized the color line. Early in 1951, Bledsoe delivered the document to the U.S. District Court in Topeka.

In late June, Robert Carter and Jack Greenberg of the national NAACP arrived in Topeka to meet with local attorneys and prepare for the hearing. Carter and Greenberg swept aside the local chapter's strategy in favor of their own. The local attorneys wanted to showcase the geographical and physical grievances of the plaintiffs, as reflected in Bledsoe's original complaint. Carter made it clear that the team would emphasize the testimony of expert witnesses who would undermine the general concept that segregated education was equal. The NAACP attorneys would not focus on the place-specific complaints particular to the Topeka case.[83]

On June 25, a panel of three judges, all of them white, began to hear *Oliver Brown et al. v. Board of Education of Topeka, Kansas*. After establishing that the Board of Education had divided the city into eighteen "territories" for white elementary schools and four "negro districts" or "territories" for black schools, Carter and his associates called a series of witnesses who described the disruptions and inequities that such a spatial system caused. Lena Mae Carper and her daughter, Katherine, lived in west Topeka, much closer to Randolph Elementary, a white school, than to Buchanan, which Katherine attended. Each weekday morning before she headed off to work, Lena Mae accompanied Katherine four blocks to the school bus stop. On mornings when cold weather forced them to take shelter in a nearby grocery store, Lena Mae had to run outside and hail the bus as it passed. When Katherine climbed on board for the twenty-block ride, the bus was often so heavily "loaded," the girl testified, that "there is no place to sit." Oliver Brown briefly described his daughter's departure for school at 7:40 a.m.; Darlene Watson, a white woman who lived across the street from the Browns, then reported that her son left home at 8:40 to attend Sumner School. Lucinda Todd explained that her child had to attend Buchanan School ten blocks from home, but that Lowman Hill School was only three blocks distant. Numerous other plaintiffs and witnesses—Alma Galloway, Sadie Emanuel, Shirley May Hodison, James Richardson, Marguerite Emerson, Zelma Henderson, Silas Fleming—similarly attested to the physical inequities that arose when school officials tried to impose a simple color line on a complex geography.[84]

Then Greenberg called the expert witnesses, academic scholars in education, psychology, and sociology—although none in geography, which might have provided an environmental perspective—to discredit segregation's separate-but-equal premise. The scholarly contribution to the trial record shifted the plaintiff's case from grounded local concerns toward theoretical, abstract arguments that were more useful to the NAACP's national strategy. Both Hugh Speer of the University of Kansas City and James Buchanan of Kansas State Teacher's College discovered subtle physical differences between Topeka's black and white schools. Buchanan, for example, asserted that a "beautiful environment" improved learning, and that the black schools were not as attractively landscaped as the white institutions. But little of the two men's testimony addressed physical conditions specific to the city and its schools. "I don't think we can answer [a question of] educational opportunity purely on physical features," Dr. Speer stated as he defined "the total school experience," which included students' "associations with the other children." Although he had not studied the total school experience of Topeka's black children, Speer was certain that segregation automatically introduced an element of inequality into it.[85]

Each subsequent expert witness elaborated on Speer's assertion. Drawing on "thousands of experimental studies" across the United States, R. S. B. English of Ohio State University argued that segregation, "based upon a fallacy of difference," created "the very difference which it assumes to have been present to begin with." Wilbur Brookover of Michigan State College testified that the disjuncture between segregation and America's "model of democratic equality" confused and frustrated "the negro child" and provoked "delinquent," "criminal," or "socially abnormal behavior." Louisa Holt of the University of Kansas contended that legal segregation induced "a sense of inferiority" in young black children and weakened their motivation to excel. A doctoral candidate from the University of Chicago, Bettie Belk, suggested that delaying integration until junior high school imposed enormous stress on adolescent black children.[86]

By the time Belk left the witness stand, *Brown v. Board* had moved far from West First Street and Mudtown, from cold mornings at the bus stop and long rides to school, from actual children such as Katherine Carper and Linda Brown. The expert testimony assumed that space, proximity, and surroundings—"environment," in psychological parlance—influenced child development and learning. John Kane of Notre Dame University stated that segregation cut down on "communication among people" and erected "a barrier" that made black children feel inferior and deprived them of human associations important to their personal advancement.[87] Yet the environment that Kane and other scholars described was a generic condition, a virtual geography centered on the psychological state of an abstract, essential type, "the negro child." Scientific surveys and observations supported some of the experts' generalizations, but none of those studies focused on children or schools in Topeka. The LDF had taken the argument against the color line to a larger, more abstract landscape. Along the way, the local and the concrete—specific lives in specific environments and places—had faded from the picture.

On August 3, Justice Walter Huxman delivered the unanimous opinion of the court. Despite the plaintiffs' claims, the educational facilities and services for black and white children in Topeka were essentially equal. Huxman noted that the plaintiff's attorneys had placed relatively little emphasis on physical conditions. Instead, "they relied primarily upon the contention that segregation in and of itself . . . violates [the plaintiffs'] rights guaranteed by the Fourteenth Amendment." After reviewing legal precedents, including the Supreme Court's decision in *Plessy v. Ferguson* in 1896, the legal basis of the color line, Huxman concluded that the equal protection clause of the Fourteenth Amendment still permitted the state of Kansas to separate school children by race. Huxman and the other justices found the expert testimony persuasive, but they determined that only the Supreme Court had the authority to overrule *Plessy*. So they did something that allowed the LDF to keep *Brown v. Board* alive: they attached to their decision a brief "finding of fact" bluntly stating that segregation "has a detrimental effect upon the colored children," especially when "it has the sanction of law." The NAACP team, led by Carter and Greenberg, made Huxman's finding of fact the basis of an appeal.[88] A local grievance was about to become a fully national issue.

When Huxman handed down the Kansas opinion, the NAACP added it to a suite of local cases that together composed a single coordinated challenge to the color line. In Delaware, the District of Columbia, Virginia, South Carolina, and now Kansas, the organization had sponsored lawsuits that it intended to bring before the Supreme Court, each a piece of its overall assault on segregation.[89]

As argued by the LDF, each additional case transcended its roots in local geography. The LDF attorneys apparently realized the importance of that geography. "If the [school attendance] lines are drawn on a natural basis, without regard to race or color," Marshall had said, "then I think that nobody would have any complaint." But the LDF did not use geographical analysis to build its larger argument. This may have reflected the fact that few professional geographers, if any, during the 1950s studied racial problems.[90] More important, another branch of social science, psychology, provided Marshall and his colleagues with a sharper, more effective argument. Although psychology emphasized abstract types—"the negro child"—that abstractness gave the discipline a universal appeal and thus made its findings widely applicable, regardless of geography. Mapping, spatial analysis, and other geographical techniques exposed each community's social and natural landscape and the distribution of people within it, even though drawing lines on the basis of that complexity would not have been as simple and "natural" as Marshall suggested. Psychology, in contrast, cut through the messiness of geography to what seemed the core issue: the essential condition of black children everywhere.

The research most useful to the LDF came from Kenneth and Mamie Clark, African American psychologists from New York. During the 1940s, the Clarks undertook a series of simple experiments called the Dolls Test. Using brown and white dolls, or crayons and blank human forms, they asked black children to express racial preferences: "Give me the doll that you like best"; "Give me the doll that looks bad"; "Give me the doll that is a nice color." A substantial number of subjects were perfectly happy with dark skin, which they demonstrated in their choices, but a disturbing proportion of the children—up to two-thirds in some instances—made choices that suggested a negative sense of self. Many children indicated that they liked the white doll best, or that the brown doll looked bad. The source of their self-rejection was unclear, but something in their experience—the obvious factor was the attitudes and structures of a segregated society—caused them to feel inferior.[91]

Difficult questions remained. Save for one instance, no children implicated in a lawsuit had taken the test—could judges accept generalizations from such a sample? To what degree was school segregation alone responsible for the negative self-perception of black children? Why did the Clarks' findings clash with the experiences of black teachers, who insisted that they, better than anyone, understood black children and best nurtured them? And if black children were placed in integrated schools in the company of white children, wouldn't they still be vulnerable to racism?[92]

Nevertheless, the test results were emotionally devastating and had tremendous persuasive potential. Despite their seasoned professionalism, even the Clarks struggled to retain their composure while observing the agony their questions provoked in their subjects. Some children, they reported, "broke down and cried." Two "ran out of the testing room, unconsolable, convulsed in tears." One boy tried to explain that he was actually white. "I look brown because I got a suntan this summer," he said.[93] The political and legal implications of the Dolls Test were unavoidable, as was its emotional power. What kind of person would not be saddened or angered by the psychological turmoil of innocent children?

In 1952 and 1953, the Supreme Court heard oral arguments on the combined cases, now jointly listed under *Brown v. Board of Education of Topeka*. After lengthy deliberation, the court delivered its unanimous decision on May 17, 1954. Reading from the text, and referring specifically to "the Kansas case," Chief Justice Earl Warren explained that arguments based on "physical facilities" and "tangible factors" alone were not enough to overturn school segregation. Rather, "intangible considerations" that shaped the child and helped "him to adjust normally to his environment" must determine the law. Citing the "modern authority" of "psychological knowledge," Warren then laid down the court's opinion, as hard and concrete as the marble temple in which the justices sat. "We conclude," he stated, "that in the field of public education the doctrine of 'separate but equal' has no place. Separate educational facilities are inherently unequal."[94]

A triumphant Thurgood Marshall predicted that school segregation across the nation would cease within five years. Even before the Supreme Court's decision, Topeka had begun to dismantle the system. Kenneth McFarland, the segregationist superintendent, was gone, driven out by charges of financial improprieties and racism, and in 1953, a new Board of Education had voted to abolish segregation in the city's elementary schools. The Supreme Court's ruling gave Topeka's blacks further cause for celebration. "It makes me feel that I'm an American citizen in the true sense of the word," said McKinley Burnett, president of the local NAACP. "It will enable me to sing 'My country, 'tis of thee, sweet land of liberty' without making myself a hypocrite." Oliver Brown said that the decision would lead to "a better future" in which the "unity" of Americans—based on a "love for one another" that "God instituted into human hearts through Jesus Christ"—would prevent "Communism" from trying to "creep in."[95] In Topeka and throughout America, the color line was in its death throes.

Or so it seemed. The court's decision was crystal clear: school segregation was inherently unequal; therefore, all schools must integrate. But in the messy landscape of streets, houses, neighborhoods, long bus rides to distant schools, and frustrated parents, implementing the law would not be so easy. Lucinda Todd, one of the plaintiffs, anticipated the difficulties that lay ahead. Although she applauded the ruling, she acknowledged that "we may have a long time to go before segregation is actually abolished" and that a "machinery . . . must now be set up" to accomplish it.[96] The problem lay in the complexities of Topeka's geography. There, the color line would not simply disappear.

ON A NATURAL BASIS

By the time the Supreme Court rendered its decision, Linda Brown was finishing the sixth grade at McKinley School in north Topeka. In 1953, her father had accepted a position as pastor of St. Mark's African Methodist Episcopal, a north-side church, and had moved the family across the river to Sandtown. Although Linda played with white children who lived across the railroad tracks from the family home, most of her friends were black.[97]

The Brown family upheld its commitment to transcend the color line. Oliver Brown became friends with Maurice Lang, a white minister, and he officiated at a remarkable service in 1957 in which Lang and his wife converted to the AME faith. The two men were close. Traveling in Lang's automobile one evening in 1961, Oliver suddenly grew ill. He asked Lang to pray with him, and the two men clasped hands. Somewhere on the darkened prairie, as Lang sped toward the hospital, Oliver died.[98]

Leola, Linda, Terry Lynn, and Cheryl moved back to the old neighborhood on West First Street, where Cheryl attended Sumner Elementary, the school that had refused to admit her sister. Cheryl and Linda remained staunch proponents of integration. As they went to college and started families of their own, they matured into conscientious, outspoken women who advocated a society without racial boundaries.[99]

After 1954, schools in Topeka and many other communities failed to meet the mandate laid down by the *Brown* decision. The Supreme Court's unanimity did not reflect a national consensus on race relations. Many white Americans remained hostile to racial equality, and they rejected the court's instruction to proceed "with all deliberate speed" in opening their schools to black children. In a coordinated act of "massive resistance," southern states stonewalled *Brown* and, despite dramatic confrontations with the federal government, kept schools segregated for decades.[100]

Conditions were not much better elsewhere in the country, as most states practiced an informal, disguised, de facto segregation that was difficult to expose in court. During the 1970s, however, civil rights activists began to win important local cases, victories that coincided with threats from the U.S. Department of Health, Education, and Welfare (HEW) to withdraw federal money from school districts that refused to comply with *Brown*.[101] Still, even sympathetic school officials had difficulty meeting court orders and HEW demands. Merely opening the doors to all, regardless of color, they learned, would not necessarily produce a mix of races proportional to their numbers in society. Residential patterns often determined school attendance; no matter the official racial policy, a school in an all-white neighborhood would enroll an all-white student body. It meant one thing to desegregate a school, but quite another to integrate it. However subtle the distinction seemed, it posed an overwhelming problem.[102]

Around the nation, judges and public officials concluded that they had no choice but to achieve racial integration by radically redrawing school boundaries. Rather than draw the lines "on a natural basis, without regard to race or color," as Thurgood Marshall had suggested, officials drew them with an exceedingly keen eye for those markers. The lines they inscribed were as unnatural as the ones on any segregationist map. Slicing through neighborhoods to encompass just the right mix of black and white children, the irregular boundaries revealed the contortions of a society struggling to make its tangible self conform to an abstract ideal of what it should become. Ironically, implementing a Supreme Court decision based on the irrelevance of local geography required school officials to entangle themselves deeply in it.[103]

The necessary consequence of those contorted boundaries—busing children on long rides outside their home neighborhoods—compounded the irony, as it threatened to replicate the very conditions that had provoked the Browns' and others' grievances in the first place. To be sure, busing produced some striking examples of harmonious integration and improved academic performance among children both white and black, but such successes contrasted with many other instances in which busing contributed to painful social strife. The sense of place—a person's feeling of connection to the landscape in which he or she lives—was a powerful source of identity and security. As Linda Brown, her mother, and many other children and parents knew, busing violated it. Although many African Americans supported busing, many also opposed it or were ambivalent.[104]

White people especially rejected busing, and not just because it took their children away from the home neighborhood. For many whites, the absence of blacks was integral to their sense of place. To them, whiteness signified prosperity, cleanliness, and safety; blackness promised just the opposite. Resentful of blacks, school officials, judges, and liberal politicians, millions of people joined the national "white flight" from the interracial cities to the suburbs, accelerating a trend that already was changing neighborhoods and their schools. At the end of the twentieth century, the downside of *Brown* and busing was clear: many urban schools and neighborhoods were so black or so white as to be virtually segregated. Americans had reproduced the color line.[105]

Topeka experienced its own version of the events that played out in thousands of communities across the United States. There were notable successes, but even as integration transformed parts of the city, problems developed. As the population increased during the 1950s, white residents once again moved to new housing developments on the geographically open west side. The schools they left behind, including elementary schools, consequently had greater proportions of black youths relative to white. At Topeka High School, space grew tight as burgeoning numbers of students, white and black, packed its seats. The Board of Education might have relieved the pressure by shifting some black students to fill hundreds of empty seats at Highland Park High School on the southeast edge of the city. A simple, relatively painless boundary change would have done the job. But in 1960 the board made a revealing decision: it built a new high school, Topeka West, which would enroll 702 white and 2 black students.[106]

The revival of the color line in the schools was matched by its resurgence in other parts of Topeka's landscape. During the late 1950s, city and federal officials inaugurated massive urban renewal and freeway projects. The Topeka board of commissioners stated that the "rehabilitation, conservation or redevelopment" of "slum or blighted areas" was "in the interest of the public health, safety, morals, or welfare" of the city's residents. Commercial and labor organizations supported the plan. The president of the Topeka Real Estate Board pledged "the enthusiastic willingness" of realtors "to help improve housing conditions and the neighborhood environment." When the bulldozers and wrecking cranes finally went to work in 1962, they crashed through the city's lowest, most marginal environments. In the Bottoms, a swath of buildings and structures—decrepit but nonetheless significant repositories of the city's African American culture and history—disappeared. Interstate 70 furthered the destruction, wiping out a good portion of black businesses along with numerous residences, including the Brown family's old stone house at 511 West First Street.[107]

Demographic, economic, and environmental changes gradually transformed Topeka's racial geography. As time passed, fewer people remembered that places such as the Bottoms and Mudtown had existed. Instead, Topeka residents simply thought in terms of west Topeka and east Topeka. West Topeka was mostly white and better off, with finer houses and newer, better schools. East Topeka was mostly black and poor, with aging houses and old schools, many of them in a topographically low landscape devoid of the economic activity characteristic of an earlier time.[108] West Topeka and east Topeka: the distinction demarcated the new shape of the color line.

Resistance was assured. The local NAACP decried the wreckage of urban renewal and a plan to relocate displaced black citizens in segregated housing. By the 1970s, some blacks no longer could tolerate the resegregation of the schools. Complaints centered on the creation of "a racially segregated environment," but school officials asserted "that geographic boundaries had been established without unlawful racial discrimination or segregation." From 1973 to 1979, lawsuits and HEW threats forced Topeka to address the problem, and the city proposed a controversial program of school closures and busing. The last legal challenge was not settled until 1994, forty years after *Brown*, but even then it wasn't completely dead.[109] One of the lead plaintiffs in that interminable case, weary but resolute, was none other than Linda Brown.

On the thirtieth anniversary of what became known as *Brown v. Board of Education*, as the latest lawsuit dragged on, a journalist asked Linda Brown Smith for her thoughts. Then forty-one and with her own children in de facto segregated schools, she reflected on the time when her weekday morning steps had carried her through a landscape in which the choices had seemed clear, as only a child could perceive them. Life had turned on small but fundamentally important matters of basic fairness, such as who had to stand in the cold and who did not and whether or not you could experience the fullness of life in the company of your friends. "I only wanted to go to school with Mona and Guinevere because that's who I played with every day," Linda said. The road had been long and hard, she seemed to suggest, and the Supreme Court ruling "was not the quick fix we thought it would be."[110] In Topeka, as in many other American communities, the color line was alive and well, and its future was uncertain. ★

NINE

IT'S A GAS

The United States and the Oil Shock of 1973–1974

Norman Reichbach and his cus-
tomers probably had given little thought to the limitations the natural world
imposed on them. Riding on rubber tires and pavement in pursuit of their
dreams, they sped over hills and rivers, sliced through snow, rain, and darkness,
and collapsed time. In negating environmental obstacles with their machines,
they minimized the impediment of their bodies. No matter how flabby, infirm,
aged, injured, or ill, they crossed the landscape with ease. Their mechanical
mastery of nature afforded them a luxury that they often took for granted:
insulated from the scenery, they more fully enjoyed it.

Then their world and their perception of it changed. The movement of oil
from its underground sources slowed by 1973, and thousands of service station
operators across America—Norman Reichbach and many others—no longer
had as much gasoline to sell. No longer were they and their customers so free;
no longer could they ignore so easily the number and cost of their trips and
the potential consequences if they ran out of gas. As the needles on their fuel
gauges inclined toward empty, nature mattered a little more. Hills appeared
higher, winter winds felt colder, and distances seemed greater—all because
they no longer could assume the availability of a fuel that was little more than
a processed fossil soup.

As dealers ran dry and shut down their pumps, drivers formed long lines
at the stations that remained open, including Reichbach's City Line Flying A
at 1 Central Park Avenue in Yonkers, New York. The lines were not simply a
function of shortage. Doubts and fears also impelled motorists to the pumps.

Worried that they might not find gas when they needed it, they took every opportunity to top off their tanks. The intensity of their demand prompted some states to pass laws intended to distribute the flow evenly. New York mandated that dealers not favor regular customers, fill tanks on alternate days depending on odd- and even-numbered license plates, and serve only motorists whose tanks were less than half full. Still, the regulatory measures did not calm anxious drivers.[1]

Reichbach felt the strain no less than did his customers. He had never had much reason to anticipate a shortage. Perhaps he recalled that the federal government had rationed fuel during the Second World War, but he had been a boy then, and his more recent experience of postwar abundance probably dominated his consciousness. He and a partner, Philip Guidano, had opened City Line Flying A in 1962, when oil flowed freely, the economy expanded, and people purchased automobiles as never before. For some ten years, the two men profited from their small enterprise, but late in 1973, their circumstances suddenly changed. Getty Oil, their gasoline supplier, reduced its deliveries by 30 percent. Although Reichbach and Guidano charged their customers more per gallon, the price increase could not compensate for the drop in sales.[2]

As the gasoline supply dwindled, Reichbach's cordial relationship with his customers deteriorated. They began to pressure him, not only to ensure that he sold them gas but also to persuade him to sell more than the law allowed. Some tried a soft approach, offering him liquor, neckties, money, and other gifts. Others tried to ingratiate themselves by assuming a creepy, unwelcome familiarity. "Hi ya Normie," they greeted him. "Give my regards to your wife." A few women proposed an unsettling form of intimacy, offering their bodies in exchange for fuel. Other customers were subtler and more devious in their manipulations, such as those who disconnected their fuel gauges so that their tanks appeared to be empty. Many were downright aggressive, telephoning Reichbach incessantly, even at home, hounding him with their requests—their demands—for gasoline.[3]

The pressure rattled Reichbach, and he did not like what he saw in his customers or in himself. "My temper is short," he remarked. "I'm irritated easily. That's not my nature." Sometimes he just snapped. One day he noticed his wife in the line of cars. She was reluctant to cut in front of the other drivers, but he waved her ahead anyway. When a man behind her complained, he couldn't take it anymore. "Look, buddy," he shouted, "I sleep with her, not with you." Among all the behaviors that the beleaguered service station operator witnessed, violence alarmed him the most. A driver attempted to make a right turn through the line that snaked from the pumps into the street. Motorists in the line mistakenly assumed that he was trying to cut in, and three of them leaped from their vehicles, fists clenched, ready to beat him. "Animals!" Reichbach exclaimed. "People get to be animals for gas."[4]

The gasoline shortage induced in Norman Reichbach an emotional and physical reaction that epitomized the modern condition: nausea. Surely he thought himself lucky that his house stood across the street from his service station. Unlike his customers, he did not have to burn fuel to get to work. Yet that proximity also prevented him from escaping the source of his distress. "When I get up and go into the bathroom to brush my teeth," he said, "I can see them lining up in their cars with their lunch and their thermoses, like they're going on an outing. And I get sick."[5]

Until 1973, Americans were unaware of how dependent they were on oil and its derivatives and how powerless they could feel when their tanks ran dry. Like Norman Reichbach and his customers, they took for granted the machines and the fuel that insulated them from the vicissitudes of nature and the wearisome challenges of movement across the landscape. For most people, the internal combustion engine and the automobile had symbolized all that was great and promising about the United States: material abundance, economic prosperity, technological progress, individual opportunity, and freedom of movement. But like Reichbach and his customers, they discovered that the mere slowing— not stoppage—of oil forced them to confront the underside of the American Dream.

In that shadowy netherworld, virtually every marker of national greatness had an alternate, ignominious face. Instead of inexhaustible abundance, Americans now experienced limits. Rather than endless prosperity, they coped with economic contraction. If they once foresaw boundless technological progress, they now reckoned with machines that made them weak and vulnerable. Instead of ambitious, optimistic, go-getting individualists, they turned out to be anxious, alienated, desperate creatures capable of behaving like animals. If the automobile symbolized the confidence of an era when gasoline was cheap and seemingly limitless, then the line of cars at the service station stood for its opposite, a time when doubt, anger, and fear—not dreams of unlimited prosperity—issued from the pumps.

The travails of Norman Reichbach and his customers belong to a much larger story, a "big history," centered on the system by which the United States tapped the flow of energy—often measured in light, heat, and motion—that defined the very form and function of the universe.[6] By the twentieth century, the United States had increased its diversion of that flow by drawing oil from deep within the Earth and turning it into gasoline and diesel fuel at service station pumps. Composed of underground deposits, wells, pipelines, ships, refineries, storage tanks, railroads, highways, trucks, service stations, and the corporations and government agencies that ran them, the system poured oil into the U.S. economy, making the nation wealthy and powerful.

But in the early 1970s, at the very moment that U.S. oil consumption dramatically increased, the rate of extraction from the nation's domestic reserves peaked and went into decline. To make up for the deficit, the United States drew from overseas sources as never before. This reliance on imported oil left the nation vulnerable to manipulation by foreign governments. In October 1973, after the United States supported Israel in a war with Egypt and Syria, a group of Middle East countries retaliated against the nation with an oil embargo. The consequences were telling. As the vast system that linked ancient underground deposits to modern service station pumps shut down, incidences of frustration, manipulation, violence, and nausea shot up.[7]

The story of the oil shock of 1973–1974 would be important if it consisted only of shortage, embargo, and the resulting social and economic turmoil, but it has a deeper significance that speaks to the environmental basis of life in the United States and all other places. More than ever before, Americans had to confront the absolute limits of a crucially important energy source. Nature had not distributed oil uniformly or in unlimited abundance beneath the Earth's surface, and by the early 1970s, extraction within the geographical boundaries of the United States had begun to slow. Yet the energetic pinch that citizens felt was the consequence not simply of finite reserves in American territory or of the nation's desire for foreign oil. The pinch of 1973–1974 was not just a national, transnational, or international problem—it was a manifestation of a universal law of physics that conditioned the existence of all living things.[8]

The 1973–1974 oil shock tested Americans' capacity to recognize this truth and modify their behavior accordingly. Did the nation and its citizens learn anything from the experience? If so, what did they learn? Did they act on those hard lessons? From the perspective of the lines of motorists at City Line Flying A and other service stations, the initial answers are troubling. All too often, the oil shock evoked Americans' propensity for selfishness, greed, deceit, denial, anger, and violence. Many people could not see or did not want to see past their immediate concerns to the underlying causes of their predicament. They were too invested in oil to do otherwise.

Yet there is another side to the story, barely discernable at places like City Line Flying A. Not all Americans were helpless, mindless, self-absorbed victims willing to debase themselves for a few gallons of gas. In response to the crisis, many questioned their presumptions about the world and their place in it. A few tried to understand the environmental basis of what was happening to them, and some attempted alternative courses of action. It was difficult, if not impossible, for them to do anything without using oil, so heavily did they rely on it for food production, transportation, education, and myriad other economic, political, and cultural activities. Some tried to maneuver more freely within the system, and they recognized that cooperative behavior, not individualism and greed, furthered their objectives. Others sought to minimize their dependence on oil, if not break free of it altogether. A substantial number turned to the human body, a natural reserve once thought to be a major constraint on mobility. Of those Americans who opened themselves to the body's energetic potential, perhaps some had waited in line at City Line Flying A. Perhaps Reichbach himself considered its possibilities when he walked across the street to his house. But whether or not he and his customers recognized bodies as an alternative energy source, bodies were abundant everywhere—as abundant, in fact, as oil was scarce.

Americans often showed the worst side of themselves in 1973–1974. Because the nation still is dependent on oil, it might be worthwhile to remember how its citizens behaved when they first realized that oil and automobiles were not necessarily the best means by which to conserve their liberty. Revisiting the past might reveal choices—if not exits—at every turn.

THE ENTROPIC DRAMA OF THE UNIVERSE

The predicament in which Americans found themselves in 1973–1974 was the consequence of a cosmic condition that has bedeviled humankind from time immemorial. All forms of life, humans included, must capture a portion of the energy that flows through the universe. For the most part, living things do this by consuming other living things. In the abstract, the process seems straightforward. Grass absorbs sunlight. Cows eat grass. Humans drink cow's milk, converting its calories into physical movement and body heat. In reality, energy capture and conversion are anything but simple. The flow of light and heat across the Earth is finite, uneven, and evanescent, and it has taxed the powers of humankind to divert and use even a fraction of it. When people figured out how to transform petroleum—oil—into gasoline and other fuels, they tapped the flow as never before. The fossilized remains of countless organisms, oil and coal powered the development of modern industrial civilization. But if the hydrocarbon economy enabled people to accomplish great things, it did not exempt them from the constraints that the flow of energy imposed. At no moment was this more obvious than during the oil shock of 1973–1974. Norman Reichbach's nausea, it seems, was a telling register of humanity's cosmic energy predicament.

The basic conditions for that predicament appeared at the beginning of the universe. In a scientific or historical sense, no one knows what came before. The primary origin of everything will remain a problem for philosophy and theology, not history. What matters to history is what happened at the inception of galaxies, stars, planets, and the rest—and what came afterward. This much is reasonably clear: from the start, the quantity of energy was fixed. No ultimate energy source, no giant furnace, would forever pulse fresh waves of light and heat into the darkness; the universe's warmth was a one-time, one-shot proposition. The beginning was hot—very hot. From that moment onward, the flow was in one direction only, from higher temperature to lower. The shine of a star and the streak of a meteor, the rotation of a planet and the eruption of a volcano, the rush of a river and the crash of a wave—these and an infinite number of other physical motions dissipated heat from warmer conditions to cooler ones. Now known as entropy, the process never stopped or reversed. And its irreversibility pointed toward an inescapable conclusion. Eventually, at some distant moment, heat would dissipate until there would be no more hot and cold, but only a bland gray equilibrium—an undifferentiated mean—in which everything would be the same temperature. When the universe finally achieved its thermal destiny, all movements and struggles—all history—would cease.[9]

Life became the tragic protagonist in the entropic drama of the universe, the beneficiary and prisoner of the gradient down which heat and time flowed. Between three billion and four billion years ago, on a lonely planet alternately bathed in light and shrouded in darkness, microscopic organisms appeared. Radiant energy from the nearest star, the sun, enabled those organisms to combine carbon dioxide, water, and minerals into the compounds that formed their tissues. Over eons, the process fostered an astonishing diversity of plants and animals, each capable of conserving a tiny portion of the sunlight that washed across them. In effect, the carbon-based substance of each organism—a cell, a seed, or an egg, for example—served as a temporary energy reservoir, a fatty, oleaginous pool along the universe's unstoppable journey toward its undifferentiated mean. Eventually, the energy in each pool became physical movement—the reservoir spilled its contents—and the flow of heat continued. The cell divided and became two; the seed germinated and a tree arose; the egg cracked open and a reptile emerged. Yet renewal, growth, and storage were only temporary, for no matter how cunning or artful the adaptation—no matter how deep the oleaginous pool—the outcome was inevitable. Sooner or later, every reservoir emptied. And at the end of time, reservoirs would be no more.

Until that moment, pools of energy accumulated and dissipated, alternately holding and releasing heat—or the potential for heat—as it rippled through the ages. One of the purest accumulations of energy was a hydrogen and carbon compound that formed beneath the Earth's surface. Over millions of years, countless generations of organisms died and drifted down to oxygen-depleted zones on the ocean floor. One-celled aquatic plants called phytoplankton formed most of that rich benthic slime. Animal plankton that ate the phytoplankton also composed it, as did their excrement, the excrement of fishes, and odd bits of bird guano, dinosaur tissue, fish scale, gingko leaf, and anything else organic that reached the bottom before bacteria or plankton consumed it. Erosion added sand and mud to the gooey mixture, which, over additional millions of years, solidified into rock. Between seventy-five hundred and fifteen thousand feet below the earth's surface, intense pressure and moderate heat, about 180 degrees Fahrenheit, then slowly cooked the organic residue into oil. Viscous, slippery, and light, it gradually flowed upward into formations of sandstone and other porous rock, where it sometimes floated above remnant saltwater and below layers of dense, impervious stone or minerals. Some of it gradually seeped to the surface, where it occasionally gathered in pools that blackened in the air and under the rays of the sun.[10]

The Earth's living organisms mostly were indifferent to the oil in those pools. A few strains of bacteria developed the capacity to consume minute quantities of it. Larger organisms—insects and camels and saber-tooth cats—sometimes stumbled into the pools and died, their tissues merging with the energetic mass of the millions that had gone before. Eventually, a few humans discovered oil. Some used it as a salve or swallowed it in small doses, hoping to benefit from its medicinal powers. Others gathered it for fuel. In a humble smudge pot now lost to memory, a drop ignited, the reservoir opened, and once more the past flowed toward the future.

For millennia, people mostly ignored the hydrocarbon that oozed to the surface, for they were preoccupied by their pursuit of the more accessible and alluring oleaginous pools that surrounded them. They ached for those rich deposits, for the plump doe and fat cow, the juicy armadillo, chuckwalla, salmon, and conch, the greasy cricket and unctuous grasshopper. Some societies became unusually efficient at capturing the flow of energy, and they amassed extraordinary surpluses of calorie-laden substances: wheels of cheese and sides of bacon, piles of grain and slabs of wax, jars of olive oil and pots of honey, and bottles—endless bottles—of fermented drink. All of that concentrated energy served important purposes. It made possible an unprecedented degree of economic specialization and social differentiation, such that artisans, scholars, priests, bureaucrats, and soldiers could perform their duties unencumbered by the daily quest for food and warmth. The surplus, furthermore, energized political and military power, including the buildup of empires. Finally, caloric abundance fueled illusions characteristic of—perhaps necessary to—complex societies. Chunks of bread and trenchers of stew, not to mention tankard upon tankard of beer, deposited body fat and encouraged the belief—the faith—that the future would bring more of the same. And at night when the fire burned low and a chill settled over the room, the fat metabolized into heat, the body relaxed, and the mind gave flight to dreams.[11]

For centuries, life went on like this. Yet the world was not in stasis. By the nineteenth century, demographic, environmental, and economic changes had intensified humanity's hunt for additional pools of energy and the potential heat they contained. As the human population grew, the pools emptied. Near cities and on islands, entire forests went down, consumed in the fires of innumerable hearths. In the oceans, whales began to disappear, their oil and blubber dissipating as light and heat in millions of lamps around the globe. As those reservoirs ran out, people increased their drafts on other sources. They expanded their use of animal power and animal fats. Where forests still grew, they distilled the rich oleoresins of pine trees into turpentine, which, when mixed with alcohol, made an excellent lamp illuminant. They pressed oil from vegetable seeds, and they boosted and perfected their capacity to distill alcohol from wood, grain, and other plant matter.[12] But of all the energy reservoirs that humanity tapped intensively, none was as momentous as those that lay beneath the ground.

By excavating coal, humanity transformed the fossilized past into a revolutionary present. With their picks, shovels, cutters, and blasting powder, miners liberated the energy packed into dense seams of ancient fern, horsetail, club moss, gingko, and pine. Although the fallen and flattened vegetation no longer could spring to life, it retained the capacity to burst into flame—in the fireboxes of steam engines, the furnaces of power plants, and the stoves that warmed the homes and bodies of people across the land.[13] No longer were humans entirely dependent on each day's sunlight and the plants and animals that it invigorated. Now they tapped the energy reservoirs of bygone times. The world would never be the same.

If coal started the hydrocarbon revolution, then oil perfected it. By the 1850s, chemists had figured out how to create illuminating fuels—collectively known as kerosene—from coal and from the liquid hydrocarbon that seeped from cracks in the ground. No one knew much about the vast petroleum reservoirs from which those seeps or "springs" issued. In some places, common knowledge had it that "rock oil" was merely the liquid residue, the drippings, of coal beds. Some entrepreneurs thought differently and hired well drillers to find out. In 1859, along Oil Creek near Titusville, a poor timber community in northwestern Pennsylvania, William A. "Uncle Billy" Smith and his sons, working for Edwin L. Drake, erected a wooden derrick for their drilling apparatus. Using a steam engine, they drove their bit into the Earth and at a depth of only sixty-nine feet found what they were looking for. Then they pumped the oil into barrels once used for holding another kind of energy-packed liquid, whiskey. As word spread, land values around Titusville skyrocketed and whiskey barrels grew scarce. The world's first oil boom was on. A vast planetary pool began to empty.[14]

A series of strikes in the southern and western United States dramatically increased the flow of oil into the nation's expanding economy. Ohio, Indiana, Illinois, Kentucky, Virginia, and Louisiana all experienced booms, but the largest and most important discoveries were in Texas, Oklahoma, and California. One of the richest and most famous oil fields was the storied Spindletop in southeast Texas, located on a dome of ancient salt that capped an immense hydrocarbon reserve. Opened in 1901, Spindletop encompassed all of 170 acres, slightly more than one-quarter of a square mile. Those 170 acres were productive beyond belief. The first six wells yielded more oil than the world's other wells combined. One 7.5-acre area alone bristled with some 200 derricks, the legs of which overlapped because they stood so close together. By the end of

1902, roughly 400 structures clustered on the Spindletop patch; by 1904, the number had grown to approximately 1,200. Because geological forces subjected the underlying oil to intense pressure, pumping was unnecessary. Promoters impressed investors by opening wells and sending "gushers" an estimated 125 feet into the air. Much as tourists gathered around Old Faithful Geyser in Yellowstone National Park, so onlookers came to Spindletop to witness the sublime spectacle of the gushers. In September 1901, 12 open wells delighted a crowd of perhaps 15,000 people.[15]

The sudden release of this enormous natural abundance gave rise to new corporations of unprecedented power and size. Standard Oil dominated the Pennsylvania fields and by 1879 owned 90 percent of the nation's refining capacity. To its competitors and to antitrust reformers, the corporation became a hydra-headed monster that used ruthless and unscrupulous business practices to dominate the industry. The legal effort to break it down, however, merely recreated the beast in new forms: Standard Oil of New Jersey (later Exxon), Standard Oil of New York (Mobil), Standard Oil of California (Chevron), Standard Oil of Ohio (Sohio, later the American arm of British Petroleum, later BP), Standard Oil of Indiana (Amoco), Continental Oil (Conoco), and Atlantic Richfield (ARCO).[16] Gulf, Sun, Texaco, Shell, Unocal, and other corporations soon appeared, each the creature of a field from which it channeled petroleum into the homes, farms, factories, and machinery of a restless nation.[17]

By the early 1900s, less of that rich flow went into illumination than into the nation's expanding transportation network. The development of electrical generation and transmission systems enabled increasing numbers of people to substitute light bulbs for kerosene. Much of the Spindletop output, furthermore, was thick and heavy and best suited for stoves and steam engine fireboxes, not lamps. Most important, the sheer volume of Spindletop oil and its consequent rock-bottom price made it an ideal source of mechanical power. In 1901, a barrel of Spindletop crude—44 gallons—sold for three cents, a price that encouraged the conversion of railroad and steamship transportation networks from coal to oil. In 1901, the Santa Fe Railway operated one oil-burning locomotive; by 1905, it ran 227.[18] A massive shift in the industrial system of the United States had begun.

The shift to oil continued with the development of refining processes that made possible the production of a light fuel necessary to the internal combustion engine. In 1908, Henry Ford introduced the prototype Model T. At that time, oil refineries manufactured gasoline by distillation. Workers heated crude oil in a large vertical cylinder called a distillation tower. As the different molecular components of oil reached their boiling points and vaporized, they passed into pipes. When the vapors cooled, they condensed into their distinctive liquid forms, one of which was gasoline. At most, distillation transformed 20 percent of each barrel of crude oil into the fuel. William Burton, a chemist with Standard Oil of Indiana and the holder of a Ph.D. from Johns Hopkins University, set out to increase the proportion. In 1909, he and his assistants introduced thermal cracking. By subjecting crude oil to extremely high pressure and temperature—650 degrees Fahrenheit or more—they fractured or "cracked" the oil's long chains of carbon molecules, thereby turning as much as 45 percent of each barrel into gasoline. During the late 1930s, catalytic cracking—the use of mineral catalysts to hasten the cracking process—further improved production.[19]

The torrent of gasoline that poured from the refineries fueled an ever-expanding fleet of vehicles, the majority of which traveled on paved, all-weather streets and highways. In 1912, Americans operated some one million registered automobiles. By 1920, they drove about eight million, and by the end of the decade, the number increased to approximately twenty-seven million. During the 1920s, farmers purchased approximately 650,000 tractors, displacing millions of horses and bringing the hydrocarbon revolution to the rural landscape. A growing network of improved roads helped launch the United States into the auto-industrial age. The Federal Aid Road Act of 1916, the Federal Highway Act of 1921, and gasoline sales taxes imposed by the states paid for a highway system that, by the 1930s, extended some 407,000 miles.[20] Although gravel, brick, and concrete composed many miles of pavement, an increasing proportion of the total—eventually more than 90 percent—was made from asphalt, the thick, sticky tar left over from fuel manufacture. Much of the nation's early highway asphalt came from the area that first opened the country to the transportation possibilities of oil. In 1920, Port Neches, Texas, just down the road from Spindletop, boasted "the largest asphalt refinery in the world."[21]

Americans soon developed powerful attachments to the machines that tapped the world's ancient petroleum reserve. During the 1920s, Robert and Helen Lynd, a husband-and-wife team of sociologists, carried out a study of life in Muncie, Indiana, a place they called "Middletown." In effect, the Lynds went to Muncie and took a snapshot of America. Some of their findings offered striking insights into the social changes that were transforming the nation. Their surveys and interviews, for example, revealed that community members placed an exceptionally high value on automobiles. For many people, the new technology was not a luxury but a necessity, and they were willing to pay for it. A number of families had mortgaged their homes so that they could purchase their vehicles. For others, the potential sacrifices were even more basic. "We'd rather go without clothes than give up the car," one woman asserted. "I'll go without food before I see us give up the car," said another.[22]

Muncie residents used their vehicles for various purposes, but increasingly for recreation and leisure, especially trips in search of undeveloped rural nature. Many went on Sunday drives away from the town, and those who could afford annual vacations often enjoyed automobile excursions into the countryside.[23] That kind of travel was becoming a national trend. By the 1920s, growing numbers of Americans were going "back to nature," and state and federal government agencies—the National Park Service and others—assisted them by building roads through forests, mountains, seashores, and other beautiful landscapes. Tourists thus participated in a broad pattern of economic activity and geographic movement that refashioned America along hydrocarbon lines. Because of oil fields such as Spindletop, the people of Middletown could enjoy relatively untrammeled places like Yellowstone.[24]

Given this history of oil strikes, pavement, and automobile enthusiasm, it is tempting to imagine that the adoption of the internal combustion engine and the gasoline that it burned were inevitable to the development of the United States. It is easy to conclude that the people who claimed they would give up clothing and food before abandoning their cars were the direct progenitors of the anxious consumers who waited in line for hours at Norman Reichbach's service station.

Such a view of the past is not necessarily wrong—Middletown consumers who saw their cars as necessities did anticipate later Americans who formed long lines at service station pumps. It would be a mistake, however, to conclude that automobiles and oil were as ineluctable as they now might seem. The triumph of gasoline-powered motor vehicles obscured other roads that Americans might have followed into the future. By 1973–1974, most people had forgotten—if they ever knew—that some of their predecessors had resisted incurring the debt necessary to buy automobiles. "No sir, we've *not* got a car," one Muncie citizen told the Lynds. "*That's* why we've got a home."[25] And most Americans who waited in line for gasoline during the early 1970s oil shock had forgotten—if they ever knew—that oil had been only one among several energy reservoirs from which earlier citizens had drawn.

Well into the twentieth century, the future of automobiles and hydrocarbons was not settled. Animal power, which tapped the flow of solar energy that passed through forage and into the guts and muscles of horses, remained widespread. Nationally (and globally), the number of draft animals peaked in about 1920. As late as the 1930s, milk and other commodities came to the doorsteps of consumers by horse-drawn wagon. And despite the massive adoption of tractors during the 1920s, horses did not completely disappear from farms until after the Second World War.[26] Human muscle power also remained important; solar energy that flowed through plants and animals eventually made its way into the bodies of people, most of whom still walked an extraordinary number of miles. Many Americans also applied muscular effort to bicycle pedals, an efficient and healthy means of converting food into mechanical power. Bicycling became popular during the late nineteenth century, and bicyclists were the earliest and most vociferous proponents of paved roads. By 1915, Americans owned some six million two-wheelers—more than the number of cars.[27]

Nor was oil fated to be the only source of automobile energy. Until the 1930s, oil refiners faced competition from companies that produced fuel from plants. The early diesel engine ran on peanut oil, not petroleum, and gasoline engines ran well on alcohol derived from fermented vegetable matter. Distillers filled large tanks with plant material such as grain, potatoes, sugar beets, and molasses. Yeasts and other microorganisms consumed starches and sugars in the "mash" and in the process exuded alcohol. Distillers then heated the mash, vaporizing the alcohol and driving it into tubes, where it cooled and condensed into its purified form.[28] By the early twentieth century, alcohol appeared to have great promise as an illuminant and engine fuel. In 1906, the same year his administration began antitrust proceedings against Standard Oil, President Theodore Roosevelt signed into law a measure repealing an alcohol tax that had been imposed forty-four years before to help pay for the Civil War. Alcohol suddenly was much cheaper. Huge crop surpluses and a growing market for fuel in Europe made its prospects even brighter.[29]

Perhaps alcohol's greatest advantage was that petroleum supplies were so uncertain. In keeping with energy's universal limit, every oil field, even the vaunted Spindletop, proved finite. Growing numbers of oil-burning engines, including those used by the armies and navies of the First World War (1914–1918), soon reduced the glut. Yet consumption alone did not account for depletion; so did waste. Gushers impressed investors and onlookers, but well owners could not recover the oil that sprayed across the Texas sky. Spectacular fires matched the sublime spectacle of the gushers. One Spindletop conflagration destroyed sixty-two derricks and sent flames a thousand feet into the air. Much of the waste resulted from a legal principle that governed early oil extraction. According to the "rule of capture," oil from a common underground pool belonged to those who pumped it out, and drillers spilled huge volumes in their pell-mell rush for the valuable substance. Rather than directing the flow into pipes, tanks, and impervious reservoirs, for example, they channeled it into unlined earthen ditches and catchments. The losses were staggering. The geologist Wallace Pratt later estimated that producers squandered some 75 percent of the oil and natural gas they discovered.[30] Anthony Lucas, who drilled the first Spindletop well, referred to another kind of oleaginous pool when he explained what had happened. "The cow was milked too hard," he said, "and she was not milked intelligently."[31]

The reaction to depletion took different forms, including conservation, exploration, and more attention to alcohol. In 1910, Congress authorized the president to withdraw from development oil and coal lands in the American West. Much like national forests, below-ground petroleum reserves would conserve a finite natural resource of enormous value to the nation. By 1916, presidents had created fifty of them, and they had designated some, such as Teapot Dome Reserve No. 3, as strategic supplies for the U.S. Navy. Federal policy did not end with conservation, however; during the 1920s, the State Department encouraged oil companies to search for oil deposits abroad.[32] In the meantime, popular and corporate interest in fuel alcohol increased. In 1925, no less than Henry Ford predicted that alcohol would be "the fuel of the future" and would be made "from fruit like that sumac out by the road, or from apples, weeds, sawdust—almost anything. There is fuel in every bit of vegetable matter that can be fermented."[33]

Other automobile producers shared Ford's interest. During the early 1920s, three engineers at General Motors (GM)—Thomas Midgley, T. A. Boyd, and vice president of research Charles Kettering—conducted extensive analyses of the fuel. They concluded that it could serve as a partial, if not complete, substitute for oil, which they believed must come, some day, from foreign sources. They also recognized that alcohol could alleviate a technological problem that was inherent in engines larger and more powerful than the first models. When an engine piston compressed the air and fuel mixture in a cylinder, the mixture often exploded instead of burning evenly. This premature, incomplete combustion wasted fuel, reduced engine power, and caused a distinctive and troubling sound, called engine knock. Engineers such as Midgley, Boyd, and Kettering learned that gasoline composed of highly branched hydrocarbon molecules—high-octane gasoline—withstood extreme compression, burned more efficiently, and did not cause engine knock. They also discovered that certain compounds dissolved in gasoline increased its octane level and anti-knock properties. One of those compounds, they found, was alcohol.[34]

Yet the "fuel of the future" never achieved its promise. For one thing, it had significant drawbacks. Gallon-for-gallon, alcohol contained perhaps 30 percent less energetic potential than gasoline. Manufacturing it, furthermore, required significant quantities of energy. To harvest and transport plant matter, farmers had to burn fuel or metabolize the calories in animal fodder. Distillers then had to heat the mash with fuel, perhaps coal or oil. In the end, alcohol might not have yielded as much energy as was necessary for its production; it might have entailed, in short, a net loss.[35]

But there was another reason the alcohol future never arrived. In 1921, at the very moment he was experimenting with alcohol, Thomas Midgley discovered that a form of lead—tetraethyl lead—raised the octane level of gasoline. In concert with the DuPont Corporation and Standard Oil of New Jersey, GM touted tetraethyl lead as the least expensive, most efficient octane enhancer available. GM then joined with Standard Oil to create the Ethyl Corporation, which manufactured the compound. Tetraethyl lead imposed an enormous environmental and economic cost on American society. The microscopic particles of dull gray metal sickened factory workers and, when spewed from automobile tailpipes, damaged the nervous systems of children and contributed to a public health disaster that went unmitigated for some five decades. During that time, GM and its corporate allies downplayed, suppressed, or disputed information on the benefits of alcohol and the detriments of lead.[36]

One final factor ensured alcohol's demise. By the end of the 1920s, the oil shortage turned into an oil glut. Major discoveries in Oklahoma (1927) and California (1928, 1929) flooded the market with the substance. Then, in October 1930, a shabby old wildcatter named Columbus "Dad" Joiner sank a well on the east Texas farm of Daisy Bradford. Geologists laughed at Dad Joiner, and one critic (a Texaco employee) boasted that he would drink every barrel from Daisy Bradford No. 3. The gusher that roared out of the hole proved the geologists wrong. A vast new oil field—the Black Giant—soon encompassed 145,000 acres and some 3,500 wells that eventually yielded 7 billion barrels. The largest field discovered in the lower 48 states, the Black Giant drove prices to rock bottom levels. Oil that had sold for $3 per barrel in 1919 fell, by late May 1931, to $0.15, then to $0.06, and finally to $0.02.[37] The British economist John Maynard Keynes later observed that the crisis of American capitalism was one of abundance, not poverty. The deeply distressed prices of May 1931 underscored his point and revealed in stark detail the oleaginous face of the Great Depression.[38] Alcohol could not compete against the hydrocarbon surplus that engulfed the nation's service stations. The future belonged to oil.

In reaction to the price collapse, the United States installed a regulatory system that maximized the economic benefits of its petroleum superabundance. As prices tumbled, Oklahoma, Texas, and other oil-producing states replaced the rule of capture with a regulatory program called prorationing.[39] By restricting the daily output of each well, prorationing slowed depletion, kept oil off the market, and thereby boosted prices. The Texas Railroad Commission (TRC) became the most celebrated practitioner of prorationing. Founded in 1891 to oversee railroad rates, the TRC managed oil pipelines during the First World War and, in the 1920s, determined the spacing of wells. Those policies anticipated prorationing, which the TRC instituted in 1931 and 1932. Oil regulation was not limited to state agencies such as the TRC, moreover. In 1932, Congress imposed a tax on imported oil and fuels, a policy that protected domestic producers. Three years later, it prohibited the shipment of nonprorated petroleum across state lines and established the Interstate Oil Compact Commission to coordinate prorationing. The state-federal regulatory system served its purpose. The price of oil soon rose above $1 per barrel and remained there for the rest of the decade.[40]

The flow of liquid hydrocarbon—and government regulation of it—increased over the next three decades. Major discoveries during the 1940s and early 1950s added to the magnificent finds of the 1930s. In 1948, for example, drillers opened ancient ocean reefs below Scurry County, Texas, and began to extract a pool that eventually amounted to some two billion barrels. Twenty years later, Atlantic Richfield (ARCO) stumbled on an immense field of some nine billion barrels—the largest in American history—at Prudhoe Bay on Alaska's North Slope. Numerous wells off the Pacific and Gulf coasts augmented the total. Oilfield workers—drillers, roughnecks, roustabouts, geologists, and engineers—reveled in the abundance. "We're cuttin' up a fat hawg," they often said, evoking the culture of the Texas and Oklahoma oil patches. The richness was great, and the United States took additional steps to shield it from a worldwide glut that drove down import prices and undercut the domestic market. In

1959, President Dwight Eisenhower imposed an import quota pegged at 12.2 percent of U.S. demand. He might have allowed more foreign oil into the country, which would have closed domestic wells and conserved the nation's deposits, but he and his advisers, believing that national security required those wells to be in operation, decided against it. In consequence, domestic oil gushed forth as never before.[41]

America's natural petroleum bounty transformed the nation and its fortunes. Some six billion barrels fueled the World War Two struggle (1941–1945) against Germany and Japan. During the Cold War (1945–1989) and the conflicts in Korea (1950–1953) and Vietnam (1964–1973), the United States continued to mobilize its petroleum reserves to build military power. Domestically, oil profoundly altered life and landscape. By 1945, the number of cars stood at some 25 million, and within five years the figure had risen to 54 million. In 1965, three years after Norman Reichbach opened City Line Flying A, the count was 75 million, and by 1968, the total had climbed to 100 million. This vast fleet enabled—and benefited from—the 1956 Interstate Highway Act, which used revenue from a gasoline tax to construct some 41,000 miles of freeways. Many of those miles encouraged housing construction on the urban fringe, until by 1960, more Americans lived in suburbs than in cities. Virtually every suburban dwelling had a lawn that was regularly trimmed by a gasoline-fueled mower. From the B-52 bombers that patrolled the skies to the grass on which children played, twentieth-century America became a fully petroleum-powered, auto-mobilized society.[42]

The intensive use of oil profoundly shaped social relationships and culture in the hydrocarbon nation. The mass migration to auto-dependent suburbs reinforced a powerful gender ideology that idealized women as homemakers—as wives and mothers centered in single-family dwellings and oriented to domestic routines in which they drove to shopping centers, Tupperware parties, Parent-Teacher Association meetings, and, with their children, Little League games and music lessons. A rising level of affluence, itself a function of increasing petroleum use, gave husbands and wives a level of economic security that encouraged them to produce some seventy-five million children between 1946 and 1964. Most Americans probably did not draw a connection between the nation's energetic basis and the baby boom, but the demographic surge indeed was underwritten in oil. The popular culture of the growing boomers said as much. In "409," "Fun Fun Fun," "Little Deuce Coup," "Surfin' Safari," and other songs, the Beach Boys, one of the most popular rock and roll groups of the early 1960s, celebrated the joyful liberation that gasoline and internal combustion engines bestowed on California's sun-splashed youths.[43]

Yet in the midst of this vast environmental, economic, and social transformation—a transformation of world-historical significance—problems appeared. The flow of oil, the ostensible means of American strength, also proved to be a source of weakness. Some of that weakness was measured in environmental consequences. From its inception, oil extraction polluted the nation's waterways and coastlines. In December 1862, for example, ice in a Pennsylvania stream broke apart 150 oil boats, spilling the contents of some thirty thousand barrels. By the mid-twentieth century, such spills were commonplace. Oil use also sent pollutants into the air. As early as the 1940s, the inhabitants of Los Angeles noticed a yellow-brown haze that stung their eyes. Their circumstances gradually worsened until, in 1962, they reported eye irritation on 212 days. The source of their discomfort was the combustion of gasoline in their automobile engines, which yielded chemical compounds—nitrogen oxide, carbon monoxide, ozone, and others—that inflamed eyes, bronchial passages, and lungs. Lead particles added to the national pollution problem by damaging the mental capacities of children—especially poor children who lived close to streets—and depriving society of their intellectual, social, and economic potential.[44]

Social problems accompanied the harmful biophysical consequences of increased petroleum use. In 1948, a group of disaffected California men, some of them World War Two veterans, formed the Hell's Angels, a notorious outlaw motorcycle gang as "tough, mean, and potentially dangerous as packs of wild boar," according to journalist Hunter Thompson. Feelings of profound unhappiness, alienation, and boredom plagued the nation's young people, revealing a dark underside to the golden youth depicted in Beach Boys music. In *Rebel without a Cause* (1955), James Dean played a sullen teenager fed up with his parents and other authority figures and for whom automobiles became instruments of mischief and rebellion. Dean's real-life death in a car crash only heightened the popular appeal of his celluloid persona. Frustration and unhappiness similarly began to overtake women who were supposed to be happy suburban housewives. In *The Feminine Mystique* (1963), Betty Friedan argued that suburbs were "comfortable concentration camps" in which women confronted "the problem that has no name," the tension between their desire for personal fulfillment and the deadening reality of their domestic roles. Friedan and other women were not alone in feeling trapped. Hindered by pervasive discrimination, few

African Americans migrated from cities to suburbs, and fewer still found jobs with the corporations that concentrated on the urban fringe. As their incomes fell, the municipal tax base collapsed, and schools and other infrastructure crumbled, they grew angry and bitter.[45]

No less worrisome than such environmental and social problems, new discoveries of petroleum only delayed the moment of reckoning when the nation's military and economic expansion would outstrip the capacity of its reserves. None of the later discoveries matched the overall quantity of the 1930s finds, and none kept up with consumption. The Second World War burned an amount of oil equivalent to the Black Giant, and the Vietnam War expended another five billion barrels, canceling a good portion of the Prudhoe Bay find. Much of what remained ended up in cars and trucks. Overall, the use of oil and other energy sources doubled between the 1950s and 1970s, a rate far in advance of the nation's population growth.[46]

A few petroleum experts recognized that the fat was dissipating and the country was headed for trouble. Among them was a scientist named M. King Hubbert. A native of Texas, Hubbert had a Ph.D. in geology from the University of Chicago and worked for Shell Oil at its research laboratory in Houston. In 1956, the same year Congress passed the Interstate Highway Act, he made a startling prediction: in the near future, U.S. oil production in the lower forty-eight states would cease growing—it would peak, in other words—and then decline forever. Using statistics on past production and proven reserves, he calculated a total domestic supply—the amount that nature created and Americans had the means to get—of 150 billion to 200 billion barrels. By extrapolating from the rates of discovery and extraction, he then determined that at some moment between 1965 and 1972, the cumulative amount pumped from the ground would reach half the grand total. After that, the rate of extraction would fall, and rising consumption would strain against increasing scarcity. Minutes before he presented his findings to a meeting of the American Petroleum Institute, Shell officials telephoned and asked him to reconsider. A stubborn, curmudgeonly man, he refused.[47]

Events proved Hubbert correct. In 1970, U.S. oil production peaked at nine million barrels per day and then went into permanent decline. The following year, the Texas Railroad Commission announced that it would allow wells to be pumped at 100 percent of their capacity. In 1972, the commission ended production rationing altogether. By then, the domestic market was absorbing all the petroleum the nation's wells could deliver, and then some. For his efforts,

Hubbert became a hero to conservationists and other people who demanded that the United States face up to the dangers of its petroleum consumption. Their esteem only increased when he made another controversial prediction: worldwide production would peak early in the twenty-first century.[48]

What made Hubbert's peak especially unsettling—and what made it a portent of vulnerability—was that the increasing consumption that caused it also compelled the nation to rely on imports. By accidents of geological and political history, other countries—Canada, Mexico, Venezuela, and the Soviet Union, for example—had world-class deposits of oil. So did countries in the Middle East, especially those bordering the Persian Gulf. Kuwait had the immense Burgan field, discovered in 1938, which contained some seventy billion barrels. No nation on Earth, however, matched Saudi Arabia's endowment. The showpiece of Saudi oil, the basis of the kingdom's economy and the means of its political power, was the fabulous Ghawar field. Discovered in 1948, it held a gargantuan eighty-seven billion barrels. And not only were Ghawar and other Persian Gulf fields of enormous size, but they also boasted the finest—the most easily refined—light sweet crude.[49] In 1970, the United States imported some 483 million barrels of crude oil, about 12 percent of the total available to the nation that year; in 1973, the figure rose to 1.184 billion barrels, about 26 percent. Although Canada and Venezuela contributed most of the imported petroleum, an increasing proportion came from the Middle East. In 1970, Saudi Arabia and other Middle East states supplied some 18 percent of the oil imported to the United States, and three years later, they furnished roughly 42 percent.[50]

By that time, Saudi Arabia and its allies had attained an influential position in world and U.S. oil markets. Saudi Arabia's entry into the petroleum age had begun in 1933, when Standard Oil of California (Socal, later Chevron) set up the California-Arabian Standard Oil Company (Casoc) to extract Saudi petroleum and return some of the proceeds to the kingdom. In 1936, the Texas Company (later Texaco) acquired an interest in Casoc, and Socal and Texas created Caltex to help market Saudi oil, commercial quantities of which Casoc struck in 1938. In 1944, Casoc became the Arabian American Oil Company, known as Aramco. Three years later, Socal and Texaco admitted Standard Oil of New Jersey (Exxon) and Socony-Vacuum (Mobil) into Aramco, and in 1950, the participants began to split profits fifty-fifty with the Saudis. Yet the world glut and falling prices had disappointed the Saudis and other exporters, and they decided to take action. In 1960, two years before Norman Reichbach opened his Yonkers service station, representatives of Kuwait, Iran, Iraq, Venezuela, and

Saudi Arabia met in Baghdad to form the Organization of Petroleum Exporting Countries, or OPEC. Like the Texas Railroad Commission, OPEC sought to match production with demand as a means of boosting prices and profits. Within a decade, the organization was poised to exert considerable leverage on the United States. In April 1973, President Richard Nixon ended the import quotas. Demand surged ahead of domestic production that summer, and lines appeared at Norman Reichbach's service station and others across the country. Saudi Arabia and the other OPEC members had the spare capacity that the United States lacked, and they knew this gave them unprecedented power.[51]

They wielded that power in October. The pretext was a war between Israel and two of its neighbors, Egypt and Syria. The United States had supported Israel since 1948, the year that Jewish refugees, settlers, and intellectuals founded the state—and the same year that geologists discovered the Ghawar field in Saudi Arabia. Israel and surrounding Arab nations had battled each other several times over territory, the plight of Palestinian Arabs under Israeli occupation, and Israel's very existence. In early October 1973, in an attempt to regain territory lost in earlier conflicts, Egypt and Syria attacked Israel. When the Soviet Union sent military supplies to the Arab combatants, the United States rushed war materiel to its ally. In retaliation, OPEC raised the price of crude from $3.00 to $5.11 per barrel. Days later, Saudi Arabia and the other Arab OPEC members embargoed petroleum shipments to the United States. Domestic prices spiraled upward; oil that had sold for $2.90 per barrel before the embargo reached $11.65 in December. Prices at the pump rose accordingly. A gallon of gasoline that cost $0.27 in September reached $0.51 and higher by the end of the year.[52]

The fortunes of the United States shifted with the flow of energy. The nation had enjoyed a privileged position along the entropic channels that ran through the universe. More than the borders of most countries, America's had encompassed substantial underground pools that contained the radiant energy of ages past. In combination with other resource endowments, the United States had used its oil to transform itself into a global superpower. Like all pockets of oleaginous wealth, however, the nation's oil deposits inevitably emptied. As M. King Hubbert noted, the "flux of energy" that passed through Earth was "unidirectional and irreversible."[53] Eventually, tectonic forces would have opened fissures from which the oil surfaced. At those places, the environment would have absorbed the slippery substance, drop by precious drop. The outcome that nonhuman nature would have accomplished in millions of years,

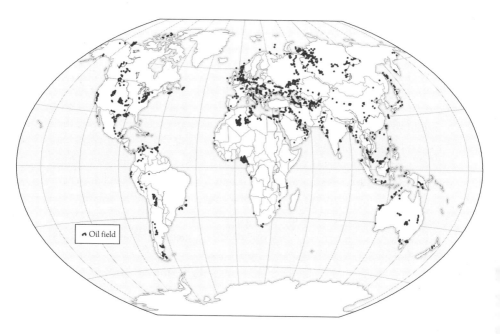

Major oil fields, 2010, showing their uneven distribution among nations, an indication of petroleum's geopolitical nature.

human nature achieved in about a hundred. In automobiles and other devices, the fossil soup momentarily flared, mechanical parts moved, and residual heat dissolved in the passage of time. Meanwhile, people in other countries tapped bigger, better pools and laid claim to greatness.

Questions remained. How would the nation respond to the oil shock? Would people everywhere degenerate into selfishness and despair, as they did at Norman Reichbach's City Line Flying A, squabbling and fighting over what little remained? Or would they question their assumptions about the world and adopt a different, more durable scale of values? Would they devise alternative ways of living and perhaps even turn to other energy sources and technologies?

GIVE ME GAS OR I WILL KILL YOU

Service station operators everywhere had much less gasoline than usual during 1973–1974. Some, like Norman Reichbach, regulated the flow by limiting the quantity of each sale, restricting the days and hours of business, or favoring well-known and trusted customers. Others pumped freely and then simply closed when their underground storage tanks ran dry. Across the nation, hand-lettered "out of gas" signs became common. As opportunities to purchase fuel diminished, the "gas line" became the symbol of a disorienting new reality. Customers often found themselves at the end of a line of maybe five or six vehicles, but those relatively short backups could grow to dozens of cars. At their most extreme, the queues attained staggering lengths. At one New York City service station, attendants counted 135 vehicles. At Ocean City, New Jersey, one motorist pulled over to wait for gas four miles from the pumps. Elsewhere, drivers waited for two or three hours to be served. No matter the length of the line, idling automobiles used enormous quantities of fuel. Consumers' Union, a nonprofit research and advocacy organization, calculated that a mile of six-cylinder engines burned 150 gallons every hour.[54]

Patience and civility vaporized along with the hydrocarbons. Service station owners and employees were not above using the situation for their own gain. A callow teenage attendant told a woman from New Jersey that she never need want for gasoline if she would "put out." Unscrupulous service station operators gouged their customers. In Chicago, motorists accused an owner—also a policeman—of a crass deception: he would give them gasoline for free, but only if they purchased mundane items—bars of soap, containers of all-purpose cleaner, rabbits' feet, standardized forms for wills, and the like—at prices that exceeded the value of the fuel. Other gasoline sellers were more straightforward—and underhanded—in their duplicity. On Long Island, a service station tricked customers by filling their tanks with less fuel than the amount indicated on the pump.[55]

But more often, service station owners and employees, Norman Reichbach and thousands more like him, had to cope with customers who seemed ready to do virtually anything for fuel. "People are trying all kinds of tricks to get in front of the line and get more gasoline," reported Haim Levi, a station owner in New York City. "Most of them have to go to the hospital, their wives are sick, they're about to have a baby. I never heard of so many babies being born and the husbands don't have gasoline." Some motorists went beyond mere pleading, cajoling, or lying. In Stamford, Connecticut, a woman with Virginia license plates offered to exchange sex for gasoline. The station owner declined, but sold her a few gallons anyway. Other customers took more aggressive action. Some cut into line, drawing the ire of the people behind them. A few behaved like petulant children. A man in New York cut in front of a line and then locked himself in his car and refused to move until the station served him. Twenty minutes later, the police finally dislodged him. Another man who had appropriated a spot at the head of the line ran into the restroom and flushed his keys down the toilet. Still another clung to a gasoline hose while attendants struggled to pull him away.[56]

The stress led to harassment and threats. Motorists in Florida cursed and insulted station owners and their employees. In Armonk, New York, a woman swore at an attendant and said that he lied when he told her the station had no gasoline. At Boopsie's Shell Station in Albany, a small, elderly woman, angry for being denied fuel, reached for a can of oil with which to hit the proprietor, George Rickert. Her threat was mild in comparison with what happened elsewhere. In Springfield, Massachusetts, "a huge bear of a man" walked into a service station and told the dealer, "You are going to give me gas or I will kill you." Angry motorists in other places confronted owners and their employees with knives, pistols, hand grenades, and worse.[57]

Some people turned to outright robbery, which they often carried out under the cover of darkness. In Salinas, California, thieves pumped eight hundred gallons from the underground storage tank of station owner Raleigh Alston. "No one would give a second thought to seeing a gas tanker at a service station in the middle of the night, would they?" observed a police officer. Farther south, in Pasadena, men armed with shotguns hijacked—or "gasjacked"—an ARCO truck when its driver arrived at a service station to make a midnight delivery of fuel. Two of the bandits bound the driver and dropped him off in a nearby town. Police found his tanker an hour later, devoid of its eighty-five hundred gallons.[58]

Service station operators and pump attendants shared Norman Reichbach's resentments. "I don't like my customers taking their frustrations out on me—threatening to kill me or to burn down the station," said Patrick Bellegrazie, a Texaco dealer in Evansville, Illinois, north of Chicago. "They're out of their minds, they're turning sick," said Alvin Garafola, co-owner of Marine Park Sunoco in Brooklyn, New York.[59] "They're worse than animals," complained one pump attendant. "The public is behaving like animals," railed another.[60] Joseph Cautela, a therapist in Natick, Massachusetts, agreed that something had changed in the minds of many drivers. "People see gasoline now in terms of basic survival," he said. "Whenever you have anything with that kind of value on it, people are going to fight for it. They do things they ordinarily would not do."[61]

To protect themselves, some service station owners and attendants began carrying firearms. In tiny Monument, Colorado, north of Colorado Springs, Morgan Porter served his regular customers ahead of the tourists who passed through on their way to see the nearby Rocky Mountains. Some of the vacationers didn't like the favoritism, and they expressed their sentiments in no uncertain terms. To "emphasize his seriousness," Porter "strapped a pistol on his hip." Although such firepower no doubt discouraged some aggressive customers, tragic gunplay also ensued. At a gas station in New Orleans, Earl Richardson protested when told that he could buy only $3 worth of gasoline. When he appeared to reach under his coat for a weapon, the pump attendant, Charles Russ, shot him to death.[62]

Chaos and violence spread beyond the service stations. As gasoline became scarcer and more expensive, stealing increased. During the night, thieves used siphons and pumps to drain the contents of automobile fuel tanks. In the morning, surprised and angry motorists headed to auto supply stores to purchase locking gas caps. Perhaps the most tragic oil shock stories concerned people who loaded up with extra gasoline and then paid dearly for it. A young Pennsylvania man filled storage cans with fifteen gallons and put them in his vehicle. He came to a fiery end when he skidded off the road and his portable reserve exploded. In Connecticut, another man burned to death when he rammed a guardrail on the Merritt Parkway, igniting the three gallons of gas that he carried in his car.[63]

Explosions, gunfire, fistfights, and other dramatic events captured popular attention, but motorists also experienced the oil shock in mundane ways. Many people quietly endured frustration, anger, disappointment, confusion, or bodily discomfort as they waited in line or curtailed trips. In Michigan one weekend, Jim and Nadine Hunt did not have enough gasoline to visit their newborn son in the neonatal intensive care unit of a distant hospital. Local service stations that might have sold them fuel were closed for the weekend. The Hunts had no recourse; they simply had to wait until Monday. In Fremont, California, Jared Orsi, a boy perhaps three or four years old, sat in the back seat of a Ford Galaxy and tried to quell the growing pressure in his bladder. The squirming youth understood that purchasing gasoline was difficult and time consuming, and he worried that a trip to the restroom might cause him and his parent to lose their place in line. Should he say something? Or should he try to hold it?[64]

The problems ramified throughout the nation's economic system. Rising prices at the pumps took a greater share of paychecks and threatened the jobs of automobile commuters and small businesses that relied on vehicles. Consumer goods of all kinds cost more, further cutting into personal capital. Citizens who had moved to distant suburbs wondered if they had made the right decision. Wives and mothers responsible for grocery shopping and transporting children worried about household budgets as money disappeared into the tanks of enormous station wagons that averaged ten or eleven miles per gallon. Near Miami, Sue Fisher drove her Ford LTD station wagon some four hundred miles per week. "I'm trying to conserve energy by saving trips," she said, "but the fuel shortage is going to affect us drastically." Ellen Jackson, of Oakton, Virginia, a suburb of Washington, D.C., acknowledged her family's automobile dependence: "It's two miles to the nearest store, and there is no public transportation of any kind. If I don't drive, my family doesn't eat."[65] In response to rising fuel costs, citizens began to purchase imported cars that got twice or more the mileage of American makes. The shift in the market devastated American manufacturers. Declining sales soon led to massive layoffs, a pattern that rippled through the steel, rubber, and glass industries.[66]

As circumstances worsened across the nation, state and federal governments attempted, with little success, to stabilize energy supplies. Legislatures restricted gasoline sales in an effort to prevent long lines, and by December 1973, twenty-one states had imposed highway speed limits of 50 or 55 miles per hour (mph), slowing speeds to burn less fuel. The federal government did more, but not much more. Congress gave President Nixon's new Federal Energy Office the authority to fix oil prices and ration gasoline. Although the agency tried to keep crude prices down, it never rationed the fuel. Perhaps the federal government's most significant conservation measure was a national 55 mph speed limit, which the president signed into law in early January 1974.[67]

Americans served up plenty of blame for "the energy crisis" and the conditions that too often provoked panicked, angry, frenzied, foolish behavior. Many citizens pointed to the Arab nations that had constricted the flow of oil, or they denounced the oil companies for using the embargo as a pretext to raise prices and gouge consumers. Others censured environmentalists for shutting down domestic wells. A few people blamed their own greed. A sizable number focused their criticism on government. These people accused public officials of ineptitude in regulating, or failing to regulate, gasoline production and sales. More fundamentally, angry citizens conflated the failure of energy policy with other national failures: the United States fought the Vietnam War because of oil fields off the Vietnamese coast; the environmental destructiveness of fossil fuel extraction was related to the war's destructiveness; President Nixon used the oil shock to divert attention from his Watergate crimes; the confusion of the oil shock and the confusion of Watergate were similar.[68]

As the problems compounded, citizens lost confidence in the direction the country was heading. Waiting their turns at the pumps, they wondered what had gone wrong with a form of transportation that once had given them such extraordinary mobility, even freedom. Now it posed so many problems, not only pollution from oil extraction and consumption but also the seemingly helpless dependence on a natural resource that increasingly came from beneath the arid domains of nations far, far away. A motorist summarized the cynicism and despair that gripped people. "You know how I feel about the environmental situation?" Kenneth Johnson asked while waiting to buy gasoline at the Hess station on Peninsula Boulevard in Hempstead, New York. "If we're all going to hell, we might as well drive there."[69]

DON'T RIDE ALONE

As the fuel crisis deepened, a substantial number of Americans searched for alternatives that might allow them to retain some control over their lives. Entropy and the dissipation of energy jarred their consciousness and opened opportunities for them to engage in cooperative behavior that countered the individualism and social atomization symbolized by the panicked, alienated, lone driver desperately seeking another tank of gas.[70] In effect, the diminution of petroleum pools invited Americans to form pools of another kind—social pools in which people united in a common effort that also benefited them individually. Because they had to build the future from the means available to them in the present, they centered their cooperative activity on petroleum fuels and motor vehicles, an effort that required them to participate in the very system that constrained them. The desire for alternatives led a few Americans to new, forgotten, or overlooked energy sources and technologies. Even these, however, were tied—if indirectly—to an increasingly global system of petroleum extraction, refinement, and distribution. The events of 1973–1974 revealed the extent to which American citizens depended on oil and how difficult it would be for them to change.

Signs of an alternative reaction to the oil shock appeared at service stations and on highways, the places most associated with acts of selfishness and desperation. Some service station customers demonstrated a capacity for civility, an essential element of cooperation and proof that not all motorists were irrational "animals." The lunches and thermoses that unnerved Norman Reichbach, for example, also might have been interpreted as evidence of well-meaning people calmly trying to make the best of an inconvenient situation. When motorists talked to each other or listened to music on their car radios, they showed a propensity for patience and restraint. Small goodwill gestures confirmed the basic decency of many drivers and also revealed an awareness of a greater public good. When Peter Russen bought fuel in New York City, he asked for only six gallons, all that he needed to get to the Berkshire Mountains in western Massachusetts. At many service stations, motorists who ran out of gas while waiting in line received a push from the car behind, or from a group of volunteers who got out of their cars and did the job with muscle power. In Tempe, Arizona, a desperate motorist siphoned gas from a stranger's parked automobile and left a $5 bill to pay for it. In San Jose, California, a group of citizen volunteers—the Radio Emergency Associated Citizens Team, or REACT—used telephones and citizens' band radios to help stranded, out-of-gas motorists find open service stations.[71]

Something other than automotive individualism was at work in American society. To realize their personal objectives, motorists drew on a rich national tradition of cooperative and associational activity centered on households, neighborhoods, schools, churches, workplaces, and technologies. Since the nineteenth century, families, fraternal associations, small business groups, labor unions, farm and consumer cooperatives, women's clubs, and charitable societies had enabled people to work together to meet the challenges of modern industrial society. The self-serving personal autonomy made possible by automobiles contrasted with—if not weakened—the social bonds that held such groups together. Yet Americans proved quite capable of adapting their cooperative strategies to the automobile and related technologies. The American Automobile Association (AAA), founded in 1902 from nine smaller clubs, lobbied for better roads and provided maps, guidebooks, towing services, and insurance to its members. Established in 1962, REACT maintained emergency communications networks among its affiliates. From local to national scales, groups helped individual drivers negotiate the complexities and hazards of the federal highway system, including its modern, multilane freeways.[72]

The cooperative use of the automobile—and the use of the automobile for cooperative purposes—also took place on an informal, grassroots level. Motor vehicles enabled rural inhabitants to overcome their isolation and gather for cultural, economic, and political activities. The Great Depression prompted citizens to combine resources, including automobile transportation, as they struggled to make ends meet. Gasoline rationing during the Second World War brought working people together to share rides and the cost of fuel. The federal government encouraged the practice; "When you ride ALONE you ride with Hitler," a poster warned. During the years of the civil rights movement, African Americans in Montgomery, Alabama, and other southern cities used churches and community associations to organize car transportation as an alternative to the segregated buses they were boycotting.[73]

Repeating these established patterns of cooperative activity, a small number of Americans in 1973–1974 began to organize car pools, a simple but effective way to mitigate rising gasoline prices. The movement began slowly. Carpooling was inconvenient for many drivers, and they were unwilling to abandon their existing practices. Many may have been constrained by an automobile-centered landscape in which workplaces, schools, grocery stores, shopping centers, hospitals, and other essential facilities were far apart. In that landscape, individuals needed a car to maintain a reasonable standard of living.[74] It was also the case that many motorists had little or no experience with cooperative activity, especially the mutual use of cars. The great age of automotive individualism was well over two decades old by 1973; with each passing year, the collective memory of sharing rides—sometimes an unpleasant memory associated with hard times and deprivation—grew dimmer. A new necessity began to bring some citizens together. Most automobile cooperatives were simple and informal as family members, friends, neighbors, and co-workers shared rides and fuel costs. State and local governments and corporations encouraged and assisted them by laying out staging areas, matching riders with rides, and offering incentives such as car pool lanes, reduced bridge and expressway tolls, and preferred parking.[75]

As the oil shock deepened, popular attention focused on one of the nation's oldest and most efficiently run co-ops, the Montclair-Riverside Car Pool (MRCP), which began in 1961 and operated out of Montclair, New Jersey, just west of New York City. Although exceptional in its age and sophistication, the organization represented the potential of automotive cooperation and contrasted starkly with the chaotic scenarios playing out at service stations such as Norman Reichbach's City Line Flying A, across the Hudson River in Yonkers.

The purpose of MRCP was to transport its members to their jobs at the Interchurch Center on Manhattan's upper west side. Dedicated in 1960, the center's massive limestone building on Riverside Drive was headquarters for Methodist, Presbyterian, Lutheran, Baptist, Catholic, and other Christian denominations and for organizations such as the National Council of Churches. In addition to administering their respective operations, the occupants of the center worked together on social, economic, and political problems. Some church personnel lived in Montclair, which appealed to them because of its hilly, wooded, suburban setting, solid middle-class homes, and highly educated population. A fair housing group, which opposed residential segregation, also attracted white and black church employees to the community. In about 1960, a few ministers began to share automobile rides to the Interchurch Center. They had tried public transportation but found the necessary combination of train, bus, and foot travel awkward and time consuming. Car travel, they decided, would be more efficient and pleasant. In 1961, the year before Reichbach opened his service station, they formally incorporated their nonprofit pool and required members to purchase at least one share of stock, then valued at a dollar.[76]

By 1973–1974, the MRCP was ideally positioned to provide its members with "a collective shield against the perils of the gasoline shortage," as one newspaper reporter wrote. By then the pool had three station wagons and some thirty members, men and women, white and black, each of whom owned at least one share worth $95 and paid $30 in monthly dues, about half the cost of public transportation to the Interchurch Center in Manhattan. Every morning at 7:30, the cars departed from Thompson's Hardware for the twenty-two-mile trip. The riders kept up a lively conversation, listened to news on the radio, and debated the issues of the day, including the 1973 Arab-Israeli war. Despite occasional heated exchanges, friendships and social bonds developed. "Oddly enough," testified Newt Thurber in *A.D. Magazine*, "I have found a Christian community in a car pool." As they sped down the highway, MRCP members could not help but contrast their situation with that of the solitary drivers and passengers on the roads. "For a good many years now we've been sorry for those people riding alone because we've been having so much fun together," said William Genne. "When we see a Cadillac with a person in the back seat by himself, we feel that is a lonely, deprived individual."[77]

The monetary and environmental benefits of sharing machinery and conserving fuel complemented the social rewards of the MRCP. Members calculated that if they drove as individuals, they would need at least twenty-five vehicles instead of three and would burn five hundred more gallons of gasoline every week. The pool also "freed up each member's family to have just one car," the Rev. J. Martin Bailey later said. The MRCP had one more benefit, perhaps the most important of all to car commuters in 1973–1974: to encourage pools, the owner of a service station near Thompson's Hardware reserved twenty-five gallons of fuel per week for the group's station wagons.[78]

The cooperative ethos manifested in the MRCP also was evident in the behavior of other motorists who rolled down the streets and highways of America. Among those motorists were independent truck drivers. Cooperation among independent truckers of necessity took a different form than it did among passenger car drivers. Car commuters transported only themselves to and from work, and they shared vehicles and split fuel costs with relative ease. Independent truckers contracted to move distinct loads (usually farm and food products) across the country in large tractor-trailer rigs. Yet the truckers still found ways to organize, and their response to the dissipation of the nation's petroleum reserves was the boldest, most daring of any group of citizens.

Independent truckers were unlikely cooperators. Many came from rural America, and they saw themselves as hard-working, virtuous, anti-authoritarian, staunchly autonomous operators on whom the well-being of the entire nation rested. Although they were hydrocarbon creatures dependent on oil companies and the federal government, they could downplay this fact as long as fuel was relatively abundant and cheap. Paragons of automotive individualism, the truckers fused rural populist values with petroleum-powered, modern industrial technology to form a unique subculture that celebrated the self-reliant man at the wheel of an enormous machine.[79] The trucker mystique found its clearest, most forceful expression in the country-and-western songs that blared from jukeboxes, radios, and tape players. Dave Dudley's "Six Days on the Road" (1963), the most famous trucker hit, celebrated the power and speed of a diesel-burning vehicle (presumably a Kenworth or Peterbilt) as its driver passed Jimmy (GMC) and White trucks, evaded the police and the ICC (Interstate Commerce Commission), and headed for home. Background vocals and instrumentals complemented Dudley's rich baritone, conveying a sense of mechanical rhythms and the whine of a shifting engine.[80]

The oil shock of 1973–1974 hit the independent truckers hard and challenged the individualist mystique they had built up around themselves. Diesel prices rose some 50 percent that winter, from about $0.25 to $0.50 per gallon in many places and, where most expensive, from $0.35 to $0.70. Fuel shortages, long waits in line, and price increases were bad enough, but the new 50–55 mph speed limits added insult to injury and seemed to be yet another form of oppressive government regulation. Truckers argued that their machines were geared to operate most efficiently at 70–75 mph, and they complained that slower travel forced them to make fewer deliveries. Less fuel at greater expense in combination with slower speeds, they pointed out, worked a hardship on them: it reduced their profits and thus diminished their ability to pay off their vehicle mortgages and support their families. At truck stops around the country, they groused over their coffee and cheeseburgers. By early December, their frustration and anger had risen to the breaking point. The paragons of automotive individualism were on the verge of organizing.[81]

The strikes began with isolated protests at truck stops and then spread to heavily traveled bottlenecks and junctions of the interstate highways. At the Tomahawk Truck Stop at Brighton, Colorado, fifteen miles northeast of Denver, drivers made known their objection to high prices and government policies by parking their rigs and refusing to move. "The Great White Fathers back in Washington don't give a damn about truck drivers," exclaimed John Welcher, a trucker from Iowa. "We're classified as the lowest form of life. We've got to shut down this country to show 'em what this is doing to us."[82] Even as Welcher spoke, truckers in at least nine other states were taking action. Some simply parked and would not budge. Others persuaded sympathetic truck stop owners to close their pumps in order to restrict the movement of all rigs, not just those of the independents. In a few key places, the protests grew to extraordinary size. Some eighteen hundred trucks blockaded the Delaware Memorial Bridge near the junction of the New Jersey Turnpike and Interstate 95, fouling traffic around Wilmington and backing up vehicles for twelve miles on the New Jersey side. On Interstate 80 a few miles south of Toledo, Ohio, at a major national crossroads, approximately three thousand trucks nearly paralyzed vehicular transportation.[83]

In these and other spontaneous actions, truckers used their citizens' band (CB) radios to maximum effect. The CB was a relatively simple technology widely adopted after 1958, when the Federal Communications Commission set aside a band of radio frequencies for use by ordinary Americans. In the hands of independent truckers, the CB became a tool for mobilizing and coordinating mass protest. Reaching out to one another on invisible waves of energy generated by the mechanical movement of their petroleum-fired engines, the truckers sensed their collective potential to change the hydrocarbon system that both benefited and constrained them. "The smallest trucking company in the world has finally spoken," Don Miller said of himself and each of his fellow independents while he sipped coffee at the Toledo ARCO Truck Stop. "Now he's the biggest trucking company in the world."[84]

In reality, Miller and his compatriots less resembled a giant corporation than a grassroots movement. Imagining himself a partner in a giant company perhaps seemed a logical extension of his identity as a businessman, but Miller and his fellows more strongly harked back to the farmers' alliances of an earlier time. Perhaps they even resembled a labor union, which was ironic in light of their resentment of the Teamsters, the nation's largest organization of truck driver employees. The similarities became stronger when independent truckers redoubled their protests in mid-December and again in January and February 1974. In mid-December, they parked their rigs at the pumps of uncooperative truck stop owners, shutting them down. Whether at truck stops or on the highways, stalling or blocking machinery was a version of the laborer's sit-down strike. Truckers also sabotaged the vehicles of uncooperative independents, recalling the Farm Holiday of the 1930s, when agrarians intercepted and destroyed produce shipments in an effort to constrict supply and raise prices. Angry striking truckers attacked—and in two instances killed—stubborn independents, actions that likened the assailants to laborers who beat non-union "scabs." Early in 1974, owner-operators resorted to another labor tactic: they blocked shipments of food and steel, forcing consumers and factory workers as well as business owners to share their pain.[85]

State and federal governments had to address the truckers' revolt, which hurt the economy and, when violent, verged on insurrection. In February 1974, William Simon, head of the Federal Energy Office, and three other Nixon administration officials judged the shutdown "a serious threat to the nation's economic well-being and safety" and called on state governors for assistance in "restoring order and commerce." In response, several governors mobilized National Guard units to protect trucking companies and their employees and to keep highway traffic flowing. The Nixon administration also opened negotiations with the owner-operators. William Usery Jr., a federal mediator and labor adviser to the president, soon began deliberations with the Truckers Unity Council, formed the previous month by the Council of Independent Truckers, the Fraternal Association of Steel Haulers, and other representatives of owner-operators. The truckers wanted lower diesel prices, a guaranteed fuel supply, an investigation of the oil companies, and the repeal of the government regulations that frustrated them, including rigid load requirements and the 55 mph speed limit.[86] Flexing their muscles, the owner-operators appeared to be in a strong position to reshape energy distribution in their favor.

Their unity soon inspired another trucker hit, "Convoy" (1975), by C. W. McCall, the pseudonym of William Fries. Irreverent, tinged with humor and self-parody, "Convoy" told of two truckers with the CB "handles" of Rubber Duck and Pig Pen who led a thousand vehicles across the nation in defiance of the federal speed limit, state police forces, and the National Guard. In the song of the convoy, the owner-operators found a powerful symbol of independent men joining together in a demonstration of collective masculine strength. Rooted in agrarian, labor, and protest traditions, it expressed a desire to claim a central place in the political economy of America.[87]

In the end, the independent truckers could not mobilize enough power to attain their goals. Numbering perhaps seventy-five thousand, they lacked the size and influence necessary to overcome the forces arrayed against them. Grocery stores and steel companies had a vested interest in keeping the goods moving, as did corporate truckers and the Teamsters union, state governors and the Nixon administration. Perhaps more important, the contradiction between the independent truckers' automotive individualism and their need for coordinated action was too great. The final settlement momentarily froze diesel prices and compensated independents with a 6 percent surcharge on goods hauled under contract to trucking companies, but these measures did little to help most owner-operators. Many rejected the agreement as a sellout, and they vowed to continue the strike. But without the resources to sustain them in the absence of regular income, they could not continue. Gradually, they gave up and went back to work.[88]

The outcome of the truck drivers' strikes of 1973–1974 was mixed. The truckers contributed to the political pressure that in the 1980s loosened ICC regulations and repealed the 55 mph speed limit.[89] Beyond that, their overall effect on energy policy was negligible. Although they had mobilized a dramatic effort to redirect the flow of energy through the country, they were too technologically and economically fragmented to prevail. Machines and oil, once the means of their freedom, had become the instruments of their division and dependency.

Those Americans who best recovered a measure of personal autonomy at the time did so by making use of transportation other than motor vehicles. The oil shock of 1973–1974 taught a powerful lesson to those willing and able to absorb it: the car could be a trap, and degrees of freedom lay somewhere beyond it. Other technologies beckoned to people frustrated by high fuel prices, long lines at service stations, and traffic jams. For some, the solution involved not just the choice of machine, but the cultivation and use of the human body.

The oil shock enabled two surprising reversals of long-term social and economic trends. One centered on the use of subways, streetcars, trains, and buses. For decades, car manufacturers and oil companies had gone to extraordinary lengths to discredit and weaken public transportation, all the while reshaping public policy and infrastructure to accommodate private automobiles. Federal law, reflecting corporate influence on Congress, stipulated that revenue from gasoline taxes must be used only for federal highway construction and maintenance. Massive federal spending on highways in turn stimulated sales of cars and gasoline and filled corporate coffers. The reshaping of America in the image of the automobile had dire consequences for public transportation. For nearly three decades after the Second World War, the number of people who patronized rail and bus systems had spiraled downward. The oil shock induced a striking turnabout. In August 1973, even before the OPEC embargo, rising fuel prices and congested roadways encouraged Congress to pass a historic measure stipulating that a portion of the Federal Highway Trust Fund (filled with revenue from gasoline taxes) must be devoted to mass transportation.[90] Over the coming year, citizens proved that senators, representatives, and President Nixon had made the right decision. A survey of 120 cities showed that between October 1973 and October 1974, the average number of riders had risen by 7.8 percent. In some localities, the increases were dramatic: 11.8 percent in Pittsburgh, 18 percent in San Diego, 22.5 percent in Jacksonville, Florida.[91] Such figures demonstrated the willingness of many citizens to leave their cars at home and take public transportation when oil and automotive individualism failed to serve their needs.

The second major socioeconomic reversal that accompanied the oil shock was a reawakened popular interest in the bicycle. Awash in cheap oil and gasoline, citizens had abandoned the bicycle as a practical mode of transportation. Most people had forgotten that the device had once opened new opportunities for mobility and that bicyclists—the League of American Wheelmen (LAW), founded in 1880—had been the first proponents of paved roads. Low membership had forced the dissolution of LAW in 1955. By the 1960s, manufacturers and most Americans thought of the bicycle as a child's toy; as late as 1969, only about 12 percent of the models sold were designed for adults. A conjunction of events in the 1960s and 1970s, however, stimulated a bicycle revival. A desire for healthy exercise and the experience of nature inspired Americans to take up hiking, mountain climbing, and skiing, but also bicycling. Many outdoor recreationists were baby boomers who carried their childhood enthusiasm for two-wheelers into their teenage and adult years. Manufacturers and importers offered them a sophisticated new machine: the narrow-wheeled, multigeared, lightweight ten-speed. For young people without access to cars, the ten-speed enabled efficient travel over relatively long distances in and out of auto-dependent suburbs, to and from schools, and around college campuses. Bicycle sales, especially of adult models, began to climb.[92]

The bicycling trend became a full-blown boom with the advent of the environmental movement and especially Hubbert's peak and the 1973–1974 oil shock. In 1971, dealers sold roughly nine million machines; two years later, some sixteen million rolled from the shops. In 1972, dealers sold more adult bikes than juvenile ones; by 1975, adult models accounted for some 65 percent of sales. Most telling, perhaps, was that Americans during the early 1970s bought more bicycles than cars. As bicycling became more widespread, enthusiasts began to reflect on the human body's energetic potential when applied to pedals. Together, the body and the bicycle efficiently converted food into mechanical movement. Multiple benefits followed: decreased oil use, increased blood flow, improved health, and peace of mind. "The novice and the regular both know the cyclist's high," bragged one commentator. "It derives, in part, from the knowledge that the energy comes from a live body, not from fossil fuels. The legs pump, the heart answers."[93]

Enthusiasm for the bicycle could be overstated, to be sure. In spite of its environmental, physiological, and psychological benefits, it still could not completely liberate citizens from oil; carbohydrates could not completely replace hydrocarbons. From resource extraction to manufacture, distribution, sale, and operation, bicycles, like any other industrial product, needed inputs of petroleum and coal: for refining metal, synthesizing rubber, electrifying factories, fueling delivery trucks and workers' personal automobiles, lubricating ball bearings and chains, and laying asphalt and concrete pavement. Nor did bicyclists give up their cars; only the rare individual completely abandoned one for the other. The United States remained an automobile-centered nation tightly connected to the underground residuum of the Earth's deep organic past. The car-mounted bicycle carrier epitomized the position of the two-wheeler in America. The simple, lightweight device, many versions of which appeared on the market in the early 1970s, allowed a motorist to carry a bike to a repair shop and to "take-off points."[94] The bicycle was an appendage to, an outgrowth of, hydrocarbon society.

Yet the bicycle still had the potential to transform the system. At local and state levels, Americans tapped the flow of oil to build the first pieces of a new order that, if it would not eliminate the need for petroleum, at least would reduce it. In 1971, the state of Oregon passed a "Bicycle Bill" that allocated—or, in the telling phrase of a journalist, "siphoned off"—1 percent of its gasoline taxes to pay for the construction of bikeways. The next year, Washington state diverted 0.5 percent of its transportation funds for the same purpose.[95] It was a small start to a trend that might modify the nation's energy use over the long term. In the aftermath of Hubbert's peak, local, state, and federal policymakers began to pay more attention to bicycles. In 1973, thirty-one states considered some two hundred bills regarding bikeways and bicycle registration and regulation. At the opening of Bicycles USA, a federally sponsored national conference held in Cambridge, Massachusetts, in May 1973, John Hirten, an official in the U.S. Department of Transportation, declared that it was time for bicycles to assume a "rightful place in the multi-modal mix." The federal government's interest was more than just talk; the 1973 Federal Aid Highway Act provided $120 million for bikeways.[96] That was a small sum in comparison with the amount devoted to highway construction and maintenance that year—but it was large in light of the total bikeway budget in 1972: zero.

Other sectors of American society also sensed the growing importance and potential of two-wheeled transportation. The most surprising included the very entities that had invested so much in gasoline consumption and had become the focus of so much customer anger: service stations and the oil companies to which they were subsidiary. In the midst of the oil shock, the Liberty Bell Tire Corporation, which distributed automobile tires and parts to service stations in Philadelphia and its vicinity, began delivering bicycles to its clients for sale to drivers interested in alternative transportation.[97]

More startling still, the Sun Oil Company, headquartered outside Philadelphia, experimented with bicycle sales and service. The corporation's Suncrest division contracted with Stelber Industries of Brooklyn, New York, for a supply of two-wheelers. Operators of Sunoco stations who paid franchise fees and completed training seminars then sold and serviced the "Suncrest" line, modestly priced at $50 to $100. The Suncrest bicycle program went into effect at twelve Sunoco stations in November 1973; the following spring, the corporation extended the program to dealers in seven states. Angelo Sutera, who owned a Sunoco station in Media, Pennsylvania, southwest of Philadelphia, converted an underused repair bay to a bicycle operation and put his daughter Janice in charge of it during her summer break from college. It proved to be a lucrative enterprise; Sutera estimated that it had netted him a $3,000 profit by early September. Bicycle repair, moreover, reinforced automobile service. After hauling in their bikes, Sutera's customers often purchased gasoline for their cars.[98]

This corporate shift toward bicycles was modest and incremental. Liberty Bell and Sunoco already sold automobile parts and other mechanical merchandise, so the addition of bicycles merely broadened the scope of their existing operations. Service stations were already well known for sales gimmicks, and they had employees, tools, and spaces easily adapted to bicycle maintenance and repair. Two bicycle mechanics, in fact, Charles and Frank Duryea, had built and operated the first American automobile in 1891.[99]

In one important respect, service station bicycles represented an extraordinary departure from the conventional practices of automobile-centered companies. To the extent that two-wheelers substituted for cars or offered the potential for such a substitution, they were an unprecedented development, a bold step toward an alternative future only beginning to take shape in 1973–1974. From the vantage of a garage bay converted to the assembly, maintenance, and repair of two wheelers, a citizen—without a trace of utopianism—could catch a fleeting glimpse of a very different world.

Americans in fact had options other than automotive individualism and its attendant despair, but whether or not people would continue to pursue those alternatives once the oil embargo ended was an open question. Would they still experiment with energy sources other than fossil fuels? Would they persist in their search for technologies that more efficiently converted energy into mechanical movement? Would they continue to seek the cooperative forms of social organization that gave them greater control over their lives? Perhaps—or perhaps not. Perhaps, in reckless haste, they would continue to spill the precious ancient reservoirs they had found along the universe's entropic highway. Perhaps the nightmare of the gas line—or worse—would become the norm.

THE PICNIC'S OVER

The First Great Oil Shock concluded in late March 1974 when the Arab members of OPEC voted to end their embargo against the United States. Egypt, Syria, and Israel, with U.S. assistance, had been negotiating a temporary settlement to the October 1973 war. Satisfied that Israel would withdraw from contested areas on Egypt's Sinai Peninsula, the Arab OPEC states once more opened their wells to American consumers.[100] As the oil gushed forth, fuel prices came down, and the lines of cars at service stations disappeared as quickly as they had formed.

Yet the days of carefree hydrocarbon consumption were over. As M. King Hubbert had pointed out, although geological processes still shaped the Earth, new petroleum deposits would not form for hundreds of millions of years.[101] The amount of oil available to humanity was finite, and in the United States, the rising rate of extraction had stalled against that natural limit. The offshore and Alaska discoveries briefly reenergized the country, yet even the rate of extraction from those rich pools soon went into decline.[102] There would be no return to the golden age of automotive individualism; Norman Reichbach and other citizens would never again enjoy the sheer abundance of the seventy years that separated Spindletop from Hubbert's peak and that made America a global superpower.

After 1970, the nation entered a period of environmental, economic, and political turmoil that extended into the twenty-first century. Although no single cause accounted for the tumult, much of it resulted from a fundamental geopolitical condition: the United States consumed more petroleum than it could supply from reserves within its territory. The oil shock of 1973–1974, and then the shock of 1979, when Iran underwent a political revolution that curtailed its petroleum exports, contributed to economic contractions and restructurings that went on for two decades. Those events also sharpened the nation's claim to Middle East oil. In 1980, following the Soviet Union's invasion of Afghanistan, President Jimmy Carter announced that the United States would resist militarily any threat to its interests in the Persian Gulf region.[103] Eleven years later, President George H. W. Bush, with the approval of Congress, mobilized the U.S. armed forces to repel Iraq's attempted takeover of oilfields in Kuwait. Fought at a time of economic contraction, the Persian Gulf War of 1991 was an outright struggle for petroleum that both anticipated and helped to ensure future conflict.[104]

Economic prosperity briefly visited the United States in the aftermath of its first oil war, but it also brought problems. The adoption of computers and the Internet stimulated production and a rise in personal incomes. In 1995, for the first time in twenty-two years, real wages—a measure of consumer buying power—began to climb.[105] The good times, however, took an environmental toll, because they intensified the extraction and consumption of natural resources, including fossil fuels. Although computers used less energy and emitted less pollution than did technologies associated with earlier booms, electricity and petroleum still went into their manufacture, distribution, and operation. Consumers with rising incomes also purchased millions of new automobiles, the large sizes of which required more fuel than smaller models. Americans spent more time on the road, often traveling to and from sprawling developments of single-family houses. Increased road time and the consumption of calorie-laden foods—calories packed there by petroleum-intensive production and processing methods—in turn contributed to a growing national problem with obesity. The automobile, it seemed, converted oil deposits not only into mechanical movement but also into ever-deeper reservoirs of human fat.[106]

Troubling events linked to America's hydrocarbon predicament also accompanied the boom—and its conclusion. On April 19, 1995, two American terrorists—one of them a disgruntled, psychopathic veteran of the Gulf War—bombed the Alfred P. Murrah Federal Building in Oklahoma City, killing 168 people. The terrorists constructed their weapon from simple materials readily available to any American. They packed an explosive mixture of diesel fuel and synthetic fertilizer (a petroleum derivative) into the back of a small truck, drove the vehicle to the Murrah Building, and detonated it.[107] The anger and insecurity that compelled that act faded during the next four years of prosperity, but in 1999, signs of shakiness reappeared. That spring, the increasing global demand for oil drove gasoline prices to well over $2.00 per gallon.[108] A year later, overextended Internet companies experienced a dramatic contraction that destroyed fortunes and stalled careers.

While the economy slumped, foreign terrorists mobilized an unprecedented attack on the United States—an attack directly related to the nation's consumption of oil. Many Muslims resented the United States because of its support for Israel and its interventions in the affairs of Middle East nations. An American military force—what some considered an infidel army—on Saudi Arabian soil during the Persian Gulf War intensified their anger. Wealthy Saudis, their bank accounts enriched by petroleum, funded the al-Qaeda terrorist network, which began to strike American targets. On September 11, 2001, nineteen men, most of them from Saudi Arabia, hijacked four airliners leaving Boston, New York, and Washington, D.C., on transcontinental flights.

The hijackers' mission was to destroy prominent buildings and incite world-wide Muslim resistance to the United States and its policies. Passengers forced the terrorists to crash one plane in the Pennsylvania countryside, sparing the United States Capitol, but the hijackers slammed a jet into the Pentagon and plunged two more into the twin towers of the World Trade Center in New York City. All the aircraft had wide bodies and large storage tanks filled with aviation fuel. The infernos that erupted on impact contributed to the death toll—some three thousand—and demonstrated how easily petroleum-powered technologies could become extraordinarily lethal weapons.[109]

In the aftermath of 9/11, as it became known, America's hydrocarbon predicament worsened. The destruction of the World Trade Center shook national and global markets, producing record losses. Stalled traffic and falling ticket sales hurt airlines and further slowed economic activity. Soon the United States was at war with the Taliban regime in Afghanistan, which harbored al-Qaeda and its operatives. And in the spring of 2003, President George W. Bush, with the near-unanimous approval of Congress, took the nation into war against Iraq. President Bush and his administration asserted that the regime of Saddam Hussein was tied to the terrorists and posed a direct threat to U.S. security. As those rationales collapsed in the absence of evidence, and as the war evolved into a conflict with various tribal, sectarian, and anti-American forces, Bush and his advisers claimed that the nation was fighting for the cause of freedom. Still, there remained a basic material fact: Iraq contained world-class petroleum reserves and occupied a strategically important position on the Persian Gulf. The United States, it seemed, was embroiled in its second oil war.[110]

As the increasingly costly military ventures in Afghanistan and Iraq dragged on, the nation crossed important hydrocarbon thresholds. M. King Hubbert had forecast in 1969 that world oil production would peak around 2000.[111] By that time, economic expansion and industrialization in China and India were absorbing more and more of the world's petroleum, driving prices up. Some analysts also claimed that the rate of production in Saudi Arabia's Ghawar field had begun to decline, although the Saudis vehemently denied it.[112] Regardless, by 2004, evidence suggested that the world had reached, or was about to reach, Hubbert's peak. That year, oil prices shot up 30 percent. But the worst was yet to come. World production stopped growing in 2005, and oil rose from $45 to $150 per barrel. By the summer of 2006, gasoline in the United States had surged above $3 per gallon at the pump. By the summer of 2008, the price had gone beyond $4. Princeton University geology professor Kenneth

Deffeyes, a proud son of the Oklahoma oil patch and an outspoken proponent of Hubbert's theory, pinpointed December 16 or 17, 2005, as the precise moment of the global peak. Hubbert, he proclaimed, had been right again.[113]

Many economists and other white-collar analysts disagreed with Deffeyes. The world had nothing to fear, they said. Additional petroleum was hidden in the folds of the abundant Earth, but more important, rising prices would stimulate technological innovations that would enable more thorough extraction from existing fields.[114] Deffeyes and the other "Hubbertians" would have none of it. They tended to be scientists and engineers close to the ground, practical people to whom natural limits were a geophysical reality that neither academic theory nor political ideology could deny. "World oil production has now ceased to grow," Deffeyes declared in 2006. "Decline is the next step. The picnic's over."[115]

The United States crossed a second hydrocarbon threshold at virtually the same time the controversy over Hubbert's peak intensified. Despite the oil shock of 1973–1974, Americans in subsequent years had not curtailed their driving; they actually had driven more. Between 1970 and the early twenty-first century, the number of motor vehicles more than doubled. By 2006, some 230 million of them—more than one for every American aged eighteen and older—rolled down the nation's streets and highways. The saturation of the automobile market had costly consequences. In 2008, the United States experienced its worst economic downturn since the Great Depression of the 1930s. Mortgage defaults on millions of single-family houses in the nation's sprawling, auto-dependent suburbs contributed to the problem. But so did cars—especially the sheer number of them. Americans had lost interest in the "gas-guzzlers" that had been the specialty of U.S. automakers since the late 1990s, and many other people simply could not afford new vehicles. Most important, they could get on with their lives without new vehicles, at least for the time being. By 2009, the automobile companies—including General Motors, once the wealthiest corporation in the world—were in deep financial trouble, if not already bankrupt.[116]

In combination with war and economic contraction, oil-derived environmental problems hurt the United States. In the spring of 2010, a BP deepwater well off the coast of Louisiana blew out. The resulting spill, the worst in the nation's history, fouled the Gulf coast and exacted an enormous toll on marine life, wetlands and estuaries, and the fishing communities that depended on them. Not only was the disaster a severe financial blow and a public relations nightmare for BP, but the negative consequences for President Barack Obama's administration showed how easily the intensive use of petroleum created problems that could deflect the course of national politics.[117]

As damaging as the 2010 spill was, its destructiveness paled in comparison with other potential environmental consequences of humanity's vast consumption of fossil fuels. The greatest of these, perhaps, was global climate change. As oil from the 2010 blowout gushed into the Gulf of Mexico, evidence mounted that carbon dioxide from the burning of oil and coal was contributing to rising temperatures around the planet. In combination with methane, water vapor, and other "greenhouse" gases, CO_2 trapped the sun's warmth, increasing the temperature of the biosphere, altering climate and weather patterns, and wreaking ecological havoc.[118] In addition to military conflicts and economic downturns, such environmental devastation offered compelling evidence that the Age of Oil—an age synonymous with the "American Century"—was coming to a close.

Yet the story of America's rise to greatness did not have to end in the hydrocarbon trap and the war, indebtedness, bankruptcy, and ecological devastation that accompanied it. Americans, it seemed, still had the means to shape a favorable outcome. Despite their devotion to automotive individualism, they never completely forgot the lessons of 1973–1974 nor entirely dispensed with the policies and practices that it had inspired. Perhaps the most important legacy of the first great oil shock was a revived and persistent conservation ethic that reminded citizens that they could not sustain their hydrocarbon habits over the long term and that they needed to try something different.

Evidence for that conservation legacy was everywhere. Although the vast majority of Americans still drove to work alone, and many struggled to organize group automobile commutes, the nation never abandoned the practice of carpooling.[119] Local, state, and federal governments also retained the concept, as designated car pool lanes on the freeways of every major city evidenced. Mass transit continued as well, supported by citizens who insisted that their tax monies go to subways, streetcars (known as "light rail"), and buses, not just automobiles and pavement. Cars themselves bore the mark of the first great oil shock. In 1975, Congress passed the Energy Policy and Conservation Act, which established "corporate average fuel efficiency" (CAFE) standards for automobiles.[120] Although loopholes allowed automakers to manufacture and sell millions of light trucks and sport utility vehicles (SUVs) with larger, less efficient engines, the CAFE program remained in place and offered guidelines by which Congress might reduce the overall quantity of gasoline and diesel that people burned. Many Americans, furthermore, continued to buy and drive small cars, not just "gas hogs," and their desire for automobile efficiency matched that of researchers and conservationists who revived the moribund, nearly forgotten experiment with fuels—alcohol, biodiesel, and others.

Not the least important conservation legacy of 1973–1974 was a persistent interest in bicycles. Saturated markets, cheap gasoline, and conservative opposition stalled the expansion of bicycling from the 1970s to the 1980s, but around 1990 the trend picked up again. In part, consumers powered the movement. Although few Americans rode to work on two-wheelers, they once more purchased large numbers of them, including the fat-tired, multigeared mountain bike. Federal legislation once again funded bicycle infrastructure and programs. In 1991 and 1998, bicycling activists and their supporters in Congress defeated political opponents and reauthorized substantial expenditures of funds for alternative transportation. Between 1998 and 2009, appropriations allocated some $6.5 billion to bicycle and pedestrian projects. Local and national interest groups assisted local efforts to make way for bikes. The League of American Wheelmen, reorganized in 1965 and renamed the League of American Bicyclists (LAB) in 1994, instituted a Bicycle Friendly America Program. Participating communities demonstrated minimum commitments of infrastructure and other resources to encourage the use of two-wheelers. By 2010, some 140 communities met LAB standards at the bronze, silver, gold, or platinum level.[121]

Activists also drew on earlier state laws for legal leverage against policymakers and officials reluctant to make way for bicycles. In Portland, Oregon, an LAB platinum community, citizens used the 1971 state Bicycle Bill as the basis for a lawsuit that compelled the city to put in bikeways and sidewalks on major street projects. In Portland and other municipalities, planners discovered that bicycle-friendly infrastructure enabled an increase in bicyclists.[122] In keeping with this reorientation of urban landscapes, Americans bought two-wheelers in large numbers, often prompted by the rising price of gasoline. In 2005, the year of global Hubbert's peak, bicycle purchases spiked, rising to some 20 million from 18.5 million two years before. By then, approximately 100 million Americans, one-third of the population, owned two-wheelers.[123] There were good reasons to be skeptical that citizens could reorient their lives and landscapes to the bicycle, but the potential for the machine to substantially alter energy use was undeniable.[124] A pedal-powered future was within reach.

America's hydrocarbon predicament has been and always will be a function of a universal thermodynamic condition. Impossible to stop or reverse, the dissipation of light and heat—the unstoppable flow of energy that marks the passage of time—is a harsh taskmaster, the driver of history and the maker of tragedy. Although the fundamental human problem is to live reasonably within its dictates, there is no perfect way to do that—there is, in short, no trouble-free route to life, liberty, and happiness. Every option, if not bad, is less than perfect—and thus inherently tragic. The challenge is to see through the tragedy to the choices that ensure the greatest range of flexibility and that enable the best, rather than the worst, of human tendencies.

The route to that optimal future begins in the past, at places like Norman Reichbach's City Line Flying A. It begins in half-empty gas tanks and lighter wallets, in stalled vehicles, pounding hearts, clenched fists, gunfire, and burning buildings. It begins in the odor of volatile hydrocarbon compounds that have the power to arouse equally volatile human tempers. It begins in oil spots on smooth concrete, grime beneath fingernails, queasy feelings deep in the gut, full bladders, frenzied family schedules, and human fat. And it begins wherever Americans come together to imagine possibilities they have forgotten or never known existed. There, the ability to find a way forward is most powerful. There, amid reinvigorated lives, renewed purpose, and restored dreams, another future, perhaps better than the last, begins to take shape. ★

PATHS THAT BECKON

IT IS A TRUISM THAT WE SEE WHAT we want to see. "The moment a person forms a theory," Thomas Jefferson wrote in 1787, "his imagination sees, in every object, only the traits which favor that theory."[1] Perhaps it is hazardous to look for nature at every step in the American past, in every idea, activity, conflict, person, and thing. The theory yields the evidence that confirms it; the environmental historian loses sight of all else. Yet if the journey from the Lincoln Memorial risks tunnel vision, it also carries a reward: the experience, almost like discovery, of wonders that the eyes have missed because the viewer has not known how to see. The surprises appear at every turn. Words and images come back to life. Distinctions between mind and matter dissolve. Seemingly unrelated events unite in vivid stories that reorient time, space, and relationships. Together, the pieces reveal the totality of a forgotten material force that shaped the founding and development of the republic.

Recovering the nature of American history is a demanding project that requires the effort of many scholars. The paths are many; the method is straightforward. Choose a topic. Ask the question: How did nature matter? Gather evidence. Think about it. And begin.

ALL NATURE IS FULL OF GOD

During the 1730s and 1740s, the American colonies experienced a religious revival known as the Great Awakening. Grassroots preachers, farmers, artisans, women, and boys, often unlettered, called on people to repent their sins, accept God's power and grace, and open themselves to Jesus's love. Although the spiritual fervor that resulted was an important moment in American religious, intellectual, cultural, political, and social history, it powerfully illustrated the importance of nature to the colonists' lives and experiences.[2]

On the one hand, the Great Awakening posited a universal human nature in which all people, including men, women, and members of different races, were equal in God's eyes. This egalitarian condition, evangelical Christians believed, authorized individual people to seek salvation apart from established social hierarchies. The Baptist preacher Isaac Backus expressed this sentiment in terms of the earthly—and potentially revolutionary—notion of rights. "Does not the course of all this difficulty lie in this," he asked, "that the common people claim as good a right to judge and act for themselves in matters of religion as civil rulers or the learned clergy?"[3]

On the other hand, the Great Awakening described human nature as part of the fallen nature of Earth in general. "The God that holds you over the pit of Hell," exclaimed the famous evangelist Jonathan Edwards, "much as one holds a spider or some loathsome insect over the fire, abhors you, and is dreadfully provoked; his wrath towards you burns like fire; he is of purer eyes than to bear to have you in his sight; you are ten thousand times so abominable in his eyes as the most hateful venomous serpent is in ours." Many colonists agreed with Edwards, and they associated the depravity of human nature with the depraved nature of nonhuman creatures. "By nature I am half a devil and half a beast," said Deborah Prince, a young woman drawn into the fervor; "I know that in me, that is in my flesh, dwells no good thing."[4]

Although the Great Awakening called on people to reject their fallen natures for an otherworldly promise, perhaps the evangelical Christian message was popular because it seemed authentic, organic, and natural, and therefore true. Evangelical sermons were sensational, but their sensationalism involved more than just their drama, as preachers appealed to people's bodily senses, to their fears, anxieties, and aversion to pain, and to their deep desire for the ecstatic emotional release of salvation. Evangelical experiences were physical, kinesthetic, and environmental. People moaned, cried, wept, writhed, trembled, and twitched. Bodily intimacy among seekers and believers was important, and participants laid hands on the afflicted and washed each other's feet. The converted underwent baptism in water, a "New Birth" that they believed would fend off sickness and that gave them hope for an eternal life in heaven, an environment as beautiful and delightful as hell was ugly and terrifying. Evangelical sermons and rituals took place in streets, barns, fields, parks, groves, and rivers, away from the artificial, false hierarchy embodied in the church buildings of established denominations. "All nature is full of God," said one evangelist, "full of his perpetual, moving, guiding, and over-ruling influence." Even the informal name of an early evangelical seminary conveyed naturalness and organic authenticity: the Log College.[5]

Basic questions can guide a deeper inquiry into the environmental history of the Great Awakening. Did rapid population growth and increasing commercialism put pressure on natural resources and incite feelings of physical and spiritual vulnerability? Did migration over rough roads beyond the bounds of existing settlements leave colonists isolated from established churches and hungry for spiritual fulfillment? Did environmental conditions in towns and cities incline colonists toward the evangelical message? Did disease, shifts in climate, crop failures, food or fuel shortages, or other environmental circumstances influence their outlook? Did they turn to evangelists whose naturalistic figures of speech expressed the biophysical precariousness of their lives? Did the widespread availability of land encourage spiritual egalitarianism, or did conflict over land lead colonists to the evangelical message? To what extent did the Great Awakening partake of Enlightenment notions of universal human nature and rights? To what extent did it reject Enlightenment ideas that nature, including human nature, was innately good? Did Enlightenment thinkers explicitly reject the evangelical concept of a fallen, depraved nature, including human nature? How did notions of gender, in particular the nature of women, figure in this dialectic of evangelical and Enlightenment ideas?[6]

The theologian Reinhold Niebuhr once observed that human beings are rooted in nature yet seek to transcend it spiritually. According to Niebuhr, "man is a child of nature, subject to its vicissitudes, compelled by its necessities, driven by its impulses, and confined within the brevity of the years which permits its varied organic form, allowing them some, but not too much, latitude." And man is something else besides, "a spirit who stands outside of nature, life, himself, his reason and the world."[7] In the Great Awakening, the colonists' physical experience of their earthly home inspired them to seek communion with a transcendent, divine power, although it was a power that they felt in their physical bodies and described in the most natural of terms. Might Niebuhr's insight serve as an opening into the environmental history of other pivotal moments in the development of American religion?

Beginning in the eighteenth century, environmental circumstances influenced the creation, growth, power, and weakness of the United States. The process was not a crude determinism in which the nature of North America made the nation what it was. Rather, contingent combinations of human choices and environmental conditions shaped the founding and development of the republic. The nation had a nature that was the product of history.

The Seven Years' War, the struggle between Britain and France for North America, redirected and intensified the environmental and historical processes that eventually created the United States. Britain gained strength from the resources of its colonies. In particular, its hold on terrestrial and marine environments gave it access to significant sources of food, fuel, and soldiers. France's colonial environmental situation, in contrast, weakened it. Its dependence on the St. Lawrence River rather than on a long coastline made it especially vulnerable to naval pressure. Its reliance on Indian trading partners and allies collapsed when a smallpox epidemic devastated the tribes. Its agriculture was too small, too limited by growing season, and too subject to bad weather and harvest failures to produce enough food to provision its military forces. France might have devoted more maritime and naval power to ensuring food shipments, but instead it chose to protect the islands of Guadeloupe and Martinique and their lucrative sugar plantations.[8] Environment in conjunction with strategy, not just strategy alone, enabled Britain's North American triumph.

Some of the same environmental conditions that influenced the Seven Years' War enabled the movement for independence. The experience of land and war changed many colonists in New England, the Mid-Atlantic region, and the South and encouraged them to believe that they were Britain's partners, not its subordinates, in the empire. Their growing population, ambition to expand westward, and increasing political autonomy heightened their sense that colonial legislatures were free-standing political bodies. Eventually, their access not only to land but also to temperate climate, arable soil, and food allowed them to break away. Their environmental circumstances differed from those of Canada and the British Caribbean, where the experiences of climate and geography fostered a greater dependence on empire.[9]

After the Revolution, the United States molded itself into the material expression of its theoretical design. Its founders tried to establish a republic according to a Newtonian order fixed in the nature of things yet flexible enough to take into account the geographical extent, variability, and malleability of the American landscape.[10] Gradually, the founders and their descendants turned the United States government into an instrument for converting resources, through land sales and various forms of taxation, into money, armies, canals, banks, government officials, buildings, Washington, D.C., even a rapidly growing population. In sum, the physical form and function of the American state embodied its fundamental purpose: the transformation of nature into wealth and power.[11]

Over the decades, the United States gained and lost power in relation to its territorial extent and resource use. During the early nineteenth century, it acquired a vast amount of land that contained an extraordinary array of natural resources and internal markets. This geography at first dispersed the population, fragmented political authority among the states, checked the growth of the federal government, and contributed to the conflict that culminated in the Civil War. Beginning in the late nineteenth century and accelerating in the twentieth, the nation transformed itself. Using coal and oil, it intensified its extractive activities, developed its steel-making and other manufacturing and infrastructural capacities, and built national transportation networks centered first on railroads and then on highways and automobiles. These developments enabled it to consolidate its hold on domestic and international markets, produce a staggering array of mass consumer goods, and strengthen the federal government to an unprecedented degree. In the process, the nation became a global economic, political, and military force without peer.[12]

By the early twenty-first century, shifting circumstances turned the environmental advantages of the United States into liabilities. The rising cost of energy needed to transport people and goods absorbed more and more resources and wealth. The expense of maintaining an enormous, inefficient, auto-centered transportation infrastructure became exorbitant. Capital that might have paid for research and education instead went into overseas oil and a huge military. The nation suffered economic disadvantages in competition with spatially compact places such as Hong Kong and Singapore. Geographic space—the vaunted American frontier—had been an asset in an agricultural and industrial age; it became a burden in a global economy centered on advanced technology, finance, the flow of electronic information, and a well-educated population. While the nation tried to maintain its creaking infrastructure and overextended military, it struggled with the environmental consequences—toxic pollution, obesity, disease—of its government-subsidized, mass production and consumption economy.[13]

The environmental basis of the United States brings to mind Frederick Jackson Turner and other historians who once boldly accorded nature a prominent place in the nation's past. Although a plethora of new approaches modified if not superseded their interpretations, perhaps scholars once again might attempt an American history with nature at its core. They might ask fundamental questions about the expansion and contraction of national power in relation to changing environmental circumstances. How did land and other natural resources influence the nation's development? In what ways did the nation's territory and resources make possible its global power? To what extent did its sheer size and natural richness contribute to its weakness? In the historical accounts that follow from such questions, nature will not be monolithic, static, or abstract, but complex, active, and material, a multifarious biophysical reality that both enabled and limited people's efforts to shape the future. Such histories might fully realize the intellectual promise implicit in the title of one of Perry Miller's most famous works, *Nature's Nation*.[14]

NATURAL RULE OR NATURAL SOCIABILITY?

In the election of 1800, Thomas Jefferson, incumbent President John Adams, and their respective parties, the Republicans and the Federalists, were locked in a bitter dispute over the nation's development. The election was complicated because Jefferson, the Republican presidential contender, and Aaron Burr, the party's vice presidential candidate, received the same number of votes in the Electoral College.[15] At that time, the Constitution stipulated that the candidate with the majority of electoral votes would become president, and the one with the second greatest number, vice president. According to the Constitution, the House of Representatives had to break the deadlock. Each state had one vote, but neither party could muster the nine of seventeen votes necessary for a majority. Federalists who disliked Jefferson contemplated throwing the election to Burr. After weeks of political machinations, on the thirty-sixth ballot, the House finally elected Jefferson, and Burr became vice president, as the Republicans had intended. The transfer of power was peaceful, established the principle that the popular vote should determine the voting of electors, and began the permanent decline of the Federalists.[16] The "Revolution of 1800" was one of the most important political contests in American history—and it was firmly grounded in the nature of the early republic.

In crucial respects, environmental conditions affected the nation's political development. A sprawling land base, temperate climate, and general healthful conditions enabled European American men and women to marry relatively early, acquire property and establish farms, and have large families. The dispersal of a rapidly growing population across a vast geography posed enormous problems for the republic's political cohesion. The authors of the 1787 Constitution tried to address those problems by creating a framework of government that distributed power among federal and state branches. A small but nonetheless important part of the framework was the Electoral College. In such an enormous country, environmental obstacles—great distances, dense forests, innumerable rivers, inclement weather, and miles of muddy roads or tracks—hindered communication and prevented many citizens from knowing much if anything about presidential candidates. Although the people voted in presidential contests, electors with powers separate from those of Congress and the people met, weighed the virtues of the candidates, and made the final decision.[17]

Within this political structure, each party made distinctive assumptions about the nature of the republic and its citizens, and each accordingly attempted a distinctive political strategy. In general, the Federalists assumed an aristocratic hierarchy of human nature according to which a few talented and virtuous people—"natural rulers"—would govern on behalf of the mediocre mass democracy. Federalist political strategy was profoundly local: through patronage and the display of disinterested political virtue, its candidates would win the loyalty of the ordinary people among whom they lived. Yet the Federalists would harness this local influence to national purposes: they would build a strong federal government—military, national bank, bureaucracy, and a monarchical presidency—that would become the focus of citizens' identity and would make the United States a global power.[18]

The Republicans thought and acted differently. Republicans assumed a "natural sociability" among people that would encourage them to set aside their personal differences and interests and behave virtuously on behalf of the nation. Republicans despised Federalist elitism, and in contrast to Federalist localism and personal connections, the Republicans made extensive use of newspapers to project their message to the many people dispersed across the nation's vast domain. And whereas the Federalists would use localism to build national power, the Republicans would use their national stature to weaken the federal government and fragment power downward. The United States would be a nation of global influence, the Republicans believed, but that influence would rest on the natural sociability of humankind and the peaceful international commerce that would flow from it.[19]

Neither the Federalist nor the Republican approach to politics was perfect, but the Republican program more accurately described the nature of the United States and the nature of its citizenry—at least, the way the preponderance of those white male citizens understood it. The Republicans espoused a political ideology that spoke to a growing, westward-moving population that continuously migrated beyond the bounds of local settings. The people who composed that population tended to dislike the elitism of the Federalists, and the availability of land and economic opportunity enabled them to acquire property and to challenge Federalist claims to greater wealth, intellect, and virtue. A social order fixed on a limited amount of land and dependent upon aristocratic patrons never came into being, and the Federalists often found themselves struggling to earn a living in competition with the very people to whom they felt superior.[20] Not just the political choices of the Federalists and Republicans but also the biophysical nature in which they made those choices transformed American politics and governance.

Questions can cast additional light on the environmental basis of the 1800 election and, for that matter, virtually any other political contest. To what degree did weather, disease outbreaks, or shifts in climate affect the process and its outcome? What of the Republicans' astute use of newspapers to project their political message and build a political majority? Was newsprint widely available, and was its availability related to the general abundance of land, forests, cotton, and other paper-making resources in the United States? What were the environmental conditions of papermaking and of the domestic and international paper trade? Did the Republicans succeed because they assumed nature to be abundant, open, and dynamic, and did the Federalists fail because they assumed nature to be limited, restricted, and static? What environmental circumstances and ideas of nature contributed to the history of democratic politics?

RECONSTRUCTING LANDSCAPES, BODIES, AND BODIES POLITIC

During and immediately after the Civil War, the United States faced the problem of how to restore the Union politically, socially, and economically. Reconstruction, as people called the process, had important achievements. The U.S. Constitution's Thirteenth, Fourteenth, and Fifteenth amendments (1865, 1868, and 1870) prohibited slavery, extended citizenship to the freed people, and recognized black men's right to vote. Southerners of all kinds drew up new state constitutions; convened new state legislatures that instituted educational, economic, and other reforms; and elected new governors and members of Congress, some of whom were African Americans. The freed people, meanwhile, reestablished family and community bonds torn apart by slavery, and they took steps toward economic independence. But that was as far as Reconstruction got, for reactionary southern whites used violence, intimidation, and fraud to reassert their dominance over black people and their white Republican allies. In 1877, after the national Republican Party abandoned its commitment to reforming the Union on the basis of racial equality, Reconstruction came to an end.[21]

Reconstruction was one of the most important events in the nineteenth century, and it can be explained as environmental history. Efforts to remake people's relationships to one another often have involved efforts to remake their relationships to nature, and Reconstruction was no exception. The environmental history of Reconstruction centered on the just landscape that the freed people desired and the racially repressive and exploitative landscape that reactionaries tried to impose.[22]

To the freed people, rights were not abstract but were grounded in the biophysical experience of space and place. They insisted on the right to move freely through the reconstructed landscape and to own dogs and firearms for subsistence hunting and self-defense. Most important, they wanted the natural resources that would secure their economic, and thus political, independence. According to long-standing Southern custom, they wanted to hunt, fish, and run cattle and other livestock on unenclosed property that belonged to others. Above all, they wanted land. Garrison Frazier, a Baptist minister in Savannah, Georgia, and a former bondman, spoke of slavery and freedom in the idiom of universal natural rights. Slavery meant "receiving . . . the work of another man, and not by his consent." Freedom, in contrast, meant "placing us where we could reap the fruit of our own labor," where black people could "have land, and turn it and till it by our own labor." African Americans tried mightily to reconstruct the landscape along those lines. When the Civil War ended, many of them seized plantation land and converted it to the production of food. Through their participation in politics, they helped repeal legislation that closed the open range and restricted hunting and fishing. And by the thousands, they applauded and tried to benefit from the early efforts of the army and the Freedmen's Bureau to redistribute farm and plantation land on which, as slaves, they had labored so long and so hard.[23]

Almost from the start, however, a powerful countervailing movement worked against the freed people's dream. As federal government efforts to redistribute land faltered, the reactionaries acted swiftly and violently to seize legislative and police power and impose their alternative landscape vision. Draconian punishments for misdemeanors and petty felonies forced many African American men into prisons and enabled convict leasing programs in which private contractors rented prisoners for labor on plantations, in mines, and in lumber camps. State laws closed the open range, made hunting and fishing difficult or impossible, and prohibited trespass. A black person hunting partridges, herding a cow, or gathering nuts was no longer legally provisioning the family but committing a crime. And instead of independent landowners, African Americans became tenants or sharecroppers who worked a portion of a plantation in exchange for cash rent or a "share" of the crop. Some black farmers hoped that renting or sharecropping might be a step toward landed independence. But as time passed, more and more of them fell into a condition of permanent indebtedness that subjected them to the tyrannical dictates of planters. A landscape that once promised freedom became a tool of repression and exploitation.[24]

In what other ways might Reconstruction have been a moment in American environmental history? That large question invites others. How did the freed people and their allies think about nature, and how did they represent the landscape in art, song, and story? Did the freed people's efforts to remake their relationship to the land also involve an attempt to gain control over their bodies, labor, health, and reproduction? Did the reconstruction of the body politic, as the historian Steven Hahn called it, necessitate a reconstruction of human bodies and the landscapes that sustained them?[25] Did African Americans' understanding and experience of nature shape their efforts to work the land and participate in politics along family and community lines? Did environmental problems weaken their efforts to achieve bodily autonomy, economic independence, and political equality? Did livestock diseases before and during the Civil War detract from their ability to travel, plow the soil, and produce food? Did wildlife diseases or other environmental conditions diminish important food sources upon which they relied?

What about the reactionaries? Did weather, climate, soil conditions, or human diseases strengthen their challenge to the freed people? What ideas of nature coursed through their minds? Did they imagine African American bodies as physical resources to be controlled, much as land was a resource to be controlled? Did they exploit African American bodies the way they exploited the land? Did they use food and hunger as tools to force the freed people back into a condition of servitude and dependency? Such questions can lead to explanations of how contingent biophysical circumstances affected Reconstruction and how that event involved a profound struggle over the environmental as well as the political, social, and economic conditions of Southern life.

A MIGHTY RESERVOIR

One of the most powerful instruments of racial repression in post-Reconstruction America was the color line, which deprived African Americans of the resources and environments—sunlight, soil, schoolrooms, and more—that they needed to fulfill their potential as human beings and citizens. W. E. B. Du Bois was a Progressive-era historian, socialist, and civil rights activist who experienced the color line and devoted himself to its defeat. Although few scholars have associated him with environmental history, in fact he said much about the importance of nature to the color line and to the people who opposed its tyranny.

Modern world history, Du Bois asserted in *Darkwater* (1920), involved an epic contest among European nations, the United States, and the world's wealthiest people to conquer, colonize, and exploit land and "raw materials." To produce agricultural commodities, harvest timber, extract minerals, and engage in other profitable economic activities, these elites needed labor, in particular the inexpensive labor of the world's colored peoples. To control that labor and justify its exploitation, the global elite promoted ideas of racial difference and hierarchy. They denied or ignored evidence, Du Bois pointed out, that "all men, black and brown and white, are brothers," and they claimed that economic inequality was "'natural'—a part of our inescapable physical environment." To protect their interests, the wealthy and the powerful perpetuated the color line, which confined the vast majority of African Americans to menial work and inferior living spaces. As Du Bois observed, "race is a part of the economic and social organization of the land."[26]

Du Bois recognized that the color line impoverished African Americans not only economically but emotionally and spiritually, too, by obstructing their efforts to enjoy "the glory of physical nature." In *Darkwater*, he wrote in rapturous terms of his visits to some of the nation's most beautiful landscapes. "God molded his world largely and mightily off this marvelous coast," he said of the Maine shoreline that soon became Acadia National Park, "and meant that in the tired days of life, men should come and worship here and renew their spirit." Of all the places Du Bois visited in his journeys, none moved him more than the Grand Canyon: "One throws a rock into the abyss. It gives back no sound. It falls on silence—the voice of its thunders cannot reach so far. It is not—it cannot be a mere, inert, unfeeling, brute fact—its grandeur is too serene—its beauty too divine!"[27] As much as all humans needed and craved natural beauty, Du Bois recognized that race prejudice and the indignities of Jim Crow transportation dissuaded if not prohibited black people from experiencing it. "I should think you would like to travel," a white person said to Du Bois and some of his African American friends. "No," one member of the group politely responded, "we don't travel much."[28]

Du Bois challenged the environmental inequities of the color line in the language of conservation. Later generations of Americans would associate conservation almost exclusively with the stewardship of forests, water, wildlife, beautiful landscapes, and other nonhuman natural resources. Around the turn of the twentieth century, public figures such as Du Bois asserted that people should be conserved, too, and that the purpose of conservation was to uplift humanity. As early as 1897, in "The Conservation of Races," he called on African Americans to conserve their moral and physical integrity—their mental well-being and bodily health—so that when ready, they might transmit their great gift to humankind: the story of their struggle to sustain themselves in the African diaspora that had carried them to the western hemisphere and to the far corners of the globe.[29] Later, Du Bois argued that the nation's natural resources and productive capacities should privilege the needs of the many rather than the interests of the few. "America is conceived as existing for the sake of its mines, fields, and factories," he wrote in *Darkwater*, "and not those factories, fields, and mines as existing for America." He called for an "industrial democracy" in which people assumed control of land and other means of production in order "to secure the greatest good of all." Borrowing a concept from water conservation, he described humanity as a "mighty reservoir of experience, knowledge, beauty, love, and deed" that, properly cared for, could benefit all.[30]

One portion of humanity in particular inspired Du Bois's reservoir analogy. How, he asked, might people "increase the knowledge of experience of common men and conserve genius for the common weal?" How might "a more careful conservation of human ability and talent" help a democratic society "accomplish its greater ends"? The answer to those questions, he believed, was the proper nurturance and education of children: "All children are the children of all and not of individuals and families and races. The whole generation must be trained and guided and out of it as out of a huge reservoir must be lifted all genius, talent, and intelligence to serve all the world."[31]

Reading Du Bois in light of nature raises questions about how American historians have depicted the past. Why are the stories of his visits to the Maine coast and the Grand Canyon not in our national park histories? Why do they not appear in our histories of race? How did Du Bois's emphasis on moral strength and bodily health compare with or challenge conventional ways of thinking about nature during the Progressive era? An important part of that thought concerned human health and the nature of human bodies; why have histories of conservation given those topics little or no attention? Why do the pages on conservation in virtually every U.S. history textbook focus almost exclusively on Theodore Roosevelt? Is it possible that in confining race and nature to separate analytical categories, scholars have unwittingly perpetuated an intellectual form of the color line?[32]

Such questions deepen the more one reads of Du Bois. A chapter in *The Souls of Black Folk* (1903), his classic meditation on race, recounts his railroad trip through the Black Belt counties of Georgia. A lyrical description of the beauty, degradation, and poverty of the landscape and its people, "Of the Black Belt" is comparable in style to Aldo Leopold's "Illinois Bus Ride," in *A Sand County Almanac* (1949), one of the nation's most famous examples of nature writing.[33] Placing Du Bois in the company of Leopold or John Muir suggests an alternative perspective on the nature writing genre. If readers go back to nature with Muir, the founder of the Sierra Club and defender of Yosemite National Park and the Sierra Nevada, they arrive in a high, windswept, beautiful environment, a place of trees, rock, ice, wildlife, and few people—and a place that is pretty much racially and ethnically white. If they go with Leopold, they travel through wilderness but ultimately come to a rural world of farms and ranches—and a place that is pretty much racially and ethnically white.[34] If they go with Du Bois, the journey leads to rural and urban environments in which black people struggle for their lives. Many readers have accompanied Muir and Leopold into the American landscape. Might they travel with Du Bois, too? The trip would be different from those taken with other writers, but it might have just as much to teach, in its own way, about nature and society's place in it.

I am not alone in thinking about Du Bois and related topics in these terms. In 2007, Kimberly Smith published *African American Environmental Thought*, a work of remarkable erudition that recovered and analyzed the many ways in which Du Bois and other black intellectuals experienced, imagined, and represented nature. The events that motivated Smith to write her book were strikingly similar to those that prompted me to think about iconic moments in the American past as environmental history. Smith had offered a college course on American environmental thought, which featured the work of Thoreau, Muir, Leopold, and other figures in the nature writing canon. On the first day of class, a student had asked a provocative question: Why were there no African Americans on the syllabus?[35]

Is it possible to dismantle conventional categories and genres and reassemble the parts into new histories that do not separate nature from race? Is it possible to overcome the intellectual segregation that has confined nature to a separate box and prevented Americans from seeing things whole? Will more students challenge their professors with simple but powerful questions?

"I believe in Liberty for all men," Du Bois wrote in *Darkwater*: "the space to stretch their arms and their souls, the right to breathe and the right to vote, the freedom to choose their friends, enjoy the sunshine, and ride on the railroads, uncursed by color; thinking, dreaming, and working in a kingdom of beauty and love."[36] Will scholars open their minds and follow Du Bois's lead?

ASSEMBLING NATURE

By late 1936, thousands of assembly-line workers at General Motors (GM) were on the verge of rebellion. They were fed up with accelerating assembly lines, periodic layoffs, foremen and company police who used violence to enforce discipline, and managers who refused to hear their grievances. Unable to endure the abuse any longer, they finally stopped production. Borrowing a technique from disgruntled employees in rubber factories, they sat down at their work stations and refused to budge until GM listened to them. The sit-down strike, as it was called, proved effective. Its profits falling because of the stoppage, GM agreed to bargain with the strikers and their union, the United Auto Workers (UAW). GM's capitulation began a trend, and soon other corporations recognized still more unions representing thousands upon thousands of additional workers who toiled under exploitative conditions across the land.[37]

Although historians have pointed out that the sit-down strikers were heroes who exercised agency, courageously seized control of machinery, and thereby bettered their futures, the nature of the industrial system conditioned their choices and actions. Ultimately, the sit-down strike originated in the minds, hearts, and bodies of working men and women and, deep underground, in coal seams, iron formations, and oil deposits.

Industrialization required energy, energy required labor, and labor devoted to energy had important social and cultural consequences. By the early twentieth century, most industrial energy came from coal. By its nature, coal was dense, heavy, and chunky, and thus extracting it in mass quantities required the muscular effort, intelligence, and skill of many workers.[38] By their nature, miners were sociable. To extract the coal and better their lives, they had to talk to each other, work together, and overcome their ethnic and linguistic differences. They and their families also lived near each other, intermarried, attended the same churches, and sent their children to the same schools. From these experiences, the miners and their families developed a sense of solidarity, the awareness that they were alike in their values, purposes, and identity. Coal did not determine solidarity. Rather, solidarity resulted from the mobilization and intermixing of two kinds of nature—coal and people—under industrial capitalism.[39]

John L. Lewis, an Iowa coal miner and president of the United Mine Workers (UMW), recognized that labor solidarity could be an enormously powerful tool. Aroused by pain, sorrow, resentment, and anger and fueled by coal, it could motivate workers to unionize, changing forever the face of industrial America. In 1935, Lewis and other union leaders created the Committee for Industrial Organization (CIO) to put his plan into action. Federal laws in 1933 and 1935 acknowledged the right of industrial workers to form unions without harassment from employers; under Lewis's direction, the UMW boosted its rolls and allocated a portion of each member's dues to a CIO organizing fund. By 1936, the fund totaled $2.5 million, a small amount by today's standards but a large sum during the Great Depression. Most of the fund came from the UMW, and so its dollars represented organized labor's foundational connection to nature. The dollars stood for so many tons of coal but also for so many hours of labor expended on the extraction of those tons. Coal and labor—nonhuman and human nature—thus would subsidize the unionization of other industries. The money would cover the wages of organizers and the cost of union offices. And should a strike occur, it would pay for food and rent so that the families of workers would not go hungry and homeless.[40]

Lewis and other CIO officials decided to organize the people who toiled in the nation's steel mills and, after that, the ones who worked in automobile factories. Whether Lewis and his allies realized it or not, nature shaped the circumstances in which they made that decision. To achieve its objectives, the CIO had to focus its efforts on industries that concentrated the largest numbers of laborers.[41] By its nature, the industrial transformation of iron, silica, rubber, and other solid substances into steel, glass, tires, and automobiles required giant mills and factories, mind-boggling amounts of coal, and vast quantities of labor. It was no coincidence that Lewis and the CIO did not carry their campaign to the drillers, roughnecks, roustabouts, and refinery workers who extracted and processed petroleum, the nation's other great energy source. By its nature, the industrial transformation of oil into motor fuel was not conducive to massed labor. Oil was light and fluid, often emerged from wells under natural pressure, and flowed through pipelines that relied on gravity, and thus it required relatively few workers to extract, move, and process it.[42] In contrast, large numbers of laborers came together to make steel, glass, tires, and the engines and automobiles that would convert oil into mechanical movement.

Automobile manufacture, it turned out, and not steel, became the site at which the CIO had to begin its organizing drive. Before the CIO moved into the steel mills and towns, the UAW and its members at Flint, Michigan, and Cleveland, Ohio, revolted against the tyranny of the assembly line and its controllers, forcing the CIO to shift its priorities. The autoworkers went on strike in reaction to conditions shaped by nature. Automobile manufacture, labor historians have pointed out, followed a "seasonal production cycle" in which "employees worked long, hard hours during the winter and spring, only to be laid off for up to three months when the company retooled the factories during the off season." Autoworkers resented the seasonal layoff because it lowered their annual incomes. The sources of their discontent, however, lay even deeper in the nature of the industrial production system. Electrical plants burned coal to create steam that drove turbines and generators and sent a stream of electrons through copper wires to the motors of assembly lines. With the flip of a switch or the turn of a knob, factory managers could speed up the conveyors and increase output and profits. Autoworkers detested the speed-up because of the bodily fatigue, discomfort, pain, and mental strain it caused them. GM's disciplinary practices enflamed them even more. To force them to behave as if they were cogs in the machinery, foremen and company police shoved, struck, and beat them.[43]

But if the nature of the assembly line gave the automobile companies a powerful tool with which to regiment workers' bodies, it also gave the workers a potent weapon with which to resist. "The logic of the sit-down strike," the historian David Kennedy wrote, "called for identifying a critical pressure point in the ganglia of the huge automaking system and pinching off production at that strategic point."[44] In the act of sitting down, the autoworkers exploited the system's vulnerability and stalled the flow of earthen resources—coal and iron and electrons—that had damaged their bodies, taxed their sanity, and enriched the wealthiest corporate shareholders. The automakers had mastered nature on an unprecedented scale, from deep mines to sales lots in cities and towns. Their control of one critical component, however, failed: they could not turn people into machines. The means of their mastery became the instrument of their defeat.

Thinking about the sit-down strike as environmental history raises a host of questions about labor history during this pivotal time. Historians have written about the environmental problems of rural America during the Great Depression and New Deal period.[45] How might a similar approach be applied to factory work sites? To what extent were the production rhythms of industries related to those in the countryside? Was the seasonal production cycle in the automobile factories tied to the seasonal production cycle in the agricultural sector? Henry Ford was a notoriously autocratic industrialist unable to let go of his rural past and values; was the seasonal production cycle a holdover from an earlier time? How might the factory be imagined as an environment as important to industrial laborers as agricultural landscapes were to farmers and field hands?[46] Did factory workers come from rural, agricultural backgrounds, and did this affect their adaptation and resistance to industrial discipline? Did New Deal policies regarding agricultural environments and landscapes alter the movement of rural people into factories? The nature of coal production affected the environmental history of automobile factories; what about other industries? How did electrical production change industrial manufacturing? What were the environmental connections among agricultural, electrical energy, and factory production? Did the struggle to control the pace of factory work involve a struggle over the work environment itself?[47] Did the nature of work—analytical "brain" work as opposed to repetitive or brute force bodily labor—shape the schism between the skilled craftsmen in the American Federation of Labor and the industrial employees in the CIO?

By conventional standards, Betty Friedan was not a nature writer. Her classic work on modern American women, *The Feminine Mystique* (1963), did not call on readers to contemplate the natural world as a means to perceive ultimate truths, nor did it draw attention to the environmental problems of modern industrial society. Mountains, woodchucks, wildflowers, and clear-running streams did not appear in the pages she wrote, and neither did pesticides, bull-dozers, smokestacks, and sewage. Betty Friedan, in short, was no Mary Austin, Rachel Carson, or Annie Dillard. Her book was about women, especially white, middle-class women, and the inner turmoil they felt—"the problem that has no name"—as their personal aspirations and ambitions clashed with social expectations that they focus their energies on husbands, children, and homes.[48] The book became one of the foundational texts of modern feminism. Strange it might seem, then, that Friedan, *The Feminine Mystique*, and the entire women's movement were important to American environmental history. In talking about women, Friedan necessarily had to talk about nature, too.

The nature that Friedan addressed was human nature, and particularly the nature of women. Like many other thoughtful, well-educated, articulate people, she believed that personal experience and scientific research confirmed "the enormous plasticity of human nature." All human beings shared an inborn potential for intelligence and creativity; men and women were equal in this regard. Yet, Friedan argued, a reactionary idea had pervaded American society after the Second World War. According to this line of thought, women did not share with men a "limitless human potential" that invited them to pursue their individual intellectual, artistic, political, and economic ambitions. Rather, women's essential nature was to be passive, dependent, and maternal, to be housewives and mothers, not scientists, writers, artists, senators, or executives. Consequently, Friedan charged, women who acted on their internal drive to grow and realize their intrinsic potential "had to fight the conception that they were violating the God-given nature of woman," that they were "unnatural monsters" and "man-eaters" whose ambitions tended to destroy the opposite sex.[49]

Friedan believed that people's environmental experiences and the rearrangement of the American landscape reinforced this reactionary view of women. Men and women who had suffered the destruction, deprivation, and loneliness of war and then endured the threat of atomic conflict sought security in marriage, numerous children, and suburban homes. Suburbs and their large, open-plan houses, Friedan argued, composed a sprawling, inefficient environment that encouraged (if not compelled) housewives to devote more and more labor and time to an ever-growing array of appliances, fixtures, cleaners, and other household consumer goods. Trapped in automobiles, shopping centers, and homes, oriented to their children's and husbands' needs and wants, suburban housewives and mothers seemed to confirm their essential domestic nature.[50]

The consequences, Friedan observed, were telling. Women who lost their autonomous, future-oriented, fully realized selves became bored and listless. Their mental and physical health deteriorated as they ate too much, struggled with obesity, sedated themselves with alcohol, tranquilizers, and sleeping pills, and suffered from the frustration and despair of restless sexual appetites that offered them the only outlet for their inner drives. The damage was not confined to women alone. Smothered by too much maternal attention, children grew passive, dependent, without ambition, unfulfilled. Burdened by their unsatisfied, anxious wives, men became resentful and sought escape from the responsibilities of fatherhood and marriage. Not warmth and tranquility, then, but domestic turmoil and profound unhappiness were the ultimate consequences of the feminine mystique.[51]

To escape the trap, Friedan argued, women needed "a new life plan" that would enable them to be who they really were—in essence, to be true to human nature. They must reject the constricted housewife role, Friedan instructed, in favor of a domestic egalitarianism in which husbands and wives shared responsibilities. They must seek educational and constructive outlets for their talents and ambitions. The possibilities were unlimited. "Who knows what women can be," Friedan concluded, "when they are fully free to become themselves?... It has barely begun, the search of women for themselves. But the time is at hand when the voices of the feminine mystique can no longer drown out the inner voice that is driving women on to become complete."[52]

How else might a historian imagine Friedan, *The Feminine Mystique*, and the modern women's movement as environmental history? A range of possibilities exists. Was the postwar treatment of women connected to the treatment of landscape? Were the application of DDT to the landscape and the prescription of tranquilizers, sleeping pills, and other medicines to women related parts of the same technological shift that saturated the American environment with chemicals? Did Friedan's suburban women also experience the spraying of their homes with DDT? Did they associate their treatment and health with the landscape's treatment and health? "You have done for women," the feminist historian Gerda Lerner wrote to Friedan early in 1963, "what Rachel Carson did for birds and trees."[53] Was Friedan's focus on a seemingly inexplicable social malady, "the problem with no name," analogous to Carson's emphasis on a mysterious ecological one—the "silent spring"? Was Friedan's insistence that readers contemplate the ultimate truth of a transcendent nature—albeit a human nature—similar in style and purpose to conventional nature writing?

Finally, how did the deep structure of energy use in the second half of the twentieth century influence the rise of modern feminism? The nation's oil economy fueled the expansion of automobile suburbs that trapped women; did that energy abundance—and the environmental abundance in general of the United States—underwrite the wealth, education, discretionary time, and automobility that enabled those women to become feminists?[54] To what extent were modern contraceptive technologies based on the chemical transformation of petroleum? The founding of the National Organization for Women (NOW) in 1966 took place at the zenith of the nation's petroleum exuberance. Was this a coincidence? Was the growing crisis in gender relations related to the looming crisis in the nation's use of oil? What consequences did Hubbert's peak and the oil shock of 1973–1974 have for gender relations, feminism, and NOW's political program? Did economic and social dislocations resulting from Hubbert's peak and the oil shock strengthen feminism, or did they empower the conservative backlash against it?

CONSERVATIVE NATURE

During the 1980s, an epidemic swept through a significant portion of American society, ravaging its victims' immune systems and leaving them vulnerable to infections. Scientists labeled the scourge AIDS, acquired immunodeficiency syndrome, and by 1984 they had identified its agent: human immunodeficiency virus, or HIV. As the end of the decade neared, the Centers for Disease Control reported some eighty-two thousand cases and forty-six thousand deaths; the agency also estimated that the actual number of infected people might have been ten times as large. Like many other diseases, HIV killed people indiscriminately, but during the 1980s, gay men suffered the most by far. For many conservative Americans, the AIDS epidemic was not simply a public health crisis; it was also a symptom of a more basic, elemental problem. "The poor homosexuals," wrote the political commentator Patrick Buchanan. "They have declared war on nature and now nature is exacting an awful retribution."[55]

The history of AIDS and comments such as Buchanan's serve as the starting point from which to envision an environmental history of modern conservatism, one that reaches beyond the movement's opposition to environmental laws and regulations. Conservatism gathered political power from the transformation of the American landscape and in reaction to the environmental, economic, social, and political crises generated by that transformation. At its core, conservatism articulated a set of convictions, sometimes contradictory, about the nature of the world and the nature of humans. As evidenced by Buchanan's indictment of gay men, the modern conservative movement might be understood fundamentally as an argument about nature.[56]

The political reaction that triumphed in 1980 with the election of Ronald Reagan to the presidency was, in part, an outgrowth of the nation's extravagant use of land and other natural resources. During the twentieth century, backed by an astonishing assertion of federal government power, expertise, and largesse, Americans extracted immense quantities of oil, minerals, food, and lumber from the Earth. The conversion of these substances into highways, dams, hydroelectric plants, industries, chemicals, weapons, suburbs, consumer goods, and ultimately more children and larger families enabled the production and democratization of wealth on an unprecedented scale. To a substantial number of citizens, this prosperity represented the fulfillment of the American promise and the beginning of an unending enlargement of national power and greatness.[57]

Yet this enormous expansion of national productivity and wealth also brought social, economic, and environmental changes that, in various ways, provoked conservative political reactions. The liberation and intensive use of natural resources—fossil fuels in particular—stimulated the migration of African Americans and encouraged them to claim their civil rights, including rights of access to places such as parks, suburbs, and schools. Fearing the consequences of this social and environmental reorientation, white citizens took steps to isolate themselves and protect their interests. Aided by measures such as California's Proposition 14 (1964), which repealed a fair housing law that prohibited racial discrimination in real estate sales, they congregated in suburbs, neighborhoods, and schools. Confined to inner cities, black people watched as corporations, aided by the construction of the interstate highway system, moved to the urban fringe. As white flight and corporate relocation shrank municipal tax revenues, infrastructure decayed and urban environments became inhospitable. Riots by aggrieved African American citizens and rising crime rates further deteriorated life in the urban landscape. Government efforts to alleviate the crisis—federal funding of mass transit and court-ordered busing to achieve school desegregation, for example—provoked another powerful reaction among white Americans that further contributed to the rise of conservative politics.[58]

Related to this reorientation of the American landscape was a broader environmental crisis, the reaction to which boosted conservatism still more. In the 1960s and 1970s, air and water pollution, toxic substances, the destruction of wildlife, energy problems, and the development of prized parts of the landscape—the consequence of the nation's intensive use of land and other natural resources—gave rise to environmentalism and legislation intended to curb the worst abuses. Substantial numbers of Americans, however, conditioned by their experience of ever more massive resource extraction and wealth, refused to accept the notion that conditions were worsening or that extraction and consumption must be limited. Economic dislocations and restructurings in the aftermath of the boom unsettled those citizens still more, and they blamed African Americans, "big government," and environmentalists. In cities and suburbs, they reacted against mass transit, school busing, regulation of business, and curbs on property rights. In rural areas, they objected to wildlife policies, management of public land, and restrictions on private property.[59]

The rise of conservatism, however, was not only a materialistic, self-interested reaction against the consequences of land and resource use. Integral to the movement was a set of ideas about nature of which Patrick Buchanan's comment was only the tip. Like everyone else, conservatives had an idea of what was "natural" and therefore right. They did not always agree on the particulars, and individuals sometimes held inconsistent ideas, but in general they subscribed to what might be called a conservative environmental ideology. In their view, people had a God-given natural right to take as much as possible from the Earth, which had more resources and was more resilient than environmentalists allowed. In one sense, Americans, aided by the government, had the right to exert their power over nature, even to the point of destroying parts of it. In another sense, this exertion of power itself was natural. In particular, capitalism was natural, because it expressed people's innate impulses, desires, and behaviors. Society itself was naturally hierarchical, because some people were intrinsically more capable than others in acquiring wealth. A few conservatives even came close to arguing that certain groups, not just individuals, were naturally less intelligent and capable.[60]

By defining what was natural, conservatives defined what was unnatural. Even though the empirical evidence for Darwinian natural selection—evolution—was overwhelming, and even though evolutionary concepts formed the basis of epidemiology and medicine that saved millions of lives, evolution contradicted the God-given order of things and therefore was unnatural and false. Other unnatural errors centered on the human body. A woman without a husband and children was potentially unnatural. Abortion was unnatural, "pro-life" conservatives argued. Above all, despite claims that the feelings of gays and lesbians were innate and their behavior the expression of their natural right to do as they pleased with their bodies, homosexual sex, especially between men, was unnatural. If there was a war on nature, as Patrick Buchanan said, that war was waged by gay men against the nature of their bodies.[61]

What questions might guide an environmental history of conservatism? Ideas of natural rights and natural law have been central to conservative thought. How might a deeper understanding of those ideas illuminate the way conservatives saw the natural world, human and nonhuman? What insights might result from rereading classic texts such as Friedrich Hayek's *The Road to Serfdom* (1944) and Russell Kirk's *The Conservative Mind* (1953) in light of environmental history? Did conservatives always agree about nature? Did they ever subscribe to notions of conservation? Did conservative Christians believe that the beauty of nature was evidence of God's consecration of it? Did conservatives think that the unrestrained economic market weakened the organic wholeness of communities and the landscapes on which they relied? Did they share liberal environmentalists' objections to large-scale, statist manipulations of the environment, not only massive "urban renewal" projects but also large dams and interstate highways?[62] How did conservatives experience nature, and what did they say about those experiences? Did environmental factors influence the spatial distribution of conservatives across the nation's landscape? Many conservative citizens were concentrated in centers of aerospace production in the South and West; how did this demographic shift toward the "Sun Belt" shape conservatives' experience and understanding of the environment? Conservatism remains one of the least studied and appreciated historical subjects, and the environmental history of conservatism all the more so.[63]

During the early years of the United States, improvement in its fullest sense meant the fulfillment of nature's potential to nurture and sustain human life and a republican society and government. As important as improvement was, and as much as historians have said about it, its story remains incompletely told. Although it disappears from the pages of history books after Lincoln, it did not die with the rail splitter. Rather, in response to environmental changes, technological innovations, and other events, Americans redefined it and pushed it in new directions. Tracing its legacies in the 150 years after Lincoln might be instructive to Americans as they confront the problems of their own time.

Improvement did not necessarily lead to the productive, peaceful, happy future that Abraham Lincoln and his contemporaries envisioned. A student named Michael Shepherd once asked me if improvement also had disastrous consequences, such as strip mining. He was correct, of course, and his insight explains why some people today speak of "improvement" in a cynical, ironic sense, as synonymous with the unchecked, destructive use of nature. Certainly many Americans from Lincoln's time onward wrecked land and life in the name of improvement. They saturated the environment with chemicals and toxic waste, sterilized and experimented on people, and developed machines that scarred the landscape, tore minerals and organic material from the Earth, and threatened human life. And the possible outcomes of improvement could be worse still. Without distorting the past, the historian might draw a line from Lincoln's interest in improved weaponry to the nuclear bombs of the Second World War and beyond. Improvement, in short, might have ended—and still might end—in ultimate destruction. Perhaps that is why improvement disappears from the textbooks after Lincoln. A century and a half of despoliation and conflict, from the Civil War to the war on terror, gradually weakened the belief that improvement was an unqualified achievement and evidence of national progress.[64]

Yet improvement also had positive trajectories. It led to a profusion of technologies and practices that bettered human and environmental health, eased suffering, and saved lives: water purification and sewage treatment systems, modern medicines, wind and solar power, high speed trains, perennial polyculture, ecologically based farming, and much more. In the aftermath of war and destruction, some people redirected the flagging energies of improvement into vigorous programs for conservation, and they tried to rescue natural resources of immense environmental, economic, and patriotic value. The landscape architect Frederick Law Olmsted exemplified this transformation. In 1865, in reaction to the Civil War, Olmsted argued that the protection of Yosemite's natural beauty in a public park would enable the "reinvigoration" of the health, intelligence, well-being, and happiness of "the great body of the people."[65] Equally important, improvement advanced the cause of human rights in the United States and around the planet. Reconstruction, the Thirteenth, Fourteenth, and Fifteenth amendments to the Constitution, the Four Freedoms, the Atlantic Charter, and other programs and statements anticipated a world in which all people enjoyed the blessings of liberty precisely because they fulfilled nature's potential to nurture and sustain human life and representative government.[66]

Recovering the history of improvement requires the recognition that a moral or ethical standard was implicit in the concept. Americans decided that a more efficient tool was an improvement because it produced more food, alleviated suffering, or furthered democracy. Such a standard enabled them to determine whether an instrumental technique had been misused or had gone wrong—whether or not toxic chemicals, gas chambers, and bombs represented "the corruption of improvement," as the historian Robert Friedel called it.[67] Such a standard also equipped Americans to recognize—without cynicism—the irony in their history: for example, that their fossil fuels and nuclear arsenal were sources of both enormous strength and profound vulnerability, and that a calamity such as war also yielded antibiotics and other medicines of incalculable value. An ethical standard, finally, gave Americans the means to recognize tragedy, as in a political leader's agonized decision to preserve the possibility of improvement by exercising its antithesis.[68]

Abraham Lincoln understood the tragic nature of improvement. Although he advocated better weaponry, he did so because he wanted to save the United States and bring the Civil War to a quick end. Human life and liberty and the republic that guaranteed them ranked above all else, but to perpetuate the Union and its citizens and ensure their improvement, he engaged in acts of utter destruction. He grieved for the soldiers he sent to their deaths, some of whom he knew but most of whom represented the nation's anonymous democratic mass. He was a heroic but tragic figure who knew that his actions were no less terrible because they were necessary.

Lincoln's struggle is an important reminder that the path to improvement often was frustrating, painful, and fraught with danger. Before and after

Lincoln, Americans often wished for clear standards on which they could agree. The reality, of course, was conflicted and contentious. As Lincoln recognized, improvement sometimes required terrifying acts of destruction. Perhaps more important, Americans fought over improvement's very meaning. What was morally grounded improvement to one was amoral, if not immoral, destruction to another. Would the dam fulfill the valley's natural potential to become a reservoir, thereby bringing water and prosperity to the citizenry? Or would it forever destroy the river's rhythms and wreak havoc on flora and fauna the value which could not be calculated?

Despite their declining confidence in improvement, some Americans returned to it like a thirsty traveler to a spring, there to refresh themselves before resuming their search for a better path into the future. One noteworthy seeker was the scientist, writer, and environmentalist René Dubos. Born in France in 1901, Dubos immigrated to the United States in 1924, became a scientist and a professor at Rockefeller University, and eventually settled on a ninety-acre abandoned farm near Garrison, New York. A microbiologist who developed antibiotics from soil organisms, he took improvement seriously. He acknowledged environmental damage and the importance of wilderness, but he also believed that humanity had choices other than the stark dichotomy of either destroying nonhuman nature or preserving it untouched.[69]

In 1980, inspired by Thomas Jefferson and the Indian writer, intellectual, and humanitarian Rabindranath Tagore, Dubos called for "the wooing of Earth." By applying labor, intelligence, imagination, and love to bettering the places in which they lived, people might draw out the "potentialities" latent in nature and provide for human needs. "We can improve on nature," he wrote, "to the extent that we can identify these unexpressed potentialities and can make them come to life by modifying environments, thus increasing the diversity of the Earth and making it a more desirable place for human life." He believed that the human potential to shape the future was "the most impressive manifestation of freedom" and was essential to the pursuit of happiness. "The right to a good environment," he concluded, "is coming to be regarded as one of the fundamental inalienable rights."[70]

As a historical topic and as a program for action, improvement still appeals to the thirsty traveler much as it appealed to René Dubos. What were its cultural and intellectual sources? How might it reveal the ways in which nature— as ideal and physical reality—mattered to the formation and development of the United States? Did it flow from the nation's deep commitment to birth, growth, fruition, and rebirth—organic processes of which Lincoln spoke so eloquently? Did it express the principle that the regeneration of life and the regeneration of liberty were closely connected, if not one and the same? Was it intrinsic to the American Revolution? What happened to it after the Civil War? What was its relationship to Reconstruction, conservation, civil rights, and other important events and movements? Was it reborn as sustainability in the late twentieth century? Might it still offer Americans a means by which to make sense of their problems? Might it offer them a cool, clarifying, reinvigorating drink on their way into the future?

The paths that circle through the nature of American history are endless. Winding through time and experience and across vast expanses, they lead again and again to the events that have defined the United States and its place in the world. I have explored some in this book: the darkest fears of colonists who struggled to make the biophysical world conform to their faith; a revolutionary idea enabled by the North American environment; the efforts of nearly powerless people to carve a measure of freedom from the life cycle of a plant; a president's noble but tragic project to fulfill the republic's inherent potential; an earth-shaking battle arising from the organic possibilities of the land; machines brought about by massed muscular exertion; a scientific quest that led to both mountain majesties and horrific explosions; prejudice materialized in a line that divided the nation as well as a heartland city; the striving for unlimited power in a universe that strictly limits its physical basis.

Much more might be said about the environmental history of these and other iconic chapters in the American experience. What comes next is undecided. The paths beckon. A venerable temple in the nation's capital speaks to you, and you respond with a simple question: How did nature matter? That question prompts a second, and a third. How does nature matter now? How will it matter in the future? The marble calls to you—and you go. ★

ACKNOWLEDGMENTS

I could not have completed this book without the help of many people and institutions. Scott Casper, Jim Davidson, Karl Jacoby, Marianne Keddington-Lang, Jane Kepp, Janet Ore, and Jared Orsi read the entire manuscript in one form or another, and I am grateful for their criticisms, suggestions, and encouragement. John Albright, Ruth Alexander, SueEllen Campbell, Nate Citino, Robert Gudmestad, Adrian Howkins, and Ann Little each read major portions and provided critical comments and advice, and I thank them for their help. I have superb colleagues in the Department of History at Colorado State University; in particular, I thank Janet, Jared, Ruth, Nate, Robert, Adrian, and Ann.

Bill Cronon, Julidta Tarver, and Marianne Keddington-Lang, my sponsoring editors at the University of Washington Press, helped me transform an amorphous idea into a concrete product. Bill's influence on my work is considerable, and I am grateful for his wisdom, guidance, and patience. Julidta encouraged the project from the start. Marianne edited the manuscript line-by-line, insisted that I privilege the needs and interests of the nonspecialist reader, and guided me through some rough moments with her characteristic intelligence, warmth, and sensitivity. I thank Pat Soden, Marilyn Trueblood, Tom Eykemans, and other staff at the University of Washington Press for their generous support, and I acknowledge the expert help of Tanya Buckingham and the University of Wisconsin-Madison Cartography Lab in the preparation of the maps.

For their critical reaction to portions of my work and for their help and encouragement, I am grateful to Thomas Andrews, Sue Armitage, Mart Bailey,

Lisa Brady, Mary Braun, Karl Brooks, Michael Burlingame, Maren Bzdek, Phil Cafaro, John Calderazzo, Gerry Callahan, Jonathan Cobb, Pattie Cowell, Greg Cushman, Sue Doe, Ron Doel, Tom Dunlap, Sterling Evans, Steve Fountain, Phil Garone, David Goodstein, Shane Hamilton, Blane Harding, Mark Harvey, Todd Henry, Eric Hinderaker, Greg Hobbs, Dave Hsiung, Jon Hunner, Phyllis Hunter, Nancy Scott Jackson, Fredrik Jonsson, Bob Keller, Ari Kelman, Jack Kirby, Bill Kovarik, Prakash Kumar, Mike Lansing, Jim Leiker, Patty Limerick, Dick Lowitt, Mark Lytle, Neil Maher, Peter Mallios, Dale Martin, Dave Mogen, Kathy Morse, Mary Murphy, Linda Nash, Tim Orr, Dick Orsi, Jeff Pappas, Don Pisani, Steve Pyne, Fred Quivik, Harry Ritter, Bruce Ronda, Ed Russell, Jeff Sanders, Adam Sowards, Mart Stewart, Steven Stoll, Ellen Stroud, Paul Sutter, Lou Swanson, Bill Timpson, Sam Truett, Richard Tucker, Jeremy Vetter, Louis Warren, Marsha Weisiger, Richard White, Stewart Winger, Bob Wilson, Don Worster, Graeme Wynn, Doug Yarrington, and Rick Zier.

A book of this sort necessarily relies heavily on the productions of other scholars. I am grateful to historians and other writers and intellectuals for the mountain of articles, books, and documents they have created and on which I have drawn. I have thanked a few of them in person or in writing, and I wish I could do the same for the rest. The chapter notes and the reference list suggest the magnitude of my debt. If my book accomplishes anything, it is because of them.

Space precludes me from acknowledging by name every student from whom I have learned and who inspired or helped with this book, but in particular I would like to thank Avana Andrade, Shane Armstrong, Alan Barkley, Craig Boardman, Brian Collier, Rolly Constable, Mike Eckhoff, Heather Craig Everett, Rose Gaudio, Mike Geary, Chelsea Gilmore, Dirk Hobman, Tristan Kenyon-Schultz, Cori Knudten, Andy Kruse, Tom Latousek, Carol Hutton Lucking, Jake McMahon, Lori Walker Mentink, Emmie Miller, Tracy Miller, Burr Neely, Brad Patterson, Nellie Pierson, Eric Saulnier, Emilie Sniteley (also my niece), Ted Snyder, Sierra Standish, Paul Stock, Clarissa Janssen Trapp, Ted Veggeberg, and all my students—past, present, and future—in HY464-HIST355 American Environmental History.

At Colorado State University, I received invaluable support from the College of Liberal Arts, Morgan Library, the Department of History, and the William E. Morgan Chair of Liberal Arts. In particular, I thank college deans Bob Hoffert and Ann Gill, department chairs Ruth Alexander, Doug Yarrington, and Diane Margolf, administrative assistants Lorraine Dunn and Robin

Troxell, and the benefactors of the Morgan Chair. Like other underfunded public institutions, Colorado State University struggles to fulfill its mission, and I am grateful for its efforts to support the people and provide the resources that make it an appealing place to teach, research, and write.

The Walter Hines Page Fellowship at the National Humanities Center in Durham, North Carolina, gave me the time, space, and resources to complete a sizable portion of the manuscript. I thank the Research Triangle Foundation of North Carolina for its support and the fellows and staff members of the center for their assistance.

I presented portions of my work at Colorado State University; University of California, Davis; University of Colorado, Boulder; University of Colorado, Denver; University of Georgia; University of Illinois, Springfield; University of Kansas; Washington State University; Western Washington University; Colorado Historical Society; Lincoln Home National Historic Site; National Humanities Center; and meetings of the American Society for Environmental History and the Society for Historians of American Foreign Relations. I am grateful to the organizers of these events, and I thank participants and audiences for their questions, criticisms, suggestions, and encouragement.

Portions of the manuscript originally appeared in *Environmental History*, under the editorship of Marc Cioc, and in *Natural Enemy, Natural Ally*, edited by Richard Tucker and Ed Russell. I am grateful to the American Society for Environmental History and Oregon State University Press to republish them here.

One of the pleasures of this project was the many hours I spent in independent bookstores around the country. Those that helped me the most and that I enjoyed the most include Jade Creek, Old Corner, Old Firehouse, Reader's Cove, and Stone Lion in Fort Collins, Colorado, and—home away from home, gone but not forgotten—Magpie Books in Three Forks, Montana.

I am fortunate for friends and family members who sustained me at critical moments. Scott Casper and Jared Orsi have national reputations for their scholarship, extraordinary intelligence, and most of all their generosity and compassion, and both came through when I needed them most. Louis Warren, SueEllen Campbell, Mike Lansing, David Lewis, Jay Taylor, and Neil Maher understood the challenge of writing this book and helped me in more ways than they will ever know. Maren Bzdek went from student to colleague and friend, and I'm grateful for her assistance and support and for how much I have learned from her over the years. David Lewis, Greg Smoak, Jay Taylor, Matt

Klingle, Mike Lansing, and Bob Wilson left no claim unchallenged. The Ore family included me in its small but unbreakable circle. My sister, Gale Fiege, and my brother-in-law, Jon Bauer, know the pressures of writing, and their encouragement buoyed me when I was down. My mother, Phyllis Fiege, took pride in me and my work, as always. Although my father, Gene Fiege, died long before I began this book, his sizable personal library and my memories of him helped me to complete the project. Conversations with my uncle, Mike Eckstein, were too brief and too few, but sufficient for me to draw his spirit into these pages. Greg Silkensen accompanied me along the old transcontinental railroad line from Sherman Summit to Donner Pass. In the desert north of the Great Salt Lake, a hump in the unpaved road warranted the application of brakes, but—I still don't know why I did it—I stomped on the accelerator instead. I will never forget the look on Greg's face after we returned to earth, but he laughed and forgave me and we made it to Reno intact.

My colleague, companion, and wife, Janet Ore, spent countless hours discussing history with me, read and critiqued every chapter more times than I can remember, endured my absences, and believed in me during the hard times when I lost faith in myself. I could not have written this book without her help, and I can never repay her for her intelligence, kindness, devotion, and love. Alexandra Ore, who once referred to the book as my "second child," helped and inspired me with her patience, good humor, sensitivity to the human predicament, and endless enthusiasm for the written word. I could not ask for a better daughter; the dedication expresses the depth of my love and appreciation. ★

NOTES

In some direct quotations, I have silently corrected archaic or awkward spelling, grammar, and punctuation when these threatened to interfere with narrative flow. Readers are encouraged to consult the original sources.

LAND OF LINCOLN

1   For a classic essay on the journey as a means to understand American environmental history, see Cronon, "Kennecott Journey."

2   Whitman quoted in White, *A. Lincoln*, 3.

3   See Trouillot, *Silencing the Past*, 29–30.

4   C. Thomas, *Lincoln Memorial and American Life*, is an outstanding history of the monument. See also C. Thomas, "Lincoln Memorial and Its Architect"; USDI/ NPS, *Lincoln Memorial*; and Concklin, *Lincoln Memorial*. On the history and physical condition of the memorial's stone, see Prescott, *Lincoln Memorial Stone Survey*, and McGee, *Colorado Yule Marble*. "An accurate knowledge of the origin of the arts," Alexander von Humboldt observed, "can be acquired only from studying the nature of the site where they arose." See Walls, *Passage to Cosmos*, 7.

5   Thomas, *Lincoln Memorial and American Life*, 101–7, 113–16.

6   Ibid.; USDI/NPS, *Lincoln Memorial*, 4–14, 34–41.

7   Thomas, *Lincoln Memorial and American Life*, 138–40.

8   Ibid., 113–22, 139; Vandenbusche and Myers, *Marble, Colorado*, 24–105.

9   Thomas, *Lincoln Memorial and American Life*, 128–29, 152–62; Boime, *Unveiling of the National Icons*, 253–306; Sandage, "Marble House Divided"; Concklin, *Lincoln Memorial*, 78–81 (quotation 79).

10   Sometimes the surprises are buried. The National Park Service offers occasional tours of the memorial's foundations, referred to as "the caves" or "the

catacombs." I thank my colleague Jeff Pappas, an NPS ranger, for bringing this to my attention. See also Thomas, "Lincoln Memorial and Its Architect," 2:582–83.

11 For historiographical and theoretical assessments of American environmental history, see, among many others, Worster, "History as Natural History"; White, "American Environmental History"; "A Round Table: Environmental History"; Cronon, "A Place for Stories"; McEvoy, "Working Environments"; White, "Are You an Environmentalist or Do You Work for a Living?"; Stine and Tarr, "At the Intersection of Histories"; Sellers, "Thoreau's Body"; "Forum: Environmental History, Retrospect and Prospect," especially White, "Environmental History," 103–11; Rome, "What Really Matters in History?"; Russell, "Evolutionary History"; Scharff, "Man and Nature!"; Environment and History Theme Issue, *History and Theory* 42, especially Stroud, "Does Nature Always Matter?" 75–81; White, "From Wilderness to Hybrid Landscapes"; Stewart, "If John Muir Had Been an Agrarian"; Pyne "End of the World"; "AHR Conversation: Environmental Historians and Environmental Crisis"; and Russell et al., "Nature of Power." For recent, sophisticated elaborations of environmental history methodology in book form, see, among many other examples, Orsi, *Hazardous Metropolis*, 1–10, 165–83; Andrews, *Killing for Coal*, 123–53; LeCain, *Mass Destruction*, 1–23; Walker, *Toxic Archipelago*, xii–xv, xvii–xviii, 3–21. Walls, *Passage to Cosmos*, is an important effort to recover the nearly forgotten legacy of an original environmental-historical thinker.

12 Many sources have influenced my concept of nature, but see White, *Organic Machine,* and Nash, *Inescapable Ecologies.*

13 Hughes, *Human-Built World,* is a useful introduction to a vast literature on the developments described here. See also Cronon, *Nature's Metropolis.*

14 These themes are elucidated in Niebuhr, *Nature and Destiny of Man,* vol. 1, *Human Nature,* and vol. 2, *Human Destiny.*

15 The classic statement about ideas of nature is Williams, "Ideas of Nature." On ideas as products of people's interactions with their environments, see especially Nash, "The Agency of Nature or the Nature of Agency?" On the materiality of ideas and their relationship to people and culture, see Lansing, "The Significance of Nonhumans in U.S. Western History," 152–59. See also, for example, Watt-Cloutier, "The Inuit Right to Culture Based on Ice and Snow."

16 Agency and determinism, along with contingency, are fundamental problems in history. For a concise discussion, see "Determinism," in Ritter, *Dictionary of Concepts in History,* 104–12.

17 On irony and tragedy in American history, see Niebuhr, *Irony of American History.*

18 In the field of environmental history, my work is complementary to, but ultimately different from, a large body of scholarship. For overviews that synthesize much of the best work in the field, see, for example, Opie, *Nature's Nation*; Penna, *Nature's Bounty*; Magoc, *So Glorious a Landscape*; Merchant, *American Environmental History*; Steinberg, *Down to Earth.*

19 See, for example, Boorstin, *Lost World of Thomas Jefferson,* especially the chapter titled "The Natural History of a New Society."

20 See Price, *Flight Maps*, xvii, xx, xxi, 163.

21 Boorstin, in *Lost World of Thomas Jefferson*, 246–48, suggested that urban life, the philosophy of pragmatism, and modern technologies such as the internal combustion engine unmoored Americans from nature and encouraged them to believe that culture alone defined them and their place in the world. Compare Boorstin with Worster, "Seeing Beyond Culture."

22 See White, "Environmental History," in "Forum: Environmental History," 110.

1. SATAN IN THE LAND

1 Boyer and Nissenbaum, *Salem Witchcraft Papers*, 1:189.

2 Ibid., 1:190.

3 Ibid., 1:192–94.

4 Miller, *Errand into the Wilderness*, 1–15. On the colonial problem of shaping and being shaped by the environment, see Finch, "'Civilized' Bodies and the 'Savage' Environment of Early New Plymouth."

5 Karlsen, *Devil in the Shape of a Woman*, 98–101; Norton, *In the Devil's Snare*, 182.

6 Boyer and Nissenbaum, *Salem Witchcraft Papers*, 1:192–93.

7 Ibid., 1:192–94.

8 The literature on New England witchcraft is large, but I have benefited especially from Demos, *Entertaining Satan*; Norton, *In the Devil's Snare*; Karlsen, *Devil in the Shape of a Woman*; Godbeer, *Devil's Dominion*; Godbeer, *Escaping Salem*; Reis, *Damned Women*; and Boyer and Nissenbaum, *Salem Possessed*.

9 On Puritan beliefs about women and women's bodies being especially vulnerable to Satan, see Reis, *Damned Women*, 93–120. On the Puritans' quest for control and their fear of disorder, see Nash, *Red, White, and Black*, 81–82.

10 Demos, *Entertaining Satan*; Lepore, *In the Name of War*; and Little, *Abraham at Arms*, in particular have shaped my understanding of colonial New England history. Behringer, in *Witchcraft Persecutions in Bavaria*, 91–114, attributed witchcraft disturbances to an "agrarian crisis" during the sixteenth and seventeenth centuries, when environmental conditions contributed to human and livestock diseases, harvest failures, increasing food prices, and hunger during a time of population growth. Behringer did not argue that these events alone caused the unrest, but he did say they were important.

11 Jameson, *Johnson's Wonder-Working Providence*, 168.

12 Kupperman, *Indians and English*, 110–41; Cave, *Pequot War*, 24–29; Salisbury, *Manitou and Providence*, 37, 39; Chaplin, *Subject Matter*, 261.

13 Jameson, *Johnson's Wonder-Working Providence*, 168 (quotation); Cave, *Pequot War*, 24–29; Cave, "Indian Shamans and English Witches in Seventeenth-Century New England."

14 Fischer, *Albion's Seed*, 125; Wills, *Head and Heart*, 29–34; Cave, *Pequot War*, 13–48. See also Carroll, *Puritanism and the Wilderness*.

15 Mather, *Magnalia Christi Americana*, 118.

16 Cronon, *Changes in the Land*, 109; Taylor, *American Colonies*, 194.

17 Fischer, *Albion's Seed*, 16–17, 17n7; Taylor, *American Colonies*, 164–66.

18 Bradford, *Of Plymouth Plantation*, 253.

19 Cronon, *Changes in the Land*, 54–81, compares and contrasts the property systems of Indians and English.

20 Cronon, *Changes in the Land*, 55-57; Tomlins, *Freedom Bound*, 133-56 (quotations 150, 151). See also *Winthrop Papers*, ed. Ford et al., 2:111-49. I have modernized the spelling of the quotations for readability.

21 Crosby, "'God . . . Would Destroy Them'"; Cave, *Pequot War*, 84–86; Cronon, *Changes in the Land*, 90 (quotation). Jones, in *Rationalizing Epidemics*, 21–67, stressed the complexity of English responses to Indian deaths but also showed that a belief in providence was an important feature of colonists' explanation of events.

22 Steele, *Warpaths*, 89–90; Cave, *Pequot War*, 49–98.

23 Steele, *Warpaths*, 89–91; Anderson, *Creatures of Empire*, 181–82; Taylor, *American Colonies*, 194–95; Carroll, *Puritanism*, 90; Cave, *Pequot War*, 69–121.

24 Steele, *Warpaths*, 91–93; Carroll, *Puritanism*, 77 (quotation).

25 Hart, *American History Told by Contemporaries*, 1:439–49 (quotations, 442, 443); Kupperman, *Indians and English*, 229–34. See also Cave, *Pequot War*, 98–163.

26 Hall, *Puritans in the New World*, 246–54 (quotations, 251).

27 Steele, *Warpaths*, 94; Cave, *Pequot War*, 153–63.

28 Carroll, *Puritanism*, 90–91; Bradford, *Of Plymouth Plantation*, 296.

29 Steele, *Warpaths*, 94.

30 Schutte, "'Such Monstrous Births,'" 86–88 (first quotation, 88); Hall, *Worlds of Wonder, Days of Judgment*, 95–97, 140–41 (second quotation, 140); LaPlante, *American Jezebel*, 88; Karlsen, *Devil in the Shape of a Woman*, 71, 166–67; Demos, *Circles and Lines*, 19–20.

31 Schutte, "'Such Monstrous Births,'" 90–91; LaPlante, *American Jezebel*, 88.

32 Schutte, "'Such Monstrous Births,'" 89, 89–90n11; LaPlante, *American Jezebel*, 88–89; Winthrop, *Journal of John Winthrop*, 254 (quotation). Puritans were attuned to portents in the material world. See, for example, Hall, "Mental World of Samuel Sewall."

33 Hall, *Antinomian Controversy*, 3–20; Wills, *Head and Heart*, 57–61.

34 Hall, *Antinomian Controversy*, 3–20, 311–88; Hall, *Worlds of Wonder*, 95–101 (quotation, 96).

35 Karlsen, *Devil in the Shape of a Woman*, 120–22, 149–50; Hall, *Worlds of Wonder*, 95–101.

36 Schutte, "'Such Monstrous Births,'" 88–89; Hall, *Antinomian Controversy*, 281–82 (quotations).

37 Schutte, "'Such Monstrous Births,'" 88–90; LaPlante, *American Jezebel*, 217.

38 Schutte, "'Such Monstrous Births,'" 94, 103.

39 Hall, *Antinomian Controversy*, 214–15, 280–82 (quotations, 214, 280–81); Wills, *Head and Heart*, 30–31; Karlsen, *Devil in the Shape of a Woman*, 14–19.

40 Hall, *Witchhunting in Seventeenth-Century New England*, 19–20.

41   LaPlante, *American Jezebel*, 228–45 (quotations, 244).

42   Karlsen, *Devil in the Shape of a Woman*, 122–25; Godbeer, *Escaping Salem*, 193–97 (quotation, 196); Wills, *Head and Heart*, 20–21.

43   Hall, *Witchhunting*, 171–72.

44   Ibid., 183.

45   Demos, *Entertaining Satan*, 357–62 (first quotation, 359); Hall, *Witchhunting*, 173–75, 178–79 (second quotation, 174).

46   Hall, *Witchhunting*, 180.

47   Ibid., 172–73, 176, 177 (quotations), 180.

48   Ibid., 181.

49   Ibid., 179–81 (quotations, 180, 181). See also Taylor, *Witchcraft Delusion*, 47–61.

50   Demos, *Entertaining Satan*, 373–76.

51   See, for example, ibid., 340–45, 368–86; Philbrick, *Mayflower*, 183–87.

52   Demos, *Entertaining Satan*, 402–6; Karlsen, *Devil in the Shape of a Woman*, 20.

53   Hall, *Witchhunting*, 146–63 (quotations, 153, 156).

54   Karlsen, *Devil in the Shape of a Woman*, 24–25 (Greensmith first and second quotations, 25); Demos, *Entertaining Satan*, 349–52, 405 (Greensmith third and fourth quotations, 352).

55   Demos, *Entertaining Satan*, 355–59; Karlsen, *Devil in the Shape of a Woman*, 4–14, 63–71, 75, 80–89, 115–16, 119–46, 160–81, 214–17, 297–98, 308–9.

56   Anderson, *Creatures of Empire*, 75–105; Karlsen, *Devil in the Shape of a Woman*, 6–9. See also Rosenthal, *Salem Story*, 121.

57   Hall, *Witchhunting*, 151, 171–72, 183–84; Karlsen, *Devil in the Shape of a Woman*, 86–89 (first quotation, 87); Demos, *Entertaining Satan*, 362–63 (second quotation, 363).

58   Hall, *Witchhunting*, 183–84; Demos, *Entertaining Satan*, 362–63.

59   Norton, *In the Devil's Snare*, 86–87; Lepore, *In the Name of War*, 74–76.

60   Melvoin, *New England Outpost*, 101–3.

61   Lepore, *In the Name of War*, 71–72, 78–79, 95–96, 132; Anderson, "King Philip's Herds," 622–23; Slotkin and Folsom, *So Dreadful a Judgment*, 115.

62   Lepore, *In the Name of War*, 105; Hubbard, *History of the Indian Wars in New England*, 1:67–72.

63   Lepore, *In the Name of War*, 126–27; Slotkin and Folsom, *So Dreadful a Judgment*, 323–25.

64   Historians' assessments vary, but all agree that the destruction was extraordinary. See Steele, *Warpaths*, 103, 107–8; Taylor, *American Colonies*, 200, 202; Slotkin and Folsom, *So Dreadful a Judgment*, 3–4; Lepore, *In the Name of War*, xii.

65   Taylor, *American Colonies*, 203; Steele, *Warpaths*, 96–97; Nash, *Red, White, and Black*, 118–22; Anderson, "King Philip's Herds," 602, 607–8, 618, 619–20; Philbrick, *Mayflower*, 213–15.

66   Anderson, "King Philip's Herds," 609–21.

67   Taylor, *American Colonies*, 199–200; Steele, *Warpaths*, 99–101; Nash, *Red, White, and Black*, 118–20; Philbrick, *Mayflower*, 198–258.

68 Slotkin and Folsom, *So Dreadful a Judgment*, 86, 88, 90–91, 93, 101–6, 116 (quotation), 121; Lepore, *In the Name of War*, 6–7, 11, 12 (quotation), 13, 108 (quotation); Nash, *Red, White, and Black*, 121–22; Philbrick, *Mayflower*, 263 (quotation); Taylor, *American Colonies*, 200; Steele, *Warpaths*, 103. See Wills, *Head and Heart*, 43–50, for additional analysis of Puritan views of Indians as instruments of Satan.

69 Slotkin and Folsom, *So Dreadful a Judgment*, 63–64, 99–100, 179–80 (quotations); Nash, *Red, White, and Black*, 121–22.

70 Taylor, *American Colonies*, 200; Slotkin and Folsom, *So Dreadful a Judgment*, 86, 88, 90–91, 93, 106, 119.

71 Philbrick, *Mayflower*, 258–83; Steele, *Warpaths*, 102.

72 Norton, *In the Devil's Snare*, 92–93 (first quotation, 92); Philbrick, *Mayflower*, 261–62, 405 (second quotation, 262, 405), 338. Cf. Taylor, *American Colonies*, 201.

73 Taylor, *American Colonies*, 201; Steele, *Warpaths*, 99–102.

74 Taylor, *American Colonies*, 201–3; Steele, *Warpaths*, 101–3, 106–9; Philbrick, *Mayflower*, 244–45, 270–83.

75 Philbrick, *Mayflower*, 263; Taylor, *American Colonies*, 201; Steele, *Warpaths*, 107, 109.

76 Steele, *Warpaths*, 108–9.

77 Burr, *Narratives of the Witchcraft Cases*, 177, 360.

78 Boyer and Nissenbaum, *Salem Witchcraft Papers*, 1:190–92 (quotations, 190, 192).

79 Ibid., 2:342–43, 522–25 (first quotation, 523; second quotation, 523, 525).

80 Ibid., 1:184–87, 194–96 (quotations, 185).

81 Ibid., 1:197–98 (first quotation, 197; fourth quotation, 198), 2:527–30 (second and third quotations, 528).

82 Ibid., 1:201–3.

83 See, for example, Norton, *In the Devil's Snare*; Rosenthal, *Salem Story*; Godbeer, *Devil's Dominion*, 179–222; Davidson and Lytle, *After the Fact*, 23–47; and Boyer and Nissenbaum, *Salem Possessed*.

84 Hansen, "Andover Witchcraft and the Causes of the Salem Witchcraft Trials," 39, 52–53.

85 Boyer and Nissenbaum, *Salem Witchcraft Papers* 1:308, 3:767–69; Rosenthal, *Salem Story*, 52, 62.

86 Norton, *In the Devil's Snare*, 3–4, 327n2; Boyer and Nissenbaum, *Salem Possessed*, 5; Boyer and Nissenbaum, *Salem Witchcraft Papers*, 3:771–74.

87 Wills, *Head and Heart*, 32–33, 37–53; Boyer and Nissenbaum, *Salem Possessed*, 214–16; Norton, *In the Devil's Snare*, 161; Davidson and Lytle, *After the Fact*, 26–27.

88 See Boyer and Nissenbaum, *Salem Possessed*, 193–94, for the case of Sarah (Prince) Osborne.

89 Norton, *In the Devil's Snare*, 93–111, 263; Godbeer, *Devil's Dominion*, 184–86, 197; Demos, *Entertaining Satan*, 380–81; Kences, "Some Unexplored Relationships of Essex County Witchcraft to the Indian Wars of 1675 and 1689."

90 The classic account is Boyer and Nissenbaum, *Salem Possessed*, 80–109. Prominent colonial historians reprise their challenges to the work in Kamensky, "Forum: Salem Repossessed."

91 Greven, *Four Generations*, 50–64.

92 Ibid., 107, accepts the claims of Andover residents that the Carrier family was responsible for bringing smallpox to the town. Fenn, *Pox Americana*, 13–43, explains the nature of the disease.

93 Boyer and Nissenbaum, *Salem Witchcraft Papers*, 1:193.

94 Ibid., 3:767–68 (quotations).

95 Norton, *In the Devil's Snare*, 58–59.

96 Carlson, in *A Fever in Salem*, made a vigorous case that an animal-borne disease, *encephalitis lethargica*, infected colonial livestock and their keepers, inducing physical maladies and hallucinations that in turn became the subject of the witchcraft accusations and trials. Norton, in *In the Devil's Snare*, 327n3, refuted the argument as oversimplistic and reductive and briefly reviewed the literature surrounding a similar interpretation in which ergot, a grain-borne fungus, caused the crisis. It is reasonable to read the historical record, however, for evidence of diseases that gave rise to popular fears of witchcraft. See, for example, Demos, *Entertaining Satan*, 346–48, 370, 373, 382–84. It is just as reasonable to assume that livestock, no less than people, suffered from maladies that contributed to the witchcraft alarm and to find evidence of that in the historical record. To assume the opposite—that illness felled people while cattle and other domesticates enjoyed complete health—does not seem credible.

97 Boyer and Nissenbaum, *Salem Witchcraft Papers*, 1:59, 100, 105, 106, 124, 135, 202, 217; Norton, *In the Devil's Snare*, 77. This is but a sample of the supernatural animal stories contained in the historical record.

98 Boyer and Nissenbaum, *Salem Witchcraft Papers*, 2:523.

99 Ibid., 101, 195–98; 200–202; Rosenthal, *Salem Story*, 45–46, 115–20; Norton, *In the Devil's Snare*, 71–72, 116–17, 158, 242–43.

100 Norton, *In the Devil's Snare*, 159–60, 372n9; Karlsen, *Devil in the Shape of a Woman*, 242–43; Boyer and Nissenbaum, *Salem Witchcraft Papers*, 1:211 (quotations).

101 Norton, *In the Devil's Snare*, 120–32; Rosenthal, *Salem Story*, 129–34; Boyer and Nissenbaum, *Salem Witchcraft Papers*, 2:523.

102 Rosenthal, *Salem Story*, 113; Norton, *In the Devil's Snare*, 216–17.

103 Burr, *Narratives of the Witchcraft Cases*, 362–64 (quotations, 363).

104 Davidson and Lytle, *After the Fact*, 27; and especially Rivett, "Our Salem, Our Selves."

105 Davidson and Lytle, *After the Fact*, 27; Boyer and Nissenbaum, *Salem Possessed*, 9–21.

106 Burr, *Narratives of the Witchcraft Cases*, 361.

107 Ibid., 177, 361 (quotation); Norton, *In the Devil's Snare*, 256–57.

2. BY THE LAWS OF NATURE AND OF NATURE'S GOD

1 Miller, *Jefferson and Nature*, 1–55; Peterson, *Jefferson: Writings*, 1467 (quotation).

2 On Jefferson, see Boorstin, *Lost World of Thomas Jefferson*; Cohen, *Science and*

the Founding Fathers; Dugatkin, *Mr. Jefferson and the Giant Moose*; Ellis, *American Sphinx*; Gordon-Reed, *Hemingses of Monticello*; McLaughlin, *Jefferson and Monticello*; Miller, *Jefferson and Nature*; Scharff, *Women Jefferson Loved*; Stein, *Worlds of Thomas Jefferson at Monticello*; Stein et al., *Monticello*; Wills, *Inventing America*; and Wills, *Mr. Jefferson's University*.

3   Miller, *Jefferson and Nature*, 116–17; McLaughlin, *Jefferson and Monticello*, 7, 52–55, 64, 248–52, 282, 376–77, 387–88; Wills, *Inventing America*, 128–29.

4   Stein, *Worlds of Thomas Jefferson*, 50–116 (second quotation, 63), 128–29 (first quotation, 128), 374–81, and passim; Wills, *Inventing America*, 93–131; Cohen, *Science and the Founding Fathers*, 56–72; McLaughlin, *Jefferson and Monticello*, 339–74.

5   Stein, *Worlds of Thomas Jefferson*, 34–35 (quotation, 34), 69, 162; McLaughlin, *Jefferson and Monticello*, 363; Miller, *Jefferson and Nature*, 86. Asher Durand's engraving became the basis of the print that Jefferson displayed in the entrance hall.

6   The structural equation of Monticello and the Declaration of Independence draws from Stein, *Worlds of Thomas Jefferson*, 193–95; McLaughlin, *Jefferson and Monticello*, 276; Cohen, *Science and the Founding Fathers*, 108–34; and Miller, *Jefferson and Nature*, 165–68. On the Declaration of Independence, see Becker, *Declaration of Independence*; Ellis, *What Did the Declaration Declare?*; Maier, *American Scripture*; and Wills, *Inventing America*. On the connections between ideas and artifacts, see, for example, Deetz, *In Small Things Forgotten*, 2–25, and Glassie, *Folk Housing in Middle Virginia*, 8–18.

7   On the Declaration's worldwide appeal, see Armitage, *Declaration of Independence*.

8   Peterson, *Jefferson: Writings*, 882.

9   Wills, *Mr. Jefferson's University*, 73–77 (quotation, 73).

10 McLaughlin, *Jefferson and Monticello*, 35–36, 156, 250–52 (first quotation, 251), 265–66, 286–88; Stein et al., *Monticello*, 56 (second and third quotations), 58.

11 Gordon-Reed, *Hemingses of Monticello*, 100, 111–15, 141, 267–68, 271–72, 509–10, 571–83; McLaughlin, *Jefferson and Monticello*, 65–145.

12 Gordon-Reed, *Hemingses of Monticello*, 613–15 (quotations, 613, 614); McLaughlin, *Jefferson and Monticello*, 255–57, 298.

13 On the American Revolution, I have benefited especially from Amar, *America's Constitution*; Appleby, *Capitalism and a New Social Order*; Bailyn, *Ideological Origins of the American Revolution*; Becker, *Declaration of Independence*; Breen, *American Insurgents, American Patriots*; Commager, *Empire of Reason*; Countryman, *American Revolution*; Dworetz, *Unvarnished Doctrine*; Ellis, *Founding Brothers*; Foner, *Story of American Freedom*; Foner, *Tom Paine and Revolutionary America*; Holton, *Unruly Americans and the Origins of the Constitution*; Hunt, *Inventing Human Rights*; Kerber, *Women of the Republic*; Klepp, *Revolutionary Conceptions*; Maier, *American Scripture*; McCoy, *Elusive Republic*; McDonald, *Novus Ordo Seclorum*; Nash, *Unknown American Revolution*; Norton, *Liberty's Daughters*; Oakes, *Ruling Race*; Oakes, *Slavery and Freedom*; Tomlins, *Freedom Bound*; Waldstreicher, *Runaway America*; Wilentz, *Rise of American Democracy*; Wood, *American*

Revolution; Wood, *Creation of the American Republic, 1776–1787*; Wood, *Empire of Liberty*; and Wood, *Radicalism of the American Revolution*.

See also Gibson, *Interpreting the Founding and Understanding the Founding*, for an analysis of the literature. Of the schools of thought that Gibson outlined, my interpretation conforms most closely to the "liberal tradition." See Gibson, *Interpreting the Founding*, 13–21, 54–59, 125–29, and Appleby, *Capitalism and a New Social Order*. Readers also should be aware that a recent work, Tomlins, *Freedom Bound*, challenges liberal historiography.

Useful collections of documents include Bailyn, *Pamphlets of the American Revolution*; Commager and Morris, *Spirit of 'Seventy-Six*; Davis and Mintz, *Boisterous Sea of Liberty*; Ellis, *What Did the Declaration Declare?*; Greene, *Colonies to Nation*; Jensen, *Tracts of the American Revolution*; and Patrick, *Founding the Republic*.

14 Paine, "Common Sense," in Jensen, *Tracts of the American Revolution*, 423, 427; Jefferson quoted in Commager, *Empire of Reason*, 164. Jefferson made virtually the same point in his inaugural address; see Ellis, *American Sphinx*, 217.

15 Henretta et al., *America's History*, 21–24; Taylor, *American Colonies*, 24–25, 45–46, 119–23, 159–67.

16 Taylor, *American Colonies*, 119–22.

17 Henretta et al., *America's History*, 23–30, 41–49, 51–59; Taylor, *American Colonies*, 133–37, 139–46, 159–86.

18 Taylor, *American Colonies*, 39–49, 127–37, 188–203, 231–36, 264–69; Murrin, "Beneficiaries of Catastrophe." See also, for example, Anderson, "King Philip's Herds"; Cronon, *Changes in the Land*; Crosby, *Ecological Imperialism*; and Lemon, *Best Poor Man's Country*.

19 Taylor, *American Colonies*, 39–46, 133–37, 144–57, 323–37.

20 Ibid., 39–46, 130–31, 144–45, 170, 269; Wood, *American Revolution*, 6–7; Klepp, *Revolutionary Conceptions*, 3–4, 56–77, 107. See also Franklin, "Observations Concerning the Increase of Mankind" (1751) in Franklin, *Silence Dogood, The Busy-Body, and Early Writings*, 367–74.

21 See Boorstin, *Lost World of Thomas Jefferson*, 98–108; Cohen, *Science and the Founding Fathers*, 72–88; Commager, *Empire of Reason*, 42–108 (first quotation, 88); and Dugatkin, *Mr. Jefferson*, especially 10–100 (second quotation, 45).

22 Commager, *Empire of Reason*, 88 (first quotation); Dugatkin, *Mr. Jefferson*, 45–46 (second quotation). Gemery, in "The White Population of the Colonial United States, 1607–1790," and Walsh, in "The African American Population of the Colonial United States," summarized the literature on demography, living standards, and stature. See also Steckel, "Stature and the Standard of Living"; Tadman, "Demographic Cost of Sugar"; and Oakes, *Slavery and Freedom*, 35.

23 Cronon, *Changes in the Land*; Merchant, *Ecological Revolutions*.

24 Taylor, *American Colonies*, 137, 140, 165, 170–72, 225–26, 242–43, 246–48, 276, 285–88, 441; Henretta et al., *America's History*, 45–46, 57, 59; Wood, *American Revolution*, 94–95, 117–19; Dunn, *Age of Religious Wars*, 191; and especially the

remarkable analysis by Wood in *Radicalism of the American Revolution*, 109–89, 271–305. See also Meinig, *Shaping of America*, 295–307, and Cronon, Miles, and Gitlin, "Becoming West," 3–27. Tomlins, in *Freedom Bound*, stressed the connections between freedom and slavery under environmental conditions that fostered and enabled both.

25 Taylor, *American Colonies*, 276 (quotation).

26 Ibid., 166–70 (quotations, 168–69).

27 Henry quoted in Bridenbaugh, *Spirit of '76*, 3. See especially Main, *Peoples of a Spacious Land*.

28 The authoritative text on the Seven Years' War is Anderson, *Crucible of War*. See also Wood, *American Revolution*, 3–44.

29 Anderson, *Crucible of War*, 453–56, 518–28, 557–616, 641–713; Dunn, "America in the British Empire."

30 Anderson, *Crucible of War*, 453–56, 518–28, 557–616, 641–713; Dunn, "America in the British Empire."

31 Anderson, *Crucible of War*, 453–56, 518–28, 557–616 (quotation, 615), 641–713.

32 Ibid., 560–71; Wood, *American Revolution*, 17–24.

33 Breen, *American Insurgents*, 25–27, 52–53, 275–300.

34 Sabine and Thorson, *History of Political Theory*, 39–44, 148–51, 154–58, 161–64, 176–77, 386–88, 392–98, 400–401, 485–88, 493–94, and the sources listed in note 43; Cohen, *Science and the Founding Fathers*, 111.

35 Appleby, *Capitalism and a New Social Order*, 25–50 (quotations, 31, 32).

36 Willey, *Eighteenth Century Background*, 14–42; Becker, *Declaration of Independence*, 24–79; Dunn, *Age of Religious Wars*, 199–216; Sabine and Thorson, *History of Political Theory*, 386–88, 392–94, 400–401.

37 Dunn, *Age of Religious Wars*, 152–98.

38 Becker, *Declaration of Independence*, 24–134; McDonald, *Novus Ordo Seclorum*, 57–96. See also, for example, Otis, "The Rights of the British Colonists Asserted and Proved," in Bailyn, *Pamphlets of the American Revolution*, 426. The authoritative edition of Locke's work is Locke, *Two Treatises of Government*.

39 Locke, *Two Treatises of Government*, 287–88, 360–61, 412–13.

40 Ibid., 301; Becker, *Declaration of Independence*. See also, for example, Jefferson, "A Summary View of the Rights of British America," in Jensen, *Tracts of the American Revolution*, 256–76; Otis, "The Rights of the British Colonists Asserted and Proved"; and Paine, "Common Sense."

41 Berlamaqui, *Principles of Natural and Politic Law*, ix–xix (first quotation, x), 112 (second quotation). For a summary of the diffusion of Lockean thought through the American colonies during the Revolution, see Dworetz, *Unvarnished Doctrine*.

42 Nash, *Unknown American Revolution*, 96; Becker, *Declaration of Independence*, 24–279 (quotation, 72); Dworetz, *Unvarnished Doctrine*.

43 Otis, "The Rights of the British Colonists Asserted and Proved." For general discussions of natural law and rights during the Revolution, see Becker, *Declaration*

of Independence, especially chapter 2, "Historical Antecedents of the Declaration: The Natural Rights Philosophy"; Willey, *Eighteenth Century Background*, chapter 2, "Natural Law"; Barker, "Natural Law and the American Revolution"; and Weinberg, *Manifest Destiny*, chapter 1, "Natural Right."

44   Davis and Mintz, *Boisterous Sea of Liberty*, 156–57, 177–78 (McDougall and Warren); Jensen, *Tracts of the American Revolution*, 235 (Adams); Becker, *Declaration of Independence*, 116–17 (Jefferson); Maier, *American Scripture*, 47–96 (Pennsylvania, 88–89).

45   Paine, "Common Sense," 423. See also Foner, *Tom Paine and Revolutionary America*.

46   Maier, *American Scripture*, 3–46, 97–153; Becker, *Declaration of Independence*, 25–26 (Jefferson), 135–93.

47   See especially Hsiung, "Food, Fuel, and the New England Environment in the War for Independence, 1775–1776"; Fenn, *Pox Americana*; Bodle, *Valley Forge Winter*; and Nash, *Unknown American Revolution*, 216–23.

48   See, for example, Klepp, *Revolutionary Conceptions*, 88–127.

49   Nash, *Unknown American Revolution*, 215.

50   Bellesiles, *Revolutionary Outlaws*, 1–79, 156–89.

51   Shapiro, "Ethan Allen" (first quotation, 242–43); Bellesiles, *Revolutionary Outlaws*, 52–111 (second quotation, 106; third quotation, 94); Nash, *Unknown American Revolution*, 110–14, 280–83.

52   Nash, *Unknown American Revolution*, 280–83 (quotations, 281, 282).

53   Ibid., 5, 282–83, 443–48. See also, for example, Bellesiles, *Revolutionary Outlaws*, 301n2, and Taylor, *Liberty Men and Great Proprietors*.

54   Otis, "The Rights of the British Colonists Asserted and Proved," 420–22. On implications of the Revolution for women, see especially Zagarri, *Revolutionary Backlash*, 1–45.

55   Berkin, *First Generations: Women in Colonial America*, 165–94 (quotation, 182); Henretta et al., *America's History*, 196; Gunderson, *To Be Useful to the World*, 149–68 (quotation, 162); Kerber, "'History Can Do It No Justice,'" 6–8, 18–20; Kerber, "Republican Mother," in Kerber and De Hart, *Women's America*, 41–62; Kerber, *Women of the Republic*, 15–67; Woloch, *Women and the American Experience*, 80–84; Norton, *Liberty's Daughters*, 125–51, 155–94.

56   Berkin, *First Generations*, 186–191; Gunderson, *To Be Useful to the World*, 164–67; Kerber, "'History Can Do It No Justice,'" 7–16; Woloch, *Women and the American Experience*, 80.

57   Nash, *Unknown American Revolution*, 133–46 (first quotation, 141), 232–38; Berkin, *First Generations*, 184; Gunderson, *To Be Useful to the World*, 155–59 (second quotation, 156).

58   Warren quoted in Kerber, *Women of the Republic*, 82; Murray quoted in Klepp, *Revolutionary Conceptions*, 102.

59   Wollstonecraft, *A Vindication of the Rights of Woman*, 13, 16; Nash, *Unknown American Revolution*, 450–53.

60 Nash, *Unknown American Revolution*, 452 (Boudinot quotation); Klepp, *Revolutionary Conceptions*, 1–19, 56–127 (Hopkins quotation, 87), 179–214.

61 Nash, *Unknown American Revolution*, 288–90, 450–53.

62 Kerber, "The Republican Mother: Women and the Enlightenment," 43–45, 52; Kerber, *Women of the Republic*, 15–32.

63 Berkin, *First Generations*, 173–74; Gunderson, *To Be Useful to the World*, 169–70, 178–79; Woloch, *Women and the American Experience*, 72–76; Scharff, *Women Jefferson Loved*, 195–97 (first quotation, 197); Miller, *Jefferson and Nature*, 76–79; Norton, *Liberty's Daughters*, 110–24 (second quotation, 114), 192–94. See especially Zagarri, *Revolutionary Backlash*.

64 Kerber, "Republican Mother," 90–91 (quotations); Kerber, "Daughters of Columbia," 49–50; Jacobs, *Fables of Aesop*, "The Jay and the Peacock," unpaginated; Keller and Keating, *Aesop's Fables*, 83–84 (quotation). On the varied uses of Aesopian fables in English culture, see Lewis, *English Fable*.

65 Gunderson, *To Be Useful to the World*, 169–83; Kerber, "'History Can Do It No Justice,'" 34–42; Kerber, *No Constitutional Right to Be Ladies*, xxiii–xxiv, 8–29; Woloch, *Women and the American Experience*, 72–84.

66 Paine quoted and discussed in Kerber, *No Constitutional Right*, 10–11, and Kerber, "'History Can Do It No Justice,'" 31–32; Nash, *Unknown American Revolution*, 289.

67 Akers, *Abigail Adams*, 48 (Adams first quotation); Woloch, *Early American Women*, 168–70, 186–90; Nash, *Unknown American Revolution*, 206 (Adams second quotation). See also Woloch, *Women and the American Experience*, 84–86. On women's resistance to gender conservatism generally, see Akers, *Abigail Adams*, 35–52; Gunderson, *To Be Useful to the World*, 170; Kerber, "Republican Mother," 90–92; Norton, *Liberty's Daughters*, 188–94, 256–94; and Zagarri, *A Woman's Dilemma*.

68 Kerber, "Republican Mother: Women and the Enlightenment," 41–62; Kerber, "Republican Mother," 87–95; Kerber, "'History Can Do It No Justice,'" 30–42; Gunderson, *To Be Useful to the World*, 169–83.

69 Kerber, "Republican Mother: Women and the Enlightenment," 53–55; Norton, *Liberty's Daughters*, 110–24; Woloch, *Women and the American Experience*, 73, 84–86.

70 Quoted in Kerber, "Republican Mother," 90; cf. Stanton, "Declaration of Sentiments and Resolves," from the 1848 women's rights meeting in Seneca Falls, New York, 427–30. See also Isenberg, *Sex and Citizenship in Antebellum America*, "Natural Law and National Citizenship," 28–32.

71 Locke, *Two Treatises*, 283, 367. The literature on African Americans in the Revolution is large. I have benefitted from Bailyn, *Ideological Origins of the American Revolution*, 230–319; Berlin, *Many Thousands Gone*, 219–365; Davis, *Problem of Slavery in the Age of Revolution*; Frey, *Water from the Rock*; Nash, *Race and Revolution*; Quarles, *Negro in the American Revolution*; and Quarles, "The Revolutionary War as a Black Declaration of Independence."

72 Waldstreicher, "Capitalism, Slavery, and Benjamin Franklin's American

Revolution," 183–235; Waldstreicher, *Runaway America*; Nash, *Unknown American Revolution*, 32–29, 59–62, 116 (quotation), 121–24; Gordon-Reed, *Hemingses of Monticello*, 99–100 (quotation, 100), 682n26. The accounts of Nash and Gordon-Reed differ somewhat; for example, Nash refers to Howell as "Thomas," whereas Gordon-Reed refers to him as Samuel. On this and other details I have deferred to Gordon-Reed.

73 Bailyn, *Ideological Origins*, 232–46 (quotations, 232–33, 234).

74 Otis, "The Rights of the British Colonists Asserted and Proved," 439; Paine quoted in Berlin, *Many Thousands Gone*, 220.

75 Berlin, *Many Thousands Gone*, 361.

76 Berlin, *Many Thousands Gone*, is the authoritative study of slavery in the colonial era; see especially 29–215.

77 Ibid., 219–85; Nash, *Unknown American Revolution*, 223–32, 336, 339; Gordon-Reed, *Hemingses of Monticello*, 134–35. On embodied knowledge, see Andrews, *Killing for Coal*, 163.

78 Wood, "'Liberty Is Sweet,'" 149–84 (quotation, 152). See Johnson, "On Agency," for a trenchant critique of historians' tendency to frame historical explanations of enslaved Americans in terms of liberal rights. It might be a mistake, however, to go to the opposite extreme and deny or overlook the potential of enslaved and emancipated people to think about themselves in those terms.

79 Bruns, *Am I Not a Man and a Brother*, 306–8, 454–56 (Wheatley and Cuffe quotations); Nash, *Unknown American Revolution*, 223–24 (Haynes quotation).

80 Patrick, *Founding the Republic*, 102–5; Peterson, *Jefferson: Writings*, 982–83; and see Gordon-Reed, *Hemingses of Monticello*, 474–79.

81 Berlin, *Many Thousands Gone*, 140, 160 (first and third quotations); Nash, *Unknown American Revolution*, 60–61 (second and fourth quotations).

82 Aptheker, *Documentary History of the Negro People in the United States*, 8–9, 9–10, 10–12; Nash, *Unknown American Revolution*, 320–22.

83 Berlin, *Many Thousands Gone*, 219–324; Franklin, "Observations Concerning the Increase of Mankind," in Franklin, *Silence Dogood*, 369–70 (quotations, 370).

84 Bailyn, *Ideological Origins*, 245–46; Ellis, *What Did the Declaration Declare?* 10.

85 Berlin, *Many Thousands Gone*, 229–35, 278–79, 280 (quotation); Wood, *Empire of Liberty*, 522.

86 Berlin, in *Many Thousands Gone*, 286, discussed name changes that the Revolution inspired.

87 Ibid., 228–365.

88 Ibid., 224, 234, 279, 309, 363; Hunt, *Inventing Human Rights*, 186–88, 190; Wood, *Empire of Liberty*, 508; Frey, *Water from the Rock*, 236 (quotation). As Edmund Morgan argued, Virginia planters enjoyed a purer republican way of life because institutionalized racial slavery defused the class discontent that might have undermined notions of equality. Morgan, *American Slavery, American Freedom*, 363–87.

89 Jefferson, *Notes on the State of Virginia*, 137–43 (quotations, 142, 143). See also

Miller, *Jefferson and Nature*, 66–76, and Jordan, *White over Black*, 403–582.

90 Jefferson, *Notes on the State of Virginia*, 143.

91 Nash, *Unknown American Revolution*, 161–66, 327–39; McNeil, *Mosquito Empires*, 198–234.

92 Wood, *Empire of Liberty*, 508–42; Jordan, *White over Black*, 403–26, 573–82; Foner, *Story of American Freedom*, 29–45. Berlin, in *Many Thousands Gone*, 278, called the state laws "half-measures." On Washington, Madison, Jefferson, and the other founding fathers and slavery, see Rodehamel, *George Washington: Writings*, 1022–42; Berlin, *Many Thousands Gone*, 259; Ellis, *Founding Brothers*, 81–119; and Nash, *Unknown American Revolution*, 122–24, 320–27. See also Waldstreicher, *Runaway America*.

93 Maier, *American Scripture*, 146–47; Ellis, *American Sphinx*, 56, 60–61. Kerber speculated that the conservatism of the Revolution perhaps spared it from political instability but ensured that Americans for decades would avoid its most radical implications. Kerber, "'History Can Do It No Justice,'" 41–42. The Naturalization Act of 1790 appears in Peters, *Public Statutes at Large of the United States of America*, 103–4.

94 Lincoln, "Address at the Gettysburg National Cemetery," 19 November 1863, 788; King, "I Have a Dream," 28 August 1963, 449–53.

95 Useful works on the expansion of the Revolutionary republic include Anderson, *Crucible of War*, 709–46; Hinderaker, *Elusive Empires*, 185–267; Onuf, *Jefferson's Empire*; Seelye, *Beautiful Machine*; Stephanson, *Manifest Destiny*, 3–27; Weeks, *Building the Continental Empire*, ix–29; and Weinberg, *Manifest Destiny*, 1–223.

96 Weinberg, *Manifest Destiny*, 1–42 (quotations, 22, 25).

97 Quotations in Ellis, *Founding Brothers*, 133, 135; Seelye, *Beautiful Machine*, 87; Weinberg, *Manifest Destiny*, 31.

98 I draw this conceptualization from McCoy, *Elusive Republic*.

99 Ibid.; Onuf, *Jefferson's Empire*; Ellis, *American Sphinx*, 240–53 ("Western Magic"), 321 (Jefferson's "diffusion" theory); Peterson, *Jefferson: Writings*, 1484–87.

100 Hamilton, Jay, and Madison, *The Federalist*, nos. 5–9, 17–41 (quotation, 39). See also, for example, Anderson, *Crucible of War*, 745–46, and Meinig, *Shaping of America*, 338–418.

101 Henretta et al., *America's History*, 195–207; Holton, *Unruly Americans*; Hamilton, Jay, and Madison, *The Federalist*, no. 15, 68–75 (quotations, 70–71, 75).

102 On the background of these developments, see Wood, *Empire for Liberty*, 116, 121–22, 141–43; Henretta et al., *America's History*, 201–2; Johnson, *Order upon the Land*, 40–49; and Opie, *Law of the Land*, xi–xxi, 1–29.

103 The literature on the Constitution is enormous and beyond the scope of this brief treatment, but see Amar, *America's Constitution*, 22, 36, 40–53, 249–72; Wood, *Radicalism of the American Revolution*, 243–70; Wood, *Empire of Liberty*, 5–139; McDonald, *Novus Ordo Seclorum*; Holton, *Unruly Americans*; and Hamilton, Jay, and Madison, *The Federalist*, especially Madison, no. 10, 42–49.

104 Hamilton, Jay, and Madison, *The Federalist*, nos. 11–14, 49–67 (quotations 63, 67);

Amar, *America's Constitution*, 40–53; Beeman, *Penguin Guide to the United States Constitution*, 33.

105 Richter, *Facing East from Indian Country*, 110–253; Calloway, *American Revolution in Indian Country*, xi–64, 272–301; White, *Middle Ground*, 223–523; Hinderaker, *Elusive Empires*, 176–270; Wallace, *Jefferson and the Indians*.

106 Richter, *Facing East*, 151–236; also Calloway, *New Worlds for All*.

107 Richter, *Facing East*, 189–236; Calloway, *World Turned Upside Down*, 162–66, 170–77.

108 Only later, when conquered Indians struggled for sovereignty within the larger American republic, did they adopt the language of natural rights and lay claim to the principles embodied in the Declaration of Independence. In 1833, for example, the Mashpee of New England issued an "Indian Declaration of Independence," asserting that "we, as a tribe, will rule ourselves, and have the right to do so; for all men are created equal, says the Constitution of the country." Richter, *Facing East*, 240.

109 Ibid., 224–36.

3. KING COTTON

1 Northup, *Twelve Years a Slave*, in Osofsky, *Puttin' On Ole Massa*, 229, 231, 263, 332, 342, 344 (quotation), 361, 383. Save for the "Virginia Reel," there is no mention of the tunes Platt Epps played. The additional pieces listed here were popular in the nineteenth century. Derby and Miller of Auburn, New York, first published *Twelve Years a Slave* in 1853. For a useful annotated edition, see Northup, *Twelve Years a Slave*, eds. Sue Eakin and Joseph Logsdon. All subsequent references are to the version in Osofsky, *Puttin' On Ole Massa*, unless noted otherwise.

2 Northup, *Twelve Years a Slave*, 314 (first quotation), 321–22 (second, third quotations, 322). On the relationship between workers' bodies and the labor they performed, see Sackman, "Nature's Workshop."

3 Northup, *Twelve Years a Slave*, 322 (quotation). I have constructed the master's dialogue from references to his cursing (pp. 312–13, 322–23, 325, 350–51) and from a quotation (p. 322): "Practice and whipping were unavailing, and [the master], satisfied of it at last, swore I was a disgrace—that I was not fit to associate with a cotton-picking 'nigger.'"

4 Northup, *Twelve Years a Slave*, 322–24 (quotations, 323, 324).

5 Ibid., 344.

6 On the themes and achievements of the conventional historiography, see, for example, Parish, *Slavery*; Berlin, *Many Thousands Gone*; and Berlin, *Generations of Captivity*. For an outstanding environmental history of slavery in the low country of Georgia, see Stewart, *"What Nature Suffers to Groe."* In two essays, "If John Muir Had Been an Agrarian" and "Slavery and the Origins of African American Environmentalism," Stewart challenged historians to examine the environmental history of the South and southern slavery. Since Stewart's, numerous other

outstanding works on southern slavery have addressed space, time, healing, hunting, reproduction, labor, physical skill, and other themes pertinent to environmental history, although they tend to focus more on culture and economy than on nature. See Smith, *Mastered by the Clock*; Schwartz, *Born in Bondage*; Fett, *Working Cures*; Proctor, *Bathed in Blood*; Camp, *Closer to Freedom*; Follett, *Sugar Masters*; Berry, "*Swing the Sickle for the Harvest Is Ripe*"; Kaye, *Joining Places*; and Knight, *Working the Diaspora*. Morris, in "A More Southern Environmental History," offered an insightful survey but did not address the extent to which scholars such as Smith, Schwartz, Fett, Proctor, Camp, Follett, Berry, Kaye, and Knight addressed environmental topics.

7   On the intertwined histories of people and plants, see Pollan, *Botany of Desire*, xiii–xxv, and Hobhouse, *Seeds of Change*, 141–87. On the international political economy of cotton production, see Schoen, *Fragile Fabric of Union*, 1–10, 23–60, 100–145, and Kaye, "Second Slavery."

8   Meinig, *Shaping of America*, 23–40, 58–102, 128–57, 285–96; Lakwete, *Inventing the Cotton Gin*, 47–96; Rothman, *Slave Country*; Deyle, *Carry Me Back*, 40–62; Watkins, *King Cotton*, 29–30; Hilliard, *Atlas of Antebellum Southern Agriculture*, 67–71; Schoen, *Fragile Fabric of Union*, 2. See also Oakes, *Slavery and Freedom*, 97–106, and Oakes, *Ruling Race*, 69–95.

9   Deyle, *Carry Me Back*, 15–62, 94–173, 245–75; Rothman, *Slave Country*, 1–35; Oakes, *Ruling Race*, 3–34; Oakes, *Slavery and Freedom*, 34–35 (quotation, 34); Meinig, *Shaping of America*, 288; Hilliard, *Atlas*, 29–34; Gudmestad, *A Troublesome Commerce*. Sale of a spouse or child fragmented an estimated one-half of all upper South enslaved families. Deyle, *Carry Me Back*, 246. For overall figures, which I have rounded, see Tadman, *Speculators and Slaves*, 11–12, and Wright, *Slavery and American Economic Development*, 58–61.

10 Northup, *Twelve Years a Slave*, 233–311 (quotation, 270), 371. On the drugging of Northup, see Northup, *Twelve Years a Slave*, eds. Eakin and Logsdon, 18n1. On the kidnapping of free people, see Wilson, *Freedom at Risk*, 1–39, and Deyle, *Carry Me Back*, 17, 29, 31, 51, 178. The number of abductions may have been few, but that they occurred at all suggests the extraordinary influence of cotton production on American society.

11 See Pollan, "When a Crop Becomes King."

12 On the importance of cycles to environmental history, see Cronon, "Kennecott Journey," 35.

13 Hughes, *Thirty Years a Slave*, 36–37; Williams, *Narrative of James William*, 46–47; Miller, "Plantation Labor Organization and Slave Life on the Alabama-Mississippi Black Belt," 158–62.

14 Thorpe, "Cotton and Its Cultivation," 171; Brown, *Slave Life in Georgia*, 173; Hughes, *Thirty Years a Slave*, 27–28; Northup, *Twelve Years a Slave*, 313; Williams, *Narrative of James Williams*, 46. See also Gray, *History of Agriculture in the Southern United States to 1860*, 2:700–701, and Monette, "Cotton Crop."

15 Smith, in *Mastered by the Clock*, 94–125, described the masters' insertion of

modernist, market-driven, mechanical clock time into the biological rhythms of agriculture as a means of regulating the enslaved labor force. Camp, in *Closer to Freedom*, 12–34, documented the "geographies of containment" by which masters manipulated space to control plantation labor. Kaye, in *Joining Places*, 96–106, explained that agricultural reform in response to environmental problems and economic downturns placed additional burdens on enslaved workers.

16   Hughes, *Thirty Years a Slave*, 27.

17   Thorpe, "Cotton and Its Cultivation," 171–72; Brown, *Slave Life in Georgia*, 172–73; Hughes, *Thirty Years a Slave*, 27.

18   Thorpe, "Cotton and Its Cultivation," 172; Olmsted, *Cotton Kingdom*, 408 (quotation), 494–95. Sampson Low, Son and Company of London originally published *The Cotton Kingdom* in two volumes in 1861.

19   Ball, *Fifty Years in Chains*, 88–89. John S. Taylor of New York originally published Ball's story in 1837 under the title *Slavery in the United States: A Narrative of the Life and Adventures of Charles Ball, a Black Man*. See also Olmsted, *Cotton Kingdom*, 432.

20   Ball, *Fifty Years in Chains*, 145–50.

21   Olmsted, *Cotton Kingdom*, 407–8.

22   Hughes, *Thirty Years a Slave*, 22–24 (quotation, 23); Northup, *Twelve Years a Slave*, 314; Williams, *Narrative of James Williams*, 37–68; Ball, *Fifty Years in Chains*, 159; Olmsted, *Cotton Kingdom*, 452–53; Brown, *Slave Life in Georgia*, 129–31, 196–97 (quotation, 197), 174.

23   Northup, *Twelve Years a Slave*, 349–50; Williams, *Narrative of James Williams*, 37–68 (quotation, 48).

24   My analysis differs from the argument that lackadaisical slaves had no incentive to care for draft animals and tools or that they resisted domination and struck back at their masters by abusing draft animals and mishandling tools. For the classic interpretation, see Genovese, *Political Economy of Slavery*, especially 54–55, 60, 110–13, and Franklin and Schweninger, *Runaway Slaves*, 2–3. No doubt such carelessness and sabotage took place, but the evidence also suggests that the situation could be more complicated.

25   Brown, *Slave Life in Georgia*, 28.

26   Ibid., 29–30. See also Hughes, *Thirty Years a Slave*, 23–24.

27   Williams, *Narrative of James Williams*, 61–64, 82 (quotations, 63, 82).

28   Thorpe, "Cotton and Its Cultivation," 172; Brown, *Slave Life in Georgia*, 196–97.

29   Thorpe, "Cotton and Its Cultivation," 172; Brown, *Slave Life in Georgia*, 196–97; Williams, *Narrative of James Williams*, 49; Stampp, *Peculiar Institution*, 113–14; Norton et al., *A People and a Nation*, 316.

30   Olmsted, *Cotton Kingdom*, 445–56 (quotation, 455); Williams, *Narrative of James Williams*, 53–60 (quotations, 59).

31   Thorpe, "Cotton and Its Cultivation," 175; Northup, *Twelve Years a Slave*, 315.

32   Thorpe, "Cotton and Its Cultivation," 173–74; Gray, *History of Agriculture*, 2:703–4; Hughes, *Thirty Years a Slave*, 28–30 (quotation, 30).

33 Thorpe, "Cotton and Its Cultivation," 174 (first quotation); Gray, *History of Agriculture*, 2:704 (second and third quotations).

34 Thorpe, "Cotton and Its Cultivation," 174.

35 Northup, *Twelve Years a Slave*, 329–32 (quotation, 332); Watkins, *King Cotton*, 195. Follett, in *Sugar Masters*, 10–13, 39–40, 92–117, addressed environmental circumstances affecting sugar cane production.

36 Northup, *Twelve Years a Slave*, 332–35.

37 Thorpe, "Cotton and Its Cultivation," 174–75; Ball, *Fifty Years in Chains*, 213–18; Brown, *Slave Life in Georgia*, 175–76; Hughes, *Thirty Years a Slave*, 31–32 (quotation, 32).

38 Hughes, *Thirty Years a Slave*, 31–32 (quotation, 31); Brown, *Slave Life in Georgia*, 128–31 (quotation, 131), 172–76; Monette, "Cotton Crop," 320–22.

39 Ball, *Fifty Years in Chains*, 314; Brown, *Slave Life in Georgia*, 129 (quotation), 176; Northup, *Twelve Years a Slave*, 327–28 (quotation, 328).

40 On failed attempts to build mechanical pickers, see Gray, *History of Agriculture*, 2:689, 702.

41 Moore, "Cotton Breeding in the Old South," 95; Campbell, "As 'a Kind of Freeman'?" 246–48.

42 Monette, in "Cotton Crop," 321, described whippings "performed with as much care and humanity as the nature of the case will permit," although plantation overseers perhaps administered soft whippings for economic more than humanitarian reasons.

43 Campbell, "As 'a Kind of Freeman'?" 246–48. See also Follett, *Sugar Masters*, 10–13, 195–215.

44 Moore, "Cotton Breeding," 95–104. See also Moore, *Emergence of the Cotton Kingdom in the Old Southwest*, 11–13; Campbell, "As 'a Kind of Freeman'?" 246–48; Thorpe, "Cotton and Its Cultivation," 174; Gray, *History of Agriculture*, 2:689–90.

45 Campbell, "As 'a Kind of Freeman'?" 249.

46 Gray, in *History of Agriculture*, 2:696–700, charted the price trends, although he did not pinpoint the connection between falling prices and the adoption and spread of superabundant Mexicanized varieties.

47 On the relationship of labor requirements and the cotton harvest, see Olmsted, *Cotton Kingdom*, 367, 501–2; Ball, *Fifty Years in Chains*, 267–74; Gray, *History of Agriculture*, 2:707; Boles, *Black Southerners*, 71.

48 Moore, "Cotton Breeding," 98–99; Campbell, "As 'a Kind of Freeman'?" 252–65; Hughes, *Thirty Years a Slave*, 32; Brown, *Slave Life in Georgia*, 194.

49 Gray, *History of Agriculture*, 2:702; Northup, *Twelve Years a Slave*, 332 (quotation), 348.

50 See, for example, Ball, *Fifty Years in Chains*, 267–69.

51 Olmsted, *Cotton Kingdom*, 502.

52 See Olmsted, *Cotton Kingdom*, 444: "It is difficult to handle simply as property, a creature possessing human passions and human feelings, however debased and torpid the condition of the creature may be; while, on the other hand, the

absolute necessity of dealing with property as a thing, greatly embarrassed a man in any attempt to treat it as a person. And it is the natural result of this complicated state of things, that the system of slave management is irregular, ambiguous, and contradictory; that it is never either consistently humane or consistently economical."

53 White, *Ar'n't I a Woman?*, 67–69, 98–99; Deyle, *Carry Me Back*, 27–29, 46–49, 52–53. Deyle pointed out that raising slaves for sale in the manner of livestock was uneconomical, given that humans had relatively long childhoods during which they could provide little labor, if any.

54 Perrin, "Resisting Reproduction: Reconsidering Slave Contraception in the Old South," 255–74 (quotation, 262). Perrin also explained the uncertain demographic effects of contraceptive practices.

55 White, *Ar'n't I a Woman?* 69–70, 85–87, 110; Brown, *Slave Life in Georgia*, 131–32; Steckel, "African American Population of the United States, 1790–1920," 450; Schwartz, *Born in Bondage*, 1–106. See also Williams, *Narrative of James Williams*, 64–65.

56 Steckel, "African American Population," 450–51; Rathbun and Steckel, "Health of Slaves and Free Blacks in the East," 220; Schwartz, "'At Noon, Oh How I Ran,'" 241–59; Schwartz, *Born in Bondage*, 48–106, 131–54; Olmsted, *Cotton Kingdom*, 431.

57 Schwartz, "'At Noon, Oh How I Ran,'" 242–51; Schwartz, *Born in Bondage*, 48–106, 131–54; White, *Ar'n't I a Woman?* 69–70, 99–100, 113; Steckel, "African American Population," 449–51; Rathbun and Steckel, "Health of Slaves," 209, 214, 220.

58 Steckel, "African American Population," 451–52; Northup, *Twelve Years a Slave*, 317–18.

59 Boles, *Black Southerners*, 71–72, 88–89; Hilliard, *Atlas*, 57–67; Hughes, *Thirty Years a Slave*, 33–34.

60 Boles, *Black Southerners*, 72, 88; Northup, *Twelve Years a Slave*, 318–19. The distribution of hogs across the South loosely followed the distribution of cotton. See Hilliard, *Atlas*, 47, 49, 50, 68–71.

61 Covington, *Diary (1829–1830)*, 179.

62 Northup, *Twelve Years a Slave*, 316–17; Ball, *Fifty Years in Chains*, 85, 106, 109–21, 187–89; Brown, *Slave Life in Georgia*, 19.

63 Kiple and Kiple, "Black Tongue and Black Men," 411–28.

64 Ball, *Fifty Years in Chains*, 44 (quotation), 67, 82, 497; Brown, *Slave Life in Georgia*, 20–21; Kiple and Kiple, "Black Tongue and Black Men."

65 Ball, *Fifty Years in Chains*, 199–200

66 Brown, *Slave Life in Georgia*, 128, 177 (quotations).

67 Owens, *This Species of Property*, 52–54.

68 Camp, in *Closer to Freedom*, 7, borrowing from Edward Said, described the "rival geography" that enslaved people created in resistance to the planters' "geography of containment." Kaye, in *Joining Places*, 21–23, described enslaved people's

neighborhoods, which functioned in opposition to the controlled landscapes of the plantations.

69 Ball, *Fifty Years in Chains*, 166 (quotation), 139, 166–67 (quotation, 166); Olmsted, *Cotton Kingdom*, 79–80, 433–34, 447, 482; Berlin and Morgan, "Labor and the Shaping of Slave Life in the Americas," 29–35, 39; Reidy, "Obligation and Right," 143–48; Boles, *Black Southerners*, 89–91; Owens, *This Species of Property*, 52–54.

70 Berlin and Morgan, "Labor and the Shaping of Slave Life," 30–31; Reidy, "Obligation and Right," 149; Olmsted, *Cotton Kingdom*, 79, 447. On the proportion of undeveloped land in the South, see McDonald and McWhiney, "The South from Self-Sufficiency to Peonage," 1099.

71 Ball, *Fifty Years in Chains*, 145, 223, 229, 230, 233, 262–63, 276–83, 324, 428, 429, 435, 443; Olmsted, *Cotton Kingdom*, 448; Brown, *Slave Life in Georgia*, 198–99; Foster and Duke, *Field Guide to Medicinal Plants*, 216; Northup, *Twelve Years a Slave*, 334–36 (quotations, 335); Proctor, *Bathed in Blood*, 144–68.

72 Olmsted, *Cotton Kingdom*, 448; Northup, *Twelve Years a Slave*, 335–36; Ball, *Fifty Years in Chains*, 223, 229, 233, 276–77, 324, 435, 443. See also Giltner, "Slave Hunting and Fishing in the Antebellum South," 21–36.

73 Ball, *Fifty Years in Chains*, 324–25.

74 Campbell, "'My Constant Companion,'" 53–76 (quotation, 54); Ball, *Fifty Years in Chains*, 352–56, 389.

75 For example, Campbell, "'My Constant Companion,'" 65; Olmsted, *Cotton Kingdom*, 482; Miller, "Plantation Labor Organization," 167.

76 Campbell, "'My Constant Companion,'" 56–58.

77 Ibid., 59, 66–67; Reidy, "Obligation and Right," 148; Olmsted, *Cotton Kingdom*, 430–31.

78 Reidy, "Obligation and Right," 149; Olmsted, *Cotton Kingdom*, 447, 482.

79 Ball, *Fifty Years in Chains*, 276–79, 292–95.

80 Ibid., 295–318 (quotations, 297, 317).

81 Brown, *Slave Life in Georgia*, 192 (quotation). See also Ball, *Fifty Years in Chains*, 298–99, and Hughes, *Thirty Years a Slave*, 20: "The idea never seemed to occur to the slave holders that these slaves were getting no wages for their work and, therefore, had nothing with which to procure what, at times, was necessary for their health and strength—palatable and nourishing food. When the slaves took anything the masters called it stealing, yet they were stealing the slaves' time year after year."

82 See, for example, Olmsted, *Cotton Kingdom*, 409–10, 418, 419, 437, 450, 454; Ball, *Fifty Years in Chains*, 262, 324, 387–465; and Northup, *Twelve Years a Slave*, 358–63.

83 Northup, *Twelve Years a Slave*, 358–59, and see 361–62 for the remarkable story of Celeste, who claimed to share "a secret" with the dogs, which would not obey the overseer's "devilish orders" to pursue her; Williams, *Narrative of James Williams*, 81–99; James Smith interview by Henry Bibb, 1852, in Blasingame, *Slave Testimony*, 280–83.

84 Berlin and Morgan, "Labor and the Shaping of Slave Life," 39; Reidy, "Obligation

and Right," 149; Owens, *This Species of Property*, 52–54; Ball, *Fifty Years in Chains*, 262–63, 276; Brown, *Slave Life in Georgia*, 70; Northup, *Twelve Years a Slave*, 358–59.

85 Reidy, "Obligation and Right," 148–54; Miller, "Plantation Labor Organization," 166–69; Campbell, "As 'a Kind of Freeman'?" 259, 264–71; Olmsted, *Cotton Kingdom*, 448; Campbell, "'My Constant Companion,'" 53, 67–70.

86 Ekirch, in *At Day's Close*, suggested some of the ways in which historians might recover the night as a meaningful subject of historical analysis. See especially 155–84, 227–58. See also Rawick, *From Sundown to Sunup*.

87 See, for example, Hughes, *Thirty Years a Slave*, 35, 39–40; Northup, *Twelve Years a Slave*, 316–17; and Williams, *Narrative of James Williams*, 47, 55.

88 Brown, *Slave Life in Georgia*, 45–48. Hamilton then attempted to profit from his discovery by marketing pills (consisting simply of flour) that he claimed would work only when administered with cayenne-pepper tea. After the sunstroke experiments, Hamilton subjected Brown to another set of tests, this time to determine the depth of the pigmentation in his skin.

89 Owens, *This Species of Property*, 27–33; Boles, *Black Southerners*, 95–104. See also Kiple and King, *Another Dimension to the Black Diaspora*.

90 Olmsted, *Cotton Kingdom*, 283; Northup, *Twelve Years a Slave*, 320–21.

91 Owens, *This Species of Property*, 31–37, 42–44; Northup, *Twelve Years a Slave*, 321. See also Fett, *Working Cures*, on enslaved people's use of folk cures and medicines to enhance their autonomy.

92 Owens, *This Species of Property*, 30, 37, 39; Northup, *Twelve Years a Slave*, 321; Olmsted, *Cotton Kingdom*, 449.

93 Northup, *Twelve Years a Slave*, 365–66.

94 Ibid., 310–11 (quotations, 310, 311).

95 Ibid., 366–68 (quotation, 368).

96 Ibid., 371. See pp. 352–55 for Northup's account of an earlier escape attempt, in which seasonal change, night, and foraging skills influenced his actions.

97 Ibid., 371–72 (quotations, 371, 372).

98 Ibid., 373–80 (quotations, 375, 376, 378).

99 Ibid., 381–86.

100 Ibid., 259–60, 387–96 (quotations, 395, 396).

101 Ibid., 397–99 (quotations, 398–99).

102 Ibid., 399–405.

4. NATURE'S NOBLEMAN

1 Burlingame, *Abraham Lincoln*, 1:310; Donald, *Lincoln*, 143, 145; Townsend, "Lincoln in Illinois," 78–81, 85, 87, 102–3, 114–15, 133; Angle, "*Here I Have Lived*," 73–75, 174–83.

2 See Mill, *Principles of Political Economy*, 1:xciii (second quotation), 28 (first quotation), 47, 189, and passim. The 1965/2006 edition reproduces the 1871 edition of

the work, which is substantially the same as the first edition published in 1848. On the books in the law office library, see Guelzo, *Abraham Lincoln: Redeemer President*, 105–8.

3 Angle, *"Here I Have Lived"*; Davis, *Frontier Illinois*, 201–81, 355–428; Gobel-Bain, "From Humble Beginnings," 5–26.

4 Basler, *Collected Works of Abraham Lincoln* (hereafter CW), 2:437. For an astute description and analysis of the speech and its history, see Emerson, *Lincoln the Inventor*, 35–51, 90n74. Scholars once thought that Lincoln had two speeches on discoveries and inventions but now believe them to be two parts of the same speech. Both are reproduced in Appendix 2 of Emerson's book. I treat them as related parts of a larger whole. For an important, insightful analysis of Lincoln and the lyceum system of public lectures and education, see two articles by Winger, "High Priests of Nature" and "Lincoln's *Alma Mater*."

5 CW 2:437–42 (quotations, 437, 441–42).

6 Fehrenbacher, *Abraham Lincoln: Speeches and Writings* (hereafter SW), 2:5–10 (quotations, 5, 6, 10).

7 Emerson, *Lincoln the Inventor*, 35–36, 46–53.

8 "The rough conditions in which Lincoln was raised and made his way as a young man are undeniable," the Lincoln scholar Douglas Wilson wrote, "but they are all too easily rationalized as what he rose above, rather than what stamped his character." Wilson, *Honor's Voice*, 4. On the importance of public lectures and the lyceum system to Lincoln, see Winger, "Lincoln's *Alma Mater*."

9 Burlingame's superb two-volume biography, *Abraham Lincoln*, is the essential guide to Lincoln. Also see Boritt, *Gettysburg Gospel*; Boritt, *Lincoln and the Economics of the American Dream*; Burlingame, *Inner World of Abraham Lincoln*; Donald, *Lincoln*; Emerson, *Lincoln the Inventor*; Epstein, *Lincoln and Whitman*; Foner, *Fiery Trial*; Foner, *Our Lincoln*; Fornieri and Gabbard, *Lincoln's America*; Fraysse, *Lincoln, Land, and Labor*; Fredrickson, *Big Enough to Be Inconsistent*; Guelzo, *Abraham Lincoln*; Guelzo, *Abraham Lincoln as a Man of Ideas*; Guelzo, *Lincoln*; Guelzo, *Lincoln's Emancipation Proclamation*; Kaplan, *Lincoln*; McPherson, *Abraham Lincoln*; McPherson, *Abraham Lincoln and the Second American Revolution*; McPherson, *Tried by War*; Miller, *Lincoln and His World*, vol. 1, *The Early Years*, and vol. 2, *Prairie Politician*; Oakes, *The Radical and the Republican*; Paludan, *Presidency of Abraham Lincoln*; Thomas, *Lincoln's New Salem*; White, *A. Lincoln*; Wills, *Lincoln at Gettysburg*; Wilson, *Honor's Voice*; and Winger, *Lincoln, Religion, and Romantic Cultural Politics*.

10 See Foner, *Free Soil, Free Labor, Free Men*.

11 On the importance of environment to the way historians write about the lives of important figures in American history, see Worster, "When Writing about John Muir, I Had to See What He Saw." On the importance of Lincoln's environment to his thought and speech, see McPherson, *Abraham Lincoln and the Second American Revolution*, 95.

12 Fraysse, *Lincoln, Land, and Labor*, 7–9; Boritt, *Lincoln and the Economics of the American Dream*, 285.

13 Fraysse, *Lincoln, Land, and Labor*, 27–28; SW 2:161 (quotation), 162; Donald, *Lincoln*, 34, 36; Kaplan, *Lincoln*, 47. See also Faragher, *Sugar Creek* and Davis, *Frontier Illinois*.

14 Howells, *Life of Abraham Lincoln*, 21. This is a reprint of the original 1860 edition, which Lincoln corrected and which appeared in *Lives and Speeches of Abraham Lincoln and Hannibal Hamlin*. On the importance of labor and nature, see White, "Are You an Environmentalist or Do You Work for a Living?" 171–85, and White, *Organic Machine*.

15 Fraysse, *Lincoln, Land, and Labor*, 27–28.

16 Valenčius, *The Health of the Country*, is representative of several important studies that have dissolved the scholarly boundary between the body and its environment. Valenčius observed (pp. 3–4) that in the nineteenth century, "people were influenced by their environments in direct and powerful ways, and the exterior world and the human body were not as separate as they are now. . . . It is thus in the everyday places and everyday occupations of nineteenth-century Americans that some of their most profound beliefs and ways of understanding the world came to the fore." Not only does this insight help to explain Lincoln, but it also suggests the need to join environmental history and its emphasis on ecology with political history and its emphasis on economy and ideology.

17 Donald, *Lincoln*, 64 (quotation), 245; Thomas, *Lincoln's New Salem*, 131.

18 Donald, *Lincoln*, 575.

19 Ibid., 32–33, 37, 47; Burlingame, *Inner World*, 39; Fraysse, *Lincoln, Land, and Labor*, 26–34, 46; CW 2:440 (quotation). Cf. Kaplan, *Lincoln*, 43–44.

20 Burlingame, *Inner World*, 37 (quotation), 53n130; Donald, *Lincoln*, 32–33, 34, 36, 152.

21 Burlingame, "'I Used to Be a Slave': The Origins of Lincoln's Hatred of Slavery," in *Inner World*, 22–56 (quotation, 36), is the classic analysis. See also Fredrickson, *Big Enough to Be Inconsistent*, 48–49, and Oakes, *The Radical and the Republican*, 57–58.

22 SW 2:585 (first quotation), 1:302 (second quotation).

23 For general studies of improvement in this period, see Drayton, *Nature's Government*, and Nye, *America as Second Creation*. According to Howe, in *What Hath God Wrought*, 244, John Quincy Adams "believed that knitting the Union together, strengthening it economically and culturally, fulfilled the promise of the Revolution. The whole point of liberation from foreign domination, Adams asserted, was so that Americans could pursue the goal of human improvement, for their own benefit and for the benefit of mankind." See also Sheriff, *Artificial River*, 25.

24 Howe, *What Hath God Wrought*, 211–84, especially 244. See also Nye, *America as Second Creation*; Stoll, *Larding the Lean Earth*; Cohen, *Notes from the Ground*; and Howe, *Making the American Self*.

25 Howe, *What Hath God Wrought*, 211–84; Larson, *Internal Improvement*; Sheriff, *Artificial River*; SW 1:1–5, 187–98 (quotation, 198).

26 Howe, *What Hath God Wrought*, 244–45.

27 Boritt, in *Lincoln and the Economics of the American Dream*, explained in detail Lincoln's commitment to internal improvement and his relationship to the political movement that supported it. According to Howe, in *Making the American Self*, 139, "the internal improvements that the Whig party favored were human as well as material." Of John Quincy Adams, an early Whig, Howe, in *What Hath God Wrought*, 245, remarked: "Adams envisioned the American republic as the culmination of the history of human progress and the realization of the potential of human nature."

28 Burlingame, *Inner World*, 39–40; Kaplan, *Lincoln*, 3–98; Wilson, *Honor's Voice*, 54–58, 62–67, 103–4. "We do require dimensions of our brains," according to the philosopher Holmes Rolston, "that are specified by genetics, as in hearing and seeing. But our brains are also quite plastic, forging properties enabled by our genes but shaped by our experience, environmental and social." See Rolston, *Three Big Bangs*, 92–97 (quotation, 96).

29 Groves, "The Book Trade Transformed"; Casper, "Antebellum Reading Prescribed and Described," 109, 135–36; McGaw, *Most Wonderful Machine*, especially 27–30, 43, 74–76, 109–10, 197. See also "Look Away," my portion of Fiege and Mihm, "On Bank Notes."

30 Donald, *Lincoln*, 38; Thomas, *Lincoln's New Salem*, 134.

31 Wilson, *Honor's Voice*, 28 (second quotation), 64–65 (first quotation).

32 Constantin de Volney quoted in Wilson, *Honor's Voice*, 79; Paine, *Age of Reason*, 153; Blackstone, *Commentaries on the Laws of England*, 1:38–40, 125. On Blackstone, see also Guelzo, *Abraham Lincoln: Redeemer President*, 77. Kaplan, *Lincoln*, is the most complete evaluation of what Lincoln read. Bray, "What Abraham Lincoln Read," is an essential guide to the subject. See also Wilson, *Honor's Voice*, 54–85. Winger, in "High Priests of Nature" and "Lincoln's *Alma Mater*," stressed the importance of the lyceum system to Lincoln's program of self-improvement.

33 Donald, *Lincoln*, 38–39; Thomas, *Lincoln's New Salem*, 59–61.

34 Donald, *Lincoln*, 39; Thomas, *Lincoln's New Salem*, 60–61. On the importance of bodily strength and physical prowess to Lincoln's early political popularity, see Wilson, *Honor's Voice*, 142–43, 150–51.

35 *SW* 1:2–3 (quotations), 836–37; Donald, *Lincoln*, 38–39; Thomas, *Lincoln's New Salem*, 59–61.

36 *SW* 1:1–5 (quotations, 1–3). Cf. Sheriff, *Artificial River*. It is possible that Lincoln learned of this channel-clearing technique from an article in the *Louisville Advertiser*, 11 April 1831, which described the project of engineer Henry M. Shreve to cut through a narrow neck of land in a meander bend on the lower Mississippi River. See Gudmestad, "Steamboats and the Removal of the Red River Raft," and Gudmestad, *Steamboats and the Rise of the Cotton Kingdom*.

37 Thomas, *Lincoln's New Salem*, 74–75; Donald, *Lincoln*, 43.

38 Thomas, *Lincoln's New Salem*, 76–77; Donald, *Lincoln*, 43–44; Pratt, "Lincoln Pilots the *Talisman*," 319–29.

39   SW 1:837–38; Boritt, in *Lincoln and the Economics of the American Dream*, addressed Lincoln's commitment to the improvement program. See also the passages on Lincoln in Howe, *Making the American Self*, and Howe, *What Hath God Wrought*.

40   Fraysse, *Lincoln, Land, and Labor*, 9–14, 59–60; Donald, *Lincoln*, 51–52. Opie, in *Law of the Land*, provides an excellent description of the rectangular survey.

41   Donald, *Lincoln*, 51, 142–43. Training his brain had deleterious consequences for other parts of Lincoln's body. He studied with such zeal that he missed meals and lost weight. Receiving wages reversed the deterioration and validated the temporary sacrifice of his body in the service of improving his mind. Surveying "procured bread," he recalled, and "kept soul and body together." Miller, *Lincoln and His World*, 1:215–20 (quotation, 218).

42   SW 1:28–36 (first quotation, 35; second quotation, 31), 81–90; Donald, *Lincoln*, 118. See Howe, *Making of the American Self*, for a thorough discussion of faculty psychology and its theory of the passions.

43   Donald, *Lincoln*, 40, 45, 118.

44   SW 1: 84 (quotation); Thomas, *Lincoln's New Salem*, 48; Pratt, "Lincoln Pilots the Talisman," 326. Rorabaugh, in *Alcoholic Republic*, surveyed the production and consumption of alcohol during the nineteenth century.

45   SW 1:81–90. See also CW 4:420.

46   SW 1:36. Fraysse, in *Lincoln, Land, and Labor*, 37–38, highlighted Lincoln's objection to unwarranted emotionalism, whether manifested in dram shops or at religious revivals.

47   SW 1:81–90

48   Ibid., 1:4.

49   Ibid., 1:89–90 (quotation, 90). Cf. Boritt, *Lincoln and the Economics of the American Dream*, 138–39.

50   CW 2:32–36 (quotation, 33). In his speech on discoveries and inventions, Lincoln discussed transportation and highlighted the development of patent laws, provided for in the U.S. Constitution, "which secured to the inventor, for a limited time, the exclusive use of his invention; and thereby added the fuel of *interest* to the *fire* of genius, in the discovery and production of new and useful things." SW 2:8–9, 10–11 (quotation, 11); see also Emerson, *Lincoln the Inventor*, 24–25. Although he remained a man of the earth, his interest in the new technologies gradually led him to introduce elements of mechanism into his language. He later referred to himself as "a little engine that knew no rest," and on another occasion he asserted that the president's governmental duty was "to run the machine as it is." Donald, *Lincoln*, 81, 269.

51   Donald, *Lincoln*, 51, 142–43; SW 1:4, 2:99 (quotation); CW 3:362–63.

52   McPherson, *Ordeal by Fire*, 53–70; Wilentz, *Rise of American Democracy*, 577–667.

53   McPherson, *Ordeal by Fire*, 71–96; Wilentz, *Rise of American Democracy*, 668–706; Guelzo, *Lincoln*, 56–89.

54 Wilentz, *Rise of American Democracy*, 707–44; Tomlins, *Freedom Bound*, 512–14.

55 Guelzo, *Abraham Lincoln: Redeemer President*, 143–227.

56 On the importance of the Declaration of Independence to Lincoln, see, for example, Guelzo, *Abraham Lincoln: Redeemer President*, 193–97; White, *A. Lincoln*, 201–2, 260–61, 279–85.

57 See Oakes, *Slavery and Freedom*. On slaveholders and agricultural improvement, see Cohen, *Notes from the Ground*, 85–99, 131–33, 155–61, 224n15, and Ruffin, *Nature's Management*, 16–17, 330–31.

58 Ellis, *American Sphinx*, 321–22; Howe, *What Hath God Wrought*, 149, 264–65, 409; Paludan, *Presidency of Abraham Lincoln*, 17.

59 Howe, *What Hath God Wrought*, 129–32, 136, 148; McPherson, *Battle Cry of Freedom*, 91–103, 123, 128; Guelzo, *Abraham Lincoln: Redeemer President*, 131–32; Guelzo, *Lincoln*, 63.

60 Calhoun, *Union and Liberty*, edited by R. M. Lence, 463–76, 539–70 (first quotation, 574; second quotation, 569). According to Lence (p. 539), "Calhoun perceived that the real source of conflict between North and South was, in the final analysis, based on fundamental beliefs about human nature, and not upon principles of political practice."

61 Wilentz, *Rise of American Democracy*, 708–15; Huebner, "Roger B. Taney and the Slavery Issue," 17–39 (first quotation, 17); *Dred Scott v. Sandford* (60 U.S. 393), in Frohnen, *American Republic*, 646–64 (quotations, 646, 647, 648, 649, 655). The name was misrecorded as Sandford.

62 Fredrickson, *Big Enough to Be Inconsistent*, is a thorough analysis of this matter, but it should be tempered by a reading of the scholarship of Burlingame, Guelzo, Oakes, and Paludan, who believe that Lincoln was motivated far less by any racist beliefs he might have had than by political circumstances and his belief that the end of slavery had to be achieved by constitutional means. See, for example, Paludan, *Presidency of Abraham Lincoln*, xiii–xvii, 12–20.

63 *SW* 1:449 (second quotation), 478, 512 (fourth quotation), 585 (first quotation), 2:99; *CW* 2:440 (third quotation), 4:3.

64 *CW* 4:207 (first quotation); *SW* 1:198 (third quotation), 2:133 (second quotation).

65 *SW* 2:96–98 (first quotation, 96; second quotation, 98).

66 *CW* 2:4 (quotations); *SW* 2:90–101, 520–21; Donald, *Lincoln*, 110.

67 *SW* 1:334. Jacoby, in "Slaves by Nature?" argued that the domestication of animals and the enslavement of people began during the Neolithic period and that many of the same methods used for controlling animals were applied to the control and brutalization of human slaves. In his speech on discoveries and inventions, Lincoln did not describe slavery as an important innovation in human history. Whether he thought about its origins or not, he believed it to be immoral and antithetical to natural rights, and thus it stood outside the great story of human progress and improvement that he tried to tell.

68 *SW* 1:326.

69 *SW* 1:313, 584. See also ibid. 1:327–28, 2:139, 149.

70 CW 3:425, cited in Oakes, "'No Such Right,'" 135–50 (quotation, 141).

71 SW 1:584 (first quotation); Guelzo, *Lincoln*, 69–70 (second quotation).

72 SW 1:112 (second quotation), 808 (first quotation), 581–82 (third quotation); Donald, *Lincoln*, 234–35.

73 SW 1:323–24.

74 Ibid., 1:108 (first quotation), 330–31, 334 (fourth quotation), 581–82, 584–85; 2:132–50 (second quotation, 134), 137 (third quotation).

75 Ibid., 2:40–41.

76 Guelzo, *Lincoln*, 69.

77 SW 2:85.

78 Cassius M. Clay reminiscence of Abraham Lincoln, in Rice, *Reminiscences of Abraham Lincoln*, 297 (first quotation); SW 1:478 (second quotation).

79 SW 1:398.

80 SW 1:390–403 (first quotation, 398; second and third quotations, 397; fourth quotation, 397–98).

81 Lincoln most famously argued for restriction on constitutional grounds in his Cooper Institute address of 1860. See White, *A. Lincoln*, 311–12, and SW 2:111–30.

82 SW 1:309.

83 Ibid., 1:426, 584–85 (quotations).

84 Ibid., 2:224.

85 Davis, "Abraham Lincoln's Quest for Order"; Burlingame, "Thoughts on the Nature of Lincoln."

86 The classic statement about a large or extensive republic as a cure for the problem of faction is James Madison's in *The Federalist*, no. 10, 42–49.

87 SW 1:426.

88 Donald, *Lincoln*, 45.

89 McPherson, *Tried by War*, 2–4 (quotation, 3).

90 See ibid. for a thorough analysis of Lincoln as commander-in-chief.

91 Commager, *Documents of American History*, 410–13.

92 McPherson, *Tried by War*, 190–92; Bruce, *Lincoln and the Tools of War*, 114–15 (quotations, 115), 262–63.

93 McPherson, *Tried by War*, 57–58, 128–29. See also McPherson, *Abraham Lincoln*, x: "Only after years of studying the powerful crosscurrents of political and military pressures on Lincoln did I come to appreciate the skill with which he steered between the numerous shoals of conservatism and radicalism, free states and slave states, abolitionists, Republicans, Democrats, and border-state Unionists to maintain a steady course that brought the nation to victory—and the abolition of slavery—in the end. If he had moved decisively against slavery in the war's first year, as radicals pressed him to do, he might well have fractured his war coalition, driven border-state Unionists over to the Confederacy, lost the war, and witnessed the survival of slavery for at least another generation." On Lincoln and prudence, see Fornieri, "Introduction: Lincoln, the Natural Law, and Prudence," xix–lxiii, and Guelzo, *Lincoln's Emancipation Proclamation*, 1–11.

See Oakes, *The Radical and the Republican*, 213–17, 264–75, on a similar analysis by the African American abolitionist Frederick Douglass.

94 McPherson, *Tried by War*, 58–59 (quotation, 59), 85–86.

95 Ibid., 86–88, 103–9.

96 Ibid., 65–160; Burlingame, *Abraham Lincoln*, 2:333–418.

97 McPherson, *Tried by War*, 127–34; Burlingame, *Abraham Lincoln* 2:419–73; *SW* 2:368–70 (quotation, 368).

98 *SW* 2:403–6 (first quotation, 403; second and third quotations, 404; fourth quotation, 406).

99 *SW* 2:406–11 (first quotation, 409; second quotation, 410).

100 *SW* 2: 395 (second quotation), 411–14 (first, third, and fourth quotations, 412; fifth quotation, 413; sixth quotation, 411). See also Foner, *Fiery Trial*, 237–38. Lincoln most likely modeled his plan to end slavery and colonize freed people on an earlier Whig program advocated by the Kentucky statesman Henry Clay, his political hero. See Howe, *What Hath God Wrought*, 260–66, 409.

101 *SW* 2:414–15 (quotations, 415).

102 *SW* 2:424–25 (quotations, 425). On the historic significance of the Emancipation Proclamation, see Guelzo, *Lincoln's Emancipation Proclamation*.

103 See especially Oakes, "'No Such Right.'" Oakes argued that the Whigs, the Republicans, and Lincoln were pro-capitalist but believed that human beings, including alcoholics, families, and enslaved people, should be shielded from the market's excesses. Lincoln believed in a universal human nature, and thus his and other people's call for an end to slavery can be interpreted as one of the first federal government efforts to restrict the commercialization of nature. Cf. Nash, *Rights of Nature*, esp. 199–213, and Worster, *A Passion for Nature*, 6–11. Nash argued that society extended liberal rights to enslaved blacks and then began to extend those rights to nature. Worster similarly emphasized the expansion of liberal democratic ideals to encompass nature conservation. My point is that Lincoln and other antislavery proponents acknowledged that humans, including blacks, were a form of nature with natural rights and should be protected from privatization and reduction to the status of commodities. In this sense, the original form of nature preservation under modern liberalism was humanity, not wildlife or national parks.

104 McPherson, *Abraham Lincoln*, 48–49.

105 McPherson, *Tried by War*, 202–3 (first quotation); *SW*, 2:498 (second quotation).

106 McPherson, *Tried by War*, 247–49 (quotation, 248); McPherson, *Ordeal by Fire*, 450–56. Beginning in October 1864, the Confederacy abandoned its policy of not exchanging black prisoners.

107 Boritt, *Gettysburg Gospel*, 53, 54, 81, 83, 122, 128, 169–70, photograph after 180.

108 Oakes, *The Radical and the Republican*, 209–75 (quotation, 274); White, *A. Lincoln*, 658–67; Howe, *Making of the American Self*, 136–56. See Myers, *Frederick Douglass*, for a consideration of the political philosophy that Douglass shared with Lincoln.

109   Burlingame, *Abraham Lincoln*, 2:745–51 (first quotation, 748); Guelzo, *Abraham Lincoln: Redeemer President*, 400–403; SW 2:670 (second quotation).

110   U.S. Constitution, amend. 14, sec. 1; amend. 15, sec. 1.

111   SW 2:699.

112   Guelzo, *Lincoln*, 29–30 (first quotation, 30); SW 2:101 (second quotation, with italics added); McPherson, *Tried by War*, 267.

113   McPherson, *Tried by War*, 179 (first quotation); Burlingame, *Abraham Lincoln*, 2:717 (second and third quotations).

114   Donald, *Lincoln*, 26 (first quotation), 27 (second quotation); CW 6:16–17 (second quotation).

115   Burlingame, *Inner World*, 95–96 (quotation, 95). The quotation was from Sarah's brother-in-law.

116   Donald, *Lincoln*, 57–58, 153–54, 608–9n55.

117   Burlingame, *Inner World*, 104, 105.

118   Donald, *Lincoln*, 336–38; Goodwin, *Team of Rivals*, 415–23.

119   Donald, *Lincoln*, 15, 337; Carwardine, "Lincoln's Religion," in Foner, *Our Lincoln*, 229–32.

120   SW 2:199.

121   Burlingame, *Abraham Lincoln*, 2:356; McPherson, *Tried by War*, 111.

122   White, *A. Lincoln*, 658–66; Guelzo, *Abraham Lincoln: Redeemer President*, 416–21; Burlingame, *Abraham Lincoln*, 2:765–72; SW 2:686–87 (quotations, 687).

123   "The Almighty has His own purposes," Lincoln said in his second inaugural address. SW 2:687. On the assassination, see Kauffman, *American Brutus*, 46, 226, photograph following 240, 410n16. Steers, in *Lincoln Assassination Encyclopedia*, 176–77, states that the murder weapon was a .41 caliber cap-and-ball derringer. (Deringer's pistol became known as the derringer, with a double *r*.) Other sources state that it was .44 caliber.

124   SW 2:536. See also Wills, *Lincoln at Gettysburg*, and Boritt, *Gettysburg Gospel*.

125   On Lincoln's modern, technological, telegraphic style, see Wills, *Lincoln at Gettysburg*, 159, 169–75.

126   Boritt, *Gettysburg Gospel*, 37–39; Wills, *Lincoln at Gettysburg*, 20–23, 28–30 (quotation, 30).

127   Donald, *Lincoln*, 463 (quotation); Boritt, *Gettysburg Gospel*, 62 (quotation), 66–68. The story of the rosebuds may be more metaphorically than factually true. It appears in a remembrance of Lincoln published more than two decades after the president traveled to Gettysburg. See Rice, *Reminiscences of Abraham Lincoln*, 511. Both Donald (p. 463) and Boritt (p. 62) relate the story as factual. The original quotation appeared as "Flowrth for the President!" I have modified the spelling slightly for consistency.

5. THE NATURE OF GETTYSBURG

1   See Boritt, *Gettysburg Nobody Knows*; Catton, *Glory Road*; Coco, *Strange and*

Blighted Land; Coddington, *Gettysburg Campaign*; Frassanito, *Early Photography at Gettysburg*; Frassanito, *Gettysburg*; Glatthaar, "Common Soldier's Gettysburg Campaign"; Pfanz, *Gettysburg*; Stewart, *Pickett's Charge*; Tucker, *High Tide at Gettysburg*; and Wheeler, *Witness to Gettysburg*. Shaara, *Killer Angels*, is a historical novel that accurately represents many of the events in the battle. See also the histories and edited compilations of Gary Gallagher and Harry Pfanz. Useful works on the Civil War include McPherson, *Battle Cry of Freedom*; McPherson, *Ordeal by Fire*; Reid, *America's Civil War*; Stoker, *Grand Design*; Weigley, *A Great Civil War*; Catton, *American Heritage Picture History of the Civil War*; Ward, *Civil War*; Commager, *The Blue and The Gray*; Paludan, *A People's Contest*; and Thomas, *Confederate Nation*. McPherson addressed the motivations of Civil War soldiers in *What They Fought For*.

2   In keeping with the conventional view, James McPherson asserted that the Gettysburg battle was "the most crucial battle in American history" and "the largest and most important of the war"; see his *Ordeal by Fire*, 326, and *Battle Cry of Freedom*, 654. In contrast, Richard M. McMurry concluded that other battles were more important and that Gettysburg "had no impact on the outcome of the war." See his "The Pennsylvania Gambit and the Gettysburg Splash," 200. McMurry was correct, to a point. Vicksburg, for example, certainly was as crucial to the course of the war as Gettysburg, if not more so. But by trying to demolish the mystique of Gettysburg, McMurry understated the battle's importance. In addition, Gettysburg is attractive to the historian precisely because of its mystique and precisely because ordinary Americans know more about it than they do about other battles. The battle's very popularity makes it a compelling choice for an environmental history reinterpretation. Brian Holden Reid asserted that such critiques were overstated and that "this battle was a decisive turning point in the Civil War." See Reid, *America's Civil War*, 304.

3   Scholarship on the environmental history of the Civil War is growing. Older studies include Lonn, *Salt as a Factor in the Confederacy*; Massey, *Ersatz in the Confederacy*; Gates, *Agriculture and the Civil War*; Steiner, *Disease in the Civil War*; and Goff, *Confederate Supply*. For more recent work, see Bell, *Mosquito Soldiers*; Brady, "The Wilderness of War"; Hess, *Union Soldier in Battle*, especially chapter 3, "The Nature of Battle"; Kirby, "American Civil War"; McElfresh, *Maps and Mapmakers of the Civil War*; Sharrer, "The Great Glanders Epizootic," 79–97; Sharrer, *A Kind of Fate*; and Steinberg, *Down to Earth*, 89–98. Lisa Brady's forthcoming book on "hard war" and the Civil War promises to become the first comprehensive environmental history of the conflict.

4   I am responsible for recasting the origins of the Civil War as environmental history, of course, but in doing so I have relied on various works, including McPherson, *Battle Cry of Freedom*, 6–307; Ward, *Civil War*, 2–87; Thomas, *Confederate Nation*, 17–66; Foner, *Free Soil, Free Labor, Free Men*; and the chapters by Paul E. Johnson and James McPherson in Murrin et al., *Liberty, Equality, Power*. For provocative summaries of the recent work of cultural and human geographers,

see, for example, Mitchell, *Cultural Geography*, and Johnston et al., *Dictionary of Human Geography*.

5   Paludan, *People's Contest*, 127–69; Gates, *Agriculture and the Civil War*, 129–247; Current, "God and the Strongest Battalions," 15–32. See also Fiege, "Gettysburg and the Organic Nature of the American Civil War."

6   McPherson, in "American Victory, American Defeat," 17–42, 166–68, reviewed the historiography from which an environmental history of the Civil War might proceed. He criticized the simplistic argument that the North won because of its superior resources but acknowledged that its resources and conquest of Confederate territory and resources mattered; that in spite of the Confederacy's ability to mobilize resources, those resources still were deficient and the Confederacy less capable than the North in handling them; that shortages and malnutrition in the Confederacy weakened it; and that Lincoln's superiority as a wartime leader might be explained, in part, by the "ill health" and frequent "sickness" of Jefferson Davis. McPherson urged historians to focus on the interplay of contingent events that explain the South's defeat.

Scholars pursuing the environmental history of the Civil War might also examine older and more recent works that assess the Civil War in the broadest of contexts; see, for example, Beringer et al., *Why the South Lost the Civil War*, and McCurry, *Confederate Reckoning*. They might read the work of McPherson, Beringer, McCurry, and others in light of the conceptual thought of environmental historians. See, for example, Worster, "Transformations of the Earth," which discusses subsistence and capitalist agroecological modes of production. Although both the Union and the Confederacy relied on capitalist modes, each side's mode had distinctive economic and ecological features, and each side oriented its mode toward military ends. The Civil War might be interpreted not simply as a contest of capitalist agroecological modes but as a conflict between military modes of production.

7   McPherson, *Ordeal by Fire*, 184–88.

8   Goff, *Confederate Supply*, 31, 63, 135; Gates, *Agriculture and the Civil War*, 6–7, 13–14; Stoker, *Grand Design*, 27–28.

9   Unless otherwise specifically noted, the problems of Southern subsistence are covered in Gates, *Agriculture and the Civil War*, 3–126; Thomas, *Confederate Nation*, 1–16, 120–44, 190–214; McPherson, *Battle Cry of Freedom*, 611–25; Blair, *Virginia's Private War*, 3–107; and Massey, *Ersatz in the Confederacy*. Bell, in *Mosquito Soldiers*, 115, explained the Confederacy's inability to supply its troops with quinine, in contrast to the vast quantities supplied to Union forces.

10 Stoker, *Grand Design*, 26–27.

11 Ibid., 24; Reid, *America's Civil War*, 35; Goff, *Confederate Supply*, 17–24, 39–43, 49, 54, 65, 89, 140, 175, 184, 240–41, 242–51.

12 McPherson, *Ordeal by Fire*, 184–88; Brady, "War upon the Land."

13 Reid, *America's Civil War*, 284–86 (quotations, 285).

14 Gates, *Agriculture and the Civil War*, especially 13–27.

15 Stoker, *Grand Design*, 27–30, 104; Goff, *Confederate Supply*, 45–46.

16 For figures on the reduction of land in production and for a map depicting the Confederacy's radical loss of space to Union military forces, see Gates, *Agriculture and the Civil War*, 118, 126. Lincoln himself noted the importance of Vicksburg to the movement of resources: "We can take all the northern ports from the Confederacy, and they can still defy us from Vicksburg. It means hog and hominy without limit, fresh troops from the states of the far South, and a cotton country where they can raise the staple without interference." Quoted in Ward, *Civil War*, 212. I have drawn the term *contraction* from language that Confederates used to describe their loss of productive land. Conveying an order from General Lee, General R. H. Chilton wrote of "the contracted limits of cultivated country," for example. See *War of the Rebellion* (hereafter *OR*), series 1, vol. 25, part 2, 708. Technically, Port Hudson, Louisiana, was the last Confederate stronghold on the Mississippi River to surrender.

17 Gates, *Agriculture and the Civil War*, 57–59, 73–83, 91–95, 111–15, 118–25.

18 Ibid., 29, 56, 61, 67–68, 86–87, 90–92; Goff, *Confederate Supply*, 37, 78; Sharrer, "The Great Glanders Epizootic."

19 Gates, *Agriculture and the Civil War*, 67–68, 80–81; Lonn, *Salt as a Factor in the Confederacy*, 13–34, 188–203, 221–30.

20 Gates, *Agriculture in the Civil War*, 116; Blair, *Virginia's Private War*, 89; Massey, *Ersatz in the Confederacy*, 80–83; McPherson, *Battle Cry of Freedom*, 611–25; Weigley, *A Great Civil War*, 218; Catton, *Glory Road*, 273.

21 *OR*, series 1, vol. 25, part 2, 598, 605–6, 627, 658, 666, 680–82, 686–88, 689–90, 695, 701–2, 703, 709, 730, 735–36, 747–49, 793; Dowdey, *Wartime Papers of R. E. Lee*, 328, 400–410, 417–19, 434–35, 450–51, 551; Freeman, *R. E. Lee*, 2:415–17, 475–507, 3:245–53.

22 *OR*, series 1, vol. 25, part 2, 730; Dowdey, *Wartime Papers of R. E. Lee*, 418–19; Freeman, *R. E. Lee*, 2:494; Catton, *Glory Road*, 93–94, 122–23, 158–61; Adams quoted in Steiner, *Disease in the Civil War*, 17.

23 *OR*, series 1, vol. 25, part 2, 605–6, 627, 680–82, 689–90, 695, 701–2, 709, 747–49, 765, 793; Dowdey, *Wartime Papers of R. E. Lee*, 400–410, 551; Freeman, *R. E. Lee*, 2:417, 484, 491–92, 3:251–53; Ramsdell, "General Robert E. Lee's Horse Supply," 758–64; McPherson, *Battle Cry of Freedom*, 638–39; Coddington, *Gettysburg Campaign*, 16. See also Greene, *Horses at Work*, 118–63.

24 Blair, *Virginia's Private War*, 73–76; Thomas, *Confederate Nation*, 202–6; McPherson, *Battle Cry of Freedom*, 617–19.

25 *OR*, series 1, vol. 25, part 2, 684–85, 700–701, 710–12, 724–26; McPherson, *Battle Cry of Freedom*, 638–39; Gates, *Agriculture and the Civil War*, 95–96; Freeman, *R. E. Lee*, 2:492.

26 Blair, *Virginia's Private War*, 86–87; Coddington, *Gettysburg Campaign*, 3–25; McPherson, *Battle Cry of Freedom*, 638–48; Tucker, *High Tide at Gettysburg*, 17–20; Ward, *Civil War*, 214; Weigley, *A Great Civil War*, 229–30; Wheeler, *Witness to Gettysburg*, 1–18. In late summer 1862, Lee had attempted a similar strategy by

leading his army into Maryland and ultimately to the battle of Antietam. Commager, *The Blue and the Gray*, 1:171.

27 Catton, *American Heritage Picture History of the Civil War*, 291–92, 297–306; McPherson, *Battle Cry of Freedom*, 639–47; Ward, *Civil War*, 201–11; Weigley, *A Great Civil War*, 223–29.

28 "Terrain is not neutral—it either helps or hinders each of the opposed forces." U.S. Army, *Field Manual 100-5* (Washington, D.C.: Department of the Army, 1993), quoted in Winters et al., *Battling the Elements*, 113. For an earth scientist's view of Gettysburg, see Brown, *Geology and the Gettysburg Campaign*. See also Winters et al., *Battling the Elements*, 126–23.

29 The planning and execution of the Gettysburg campaign are covered in Coddington, *Gettysburg Campaign*, 3–25, 47–102, 105–7, 125. Lee and his commanders also had to deal with the problems of resource scarcity and supply on their way north. See Coddington, *Gettysburg Campaign*, 17, 22–23, 105–7, 603–4n31; Dowdey, *Wartime Papers of R. E. Lee*, 510, 520–30.

30 Miller, *Mapping for Stonewall*, is the single best source. McElfresh, in *Maps and Mapmakers of the Civil War*, superbly covered the work of engineers and mapmakers in relation to topography and other environmental conditions. Hotchkiss's map is reproduced on pp. 128–29. For engineers' attitudes toward nature, see, for example, Merritt, *Engineering in American Society*, especially chapter 5, "The Manipulators of Nature."

31 OR, series 1, vol. 25, part 2, 810–11; Coddington, *Gettysburg Campaign*, 11, 22, 125.

32 Coco, *Strange and Blighted Land*, 2; Commager, *The Blue and the Gray*, 2:595; Glatthaar, "Common Soldier's Gettysburg Campaign," 9; Glatthaar, *General Lee's Army*, 269–73; Mitchell, *Civil War Soldiers*, 148–57.

33 The best account is Brown, *Retreat from Gettysburg*, 12–36, but see also Coddington, *Gettysburg Campaign*, 23, 153–79; Commager, *The Blue and the Gray*, 2:594–96; Frassanito, *Early Photography at Gettysburg*, 150–52; Glatthaar, "Common Soldier's Gettysburg Campaign," 7–11; Glatthaar, *General Lee's Army*, 271–72; Magner, *Traveller and Company*, 17–21; McPherson, *Battle Cry of Freedom*, 649–50; and Tucker, *High Tide at Gettysburg*, 27–30. The Pennsylvania woman is quoted in Ward, *Civil War*, 215.

34 Furtwangler, *Acts of Discovery*, 108. The title of chapter 5, "Ingesting America," is suggestive. On Lee and plundering, see, for example, Brown, *Retreat from Gettysburg*, 33, 35.

35 Coddington, *Gettysburg Campaign*, 26–133.

36 Brown, *Retreat from Gettysburg*, 17–36.

37 Reid, *America's Civil War*, 285–302, 310n44; Stoker, *Grand Design*, 296–98; Brown, *Retreat from Gettysburg*, 31–40, 47–66.

38 Historians have described, analyzed, and debated the battle of Gettysburg in extraordinarily fine detail. Unless otherwise noted, I have drawn information for my narrative from the following sources: Coddington, *Gettysburg Campaign*, 180–574; Commager, *The Blue and the Gray*, 2:596–639; Frassanito, *Gettysburg*;

Luvaas and Nelson, *Guide to the Battle of Gettysburg*; McPherson, *Battle Cry of Freedom*, 646–65; Pfanz, *Gettysburg*; Stewart, *Pickett's Charge*; Ward, *Civil War*, 214–37; Wheeler, *Witness to Gettysburg*, 77–258; and Weigley, *A Great Civil War*, 236–56. In particular, see Brown, *Retreat from Gettysburg*, 12–49, and Reid, *America's Civil War*, 265–305. Also see Sears, *Gettysburg*, and Trudeau, *Gettysburg*.

39 Howard's description of the terrain is typical of post-battle reports and reveals the importance of topography to military tactics: "After an examination of the general features of the country, I came to the conclusion that the only tenable position for my limited force was the ridge to the southeast of Gettysburg, now so well known as Cemetery Ridge. The highest point at the cemetery commanded every eminence within easy range. The slopes toward the west and south were gradual, and could be completely swept by artillery. To the north, the ridge was broken by a ravine running transversely." OR, series 1, vol. 27, part 1, 702. Dawn the following day brought sufficient light for Lee and Longstreet to study the Union positions and gain "a general idea of the nature of the ground." Quoted in Trudeau, *Gettysburg*, 279.

40 OR, series 1, vol. 27, part 2, 299, 307–8, 309, 318; Wheeler, *Witness to Gettysburg*, 171–73; Weigley, *A Great Civil War*, 246; McPherson, *Ordeal by Fire*, 38; Sears, *Gettysburg*, 234–39; Trudeau, *Gettysburg*, 252–53, 267–68, 278–79.

41 OR, series 1, vol. 27, part 2, 299, 307–8 (Lee first quotation, 308), 309, 318; Stoker, *Grand Design*, 297–98; Brown, *Retreat from Gettysburg*, 38; Reid, *America's Civil War*, 301–2; McPherson, *Ordeal by Fire*, 328; McPherson, *Battle Cry of Freedom*, 656 (Lee second quotation).

42 Weigley, *A Great Civil War*, 245, 246, 248–49; McPherson, *Battle Cry of Freedom*, 657; Reid, *America's Civil War*, 293–94; Brown, *Retreat from Gettysburg*, 44.

43 For good descriptions of Little Round Top's topography, see OR, series 1, vol. 27, part 2, 391–416 (Hillyer's words appear on 399–400), and passim; and Frassanito, *Early Photography at Gettysburg*, 242–43. "In fact," General John Bell Hood remembered, "it seemed to me that the enemy occupied a position by nature so strong—I may say impregnable—that, independently of their flank-fire, they could easily repel our attack by merely throwing and rolling stones down the mountain side as we approached." See Hood's account in Commager, *The Blue and the Gray*, 2:608–12. See also the account of Joshua Lawrence Chamberlain in Nesbitt, *Through Blood and Fire*, 64–115.

44 OR, series 1, vol. 27, part 1, 824–32, 855–57, part 2, 504; Frassanito, *Early Photography at Gettysburg*, 194–211; "Defense of Culp's Hill," National Park Service interpretive sign at Culp's Hill, Gettysburg National Military Park, Pennsylvania.

45 Quotation in Stewart, *Pickett's Charge*, 69.

46 Quotations in ibid., 183, 204; Ward, *Civil War*, 232; and Commager, *The Blue and the Gray*, 2:631. See also Rollins, *Pickett's Charge*.

47 Quotation in Stewart, *Pickett's Charge*, 199.

48 Casualty figures differ somewhat. See, for example, McPherson, *Ordeal by Fire*, 331; Stoker, *Grand Design*, 298; Sears, *Gettysburg*, 496, 498, 513; and Trudeau,

Gettysburg, 529. Scholars also disagree in their overall assessments of the campaign. "The Gettysburg campaign was a disaster for the Confederacy and gained them nothing," according to Stoker, *Grand Design*, 302. "Although the battle of Gettysburg indeed was a Confederate loss," concluded Brown in *Retreat from Gettysburg*, 387–88, "the invasion of Pennsylvania may not have been."

49 Quotation in Coco, *Strange and Blighted Land*, 40. Unless otherwise noted, my account of the battle's aftermath draws from Coco and from Frassanito, *Early Photography at Gettysburg*. Coco's work features page after page of extremely graphic descriptions of the battlefield after the fighting, often employing extended quotations from primary sources. On the nation's experience of Civil War death, see Faust, *This Republic of Suffering*.

50 The contents of Confederate haversacks are described in Coco, *Strange and Blighted Land*, 26, 29, 31, 33, 41, 51, 52, 60, 77, 277–79, 363.

51 Battlefield descriptions, including those of bodies, tears, vomiting, flies, hogs, and wounded men, are from Coco, *Strange and Blighted Land*, 6–84, and Frassanito, *Early Photography at Gettysburg*, 331–32, 340–41. The figure of about three thousand dead horses is probably conservative. On horses, see Magner, *Traveller and Company*, 35–40; Frassanito, *Gettysburg*, 150; and Coco, *Strange and Blighted Land*, 313–15. Coco calculated the total weight of dead humans and animals to have been about six million pounds, or three thousand tons.

52 Coco described the field hospitals in *Strange and Blighted Land*, 153–253. On Civil War medicine, see Adams, *Doctors in Blue*, and Cunningham, *Doctors in Gray*. My narrative is based closely on General Carl Schurz's description in Commager, *The Blue and the Gray*, 2:790–91.

53 Nobody knows exactly what the dying men thought about, of course, but in their delirium they might have imagined peaceful places. See, for example, General "Stonewall" Jackson's final words after receiving a mortal wound at Chancellorsville: "Let us cross the river and rest under the shade of the trees." Quoted in Ward, *Civil War*, 211. Nineteenth-century people viewed death as a passage or journey. Colonel Joshua Lawrence Chamberlain, for example, wrote of "the bridge of life and death" and recalled a brave dead soldier whom he looked forward to meeting again "on whatever shore." Nesbitt, *Through Blood and Fire*, 66, 72.

54 Coco, *Strange and Blighted Land*, 17–18, 48 (quotation), 52.

55 Linenthal, *Sacred Ground*, 89.

56 I have constructed this interpretation using Steiner, *Disease in the Civil War*, 13, 33–34; Adams, *Doctors in Blue*, 223; Cunningham, *Doctors in Gray*, 165–66; and Catton, *Glory Road*, 122–23.

57 On railroads in the Gettysburg campaign, see Coddington, *Gettysburg Campaign*, 22–23, 148, 170–72; in the Civil War, see Turner, *Victory Rode the Rails*. In fact, the failure of railroads to move supplies exacerbated the resource scarcity and crisis that culminated in the Gettysburg campaign. See, for example, Massey, *Ersatz in the Confederacy*, 15–16, 125–27, 133–34, and Ramsdell, "General Robert E. Lee's Horse Supply," 760, 764.

58   Lee quoted in Tucker, *High Tide at Gettysburg*, 18. See also Coddington, *Gettysburg Campaign*, 159, and Sellers, "Thoreau's Body," 486–514.

59   Catton, *Glory Road*, 40, 42–43, 123–24, 179–80, 254–62. On the Union's production and supply systems, see Wilson, *Business of Civil War*, and Bacon, *Sinews of War*.

60   Brown, *Retreat from Gettysburg*, 45, 47. The Union furnished its armies with some one million horses and mules at a cost of "well over $100 million." The cost of acquiring and maintaining large numbers of horses and mules "account[ed] for a large fraction of the army budget." Wilson, *Business of War*, 1, 140, 204, 267n95.

61   Catton, *Glory Road*, 180; Blair, *Virginia's Private War*, 86; McPherson, *Ordeal by Fire*, 186. President Lincoln and some of his generals complained about the material "impedimenta" that constrained the movement of Union forces. Eventually, the exigencies of war and Lincoln's desire for faster, more aggressive campaigns favored commanders such as Ulysses Grant, whose personal habits were consistent with his military practice. During one campaign, an observer noticed that his "entire baggage consisted of a tooth-brush." See McPherson, *Tried by War*, 137 (first quotation), 155, 170 (second quotation). On the Confederacy's demise, see Thomas, *Confederate Nation*, chapter 7, "The Death of the Nation."

62   Unless otherwise noted, my account of Gettysburg's commemoration draws from Coco, *Strange and Blighted Land*, 367–73; Frassanito, *Early Photography at Gettysburg*, 142–46, 257, 265; Kinsel, "From Turning Point to Peace Memorial," 203–22; and especially Linenthal, *Sacred Ground*, 87–126.

63   The contrasts as well as the similarities between the historic and modern Gettysburg landscapes are most strikingly revealed through the juxtaposition of old and new photographs, using the technique of repeat photography; see Frassanito, *Gettysburg*, and Frassanito, *Early Photography at Gettysburg*. On tourists at Culp's Hill, see Frassanito, *Early Photography at Gettysburg*, 195.

64   Catton, *Glory Road*, 345; Sellars, "Granite Orchards of Gettysburg," 21.

65   Linenthal, *Sacred Ground*, 117.

66   This paragraph is based on personal experience and on conversations with people who have visited the battlefield.

67   Weigley, *A Great Civil War*, xiv. See also McPherson, "Gettysburg."

6. IRON HORSES

1   Among the many histories of the transcontinental railroad, I have consulted Ames, *Pioneering the Union Pacific*; Athearn, *Union Pacific Country*; Bain, *Empire Express*; Best, *Iron Horses to Promontory*; Combs, *Westward to Promontory*; Davis, *Union Pacific Railway*; Galloway, *First Transcontinental Railroad*; Griswold, *Work of Giants*; Hogg, *Union Pacific*; Howard, *Great Iron Trail*; Klein, *Union Pacific*; Kraus, *High Road to Promontory*; Mayer and Vose, *Makin' Tracks*; McCague, *Moguls and Iron Men*; Raymond and Fike, *Rails East to Promontory*; Sabin, *Building the Pacific Railway*; Utley and Ketterson, *Golden Spike National Historic Site*; and Williams,

Great and Shining Road. I also relied on Beebe and Clegg, *Hear the Train Blow*, and Kratville, *Golden Rails*, both masterpieces of the pictorial history genre. Finally, there are a number of excellent World Wide Web sites with photographs, maps, documents, articles, and books on the first transcontinental railroad. See, for example, the sites for the Central Pacific Photographic History Museum, http://cprr.org/, and the Golden Spike National Historic Site, www.nps.gov/gosp/home.html. Orsi, *Sunset Limited*, 3–17, is the single best summary of the Central Pacific's construction and a model environmental history of the corporation that evolved into the Southern Pacific. Briggs, in *Power of Steam*, provides a global perspective.

    For detailed discussions of the Promontory Summit ceremony, see Anderson, "Driving of the Golden Spike"; Best, "Rendezvous at Promontory," 69–75; Bowman, "Driving the Last Spike at Promontory," 76–101; Ketterson, "Golden Spike National Historic Site," 58–68; Bain, *Empire Express*, 645–72; Klein, *Union Pacific*, 217–28; Kraus, *High Road to Promontory*, 262–85; Williams, *Great and Shining Road*, 244–68; and especially Francaviglia, *Over the Range*, 101–42.

2   Williams, *Great and Shining Road*, 264 (quotation). Okihiro, in *Common Ground*, especially chapter 1, "West and East," laid out themes that suggest how the transcontinental railroad might be imagined as an episode in imperial and transnational history.

3   See especially Bain, *Empire Express*, 658–59; Best, "Rendezvous at Promontory"; Bowman, "Driving the Last Spike"; Ketterson, "Golden Spike National Historic Site"; and Kraus, *High Road to Promontory*, 262–85. On basic features of steam-powered locomotives, including the American Standard 4-4-0, see White, *American Locomotives*, 25–27, 93–235, 422–26.

4   Todd quoted in Kraus, *High Road to Promontory*, 274.

5   Dodge quoted in Bain, *Empire Express*, 666. See also Kraus, *High Road to Promontory*, 279; Mayer and Vose, *Makin' Tracks*, 195; and Sabin, *Building the Pacific Railway*, 220.

6   Bain, *Empire Express*, 662–63, 756n31; Bowman, "Driving the Last Spike"; Orsi, *Sunset Limited*, 17.

7   Bain, *Empire Express*, 663–69; Kraus, *High Road to Promontory*, 279–81; Sabin, *Building the Pacific Railway*, 223–24; Williams, *Great and Shining Road*, 267.

8   The photograph appears in virtually every book on the Pacific railroad and in many texts on U.S. and western U.S. history. See, for example, Mayer and Vose, *Makin' Tracks*, 202–3. Bain described the moment in *Empire Express*, 667.

9   Schobert, *Energy and Society*; 114–26; Lamb, *Perfecting the American Steam Locomotive*, 1–3, 15–24, 33–46, 175–81, especially chapter 3, "The Physics of Steam Power"; Francaviglia, *Over the Range*, 116–21.

10   Pyne, in *Fire in America*, 3–5, 34–44, described the ecological complexity of fire and the "confined forms of fire" characteristic of machinery, and in the process suggested other connections between railroads and the Earth's substances and processes. Orsi, in *Sunset Limited*, 169–72, proposed water, the other major

component of steam, as a principle theme of western railroad history. The Central Pacific's and Union Pacific's reliance on wood influenced the last spike ceremony in subtler ways. The Central Pacific originally scheduled the *Antelope* for the ceremony, but workmen in the Sierra Nevada, unaware of the locomotive's approach, rolled a log down a slope and it landed on the tracks. The resulting collision damaged the *Antelope* and took it out of commission, so Central Pacific officials assigned the *Jupiter* to the ceremony. The Union Pacific, too, had scheduled another locomotive for the event, but hundreds of striking tie cutters in Wyoming surrounded and delayed the engine, preventing its participation and opening the way for the *No. 119*. See USDI/NPS, *Everlasting Steam*; Bain, *Empire Express*, 646–50.

11 On the importance of muscle power, see Schobert, *Energy and Society*, 1–32, and Smil, *Energy in Nature and Society*, 119–80. The inventor James Watt derived the concept of horsepower from the amount of work a large draft horse—a brewery horse—could do in pulling or lifting a load. In Watt's calculus, work was the product of force and distance, and power was the rate of doing work. One horsepower, therefore, was a "unit of power equal to 746 watts or 33,000 foot pounds per minute." See Nye, *Consuming Power*, 22, and Schobert, *Energy and Society*, 123, 625.

12 On the various motivations and plans for a Pacific railroad, see Bain, *Empire Express*, 3–77; Francaviglia and Bryan, "'Are We Chimerical in This Opinion?'" (quotations, 196); Galloway, *First Transcontinental Railroad*, 27–51; Haney, *A Congressional History of Railways in the United States*; Meinig, *Shaping of America,* vol. 3, *Transcontinental America*, 3–28; Sabin, *Building the Pacific Railway*, 13–40; Utley and Ketterson, *Golden Spike*, 1–4; and Williams, *Great and Shining Road*, 6–19. For a volume that examines the concept of railway imperialism but overlooks the U.S. transcontinental railroads as examples of this phenomenon, see Davis and Wilburn, *Railway Imperialism*.

13 Bain, *Empire Express*, 28 (Whitney quotation); Haney, *Congressional History*, 1:248 (*Public Ledger* quotation); Gilpin, "Observations on the Pacific Railroad," 261. White, in *It's Your Misfortune and None of My Own*, 61–210, covered these and other major events in U.S. westward expansion.

14 Boime, *Magisterial Gaze*; Sabin, *Building the Pacific Railway*, 19 (Benton quotation).

15 Bain, *Empire Express*, 26–53; Meinig, *Transcontinental America*, 8–19; Potter, *Impending Crisis*, 145–76; Williams, *Great and Shining Road*, 6–28.

16 Goetzmann, *Army Exploration in the American West*, 262–63.

17 Ibid., 262–304, covers the railroad surveys and the resulting paralysis.

18 Klein, *Union Pacific*, 11–13; Meinig, *Transcontinental America*, 6–7 (quotation, 7).

19 Ames, *Pioneering the Union Pacific*, 11–17, 30–32; Bain, *Empire Express*, 104–18; Orsi, *Sunset Limited*, 9–14; Haney, *Congressional History*, 2:49–75; Kraus, *High Road to Promontory*, 40–49; Utley and Ketterson, *Golden Spike*, 4–8; Williams, *Great and Shining Road*, 42–48; Commager, *Documents of American History*, 411–12.

20 The tougher nature became, the greater the difficulty and expense of completing the miles of track that would bring the government loans, acres of public land, confidence of investors, and ultimately revenue from passenger tickets and freight charges. On this general feature of capitalism and nature, see Henderson, *California and the Fictions of Capital*, ix–80; on its relationship to the building of the Pacific Railroad, see, for example, Bain, *Empire Express*, 246–47; Griswold, *Work of Giants*, 20–61; and Williams, *Great and Shining Road*, 46, 203–7. According to Orsi, in *Sunset Limited*, 14, "the 1864 law reduced the federal bond loan to a second mortgage and allowed the railways to sell their own first-mortgage bonds equal in amount to the government subsidy, thereby doubling the companies' potential construction capital."

21 Dodge quoted in Bain, *Empire Express*, 158, and Griswold, *Work of Giants*, 49.

22 Bain, *Empire Express*, 57–84; Kraus, *High Road to Promontory*, 13–31.

23 Bain, *Empire Express*, 85–103 ("most difficult country," 97); Kraus, *High Road to Promontory*, 32–38. See also Judah, *A Practical Plan for Building the Pacific Railroad*, 6–8 (quotations).

24 Bain, *Empire Express*, 94–102 (quotation, 100); Judah, *Practical Plan*, 18–19.

25 Judah originally projected the line to run 81 miles from Sacramento to the summit, with a total elevation gain of 7,027 feet above the top of the levee at Sacramento. Deviating somewhat from Judah's original plan, the completed railroad line ran 105.5 miles to Summit Tunnel at the top of Donner Pass. Bain, *Empire Express*, 99, 102; Kraus, *High Road to Promontory*, 36 (quotation), 46–47, 55, 70, 75.

26 Griswold, *Work of Giants*, 30–32; Bain, *Empire Express*, 134–42.

27 Griswold, *Work of Giants*, 37; Bain, *Empire Express*, 144–42.

28 Klein, *Union Pacific*, 17–64; Utley and Ketterson, *Golden Spike*, 6–7.

29 Klein, *Union Pacific*, 51–64, 76–79, 99–107, 117–21, 151–52; Bain, *Empire Express*, 192; Dodge, *How We Built the Union Pacific Railway*, 11–13.

30 Klein, *Union Pacific*, 51–64, 76–79, 99–107, 117–21; Bain, *Empire Express*, 232; Dodge, *How We Built the Union Pacific Railway*, 13.

31 Klein, *Union Pacific*, 52–54 (quotations 53, 54); Bain, *Empire Express*, 184 (quotation). See also the photograph in Kraus, *High Road to Promontory*, 180, of James Strobridge, the Central Pacific's construction superintendent, and his children in a boat on Donner Lake in the Sierra Nevada. To say that railroads swept wilderness aside is, of course, a relative judgment. Although they were responsible for massive environmental changes in the West, some railroads also promoted wilderness preservation. See, for example, Orsi, *Sunset Limited*, 349–75.

32 Klein, *Union Pacific*, 78; Bain, *Empire Express*, 158 (Dodge quotation), 232–33. Evidently, locating the eastern base of the Rockies was not as great an issue for the Union Pacific as determining the western base of the Sierra Nevada was for the Central Pacific. The Pacific Railway Act stipulated that the mountain miles of the Union Pacific would begin somewhere in Wyoming Territory. See Bain, *Empire Express*, 118, 303.

33 Kraus, *High Road to Promontory*, 58, 60, 72, 78, 87, 93, 107, 114–15; Bain, *Empire Express*, 173, 219.

34 Ames, *Pioneering the Union Pacific*, 41, 45; Griswold, *Work of Giants*, 95; Klein, *Union Pacific*, 65, 70, 71, 74, 76.

35 On the complex connections among sites of extraction, production, construction, and consumption, see Cronon, *Nature's Metropolis*, and Tucker, *Insatiable Appetite*.

36 Gordon, *American Iron*, 7–170; Gordon and Malone, *Texture of Industry*, 57–175; Warren, *American Steel Industry*, 1–64. On ironmaking and the environment in a specific place, see Gordon, *A Landscape Transformed*.

37 On the manufacture of Pacific Railroad locomotives, rails, and other iron material, see Bain, *Empire Express*, 175, 177, 279; Best, *Iron Horses to Promontory*, 163–84; Griswold, *Work of Giants*, 22–23, 82–83, 113; Klein, *Union Pacific*, 137; and Kraus, *High Road to Promontory*, 51, 69; USDI/NPS, *Everlasting Steam*.

38 Bain, *Empire Express*, 65, 472; Griswold, *Work of Giants*, 22–23, 38, 82–83; Mayer and Vose, *Makin' Tracks*, 16; Sabin, *Building the Pacific Railway*, 98–100.

39 Williams, in *Americans and Their Forests*, 344–52 (quotation, 352), explained the intensive use of wood by American railroads during the nineteenth century.

40 Bain, *Empire Express*, 223, 239, 363, 429, 430; Sabin, *Building the Pacific Railway*, 185; Galloway, *First Transcontinental Railroad*, 142, 143; Griswold, *Work of Giants*, 22, 117; Williams, *Great and Shining Road*, 109, 115, 130, 163–64, 185–86; *Sacramento Daily Union*, 1 May 1865, www.cprr.org/Museum/Newspapers.

41 Klein, *Union Pacific*, 69, 137, 138, 160, 192, 193; Bain, *Empire Express*, 182, 241–42, 259, 304, 377, 430; Ames, *Pioneering the Union Pacific*, 118, 157, 289; Sabin, *Building the Pacific Railway*, 100, 143, 155, 172; Athearn, *Union Pacific Country*, 43–44 (quotation, 43); Galloway, *First Transcontinental Railroad*, 271–73, 276–77; Griswold, *Work of Giants*, 136; Williams, *Great and Shining Road*, 147, 197.

42 Ames, *Pioneering the Union Pacific*, 118, 157; Bain, *Empire Express*, 182, 241–42, 514, 586–87; Galloway, *First Transcontinental Railroad*, 271–73; Klein, *Union Pacific*, 69, 137, 138, 192, 193; Sabin, *Building the Pacific Railway*, 143; Cronon, *Nature's Metropolis*, 148–206.

43 See especially Wrigley, *Continuity, Chance, and Change*, 7–97. See also Marks, *Origins of the Modern World*, 22–32, 38–39, 101–2, 104–5, 106, 110–11, 118, 126, 135, 136, 148, 156, 160; Braudel, *Civilization and Capitalism*, 1:157–69, 224–35; Hunter, *History of Industrial Power in the United States*, 2:412–15; Burke, "The Big Story"; Jones, "Landscape of Energy Abundance"; Nye, *Consuming Power*, 39–40, 43–68, 75–83; and Sieferle, *Subterranean Forest*, 78–137.

44 On these technological changes generally, see Smil, *Energy in Nature and Society*, 180–88, 196–202, and Belich, *Replenishing the Earth*, 9–10, 106–14, 555–56.

45 On the history of muscle power (sometimes called animate power), see Braudel, *Civilization and Capitalism*, 1:337–52; Hunter and Bryant, *History of Industrial Power in the United States*, 3:3–52; Smil, *Energies*, 110–17; and Smil, *Energy in World History*, 40–47, 92–102. See also White, *Organic Machine*. Andrews, in *Killing for*

Coal, 163, discussed "the embodied knowledge of mineworkers and mules." In Hard Traveling, especially the chapter "Human Machines," Schwantes interpreted massed muscle power in the context of mechanization, as did Montgomery in Fall of the House of Labor, 60–63. For general descriptions of Pacific railroad labor, see Bissell, "Reminiscences of Hezekiah Bissell"; Dick, Vanguards of the Frontier, 368–89; Gilliss, "Tunnels of the Pacific Railroad," 155–71; Haycox, "'A Very Exclusive Party,'" 20–35; Kraus, "Central Pacific Construction Vignettes," 45–61; Kraus, "Chinese Laborers and the Construction of the Central Pacific," 41–57; Lockwood, "With the Casement Brothers while Building the Union Pacific," 3–4, 24, 36; Saxton, "The Army of Canton in the High Sierra," 27–36; and Yen, "Chinese Workers and the First Transcontinental Railroad of the United States of America." For descriptions of work processes and construction activities, see Ames, Pioneering the Union Pacific; Bain, Empire Express; Kraus, High Road to Promontory; Klein, Union Pacific; Mayer and Vose, Makin' Tracks; and Kibbey, Railroad Photographs of Alfred A. Hart.

46 Williams, in Great and Shining Road, 178, explained the Union Pacific's transition to using coal as an energy source. See also Bain, Empire Express, 156, 303, 430, 474, 508, 595; Klein, Union Pacific, 55–56, 78, 116, 149, 161, 171. On the use of wood and coal by the railroads, and on the locomotive technologies designed for each fuel, see White, American Locomotives, 83–90, 102, 114. See also Melosi, Coping with Abundance, 24–27; and Nye, Consuming Power, 77–78.

47 Industrialization and railroad locomotion increased rather than decreased urbanizing America's need for horse power, and the United States' horse population increased from some 8.7 million animals in 1870 to some 24 million in 1900. See McShane and Tarr, "Centrality of the Horse in the Nineteenth Century American City," 105–30, and Briggs, Power of Steam, 107-108. See also Greene, Horses at Work, 164–99, and Essin, "Mule," 747. Barclay, in Role of the Horse in Man's Culture, 157–61, 339–40, focused on the global picture and observed (p. 339) that the population of domesticated horses worldwide "probably reached its peak about 1910–1920 when it was in the neighborhood of 110 million." The number of farm horses and mules in the United States followed a similar trend, reaching a peak of some 25.2 million animals in 1920. Thereafter the number steadily fell. See U.S. Department of Commerce, Fifteenth Census of the United States, 562.

Craig, in "Horse Soldiers," showed that stereotypically modern, industrialized conflicts used substantial quantities of animal power. Keegan, in Illustrated History of the First World War, 162, pointed out that the conflict stimulated horse production and that fodder for horses "was the largest single item, by bulk, of stores shipped by all armies throughout the war." Essin, in "Mule," surveyed the history of mules in the American West and called the animals "empire builders" (p. 745) but offered little information about their importance to railroad construction. On common laborers in the world's industrial capitalist economy, see Wolf, Europe and the People without History, 354–83; Montgomery, Fall of the House of Labor, 58–111; and Schwantes, Hard Traveling, xi–78. White, in Organic Machine (e.g., 108–13), suggested the ways in which machines are not just metaphorically organic (the "iron horse") but are literal embodiments of complex relationships between human activities and nature, including organic nature.

48 Marks, *Origins of the Modern World*, 102–7; Marks, "Commercialization without Capitalism," 56–82; Kraus, "Chinese Laborers and the Construction of the Central Pacific"; Chan, *This Bittersweet Soil*, 7–31; Chen, *Chinese of America*, 3–78; Williams, *Great and Shining Road*, 95; McCaffrey, *Irish Diaspora in America*, 59–69; Warrin and Gomes, *Land, as Far as the Eye Can See*, 18–32, 77–83, 134–39. On the environmental circumstances of the Civil War, see chapter 5.

49 See, for example, Bain, *Empire Express*, 221–22, 307, 331, 376, 448, 501, 520–21; Bissell, "Reminiscences," 64–65; Klein, *Union Pacific*, 150–51, 161, 180; Kraus, "Central Pacific Construction Vignettes"; Mayer and Vose, *Makin' Tracks*, 32, 38, 84–85; and Williams, *Great and Shining Road*, 96–99, 124, 125, 126.

50 Bain, *Empire Express*, 606–7; Klein, *Union Pacific*, 100–101; Kraus, *High Road to Promontory*, 221; Mayer and Vose, *Makin' Tracks*, 78 (Warman quotation); Williams, *Great and Shining Road*, 126–27.

51 The numbers of laborers given by historians are inconsistent. See, however, Galloway, *First Transcontinental Railroad*, 302; Kraus, *High Road to Promontory*, 125, 141; Sabin, *Building the Pacific Railway*, 170–71; Utley and Ketterson, *Golden Spike*, 17, 21; Yen, "Chinese Workers," 114; and Orsi, *Sunset Limited*, 16, which says that "more than 14,000 men" worked on the Central Pacific. See also the descriptions of massed human and animal muscle power in "Building of the Iron Road" and in Kraus, "Union Pacific Construction Vignettes." On the Civil War and military influence, see Francaviglia, *Over the Range*, 56; Nye, *Consuming Power*, 107; Bain, *Empire Express*, 158–62, 253–55, 261–65, 307, 370–71, 389, 527–28, 639–40; and Dodge, *How We Built the Union Pacific Railway*, 13–14 (quotation), 29–32.

52 John Charles Currier diary, 7 May 1869; the account of the journalist is in Mayer and Vose, *Makin' Tracks*, 76.

53 Bain, *Empire Express*, 272–75, 315–16, 320–21; Kraus, *High Road to Promontory*, 135–36, 151–52, 238; *Auburn Placer Herald*, 24 April 1866, in "California Newspapers, 1865–66."

54 Currier diary, 7 May 1869; Bain, *Empire Express*, 527. Horses and mules also died in explosions during rock removal. See, for example, *Salt Lake City Daily Telegraph*, 14 April 1869, quoted in Utley, "Dash to Promontory," 105.

55 For a description of pile driving on the Union Pacific, see Bissell, "Reminiscences," 80, 85–86. See also Griswold, *Work of Giants*, 22.

56 See, for example, *San Francisco Alta, California*, 1, 3 May 1869; *Salt Lake City Deseret News*, 23 April 1869; and *San Francisco Evening Bulletin*, 28 April 1869, all in "Newspaper Accounts of Track Laying." See also Kraus, "Central Pacific Construction Vignettes"; Mayer and Vose, *Makin' Tracks*, 74–75; and Dodge, *How We Built the Union Pacific Railway*, 31 (quotation).

57 On Jack Casement, see Ames, *Pioneering the Union Pacific*, 123; Klein, *Union Pacific*, 71; Williams, *Great and Shining Road*, 122; and Mayer and Vose, *Makin'*

Tracks, 70–71. On China herders, see Kraus, *High Road to Promontory*, 134.
On Crocker's pets, see Sabin, *Building the Pacific Railway*, 111. On Strobridge,
Crocker, and their exchange, see Bain, *Empire Express*, 207–8; Griswold, *Work of
Giants*, 91–92; and Williams, *Great and Shining Road*, 130. The business adversaries of Collis P. Huntington, another of the Central Pacific's aggressive Big Four,
thought of him as a shark. Prostitutes who serviced the laborers were sometimes
called soiled doves. On preindustrial animal analogies, see Nye, *Consuming
Power*, 89–90. On Crocker, Huntington, Strobridge, and other people as bulls,
sharks, soiled doves, and so forth, see Bain, *Empire Express*, 89, 207–8, 607, and
Howard, *Great Iron Trail*, 21. Conversely, laborers sometimes ascribed human
qualities to the animals with which they worked. See, for example, the story of
the "powerful bay horse named Tom," in Haycox, "'A Very Exclusive Party',"
27. Animal vitality also seemed appropriate for making sense of machines.
Tracklayers boarded in special cars that they called sowbellies, because the
sagging midsections of the sleepers reminded them of the teats on female hogs.
Workmen sometimes affixed elk or deer horns to the front of their locomotives,
turning them into symbols of aggressive masculine power. On sowbellies, see
Combs, *Westward to Promontory*, 39; on locomotives with antlers, see Klein, *Union
Pacific*, 75, and Mayer and Vose, *Makin' Tracks*, 82–83; on iron horse, see Bain,
Empire Express, 306. The term *iron horse* arose from the fact that horses literally
pulled the first railroad cars. "Since the cars on railroads were originally pulled
by horses," wrote Stuart Berg Flexner, "it was also natural to call a locomotive
an *iron horse* (1830s) or even a *steam horse* (1840s)." Flexner, *I Hear America Talking*,
203.

58   Ames, *Pioneering the Union Pacific*, 271–98; Klein, *Union Pacific*, 69 (quotation),
100, 104, 137, 150. Righter, in *Wind Energy in America*, discussed the importance of
wind energy to the American settlement and development of the West. For the
importance of wind power for pumping water from wells for the Pacific railroad,
see especially 24–25. For some of the difficulties involved in securing that water,
see Bain, *Empire Express*, 463, 464.

59   Kraus, *High Road to Promontory*, 90, 91, 93, 107, 114, 116, 121, 136, 141; Mayer and
Vose, *Makin' Tracks*, 24–25.

60   Williams, *Great and Shining Road*, 100 (quotation), 113–14.

61   Bain, *Empire Express*, 298–99; Gilliss, "Tunnels of the Pacific Railroad," 161–62;
Kraus, "Central Pacific Construction Vignettes," 53–55; Kraus, *High Road to Promontory*, 152–53; Williams, *Great and Shining Road*, 131.

62   Bain, *Empire Express*, 332; Kraus, *High Road to Promontory*, 153, 157; Kraus, "Central
Pacific Construction Vignettes," 53–54; Williams, *Great and Shining Road*, 131–32,
161; Yen, "Chinese Workers," 127–28.

63   On the general labor problem of railroad building and the use of Chinese labor,
see Griswold, *Work of Giants*, 108–25, and Kraus, "Chinese Laborers and the
Construction of the Central Pacific." The labor problem was part of a larger
set of difficulties the railroads faced in expending and accumulating capital in

relation to obstacles posed by nature.

64 Bain, *Empire Express*, 205–8, 222, 277–78; Griswold, *Work of Giants*, 109–11 (quotation, 111); Williams, *Great and Shining Road*, 96; Saxton, "Army of Canton in the High Sierra."

65 Yen, "Chinese Workers," 121–30 (quotation, 129); Bain, *Empire Express*, 245–46, 317–18, 320, 332, 369–70, 428–29, 439; Gilliss, "Tunnels of the Pacific Railroad," 155–61; Kraus, *High Road to Promontory*, 182–83.

66 Bain, *Empire Express*, 360–62; Yen, "Chinese Workers," 130–31.

67 Bain, *Empire Express*, 360–62; Griswold, *Work of Giants*, 115; Williams, *Great and Shining Road*, 90, 94, 115; Yen, "Chinese Workers," 131. According to Foner, in *Reconstruction*, 419–20, southern planters envisioned using "indentured laborers from China, whose 'natural' docility would bolster plantation discipline and whose arrival, by flooding the labor market, would reduce the wages of blacks."

68 Adas, *Machines as the Measure of Men*, 1–16, 199–270.

69 West, *Way to the West*; West, *Contested Plains*; White, "Winning of the West," 319–43; Hämäläinen, "Rise and Fall of Plains Indian Horse Cultures" (quotation, 843). On the concept of dependency, see White, *Roots of Dependency*, xii–xix.

70 Bain, *Empire Express*, 349, 350–51, 479; Bissell, "Reminiscences," 70; Klein, *Union Pacific*, 99–100; Ames, *Pioneering the Union Pacific*, 215–22 (quotation, 215), 263, 264.

71 Porcupine's story, recorded by George Bird Grinnell, appears as "An Indian's Account of the Plum Creek Wreck," in Botkin and Harlow, *Treasury of Railroad Folklore*, 117–19. Bain, *Empire Express*, 386–388, and Griswold, *Work of Giants*, 220–22, provide standard accounts of the event.

72 Bain, *Empire Express*, 182, 354–58; Brinkerhoff, "Native Americans and the Transcontinental Railroad," 8; Griswold, *Work of Giants*, 95; Bissell, "Reminiscences," 43; *San Francisco Chronicle*, 10 September 1868, quoted in Kraus, "Chinese Laborers and the Construction of the Central Pacific." For additional information on the ambivalent relationship of the Pawnees to the railroad, see Bain, *Empire Express*, 355, and Haycox, "'A Very Exclusive Party,'" 28. For a discussion of the environmental problems and the consequent dependency of the Pawnees, see White, *Roots of Dependency*, 147–211, especially 199–211. Littlefield and Knack, in *Native Americans and Wage Labor*, discussed some of the means by which Indians entered the wage system. In 1866, the Union Pacific hired Pawnees to stage a sham attack on a party of dignitaries and to perform wild West shows for the group, thus highlighting the irony and tragedy of the Pawnees' predicament. These events are described in Bain, *Empire Express*, 292–93, although the interpretation is mine.

73 For example, Cecil B. DeMille and Paramount Pictures reenacted the Plum Creek raid in *Union Pacific*. See Best, *Iron Horses to Promontory*, 102.

74 Lockwood, "With the Casement Brothers," 24. Spotted Tail's deeper motivations, if any, are impossible to discern from Lockwood's account. Spotted Tail had a complicated relationship with Americans. In 1866, he signed a peace treaty

with the United States, primarily so that his band could maintain its cultural and subsistence practices while focusing its military power on fighting its Pawnee enemies. Spotted Tail also maintained friendships with some U.S. Army officers and their families at Fort Laramie and other posts. See Hyde, *Spotted Tail's Folk*, 71–129. For similar events involving Pawnee Indians, see Bain, *Empire Express*, 269–70. The propensity of European and European American colonists to use technology as a point of comparison between themselves and natives long antedated their obsession with locomotives and other modern machinery. Chaplin, in *Subject Matter*, 79–115, described the English colonists' obsession with archery and how the English used archery to gauge their cultural development relative to Indians. In the seventeenth century, a shared knowledge of archery established commonality between Anglo Americans and American Indians. By the nineteenth century, Lockwood's account suggests, Anglo Americans viewed American Indian archery as a savage art that contrasted with modern machines such as locomotives.

75 The quotations and examples are from, in order, Williams, *Great and Shining Road*, 49; Boime, *Magisterial Gaze*, 130, 131; and Bain, *Empire Express*, 671. See also Thomas Durant, quoted in Bain, *Empire Express*, 294–95, and Adas, *Machines as the Measure of Men*, 221–36. In at least one incident, a locomotive purportedly smashed through a group of Indians. See Williams, *Great and Shining Road*, 151. This theme appeared again and again in American arts, letters, and lore, even into the twentieth century. In 1941, the historian Everett Dick repeated a story, probably exaggerated if not outright false, that recapitulated the modern machine's defeat of primitive man. "The Indians . . . determined to wreck a train by stretching a rawhide lariat across the track with thirty braves on each side," Dick wrote of an incident during the Pacific railroad construction. "Needless to say, they were an astonished crowd of Indians when they saw with what ease the engine pulled the rope through their scorched hands." Dick, *Vanguards of the Frontier*, 381. The artist Arnold Blanch created a similar scene in an illustration that appeared in Morgan, *The Humboldt*, 288.

76 Utley, "Dash to Promontory."

77 Kraus, *High Road to Promontory*, 190–91 (quotation, 191); Orsi, *Sunset Limited*, 386–87. On railroads as a source of wildland and rural fires, see Pyne, *Fire in America*, 57, 60, 161, 199–200, 226, 252, 502–3.

78 Bain, *Empire Express*, 370, 412, 520; Kraus, *High Road to Promontory*, 182–83, 186–88, 191, 194, 196, 198; Williams, *Great and Shining Road*, 184–85, 209–10.

79 Kraus, *High Road to Promontory*, 201, 203; Williams, *Great and Shining Road*, 206–7, 239; Bain, *Empire Express*, 520–21 (quotations).

80 Bain, *Empire Express*, 493; Kraus, *High Road to Promontory*, 186, 201.

81 Kraus, *High Road to Promontory*, 200–227; Williams, *Great and Shining Road*, 207–8.

82 Bain, *Empire Express*, 471; Brinkerhoff, "Native Americans and the Transcontinental Railroad"; Kraus, *High Road to Promontory*, 186, 204, 208, 221, 226, 227,

234. Knack, in "Nineteenth-Century Great Basin Indian Wage Labor," 144–76, emphasized agricultural wage labor, not railroad wage labor.

83 Kraus, *High Road to Promontory*, 200–227.

84 Bain, *Empire Express*, 595, 604; Kraus, *High Road to Promontory*, 188, 191, 194, 196, 212, 227; Williams, *Great and Shining Road*, 249, 251. For mileages, see Best, *Iron Horses to Promontory*, 189–90.

85 Ames, *Pioneering the Union Pacific*, 238–337 (for mileages, see 295, 336); Bain, *Empire Express*, 476–81, 494–501, 506–18, 527–37, 581–85, 618–20, 648–51.

86 See Arrington and Bitton, *Mormon Experience*, 109–26, and May, "Economic Beginnings" and "Towards a Dependent Commonwealth." For overviews of, and insights into, Utah's environmental history, see Flores, "Zion in Eden," and Alexander, "Stewardship and Enterprise." Bagley, in *Blood of the Prophets*, 95–103, 106, 109, 111–12, 120–21, demonstrated that conflicts over livestock forage contributed to the tensions between Utah pioneers and overland migrants that culminated in the Mountain Meadows Massacre. For similar events in Colorado that culminated in the Sand Creek Massacre, see West, *Contested Plains*. Andrews, in *Killing for Coal*, 35–42, described Colorado as a "stagnant frontier" suffering from an organic energy crisis that coal and railroads eventually alleviated; perhaps the Mormons of Utah experienced a similar problem and found a similar solution. On Utah Mormons, the Pacific railroad, and Utah's environmental and economic conditions, see Athearn, "Contracting for the Union Pacific," 17–40; Bain, *Empire Express*, 364–65, 489, 495–97, 502, 509–10, 532–33, 551–52, 554, 556, 564, 619–20, 631–32, 659–60; and Cowan, "Steel Rails and the Utah Saints," 177–96. On the dilemma of religious idealism, see Morgan, *Puritan Dilemma*. In this regard, see Hirshson, *Grenville M. Dodge*, 164, for the observations of General William T. Sherman on the likely consequences of the railroad for Mormon culture.

87 Ames, *Pioneering the Union Pacific*, 238–337; Klein, *Union Pacific*, 158–220; Kraus, *High Road to Promontory*, 228–61; Utley, "Dash to Promontory." For mileages, see Ames, *Pioneering the Union Pacific*, 295, 336; and Best, *Iron Horses to Promontory*, 191–92.

88 Kraus, *High Road to Promontory*, 241, 244; Utley, "Dash to Promontory," 106–7.

89 Kraus, *High Road to Promontory*, 248–49, 252; Bain, *Empire Express*, 539, 638–40.

90 Kraus, *High Road to Promontory*, 248–49, 252; Bain, *Empire Express*, 638–40; Sabin, *Building the Pacific Railway*, 200–204; Utley, "Dash to Promontory," 108–9; Williams, *Great and Shining Road*, 260–63.

91 Bain, *Empire Express*, 639 (first quotation); Utley and Ketterson, *Golden Spike*, 40 (second quotation); Kraus, *High Road to Promontory*, 249 (third quotation). See also Arthur M. Johnson's foreword to Ames, *Pioneering the Union Pacific*, vii–viii.

92 "It should be remembered," wrote Hezekiah Bissell in his recollection of the Union Pacific construction, "that this was done before the days of track-laying machines, and everything in that line was done by main strength and cussedness." Bissell, "Reminiscences," 65. Beebe and Clegg similarly resisted the anachronistic tendency to see railroad labor as the inception of modern automation.

"In an age innocent of earth-moving machinery," they wrote, "the vast fills essential to mountain railroading were built by Chinese laborers with hand barrows and mule-drawn tipcarts." Beebe and Clegg, *Hear the Train Blow*, 140.

93 Kraus, *High Road to Promontory*, 252; Sabin, *Building the Pacific Railroad*, 200–202, 202n1, 202–4; Williams, *Great and Shining Road*, 261–63; Bain, *Empire Express*, 638–40, 754n99; Hanover, "All in a Day's Work," 9; Heath, "A Railroad Record That Defies Defeat," 3–5. Many sources claim that a team of eight Irishmen handled all 3,520 rails. There is reason to be skeptical. Bain mentions the story in a citation, but his text (p. 639) says only that "teams of Irishmen fairly ran the five-hundred-pound rails and hardware forward."

94 On the environmental legacies of the western railroads, see Orsi, *Sunset Limited*, and White, *Railroaded*.

7. ATOMIC SUBLIME

1 Brode, *Tales of Los Alamos*, 6, 10, 11, 15. Hunner, *Inventing Los Alamos*, 3–80, is the best history of the town's development.

2 Brode, *Tales of Los Alamos*; quotation from Goodchild, *Edward Teller*, 287. Goodchild, *Edward Teller*, and Teller, *Memoirs*, are the best sources on Edward and Mici. For Teller's early devotion to the hydrogen bomb, see Rhodes, *Making of the Atomic Bomb*, 543, 545–46.

3 Brode, *Tales of Los Alamos*, 11, is the source of the story.

4 Brode, *Tales of Los Alamos*, 11. See also Teller, *Memoirs*, 170–71.

5 Palevsky, *Atomic Fragments*, 106; Sherry, *Rise of American Air Power*, 201–3, 234–35, 251–55. See also DeGroot, *The Bomb*, x.

6 The best explanation of instrumental reason and nature is in Worster, *Rivers of Empire*, 54–58; but see also Sherry, *Rise of American Air Power*, 219–55.

7 See Teller, *Memoirs*, 4, 7, 36 (quotation), 40, 48, 70, 132–33, 135–36, 189, 246n16, 328–29, and Goodchild, *Edward Teller*, xix–xxv, 29, 162.

8 *Compartmentalization* conventionally referred to the army's policy of secrecy, in which lower-level functionaries in the Manhattan Project knew little or nothing of its organizational parts other than the specific ones in which they worked. See Hales, *Atomic Spaces*, 118–19. Dyson, in *Disturbing the Universe*, 63, used the concept of compartmentalization to describe discrete, unrelated processes and phenomena in nature. And indeed, one of the problems of physics has been that matter and energy function differently at planetary and atomic scales. See, for example, Rhodes, *Making of the Atomic Bomb*, 53–77.

9 For an alternative version of this story, see Fiege, "The Atomic Scientists, the Sense of Wonder, and the Bomb." That article and this chapter are similar, and the one informs the other, but they differ in interpretive emphasis and narrative structure. For the most complete list of primary and secondary sources, see the citations in the article. In general, I have relied on Bird and Sherwin, *American Prometheus*; Conant, *109 East Palace*; Davis, *Lawrence and Oppenheimer*; DeGroot,

The Bomb; Gleick, *Genius*; Herken, *Brotherhood of the Bomb*; Jungk, *Brighter than a Thousand Suns*; Lamont, *Day of Trinity*; Norris, *Racing for the Bomb*; Palevsky, *Atomic Fragments*; Rhodes, *Making of the Atomic Bomb*; Szasz, *Day the Sun Rose Twice*; Takaki, *Hiroshima*; and Thorpe, *Oppenheimer*.

10   See Rhodes, *Making of the Atomic Bomb*, 29–232, and DeGroot, *The Bomb*, 1–32. Clark, *Matter and Energy*, is a useful guide for the nonspecialist. See also Brown and MacDonald, *Secret History of the Atomic Bomb*.

11   See especially Rhodes, *Making of the Atomic Bomb*, 29–77 (quotation, 77).

12   DeGroot, *The Bomb*, 5–6 (quotations).

13   Ibid., 6.

14   Rhodes, *Making of the Atomic Bomb*, 31–36, 782; DeGroot, *The Bomb*, 8–12, 17; Badash, *Scientists and the Development of Nuclear Weapons*, 7–10.

15   Rutherford quoted in Jungk, *Brighter than a Thousand Suns*, 58–59. See also Bethe, "Brighter than a Thousand Suns," 426–28.

16   Carson, *Sense of Wonder*, 42, 88–89. The nature study movement shaped the childhood experiences of several atomic scientists. See Fiege, "The Atomic Scientists, the Sense of Wonder, and the Bomb," 584–87, 606n13, 607n14. On the nature study movement generally, see Armitage, *Nature Study Movement*, and Kohlstedt, "Nature, Not Books."

17   Bernstein, "Physicist—I: I. I. Rabi," 49; Cassidy, *J. Robert Oppenheimer and the American Century*, 16–17; Bird and Sherwin, *American Prometheus*, 14–15, 21, 23; Lanouette, *Genius in the Shadows*, 23; Teller, *Memoirs*, 7. Niels Bohr resembled the other atomic scientists in this regard. "To be able to fully understand Bohr's rare nature," observed a friend, "one must be clear that through the years he has retained the boy in him, retained the boy's love of play and the boy's curiosity, the latter of course being a very important thing for a researcher in science." Blaedel, *Harmony and Unity*, 145–46. Rabi also observed that "physicists are the Peter Pans of the human race. They never grow up, and they keep their curiosity." Bernstein, "Physicist—II: I. I. Rabi," 58.

18   Gleick, *Genius*, 28–29 (first quotation, 28), 396–401; Dyson, "Wise Man," 6; Fiege, "Atomic Scientists," 586 (second quotation).

19   See Nicolson, *Mountain Gloom and Mountain Glory*.

20   DeGroot, *The Bomb*, 12 (Weisskopf quotation); Bernstein, "Physicist—I: I.I. Rabi," 50 (Rabi first quotation); Rigden, "Isidor Isaac Rabi" (Rabi second quotation).

21   Rhodes, *Making of the Atomic Bomb*, 571–72; Bird and Sherwin, *American Prometheus*, 90–91, 99–102, 373–75 (first quotation, 373); Gleick, "Fallout," (second quotation).

22   Blaedel, *Harmony and Unity*, 3–8 (quotation, 7), 144–55. See also Bohr, *Atomic Theory and the Description of Nature*.

23   Bird and Sherwin, *American Prometheus*, 25, 39, 70–73, 80–81 (quotation, 80), 103–4.

24   Blaedel, *Harmony and Unity*, 3–8, 144–63.

25   Teller, *Memoirs*, 168; Brode, *Tales of Los Alamos*, 44; Goodchild, *Edward Teller*, 28. On the similarities between scientists and artists, see Rhodes, *Making of the Atomic Bomb*, 143, 173. See also Bernstein, "Physicist—I: I. I. Rabi," 105, 108; Bernstein, "Physicist—II: I. I. Rabi," 56, 58; and the reflections of Robert Oppenheimer in Bird and Sherwin, *American Prometheus*, 53–54.

26   Gleick, *Genius*, 105, 173, 176 (first quotation), 185, 241–51 (second quotation, 244), 272–77 (third quotation, 275), 285–86; Dyson, *Disturbing the Universe*, 54–56 (fourth quotation, 55), 62 (fifth quotation). See also Dyson, "Wise Man," 4.

27   Bird and Sherwin, *American Prometheus*, 70 (first quotation), 79 (second quotation), 96, 217, 258; Herken, *Brotherhood of the Bomb*, 11, 13.

28   Bird and Sherwin, *American Prometheus*, 214 (quotation); Norris, *Racing for the Bomb*, 61, 78, 94, 102, 106–7, 210 (quotation), 325, 347, 544.

29   Rhodes, *Making of the Atomic Bomb*, 198–449; Norris, *Racing for the Bomb*, 6–7, 170 (quotation), 242–43; Bird and Sherwin, *American Prometheus*, 185.

30   Groves, *Now It Can Be Told*, 65–67; Bird and Sherwin, *American Prometheus*, 185–86, 205–7; Hunner, *Inventing Los Alamos*, 12–17; Rhodes, *Making of the Atomic Bomb*, 449–51.

31   Rhodes, *Making of the Atomic Bomb*, 168–97, 303–14; Bird and Sherwin, *American Prometheus*, 187–88, 209, 221, 268; DeGroot, *The Bomb*, 14.

32   Goodchild, *Edward Teller*, xix–xxv, 1–33; Teller, *Memoirs*, 3–41.

33   Bird and Sherwin, *American Prometheus*, 210–11, 268–76 (quotation, 270), 495; Rhodes, *Making of the Atomic Bomb*, 308, 524–38; DeGroot, *The Bomb*, 38.

34   Norris, *Racing for the Bomb*, 187–229; Rhodes, *Making of the Atomic Bomb*, 486, 497. Historians of science often refer to massive projects involving scientists, government agencies, corporations, and extensive laboratory and production facilities as "big science." They interpret the Manhattan Project as an important moment in the development of this kind of enterprise. See Hughes, *Manhattan Project*.

35   Norris, *Racing for the Bomb*, 71–183 (quotation, 127). On the concept of brute force technology, see Josephson, *Industrialized Nature*, 1–68.

36   Groves, *Now It Can Be Told*, 415.

37   Rhodes, *Making of the Atomic Bomb*, 453–55, 502–10, 542–43; Bird and Sherwin, *American Prometheus*, 211, 217, 218, 225–27, 229–30; Norris, *Racing for the Bomb*, 231–52; Lanouette, *Genius in the Shadows*, 237–38 (quotation, 238); DeGroot, *The Bomb*, 36.

38   Oppenheimer, "Memorandum of the Los Alamos Project," 10.

39   Lanouette, *Genius in the Shadows*, 255.

40   Wilson, "Not Quite Eden," 43–55; Bird and Sherwin, *American Prometheus*, 207 (Oppenheimer quotation), 256; Mark, "A Roof Over Our Heads," 34. The richly descriptive reminiscences in Wilson and Serber's *Standing By and Making Do* are among the best primary sources on life in wartime Los Alamos, but see also Hunner, *Inventing Los Alamos*, 12–80.

41   Hunner, *Inventing Los Alamos*, 24 (first quotation); Groves, *Now It Can Be Told*,

164 (second quotation); Norris, *Racing for the Bomb*, 231–52.

42 Lanouette, *Genius in the Shadows*, 38–44; Norris, *Racing for the Bomb*, 209–10; Hunner, *Inventing Los Alamos*, 95–96.

43 Bird and Sherwin, in *American Prometheus*, explained in great detail the troubled relationship between Oppenheimer and army intelligence officers. See pp. 285–87 for the spies that the army missed. Norris's scrupulously researched biography of Groves, *Racing for the Bomb*, 236, 240–43, 268–70, documents the general's confidence in Oppenheimer.

44 Rhodes, *Making of the Atomic Bomb*, 141–44; Bernstein, "Physicist—I: I. I. Rabi," 105–8.

45 Childs, *American Genius*, 23–323; Rhodes, *Making of the Atomic Bomb*, 143–48, 487–92; DeGroot, *The Bomb*, 13, 35.

46 Gleick, *Genius*, 142–44 (first quotation, 144); Bird and Sherwin, *American Prometheus* 85–87; Childs, *American Genius*, 143 (second quotation); Herken, *Brotherhood of the Bomb*, 11, 136.

47 Teller, *Memoirs*, 3, 4–5, 6, 17; Lanouette, *Genius in the Shadows*, 25–26, 30–31; Gleick, *Genius*, 17–20, 27–28, 77–79. See also Bernstein, "Physicist—I: I. I. Rabi," 53, 60–64, 105–8. And, to be sure, some of the experimentalists revealed intuitive, artistic sides that resembled the proclivities of the theoreticians. For example, Lawrence rode horses and camped with Oppenheimer, and in later years Robert Wilson became a sculptor. Herken, *Brotherhood of the Bomb*, 12, 28; Palevsky, *Atomic Fragments*, 126.

48 Bird and Sherwin, *American Prometheus*, 91, 186, 208, 217–18 (quotation, 217), 224, 278; Norris, *Racing for the Bomb*, 6–7, 240–43; Rhodes, *Making of the Atomic Bomb*, 448–49. On Oppenheimer's charisma and its role in the military-scientific bureaucracy, see Thorpe, *Oppenheimer*.

49 Bird and Sherwin, *American Prometheus*, 211.

50 Mark, "A Roof Over Our Heads," 37; Bird and Sherwin, *American Prometheus*, 215 (Bethe quotation), 255–56; Brode, *Tales of Los Alamos*, 11; Rhodes, *Making of the Atomic Bomb*, 451 (Segrè first quotation), 540 (Segrè second quotation), 543, 567.

51 Kistiakowsky, "Reminiscences of Los Alamos," 61 (quotation); "Sawyer's Hill Ski Tow Association," *Daily Bulletin*, 10 November 1944, and "Plans for Ski Tow Developed," *Los Alamos Times*, 8 November 1946, both in Lyon and Evans, *Los Alamos: The First Fifty Years*, 22, 91.

52 Brode, *Tales of Los Alamos*, 77–88; Rhodes, *Making of the Atomic Bomb*, 451, 565 (quotation), 567, 569; Bird and Sherwin, *American Prometheus*, 258.

53 Goodchild, *Edward Teller*, 77 (first quotation); Hirschfelder, "Scientific and Technological Miracle at Los Alamos," 81 (second quotation), 82; Gleick, *Genius*, 167. Joseph Weinberg, a student of Oppenheimer's, compared physics calculations to rock climbing; Bird and Sherwin, *American Prometheus*, 169–70. Leo Szilard enjoyed hiking as a young man, but it is unclear whether he hiked while at Los Alamos. After the war, however, while holding a professorship at the University of Colorado at Boulder, he enjoyed outings to nearby Rocky Mountain National

Park. There he enjoyed sitting in the rarefied air and letting his mind run free, a method he called "botching." See Lanouette, *Genius in the Shadows*, 321, photograph following 396. See also Alvarez, *Alvarez*, 14–15, for an account of a Los Alamos scientist introduced to mountaineering on a Sierra Club High Trip in 1928. And compare Weisskopf, *Joy of Insight*, 18.

54 Gleick, *Genius*, 169–70, 182, 186; Fermi, *Atoms in the Family*, 224–25 (quotations, 225). Joseph Hirschfelder recalled that Niels Bohr and his son Aage, also a physicist, "took a long walk each day," during which "they would discuss some very difficult physics problem." Hirschfelder thought the senior Bohr "was very close to God." "God and nature are simple," the great physicist told him; "it is we who are complicated!" Hirschfelder, "Scientific and Technological Miracle," 80. See also Bird and Sherwin, *American Prometheus*, 169.

55 DeGroot, *The Bomb*, 38–43; Bird and Sherwin, *American Prometheus*, 208–9, 215–17, 255–59, 323 (first quotation); Rhodes, *Making of the Atomic Bomb*, 539; Herkin, *Brotherhood of the Bomb*, 81 (second quotation) Hirschfelder, "Scientific and Technological Miracle," 78–79 (third quotation, 78); Thorpe and Shapin, "Who Was J. Robert Oppenheimer?" 545–90.

56 Brode, *Tales of Los Alamos*, 13–19, 38–54; Hunner, *Inventing Los Alamos*, 61–65; Bird and Sherwin, *American Prometheus*, 258–59.

57 Brode, *Tales of Los Alamos*, 109–19 (quotations, 109, 117); Brode, "Life at Los Alamos," 87–90.

58 Hunner, *Inventing Los Alamos*, 38–39 (quotation, 39); DeGroot, *The Bomb*, 43–44; Bird and Sherwin, *American Prometheus*, 263.

59 Hunner, *Inventing Los Alamos*, 39.

60 Norris, *Racing for the Bomb*, 1, 2, 15, 52–54, 65–66, 90–94, 98–99, 100, 105, 106–7, 108, 239, 347–48, 355. See also Scharff, "Man and Nature!" 3–19.

61 Hunner, *Inventing Los Alamos*, 39; Bird and Sherwin, *American Prometheus*, 257, 259, 262 (first quotation), 263 (second quotation).

62 Mason, *Children of Los Alamos*, 49–50 (Bainbridge quotations, 50), 64–65 (Martinez quotation, 65), and passim.

63 Ibid., 156–58 (quotations, 157, 158).

64 Groves, *Now It Can Be Told*, 33–37, 176–77, 197; DeGroot, *The Bomb*, 12–13, 18, 48; Rhodes, *Making of the Atomic Bomb*, 487–90, 600–601.

65 DeGroot, *The Bomb*, 34–35, 48–50, 53; Rhodes, *Making of the Atomic Bomb*, 486–87, 490–96, 601–4. Groves and the Corps of Engineers soon added a liquid thermal diffusion plant to supplement the other facilities; see Rhodes, *Making of the Atomic Bomb*, 550–53, 602.

66 DeGroot, *The Bomb*, 46–47, 53; Rhodes, *Making of the Atomic Bomb*, 496–500, 603–5.

67 DeGroot, *The Bomb*, 25, 27; *Encyclopaedia Britannica*, 15th ed., s.v. "Plutonium" (first and second quotations); Rhodes, *Making of the Atomic Bomb*, 353–55, 407–11, 413–15, 540, 548, 659–60 (third quotation).

68 Bird and Sherwin, *American Prometheus*, 208.

69   DeGroot, *The Bomb*, 39; Bird and Sherwin, *American Prometheus*, 211, 217, 219, 224–27; Gleick, *Genius*, 165–69, 185.

70   Bird and Sherwin, *American Prometheus*, 217. The regimentation of time is an important feature of the application of instrumental reason. See Worster, *Rivers of Empire*, 57.

71   Szasz, *Day the Sun Rose Twice*, 60–61; DeGroot, *The Bomb*, 45; Rhodes, *Making of the Atomic Bomb*, 569.

72   Bird and Sherwin, *American Prometheus*, 209–12, 287–89, 291–95.

73   Ibid., 284–85.

74   Ibid., 287–303; DeGroot, *The Bomb*, 68, 70, 72, 74, 76; Wittner, *Struggle against the Bomb*, 1:ix–xii, 3–36; Takaki, *Hiroshima*, 121–36.

75   Bird and Sherwin, *American Prometheus*, 287–303.

76   Ibid.

77   On the decision to drop the bomb, see Rhodes, *Making of the Atomic Bomb*, 617–50, 682–99; DeGroot, *The Bomb*, 72–73, 76–79; and Bird and Sherwin, *American Prometheus*, 293–303. On the historiographical controversy regarding the decision to drop the bomb, see Walker, "Recent Literature on Truman's Atomic Bomb Decision," 311–34.

78   DeGroot, *The Bomb*, 50–51; Rhodes, *Making of the Atomic Bomb*, 611 (quotation), 701–3; Manhattan Project Heritage Preservation Association, Inc., "Little Boy."

79   DeGroot, *The Bomb*, 51; Rhodes, *Making of the Atomic Bomb*, 589–90, 659–61, 739; Manhattan Project Heritage Preservation Association, Inc., "Fat Man."

80   Sherry, *Rise of American Air Power*, 202–3; DeGroot, *The Bomb*, 56, 64. Merchant, in *Death of Nature*, described the origins of this point of view.

81   See the remarkable analysis by Palevsky in *Atomic Fragments*, 238–41.

82   Howes and Herzenberg, *Their Day in the Sun*; Wilson and Serber, *Standing By and Making Do*. Those women by and large also shared the belief that the bomb was necessary and that it had saved lives. See Manley, "Women of Los Alamos during World War II," 251–66.

83   See, for example, Fermi, *Atoms in the Family*.

84   Szasz, *Day the Sun Rose Twice*, 27–41.

85   Ibid., 40–41; Bird and Sherwin, *American Prometheus*, 304; Rhodes, *Making of the Atomic Bomb*, 571–72; Torrance, *Encompassing Nature*, 141–48.

86   Szasz, *Day the Sun Rose Twice*, 79–81.

87   Ibid., 67–78; Bird and Sherwin, *American Prometheus*, 305–6; Kistiakowsky, "Trinity: A Reminiscence," 21–22.

88   Bainbridge, "Foul and Awesome Display," 43.

89   Lamont, *Day of Trinity*, 193 (quotations).

90   Szasz, *Day the Sun Rose Twice*, 82–83.

91   Ibid.; Rhodes, *Making of the Atomic Bomb*, 664–69; Bird and Sherwin, *American Prometheus*, 307–9; Groves, "Memorandum for the Secretary of War," 47–55.

92   Howes and Herzenberg, *Their Day in the Sun*, 55–56.

93   Szasz, *Day the Sun Rose Twice*, 83.

94 Wilson, "Introduction," x–xi; Szasz, *Day the Sun Rose Twice*, 79.

95 Wilson, "Introduction," x–xi.

96 Szasz, *Day the Sun Rose Twice*, 79; Lamont, *Day of Trinity*, 201–2; Groves, "Some Recollections of July 16, 1945," 26; Groves, "Memorandum," 51; Jungk, *Brighter than a Thousand Suns*, 200; Bainbridge, "Foul and Awesome Display," 44–46.

97 Jungk, *Brighter than a Thousand Suns*, 198–99.

98 Szasz, *Day the Sun Rose Twice*, 58 (quotation).

99 Groves, *Now It Can Be Told*, 296–97.

100 Groves, "Memorandum," 51; Groves, "Some Recollections," 26 (quotation).

101 Szasz, *Day the Sun Rose Twice*, 86; DeGroot, *The Bomb*, 63.

102 Szasz, *Day the Sun Rose Twice*, 82; Rhodes, *Making of the Atomic Bomb*, 669; Groves, *Now It Can Be Told*, 295–96.

103 Groves, "Memorandum," 52; Lamont, *Day of Trinity*, 226 (quotation). Bird and Sherwin, in *American Prometheus*, 308, stated that Oppenheimer was prone.

104 Rhodes, *Making of the Atomic Bomb*, 672.

105 Ibid., 670–71, 672 (first and fifth quotations), 673 (second quotation); Wilson, "Introduction," x (third quotation); Groves, "Memorandum," 53 (fourth quotation).

106 Rhodes, *Making of the Atomic Bomb*, 675.

107 Groves, "Memorandum," 48 (first and fourth quotations), 52 (third quotation); Rhodes, *Making of the Atomic Bomb*, 675 (second quotation). See also Bird and Sherwin, *American Prometheus*, 307.

108 Rhodes, *Making of the Atomic Bomb*, 673 (first quotation); Szasz, *Day the Sun Rose Twice*, 89 (second and third quotations). See also Rhodes, *Making of the Atomic Bomb*, 676, and Bird and Sherwin, *American Prometheus*, 309. For other treatments of the atomic sublime, see Ferguson, "Nuclear Sublime," 4–10, and Hales, "Atomic Sublime," 5–31.

109 Groves, "Memorandum," 52–53 (first quotation, 52–53; third quotation, 53); Rhodes, *Making of the Atomic Bomb*, 673 (second quotation), 675 (eighth quotation); Szasz, *Day the Sun Rose Twice*, 89 (fourth and fifth quotations); Wilson, "Introduction," xi (sixth quotation); Weisskopf, *Joy of Insight*, 152 (seventh quotation).

110 Rhodes, *Making of the Atomic Bomb*, 675–76; Bird and Sherwin, *American Prometheus*, 309; Szasz, *Day the Sun Rose Twice*, 90–91.

111 Szasz, *Day the Sun Rose Twice*, 89; Rhodes, *Making of the Atomic Bomb*, 675 (first quotation); Groves, "Memorandum," 49 (second quotation). See also Saint-Amour, "Bombing and the Symptom," 59–82.

112 Szasz, *Day the Sun Rose Twice*, 90–91 (first quotation, 90; second quotation, 91); Rhodes, *Making of the Atomic Bomb*, 677.

113 See Committee for the Compilation of Materials on Damage Caused by the Atomic Bombs in Hiroshima and Nagasaki, *Hiroshima and Nagasaki*, and Rhodes, *Making of the Atomic Bomb*, 712–34.

114 Rhodes, *Making of the Atomic Bomb*, 732. See also Publishing Committee for

"Children of Hiroshima," *Children of Hiroshima*.

115   Dower, "Triumphal and Tragic Narratives of the War in Asia," 1133, 1133n20; Japanese Broadcasting Corporation, *Unforgettable Fire*, 58, 104. The number of people killed is difficult to establish. See Badash, *Scientists and the Development of Nuclear Weapons*, 56; Rhodes, *Making of the Atomic Bomb*, 734–35; and Committee for the Compilation of Materials on Damage Caused by the Atomic Bombs in Hiroshima and Nagasaki, *Hiroshima and Nagasaki*, 7, 11, 14, 113.

116   Gleick, *Genius*, 156 (first quotation); Bird and Sherwin, *American Prometheus*, 316 (second quotation); Hunner, *Inventing Los Alamos*, 77 (third quotation).

117   Bird and Sherwin, *American Prometheus*, 315, 316 (first and second quotations); Feynman, *"Surely You're Joking, Mr. Feynman!"* 135; DeGroot, *The Bomb*, 104.

118   Feynman, *"Surely You're Joking"* 135–36 (first quotation, 135; second quotation, 136); Rhodes, *Making of the Atomic Bomb*, 735–36 (third quotation); Bird and Sherwin, *American Prometheus*, 316 (fourth and fifth quotations).

119   Bird and Sherwin, *American Prometheus*, 317 (first quotation); Feld, "Nagasaki Binge," 215.

120   Bird and Sherwin, *American Prometheus*, 320–21 (quotations, 321).

121   Ibid., 317–20 (first quotation, 320; second quotation, 319); Herken, *Brotherhood of the Bomb*, 139–42 (third quotation, 141); Rhodes, *Making of the Atomic Bomb*, 750–51. See also Takaki, *Hiroshima*, 137–51.

122   Isidor Rabi believed that the hierarchical, antidemocratic practices of Nazi science contributed to the failure of Germany's atomic bomb program. Bernstein, "Physicist—I: I. I. Rabi," 88, 93. It is revealing that Otto Hahn, the German scientist who won the Nobel prize for the discovery of fission and who served the Nazi regime, required the help of Lise Meitner, who already had fled the country because of her Jewish ancestry, to explain how fission worked. Once the war began, Germany's racist policies fully precluded any such collaboration. On Meitner's role, for which she should have shared the Nobel, see Rhodes, *Making of the Atomic Bomb*, 256–64.

123   Oppenheimer, "Speech to the Association of Los Alamos Scientists," 315–25 (quotations, 317, 319).

124   Palevsky, *Atomic Fragments*, 19–38, 69–72 (quotations, 28, 30, 35, 36, 72). The cultural critic, cultural historian, and World War Two veteran Paul Fussell cut to the heart of the tragedy. Like many other American servicemen, he feared that he would not survive a bloody invasion of Japan. "I was saying," he wrote of his most controversial essay on the subject, "that I was simultaneously horrified about the bombing of Hiroshima and forever happy because the event saved my life. Both at the same time." Fussell, *Thank God for the Atom Bomb, and Other Essays*, 27.

125   Bird and Sherwin, *American Prometheus*, 323–33; Palevsky, *Atomic Fragments*, 125–50; Feynman, *"Surely You're Joking"*, 136 (first quotation); Rhodes, *Making of the Atomic Bomb*, 765–66 (second quotation).

126   Bird and Sherwin, *American Prometheus*, 317, 647n316.

1   This description is drawn from Kluger, *Simple Justice*, 407–8; U.S. Commission on Civil Rights, *Twenty Years After Brown*, 1; Leola Brown Montgomery interview, 15 November 1991, 37, in *Brown v. Board of Education* Oral History Collection, Manuscript Collection no. 251, Kansas State Historical Society Library and Archives, Topeka, Kansas (hereafter *Brown v. Board* Oral History and KSHS); Sanborn Fire Insurance Map, Topeka, Kansas, 1950, Microfilm Reel 15, MS 1341; and Sanborn Fire Insurance Map, Topeka, Kansas, 1954, Microfilm Reel 18, MS 1344, KSHS (hereafter Sanborn Map or Maps).

2   For the classic analysis of the color line, see Du Bois, *Souls of Black Folk*. On early race relations in Kansas, see Woods, "Integration, Exclusion, or Segregation?" For a model historiographical analysis, see Leiker, "Race Relations in the Sunflower State." On Topeka and the *Brown* case, see Patterson, *Brown v. Board of Education*, and Kluger, *Simple Justice*. For scholarly examinations of race, ethnicity, and urban environments, see Delaney, *Race, Place, and the Law, 1836–1948*, especially 1–28; Mitchell, *Cultural Geography*; Colten, *Unnatural Metropolis*; Glave and Stoll, *To Love the Wind and the Rain*; Hurley, *Environmental Inequalities*; Kelman, *A River and Its City*; Klingle, "Changing Spaces"; Klingle, *Emerald City*; Orsi, *Hazardous Metropolis*; Seligman, *Block by Block*; Stroud, "Troubled Waters in Ecotopia"; and Washington, *Packing Them In*. Melosi, in "Environmental Justice, Political Agenda Setting, and the Myths of History" explored the complicated relationship between the environmental justice and environmental movements. My purpose in this chapter is to suggest the ways in which issues central to the civil rights movement also were deeply intertwined with environmental conditions and thus that "environmental justice" encompassed much more than the siting of toxic dumps, waste incinerators, and so forth.

3   For the development of Topeka's geography, see Sanborn Maps, 1883–1954, and Wallace and Bird, *Witness of the Times*.

4   Hall, "African American Community in Topeka, Kansas." See also Topeka–Shawnee County Regional Planning Commission, *Preliminary Land Use Plan for the Topeka–Shawnee County Regional Planning Area*.

5   Cox, *Blacks in Topeka, Kansas*, 1–45, 201.

6   On environmental, economic, and political conditions in the South, the repression of the freedmen, and the migration out, see Foner, *Reconstruction*; Hahn, *A Nation Under Our Feet*; Hahn, "Hunting, Fishing, and Foraging"; Litwack, *Trouble in Mind*; Oshinsky, *"Worse than Slavery"*; Painter, *Exodusters*; and Gregory, *Southern Diaspora*.

7   Hughes, *One Way Ticket*, 61–62.

8   See Painter, *Exodusters*; Athearn, *In Search of Canaan*; Cox, *Blacks in Topeka*, 46–81, 201; and Swan, *Ethnic Heritage of Topeka, Kansas*, 49–57.

9   Cox, *Blacks in Topeka*, 46–52; Swan, *Ethnic Heritage*, 59–65.

10 Cox, *Blacks in Topeka*, 33, 59–62, 64, 68–71; Swan, *Ethnic Heritage*, 57–61.

11 Cox, *Blacks in Topeka*, 59–61, 79–80; Swan, *Ethnic Heritage*, 57–65.

12 Cox, *Blacks in Topeka*, 59; Swan, *Ethnic Heritage*, 59–61.

13 Linda's route to school can be pieced together from Sanborn Maps, 1950 and 1954; "Bus Schedule for Colored Schools," 1950–1951, appended to Charles E. Bledsoe, Elisha Scott, John J. Scott, and Charles S. Scott, "Requested Stipulation by Plaintiffs," 22 June 1951, *Oliver Brown et al. v. Board of Education of Topeka, Shawnee County, Kansas et al.*, Civil Action no. T-316, U.S. District Court, District of Kansas, Topeka, Kansas, Microcopy no. RA-3, Roll 1, *Oliver Brown et al. vs. Board of Education of Topeka, Kansas*, Project no. 3, Regional Archives Microfilm Project, National Archives and Records Service, Kansas City (hereafter *Brown v. Board of Education* Microfilm); and "Transcript of Proceedings," 25 June 1951, 206-13, *Brown v. Board of Education* Microfilm (hereafter "Transcript," *Brown v. Board of Education* Microfilm).

14 "Transcript," 212, *Brown v. Board of Education* Microfilm; Leola Brown Montgomery interview, 9, in *Brown v. Board* Oral History. I have modified the punctuation slightly for clarity. Montgomery recalled that the school bus driver was Mr. Bryants, the same driver who had driven her bus when she herself was a student. Contemporary evidence, however, indicates that it was Clarence G. "Cap" Grimes. Montgomery may have remembered the name of a school patrol monitor who accompanied Grimes. See "Transcript," 209, 212, *Brown v. Board of Education* Microfilm.

15 On the origins and locations of Sandtown and the other black neighborhoods, see Cox, *Blacks in Topeka*, 151; Hall, "African American Community," 15, 43–45; Wallace and Bird, *Witness of the Times*, 277–78; and Swan, *Ethnic Heritage of Topeka*, 66–67. The Sanborn Maps, 1887–1954, are invaluable for determining landscape features in Topeka's black neighborhoods. Those neighborhoods were not official designations, and sources disagree on their exact boundaries. The locations I describe are drawn from various sources and are intended to describe the approximate center of each neighborhood.

16 Cox, *Blacks in Topeka*, 62–63; Wallace and Bird, *Witness of the Times*, 253–55; Swan, *Ethnic Heritage of Topeka*, 67 (quotation), 167n250.

17 Cox, *Blacks in Topeka*, 31, 62–63, 106–7, 144–51; Swan, *Ethnic Heritage of Topeka*, 67–70.

18 Swan, *Ethnic Heritage of Topeka*, 67–68 (quotation 68).

19 Joe Douglas interview, 24 October 1991, 8, and Anonymous interview, 7 February 1992, 8, 26, both in *Brown v. Board* Oral History. Like Topeka's other black neighborhoods, Mudtown had no precise boundaries; on its general boundaries, see, for example, Jack Alexander interview, 1991 (no day or month identified), 11, and Clementine Martin interview, 18 February 1992, 26, both in *Brown v. Board* Oral History; and Swan, *Ethnic Heritage of Topeka*, 66. On environmental conditions in Mudtown and other low-lying black neighborhoods, see Wallace and Bird, *Witness of the Times*, 252, 278–79, 286, 290; and Russell Sage Foundation, *Topeka Improvement Survey*, map between 22 and 23, map between 44 and 45, 48–51.

20 Jack Alexander interview, 11, *Brown v. Board* Oral History; Harland Bartholomew and Associates, *Comprehensive Plan of the City of Topeka and Shawnee County, Kansas*, 19–20.

21 Swan, *Ethnic Heritage of Topeka*, 64–65; Christina Jackson interview, 5–6, in *Brown v. Board* Oral History.

22 Wallace and Bird, *Witness of the Times*, 257–60; Cox, *Blacks in Topeka*, 137–38 (quotation, 138); Bird, *Topeka*, 55; Krause, *Impact of Water on the Development of Topeka*, part 4, pp. 2, 4, 12, 18, 21–22, 24, 29, 30–32, 50. African Americans in Topeka, perhaps also in part because of environmental conditions, suffered higher rates of diseases than did whites. See Cox, *Blacks in Topeka*, 136–38, 143; Wallace and Bird, *Witness of the Times*, 286; and Russell Sage Foundation, *Topeka Improvement Survey*, 7, 9–10, 11, 17.

23 Masters, "Life and Legacy of Oliver Brown," 41–42.

24 Du Bois, "The Upbuilding of Black Durham," 253–58 (quotation, 253).

25 Du Bois, "The Conservation of Races" (quotations, 822). For more of Du Bois's thoughts on the exploitation of nature and labor, including human bodies, and the need to conserve the physical health and intellectual talents of black people specifically and humanity generally, see, for example, Du Bois, *Darkwater*, 24–28, 48–59, 80–92, 121–27. See also Stradling, *Conservation in the Progressive Era*, 57–72; Fisher, "National Vitality, Its Wastes and Conservation," 3:620–751; *Oxford English Dictionary*, 2nd ed., s.v. "Conservation"; and especially Maher, *Nature's New Deal*. On the connections between human conservation and eugenics, see Stern, *Eugenic Nation*. Although Du Bois used terms such as *race* and *blood* to distinguish African Americans and other groups, he did not believe in the biological superiority or inferiority of any segment of humanity. On black racial destiny and progress, see especially Mitchell, *Righteous Propagation*.

26 Ducker, *Men of the Steel Rails*, 161–63; Cox, *Blacks in Topeka*, 30, 94, 115, 170–71; Wallace and Bird, *Witness of the Times*, 106–7; Russell Sage Foundation, *Topeka Improvement Survey*, 4–15. See also Anonymous interview, 13–14, 17–18, and Richard Ridley interview, 21 January 1992, 3–4, both in *Brown v. Board* Oral History.

27 Cox, *Blacks in Topeka*, 82–196, passim (quotation, 183); Kluger, *Simple Justice*, 384–88; Hall, "African American Community," 16–18, 28.

28 Cox, *Blacks in Topeka*, 82–196, passim; Hall, "African American Community," 20–22, and, for later developments, 50–55. For an outsider's view of the 1930s and 1940s, see Wilson, *A Time to Lose*, 58–61.

29 Cox, *Blacks in Topeka*, 91; Hall, "African American Community," 17, 52; Leola Brown Montgomery interview, 26–27, in *Brown v. Board* Oral History; Topeka Capital-Journal, *Topeka*, 92–93. The Kansas Industrial and Educational Institute was founded in 1895 in Mudtown. In 1900, community leaders reorganized it on the model of Tuskegee Institute. In 1919, the state of Kansas took over the school, fully funded it, and renamed it the Kansas Vocational Institute. See Cox, *Blacks in Topeka*, 142, 143, 152–58.

30 Jack Alexander interview, 20; Eugene Johnson interview, 8 and 9 November 1991,

13; and Thayer Brown Phillips interview, 20 November 1991, 44, all in *Brown v. Board* Oral History.

31 Cox, *Blacks in Topeka*, 27–28, 112–13; Carper, "Popular Ideology of Segregated Schooling"; Van Delinder, "Early Civil Rights Activism in Topeka," 45–47. See also "The Colored Schools, Pupils, and Teachers," in Retired Teachers of the School System, "Centennial History of Topeka Schools."

32 Cox, *Blacks in Topeka*, 113–14 (quotation, 114); Van Delinder, "Early Civil Rights Activism in Topeka," 47–48.

33 Jack Alexander interview, 39; Joe Douglas interview, 12, 24 (quotations); Leola Brown Montgomery interview, 9–14; Eugene Johnson interview, 53; and Julietta Parks interview, 16 October 1991, 17–19, all in *Brown v. Board* Oral History. See also "Transcript," 200–205, *Brown v. Board of Education* Microfilm, and Hall, "African American Community," 25–29, 46.

34 Christina Jackson interview, 20 September 1991, 6–10, and Joe Douglas interview, 25, both in *Brown v. Board* Oral History; Henderson, "Reaffirming the Legacy," 165–66.

35 Johnson, "Lift Every Voice and Sing."

36 "Bus Schedule for Colored Schools," 1950–1951, *Brown v. Board of Education* Microfilm. I surmise Grimes's likely route from near Washington School to Monroe School.

37 Hall, "African American Community," 47, 56. See also Eugene Johnson interview, 35–36; Clementine Martin interview, 18–19; and William Mitchell and Thayer Brown Phillips interview, 59–61, all in *Brown v. Board* Oral History. See also the lists of teacher salaries in *Brown v. Board of Education* Microfilm.

38 Miller, "Charles M. Sheldon and the Uplift of Tenneseetown"; Swan, *Ethnic Heritage of Topeka*, 72–82; Cox, *Blacks in Topeka*, 144–52.

39 Miller, "Charles M. Sheldon," 134–37; Cox, *Blacks in Topeka*, 146–49 (quotation, 149); Hall, "African American Community," 44–45, 55.

40 William Mitchell interview, 20 November 1991, 65, in *Brown v. Board* Oral History.

41 Clementine Martin interview, 25; Anonymous interview, 23; Joe Thompson interview, 25 October 1991, 13–14; William Mitchell interview, 63–64; and Berdyne Scott interview, 24 November 1991, 35, all in *Brown v. Board* Oral History. For clarity, I have modified the punctuation of the William Mitchell quotation.

42 Ida Norman interview, 1 November 1991, 15, in *Brown v. Board* Oral History; and see Hall, "African American Community," 55. At moments in the Bottoms, including in some of its illicit establishments, the color line may have disappeared. See, for example, Wilson, *A Time to Lose*, 60: "Occasionally, some of my more adventuresome colleagues spoke suggestively of real or imagined Saturday night forays among the fleshpots of the East Bottoms, where the color line grew indistinct."

43 Berdyne Scott interview, 24 November 1991, 35–36 (quotation, 35); Hall, "African American Community," 22, 43–44 (quotation, 44), 55.

44 Zelma Henderson interview, 31 January 1992, 19, in *Brown v. Board* Oral History.

45 Berdyne Scott interview, 35, and William Mitchell interview, 63, both in *Brown v. Board* Oral History.

46 Clementine Martin interview, 25, in *Brown v. Board* Oral History.

47 Quinn Evans/Architects, *Historic Structure Report: Monroe Elementary School*, 9–11, 17–18, 41–44; Hagedorn-Krass and Butowsky, "Sumner Elementary School and Monroe Elementary School"; "Transcript," 89, 94–95, *Brown v. Board of Education* Microfilm. See also Weisser, "Marking Brown v. Board of Education," 97–108.

48 On the history of the school's mudscrapers, see Quinn Evans/Architects, *Historic Structure Report*, 10–11.

49 Bryant, *History of the Atchison, Topeka, and Santa Fe Railway*, 272, 274; Hall, "African American Community," 48, 86–88; Wallace and Bird, *Witness of the Times*, 98; Masters, "Life and Legacy of Oliver Brown," 45–47; Kluger, *Simple Justice*, 395, 408; Jack Alexander interview, 43, in *Brown v. Board* Oral History.

50 Zelma Henderson interview, 4–30 (quotation, 11), in *Brown v. Board* Oral History. For other examples, and for examples of people moving from Oklahoma, Missouri, and other southern states to Topeka and expecting the city to be less segregated, see Hall, "African American Community," 94–96. On the contraction of the rural population of Kansas and the expansion of the urban, see Topeka–Shawnee County Regional Planning Commission, *Preliminary Land Use Plan for the Topeka–Shawnee County Planning Area*.

51 Hall, "African American Community," 16–19; Kluger, *Simple Justice*, 375; Wallace and Bird, *Witness of the Times*, 251. See also Anonymous interview, 19–20; Joe Douglas interview, 38–40; Claude Emerson interview, 25 October 1991, 10–11; and Eugene Johnson interview, 37, all in *Brown v. Board* Oral History. Quotations appear throughout all these sources. One important exception to whites' general aversion to blacks was in the nightlife and fleshpots of the Bottoms, where the color line momentarily grew indistinct. See, for example, Joe Douglas interview, 39–40, in *Brown v. Board* Oral History, and Wilson, *A Time to Lose*, 60.

52 William Mitchell interview, 39, and Eugene Johnson interview, 36–37 (quotation, 37), both in *Brown v. Board* Oral History. Compare Joe Douglas interview, 4, in *Brown v. Board* Oral History.

53 Kluger, *Simple Justice*, 376; Hall, "African American Community," 91–94; Van Delinder, "Early Civil Rights Activism in Topeka," 55; Van Delinder, "Border Campaigns," 135–38.

54 Wallace and Bird, *Witness of the Times*, 244; Hall, "African American Community," 45–46; Van Delinder, "*Brown v. Board of Education of Topeka*: A Landmark Case Unresolved Fifty Years Later." See also Richard and Frances Ridley interviews, 21 January 1992, 5 March 1992, 26; Constance Sawyer interview, 5–6; Dorothy Scott interview, 27 January 1992, 22; and Joe Thompson interview, 17, all in *Brown v. Board* Oral History; and Sugrue, *Origins of the Urban Crisis*, 44–46.

55 Berdyne Scott interview, 10, 12, 47 (quotation, 10), in *Brown v. Board* Oral History;

Hall, "African American Community," 45.

56 Christina Jackson interview, 5, in *Brown v. Board* Oral History.

57 Frederick Temple interview, 14 June 1992, 11, in *Brown v. Board* Oral History.

58 Joe Douglas interview, 10, 14–18 (quotations, 15, 16), in *Brown v. Board* Oral History.

59 William Mitchell interview, 45, in *Brown v. Board* Oral History. Among ordinary Americans, as the historian Robert McElvaine noted, "there was during the Depression an expansion of the more traditional, community-oriented values that have generally been in decline throughout the rest of the twentieth century." McElvaine, *Great Depression*, xxiv. Those community-oriented values often encouraged forms of family, local, and neighborhood economic cooperation but also, as some black and white people in Topeka demonstrated, greater integration in day-to-day social life.

60 Leola Brown Montgomery interview, 1–2, 6–8, 14 (quotation, 8), in *Brown v. Board* Oral History.

61 Hall, "African American Community," 29–33 (quotation, 32); Kluger, *Simple Justice*, 382. See also Jack Alexander interview, 16–43; Joe Douglas interview, 13; Eugene Johnson interview, 25–26, 28; Leola Brown Montgomery interview, 24; and Berdyne Scott interview, 19–23, all in *Brown v. Board* Oral History.

62 Berdyne Scott interview, 22, and Joe Douglas interview, 23, both in *Brown v. Board* Oral History. Cf. the story in Wilson, *A Time to Lose*, 60. And compare these views with Hall, "African American Community," 19.

63 Van Delinder, "Early Civil Rights Activism in Topeka," 52–54; Hall, "African American Community," 83–86.

64 Jack Alexander interview, 16, 21–25 (quotations, 16, 21, 22), in *Brown v. Board* Oral History.

65 Joe Douglas interview, 8–13, 23–31 (quotation, 9), in *Brown v. Board* Oral History.

66 Hall, "African American Community," 66–68. See also Joe Douglas interview, 31–36, and Berdyne Scott interview, 23, both in *Brown v. Board* Oral History.

67 Kluger, *Simple Justice*, 380–83; Van Delinder, "Border Campaigns," 142–44; Van Delinder, "Early Civil Rights Activism in Topeka," 56–57; Hall, "African American Community," 34–37.

68 Kluger, *Simple Justice*, 381–82 (second and third quotations, 382); Hall, "African American Community," 34 (fourth quotation).

69 Kluger, *Simple Justice*, 379, 382; Hall, "African American Community," 85, 108–9; Van Delinder, "Early Civil Rights Activism in Topeka," 54. At a meeting of the Board of Education, one spokesman for a group of black teachers said that "colored teachers know the psychology of the colored children better than a white teacher could," and the "time was not ripe to make a change" to white-majority schools. Wallace and Bird, *Witness of the Times*, 187.

70 Hall, "African American Community," 32; Jack Alexander interview, 25, in *Brown v. Board* Oral History.

71 Van Delinder, "Border Campaigns," 76–90, 147–48; Van Delinder, "Early Civil

Rights Activism in Topeka," 48–52; "Transcript," 206, *Brown v. Board of Education* Microfilm. See also Julietta Parks interview, 20, and Constance Sawyer interview, 5 March 1992, 4, 10, 11, 13, both in *Brown v. Board* Oral History.

72   Leola Brown Montgomery interview, 36–37 (quotation, 37), and Christina Jackson interview, 10, both in *Brown v. Board* Oral History. See also Hall, "African American Community," 76–77. Some parents whose children experienced lengthy, dangerous, inconvenient trips to school did not object to segregation but insisted that the transportation be improved. See, for example, Joe Douglas interview, 19–21, in *Brown v. Board* Oral History.

73   "Transcript," 76–77, *Brown v. Board of Education* Microfilm.

74   Hagedorn-Krass and Butowsky, "Sumner Elementary School and Monroe Elementary School"; Butowsky, "Sumner Elementary School"; Kluger, *Simple Justice*, 408–9. See also Weisser, "Marking Brown v. Board of Education."

75   U.S. Commission on Civil Rights, *Twenty Years After Brown*, 1; Kluger, *Simple Justice*, 408–9.

76   Van Delinder, "Border Campaigns," 138–45; Van Delinder, "Early Civil Rights Activism in Topeka," 54–58; Hall, "African American Community," 69–81, 97. Topeka NAACP members had been in contact with the national office and the LDF lawyers for some time; see Greenberg, *Brown v. Board of Education*, 74–75. Washburn College became Washburn University in 1941; see Wallace and Bird, *Witness of the Times*, 199–200.

77   Patterson, *Brown v. Board of Education*, 1–45; Hall, "African American Community," 103–7. The most thorough analysis of the NAACP campaign leading to the *Brown v. Board* case is in Kluger, *Simple Justice*.

78   On shifting scales and their interrelationships, see White, "Nationalization of Nature."

79   On the NAACP's strategy, see Van Delinder, "Border Campaigns," 151–54; Hall, "African American Community," 104–7; and Patterson, *Brown v. Board of Education*, 21–45.

80   Van Delinder, "Border Campaigns," 146–51; Kluger, *Simple Justice*, 395.

81   The best analysis is in Van Delinder, "Border Campaigns," 144–48.

82   Charles E. Bledsoe, "Complaint," 26 February 1951, quotation 2–3, *Brown v. Board of Education* Microfilm. Bledsoe and the Scott brothers later filed an amended complaint, which addressed the plaintiffs' geographical grievances. See Charles E. Bledsoe, Charles S. Scott, and John J. Scott, "Amended Complaint," 22 March 1951, *Brown v. Board of Education* Microfilm.

83   Van Delinder, "Border Campaigns," 151–54; and on tension reflecting different geographical scales, see especially Kluger, *Simple Justice*, 401.

84   "Transcript," 25 June 1951, 13, 19–20, 33–77 (quotations, 13, 19, 39), *Brown v. Board of Education* Microfilm.

85   Ibid., 79–145 (quotations, 114, 117, 139).

86   Ibid., 145–98 (quotations, 153, 155, 164, 172).

87   Ibid., 184.

88 Walter Huxman, "Opinion of the Court," 3 August 1951; Walter Huxman, "Findings of Fact," 3 August 1951, 3–4; Charles E. Bledsoe, John J. Scott, Charles S. Scott, Robert L. Carter, Jack Greenberg, and Thurgood Marshall, "Petition for Appeal, 1 October 1951"; Charles E. Bledsoe, Charles Scott, John Scott, Jack Greenberg, Thurgood Marshall, and Robert L. Carter, "Statement as to Jurisdiction," 1 October 1951, all in *Brown v. Board of Education* Microfilm. See also Greenberg, *Brown v. Board of Education*, 74–81.

89 The best history of the combined cases is in Kluger, *Simple Justice*. But see also Martin, *Brown v. Board of Education*.

90 Patterson, *Brown v. Board of Education*, xx, 41–42 (quotation, 41). Not until the early 1970s did an African American geographer, Harold Rose, publish significant work on race and space in the American landscape. On the absence of geography from the study of race during the 1950s and 1960s and the discipline's eventual embrace of the subject, including Rose's work, see Kobayashi, "The Construction of Geographical Knowledge—Racialization, Spatialization," 544–56.

91 See, for example, Clark and Clark, "Racial Identification and Preference in Negro Children," 169–78 (quotations, 169); and Clark and Clark, "Emotional Factors in Racial Identification and Preference in Negro Children," 341–50. For discussions of the Clarks and their work and of the influence of social science in the shaping of the *Brown v. Board* case, see Kluger, *Simple Justice*, 315–45, 353–58, 492–95, 501–5, 553–57; and Patterson, *Brown v. Board of Education*, 42–45, 66–67.

92 For a discussion of some of the inherent problems of the Dolls Test, see Patterson, *Brown v. Board of Education*, 44–45, 61, 63.

93 Clark and Clark, "Racial Identification and Preference in Negro Children," 178 (quotations); Kluger, *Simple Justice*, 318, 556.

94 The decision is discussed in Kluger, *Simple Justice*, 657–708, and Patterson, *Brown v. Board of Education*, 46–69. See also Friedman, *Brown v. Board*, 12, for the LDF's emphasis on the inherent inequality of segregated schools. The official Supreme Court decision is *Brown v. Board of Education of Topeka*, 347 U.S. 483 (1954). A copy of the complete text of the decision appears in Kluger, *Simple Justice*, 779–87. For a summation of social science findings attached to the appellants' briefs, see Clark, Chein, and Cook, "The Effects of Segregation and the Consequences of Desegregation," 495–501.

95 Kluger, *Simple Justice*, 700–747; Patterson, *Brown v. Board of Education*, 46–71; Van Delinder, "Border Campaigns," 154–57; Van Delinder, "Early Civil Rights Activism in Topeka," 57–58; Millikan, "Negroes to Mark Court Victory Tuesday Night" (quotations). See also Dudziak, "Limits of Good Faith," 69. The crumbling of the color line in the schools was accompanied by its destruction in other environments. Already black citizens and the Topeka NAACP were mounting a legal challenge to desegregate the city's swimming pools. See "Negro Swimmers Ask Use of All Pools in Topeka," and Murphy, "Motion Filed on Gage Park Pool Hearing."

96   Millikan, "Negroes to Mark Court Victory Tuesday Night."

97   Masters, "Life and Legacy of Oliver Brown," 56–58; Linda Brown Thompson interview, pp. 2–6; Johnson, *Brown v. Board of Education Oral History Collection*, 45, 63.

98   Masters, "Life and Legacy of Oliver Brown," 58–60, 105–9, 130–45.

99   See especially Cheryl Brown Henderson interview, 4 December 1991, *Brown v. Board* Oral History.

100 Patterson, *Brown v. Board of Education*, 86–117 (quotations, 99, 113). Patterson, in *Brown v. Board of Education*, 70–223, offered an excellent summary and analysis of the aftermath of the *Brown* decision. See also Kluger, *Simple Justice*, 748–78. For an excellent, wide-ranging compilation of African American opinions on the decision, see *Unfinished Agenda of Brown v. Board of Education*.

101 Patterson, *Brown v. Board of Education*, 118–69.

102 Ibid., 170–90.

103 Ibid., 152–90.

104 Ibid., 42, 156–90.

105 Ibid., 170–223.

106 Van Delinder, "*Brown v. Board of Education of Topeka*: A Landmark Case," part 1, p. 4, and part 2, pp. 3–8; Wallace and Bird, *Witness of the Times*, 188; Joe Douglas interview, 44, in *Brown v. Board* Oral History.

107 Wallace and Bird, *Witness of the Times*, 247–49; Bird, *Topeka*, 111–15; Eugene Johnson interview, p. 55, in *Brown v. Board* Oral History; "Urban Plan Wins Formal City Approval" (first quotation); Byer, "Realtors Urge Topeka Act Against Slums" (second quotation). Cf. Seligman, *Block by Block*, 69–98.

108 Jack Alexander interview, 11; Claude Emerson interview, 8; and William Mitchell interview, 37, all in *Brown v. Board* Oral History. See also Hall, "African American Community," 45–46, 55–56. The west Topeka–east Topeka division already was appearing as early as about 1940; see Wilson, *A Time to Lose*, 58–59.

109 On resistance to urban renewal, see Wallace and Bird, *Witness of the Times*, 188; "Commission Vote Comes Amid Protest"; Sheppeard, "Court Action May Halt UR"; and "Minority Housing Policy Target of NAACP Speaker." Business owners also resisted the urban renewal project; see "Another Suit Filed Against Renewal Plan." On the reaction to school segregation, see Dudziak, "Limits of Good Faith," 59–88; Kluger, *Simple Justice*, 777–78; Lamson, "Race and Schools in Topeka, Kansas," 1–9, 183, 240–41; Patterson, *Brown v. Board of Education*, 164, 190; Powell, "*Brown v. Board of Education—Johnson v. Board of Education*, 1954–1975," 76–122 (quotations, 81, 82); Wilson, *A Time To Lose*, 223–25; and Van Delinder, "*Brown v. Board of Education of Topeka*: A Landmark Case," part 2, 3–6.

110 Goodman, "Brown v. Board of Education"; Gross, "Linda Brown Reopens Her Landmark Case against Racism"; Patterson, *Brown v. Board of Education*, 190. See also Gagan, "Landscapes of Childhood and Youth," 404–19.

9. IT'S A GAS

1   Blumenthal, "Manning the Pump Is Like Manning a Battle Station."
2   Ibid.
3   Ibid.
4   Ibid.
5   Ibid.
6   Christian, *Maps of Time*.
7   Merrill, *Oil Crisis of 1973–1974*, is an excellent overview.
8   Thomas Bender, a leading opponent of national history, "rejects the territorial space of the nation as the sufficient context for a national history" and argues "for the transnational nature of national histories." Bender, *A Nation among Nations*, ix. Bender uses the word *nature* in a general sense and includes occasional references to disease, natural history, and other themes pertinent to environmental history. A fully developed environmental history perspective suggests that scholars might consider scales far beyond the political frames characteristic of the transnational methodology. See, for example, Christian, *Maps of Time*, which takes a universal approach to human history, situating it in the history of the cosmos.
9   Goodstein, *Out of Gas*, 89–98. See also Atkins, *Four Laws That Drive the Universe*. I thank David Goodstein, professor of physics and former vice provost at the California Institute of Technology, for reviewing my descriptions of thermodynamics here and at the conclusion of the chapter.
10 Deffeyes, *Hubbert's Peak*, 14–69; Deffeyes, *Beyond Oil*, 13–16. See also Stock, "One Barrel of Oil," 14–17, 38, 42–47, 48, 50, 52, 54, 58, 60, 65–66; and Adams, "A Tankful of Gas," 270–77, 282–87, 289–90, 295–304.
11 Cottrell, in *Energy and Society*, 15–78, explained the basic organic and inorganic energy sources in the "low energy society." See also Hubbert, *Energy Resources*, 1–21.
12 Wrigley, in *Continuity, Chance, and Change*, 34–67, explained the intensification of energy use in the "advanced organic economy."
13 Wrigley, *Continuity, Chance, and Change*, 68–132; Andrews, *Killing for Coal*; *Encyclopaedia Britannica*, 15th ed., s.v. "coal"; *Dictionary of Geological Terms*, 3rd ed. (1984), s.v. "gymnosperm."
14 Melosi, *Coping with Abundance*, 37–38; Yergin, *The Prize*, 26–31.
15 Melosi, *Coping with Abundance*, 40–48; Yergin, *The Prize*, 82–86.
16 Melosi, *Coping with Abundance*, 40–43, 70–71; Yergin, *The Prize*, 35–55, 96–113.
17 Melosi, *Coping with Abundance*, 43–47; Yergin, *The Prize*, 78–95.
18 Yergin, *The Prize*, 86–87.
19 Schobert, *Energy and Society*, 292–306; Yergin, *The Prize*, 111–12, 383.
20 Melosi, *Coping with Abundance*, 105–10; Flink, *Automobile Age*, 26, 78–80, 153; Famighetti, *World Almanac and Book of Facts, 2000*, 715. Sabin, *Crude Politics*, is an essential study of the political economy of oil and the role of government in the

oil market.

21 Holley, "Blacktop," 730–32.

22 Lynd and Lynd, *Middletown*, 253–63 (quotations, 255, 256); Edsforth, *Class Conflict and Cultural Consensus*, 1–96.

23 Ibid., 257, 260–63.

24 Louter, *Windshield Wilderness*; Lipin, *Workers and the Wild*, 85–115; Flink, *Car Culture*, 171–82; Edsforth, *Class Conflict and Cultural Consensus*, 16–17. The discovery of the Trenton oil and gas field contributed to Muncie's economic development, and some of the city's residents no doubt took trips to the Indiana Dunes State Park, which in 1966 became the Indiana Dunes National Lakeshore, a unit in the national park system.

25 Lynd and Lynd, *Middletown*, 255.

26 Greene, *Horses at Work*, 244–74, 278–79.

27 Schobert, *Energy and Society*, 312–14.

28 Ibid., 549–57.

29 Kovarik, "Henry Ford, Charles Kettering and the 'Fuel of the Future,'" is an outstanding article on the early history and promise of alcohol fuel.

30 Melosi, *Coping with Abundance*, 39, 44–45, 47–50, 94–96; Vietor, *Energy Policy in America since 1945*, 22; Wall, "Oil Industry," 806. See also Maurer, "Fuel and the Battle Fleet," 200–204.

31 Melosi, *Coping with Abundance*, 45.

32 Ibid., 83–84, 160–75; Ise, *United States Oil Policy*, 274–89, 309–22.

33 "Ford Predicts Fuel from Vegetation," *New York Times*, 20 September 1925.

34 Schobert, *Energy and Society*, 298–301; Kovarik, "Henry Ford, Charles Kettering,'" 12–21.

35 Kovarik, "Henry Ford, Charles Kettering," 22–23; Bill Kovarik to Mark Fiege, 7 March 2009, e-mail in possession of the author; Schobert, *Energy and Society*, 551–53.

36 Kovarik, "Henry Ford, Charles Kettering," 14–18, 21–23; Markowitz and Rosner, *Deceit and Denial*, 12–138.

37 Vietor, *Energy Policy in America*, 21; Melosi, *Coping with Abundance*, 152–53; Yergin, *The Prize*, 244–48.

38 Skidelsky, *Keynes*, 78.

39 *Prorationing* means to proration a substance on a pro rata basis—to proportionately divide, distribute, or ration a fractional part of each producer's productive capacity. See *Webster's New Collegiate Dictionary* (1977), s.v. "pro rata," "prorate," "proration"; Yergin, *The Prize*, 248–52.

40 Melosi, *Coping with Abundance*, 152–55; Yergin, *The Prize*, 248–59; Vietor, *Energy Policy in America*, 21–24.

41 Deffeyes, *Hubbert's Peak*, 54 (quotation), 137–38, 154; Yergin, *The Prize*, 87 (on the birth of oilfield language), 570–72; Vietor, *Energy Policy in America*, 91–115, 119–21; Melosi, *Coping with Abundance*, 259–61.

42 Wall, "Oil Industry," 807–8; Melosi, *Coping with Abundance*, 177–95; Yergin, *The*

Prize, 368–408, 548–54; Patterson, *Grand Expectations*, 10–11, 61–81, 274, 311–42; Famighetti, *World Almanac and Book of Facts*, 715. Nye, in *Consuming Power*, 187–246, surveyed the development and consequences of the nation's high-energy economy.

43   See Patterson, *Grand Expectations*, 61–81. In general, see Cohen, *Consumer's Republic*, and Friedan, *Feminine Mystique*.

44   Melosi, *Coping with Abundance*, 39, 266–73.

45   Thompson, *Hell's Angels*, 80–93, 95 (quotation), 196–202; Friedan, *Feminine Mystique*, 11–27, 271–98 (quotations, 11, 271); Patterson, *Grand Expectations*, 383–84, 558, 663–65.

46   Wall, "Oil Industry," 807; Melosi, *Coping with Abundance*, 282–83.

47   Deffeyes, *Hubbert's Peak*, 1–5, 133–46; Goodstein, *Out of Gas*, 16–16, 26–28. On Hubbert generally, see Doel, "Marion King Hubbert." Hubbert's classic paper was published in 1956 by the Shell Development Company as "Nuclear Energy and the Fossil Fuels." According to the historian and Harvard business professor Richard Vietor, "*Geophysical reality* is fundamental to the whole subject. The essential physical characteristic of fossil fuels is that their supply is finite. Technological innovation, higher prices, or luck may yield increased reserves, but inevitably a growing rate of extraction and consumption must result in the depletion of the earth's fixed stock." Vietor, *Energy Policy in America*, 4–5.

48   Deffeyes, *Hubbert's Peak*, 5, 146–49; Deffeyes, *Beyond Oil*, xiii, 4, 35–51.

49   Deffeyes, *Hubbert's Peak*, 22, 113–32; Yergin, *The Prize*, 300–301.

50   Production figures, in barrels, are given in the following table.

Statistic	1970	1973
Total imports	483,000,000	1,184,000,000
Total domestic field production	3,517,450,000	3,360,903,000
Total imports + domestic field production	4,000,450,000	4,554,903,000
Total imports from Middle East nations*	87,000,000	502,000,000
Imports as % of total imports + field production	12	26
Middle East imports as % of total imports	18	42
Middle East imports as % of total imports + field production	2	11

*Egypt, Iran, Kuwait, Libya, Saudi Arabia, United Arab Emirates

Sources: U.S. Bureau of the Census, *Statistical Abstract of the United States: 1974*, 512, 516; U.S. Energy Information Administration, *Monthly U.S. Imports of Crude Oil, 1920–2009*; U.S. Energy Information Administration, *Monthly U.S. Field Production of Crude Oil, 1920–2009*. Cf. Melosi, *Coping with Abundance*, 282; Yergin, *The Prize*, 591; Merrill, *Oil Crisis of 1973–1974*, 5, 23; Patterson, *Grand Expectations*, 784–85.

51   Melosi, *Coping with Abundance*, 165–71, 192–93, 241–52, 277–86; Deffeyes, *Hubbert's Peak*, 4–6; Yergin, *The Prize*, 522–25, 588–97; Vietor, *Energy Policy in America*,

193–235; Merrill, *Oil Crisis of 1973–1974*, 9–14.

52 Melosi, *Coping with Abundance*, 277–86; Yergin, *The Prize*, 588–632; Patterson, *Grand Expectations*, 784–85; Merrill, *Oil Crisis of 1973–1974*, 1, 22; "A Time of Learning to Live with Less."

53 Hubbert, *Energy Resources*, 7.

54 "Even without Gas Rationing—Headaches Pile Up for Drivers," 11–12; McFadden, "Lack of Gasoline 'Worst Ever' Here"; "Line of Idling Cars Tested for Gasoline Consumption,"; Flint, "Except in Northeast, Gasoline Is Available, but Supply Is Tightening,"; Montgomery, "Long Weekend Worsens Gasoline Situation Here."

55 Silver, "Driver Exposes Cheating Gas Pumps"; "Panic at the Pump"; Viorst, "A Day at the Pumps," 40.

56 Montgomery, "Drivers Face Another Weekend of Lines and Rising Fuel Prices"; Montgomery, "Service Stations Shut Down Early"; Ferretti, "The Way We Were."

57 Andelman, "Motorists Line Up for Gasoline Here"; Montgomery, "Drivers Hunt for Gasoline; Warning on Prices Issued"; Perlmutter, "Harried Drivers Lose Tempers"; "No End in Sight to Gas-Pump Lines." See also Montgomery, "Service Stations Shut Down Early"; Flint, "Except in Northeast, Gasoline Is Available, but Supply is Tightening"; and "Panic at the Pump," 15 (quotation).

58 "800 Gallons of 'Gas' Stolen" (quotation); "8,500 Gallons Missing in Coast 'Gasjacking'"; "Panic at the Pump."

59 "No End in Sight to Gas-Pump Lines," 14.

60 Johnston, "Pity Poor Dave, the Pump Man" (first quotation); Montgomery, "Long Weekend Worsens Gasoline Situation Here" (second quotation); Blumenthal, "Manning the Pump Is Like Manning a Battle Station," (third quotation).

61 "Panic at the Pump."

62 Sterba, "Tourists May Have a Long Wait in Gas-Dry Colorado" (quotation); "Driver Wanting to Exceed Gasoline Limit Is Slain." See also Fowler, "Motorists Begin a Grim Weekend," and Ferretti, "The Way We Were."

63 Gold, "Hot Items"; "Ingenuity of Seven Youths and a Pump Is Balked"; "Library Vans Parked in Way to Stop Siphoning"; "Storing Gasoline Can Kill You!"; "Gas in Can Proves Death Trap for Driver"; "The Dangers of Taking Precautions," 97.

64 Bird, "It's Motorist Be Nimble to Keep Gas Tank Full"; Jared Orsi, e-mails to Mark Fiege, 25, 26, and 27 May 2010, in author's possession.

65 "The Painful Change to Thinking Small," 22 (quotations); Malcom, "Fuel Rationing Could Hobble That Work Horse of Suburbia"; Stevens, "Gasoline Shortages Are Forcing Exurbanites to Readjust Their Life-Style"; King, "Energy Gap Makes It Harder to Sell a House."

66 Lichtenstein, Strasser, and Rosenzweig, in *Who Built America?* 2:683–88, offer an excellent summary of the economic consequences of the 1973–74 oil shock. I agree with the authors' judgment that the oil shock "was actually a political phenomenon" (p. 684), but I would add that other factors also need to be considered,

such as the dependence of the United States on a nonhuman, natural substance that geological processes distributed unevenly within the Earth and therefore in uneven relation to humanity's historic cultural, social, economic, political, and military configurations. To understand the political history of oil, we must first come to grips with the environmental history of oil, and most specifically with the thermodynamic history of oil. Nature, political economy, technology, and history were (and are) integral, inseparable parts of the same human problem, whether in the 1973–74 oil shock or in any other event.

67 Melosi, *Coping with Abundance*, 282–86; Merrill, *Oil Crisis of 1973–1974*, 18–20; "U.S. to Allocate All Petroleum Supplies," 108–10; "Nixon Approves Limit of 55 M.P.H." The speed limit law required states to limit highway speeds to fifty-five miles per hour on divided highways of four lanes or more as a condition of receiving federal highway trust funds, which had been set up under the terms of the 1956 Interstate Highway Act.

68 Kneeland, "Energy: Many Skeptical on Reasons for Crisis"; "Poll Finds Oil Crisis Laid to Government and Big Companies"; Cowan, "Squeeze on Fuel"; Szasz, "When History Comes Home to Roost"; Cummings, "Gasoline Users Uncertain on Return of Normalcy"; Nye, *Consuming Power*, 225–26; "A Time of Learning to Live with Less."

69 Andelman, "Motorists Line Up for Gasoline Here" (quotation).

70 "What remains striking in hindsight is the depth and complexity of the self-scrutiny that many Americans undertook to grasp what had happened. . . . The oil crisis clarified people's understanding of two powerful features of America's place in the postwar world: the environmental costs of the nation's rise to economic power, and the political conundrums that arose out of America's enormous resource needs, particularly the country's increasing dependence on foreign oil." Merrill, *Oil Crisis of 1973–1974*, 22–23. The oil shocks of 1973–74 and 1979–81 stimulated an enormous amount of scholarly research. See Smil, *Energy in Nature and Society*, 11. Cf. Nye, *Consuming Power*, 226–28.

71 Fowler, "Motorists Begin a Grim Weekend"; "Gasoline Siphoner Leaves $5 Payment in Tank"; "Coast Volunteers Check 'Gas' Stations on Sundays."

72 *Encyclopaedia Britannica*, 15th ed., s.v. "automobile club"; Flink, "American Automobile Association." AAA has come under intense scrutiny and criticism for its opposition to consumer protection, environmental policies, and public transportation. See Rivlin, "Secret Life of AAA." Edsforth, in *Class Conflict and Cultural Consensus*, and Schwantes, in "Patterns of Radicalism on the Wageworkers' Frontier," have argued that the physical, geographical, and social mobility associated with automobile ownership and use undercut working-class solidarity.

73 See, for example, Morlan, *Political Prairie Fire*, 27, 79; McElvaine, *Great Depression*; Kay, *Asphalt Nation*, 222 (quotation); Morris, *Origins of the Civil Rights Movement*, 18–19, 48–49, 56–58, 64–66, 279–86.

74 See, for example, Kay, *Asphalt Nation*.

75 Boylan, "No Rush to Car Pools, Mass Transit or Two-Wheelers"; "Nassau

Unveils 3 Car-Pool Areas—Without Drivers"; "State to Assist Cities to Set Up Car Pools"; "Gallup Poll Finds Most Still Use Car"; but see Stevens, "Americans, Hit by High Cost of Gas and Recalling Shortage, Rely Less on Autos."

76 Treaster, "In Montclair, a Car Pool Is a Corporation"; "Interchurch Center History." My sincere thanks to the Rev. J. Martin Bailey for providing additional information in e-mails and during a telephone conversation on 22 January 2009 (hereafter, Bailey conversation). See also Winerip, "A Great Car Pool: Decorum, Faith, and a Manual."

77 Treaster, "In Montclair, a Car Pool Is a Corporation" (first and third quotations); Bailey conversation; Thurber, "Caring Carpool Is Community," 39 (second quotation).

78 Treaster, "In Montclair, a Car Pool Is a Corporation"; Bailey conversation (quotation).

79 Hamilton, *Trucking Country*, especially 187–231.

80 Green and Montgomery, "Six Days on the Road"; Hamilton, *Trucking Country*, 191, 193, 195, 199.

81 United Press International (hereafter UPI), "Truck Driver-Owners Block Highways in Five States"; Lindsey, "The Angry Truck Driver: 'We've Got to Show 'em'"; Associated Press (hereafter AP), "Ohio Protest Goes On"; McElheny, "Truck 'Gas' Saving at 50 M.P.H. Found."

82 Lindsey, "Angry Truck Driver."

83 AP, "Ohio Protest Goes On"; Salpukas, "Protest Transforms Driver in Toledo into 'Biggest Truck Company' Around."

84 Salpukas, "Protest Transforms Driver in Toledo" (quotation); "Thousands of Truck Drivers Stay Off the Road to Protest Effects of Fuel Shortage"; Kates, "Citizens Band (CB) Radio"; *Encyclopaedia Britannica*, 15th ed., s.v. "citizens band radio." See also Hamilton, *Trucking Country*, 200, 217.

85 Lindsey, "Angry Truck Driver"; "Thousands of Truck Drivers Stay Off the Road"; McFadden, "Trucks Are Damaged in Protest on Fuel Situation"; UPI, "Truckers Disrupt Oil Deliveries and Harass Working Drivers"; Salpukas, "Trucker Protest Slowing Gasoline Deliveries Here"; Salpukas, "Truckers' Protest Cuts Flow of Food and Steel"; Salpukas, "Strike Has Varied Impact in Ohio"; Bird, "Effects Spreading Here"; Bird, "Meat Supplies Dip 'Dramatically' in City." See also Hamilton, *Trucking Country*, 216–18.

86 Salpukas, "Owner Driver Gives Case for Fuel Protest"; AP, "U.S. Aides Worried by Truck Protest"; Robbins, "Revised Strike Pact Sent White House by Truckers."

87 Hamilton, *Trucking Country*, 221–22; Fries, "Convoy."

88 Robbins, "Truckers Reach Accord, Leaders Ask Strike End"; "I.C.C. Orders Aid to Owner-Drivers"; Hamilton, *Trucking Country*, 218, 224–31.

89 Hamilton, *Trucking Country*, 218, 224–31.

90 "President Signs Highway Bill with Provisions for Mass Transit Assistance."

91 Lindsey, "In Mass Transit, Turnstiles Are Clicking Faster"; Lindsey, "Transit Systems Gain Customers"; Blumenthal, "Many Transport Systems Retain

Crisis-Won Riders." This turn toward public transportation followed a political reaction against the interstate highway system and the destruction that it visited on the physical fabric of American cities. See Mohl, "Interstates and the Cities," and Mohl, "Stop the Road."

92 Cleckner, "Bikeways," 7; Kanfer, "Full Circle"; Forester, "The Toy Bicycle Mentality in Government," 52–54; Mapes, *Pedaling Revolution*, 27–31. See also Hays, *Beauty, Health, and Permanence*, 2–5, 7–10, 13–14, 21–39, and Crotty, "Single Track Mind."

93 Kanfer, "Full Circle" (quotation); Waggoner, "Bike Rentals Up in Energy Crisis"; Cleckner, "Bikeways," 7; Dougherty, "The Bicycle vs. the Energy Crisis," 36–39; Hirst, "Cycling for Energy Conservation," 48–49. See also U.S. Department of Transportation, *Bicycle Transportation for Energy Conservation*, and Moran, *Bicycle Transportation for Energy Conservation*.

94 "The Marriage of Bike and Auto," 20–23 (quotation, 20). See also "History of the Bus Bike Rack."

95 Reinhold, "Federal Officials Study Pedal Power as One Alternative to Piston Power" (quotation); "Getting Our Share"; "Environmental Legislation."

96 Reinhold, "Federal Officials Study Pedal Power" (quotation); "President Signs Highway Bill with Provisions for Mass Transit Assistance"; U.S. Department of Transportation, *Bicycles USA*; Bicycle Institute of America, "Summary of 1973 Bikeways Legislation," 22–24; Cleckner, "Bikeways"; Birnbaum, "Federal-Aid Highway Funding for Bikeways." See also U.S. Department of Transportation, *Bicycling for Recreation and Commuting*. On the efforts of Davis, California, to promote bicycling as practical transportation, see Lott and Sommer, "Moving People by Bicycle," 14–15.

97 "Gas Stations Selling Bikes."

98 Retkwa, "Sun Oil Peddles Bicycles."

99 Flink, *Automobile Age*, 5, 13.

100 Merrill, *Oil Crisis of 1973–1974*, 22.

101 Hubbert, "Nuclear Energy and the Fossil Fuels."

102 Wall, "Oil Industry," 807; U.S. Energy Information Administration, *Monthly Alaska Field Production of Crude Oil*. For an excellent overview of the period, see Bacevich, *Limits of Power*, 15–66.

103 Merrill, *Oil Crisis of 1973–1974*, 24–25, 124–29.

104 Ibid., 134–35; Patterson, *Restless Giant*, 230–38.

105 Patterson, *Restless Giant*, 346–63; Yates, "Statistical Portrait of the U.S. Working Class."

106 McKee, "As Suburbs Grow, So Do Waistlines"; Manning, "The Oil We Eat," 37–45; Kolata, "For a World of Woes, We Blame Cookie Monsters"; Ehrenreich, "Fat Guzzling," 14–15.

107 Patterson, *Restless Giant*, 261.

108 Oppel, "Circumventing an Oil Crisis."

109 For specific facts and general context concerning September 11, see Foner, *Give*

Me Liberty! 1172–88; Bacevich, *Limits of Power*; Johnson, *Sorrows of Empire*; and Meyerowitz, *History and September 11th*.

110 See Bacevich, *Limits of Power*, 15–66, for a concise, cogent overview of the oil wars through September 11.

111 Deffeyes, *Beyond Oil*, xi–xvii. For a critical view of Deffeyes, but one that affirms the likelihood of an imminent peak, see Smil, "Peak Oil."

112 See Simmons, *Twilight in the Desert*; Saleri, "Dawn in the Desert"; and Maass, "Breaking Point," 30–35, 50, 56–57.

113 Deffeyes, *Beyond Oil*, xi–xvii.

114 Simon and Kahn, *The Resourceful Earth*, is the classic statement of this "cornucopian" point of view.

115 Deffeyes, *Beyond Oil*, xi–xvii, 3–4 (quotation, 4); Deffeyes, *Hubbert's Peak*, ix–xiv, 1–13.

116 Abbott, "Finally, Too Many Cars."

117 Kaufman, "Gulf Oil Plumes Again Imperil Sea Turtle No. 15"; Wald and Zeller, "Fishing Ban Is Expanded as Spill's Impact Becomes More Evident"; Cooper and Baker, "Administration Opens Inquiries into Oil Disaster"; Baker, "Regret Mixed with Resolve"; "The Latest on the Oil Spill"; Krauss, Broder, and Calmes, "Leak May Persist through August, Obama Aides Say, as Criticism Mounts"; Mouawad and Schwartz, "Rising Cleanup Costs and Numerous Lawsuits Rattle BP's Investors"; Abramson, "A Waiting Game for Fishermen on the Louisiana Water"; Randolph, "Deep Underwater, Threatened Reefs."

118 See Intergovernmental Panel on Climate Change (IPCC), *Climate Change 2007* and other documents at www.eoearth.org/article/ IPCC_Fourth_Assessment_Report.

119 See, for example, Kay, *Asphalt Nation*, 316–17. Ferguson, in "Rise and Fall of the American Carpool," surveyed the social, economic, political, and geographical factors that affected the car pool habits of drivers. See also Tavernise and Gebeloff, "Car Pools, Passé as Hitchhiking." Historians have done little to explain the history of American carpooling.

120 Merrill, *Oil Crisis of 1973–1974*, 23.

121 Mapes, *Pedaling Revolution*, 29, 45–60, 148–50; Mygatt, "Bicycle Production Remains Strong Worldwide"; League of American Bicyclists, "Bicycle Friendly America."

122 Mapes, *Pedaling Revolution*, 141–68.

123 Mygatt, "Bicycle Production Remains Strong Worldwide."

124 See, for example, Mapes, *Pedaling Revolution*, 13–14.

PATHS THAT BECKON

1 Quoted in Miller, *Jefferson and Nature*, 53.

2 See Henretta et al., *America's History*, 128–32; Butler, Wacker, and Balmer, *Religion in American Life*, 118–41; Taylor, *American Colonies*, 338–62; and Wills, *Head and Heart*, 100–117.

3 Henretta et al., *America's History*, 131–32 (quotation, 132).

4 Wills, *Head and Heart*, 110–11 (quotations).

5 Taylor, *American Colonies*, 343–60 (first quotation, 345); Henretta et al., *America's History*, 132 (second quotation); Wills, *Head and Heart*, 115–16; Nash, *Unknown American Revolution*, 7–12.

6 See especially Wills, *Head and Heart*, 100–117 (quotation, 111).

7 Niebuhr, *Nature and Destiny of Man*, 1:3. Stoll, *Protestantism, Capitalism, and Nature in America*, and Dunlap, *Faith in Nature*, are essential to any exploration of the environmental history of American Christianity.

8 Anderson, *Crucible of War*, map 3 following xxvii, 227–28, 236–39, 345–47, 411–12, 741–46.

9 A consideration of the environmental histories of colonial regions during the revolutionary period might begin with Hornsby, *British Atlantic, American Frontier*, and O'Shaughnessy, *An Empire Divided*.

10 The order was Newtonian in the sense of general laws at work in the social and political affairs of people, not of some specific law or principle derived directly from Newton's science. On this matter, and on the proclivity of Americans for an inductive, experimental style of reasoning appropriate to "a consciousness of a frontier" and "the hard facts of brute experience," see Cohen, *Science and the Founding Fathers*, especially 19–60, 237–80.

11 Novak, "The Myth of the 'Weak' American State," 752–72, and the subsequent exchange, "On the 'Myth' of the 'Weak' American State," 766–800, provide a lively debate on American state formation, although with scant reference to biophysical conditions in relation to which the state took shape. More suggestive for the environmental historian are Maier, "Consigning the Twentieth Century to History: Alternative Narratives for the Modern Era"; 807–31; Schulman, "Governing Nature, Nurturing Government"; and Smith, *Building New Deal Liberalism*. I thank my colleagues Nathan Citino and Jared Orsi for helping me think about questions related to the environmental history of U.S. state formation and national development.

12 Maier, "Consigning the Twentieth Century to History," 814–23. See also Hofstadter, *Progressive Historians*, 152–64, and Nye, *Consuming Power*, 111–28.

13 Maier, "Consigning the Twentieth Century to History," 823–31. A consideration of the changing nature of the nation might begin with works that assess the cost of highways, suburbs, consumption, and empire. See, for example, Bacevich, *Limits of Power*, 15–66, but also Stoll, *Great Delusion*; Cohen, *Consumer's Republic*; Gutfreund, *Twentieth Century Sprawl*; Schlosser, *Fast Food Nation*; and Johnson, *Blowback*.

14 Faragher, *Rereading Frederick Jackson Turner*; Miller, *Nature's Nation*.

15 Although the parties differentiated their presidential and vice presidential aspirants, the Constitution contained no provision for electors to do the same. The Republican electors had failed to coordinate their votes, and they mistakenly gave Jefferson and Burr the same number.

16 Wood, *Empire of Liberty,* 276–86.

17 Ibid., 2–3, 209–10, 315–16; Wood, *Creation of the American Republic,* 471–564.

18 Wood, *Empire of Liberty,* 53–114, 209–16, 256–68, 302–8 (quotation, 304).

19 Ibid., 140–73, 251–56, 268–71, 276–77, 286–301 (quotation, 301), 315–99.

20 Ibid., 114–39, 158–73, 216–34, 249–50, 256–62, 276–77, 305–8.

21 Foner, *Reconstruction,* and Hahn, *A Nation Under Our Feet,* are two essential sources on Reconstruction.

22 Giltner, in *Hunting and Fishing in the New South,* did not focus on Reconstruction but asked the kinds of questions that might enable a reconsideration of that event as an important moment in American environmental history. See also Hahn, "Hunting, Fishing, and Foraging," 36–64.

23 Foner, *Reconstruction,* 11–18, 50–60, 68–76 (quotation, 70), 77–78, 102–19, 228–345; Hahn, *Nation Under Our Feet,* 62–313.

24 Foner, *Reconstruction,* 124–227, 392–459, 524–601. Hahn, in *Nation Under Our Feet,* 317–464, was much more positive about African Americans' lasting achievements in the face of severe repression.

25 Hahn, *Nation Under Our Feet,* 163.

26 Du Bois, *Darkwater,* 1 (second quotation), 17–42, 47–69 (first quotation, 57), 78–92 (third quotation, 91; fourth quotation, 83).

27 Ibid. 132–40 (quotations, in order, 132, 133, 139).

28 Ibid. 134–35 (quotations).

29 Du Bois, "Conservation of Races," 815–26.

30 Du Bois, *Darkwater,* 47–59, 78–92 (second and third quotations, 80; fourth quotation, 81), 123–27 (first quotation, 123).

31 Ibid. 114–27 (quotations, 123, 127).

32 "The modern world," Charles Maier observed, "was gripped by the episteme of separation," and it divided things conceptually and spatially along national, racial, gender, class, and other lines. Maier, "Consigning the Twentieth Century to History," 819. I would argue that the episteme of separation also reinforced a deep-seated cultural predisposition to segregate race from nature and other categories of intellectual inquiry. Otherwise outstanding, well-meaning scholarship that severs social and labor history from its biophysical basis unknowingly perpetuates the anachronistic, outmoded episteme of separation. The effort of environmental historians to understand the world in terms of connections, flows, networks, and ecological relationships is consistent with, if not a product of, the episteme's breakdown. Cf. White, "The Problem with Purity."

33 Du Bois, *Souls of Black Folk,* 77–93; Leopold, *Sand County Almanac,* 124–27. See also Du Bois, *Darkwater,* 47–59.

34 Muir and Leopold were aware of race and ethnicity in relation to landscape, but this was not the point of their work as it was for Du Bois. See Worster, *Passion for Nature,* and Meine, *Aldo Leopold.*

35 Smith, *African American Environmental Thought,* ix.

36 Du Bois, *Darkwater,* 2.

37 Kennedy, *Freedom from Fear*, 288–322; Lichtenstein, Strasser, and Rosenzweig, *Who Built America?* 2:431–34, 439–48.

38 Mitchell, in "Carbon Democracy," 399–432, explained the connections between the physical nature of energy sources and the democratization of society.

39 The starting point for any consideration of coal, industrialization, and environmental history is Andrews, *Killing for Coal*.

40 Kennedy, *Freedom from Fear*, 298–300, 302–3, 305.

41 Ibid., 300, 302–5.

42 Mitchell, "Carbon Democracy," 403–9.

43 Kennedy, *Freedom from Fear*, 308–10; Lichtenstein et al., *Who Built America?* 2:440 (quotation); Nye, *Consuming Power*, 121–28, 132–33, 142.

44 Kennedy, *Freedom from Fear*, 310.

45 See, for example, Maher, *Nature's New Deal*; Phillips, *This Land, This Nation*; and Worster, *Dust Bowl*.

46 See, for example, McEvoy, "Working Environments," S145–S172, and Edsforth, *Class Conflict and Cultural Consensus*, 8, on workers' maintenance of rural, preindustrial relationships to nature as a means of coping with the rigors of industrial work.

47 On this question, see Cooper, "Custom Design, Engineering Guarantees, and Unpatentable Data," 506–36.

48 Friedan, *Feminine Mystique*, 15 (quotation). On gender and nature generally, see Scharff, *Seeing Nature through Gender*.

49 Friedan, *Feminine Mystique*, 37, 45, 54 (second quotation), 79 (third quotation), 110, 127 (first quotation).

50 Ibid., 174–246.

51 Ibid., 247–325.

52 Ibid., 326–64 (quotations, 330, 364).

53 Lerner quoted in Horowitz, "Rethinking Betty Friedan and *The Feminine Mystique*," 22; Carson, *Silent Spring*.

54 See, for example, Bacevich, *Limits of Power*, 25–27.

55 Patterson, *Restless Giant*, 179–80 (quotation, 180). On the environmental history of AIDS, see Shilts, *And the Band Played On*, 311 (quotation), and Garrett, *Coming Plague*. As Shilts wrote (p. 41), the first AIDS deaths were like "single frames of tragedy in this and that corner of the world," which "would begin to flicker fast enough to reveal the movement of something new and horrible from the earth's biological landscape."

56 For a learned, provocative analysis that says virtually nothing about conservatism's relationship to nature, environment, or material underpinnings generally, see Chappell, "The Triumph of Conservatives in a Liberal Age," 303–27.

57 In general, see Patterson, *Grand Expectations*, 61–104, 311–74.

58 Patterson, *Grand Expectations*, 375–406, 560–92, 637–77, 730–35; Foner, *Story of American Freedom*, 314–16; Patterson, *Restless Giant*, 15–44.

59 Patterson, *Grand Expectations*, 725–29; Patterson, *Restless Giant*, 15–44.

60 Patterson, *Restless Giant*, 152–78; Foner, *Story of American Freedom*, 320–30.

61 Patterson, *Restless Giant*, 78, 136–38, 251–52, 253–54, 266; Foner, *Story of American Freedom*, 318–19. On the robustness, enduring vitality, and truth of evolutionary thought, see, for example, Gould, *Bully for Brontosaurus*.

62 See, for example, Brooks, *Public Power, Private Dams*; Cannon, *President Reagan*, 530; and Drake, "The Skeptical Environmentalist."

63 An excellent entry point into the environmental history of conservatism is Frohnen, Beer, and Nelson, *American Conservatism*. See, for example, the entries under abortion, agrarianism, Burkean conservatism, capitalism, community, conservatism, environmentalism, historic preservation, natural law, new urbanism, property rights, science and scientism, Southern Agrarians, and West, American.

64 Friedel, *Culture of Improvement*, 479–501, 527–43.

65 Olmsted, *Yosemite and the Mariposa Grove*, 1–28 (quotations, 13, 18). Worster, in *Passion for Nature*, 6–11, 328, 417, 465, observed that conservation in the United States was integral to the rise of liberal democracy.

66 I addressed some of these issues in Fiege, "Land of Lincoln." See also, for example, Borgwardt, *A New Deal for the World*.

67 Friedel, *Culture of Improvement*, chapter 24, "The Corruption of Improvement." On instrumental reason and some of its consequences, see Worster, *Rivers of Empire*, 52–58, and Sherry, *Rise of American Air Power*, 219–55.

68 On irony and tragedy in American history, see Niebuhr, *Irony of American History*.

69 See Moberg, *René Dubos, Friend of the Good Earth*.

70 Dubos, *Wooing of Earth*, xv (first and second quotations), 80 (third quotation); Moberg, *René Dubos*, 172 (fourth and fifth quotations). See also Stoll, *Larding the Lean Earth*, 224–26. For an outstanding practical example of the kind of activity that Dubos described as wooing, see Sutter, "Representing the Resource," 94–96. For a critique of Dubos, see Abbey, "Thus I Reply to René Dubos." Worster's thoughts regarding humanity's place in nature might be worth considering in this context. "When set free from its bondage to money and power," he wrote, "reason can determine which uses of the earth are worthy and truly necessary, and which are not. It can show us how to escape the limits of nature, not by dominating with machines or dams, but by transcending through the development of human imagination and virtue." Worster, *Rivers of Empire*, 58.

REFERENCES

Abbey, Edward. "Thus I Reply to René Dubos." In *Down the River*, 111–21. New York: E. P. Dutton, 1982.

Abbott, Carl. "Finally, Too Many Cars." *History News Network*, 23 February 2009, http://hnn.us/articles/62948.html.

Abramson, Jill. "A Waiting Game for Fishermen on the Louisiana Water." *New York Times*, 2 June 2010.

Adams, George Worthington. *Doctors in Blue: The Medical History of the Union Army in the Civil War*. Baton Rouge: Louisiana State University Press, 1952. Reprint, Baton Rouge: Louisiana State University Press, 1996.

Adams, Nathan M. "A Tankful of Gas." *Reader's Digest*, May 1976, 270.

Adas, Michael. *Machines as the Measure of Men: Science, Technology, and Ideologies of Western Dominance*. Ithaca, N.Y.: Cornell University Press, 1989.

"AHR Conversation: Environmental Historians and Environmental Crisis." *American Historical Review* 113 (December 2008): 1431–65.

Akers, Charles W. *Abigail Adams: An American Woman*. 2nd ed. New York: Longman, 2000.

Alexander, Thomas G. "Stewardship and Enterprise: The LDS Church and the Wasatch Oasis Environment, 1847–1930." *Western Historical Quarterly* 25 (Autumn 1994): 340–64.

Alvarez, Luis W. *Alvarez: Adventures of a Physicist*. New York: Basic Books, 1987.

Amar, Akhil Reed. *America's Constitution: A Biography*. New York: Random House, 2005.

Ames, Charles Edgar. *Pioneering the Union Pacific: A Reappraisal of the Builders of the Railroad*. New York: Appleton-Century Crofts, 1969.

Andelman, David. "Motorists Line Up for Gasoline Here." *New York Times*, 2 December 1973.

Anderson, Bernice Gibbs. "The Driving of the Golden Spike: The End of the Race." *Utah Historical Quarterly* 24 (April 1956): 149–56.

Anderson, Fred. *Crucible of War: The Seven Years' War and the Fate of Empire in British North America, 1754–1766.* New York: Knopf, 2000.

Anderson, Virginia DeJohn. *Creatures of Empire: How Domestic Animals Transformed Early America.* New York: Oxford University Press, 2004.

———. "King Philip's Herds: Indians, Colonists, and the Problem of Livestock in Early New England." *William and Mary Quarterly* 51, 3rd series (October 1994): 601–24.

Andrews, Thomas. *Killing for Coal: America's Deadliest Labor War.* Cambridge, Mass.: Harvard University Press, 2008.

Angle, Paul M. *"Here I Have Lived": A History of Lincoln's Springfield, 1821–1865.* New Brunswick, N.J.: Rutgers University Press, 1935.

"Another Suit Filed against Renewal Plan." *Topeka Journal,* 20 July 1959. In newspaper clipping books, Kansas State Historical Society, Topeka.

Appleby, Joyce. *Capitalism and a New Social Order: The Republican Vision of the 1790s.* New York: New York University Press, 1984.

Aptheker, Herbert, ed. *A Documentary History of the Negro People in the United States.* New York: Citadel Press, 1951.

Armitage, David. *The Declaration of Independence: A Global History.* Cambridge, Mass.: Harvard University Press, 2007.

Armitage, Kevin C. *The Nature Study Movement: The Forgotten Popularizer of America's Conservation Ethic.* Lawrence: University Press of Kansas, 2009.

Arrington, Leonard J., and Davis Bitton. *The Mormon Experience: A History of the Latter-day Saints.* New York: Knopf, 1979.

Associated Press. "Ohio Protest Goes On." *New York Times,* 6 December 1973.

———. "U.S. Aides Worried by Truck Protest." *New York Times,* 3 February 1974.

Athearn, Robert G. "Contracting for the Union Pacific." *Utah Historical Quarterly* 37 (Winter 1969): 17–40.

———. *In Search of Canaan: Black Migration to Kansas, 1879–1880.* Lawrence: Regents Press of Kansas, 1978.

———. *Union Pacific Country.* Chicago: Rand McNally, 1971.

Atkins, Peter. *Four Laws That Drive the Universe.* New York: Oxford University Press, 2007.

Bacevich, Andrew J. *The Limits of Power: The End of American Exceptionalism.* New York: Metropolitan Books and Henry Holt, 2008.

Bacon, Benjamin W. *Sinews of War: How Technology, Industry, and Transportation Won the Civil War.* Novato, Calif.: Presidio Press, 1997.

Badash, Lawrence. *Scientists and the Development of Nuclear Weapons: From Fission to the Limited Test Ban Treaty, 1939–1963.* Atlantic Highlands, N.J.: Humanities Press, 1995.

Bagley, Will. *Blood of the Prophets: Brigham Young and the Massacre at Mountain Meadows.* Norman: University of Oklahoma Press, 2002.

Bailyn, Bernard. *The Ideological Origins of the American Revolution.* Cambridge, Mass.: Harvard University Press, 1967.

————, ed. *Pamphlets of the American Revolution, 1750–1776.* Cambridge, Mass.: Harvard University Press, 1965.

Bain, David Haward. *Empire Express: Building the First Transcontinental Railroad.* New York: Viking Penguin, 1999.

Bainbridge, Kenneth T. "A Foul and Awesome Display." *Bulletin of the Atomic Scientists* 31 (May 1975): 43.

Baker, Peter. "Regret Mixed with Resolve: President Concedes Mistakes on Oil Spill." *New York Times,* 28 May 2010.

Ball, Charles. *Fifty Years in Chains.* New York: Dover, 1970.

Barclay, Harold B. *The Role of the Horse in Man's Culture.* London: J. A. Allen, 1980.

Barker, Ernest. "Natural Law and the American Revolution." In *Traditions of Civility: Eight Essays,* 263–355. Cambridge: Cambridge University Press, 1948. Reprint, New York: Archon Books, 1967.

Basler, Roy P., ed. *The Collected Works of Abraham Lincoln.* 9 vols. New Brunswick, N.J.: Rutgers University Press, 1953, 1955.

Becker, Carl. *The Declaration of Independence: A Study in the History of Political Ideas.* New York: Vintage Books, 1958.

Beebe, Lucius, and Charles Clegg. *Hear the Train Blow: A Pictorial Epic of America in the Railroad Age.* New York: Dutton, 1952.

Beeman, Richard. *The Penguin Guide to the United States Constitution.* New York: Penguin Books, 2010.

Behringer, Wolfgang. *Witchcraft Persecutions in Bavaria: Popular Magic, Religious Zealotry, and Reason of State in Early Modern Europe.* Cambridge: Cambridge University Press, 1997.

Belich, James. *Replenishing the Earth: The Settler Revolution and the Rise of the Anglo-World, 1783–1939.* New York: Oxford University Press, 2009.

Bell, Andrew McIlwaine. *Mosquito Soldiers: Malaria, Yellow Fever, and the Course of the American Civil War.* Baton Rouge: Louisiana State University Press, 2010.

Bellesiles, Michael A. *Revolutionary Outlaws: Ethan Allen and the Struggle for Independence on the Early American Frontier.* Charlottesville: University Press of Virginia, 1993.

Bender, Thomas. *A Nation among Nations: America's Place in World History.* New York: Hill and Wang, 2006.

Beringer, Richard E., Herman Hattaway, Archer Jones, and William N. Still Jr. *Why the South Lost the Civil War.* Athens: University of Georgia Press, 1986.

Berkin, Carol. *First Generations: Women in Colonial America.* New York: Hill and Wang, 1996.

Berlamaqui, Jean-Jacques. *Principles of Natural and Politic Law.* Edited and with an introduction by Peter Korkman. Indianapolis, Ind.: Liberty Fund, 2006.

Berlin, Ira. *Generations of Captivity: A History of African American Slaves.* Cambridge, Mass.: Harvard University Press, 2003.

————. *Many Thousands Gone: The First Two Centuries of Slavery in North America.* Cambridge, Mass.: Harvard University Press, 1998.

Berlin, Ira, and Philip D. Morgan. "Labor and the Shaping of Slave Life in the Americas." In *Cultivation and Culture: Labor and the Shaping of Slave Life in the Americas*, 1–45. Charlottesville: University Press of Virginia, 1993.

Bernstein, Jeremy. "Physicist—I: I. I. Rabi." *New Yorker*, 13 October 1975, 47–110.

———. "Physicist—II: I. I. Rabi." *New Yorker*, 20 October 1975, 47–102.

Berry, Daina Ramey. *"Swing the Sickle for the Harvest Is Ripe": Gender and Slavery in Antebellum Georgia*. Urbana: University of Illinois Press, 2007.

Best, Gerald M. *Iron Horses to Promontory*. San Marino, Calif.: Golden West Books, 1969.

———. "Rendezvous at Promontory: The 'Jupiter' and No. 119." *Utah Historical Quarterly* 37 (Winter 1969): 69–75.

Bethe, Hans. "Brighter than a Thousand Suns." *Bulletin of the Atomic Scientists* 14 (December 1958): 426–28.

Bicycle Institute of America. "Summary of 1973 Bikeways Legislation." *Bicycling!* June 1973, 22–24.

Bird, David. "Effects Spreading Here." *New York Times*, 7 February 1974.

———. "It's Motorist Be Nimble to Keep Gas Tank Full." *New York Times*, 2 January 1974.

———. "Meat Supplies Dip 'Dramatically' in City." *New York Times*, 8 February 1974.

Bird, Kai, and Martin J. Sherwin. *American Prometheus: The Triumph and Tragedy of J. Robert Oppenheimer*. New York: Knopf, 2005.

Bird, Roy. *Topeka: An Illustrated History of the Kansas Capital*. Topeka: Baranski Publishing, 1985.

Birnbaum, Marie. "Federal-Aid Highway Funding for Bikeways." In *Proceedings of the Regional Symposium on Bicycling in the Rural and Urban Environment*, 28–30. N.p.: U.S. Bureau of Outdoor Recreation, Michigan Department of Natural Resources, Michigan Recreation and Park Association, 1974.

Bissell, Hezekiah. "Reminiscences of Hezekiah Bissell." Microfilm Roll H-36, Wyoming State Archives, Cheyenne.

Blackstone, William. *Commentaries on the Laws of England* [1765–69]. 2 vols. Philadelphia: J. B. Lippincott, 1893.

Blaedel, Niels. *Harmony and Unity: The Life of Niels Bohr*. Copenhagen: Carlsbergfondet, 1985. Reprint, Madison, Wis., and Berlin, Germany: Science Tech Publishers and Springer-Verlag, 1988.

Blair, William. *Virginia's Private War: Feeding Body and Soul in the Confederacy, 1861–1865*. New York: Oxford University Press, 1998.

Blasingame, John W., ed. *Slave Testimony: Two Centuries of Letters, Speeches, Interviews, and Autobiographies*. Baton Rouge: Louisiana State University Press, 1977.

Blumenthal, Ralph. "Manning the Pump Is Like Manning a Battle Station." *New York Times*, 3 March 1974.

———. "Many Transport Systems Retain Crisis-Won Riders." *New York Times*, 2 June 1975.

Bodle, Wayne. *The Valley Forge Winter: Civilians and Soldiers in War*. University Park: Pennsylvania State University Press, 2002.

Bohr, Niels. *Atomic Theory and the Description of Nature*. Cambridge: Cambridge University Press, 1934.

Boime, Albert. *The Magisterial Gaze: Manifest Destiny and American Landscape Painting, c. 1830–1865*. Washington, D.C.: Smithsonian Institution, 1991.

———. *The Unveiling of the National Icons: A Plea for Patriotic Iconoclasm in a Nationalist Era*. Cambridge: Cambridge University Press, 1998.

Boles, John B. *Black Southerners, 1619–1869*. Lexington: University Press of Kentucky, 1984.

Boorstin, Daniel. *The Lost World of Thomas Jefferson*. New York: Henry Holt, 1948. Reprint, Boston: Beacon, 1960.

Borgwardt, Elizabeth. *A New Deal for the World: America's Vision for Human Rights*. Cambridge, Mass.: Harvard University Press, 2005.

Boritt, Gabor S., ed. *The Gettysburg Nobody Knows*. New York: Oxford University Press, 1997.

———. *The Gettysburg Gospel: The Lincoln Speech That Nobody Knows*. New York: Simon and Schuster, 2006.

———. *Lincoln and the Economics of the American Dream*. Memphis, Tenn.: Memphis State University Press, 1978.

Botkin, B. A., and Alvin F. Harlow. "An Indian's Account of the Plum Creek Wreck." In *A Treasury of Railroad Folklore: The Stories, Tall Tales, Traditions, Ballads and Songs of the American Railroad Men*, 117–19. New York: Bonanza Books, 1953.

Bowman, J. N. "Driving the Last Spike at Promontory, 1869." *Utah Historical Quarterly* 37 (Winter 1969): 76–101.

Boyer, Paul, and Stephen Nissenbaum. *Salem Possessed: The Social Origins of Witchcraft*. Cambridge, Mass.: Harvard University Press, 1974.

———, eds. *The Salem Witchcraft Papers: Verbatim Transcripts of the Legal Documents of the Salem Witchcraft Outbreak of 1692*. 3 vols. New York: Da Capo Press, 1977.

Boylan, Michael J. "No Rush to Car Pools, Mass Transit or Two-Wheelers." *New York Times*, 26 December 1973.

Bradford, William. *Of Plymouth Plantation, 1620–1647*. Edited by Samuel Eliot Morrison. New York: Knopf, 1952.

Brady, Lisa. "War upon the Land: Nature and Warfare in the American Civil War." PhD dissertation, University of Kansas, 2003.

———. "The Wilderness of War: Nature and Strategy in the American Civil War." *Environmental History* 10 (July 2005): 41–447.

Braudel, Fernand. *Civilization and Capitalism, 15th–18th Century*, vol. 1, *The Structures of Everyday Life: The Limits of the Possible*. New York: Harper and Row, 1981.

Bray, Robert. "What Abraham Lincoln Read: An Evaluative and Annotated List." *Journal of the Abraham Lincoln Association* 28 (Summer 2007): 28–81.

Breen, T. H. *American Insurgents, American Patriots: The Revolution of the People*. New York: Hill and Wang, 2010.

Bridenbaugh, Carl. *The Spirit of '76: The Growth of American Patriotism Before Independence, 1607–1776*. New York: Oxford University Press, 1975.

Briggs, Asa. *The Power of Steam: An Illustrated History of the World's Steam Age.* Chicago: University of Chicago Press, 1982.

Brinkerhoff, Kerry. "Native Americans and the Transcontinental Railroad." *Transcontinental* (Golden Spike National Historic Site) 1, no. 11 (2001): 8.

Brode, Bernice. "Life at Los Alamos, 1943–45." *Atomic Scientists' Journal* 3 (November 1953): 87–90.

———. *Tales of Los Alamos: Life on the Mesa, 1943–1945.* Los Alamos, N.M.: Los Alamos Historical Society, 1997.

Brooks, Karl Boyd. *Public Power, Private Dams: The Hells Canyon High Dam Controversy.* Seattle: University of Washington Press, 2006.

Brown, Andrew. *Geology and the Gettysburg Campaign.* Educational Series 5, 7th ed. Harrisburg: Commonwealth of Pennsylvania, Department of Conservation and Natural Resources, Bureau of Topographic and Geologic Survey, 1997.

Brown, Anthony Cave, and Charles B. MacDonald, eds. *The Secret History of the Atomic Bomb.* New York: Dial Press / James Wade, 1977.

Brown, John. *Slave Life in Georgia.* Edited by L. A. Chamerovzow. London: L. A. Chamerovzow, 1855.

Brown, Kent Masterson. *Retreat from Gettysburg: Lee, Logistics, and the Pennsylvania Campaign.* Chapel Hill: University of North Carolina Press, 2005.

Brown v. Board of Education Oral History Collection. Manuscript Collection no. 251, Kansas State Historical Society Library and Archives, Topeka, Kansas.

Bruce, Robert V. *Lincoln and the Tools of War.* Indianapolis: Bobbs-Merrill, 1956.

Bruns, Roger, ed. *Am I Not a Man and a Brother: The Antislavery Crusade of Revolutionary America, 1688–1788.* New York: Chelsea House, 1977.

Bryant, Keith L., Jr. *History of the Atchison, Topeka, and Santa Fe Railway.* New York: Macmillan, 1974.

"The Building of the Iron Road." *Overland Monthly,* May 1869, 469–78. http://cprr.org/Museum/Building%20the%20Iron%20Road.html.

Burke, Edmund, III. "The Big Story: Human History, Energy Regimes, and the Environment." In *The Environment and World History,* edited by Edmund Burke III and Kenneth Pomeranz, 33–53. Berkeley: University of California Press, 2009.

Burlingame, Michael. *Abraham Lincoln: A Life.* 2 vols. Baltimore: Johns Hopkins University Press, 2008.

———. *The Inner World of Abraham Lincoln.* Urbana: University of Illinois Press, 1994.

———. "Thoughts on the Nature of Lincoln." Paper presented at the 24th Annual Lincoln Colloquium, 17 October 2009, Lincoln Home National Historic Site, Springfield, Illinois.

Burr, George Lincoln, ed. *Narratives of the Witchcraft Cases, 1648–1706.* New York: Charles Scribner's Sons, 1914. Reprint, New York: Barnes and Noble, 1952.

Butler, Jon, Grant Wacker, and Randall Balmer. *Religion in American Life: A Short History.* New York: Oxford University Press, 2003.

Butowsky, Harry A. "Sumner Elementary School." National Register of Historic Places Inventory-Nomination Form, December 1986, Kansas State Historic

Preservation Office, Kansas Historical Society, Topeka.

Byer, Gene. "Realtors Urge Topeka Act against Slums." *Topeka Journal*, 14 March 1956. In newspaper clipping books, Kansas State Historical Society, Topeka.

Calhoun, John C. *Union and Liberty: The Political Philosophy of John C. Calhoun*, edited by Ross M. Lence. Indianapolis, Ind.: Liberty Fund, 1992.

"California Newspapers, 1865–66." Central Pacific Railroad Photographic History Museum. www.cprr.org/Museum/Newspapers.

Calloway, Colin. *The American Revolution in Indian Country: Crisis and Diversity in Native American Communities*. New York: Cambridge University Press, 1995.

———. *New Worlds for All: Indians, Europeans, and the Remaking of Early America*. Baltimore, Md.: Johns Hopkins University Press, 1997.

———. *The World Turned Upside Down: Indian Voices from Early America*. Boston: Bedford Books, 1994.

Camp, Stephanie M. H. *Closer to Freedom: Enslaved Women and Everyday Resistance in the Plantation South*. Chapel Hill: University of North Carolina Press, 2004.

Campbell, John. "As 'a Kind of Freeman'? Slaves' Market-Related Activities in the South Carolina Up Country, 1800–1860." In *Cultivation and Culture: Labor and the Shaping of Slave Life in the Americas*, edited by Ira Berlin and Philip D. Morgan, 243–74. Charlottesville: University Press of Virginia, 1993.

———. "'My Constant Companion': Slaves and Their Dogs in the Antebellum South." In *Working toward Freedom: Slave Society and Domestic Economy in the American South*, edited by Larry E. Hudson Jr., 53–76. Rochester, N.Y.: University of Rochester Press, 1994.

Cannon, Lou. *President Reagan: The Role of a Lifetime*. New York: Simon and Schuster, 1991.

Carlson, Laurie Winn. *A Fever in Salem: A New Interpretation of the New England Witch Trials*. Chicago: Ivan R. Dee, 1999.

Carper, James C. "The Popular Ideology of Segregated Schooling: Attitudes toward the Education of Blacks in Kansas, 1854–1900." *Kansas History* 4 (Winter 1978): 254–65.

Carroll, Peter N. *Puritanism and the Wilderness: The Intellectual Significance of the New England Frontier, 1629–1700*. New York: Columbia University Press, 1969.

Carson, Rachel. *The Sense of Wonder*. New York: Harper and Row, 1965.

———. *Silent Spring*. Boston: Houghton Mifflin, 1962.

Casper, Scott E. "Antebellum Reading Prescribed and Described." In *Perspectives on American Book History*, edited by Scott E. Casper, Joanne D. Chaison, and Jeffrey D. Groves, 135–64. Amherst: University of Massachusetts Press, 2002.

Cassidy, David C. *J. Robert Oppenheimer and the American Century*. New York: Pi Press, 2005.

Catton, Bruce. *The American Heritage Picture History of the Civil War*. New York: American Heritage, 1960.

———. *Glory Road: The Bloody Route from Fredericksburg to Gettysburg*. Garden City, N.Y.: Doubleday, 1955.

Cave, Alfred A. "Indian Shamans and English Witches in Seventeenth-Century New England." *Essex Institute Historical Collections* 128 (October 1992): 239–54.

———. *The Pequot War*. Amherst: University of Massachusetts Press, 1996.

Chan, Sucheng. *This Bittersweet Soil: The Chinese in California Agriculture, 1860–1910.* Berkeley: University of California Press, 1986.

Chaplin, Joyce E. *Subject Matter: Technology, the Body, and Science on the Anglo-American Frontier, 1500–1676.* Cambridge, Mass.: Harvard University Press, 2001.

Chappell, David A. "The Triumph of Conservatives in a Liberal Age." In *A Companion to Post-1945 America,* edited by Jean-Christophe Agnew and Roy Rosenzweig, 303–27. Malden, Mass.: Blackwell, 2002.

Chen, Jack. *The Chinese of America*. San Francisco: Harper and Row, 1980.

Childs, Herbert. *An American Genius: The Life of Ernest Orlando Lawrence*. New York: E. P. Dutton, 1968.

Christian, David. *Maps of Time: An Introduction to Big History*. Berkeley: University of California Press, 2004.

Clark, J. O. E. *Matter and Energy: Physics in Action*. New York: Oxford University Press, 1994.

Clark, Kenneth B., Isidor Chein, and Stuart W. Cook. "The Effects of Segregation and the Consequences of Desegregation," 22 September 1952, appendix to appellants' briefs in *Brown v. Board of Education of Topeka, Kansas, Briggs v. Elliott,* and *Davis v. Prince Edward County, Virginia*. Republished in *American Psychologist* 59 (September 2004): 495–501.

Clark, Kenneth B., and Mamie P. Clark. "Emotional Factors in Racial Identification and Preference in Negro Children." *Journal of Negro Education* 19 (Summer 1950): 341–50.

———. "Racial Identification and Preference in Negro Children." *Readings in Social Psychology,* edited by Theodore M. Newcomb and Eugene L. Hartley, 169–78. New York: Henry Holt, 1947.

Cleckner, Robert M. "Bikeways: The Path of Least Resistance." In *Proceedings of the Regional Symposium on Bicycling in the Rural and Urban Environment,* 6–8. N.p.: U.S. Bureau of Outdoor Recreation, Michigan Department of Natural Resources, Michigan Recreation and Park Association, 1974.

"Coast Volunteers Check 'Gas' Stations on Sundays." *New York Times,* 15 December 1973.

Coco, Gregory A. *A Strange and Blighted Land: Gettysburg, The Aftermath of a Battle.* Gettysburg, Pa.: Thomas Publications, 1995.

Coddington, Edwin B. *The Gettysburg Campaign: A Study in Command*. New York: Charles Scribner's Sons, 1968.

Cohen, Benjamin. *Notes from the Ground: Science, Soil, and Society in the American Countryside.* New Haven, Conn.: Yale University Press, 2009.

Cohen, I. Bernard. *Science and the Founding Fathers: Science in the Political Thought of Thomas Jefferson, Benjamin Franklin, John Adams, and James Madison.* New York: Norton, 1995.

Cohen, Lizabeth. *A Consumer's Republic: The Politics of Mass Consumption in Postwar America*. New York: Knopf, 2003.

Colten, Craig. *An Unnatural Metropolis: Wresting New Orleans from Nature*. Baton Rouge: Louisiana State University Press, 2005.

Combs, Barry B. *Westward to Promontory: Building the Union Pacific across the Plains and Mountains*. Palo Alto, Calif.: American West Publishing, 1969.

Commager, Henry Steele, ed. *The Blue and the Gray: The Story of the Civil War as Told by Participants*. 2 vols. Indianapolis: Bobbs-Merrill, 1950.

——, ed. *Documents of American History*. New York: F. S. Crofts, 1935.

——. *The Empire of Reason: How Europe Imagined and America Realized the Enlightenment*. Garden City, N.Y.: Anchor Press / Doubleday, 1977. Reprint, New York: Oxford University Press, 1982.

Commager, Henry Steele, and Richard B. Morris, eds. *The Spirit of 'Seventy-Six: The Story of the American Revolution as Told by Participants*. New York: Harper and Row, 1958.

"Commission Vote Comes Amid Protest." *Topeka Capital*, 25 March 1959. In newspaper clipping books, Kansas State Historical Society, Topeka.

Committee for the Compilation of Materials on Damage Caused by the Atomic Bombs in Hiroshima and Nagasaki. *Hiroshima and Nagasaki: The Physical, Medical, and Social Effects of the Atomic Bombings*. Tokyo: Iwanami Shoten, 1979. Reprint, New York: Basic Books, 1981.

Conant, Jennet. *109 East Palace: Robert Oppenheimer and the Secret City of Los Alamos*. New York: Simon and Schuster, 2005.

Concklin, Edward F. *The Lincoln Memorial, Washington, D.C.* Washington, D.C.: Government Printing Office, 1927.

Cooper, Gail. "Custom Design, Engineering Guarantees, and Unpatentable Data: The Air Conditioning Industry, 1902–1935." *Technology and Culture* 35 (July 1994): 506–36.

Cooper, Helene, and Peter Baker. "Administration Opens Inquiries into Oil Disaster." *New York Times*, 26 May 2010.

Cottrell, Fred. *Energy and Society: The Relation between Energy, Social Change, and Economic Development*. New York: McGraw-Hill, 1955.

Countryman, Edward. *The American Revolution*. New York: Hill and Wang, 1985.

Covington, Levin. *Diary (1829–1830)*. Reprinted in *Cotton and the Growth of the American Economy: 1790–1860*, edited by Stuart Bruchey, 176–180. New York: Harcourt, Brace, and World, 1967.

Cowan, Edward. "Squeeze on Fuel." *New York Times*, 14 January 1974.

Cowan, Richard O. "Steel Rails and the Utah Saints." *Journal of Mormon History* 27 (Fall 2001): 177–96.

Cox, Thomas C. *Blacks in Topeka, Kansas, 1865–1915: A Social History*. Baton Rouge: Louisiana State University Press, 1982.

Craig, Heather Lloyd. "The Horse Soldiers: Mass Mobilization of Horses and Mules in Modern Warfare, 1914–1945." HY494 Capstone Seminar paper, Colorado State University, Fall 2003.

Cronon, William. *Changes in the Land: Indians, Colonists, and the Ecology of New England.* New York: Hill and Wang, 1983.

———. "Kennecott Journey: The Paths Out of Town." In *Under an Open Sky: Rethinking America's Western Past,* edited by William Cronon, George Miles, and Jay Gitlin, 28–51. New York: Norton, 1992.

———. *Nature's Metropolis: Chicago and the Great West.* New York: Norton, 1991.

———. "A Place for Stories: Nature, History, and Narrative." *Journal of American History* 78 (March 1992): 1347–76.

Cronon, William, George Miles, and Jay Gitlin. "Becoming West: Toward a New Meaning for Western History." In *Under an Open Sky: Rethinking America's Western Past,* edited by William Cronon, George Miles, and Jay Gitlin, 3–27. New York: Norton, 1992.

Crosby, Alfred W. *Ecological Imperialism: The Biological Expansion of Europe, 900–1900.* New York: Cambridge University Press, 1986.

———. "'God . . . Would Destroy Them, and Give Their Country to Another People.'" *American Heritage* 29 (October-November 1978): 39–42.

Crotty, Sean. "Single Track Mind: Bicycling and the Evolution of the American Nature Ideal." Master's thesis, Colorado State University, 1999.

Cummings, Judith. "Gasoline Users Uncertain on Return of Normalcy." *New York Times,* 15 March 1974.

Cunningham, H. H. *Doctors in Gray: The Confederate Medical Service.* Gloucester, Mass.: Peter Smith, 1970.

Current, Richard N. "God and the Strongest Battalions." In *Why the North Won the Civil War,* edited by David Donald, 15–32. Baton Rouge: Louisiana State University Press, 1960. Reprint, New York: Collier Books, 1962.

Currier, John Charles. "Personal Diary Account by Capt. John Charles Currier of the 21st U.S. Infantry at Promontory on May 10, 1869." www.nps.gov/gosp/research/currier.htm (accessed 25 April 2003). Copy in author's possession.

"The Dangers of Taking Precautions." *Newsweek,* 10 December 1973, 97.

Davidson, James West, and Mark Lytle. *After the Fact: The Art of Historical Detection.* 4th ed. New York: McGraw Hill, 2000.

Davis, Clarence B., and Kenneth M. Wilburn, eds. *Railway Imperialism.* New York: Greenwood, 1991.

Davis, David Brion. *The Problem of Slavery in the Age of Revolution, 1770–1823.* Ithaca, N.Y.: Cornell University Press, 1975.

Davis, David Brion, and Steven Mintz, eds. *The Boisterous Sea of Liberty: A Documentary History of America from Discovery through the Civil War.* New York: Oxford University Press, 1998.

Davis, James E. "Abraham Lincoln's Quest for Order." Paper presented at the 24th Annual Lincoln Colloquium, 17 October 2009, Lincoln Home National Historic Site, Springfield, Illinois.

———. *Frontier Illinois.* Bloomington: Indiana University Press, 1998.

Davis, John P. *The Union Pacific Railway: A Study in Railway Politics, History, and*

Economics. Chicago: S. C. Griggs, 1894.

Davis, Nuell Phar. *Lawrence and Oppenheimer.* New York: Simon and Schuster, 1968. Reprint, Greenwich, Conn.: Fawcett, 1969.

Deetz, James. *In Small Things Forgotten: The Archaeology of Early American Life.* New York: Anchor Books, 1977.

Deffeyes, Kenneth S. *Beyond Oil: The View from Hubbert's Peak.* New York: Hill and Wang, 2006.

———. *Hubbert's Peak: The Impending World Energy Shortage.* Princeton, N.J.: Princeton University Press, 2009.

DeGroot, Gerard J. *The Bomb: A Life.* Cambridge, Mass.: Harvard University Press, 2005.

Delaney, David. *Race, Place, and the Law, 1836–1948.* Austin: University of Texas Press, 1998.

Demos, John. *Circles and Lines: The Shape of Life in Early America.* Cambridge, Mass.: Harvard University Press, 2004.

———. *Entertaining Satan: Witchcraft and the Culture of Early New England.* New York: Oxford University Press, 1982.

Deyle, Stephen. *Carry Me Back: The Domestic Slave Trade in American Life.* New York: Oxford University Press, 2005.

Dick, Everett. *Vanguards of the Frontier: A Social History of the Northern Plains and Rocky Mountains from the Fur Traders to the Sod Busters.* New York: D. Appleton-Century, 1941. Reprint, Lincoln: University of Nebraska Press, 1965.

Dodge, Grenville M. *How We Built the Union Pacific Railway.* Washington, D.C.: Government Printing Office, 1910. Reprint, Ann Arbor: University Microfilms, 1966.

Doel, Ronald. "Marion King Hubbert." In *Complete Dictionary of Scientific Biography,* vol. 21, edited by Charles Gillispie, 395–400. New York: Cengage Learning, 2008.

Donald, David R. *Lincoln.* New York: Simon and Schuster, 1995.

Dougherty, Nina. "The Bicycle vs. the Energy Crisis." *Bicycling!* January 1974, 36–39.

Dowdey, Clifford, ed. *The Wartime Papers of R. E. Lee.* New York: Bramhall House, 1961.

Dower, John W. "Triumphal and Tragic Narratives of the War in Asia." *Journal of American History* 82 (December 1995): 1133.

Drake, Brian Allen. "The Skeptical Environmentalist: Senator Barry Goldwater and the Environmental Management State." *Environmental History* 15 (October 2010): 587–611.

Drayton, Richard. *Nature's Government: Science, Imperial Britain, and the "Improvement" of the World.* New Haven, Conn.: Yale University Press, 2000.

"Driver Wanting to Exceed Gasoline Limit Is Slain." *New York Times,* 13 January 1974.

Du Bois, W. E. B. "The Conservation of Races." *Occasional Papers* 2. Washington, D.C.: American Negro Academy, 1897. Reprinted in *W. E. B. Du Bois: Writings,* edited by Nathan Huggins, 815–26. New York: Library of America, 1986.

———. *Darkwater: Voices from within the Veil.* New York: Harcourt, Brace, 1920. Reprint, Mineola, N.Y.: Dover, 1999.

———. *The Souls of Black Folk.* New York: A. C. McClurg, 1903. Reprint, New York: Bantam, 1989.

————. "The Upbuilding of Black Durham." *World's Work* 13 (January 1912): 334–38. Reprinted in *W. E. B. Du Bois: A Reader*, edited by David Levering Lewis, 253–58. New York: Henry Holt, 1995.

Dubos, René. *The Wooing of Earth: New Perspectives on Man's Use of Nature*. New York: Charles Scribner's Sons, 1980.

Ducker, James H. *Men of the Steel Rails: Workers on the Atchison, Topeka, and Santa Fe Railroad, 1869–1900*. Lincoln: University of Nebraska Press, 1983.

Dudziak, Mary L. "The Limits of Good Faith: Desegregation in Topeka, Kansas." Substantial Paper Requirement, Professor Burke Marshall, Yale University Law School, 23 May 1984. In File 1003, Box 17, Record Group 21, *Brown v. Board of Education* Exhibit Files, T-316, National Archives and Records Administration, Kansas City, Missouri.

Dugatkin, Lee Alan. *Mr. Jefferson and the Giant Moose: Natural History in Early America*. Chicago: University of Chicago Press, 2009.

Dunlap, Thomas R. *Faith in Nature: Environmentalism as Religious Quest*. Seattle: University of Washington Press, 2005.

Dunn, Richard S. *The Age of Religious Wars, 1559–1715*. 2nd ed. New York: Norton, 1979.

————. "America in the British Empire." In *The Reader's Companion to American History*, edited by Eric Foner and John A. Garraty, 29–32. Boston: Houghton Mifflin, 1991.

Dworetz, Stephen M. *The Unvarnished Doctrine: Locke, Liberalism, and the American Revolution*. Durham, N.C.: Duke University Press, 1990.

Dyson, Freeman. *Disturbing the Universe*. New York: Harper and Row, 1979.

————. "Wise Man." *New York Review of Books*, 20 October 2005, 6.

Edsforth, Ronald. *Class Conflict and Cultural Consensus: The Making of Mass Consumer Society in Flint, Michigan*. New Brunswick, N.J.: Rutgers University Press, 1987.

Ehrenreich, Barbara. "Fat Guzzling." *Progressive* 72 (September 2008): 14–15.

"800 Gallons of 'Gas' Stolen." *New York Times*, 13 December 1973.

"8,500 Gallons Missing in Coast 'Gasjacking.'" *New York Times*, 16 March 1974.

Ekirch, A. Roger. *At Day's Close: Night in Times Past*. New York: Norton, 2005.

Ellis, Joseph J. *American Sphinx: The Character of Thomas Jefferson*. New York: Knopf, 1997.

————. *Founding Brothers: The Revolutionary Generation*. New York: Knopf, 2000.

————, ed. *What Did the Declaration Declare?* Boston: Bedford / St. Martin's, 1999.

Emerson, Jason. *Lincoln the Inventor*. Carbondale: Southern Illinois University Press, 2009.

"Environmental Legislation." Oregon Legislative History, Oregon Legislative Records Guide, Oregon State Archives. www.sos.state.or.us/archives/legislative/legislative_guide/legislative_guide/History.html#Environmental (accessed 10 May 2009).

Environment and History Theme Issue. *History and Theory* 42 (December 2003).

Epstein, Daniel Mark. *Lincoln and Whitman: Parallel Lives in Civil War Washington*. New York: Random House, 2004.

Essin, Emmitt M. III "Mule." In *The New Encyclopedia of the American West*, edited by

Howard R. Lamar, 745–48. New Haven, Conn.: Yale University Press, 1998.

"Even without Gas Rationing—Headaches Pile Up for Drivers." *U.S. News and World Report*, 31 December 1973, 11–12.

Famighetti, Robert, ed. *World Almanac and Book of Facts, 2000*. Mahwah, N.J.: World Almanac Books.

Faragher, John Mack, ed. *Rereading Frederick Jackson Turner: "The Significance of the Frontier in American History" and Other Essays*. New York: Henry Holt, 1994.

———. *Sugar Creek: Life on the Illinois Prairie*. New Haven, Conn.: Yale University Press, 1986.

Faust, Drew Gilpin. *This Republic of Suffering: Death and the American Civil War*. New York: Knopf, 2007.

Fehrenbacher, Don E., ed. *Abraham Lincoln: Speeches and Writings*, vol. 1, *1832–1858*, vol. 2, *1859–1865*. New York: Library of America, 1989.

Feld, Bernard T. "The Nagasaki Binge." *Bulletin of the Atomic Scientists* 22 (February 1966): 35–37.

Fenn, Elizabeth A. *Pox Americana: The Great Smallpox Epidemic of 1775–82*. New York: Hill and Wang, 2001.

Ferguson, Erik. "The Rise and Fall of the American Carpool: 1970–1990." *Transportation* 24 (November 1997): 349–76.

Ferguson, Frances. "The Nuclear Sublime." *Diacritics* 14 (Summer 1984): 4–10.

Fermi, Laura. *Atoms in the Family*. Chicago: University of Chicago Press, 1954.

Ferretti, Fred. "The Way We Were: A Look Back at the Late Great Gas Shortage." *New York Times*, 14 April 1974.

Fett, Sharla M. *Working Cures: Healing, Health, and Power on Southern Slave Plantations*. Chapel Hill: University of North Carolina Press, 2002.

Feynman, Richard P. *"Surely You're Joking, Mr. Feynman!": Adventures of a Curious Character*. New York: Norton, 1985.

Fiege, Mark. "The Atomic Scientists, the Sense of Wonder, and the Bomb." *Environmental History* 12 (July 2007): 578–613.

———. "Gettysburg and the Organic Nature of the American Civil War." In *Natural Enemy, Natural Ally: Toward an Environmental History of War*, edited by Richard P. Tucker and Edmund Russell, 93–109. Corvallis: Oregon State University Press, 2004.

———. "Land of Lincoln: Environmental History and the Sixteenth President." Lincoln Legacy Lecture Series, Center for State Policy and Leadership, University of Illinois, Springfield, 2009.

Fiege, Mark, and Stephen Mihm. "On Bank Notes." *Environmental History* 13 (April 2008): 351–59.

Finch, Martha. "'Civilized' Bodies and the 'Savage' Environment of Early New Plymouth." In *A Centre of Wonders: The Body in Early America*, edited by Janet Moore Lindman and Michele Lise Tarter, 43–59. Ithaca, N.Y.: Cornell University Press, 2001.

Fischer, David Hackett. *Albion's Seed: Four British Folkways in America*. New York: Oxford University Press, 1989.

Fisher, Irving. "National Vitality, Its Wastes and Conservation." In *Report of the National Conservation Commission*, vol. 3, edited by Henry Gannett, 620–751. Washington, D.C.: Government Printing Office, 1909.

Flexner, Stuart Berg. *I Hear America Talking: An Illustrated History of American Words and Phrases.* New York: Touchstone, 1976.

Flink, James J. "American Automobile Association." *Dictionary of American History*, 2003. *Encyclopedia.com* (July 13, 2009). www.encyclopedia.com/doc/1G2-3401800150. html.

———. *The Automobile Age.* Cambridge, Mass.: MIT Press, 1988.

———. *The Car Culture.* Cambridge, Mass.: MIT Press, 1976.

Flint, Jerry. "Except in Northeast, Gasoline Is Available, but Supply Is Tightening." *New York Times*, 11 February 1974.

Flores, Dan. "Zion in Eden: Phases in the Environmental History of Utah." In *The Natural West: Environmental History in the Great Plains and Rocky Mountains*, 124–44. Norman: University of Oklahoma Press, 2001.

Follett, Richard. *The Sugar Masters: Planters and Slaves in Louisiana's Cane World, 1820–1860.* Baton Rouge: Louisiana State University Press, 2005.

Foner, Eric. *The Fiery Trial: Abraham Lincoln and American Slavery.* New York: Norton, 2010.

———. *Free Soil, Free Labor, Free Men: The Ideology of the Republican Party Before the Civil War.* New York: Oxford, 1970.

———. *Give Me Liberty! An American History.* 2 vols., 3rd ed. New York: Norton, 2011.

———, ed. *Our Lincoln: New Perspectives on Lincoln and His World.* New York: Norton, 2008.

———. *Reconstruction: America's Unfinished Revolution, 1863–1877.* New York: Harper and Row, 1988.

———. *The Story of American Freedom.* New York: Norton, 1998.

———. *Tom Paine and Revolutionary America.* New York: Oxford University Press, 1976.

Ford, Worthington C., and George W. Robinson and Stewart Mitchell, eds. *Winthrop Papers*, vol. 2. Boston: Massachusetts Historical Society, 1931.

Forester, John. "The Toy Bicycle Mentality in Government." *Bicycling!* September 1973, 52–54.

Fornieri, Joseph R. "Introduction: Lincoln, the Natural Law, and Prudence." In *The Language of Liberty: The Political Speeches and Writings of Abraham Lincoln*, edited by Joseph R. Fornieri, xix–lxiii. Washington, D.C.: Regnery, 2003.

Fornieri, Joseph, and Sara Vaughn Gabbard, eds. *Lincoln's America, 1809–1865.* Carbondale: Southern Illinois University Press, 2008.

"Forum: Environmental History, Retrospect and Prospect." *Pacific Historical Review* 70 (February 2001): 55–111.

Foster, Steven, and James A. Duke, *A Field Guide to Medicinal Plants: Eastern and Central North America.* Boston: Houghton Mifflin, 1990.

Fowler, Glenn. "Motorists Begin a Grim Weekend." *New York Times*, 9 February 1974.

Francaviglia, Richard V. *Over the Range: A History of the Promontory Summit Route of the Pacific Railroad*. Logan: Utah State University Press, 2008.

Francaviglia, Richard, and Jimmy L. Bryan Jr. "'Are We Chimerical in This Opinion?': Visions of a Pacific Railroad and Westward Expansion Before 1845." *Pacific Historical Review* 71 (Spring 2002): 179–202.

Franklin, Benjamin. *Silence Dogood, The Busy-Body, and Early Writings*. Edited by J. A. Leo Lemay. New York: Library of America, 1987.

Franklin, John Hope, and Loren Schweninger. *Runaway Slaves: Rebels on the Plantation*. New York: Oxford, 1999.

Frassanito, William A. *Early Photography at Gettysburg*. Gettysburg, Pa.: Thomas Publications, 1995.

———. *Gettysburg: A Journey in Time*. New York: Charles Scribner's Sons, 1975.

Frayssé, Olivier. *Lincoln, Land, and Labor*. Translated by Sylvia Neely. Paris: Publications de la Sorbonne, 1988. Reprint, Urbana: University of Illinois Press, 1994.

Fredrickson, George M. *Big Enough to Be Inconsistent: Abraham Lincoln Confronts Slavery and Race*. Cambridge, Mass.: Harvard University Press, 2008.

Freeman, Douglas Southall. *R. E. Lee: A Biography*. 3 vols. New York: Charles Scribner's Sons, 1946.

Frey, Sylvia R. *Water from the Rock: Black Resistance in a Revolutionary Age*. Princeton, N.J.: Princeton University Press, 1991.

Friedan, Betty. *The Feminine Mystique*. New York: Norton, 1963. Reprint, New York: Dell, 1973.

Friedel, Robert. *A Culture of Improvement: Technology and the Western Millennium*. Cambridge, Mass.: MIT Press, 2007.

Friedman, Leon, ed. *Brown v. Board: The Landmark Oral Argument Before the Supreme Court*. New York: New Press, 2004.

Fries, William D., Jr. "Convoy." Lyrics. Performed by William D. Fries Jr. as "C. W. McCall." *Black Bear Road*. MGM Records, 1975.

Frohnen, Bruce, ed. *The American Republic: Primary Sources*. Indianapolis, Ind.: Liberty Fund, 2002.

Frohnen, Bruce, Jeremy Beer, and Jeffrey O. Nelson, eds. *American Conservatism: An Encyclopedia*. Wilmington, Del.: ISI Books, 2006.

Furtwangler, Albert. *Acts of Discovery: Visions of America in the Lewis and Clark Journals*. Urbana: University of Illinois Press, 1993.

Fussell, Paul. *Thank God for the Atom Bomb, and Other Essays*. New York: Ballantine, 1988.

Gagan, Elizabeth A. "Landscapes of Childhood and Youth." In *A Companion to Cultural Geography*, edited by James S. Duncan, Nuala C. Johnson, and Richard H. Schein, 404–19. Malden, Mass.: Blackwell, 2004.

Galloway, John Debo. *The First Transcontinental Railroad*. New York: Simmons-Boardman, 1950.

"Gallup Poll Finds Most Still Use Car." *New York Times*, 14 February 1974.

Garrett, Laurie. *The Coming Plague: Newly Emerging Diseases in a World Out of Balance*. New York: Farrar, Straus and Giroux, 1994.

"Gas in Can Proves Death Trap for Driver." *New York Times*, 17 December 1973.

"Gas Stations Selling Bikes." *New York Times*, 6 April 1974.

"Gasoline Siphoner Leaves $5 Payment in Tank." *New York Times*, 31 December 1973.

Gates, Paul W. *Agriculture and the Civil War*. New York: Alfred A. Knopf, 1965.

Gemery, Henry. "The White Population of the Colonial United States." In *A Population History of North America*, edited by Michael R. Hines and Richard H. Steckel, 143–90. Cambridge: Cambridge University Press, 2000.

Genovese, Eugene D. *The Political Economy of Slavery: Studies in the Economy and Society of the Slave South*. 2nd ed. Middletown, Conn.: Wesleyan University Press, 1989.

"Getting Our Share." *Oregon Cycling Magazine*, June 2008. www.oregoncycling.org/2008/06/getting-our-share/ (accessed 10 May 2009).

Gibson, Alan. *Interpreting the Founding: Guide to the Enduring Debates over the Origins and Foundations of the American Republic*. 2nd ed. Lawrence: University Press of Kansas, 2009.

———. *Understanding the Founding: The Crucial Questions*. 2nd ed. Lawrence: University Press of Kansas, 2010.

Gilliss, John R. "Tunnels of the Pacific Railroad." *Transactions of the American Society of Civil Engineers* 1 (1872): 155–71.

Gilpin, William. "Observations on the Pacific Railroad." In *The American Frontier: Readings and Documents*, edited by Robert V. Hine and Edwin R. Bingham, 259–65. Boston: Little, Brown, 1972.

Giltner, Scott E. *Hunting and Fishing in the New South: Black Labor and White Leisure After the Civil War*. Baltimore, Md.: Johns Hopkins University Press, 2008.

———. "Slave Hunting and Fishing in the Antebellum South." In *To Love the Wind and the Rain: African Americans and Environmental History*, edited by Dianne D. Glave and Mark Stoll, 21–36. Pittsburgh, Pa.: University of Pittsburgh Press, 2006.

Glassie, Henry. *Folk Housing in Middle Virginia: A Structural Analysis of Historic Artifacts*. Knoxville: University of Tennessee Press, 1975.

Glatthaar, Joseph T. "The Common Soldier's Gettysburg Campaign." In *The Gettysburg Nobody Knows*, edited by Gabor S. Boritt, 3–30. New York: Oxford University Press, 1997.

———. *General Lee's Army: From Victory to Collapse*. New York: Free Press, 2008.

Glave, Dianne D., and Mark Stoll, eds. *To Love the Wind and the Rain: African Americans and Environmental History*. Pittsburgh: University of Pittsburgh Press, 2006.

Gleick, James. "Fallout." *Washington Post*, 10 April 2005.

———. *Genius: The Life and Science of Richard Feynman*. New York: Random House, 1992.

Gobel-Bain, Angela. "From Humble Beginnings: Lincoln's Illinois, 1830–1861." *Living Museum* 71 (Spring 2009): 5–26.

Godbeer, Richard. *The Devil's Dominion: Magic and Religion in Early New England*. New York: Cambridge University Press, 1992.

———. *Escaping Salem: The Other Witchcraft Hunt of 1692*. New York: Oxford, 2005.

Goetzmann, William. *Army Exploration in the American West, 1803–1863*. New Haven,

Conn.: Yale University Press, 1959. Reprint, Lincoln: University of Nebraska Press, 1979.

Goff, Richard D. *Confederate Supply.* Durham, N.C.: Duke University Press, 1969.

Gold, Gerald. "Hot Items: Siphons, Gas-Tank Locks." *New York Times,* 1 January 1974.

Goodchild, Peter. *Edward Teller: The Real Dr. Strangelove.* Cambridge, Mass.: Harvard University Press, 2004.

Goodman, Walter. "Brown v. Board of Education: Uneven Results 30 Years Later." *New York Times,* 17 May 1984.

Goodstein, David. *Out of Gas: The End of the Age of Oil.* New York: Norton, 2004.

Goodwin, Doris Kearns. *Team of Rivals: The Political Genius of Abraham Lincoln.* New York: Simon and Schuster, 2005.

Gordon, Robert B. *American Iron, 1607–1900.* Baltimore, Md.: Johns Hopkins University Press, 1996.

———. *A Landscape Transformed: The Ironmaking District of Salisbury, Connecticut.* New York: Oxford University Press, 2001.

Gordon, Robert B., and Patrick M. Malone. *The Texture of Industry: An Archaeological View of the Industrialization of North America.* New York: Oxford University Press, 1994.

Gordon-Reed, Annette. *The Hemingses of Monticello: An American Family.* New York: Norton, 2008.

Gould, Stephen Jay. *Bully for Brontosaurus: Reflections in Natural History.* New York: Norton, 1991.

Gray, Lewis Cecil. *History of Agriculture in the Southern United States to 1860.* 2 vols. New York: Peter Smith, 1941.

Green, Earl, and Carl Montgomery. "Six Days on the Road." Lyrics. Performed by Dave Dudley. *Dave Dudley Sings Six Days on the Road.* Golden Ring, 1963.

Greenberg, Jack. *Brown v. Board of Education: Witness to a Landmark Decision.* New York: Twelve Tables Press, 2004.

Greene, Ann Norton. *Horses at Work: Harnessing Power in Industrial America.* Cambridge, Mass.: Harvard University Press, 2008.

Greene, Jack P., ed. *Colonies to Nation, 1763–1789.* New York: McGraw-Hill, 1967.

Gregory, James N. *The Southern Diaspora: How the Great Migrations of Black and White Southerners Transformed America.* Chapel Hill: University of North Carolina Press, 2005.

Greven, Philip J., Jr. *Four Generations: Population, Land, and Family in Colonial Andover, Massachusetts.* Ithaca, N.Y.: Cornell University Press, 1970.

Griswold, Wesley S. *Work of Giants: Building the First Transcontinental Railroad.* New York: McGraw-Hill, 1962.

Gross, Ken. "Linda Brown Reopens Her Landmark Case against Racism." *People's Weekly,* 1 December 1986), 146, 151.

Groves, Jeffrey D. "The Book Trade Transformed." In *Perspectives on American Book History,* edited by Scott E. Casper, Joanne D. Chaison, and Jeffrey D. Groves, 109–34. Amherst: University of Massachusetts Press, 2002.

Groves, Leslie. "Memorandum for the Secretary of War," 18 July 1945. In *The American Atom: A Documentary History of Nuclear Policies from the Discovery of Fission to the Present, 1939–1984*, edited by Robert C. Williams and Philip L. Cantelon, 47–55. Philadelphia: University of Pennsylvania Press, 1984.

———. *Now It Can Be Told: The Story of the Manhattan Project*. New York: Da Capo Press, 1962, 1983.

———. "Some Recollections of July 16, 1945." *Bulletin of the Atomic Scientists* 26 (June 1970): 26.

Gudmestad, Robert. *A Troublesome Commerce: The Transformation of the Interstate Slave Trade*. Baton Rouge: Louisiana State University Press, 2003.

———. "Steamboats and the Removal of the Red River Raft." *Louisiana History*, forthcoming.

———. *Steamboats and the Rise of the Cotton Kingdom*. Baton Rouge: Louisiana State University Press, 2011.

Guelzo, Allen C. *Abraham Lincoln: Redeemer President*. Grand Rapids, Mich.: Eerdmans, 1999.

———. *Abraham Lincoln as a Man of Ideas*. Carbondale: Southern Illinois University Press, 2009.

———. *Lincoln: A Very Short Introduction*. New York: Oxford University Press, 2009.

———. *Lincoln's Emancipation Proclamation: The End of Slavery in America*. New York: Simon and Schuster, 2004.

Gunderson, Joan R. *To Be Useful to the World: Women in Revolutionary America, 1740–1790*. New York: Twayne Publishers, 1996.

Gutfreund, Owen D. *Twentieth Century Sprawl: Highways and the Reshaping of the American Landscape*. New York: Oxford University Press, 2004.

Hagedorn-Krass, Martha, and Harry A. Butowsky. "Sumner Elementary School and Monroe Elementary School." National Register of Historic Places Registration Form, 20 June 1991, Kansas State Historic Preservation Office, Kansas Historical Society, Topeka.

Hahn, Steven. "Hunting, Fishing, and Foraging: Common Rights and Class Relations in the Postbellum South." *Radical History Review* 26 (October 1982): 36–64.

———. *A Nation Under Our Feet: Black Political Struggles in the Rural South from Slavery to the Great Migration*. Cambridge, Mass.: Harvard University Press, 2003.

Hales, Peter Bacon. *Atomic Spaces: Living on the Manhattan Project*. Urbana: University of Illinois Press, 1997.

———. "The Atomic Sublime." *American Studies* 32 (Spring 1991): 5–31.

Hall, David D., ed. *The Antinomian Controversy, 1636–1638: A Documentary History*. Middletown, Conn.: Wesleyan University Press, 1968.

———. "The Mental World of Samuel Sewall." In *Saints and Revolutionaries: Essays in Early American History*, edited by David D. Hall, John M. Murrin, and Thad W. Tate, 75–95. New York: Norton, 1984.

———, ed. *Puritans in the New World: A Critical Anthology*. Princeton, N.J.: Princeton University Press, 2004.

————, ed. *Witchhunting in Seventeenth-Century New England: A Documentary History, 1638–1692*. Boston: Northeastern University Press, 1991.

————. *Worlds of Wonder, Days of Judgment: Popular Religious Belief in Early New England*. New York: Knopf, 1989.

Hall, Johanna L. "The African American Community in Topeka, Kansas, 1940–1951: Crucial Years Before *Brown*." Master's thesis, University of Kansas, 1993.

Hämäläinen, Pekka. "The Rise and Fall of Plains Indian Horse Cultures." *Journal of American History* 90 (December 2003): 833–62.

Hamilton, Alexander, John Jay, and James Madison. *The Federalist*. Edited by George W. Carey and James McClellan. Washington, D.C.: Gideon, 1818. Reprint, Indianapolis: Liberty Fund, 2001.

Hamilton, Shane. *Trucking Country: The Road to America's Wal-Mart Economy*. Princeton, N.J.: Princeton University Press, 2008.

Haney, Lewis W. *A Congressional History of Railways in the United States*. 2 vols. Madison: University of Wisconsin, 1908. Reprint, New York: August M. Kelley, 1968.

Hanover, Bob. "All in a Day's Work." Golden Spike National Historic Site *Trans-Continental* 1, no. 11 (2001): 9.

Hansen, Chadwick. "Andover Witchcraft and the Causes of the Salem Witchcraft Trials." In *The Occult in America: New Historical Perspectives*. Urbana: University of Illinois Press, 1983.

Harland Bartholomew and Associates. *Comprehensive Plan of the City of Topeka and Shawnee County, Kansas*. St. Louis: Harland Bartholomew and Associates, 1945.

Hart, Albert Bushnell, ed. *American History Told by Contemporaries*, vol. 1. New York: Macmillan, 1897.

Haycox, Ernest, Jr. "'A Very Exclusive Party': A Firsthand Account of Building the Union Pacific Railroad." *Montana: The Magazine of Western History* 51 (Spring 2001): 20–35.

Hayek, F. A. *The Road to Serfdom*. Chicago: University of Chicago Press, 1944, 2007.

Hays, Samuel. *Beauty, Health, and Permanence: Environmental Politics in the United States, 1955–1985*. New York: Cambridge University Press, 1987.

Heath, Earle. "A Railroad Record That Defies Defeat." *Southern Pacific Bulletin* 16 (May 1928): 3–5. http://cprr.org/Museum/Southern_Pacific_Bulletin/Ten_Mile_Day.html#p4.

Henderson, Cheryl Brown. "Reaffirming the Legacy." In *The Unfinished Agenda of Brown v. Board of Education*, edited by the editors of *Black Issues in Higher Education*, 165–66. Hoboken, N.J.: John Wiley and Sons, 2004.

Henderson, George. *California and the Fictions of Capital*. New York: Oxford University Press, 1999.

Henretta, James A., W. Elliott Brownlee, David Brody, and Susan Ware. *America's History*. Chicago: Dorsey Press, 1987.

Herken, Gregg. *Brotherhood of the Bomb: The Tangled Lives of Robert Oppenheimer, Ernest Lawrence, and Edward Teller*. New York: Henry Holt, 2002.

Hess, Earl J. *The Union Soldier in Battle: Enduring the Ordeal of Combat*. Lawrence: University Press of Kansas, 1997.

Hilliard, Sam Bowers. *Atlas of Antebellum Southern Agriculture*. Baton Rouge: Louisiana State University Press, 1984.

Hinderaker, Eric. *Elusive Empires: Constructing Colonialism in the Ohio Valley, 1763–1800*. Cambridge: Cambridge University Press, 1997.

Hirschfelder, Joseph O. "The Scientific and Technological Miracle at Los Alamos." In *Reminiscences of Los Alamos, 1943–1945*, by Lawrence Badash, Joseph O. Hirschfelder, and Herbert P. Broida, 67–88. Dordrecht, Netherlands: D. Reidel, 1980.

Hirshson, Stanley P. *Grenville M. Dodge: Soldier, Politician, Railroad Pioneer*. Bloomington: Indiana University Press, 1967.

Hirst, Eric. "Cycling for Energy Conservation." *Bicycling!* June 1974, 48–49.

"History of the Bus Bike Rack." *Metro Online*, 2 April 2004. http://transit.metrokc.gov/tops/bike/h-bikerack.html (accessed 9 May 2009). Copy in possession of author.

Hobhouse, Henry. *Seeds of Change: Five Plants That Transformed Mankind*. New York: Harper and Row, 1986.

Hofstadter, Richard. *The Progressive Historians: Turner, Beard, Parrington*. New York: Knopf, 1968.

Hogg, Gary. *Union Pacific: The Building of the First Transcontinental Railroad*. New York: Walker, 1967.

Holley, I. B., Jr. "Blacktop: How Asphalt Paving Came to the Urban United States." *Technology and Culture* 44 (October 2003): 703–33.

Holton, Woody. *Unruly Americans and the Origins of the Constitution*. New York: Hill and Wang, 2007.

Hornsby, Stephen J. *British Atlantic, American Frontier: Spaces of Power in Early Modern British America*. Hanover, N.H.: University Press of New England, 2005.

Horowitz, Daniel. "Rethinking Betty Friedan and *The Feminine Mystique*: Labor Union Radicalism and Feminism in Cold War America." *American Quarterly* 48 (March 1996): 1–42.

Howard, Robert West. *The Great Iron Trail: The Story of the First Transcontinental Railroad*. New York: G. P. Putnam's Sons, 1962.

Howe, Daniel Walker. *Making the American Self: Jonathon Edwards to Abraham Lincoln*. Cambridge, Mass.: Harvard University Press, 1997. Reprint, New York: Oxford University Press, 2009.

———. *What Hath God Wrought: The Transformation of America, 1815–1848*. New York: Oxford University Press, 2007.

Howells, W. D. *Life of Abraham Lincoln*. Colombus, OH: Follet, Foster, 1860. Reprint, Bloomington: Indiana University Press, 1960.

Howes, Ruth H., and Caroline L. Herzenberg. *Their Day in the Sun: Women of the Manhattan Project*. Philadelphia: Temple University Press, 1999.

Hsiung, David. "Food, Fuel, and the New England Environment in the War for Independence, 1775–1776." *New England Quarterly* 80 (December 2007): 614–54.

Hubbard, William. *The History of the Indian Wars in New England, from the First*

Settlement to the Termination of the War with King Philip, in 1677, vol. 1. Edited by Samuel G. Drake. Roxbury, Mass.: W. Elliot Woodward, 1865. Reprint, New York: Kraus, 1969.

Hubbert, M. King. *Energy Resources: A Report to the Committee on Natural Resources.* National Academy of Sciences and National Research Council Publication 1000–D. Washington, D.C.: National Academy of Sciences–National Research Council, 1962.

———. "Nuclear Energy and the Fossil Fuels." Publication 95, Shell Development Company, Exploration and Production Research Division. Presented before the spring meeting of the Southern District Division of Production, American Petroleum Institute, San Antonio, Texas, March 7–9, 1956. www.energybulletin.net/print/13630 (accessed 23 March 2009).

Huebner, Timothy S. "Roger B. Taney and the Slavery Issue: Looking Beyond—and Before—*Dred Scott.*" *Journal of American History* 97 (June 2010): 17–39.

Hughes, Jeff. *The Manhattan Project: Big Science and the Atom Bomb.* New York: Columbia University Press, 2002.

Hughes, Langston. *One Way Ticket.* New York: Knopf, 1949.

Hughes, Louis. *Thirty Years a Slave.* Milwaukee, Wis.: South Side Printing Company, 1897.

Hughes, Thomas P. *Human-Built World: How to Think about Technology and Culture.* Chicago: University of Chicago Press, 2004.

Hunner, Jon. *Inventing Los Alamos: The Growth of an Atomic Community.* Norman: University of Oklahoma Press, 2004.

Hunt, Lynn. *Inventing Human Rights: A History.* New York: Norton, 2007.

Hunter, Louis C. *A History of Industrial Power in the United States, 1780–1930*, vol. 2, *Steam Power.* Charlottesville: University Press of Virginia, 1985.

Hunter, Louis C., and Lynwood Bryant. *A History of Industrial Power in the United States, 1780–1930*, vol. 3, *The Transmission of Power.* Cambridge, Mass.: MIT Press, 1991.

Hurley, Andrew. *Environmental Inequalities: Class, Race, and Industrial Pollution in Gary, Indiana, 1945–1980.* Chapel Hill: University of North Carolina Press, 1995.

Hyde, George E. *Spotted Tail's Folk: A History of the Brule Sioux.* Norman: University of Oklahoma Press, 1961.

"I.C.C. Orders Aid to Owner-Drivers." *New York Times*, 16 February 1974.

"Ingenuity of Seven Youths and a Pump Is Balked." *New York Times*, 27 February 1974.

"Interchurch Center History: The Founding Years." Interchurch Center. www.interchurch-center.org/history.html (accessed 13 July 2009).

Intergovernmental Panel on Climate Change (IPCC). *Climate Change 2007.* www.eoearth.org/article/IPCC_Fourth_Assessment_Report.

Ise, John. *United States Oil Policy.* New Haven, Conn.: Yale University Press, 1926.

Isenberg, Nancy. *Sex and Citizenship in Antebellum America.* Chapel Hill: University of North Carolina Press, 1998.

Jacobs, Joseph. *The Fables of Aesop.* New York: Macmillan, 1930.

Jacoby, Karl. "Slaves by Nature? Domestic Animals and Human Slaves." *Slavery and Abolition* 15 (April 1994): 89–99.

Jameson, J. Franklin, ed. *Johnson's Wonder-Working Providence, 1628–1651.* New York: Barnes and Noble, 1910.

Japanese Broadcasting Corporation, ed. *Unforgettable Fire: Pictures Drawn by Atomic Bomb Survivors.* Tokyo and New York: NHK and Pantheon, 1977.

Jefferson, Thomas. *Notes on the State of Virginia.* Paris: Philippe-Denis Pierres, 1785. Reprint, New York: Norton, 1982.

Jensen, Merrill, ed. *Tracts of the American Revolution, 1763–1776.* Indianapolis, Ind.: Bobbs-Merrill, 1967.

Johnson, Chalmers. *Blowback: The Costs and Consequences of American Empire.* 2nd ed. New York: Henry Holt, 2004.

———. *The Sorrows of Empire: Militarism, Secrecy, and the End of the Republic.* New York: Metropolitan and Henry Holt, 2005.

Johnson, Hildegard Binder. *Order Upon the Land: The U.S. Rectangular Land Survey and the Upper Mississippi Country.* New York: Oxford University Press, 1976.

Johnson, James Weldon. "Lift Every Voice and Sing." In *James Weldon Johnson: Writings,* edited by William L. Andrews, 874–75. New York: Library of America, 2004.

Johnson, Walter. "On Agency." *Journal of Social History* 37 (Autumn 2003): 113–24.

Johnston, Laurie. "Pity Poor Dave, the Pump Man." *New York Times,* 1 January 1974.

Johnston, R. J., Derek Gregory, Geraldine Pratt, and Michael Watts, eds. *The Dictionary of Human Geography.* 4th ed. Oxford: Blackwell, 2000.

Jones, Christopher F. "A Landscape of Energy Abundance: Anthracite Coal Canals and the Roots of American Fossil Fuel Dependence, 1820–1860." *Environmental History* 15 (July 2010): 449–84.

Jones, David S. *Rationalizing Epidemics: Meanings and Uses of American Indian Mortality since 1600.* Cambridge, Mass.: Harvard University Press, 2004.

Jordan, Winthrop W. *White over Black: American Attitudes toward the Negro, 1550–1812.* Chapel Hill: University of North Carolina Press, 1968.

Josephson, Paul R. *Industrialized Nature: Brute Force Technology and the Transformation of the Natural World.* Washington, D.C.: Island Press, 2002.

Judah, T. D. *A Practical Plan for Building the Pacific Railroad.* Washington, D.C.: Henry Polkinhorn, 1857.

Jungk, Robert. *Brighter than a Thousand Suns: A Personal History of the Atomic Scientists.* Bern: Alfred Scherz Verlag, 1956. Reprint, New York: Harcourt, 1958.

Kamensky, Jane, ed. "Forum: Salem Repossessed." *William and Mary Quarterly* 65 (July 2008): 391–534.

Kanfer, Stefan. "The Full Circle: In Praise of the Bicycle." *Time,* 28 April 1975.

Kaplan, Fred. *Lincoln: The Biography of a Writer.* New York: HarperCollins, 2008.

Karlsen, Carol F. *The Devil in the Shape of a Woman: Witchcraft in Colonial New England.* New York: Norton, 1987.

Kates, James. "Citizens Band (CB) Radio." *Dictionary of American History,* 2003. Encyclopedia.com (10 April 2009). www.encyclopedia.com/doc/1G2-3401800825.html.

Kauffman, Michael W. *American Brutus: John Wilkes Booth and the Lincoln Conspiracies*. New York: Random House, 2004.

Kaufman, Leslie. "Gulf Oil Plumes Again Imperil Sea Turtle No. 15." *New York Times*, 19 May 2010.

Kay, Jane Holtz. *Asphalt Nation: How the Automobile Took Over America and How We Can Take It Back*. Berkeley: University of California Press, 1997.

Kaye, Anthony E. *Joining Places: Slave Neighborhoods in the Old South*. Chapel Hill: University of North Carolina Press, 2007.

———. "The Second Slavery: Modernity in the Nineteenth-Century South and the Atlantic World." *Journal of Southern History* 75 (August 2009): 626–50.

Keegan, John. *An Illustrated History of the First World War*. New York: Knopf, 2001.

Keller, John E., and L. Clark Keating. *Aesop's Fables*. Lexington: University Press of Kentucky, 1993.

Kelman, Ari. *A River and Its City: The Nature of Landscape in New Orleans*. Berkeley: University of California Press, 2003.

Kences, James. "Some Unexplored Relationships of Essex County Witchcraft to the Indian Wars of 1675 and 1689." *Essex Institute Historical Collections* 120 (1984): 179–212.

Kennedy, David M. *Freedom from Fear: The American People in Depression and War, 1929–1945*. New York: Oxford University Press, 1999.

Kerber, Linda K. "Daughters of Columbia: Educating Women for the Republic, 1787–1805." In *The Hofstader Aegis: A Memorial*, edited by Stanley Elkins and Eric McKitrick, 36–59. New York: Knopf, 1974.

———. "'History Can Do It No Justice': Women and the Reinterpretation of the American Revolution." In *Women in the Age of the American Revolution*, edited by Ronald Hoffman and Peter J. Albert, 3–42. Charlottesville: United States Capitol Historical Society and University Press of Virginia, 1989.

———. *No Constitutional Right to Be Ladies: Women and the Obligations of Citizenship*. New York: Hill and Wang, 1998.

———. "The Republican Mother." In *Women's America: Refocusing the Past*, 3rd ed., edited by Linda K. Kerber and Jane Sherron De Hart, 87–95. New York: Oxford University Press, 1991.

———. "The Republican Mother: Women and the Enlightenment—An American Perspective." In *Toward an Intellectual History of Women: Essays*, 41–62. Chapel Hill: University of North Carolina Press, 1997.

———. *Women of the Republic: Intellect and Ideology in Revolutionary America*. Chapel Hill: University of North Carolina Press, 1980.

Ketterson, F. A. "Golden Spike National Historic Site: Development of an Historical Reconstruction." *Utah Historical Quarterly* 37 (Winter 1969): 58–68.

Kibbey, Meade. *The Railroad Photographs of Alfred A. Hart, Artist*. Sacramento: California State Library Foundation, 1996.

King, Martin Luther, Jr. "I Have a Dream." In *Great Issues in American History*, vol. 3, *From Reconstruction to the Present Day*, edited by Richard and Beatrice K. Hofstadter, 449–53. New York: Vintage Books, 1982.

King, Wayne. "Energy Gap Makes It Harder to Sell a House." *New York Times*, 10 March 1974.

Kinsel, Amy J. "From Turning Point to Peace Memorial: A Cultural Legacy." In *The Gettysburg Nobody Knows*, edited by Gabor S. Boritt, 203–22. New York: Oxford University Press, 1992.

Kiple, Kenneth F., and Virginia Himmelsteib King. *Another Dimension to the Black Diaspora: Diet, Disease, and Racism*. New York: Cambridge University Press, 1981.

Kiple, Kenneth F., and Virginia H. Kiple. "Black Tongue and Black Men: Pellagra and Slavery in the Antebellum South." *Journal of Southern History* 43 (August 1977): 411–28.

Kirby, Jack Temple. "The American Civil War: An Environmental View." Revised March 2001. http://nationalhumanitiescenter.org/tserve/nattrans/ntuseland/essays/amcwar.htm.

Kirk, Russell. *The Conservative Mind: From Burke to Eliot*. Chicago: Regnery, 1953. Reprint, Thousand Oaks, Calif.: BN Publishing, 2008.

Kistiakowsky, George B. "Reminiscences of Los Alamos." In *Reminiscences of Los Alamos, 1943–1945*, edited by Lawrence Badash, Joseph O. Hirschfelder, and Herbert P. Broida, 49–66. Dordrecht, Netherlands: D. Reidel, 1980.

———. "Trinity: A Reminiscence." *Bulletin of the Atomic Scientists* 36 (June 1980): 21–22.

Klein, Maury. *Union Pacific: Birth of a Railroad, 1862–1893*. New York: Doubleday, 1987.

Klepp, Susan E. *Revolutionary Conceptions: Women, Fertility, and Family Limitation in America, 1760–1820*. Chapel Hill: University of North Carolina Press, 2009.

Klingle, Matthew. "Changing Spaces: Nature, Property, and Power in Seattle, 1880–1945." *Journal of Urban History* 32 (January 2006): 197–230.

———. *Emerald City: An Environmental History of Seattle*. New Haven, Conn.: Yale University Press, 2009.

Kluger, Richard. *Simple Justice: The History of Brown v. Board of Education and Black America's Struggle for Equality*. New York: Knopf, 1976.

Knack, Martha C. "Nineteenth-Century Great Basin Indian Wage Labor." In *Native Americans and Wage Labor: Ethnohistorical Perspectives*, edited by Alice Littlefield and Martha C. Knack, 144–76. Norman: University of Oklahoma Press, 1996.

Kneeland, Douglas E. "Energy: Many Skeptical on Reasons for Crisis." *New York Times*, 23 December 1973.

Knight, Frederick C. *Working the Diaspora: The Impact of African Labor on the Anglo-American World, 1650–1850*. New York: New York University Press, 2010.

Kobayashi, Audrey. "The Construction of Geographical Knowledge—Racialization, Spatialization." In *Handbook of Cultural Geography*, edited by Kay Anderson, Mona Domosh, Steve Pile, and Nigel Thrift, 544–56. London: Sage, 2003.

Kohlstedt, Sally Gregory. "Nature, Not Books: Scientists and the Origins of the Nature-Study Movement in the 1890s." *Isis* 96 (September 2005): 324–52.

Kolata, Gina. "For a World of Woes, We Blame Cookie Monsters." *New York Times*, 29 October 2006.

Kovarik, Bill. "Henry Ford, Charles Kettering and the 'Fuel of the Future.'" *Automotive*

History Review 32 (Spring 1998): 7–27. Also available at www.runet.edu/~wkovarik/papers/fuel.html.

Kratville, William W. *Golden Rails*. Omaha: Kratville Publications, 1965.

Kraus, George. "Central Pacific Construction Vignettes." In *The Golden Spike*, edited by David E. Miller, 45–61. Salt Lake City: Utah State Historical Society and University of Utah Press, 1973.

———. "Chinese Laborers and the Construction of the Central Pacific." *Utah Historical Quarterly* 37 (Winter 1969): 41–57.

———. *High Road to Promontory: Building the Central Pacific Across the High Sierra*. Palo Alto, Calif.: American West Publishing, 1969.

Krause, Keith. *Impact of Water on the Development of Topeka: A History*. Topeka, Kans.: Topeka–Shawnee County Flood Control and Conservation Association, 1993.

Krauss, Clifford, John M. Broder, and Jackie Calmes. "Leak May Persist through August, Obama Aides Say, as Criticism Mounts." *New York Times*, 31 May 2010.

Kupperman, Karen Ordahl. *Indians and English: Facing Off in Early America*. Ithaca, N.Y.: Cornell University Press, 2000.

Lakwete, Angela. *Inventing the Cotton Gin: Machine and Myth in Modern America*. Baltimore, Md.: Johns Hopkins University Press, 2003.

Lamb, J. Parker. *Perfecting the American Steam Locomotive*. Bloomington: Indiana University Press, 2003.

Lamont, Lansing. *Day of Trinity*. New York: Atheneum, 1965.

Lamson, William D. "Race and Schools in Topeka, Kansas: A Study of the Effects of Administrative Decision-Making on the Racial Composition of the Students Attending the Individual Schools of the United School District No. 501 from 1950 to 1983." 1985. In File 219, Box 13, Record Group 21, *Brown v. Board of Education* Exhibit Files, T-316, National Archives and Records Administration, Kansas City, Missouri.

Lanouette, William. *Genius in the Shadows: A Biography of Leo Szilard, the Man Behind the Bomb*. New York: Charles Scribner's Sons, 1992.

Lansing, Michael J. "The Significance of Nonhumans in U.S. Western History." PhD dissertation, University of Minnesota, 2003.

LaPlante, Eve. *American Jezebel: The Uncommon Life of Anne Hutchinson, the Woman Who Defied the Puritans*. New York: HarperCollins, 2004.

Larson, John Lauritz. *Internal Improvement: National Public Works and the Promise of Popular Government in the Early United States*. Chapel Hill: University of North Carolina Press, 2001.

"The Latest on the Oil Spill." *New York Times*, 31 May 2010.

League of American Bicyclists. "Bicycle Friendly America." www.bikeleague.org/programs/bicyclefriendlyamerica/index.php (accessed 10 June 2010).

LeCain, Timothy J. *Mass Destruction: The Men and Giant Mines That Wired America and Scarred the Planet*. New Brunswick, N.J.: Rutgers University Press, 2009.

Leiker, James N. "Race Relations in the Sunflower State." *Kansas History* 25 (Autumn 2005): 214–36.

Lemon, James T. *The Best Poor Man's Country: A Geographical Study of Early Southeastern Pennsylvania*. Baltimore, Md.: Johns Hopkins University Press, 1972.

Lepore, Jill. *In the Name of War: King Philip's War and the Origins of American Identity*. New York: Knopf, 1998.

Leopold, Aldo. *A Sand County Almanac*. New York: Oxford University Press, 1949. Reprint, New York: Ballantine, 1970.

Lewis, Jan Elizabeth. *The English Fable: Aesop and Literary Culture, 1650–1741*. Cambridge: Cambridge University Press, 1996.

"Library Vans Parked in Way to Stop Siphoning." *New York Times*, 20 April 1974.

Licht, Walter. *Working for the Railroad: The Organization of Work in the Nineteenth Century*. Princeton, N.J.: Princeton University Press, 1983.

Lichtenstein, Nelson, Susan Strasser, and Roy Rosenzweig. *Who Built America? Working People and the Nation's Economy, Politics, Culture, and Society*. 2 vols. New York: Worth, 2000.

Lincoln, Abraham. "Address at the Dedication of the Gettysburg National Cemetery." In *The Life and Writings of Abraham Lincoln*, edited by Philip Van Doren Stern, 786–87. New York: Modern Library, 1940.

Lindsey, Robert. "The Angry Truck Driver: 'We've Got to Show 'em.'" *New York Times*, 5 December 1973.

————. "In Mass Transit, Turnstiles Are Clicking Faster." *New York Times*, 6 January 1974.

————. "Transit Systems Gain Customers." *New York Times*, 28 October 1974.

"Line of Idling Cars Tested for Gasoline Consumption." *New York Times*, 8 February 1974.

Linenthal, Edward Tabor. *Sacred Ground: Americans and Their Battlefields*. Urbana: University of Illinois Press, 1991.

Lipin, Lawrence M. *Workers and the Wild: Conservation, Consumerism, and Labor in Oregon, 1910–1930*. Urbana: University of Illinois Press, 2007.

Little, Ann. *Abraham at Arms: War and Gender in Colonial New England*. Philadelphia: University of Pennsylvania Press, 2007.

Littlefield, Alice, and Martha C. Knack, eds. *Native Americans and Wage Labor: Ethnohistorical Perspectives*. Norman: University of Oklahoma Press, 1996.

Litwack, Leon. *Trouble in Mind: Black Southerners in the Age of Jim Crow*. New York: Knopf, 1998.

Locke, John. *Two Treatises of Government*. Edited by Peter Laslett. Cambridge: Cambridge University Press, 1988.

Lockwood, E. C. "With the Casement Brothers while Building the Union Pacific." *Union Pacific Magazine* (February 1931): 3–4, 24, 36.

Lonn, Ella. *Salt as a Factor in the Confederacy*. New York: Walter Neale, 1933.

Lott, Dale F., and Robert Sommer. "Moving People by Bicycle." *Bicycling!* March 1972, 14–15.

Louter, David. *Windshield Wilderness: Cars, Roads, and Nature in Washington's National Parks*. Seattle: University of Washington Press, 2006.

Luvaas, Jay, and Harold W. Nelson, eds. *Guide to the Battle of Gettysburg*. Lawrence: University Press of Kansas, 1986.

Lynd, Robert S., and Helen Merrell Lynd. *Middletown: A Study in Modern American Culture*. New York: Harcourt Brace, 1929.

Lyon, Fern, and Jacob Evans, eds. *Los Alamos: The First Fifty Years*. Los Alamos, N.M.: Los Alamos Historical Society, 1984.

Maass, Peter. "The Breaking Point." *New York Times Magazine*, 21 August 2005, 30–35, 50, 56–57.

Magner, Blake A. *Traveller and Company: The Horses of Gettysburg*. Gettysburg, Pa.: Farnsworth House Military Impressions, 1995.

Magoc, Chris J. *So Glorious a Landscape: Nature and Environment in American History and Culture*. Wilmington, Del.: SR Books, 2001.

Maher, Neil M. *Nature's New Deal: The Civilian Conservation Corps and the Roots of the American Environmental Movement*. New York: Oxford University Press, 2008.

Maier, Charles S. "Consigning the Twentieth Century to History: Alternative Narratives for the Modern Era." *American Historical Review* 105 (June 2000): 807–31.

Maier, Pauline. *American Scripture: Making the Declaration of Independence*. New York: Knopf, 1997.

Main, Gloria L. *Peoples of a Spacious Land: Families and Cultures of Colonial New England*. Cambridge, Mass.: Harvard University Press, 2001.

Malcom, Andrew H. "Fuel Rationing Could Hobble That Work Horse of Suburbia." *New York Times*, 17 December 1973.

Manhattan Project Heritage Preservation Association, Inc. "Fat Man." http://childrenofthemanhattanproject.org/HISTORY/fat_man.htm (accessed 10 October 2005). Also available at www.mpha.org/classic/HISTORY/fat_man.htm (accessed 21 May 2011).

———. "Little Boy." www.childrenofthemanhattanproject.org/HISTORY/little_boy.htm (accessed 2 October 2005). Also available at www.mpha.org/classic/HISTORY/little_boy.htm (accessed 21 May 2011).

Manley, Kathleen E. "Women of Los Alamos during World War II: Some of Their Views." *New Mexico Historical Review* 65 (April 1990): 251–66.

Manning, Richard. "The Oil We Eat: Following the Food Chain Back to Iraq." *Harper's*, February 2004, 37–45.

Mapes, Jeff. *Pedaling Revolution: How Cyclists Are Changing American Cities*. Corvallis: Oregon State University Press, 2009.

Mark, Kathleen. "A Roof Over Our Heads." In *Standing By and Making Do: Women of Wartime Los Alamos*, edited by Jane S. Wilson and Charlotte Serber, 29–42. Los Alamos, N.M.: Los Alamos Historical Society, 1988.

Markowitz, Gerald, and David Rosner. *Deceit and Denial: The Deadly Politics of Industrial Pollution*. Berkeley: University of California Press, 2002.

Marks, Robert B. "Commercialization without Capitalism: Processes of Environmental Change in South China." *Environmental History* 1 (January 1996): 56–82.

————. *The Origins of the Modern World: A Global and Ecological Narrative.* Lanham, Md.: Rowman and Littlefield, 2002.

"The Marriage of Bike and Auto: A Survey of Carriers." *Bicycling!* February 1973, 20–23.

Martin, Waldo E., Jr. *Brown v. Board of Education: A Brief History with Documents.* Boston: Bedford / St. Martin's, 1998.

Mason, Katrina R. *Children of Los Alamos: An Oral History of the Town Where the Atomic Age Began.* New York: Twayne, 1995.

Massey, Mary Elizabeth. *Ersatz in the Confederacy: Shortages and Substitutes on the Southern Home Front.* Columbia: University of South Carolina Press, 1952, 1993.

Masters, Isabell. "The Life and Legacy of Oliver Brown, the First Listed Plaintiff of Brown vs. Board of Education, Topeka, Kansas." PhD dissertation, University of Oklahoma, 1980.

Mather, Cotton. *Magnalia Christi Americana.* Edited by Kenneth B. Murdock. Cambridge, Mass.: Harvard University Press, 1977.

Maurer, John H. "Fuel and the Battle Fleet: Coal, Oil, and American Naval Strategy." In *In Defense of the Republic: Readings in American Military History,* edited by David Curtis Skaggs and Robert S. Browning III, 185–204: Belmont, CA: Wadsworth, 1991.

May, Dean L. "Economic Beginnings." In *Utah's History,* edited by Richard D. Poll, 193–215. Provo, Utah: Brigham Young University Press, 1978.

————. "Towards a Dependent Commonwealth." In *Utah's History,* edited by Richard D. Poll, 217–41. Provo, Utah: Brigham Young University Press, 1978.

Mayer, Lynne Rhodes, and Kenneth E. Vose. *Makin' Tracks: The Story of the Transcontinental Railroad in the Pictures and Words of the Men Who Were There.* New York: Praeger, 1975.

McCaffrey, Lawrence J. *The Irish Diaspora in America.* Bloomington: Indiana University Press, 1976.

McCague, James. *Moguls and Iron Men: The Story of the First Transcontinental Railroad.* New York: Harper and Row, 1964.

McCoy, Drew. *The Elusive Republic: Political Economy in Jeffersonian America.* Chapel Hill: University of North Carolina Press, 1980.

McCurry, Stephanie. *Confederate Reckoning: Power and Politics in the Civil War South.* Cambridge, Mass.: Harvard University Press, 2010.

McDonald, Forrest. *Novus Ordo Seclorum: The Intellectual Origins of the Constitution.* Lawrence: University Press of Kansas, 1985.

McDonald, Forrest, and Grady McWhiney. "The South from Self-Sufficiency to Peonage: An Interpretation." *American Historical Review* 85 (December 1980): 1095–1118.

McElfresh, Earl B. *Maps and Mapmakers of the Civil War.* New York: Henry N. Abrams, 1999.

McElheny, Victor K. "Truck 'Gas' Saving at 50 M.P.H. Found." *New York Times,* 6 December 1973.

McElvaine, Robert S. *The Great Depression: America, 1929–1941.* New York: Times Books, 1984.

McEvoy, Arthur F. "Working Environments: An Ecological Approach to Industrial Health and Safety." *Technology and Culture* 36 (April 1995): S145–S172.

McFadden, Robert D. "Lack of Gasoline 'Worst Ever' Here." *New York Times,* 3 February 1974.

———. "Trucks Are Damaged in Protest on Fuel Situation." *New York Times,* 15 December 1973.

McGaw, Judith A. *Most Wonderful Machine: Mechanization and Social Change in Berkshire Paper Making, 1801–1885.* Princeton, N.J.: Princeton University Press, 1987.

McGee, Elaine S. *Colorado Yule Marble: Building Stone of the Lincoln Memorial.* U.S. Geological Survey Bulletin 2162. Washington, D.C.: Government Printing Office, 1997.

McKee, Bradford. "As Suburbs Grow, So Do Waistlines." *New York Times,* 4 September 2003.

McLaughlin, Jack. *Jefferson and Monticello: The Biography of a Builder.* New York: Henry Holt, 1988.

McMurry, Richard M. "The Pennsylvania Gambit and the Gettysburg Splash." In *The Gettysburg Nobody Knows,* edited by Gabor S. Boritt, 175–202. New York: Oxford University Press, 1999.

McNeil, J. R. *Mosquito Empires: Ecology and War in the Greater Caribbean, 1620–1914.* New York: Cambridge University Press, 2010.

McPherson, James M. *Abraham Lincoln.* New York: Oxford University Press, 2009.

———. *Abraham Lincoln and the Second American Revolution.* New York: Oxford University Press, 1991.

———. "American Victory, American Defeat." In *Why the Confederacy Lost,* edited by Gabor S. Boritt, 17–42, 166–68. New York: Oxford University Press, 1992.

———. *Battle Cry of Freedom: The Civil War Era.* New York: Oxford University Press, 1988.

———. "Gettysburg." In *American Places: Encounters with History,* edited by William E. Leuchtenburg, 261–67. New York: Oxford University Press, 2000.

———. *Ordeal by Fire: The Civil War and Reconstruction.* New York: Knopf, 1982.

———. *Tried by War: Abraham Lincoln as Commander in Chief.* New York: Penguin, 2008.

———. *What They Fought For, 1861–1865.* Baton Rouge: Louisiana State University Press, 1994.

McShane, Clay, and Joel Tarr. "The Centrality of the Horse in the Nineteenth Century American City." In *The Making of Urban America,* 2nd ed., edited by Raymond A. Mohl, 105–30. Wilmington, Del.: SR Books, 1997.

Meine, Curt. *Aldo Leopold: His Life and Work.* Madison: University of Wisconsin Press, 1988.

Meinig, D. W. *The Shaping of America: A Geographical Perspective on 500 Years of History,* vol. 1, *Atlantic America, 1492–1800.* New Haven, Conn.: Yale University Press, 1986.

———. *The Shaping of America: A Geographical Perspective on 500 Years of History,* vol. 2,

Continental America, 1800–1867. New Haven, Conn.: Yale University Press, 1993.

———. *The Shaping of America: A Geographical Perspective on 500 years of History,* vol. 3, *Transcontinental America, 1850–1915.* New Haven, Conn.: Yale University Press, 1998.

Melosi, Martin. *Coping with Abundance: Energy and Environment in Industrial America.* New York: Knopf, 1985.

———. "Environmental Justice, Political Agenda Setting, and the Myths of History." *Journal of Policy History* 12 (2000): 43–71.

Melvoin, Richard I. *New England Outpost: War and Society in Colonial Deerfield.* New York: Norton, 1989.

Merchant, Carolyn. *American Environmental History: An Introduction.* New York: Columbia University Press, 2007.

———. *The Death of Nature: Women, Ecology, and the Scientific Revolution.* New York: Harper and Row, 1983. Reprint, San Francisco: HarperCollins, 1990.

———. *Ecological Revolutions: Nature, Gender, and Science in New England.* Chapel Hill: University of North Carolina Press, 1989.

Merrill, Karen. *The Oil Crisis of 1973–1974: A Brief History with Documents.* New York: Bedford / St. Martin's, 2007.

Merritt, Raymond H. *Engineering in American Society, 1850–1875.* Lexington: University Press of Kentucky, 1969.

Meyerowitz, Joanne, ed. *History and September 11th.* Philadelphia: Temple University Press, 2003.

Mill, John Stuart. *Principles of Political Economy, with Some of Their Applications to Social Philosophy.* 2 vols. Edited by J. M. Robson. Toronto: University of Toronto Press, 1965. Reprint, Indianapolis, Ind.: Liberty Fund, 2006.

Miller, Charles A. *Jefferson and Nature: An Interpretation.* Baltimore, Md.: Johns Hopkins University Press, 1988.

Miller, Perry. *Errand into the Wilderness.* Cambridge, Mass.: Harvard University Press, 1956.

———. *Nature's Nation.* Cambridge, Mass.: Harvard University Press, 1967.

Miller, Richard Lawrence. *Lincoln and His World,* vol. 1, *The Early Years.* Mechanicsburg, Pa.: Stackpole Books, 2006.

———. *Lincoln and His World,* vol. 2, *Prairie Politician.* Mechanicsburg, Pa.: Stackpole Books, 2008.

Miller, Steven F. "Plantation Labor Organization and Slave Life on the Alabama-Mississippi Black Belt, 1815–1840." In *Cultivation and Culture: Labor and the Shaping of Slave Life in the Americas,* edited by Ira Berlin and Philip D. Morgan, 155–69. Charlottesville: University Press of Virginia, 1993.

Miller, Timothy. "Charles M. Sheldon and the Uplift of Tennesseetown." *Kansas History* 9 (Autumn 1986): 125–37.

Miller, William J. *Mapping for Stonewall: The Civil War Service of Jed Hotchkiss.* Washington, D.C.: Elliott and Clark, 1993.

Millikan, Mona. "Negroes to Mark Court Victory Tuesday Night." No date. In newspaper clipping books, Kansas State Historical Society, Topeka.

"Minority Housing Policy Target of NAACP Speaker." *Topeka Capital-Journal*, 14 June 1959. In newspaper clipping books, Kansas Historical Society, Topeka.

Mitchell, Don. *Cultural Geography: A Critical Introduction*. Malden, Mass.: Blackwell, 2000.

Mitchell, Michele. *Righteous Propagation: African Americans and the Politics of Racial Destiny after Reconstruction*. Chapel Hill: University of North Carolina Press, 2004.

Mitchell, Reid. *Civil War Soldiers: Their Expectations and Experiences*. New York: Simon and Schuster, 1988.

Mitchell, Timothy. "Carbon Democracy." *Economy and Society* 38 (August 2009): 399–432.

Moberg, Carol L. *René Dubos, Friend of the Good Earth: Microbiologist, Medical Scientist, Environmentalist*. Washington, D.C.: AMS Press, 2005.

Mohl, Raymond A. "The Interstates and the Cities: The U.S. Department of Transportation and the Freeway Revolt, 1966–1973." *Journal of Policy History* 20 (2008): 193–226.

———. "Stop the Road: Freeway Revolts in American Cities." *Journal of Urban History* 30 (July 2004): 674–706.

Monette, John Wesley. "The Cotton Crop." Appendix to Joseph Hold Ingraham, *The South-West, by a Yankee*, 2 vols., 2:281–91. New York: Harper and Brothers, 1835. Reprinted in *A Documentary History of Slavery in North America*, edited by Willie Lee Rose, 316–24. New York: Oxford University Press, 1976. Reprint, Athens: University of Georgia Press, 1999.

Montgomery, David. *The Fall of the House of Labor: The Workplace, the State, and American Labor Activism, 1865–1925*. Cambridge: Cambridge University Press, 1987.

Montgomery, Paul L. "Drivers Face Another Weekend of Lines and Rising Fuel Prices." *New York Times*, 5 January 1974.

———. "Drivers Hunt for Gasoline; Warning on Prices Issued." *New York Times*, 29 December 1973.

———. "Long Weekend Worsens Gasoline Situation Here." *New York Times*, 17 February 1974.

———. "Service Stations Shut Down Early." *New York Times*, 6 January 1974.

Moore, John Hebron. "Cotton Breeding in the Old South." *Agricultural History* 30 (July 1956): 95–104.

———. *The Emergence of the Cotton Kingdom in the Old Southwest*. Baton Rouge: Louisiana State University Press, 1988.

Moran, Katie. *Bicycle Transportation for Energy Conservation*. Washington, D.C.: U.S. Department of Transportation, 1980.

Morgan, Dale. *The Humboldt: High Road of the West*. New York: Rinehart, 1943.

Morgan, Edmund. *American Slavery, American Freedom: The Ordeal of Colonial Virginia*. New York: Norton, 1975.

———. *The Puritan Dilemma: The Story of John Winthrop*. Boston: Little, Brown, 1958.

Morlan, Robert L. *Political Prairie Fire: The Nonpartisan League, 1915–1922*. Minneapolis: University of Minnesota Press, 1955. Reprint, St. Paul: Minnesota Historical Society Press, 1985.

Morris, Aldon D. *The Origins of the Civil Rights Movement: Black Communities Organizing for Change.* New York: Free Press, 1984.

Morris, Christopher. "A More Southern Environmental History." *Journal of Southern History* 75 (August 2009): 581–98.

Mouawad, Jad, and John Schwartz. "Rising Cleanup Costs and Numerous Lawsuits Rattle BP's Investors." *New York Times*, 2 June 2010.

Murphy, Anna Mary. "Motion Filed on Gage Park Pool Hearing." *Topeka Capital*, 17 June 1953. In newspaper clipping books, Kansas Historical Society, Topeka.

Murrin, John M. "Beneficiaries of Catastrophe." In *The New American History*, revised and expanded edition, edited by Eric Foner, 3–30. Philadelphia: Temple University Press, 1997.

Murrin, James M., Paul E. Johnson, James M. McPherson, Gary Gerstle, Emily S. Rosenberg, and Norman L. Rosenberg. *Liberty, Equality, Power: A History of the American People.* 2 vols. Fort Worth, Tex.: Harcourt Brace, 1999.

Myers, Peter C. *Frederick Douglass: Race and the Rebirth of American Liberalism.* Lawrence: University Press of Kansas, 2008.

Mygatt, Elizabeth. "Bicycle Production Remains Strong Worldwide." *Eco-Economy Indicators*, 13 December 2005, Earth Policy Institute. www.earth-policy.org/Indicators/Bike/2005.htm (accessed 20 May 2009).

Nash, Gary. *Race and Revolution.* Madison, Wis.: Madison House, 1990.

———. *Red, White, and Black: The Peoples of Early North America.* 3rd ed. Englewood Cliffs, N.J.: Prentice Hall, 1992.

———. *The Unknown American Revolution: The Unruly Birth of Democracy and the Struggle to Create America.* New York: Viking, 2005.

Nash, Linda. "The Agency of Nature or the Nature of Agency?" *Environmental History* 10 (January 2005): 67–69.

———. *Inescapable Ecologies: A History of Environment, Disease, and Knowledge.* Berkeley: University of California Press, 2006.

Nash, Roderick. *The Rights of Nature: A History of Environmental Ethics.* Madison: University of Wisconsin Press, 1989.

"Nassau Unveils 3 Car-Pool Areas—Without Drivers." *New York Times*, 3 January 1974.

"Negro Swimmers Ask Use of All Pools in Topeka." *Topeka Journal*, 8 July 1952. In newspaper clipping books, Kansas State Historical Society, Topeka.

Nesbitt, Mark, ed. *Through Blood and Fire: Selected Civil War Papers of Major General Joshua Lawrence Chamberlain.* Mechanicsburg, Pa.: Stackpole Books, 1996.

"Newspaper Accounts of Track Laying." www.nps.gov/archive/gosp/research/track_laying.html.

Nicolson, Marjorie Hope. *Mountain Gloom and Mountain Glory: The Development of the Aesthetics of the Infinite.* Ithaca, N.Y.: Cornell University Press, 1959. Reprint, Seattle: University of Washington Press, 1997.

Niebuhr, Reinhold. *The Irony of American History.* New York: Charles Scribner's Sons, 1952.

———. *The Nature and Destiny of Man*, vol. 1, *Human Nature*. New York: Charles

Scribner's Sons, 1941. Reprint, Upper Saddle River, N.J.: Prentice Hall, 1964.

———. *The Nature and Destiny of Man*, vol. 2, *Human Destiny*. New York: Charles Scribner's Sons, 1943. Reprint, Upper Saddle River, N.J.: Prentice Hall, 1964.

"Nixon Approves Limit of 55 M.P.H." *New York Times*, 3 January 1974.

"No End in Sight to Gas-Pump Lines." *U.S. News and World Report*, 25 February 1974, 13–14.

Norris, Robert S. *Racing for the Bomb: General Leslie R. Groves, the Manhattan Project's Indispensable Man*. South Royalton, Vt.: Steerforth Press, 2002.

Northup, Solomon. *Twelve Years a Slave*. Edited by Sue Eakin and Joseph Logsdon. Baton Rouge: Louisiana State University Press, 1968.

———. *Twelve Years a Slave*. In *Puttin' On Ole Massa: The Slave Narratives of Henry Bibb, William Wells Brown, and Solomon Northup*, edited by Gilbert Osofsky. New York: Harper and Row, 1969.

Norton, Mary Beth. *In the Devil's Snare: The Salem Witchcraft Crisis of 1692*. New York: Knopf, 2002..

———. *Liberty's Daughters: The Revolutionary Experience of American Women, 1750–1800*. Ithaca, N.Y.: Cornell University Press, 1980.

Norton, Mary Beth, David M. Katzman, Paul D. Escott, Howard P. Chudacoff, Thomas G. Paterson, and William M. Tuttle Jr. *A People and a Nation: A History of the United States*. 2nd ed. Boston: Houghton Mifflin, 1986.

Novak, William J. "The Myth of the 'Weak' American State." *American Historical Review* 113 (June 2008): 752–72.

Nye, David E. *America as Second Creation: Technology and Narratives of New Beginnings*. Cambridge, Mass.: MIT Press, 2003.

———. *Consuming Power: A Social History of American Energies*. Cambridge, Mass.: MIT Press, 1998.

Oakes, James. "No Such Right: American Political Culture and the Origin of Lincoln's Rejection of the Right of Property in Slaves." In *Lincoln's America: 1809–1865*, edited by Joseph Fornieri and Susan Vaughn Gabbard, 135–50. Carbondale: Southern Illinois University Press, 2008.

———. *The Radical and the Republican: Frederick Douglass, Abraham Lincoln, and the Triumph of Antislavery Politics*. New York: Norton, 2007.

———. *The Ruling Race: A History of American Slaveholders*. New York: Knopf, 1982. Reprint, New York: Norton, 1998.

———. *Slavery and Freedom: An Interpretation of the Old South*. New York: Knopf, 1990.

Okihiro, Gary. *Common Ground: Reimagining America's Past*. Princeton, N.J.: Princeton University Press, 2001.

Oliver Brown et al. vs. Board of Education of Topeka, Kansas. Project no. 3, Regional Archives Microfilm Project, National Archives and Records Service, Kansas City, Missouri.

Olmsted, Frederick Law. *The Cotton Kingdom: A Traveller's Observations on Cotton and Slavery in the American Slave States*. Edited by Arthur M. Schlesinger. London: Sampson, Low, Son and Company, 1861. Reprint, New York: Da Capo, 1996.

———. *Yosemite and the Mariposa Grove: A Preliminary Report, 1865.* Yosemite National Park: Yosemite Association, 1995.

"On the 'Myth' of the 'Weak' American State." *American Historical Review* 115 (June 2010): 766–800.

Onuf, Peter. *Jefferson's Empire: The Language of American Nationhood.* Charlottesville: University Press of Virginia, 2000.

Opie, John. *The Law of the Land: Two Hundred Years of American Farmland Policy.* Lincoln: University of Nebraska Press, 1987.

———. *Nature's Nation: An Environmental History of the United States.* Fort Worth, Tex.: Harcourt Brace, 1998.

Oppel, Richard A., Jr. "Circumventing an Oil Crisis." *New York Times,* 4 October 2000.

Oppenheimer, J. Robert. "Memorandum of the Los Alamos Project." No date. In "The Oppenheimer Years," *Los Alamos Science* (Los Alamos National Laboratory) 4 (Winter–Spring 1983): 10.

———. "Speech to the Association of Los Alamos Scientists," 2 November 1945. In *Robert Oppenheimer: Letters and Recollections,* edited by Alice Kimball Smith and Charles Weiner, 315–25. Cambridge, Mass.: Harvard University Press, 1980.

Orsi, Jared. *Hazardous Metropolis: Flooding and Urban Ecology in Los Angeles.* Berkeley: University of California Press, 2004.

Orsi, Richard J. *Sunset Limited: The Southern Pacific Railroad and the Development of the American West.* Berkeley: University of California Press, 2005.

O'Shaughnessy, Andrew Jackson. *An Empire Divided: The American Revolution and the British Caribbean.* Philadelphia: University of Pennsylvania Press, 2000.

Oshinsky, David M. *"Worse than Slavery": Parchman Farm and the Ordeal of Jim Crow Justice.* New York: Free Press, 1996.

Owens, Leslie Howard. *This Species of Property: Slave Life and Culture in the Old South.* New York: Oxford University Press, 1976.

Paine, Thomas. *The Age of Reason* [1794]. Chicago: Belfords, Clarke, 1879.

"The Painful Change to Thinking Small." *Time,* 31 December 1973, 18–22, 25.

Painter, Nell Irvin. *Exodusters: Black Migration to Kansas after Reconstruction.* New York: Knopf, 1976.

Palevsky, Mary. *Atomic Fragments: A Daughter's Questions.* Berkeley: University of California Press, 2000.

Paludan, Phillip Shaw. *A People's Contest: The Union and Civil War, 1861–1865.* 2nd ed. New York: Harper and Row, 1986. Reprint, Lawrence: University Press of Kansas, 1996.

———. *The Presidency of Abraham Lincoln.* Lawrence: University Press of Kansas, 1994.

"Panic at the Pump." *Time,* 14 January 1974, 15–16.

Parish, Peter J. *Slavery: History and Historians.* New York: Harper and Row, 1989.

Patrick, John J., ed. *Founding the Republic: A Documentary History.* Westport, Conn.: Greenwood Press, 1995.

Patterson, James T. *Brown v. Board of Education: A Civil Rights Milestone and Its Troubled Legacy.* New York: Oxford University Press, 2001.

———. *Grand Expectations: The United States, 1945–1974*. New York: Oxford University Press, 1996.

———. *Restless Giant: The United States from Watergate to Bush v. Gore*. New York: Oxford University Press, 2005.

Penna, Anthony N. *Nature's Bounty: Historical and Modern Environmental Perspectives*. Armonk, N.Y.: M. E. Sharpe, 1999.

Perlmutter, Emanuel. "Harried Drivers Lose Tempers." *New York Times*, 30 December 1973.

Perrin, Liese M. "Resisting Reproduction: Reconsidering Slave Contraception in the Old South." *Journal of American Studies* 35 (August 2001): 255–74.

Peters, Richard, ed. *Public Statutes at Large of the United States of America*, vol. 1. Boston: Charles C. Little and James Brown, 1845. Available at http://rsb.loc.gov/cgi-bin/ampage.

Peterson, Merrill D., ed. *Jefferson: Writings*. New York: Library of America, 1984.

Pfanz, Harry W. *Gettysburg: Culp's Hill and Cemetery Hill*. Chapel Hill: University of North Carolina Press, 1993.

Philbrick, Nathaniel. *Mayflower: A Story of Courage, Community, and War*. New York: Viking Penguin, 2006.

Phillips, Sarah. *This Land, This Nation: Conservation, Rural America, and the New Deal*. New York: Cambridge University Press, 2007.

Pollan, Michael. *The Botany of Desire: A Plant's-Eye View of the World*. New York: Random House, 2001.

———. "When a Crop Becomes King." *New York Times*, 19 July 2002.

"Poll Finds Oil Crisis Laid to Government and Big Companies." *New York Times*, 10 January 1974.

Potter, David M. *The Impending Crisis, 1848–1861*. New York: Harper and Row, 1976.

Powell, Bruce R. "*Brown v. Board of Education—Johnson v. Board of Education*, 1954–1975: Segregation, an Unresolved Controversy in the Public Schools of Topeka, Kansas, and the Nation." Senior honors thesis, University of Kansas, 1975. In File 254, Box 13, Record Group 21, *Brown v. Board of Education* Exhibit Files, T-316, National Archives and Records Administration, Kansas City, Missouri.

Pratt, Harry E. "Lincoln Pilots the *Talisman*." *Abraham Lincoln Quarterly* 2 (September 1943): 319–29.

Prescott, Einhorn Yaffee. *Lincoln Memorial Stone Survey*. Washington, D.C.: Einhorn Yaffee Prescott, 1994.

"President Signs Highway Bill with Provisions for Mass Transit Assistance; Ronan Is Pleased." *New York Times*, 14 August 1973.

Price, Jennifer. *Flight Maps: Adventures with Nature in Modern America*. New York: Basic Books, 1999.

Proctor, Nicolas W. *Bathed in Blood: Hunting and Mastery in the Old South*. Charlottesville: University Press of Virginia, 2002.

Publishing Committee for "Children of Hiroshima." *Children of Hiroshima*. Tokyo, 1980. Reprint, London: Taylor and Francis, 1981.

Pyne, Stephen J. "The End of the World." *Environmental History* 12 (July 2007): 649–53.

———. *Fire in America: A Cultural History of Wildland and Rural Fire.* Princeton, N.J.: Princeton University Press, 1982.

Quarles, Benjamin. *The Negro in the American Revolution.* Chapel Hill: University of North Carolina Press, 1961.

———. "The Revolutionary War as a Black Declaration of Independence." In *Slavery and Freedom in the Age of the American Revolution*, edited by Ira Berlin and Ronald Hoffman, 283–301. Charlottesville: United States Capitol Historical Society and University Press of Virginia, 1983.

Quinn Evans/Architects. *Historic Structure Report: Monroe Elementary School, Brown v. Board of Education National Historic Site.* Ann Arbor, Mich.: Quinn Evans/Architects, 1998.

Ramsdell, Charles W. "General Robert E. Lee's Horse Supply, 1862–1865." *American Historical Review* 35 (1930): 758–64.

Randolph, John Collins. "Deep Underwater, Threatened Reefs." *New York Times*, 2 June 2010.

Rathbun, Ted A., and Richard H. Steckel. "The Health of Slaves and Free Blacks in the East." In *The Backbone of History: Health and Nutrition in the Western Hemisphere.* New York: Cambridge University Press, 2002.

Rawick, George P. *From Sundown to Sunup: The Making of the Black Community.* Westport, Connecticut: Greenwood, 1972.

Raymond, Anan S., and Richard E. Fike. *Rails East to Promontory: The Utah Stations.* Utah Office, Bureau of Land Management, Cultural Resource Series 8. N.p.: Bureau of Land Management, 1981. Reprint, Livingston, Tex.: Pioneer Enterprises, 1997.

"REACT International History, 1962–2006." www.reactintl.org/react_histry.htm (accessed 4 April 2009). Copy in author's possession. See also "REACT history, 1962–2010," wwwreactintl.org/history (accessed 20 May 2011).

Reid, Brian Holden. *America's Civil War: The Operational Battlefield.* Amherst, N.Y.: Prometheus, 2008.

Reidy, Joseph P. "Obligation and Right: Patterns of Labor, Subsistence, and Exchange in the Cotton Belt of Georgia, 1790–1860." In *Cultivation and Culture: Labor and the Shaping of Slave Life in the Americas*, edited by Ira Berlin and Philip D. Morgan, 138–54. Charlottesville: University Press of Virginia, 1993.

Reinhold, Robert. "Federal Officials Study Pedal Power as One Alternative to Piston Power." *New York Times*, 9 May 1973.

Reis, Elizabeth. *Damned Women: Sinners and Witches in Puritan New England.* Ithaca, N.Y.: Cornell University Press, 1997.

Retired Teachers of the School System. "A Centennial History of Topeka Schools, 1854–1954." 1954. In File 19, Box 9, Record Group 21, *Brown v. Board of Education* Exhibit Files, T-316, National Archives and Records Administration, Kansas City, Missouri.

Retkwa, Rosalyn. "Sun Oil Peddles Bicycles." *New York Times*, 8 September 1974.

Rhodes, Richard. *The Making of the Atomic Bomb.* New York: Simon and Schuster, 1986.

Rice, Allen Thorndike, ed. *Reminiscences of Abraham Lincoln*. New York: North American Publishing, 1886.

Richter, Daniel K. *Facing East from Indian Country: A Native History of Early America*. Cambridge, Mass.: Harvard University Press, 2001.

Rigden, John. "Isidor Isaac Rabi: Walking the Path of God." *Physics World* 12 (November 1999): 27–32.

Righter, Robert. *Wind Energy in America: A History*. Norman: University of Oklahoma Press, 1996.

Ritter, Harry. *Dictionary of Concepts in History*. Westport, Conn.: Greenwood, 1986.

Rivett, Sarah. "Our Salem, Our Selves." *William and Mary Quarterly* 65 (July 2008): 495–502.

Rivlin, Michael J. "The Secret Life of AAA." *Amicus Journal* 22, pt. 4 (Winter 2001): 13–19.

Robbins, William. "Revised Strike Pact Sent White House by Truckers." *New York Times*, 7 February 1974.

———. "Truckers Reach Accord, Leaders Ask Strike End," *New York Times*, 8 February 1974.

Rodehamel, John, ed. *George Washington: Writings*. New York: Library of America, 1997.

Rollins, Richard, ed. *Pickett's Charge: Eyewitness Accounts*. Redondo Beach, Calif.: Rank and File Publications, 1994.

Rolston, Holmes. *Three Big Bangs: Matter-Energy, Life, Mind*. New York: Columbia University Press, 2010.

Rome, Adam. "What Really Matters in History? Environmental Perspectives on Modern America." *Environmental History* 7 (April 2002): 303–18.

Rorabaugh, W. J. *The Alcoholic Republic: An American Tradition*. New York: Oxford University Press, 1979.

Rosenthal, Bernard. *Salem Story: Reading the Witch Trials of 1692*. New York: Cambridge University Press, 1993.

Rothman, Adam. *Slave Country: American Expansionism and the Deep South*. Cambridge, Mass.: Harvard University Press, 2005.

"A Round Table: Environmental History." *Journal of American History* 76 (March 1990): 1087–1147.

Ruffin, Edmund. *Nature's Management: Writings on Landscape and Reform, 1822–1859*. Edited by Jack Temple Kirby. Athens: University of Georgia Press, 2000.

Russell, Edmund. "Evolutionary History: Prospectus for a New Field." *Environmental History* 8 (April 2003): 204–28.

Russell, Edmund, James Allison, Thomas Finger, John K. Brown, Brian Balogh, and W. Bernard Carlson. "The Nature of Power: Synthesizing the History of Technology and Environmental History." *Technology and Culture* 52 (April 2011): 246–59.

Russell Sage Foundation. *The Topeka Improvement Survey*. Topeka, Kans.: Topeka Improvement Survey Committee, 1914.

Sabin, Edwin L. *Building the Pacific Railway*. Philadelphia: J. B. Lippincott, 1919.

Sabin, Paul. *Crude Politics: The California Oil Market, 1900–1907*. Berkeley: University of California Press, 2005.

Sabine, George H., and Thomas L. Thorson. *A History of Political Theory*. 4th ed. Hinsdale, Ill.: Dryden Press, 1973.

Sackman, Douglas. "Nature's Workshop: Workers' Bodies in California's Citrus Industry." *Environmental History* 5 (January 2000): 27–53.

Saint-Amour, Paul K. "Bombing and the Symptom: Traumatic Earliness and the Nuclear Uncanny." *Diacritics* 30 (Winter 2000): 59–82.

Saleri, Nansen G. "Dawn in the Desert: Saudi High Tech Paying Off at Ghawar." *Energy Tribune*, 19 September 2007. www.energytribune.com/articles.cfm?aid=627#.

Salisbury, Neal. *Manitou and Providence: Indians, Europeans, and the Making of New England, 1500–1643*. New York: Oxford University Press, 1982.

Salpukas, Agis. "Owner Driver Gives Case for Fuel Protest." *New York Times*, 31 January 1974.

———. "Protest Transforms Driver in Toledo into 'Biggest Truck Company' Around." *New York Times*, 7 December 1973.

———. "Strike Has Varied Impact in Ohio." *New York Times*, 6 February 1974.

———. "Trucker Protest Slowing Gasoline Deliveries Here." *New York Times*, 2 February 1974.

———. "Truckers' Protest Cuts Flow of Food and Steel." *New York Times*, 1 February 1974.

Sanborn Fire Insurance Maps, 1887–1954. Kansas State Historical Society, Topeka.

Sandage, Scott A. "A Marble House Divided: The Lincoln Memorial, the Civil Rights Movement, and the Politics of Memory, 1939–1963." *Journal of American History* 80 (June 1993): 135–67.

Saxton, Alexander. "The Army of Canton in the High Sierra." In *Chinese on the American Frontier*, edited by Arif Dirlik, 27–36. New York: Rowman and Littlefield, 2001.

Scharff, Virginia J. "Man and Nature! Sex Secrets of Environmental History." In *Seeing Nature through Gender*, edited by Virginia J. Scharff, 3–19. Lawrence: University Press of Kansas, 2003.

———, ed. *Seeing Nature through Gender*. Lawrence: University Press of Kansas, 2003.

———. *The Women Jefferson Loved*. New York: Harper, 2010.

Schlosser, Eric. *Fast Food Nation: The Dark Side of the All-American Meal*. Boston: Houghton Mifflin, 2001.

Schobert, Harold H. *Energy and Society: An Introduction*. New York: Taylor and Francis, 2002.

Schoen, Brian. *The Fragile Fabric of Union: Cotton, Federal Politics, and the Global Origins of the Civil War*. Baltimore, Md.: Johns Hopkins University Press, 2009.

Schulman, Bruce J. "Governing Nature, Nurturing Government: Resource Management and the Development of the American State, 1900–1912." *Journal of Policy History* 17, no. 4 (2005): 375–403.

Schutte, Ann Jacobson. "'Such Monstrous Births': A Neglected Aspect of the Antinomian Controversy." *Renaissance Quarterly* 38 (Spring 1985): 85–106.

Schwantes, Carlos Arnaldo. *Hard Traveling: A Portrait of Work Life in the New Northwest.* Lincoln: University of Nebraska Press, 1994.

———. "Patterns of Radicalism on the Wageworkers' Frontier." *Idaho Yesterdays* 30 (December 1986): 25–30.

Schwartz, Marie Jenkins. "'At Noon, Oh How I Ran': Breastfeeding and Weaning on Plantation and Farm in Antebellum Virginia and Alabama." In *Discovering the Women in Slavery*, edited by Patricia Morton, 241–59. Athens: University of Georgia Press, 1996.

———. *Born in Bondage: Growing Up Enslaved in the Antebellum South.* Cambridge, Mass.: Harvard University Press, 2000.

Sears, Stephen W. *Gettysburg.* Boston: Houghton Mifflin, 2003.

Seelye, John. *Beautiful Machine: Rivers and the Republican Plan, 1755–1825.* New York: Oxford University Press, 1991.

Seligman, Amanda I. *Block by Block: Neighborhoods and Public Policy on Chicago's West Side.* Chicago: University of Chicago Press, 2005.

Sellars, Richard West. "The Granite Orchards of Gettysburg." *National Park Service Courier*, December 1986, 20–22.

Sellers, Christopher. "Thoreau's Body: Towards an Embodied Environmental History." *Environmental History* 4 (October 1999): 486–514.

Shaara, Michael. *The Killer Angels.* New York: Random House, 1974.

Shapiro, Darline. "Ethan Allen: Philosopher-Theologian to a Generation of American Revolutionaries." *William and Mary Quarterly*, 3rd series, 21 (April 1964): 236–55.

Sharrer, G. Terry. "The Great Glanders Epizootic: A Civil War Legacy." *Agricultural History* 69 (Winter 1995): 79–97.

———. *A Kind of Fate: Agricultural Change in Virginia, 1861–1920.* Ames: Iowa State University Press, 2000.

Sheppeard, Lee. "Court Action May Halt UR." *Topeka Capital*, 6 June 1959. In newspaper clipping books, Kansas State Historical Society, Topeka.

Sheriff, Carol. *The Artificial River: The Erie Canal and the Paradox of Progress, 1817–1862.* New York: Hill and Wang, 1996.

Sherry, Michael. *The Rise of American Air Power: The Creation of Armageddon.* New Haven, Conn.: Yale University Press, 1987.

Shilts, Gary. *And the Band Played On: Politics, People, and the AIDS Epidemic.* New York: St. Martin's, 1987.

Sieferle, Rolf Peter. *The Subterranean Forest: Energy Systems and the Industrial Revolution.* Munich: C. H. Beck, 1982. Reprint, Cambridge: White Horse Press, 2001.

Silver, Roy R. "Driver Exposes Cheating Gas Pumps." *New York Times*, 5 January 1974.

Simmons, Matthew R. *Twilight in the Desert: The Coming Saudi Oil Shock and the World Economy.* New York: Wiley, 2006.

Simon, Julian, and Herman Kahn. *The Resourceful Earth: A Response to Global 2000.* New York: Blackwell, 1984.

Skidelsky, Robert. *Keynes: The Return of the Master.* New York: Public Affairs Press, 2009.

Slotkin, Richard, and James K. Folsom, eds. *So Dreadful a Judgment: Puritan Responses to King Philip's War, 1676–1677*. Middletown, Conn.: Wesleyan University Press, 1978.

Smil, Vaclav. *Energies: An Illustrated Guide to the Biosphere and Civilization*. Cambridge, Mass.: MIT Press, 1999.

———. *Energy in Nature and Society: General Energetics of Complex Systems*. Cambridge, Mass.: MIT Press, 2008.

———. *Energy in World History*. Boulder, Colo.: Westview Press, 1994.

———. "Peak Oil: A Catastrophist Cult and Complex Realities." *World-Watch* 19 (January–February 2006): 22–24.

Smith, Jason Scott. *Building New Deal Liberalism: The Political Economy of Public Works, 1933–1956*. New York: Cambridge University Press, 2006.

Smith, Kimberly K. *African American Environmental Thought: Foundations*. Lawrence: University Press of Kansas, 2007.

Smith, Mark M. *Mastered by the Clock: Time, Slavery, and Freedom in the American South*. Chapel Hill: University of North Carolina Press, 1997.

Stampp, Kenneth M. *The Peculiar Institution: Slavery in the Ante-Bellum South*. New York: Vintage, 1956.

Stanton, Elizabeth Cady. "Declaration of Sentiments and Resolves." In *American Voices, American Lives: A Documentary Reader*, edited by Wayne Franklin, 427–30. New York: Norton, 1997.

"State to Assist Cities to Set Up Car Pools." *New York Times*, 3 January 1974.

Steckel, Richard H. "The African American Population of the United States, 1790–1920." In *A Population History of North America*, edited by Michael R. Haines and Richard H. Steckel, 433–82. New York: Cambridge University Press, 2000.

———. "Stature and the Standard of Living." *Journal of Economic Literature* 33 (December 1995): 1903–40.

Steele, Ian K. *Warpaths: Invasions of North America*. New York: Oxford University Press, 1994.

Steers, Edward. *The Lincoln Assassination Encyclopedia*. New York: Harper Perennial, 2010.

Stein, Susan R. *The Worlds of Thomas Jefferson at Monticello*. New York: Harry N. Abrams and Thomas Jefferson Memorial Foundation, 1993.

Stein, Susan, Peter J. Hatch, Lucia C. Stanton, and Merrill D. Peterson. *Monticello: A Guidebook*. Charlottesville, Va.: Thomas Jefferson Foundation, 1997.

Steinberg, Ted. *Down to Earth: Nature's Role in American History*. 2nd ed. New York: Oxford University Press, 2009.

Steiner, Paul E. *Disease in the Civil War: Natural Biological Warfare in 1861–1865*. Springfield, Ill.: Charles C. Thomas, 1968.

Stephanson, Anders. *Manifest Destiny: American Expansion and the Empire of Right*. New York: Hill and Wang, 1995.

Sterba, James P. "Tourists May Have a Long Wait in Gas-Dry Colorado." *New York Times*, 29 July 1973.

Stern, Alexandra Minna. *Eugenic Nation: Faults and Frontiers of Better Breeding in*

Modern America. Berkeley: University of California Press, 2005.

Stevens, William K. "Americans, Hit by High Cost of Gas and Recalling Shortage, Rely Less on Autos." *New York Times*, 15 April 1974.

———."Gasoline Shortages Are Forcing Exurbanites to Readjust their Life-Style." *New York Times*, 7 February 1974.

Stewart, George A. *Pickett's Charge: A Microhistory of the Final Attack at Gettysburg, July 3, 1863.* Boston: Houghton Mifflin, 1959. Reprint, Dayton, Ohio: Press of Morningside Bookshop, 1983.

Stewart, Mart A. "If John Muir Had Been an Agrarian: American Environmental History West and South." *Environment and History* 11 (May 2005): 139–62.

———. "Slavery and the Origins of African American Environmentalism." In *To Love the Wind and the Rain: African Americans and Environmental History*, edited by Dianne D. Glave and Mark Stoll, 9–20. Pittsburgh: University of Pittsburgh Press, 2006.

———. *"What Nature Suffers to Groe": Life, Labor, and Landscape on the Georgia Coast, 1680–1920.* Athens: University of Georgia Press, 1996.

Stine, Jeffrey K., and Joel Tarr. "At the Intersection of Histories: Technology and the Environment." *Technology and Culture* 39 (October 1998): 601–40.

Stock, Robert W. "One Barrel of Oil." *New York Times Sunday Magazine*, 21 April 1974.

Stoker, Donald. *The Grand Design: Strategy and the U.S. Civil War.* New York: Oxford University Press, 2010.

Stoll, Mark. *Protestantism, Capitalism, and Nature in America.* Albuquerque: University of New Mexico Press, 1997.

Stoll, Steven. *The Great Delusion: A Mad Inventor, Death in the Tropics, and the Utopian Origins of Economic Growth.* New York: Hill and Wang, 2008.

———. *Larding the Lean Earth: Soil and Society in Nineteenth-Century America.* New York: Hill and Wang, 2002.

"Storing Gasoline Can Kill You!" *Better Homes and Gardens*, March 1974, 21.

Stradling, David, ed. *Conservation in the Progressive Era: Classic Texts.* Seattle: University of Washington Press, 2004.

Stroud, Ellen. "Troubled Waters in Ecotopia: Environmental Racism in Portland, Oregon." *Radical History Review* 74 (Spring 1999): 65–95.

Sugrue, Thomas J. *The Origins of the Urban Crisis: Race and Inequality in Postwar Detroit.* Princeton, N.J.: Princeton University Press, 1996.

Sutter, Paul S. "Representing the Resource: Between Nature and Culture in the Longleaf Pine." *Environmental History* 10 (January 2005): 94–96.

Swan, Robert A., Jr. *The Ethnic Heritage of Topeka, Kansas: Immigrant Beginnings.* Topeka, Kans.: Institute of Comparative Ethnic Studies, 1974.

Szasz, Ferenc Morton. *The Day the Sun Rose Twice: The Story of the Trinity Site Nuclear Explosion, July 16, 1945.* Albuquerque: University of New Mexico Press, 1984.

Szasz, Thomas. "When History Comes Home to Roost." *New York Times*, 6 March 1974.

Tadman, Michael. "The Demographic Cost of Sugar: Debates on Slave Societies and Natural Increase in the Americas." *American Historical Review* 105 (December 2000): 1534–38.

———. *Speculators and Slaves: Masters, Traders, and Slaves in the Old South*. Madison: University of Wisconsin Press, 1989.

Takaki, Ronald. *Hiroshima: Why America Dropped the Atomic Bomb*. Boston: Little, Brown, 1995.

Tavernise, Sabrina, and Robert Gebeloff. "Car Pools, Passé as Hitchhiking." *New York Times*, 29 January 2011.

Taylor, Alan. *American Colonies*. New York: Viking, 2001.

———. *Liberty Men and Great Proprietors: The Revolutionary Settlement of the Maine Frontier, 1760–1820*. Chapel Hill: University of North Carolina Press, 1990.

Taylor, John M. *The Witchcraft Delusion in Colonial Connecticut, 1647–1697*. N.p.: n.p., 1908. Reprint, Stratford, Conn.: J. Edmund Edwards, 1969.

Teller, Edward. *Memoirs: A Twentieth-Century Journey in Science and Politics*. Cambridge: Perseus, 2001.

Thomas, Benjamin P. *Lincoln's New Salem*. Rev. ed. Chicago: Americana House, 1961.

Thomas, Christopher A. "The Lincoln Memorial and Its Architect, Henry Bacon (1866–1924)." 3 vols. PhD dissertation, Yale University, 1990.

———. *The Lincoln Memorial and American Life*. Princeton, N.J.: Princeton University Press, 2002.

Thomas, Emory M. *The Confederate Nation, 1861–1865*. New York: Harper and Row, 1979.

Thompson, Hunter S. *Hell's Angels: The Strange and Terrible Saga of the Outlaw Motorcycle Gangs*. New York: Random House, 1966.

Thorpe, Charles. *Oppenheimer: The Tragic Intellect*. Chicago: University of Chicago Press, 2006.

Thorpe, Charles, and Steven Shapin. "Who Was J. Robert Oppenheimer? Charisma and Complex Organization." *Social Studies of Science* 30 (August 2000): 545–90.

Thorpe, T. B. "Cotton and Its Cultivation." *Harper's New Monthly Magazine* 8 (February 1854): 452–57, 459. Reprinted in *Cotton and the Growth of the American Economy: 1790–1860*, edited by Stuart Bruchey, 171–76. New York: Harcourt, Brace, and World, 1967.

"Thousands of Truck Drivers Stay Off the Road to Protest Effects of Fuel Shortage." *New York Times*, 14 December 1973.

Thurber, L. Newton. "Caring Carpool Is Community." *A.D. Magazine*, February 1979, 39, copied in J. Martin Bailey to Mark Fiege, 24 January 2009, e-mail in possession of the author.

"A Time of Learning to Live with Less." *Time*, 3 December 1973, 29–32.

Topeka Capital-Journal. *Topeka: A History in Pictures*. Topeka, Kans.: Topeka Capital-Journal, 2001.

Topeka–Shawnee County Regional Planning Commission. *Preliminary Land Use Plan for the Topeka–Shawnee County Regional Planning Area*. Master Plan Report 3. Topeka, Kans.: Topeka–Shawnee County Regional Planning Commission, 1962.

Torrance, Robert M., ed. *Encompassing Nature: Nature and Culture from Ancient Times to the Modern World*. Washington, D.C.: Counterpoint, 1998.

Townsend, Timothy P. "Lincoln in Illinois." In *Abraham Lincoln: A Living Legacy*, edited by Diana L. Bailey, 76–149. Virginia Beach, Va.: Donning Co. Publishers and Eastern National, 2008.

Treaster, Joseph R. "In Montclair, a Car Pool Is a Corporation." *New York Times*, 1 January 1974.

Trouillot, Michel-Rolph. *Silencing the Past: Power and the Production of History.* Boston: Beacon, 1995.

Trudeau, Noah Andre. *Gettysburg: A Testing of Courage.* New York: HarperCollins, 2002.

Tucker, Glenn. *High Tide at Gettysburg: The Campaign in Pennsylvania.* Indianapolis: Bobbs-Merrill, 1958. Reprint, Dayton, Ohio: Press of Morningside Bookshop, 1973.

Tucker, Richard. *Insatiable Appetite: The United States and the Ecological Degradation of the Tropical World.* Berkeley: University of California Press, 2000.

Turner, George Edgar. *Victory Rode the Rails: The Strategic Place of Railroads in the Civil War.* Indianapolis: Bobbs-Merrill, 1953. Reprint, Lincoln: University of Nebraska Press, 1992.

The Unfinished Agenda of Brown v. Board of Education. Edited by the editors of *Black Issues in Higher Education.* Hoboken, N.J.: John Wiley and Sons, 2004.

United Press International. "Truck Driver-Owners Block Highways in Five States." *New York Times*, 5 December 1973.

———. "Truckers Disrupt Oil Deliveries and Harass Working Drivers." *New York Times*, 30 January 1974.

"Urban Plan Wins Formal City Approval." *Topeka Journal*, 26 June 1956. In newspaper clipping books, Kansas State Historical Society, Topeka.

U.S. Bureau of the Census. *Statistical Abstract of the United States: 1974.* Washington, D.C.: Government Printing Office, 1974, 512, 516.

U. S. Commission on Civil Rights. *Twenty Years after Brown.* Washington, D.C.: Government Printing Office, 1977.

U.S. Department of Commerce, Bureau of the Census. *Fifteenth Census of the United States, 1930, vol. 4, Agriculture.* Washington, D.C.: Government Printing Office, 1932.

U.S. Department of Transportation. *Bicycle Transportation for Energy Conservation.* Washington, D.C.: Government Printing Office, 1980.

———. *Bicycles USA: Conference Proceedings.* Washington, D.C.: Government Printing Office, 1973.

———. *Bicycling for Recreation and Commuting.* Washington, D.C.: Government Printing Office, 1972.

USDI/NPS (U.S. Department of the Interior, National Park Service). *Everlasting Steam: The Story of the Jupiter and the No. 119.* www.nps.gov/gosp/historyculture/upload/jupiter%202-2.pdf (accessed 21 May 2011).

———. *Lincoln Memorial.* Washington, D.C.: U.S. Department of the Interior, 1986.

U.S. Energy Information Administration. *Monthly Alaska Field Production of Crude Oil.* http://tonto.eia.doe.gov/dnav/pet/hist/mcrfpak1m.htm (accessed 13 July 2009).

———. *Monthly U.S. Field Production of Crude Oil, 1920–2009.* http://tonto.eia.doe.gov/dnav/pet/hist/mcrfpus1m.htm (accessed 13 July 2009).

———. *Monthly U.S. Imports of Crude Oil, 1920–2009.* http://tonto.eia.doe.gov/dnav/pet/hist/mcrimus1m.htm (accessed 13 July, 2009).

"U.S. to Allocate All Petroleum Supplies." *Oil and Gas Journal* 71 (12 November 1973): 108–10.

Utley, Robert M. "The Dash to Promontory." *Utah Historical Quarterly* 29 (April 1961): 105.

Utley, Robert M., and Francis A. Ketterson Jr. *Golden Spike National Historic Site.* Washington, D.C.: U.S. Department of the Interior, National Park Service, 1969.

Valenčius, Conevery Bolton. *The Health of the Country: How American Settlers Understood Themselves and Their Land.* New York: Basic Books, 2002.

Van Delinder, Jean L. "Border Campaigns." PhD dissertation, University of Kansas, 1996.

———. "*Brown v. Board of Education of Topeka*: A Landmark Case Unresolved Fifty Years Later." *Prologue* 36 (Spring 2004): part 1, 1–5, and part 2, 1–8. www.archives.gov/publications/prologue/2004/spring/brown-v-board-1.html; www.archives.gov/publications/prologue/2004/spring/brown-v-board-2.html.

———. "Early Civil Rights Activism in Topeka, Kansas, before the 1954 *Brown* Case." *Great Plains Quarterly* 21 (Winter 2001): 45–61.

Vandenbusche, Duane, and Rex Myers. *Marble, Colorado: City of Stone.* Denver: Golden Bell Press, 1970.

Vietor, Richard H. K. *Energy Policy in America since 1945: A Study of Business–Government Relations.* Cambridge: Cambridge University Press, 1984.

Viorst, Judith. "A Day at the Pumps: A Nostalgic Look at the Energy Crisis." *Redbook,* June 1974, 40.

Waggoner, Walter H. "Bike Rentals Up in Energy Crisis." *New York Times,* 16 December 1973.

Wald, Matthew L., and Tom Zeller Jr. "Fishing Ban Is Expanded as Spill's Impact Becomes More Evident." *New York Times,* 19 May 2010.

Waldstreicher, David. "Capitalism, Slavery, and Benjamin Franklin's American Revolution." In *The Economy of Early America: Historical Perspectives and New Directions,* edited by Cathy Matson, 183–218. Philadelphia: University of Pennsylvania Press, 2006.

———. *Runaway America: Benjamin Franklin, Slavery, and the American Revolution.* New York: Hill and Wang, 2004.

Walker, Brett L. *Toxic Archipelago: A History of Industrial Disease in Japan.* Seattle: University of Washington Press, 2010.

Walker, J. Samuel. "Recent Literature on Truman's Atomic Bomb Decision: The Search for a Middle Ground." *Diplomatic History* 29 (April 2005): 311–34.

Wall, Bennett H. "Oil Industry." In *The Reader's Companion to American History,* edited by Eric Foner and John A. Garraty, 804–7. Boston: Houghton Mifflin, 1991.

Wallace, Anthony F. C. *Jefferson and the Indians: The Tragic Fate of the First Americans.*

Cambridge, Mass.: Belknap Press of Harvard University Press, 1999.

Wallace, Douglas W., and Roy D. Bird. *Witness of the Times: A History of Shawnee County.* Topeka, Kans.: Shawnee County Historical Society, 1976.

Walls, Laura Dassow. *The Passage to Cosmos: Alexander von Humboldt and the Shaping of America.* Chicago: University of Chicago Press, 2009.

Walsh, Lorena. "The African American Population of the Colonial United States." In *A Population History of North America,* edited by Michael R. Haines and Richard H. Steckel, 191–240. Cambridge: Cambridge University Press, 2000.

Ward, Geoffrey C. *The Civil War: An Illustrated History.* New York: Alfred A. Knopf, 1991.

War of the Rebellion: A Compilation of the Official Records of the Union and Confederate Armies, series 1, vol. 25, part 2. Washington, D.C.: Government Printing Office, 1889.

War of the Rebellion: A Compilation of the Official Records of the Union and Confederate Armies, series 1, vol. 27, parts 1 and 2. Washington, D.C.: Government Printing Office, 1889.

Warren, Kenneth. *The American Steel Industry, 1850–1970: A Geographical Interpretation.* London: Oxford University Press, 1973.

Warrin, Donald, and Geoffrey L. Gomes. *Land, as Far as the Eye Can See: Portuguese in the Old West.* Spokane, Wash.: Arthur H. Clark, 2001.

Washington, Sylvia Hood. *Packing Them In: Environmental Racism in Chicago, 1865–1954.* Lanham, Md.: Lexington Books, 2005.

Watkins, James L. *King Cotton: A Historical and Statistical Review.* New York: James L. Watkins and Sons, 1908.

Watt-Cloutier, Sheila. "The Inuit Right to Culture Based on Ice and Snow." In *Moral Ground: Ethical Action for a Planet in Peril,* edited by Kathleen Dean Moore and Michael P. Nelson, 25–29. San Antonio, Tex.: Trinity University Press, 2010.

Weeks, William Earl. *Building the Continental Empire: American Expansion from the Revolution to the Civil War.* Chicago: Ivan R. Dee, 1996.

Weigley, Russell. *A Great Civil War: A Military and Political History, 1861–1865.* Bloomington: Indiana University Press, 2000.

Weinberg, Albert K. *Manifest Destiny: A Study of Nationalist Expansionism in American History.* Baltimore, Md.: Johns Hopkins University Press, 1935. Reprint, Chicago: Quadrangle Books, 1963.

Weisser, Amy. "Marking Brown v. Board of Education." In *Sites of Memory: Perspectives on Architecture and Race,* edited by Craig E. Barton, 97–108. New York: Princeton Architectural Press, 2001.

Weisskopf, Victor. *The Joy of Insight: Passions of a Physicist.* New York: Basic Books, 1991.

West, Elliott. *The Contested Plains: Indians, Goldseekers, and the Rush to Colorado.* Lawrence: University Press of Kansas, 1998.

———. *The Way to the West: Essays on the Central Plains.* Albuquerque: University of New Mexico Press, 1995.

Wheeler, George. *Witness to Gettysburg.* New York: Harper and Row, 1987.

White, Deborah Gray. *Ar'n't I a Woman? Female Slaves in the Plantation South.* Rev. ed. New York: Norton, 1999.

White, John H., Jr. *American Locomotives: An Engineering History, 1830–1880.* Revised and expanded edition. Baltimore, Md.: Johns Hopkins University Press, 1997.

White, Richard. "American Environmental History: The Development of a New Historical Field." *Pacific Historical Review* 54 (August 1985): 297–335.

———. "Are You an Environmentalist or Do You Work for a Living? Work and Nature." In *Uncommon Ground: Rethinking the Human Place in Nature*, edited by William Cronon, 175–85. New York: Norton, 1995.

———. "From Wilderness to Hybrid Landscapes: The Cultural Turn in Environmental History." *The Historian* 66 (Fall 2004); 557–664.

———. *It's Your Misfortune and None of My Own: A History of the American West.* Norman: University of Oklahoma Press, 1991.

———. *The Middle Ground: Indians, Empires, and Republics in the Great Lakes Region, 1650–1815.* Cambridge: Cambridge University Press, 1991.

———. "The Nationalization of Nature." *Journal of American History* 86 (December 1999): 976–86.

———. *The Organic Machine: The Remaking of the Columbia River.* New York: Hill and Wang, 1995.

———. "The Problem With Purity." Tanner Lecture on Human Values, University of California, Davis, May 10, 1999.

———. *Railroaded: The Transcontinentals and the Making of Modern America.* New York: Norton, 2011.

———. *The Roots of Dependency: Subsistence, Environment, and Social Change among the Choctaws, Pawnees, and Navajos.* Lincoln: University of Nebraska Press, 1983.

———. "The Winning of the West: The Expansion of the Western Sioux in the Eighteenth and Nineteenth Century," *Journal of American History* 65 (September 1978): 319–43.

White, Ronald C. A. *Lincoln: A Biography.* New York: Random House, 2009.

Wilentz, Sean. *The Rise of American Democracy: Jefferson to Lincoln.* New York: Norton, 2005.

Willey, Basil. *The Eighteenth Century Background: Studies on the Idea of Nature in the Thought of the Period.* New York: Columbia University Press, 1940.

Williams, James. *Narrative of James Williams, an American Slave.* New York and Boston: American Anti-Slavery Society and Isaac Knapp, 1838.

Williams, John Hoyt. *A Great and Shining Road: The Epic Story of the Transcontinental Railroad.* New York: Times Books, 1988.

Williams, Michael. *Americans and Their Forests: A Historical Geography.* New York: Cambridge University Press, 1989.

Williams, Raymond. "Ideas of Nature." In *Problems in Materialism and Culture: Selected Essays.* London: Verso, 1980.

Wills, Garry. *Head and Heart: American Christianities.* New York: Penguin Press, 2007.

———. *Inventing America: Jefferson's Declaration of Independence.* Garden City, N.Y.: Doubleday, 1978.

———. *Lincoln at Gettysburg: The Words That Remade America.* New York: Simon and Schuster, 1992.

———. *Mr. Jefferson's University.* Washington, D.C.: National Geographic Society, 2002.

Wilson, Carol. *Freedom at Risk: The Kidnapping of Free Blacks in America, 1780–1865.* Lexington: University Press of Kentucky, 1994.

Wilson, Douglas L. *Honor's Voice: The Transformation of Abraham Lincoln.* New York: Vintage, 1999.

Wilson, Jane S. "Introduction." In *Standing By and Making Do: Women of Wartime Los Alamos,* edited by Jane S. Wilson and Charlotte Serber, x–xi. Los Alamos, N.M.: Los Alamos Historical Society, 1988.

———. "Not Quite Eden." In *Standing By and Making Do: Women of Wartime Los Alamos,* edited by Jane S. Wilson and Charlotte Serber, 43–56. Los Alamos, N.M.: Los Alamos Historical Society, 1988.

Wilson, Mark R. *The Business of Civil War: Military Mobilization and the State, 1861–1865.* Baltimore, Md.: Johns Hopkins University Press, 2006.

Wilson, Paul. *A Time to Lose: Representing Kansas in Brown v. Board of Education.* Lawrence: University Press of Kansas, 1995.

Winerip, Michael. "A Great Car Pool: Decorum, Faith, and a Manual." *New York Times,* 26 May 1989.

Winger, Stewart. "High Priests of Nature: The Origins of Illinois State Normal 'University' and the Antebellum Lyceum." *Journal of the Illinois State Historical Society* 101 (Summer 2008): 127–62.

———. *Lincoln, Religion, and Romantic Cultural Politics.* DeKalb: Northern Illinois University Press, 2003.

———. "Lincoln's *Alma Mater*: The Lyceum and the Making of a Self-Made Man." *Lincoln Lore: The Bulletin of the Lincoln Museum,* no. 1894 (Fall 2008): 41–48.

Winters, Harold A., Gerald E. Galloway Jr., William J. Reynolds, and David W. Rhyne. *Battling the Elements: Weather and Terrain in the Conduct of War.* Baltimore, Md.: Johns Hopkins University Press, 1998.

Winthrop, John. *The Journal of John Winthrop, 1630–1649.* Edited by Richard S. Dunn, James Savage, and Laetitia Yeandle. Cambridge, Mass.: Harvard University Press, 1996.

Wittner, Lawrence. *The Struggle Against the Bomb,* vol. 1, *One World or None: A History of the World Nuclear Disarmament Movement through 1953.* Stanford, Calif.: Stanford University Press, 1993.

Wolf, Eric. *Europe and the People without History.* Berkeley: University of California Press, 1982.

Wollstonecraft, Mary. *A Vindication of the Rights of Woman.* London: Joseph Johnson, 1792. Reprint, London: Penguin, 2004.

Woloch, Nancy. *Early American Women: A Documentary History.* Belmont, Calif.: Wadsworth, 1992.

———. *Women and the American Experience*. New York: Knopf, 1984.

Wood, Gordon. *The American Revolution: A History*. New York: Modern Library, 2002.

———. *The Creation of the American Republic, 1776–1787*. Chapel Hill: University of North Carolina Press, 1969.

———. *Empire of Liberty: A History of the Early Republic, 1789–1815*. New York: Oxford University Press, 2009.

———. *The Radicalism of the American Revolution*. New York: Knopf, 1992.

Wood, Peter. "'Liberty Is Sweet': African-American Freedom Struggles in the Years before White Independence." In *Beyond the American Revolution: Explorations in the History of American Radicalism*, edited by Alfred E. Young, 149–84. Dekalb: Northern Illinois University Press, 1993.

Woods, Randall B. "Integration, Exclusion, or Segregation? The 'Color Line' in Kansas, 1878–1900." *Western Historical Quarterly* 14 (April 1983): 181–98.

Worster, Donald. *Dust Bowl: The Southern Plains in the 1930s*. New York: Oxford University Press, 1979.

———. "History as Natural History: An Essay on Theory and Method." *Pacific Historical Review* 53 (February 1984): 1–19.

———. *A Passion for Nature: The Life of John Muir*. New York: Oxford University Press, 2008.

———. *Rivers of Empire: Water, Aridity, and the Growth of the American West*. New York: Pantheon, 1985.

———. "Seeing Beyond Culture." *Journal of American History* 76 (March 1990): 1142–47.

———. "Transformations of the Earth: Towards an Agroecological Perspective in History." *Journal of American History* 76 (March 1990): 1087–1106.

———. "When Writing about John Muir, I Had to See What He Saw." *History News Network*, 1 December, 2008, http://hnn.us/articles/54739.html.

Wright, Gavin. *Slavery and American Economic Development*. Baton Rouge: Louisiana State University Press, 2006.

Wrigley, E. A. *Continuity, Chance, and Change: The Character of the Industrial Revolution in England*. Cambridge: Cambridge University Press, 1988.

Yates, Michael D. "A Statistical Portrait of the U.S. Working Class." *Monthly Review* 56 (April 2005): 12.

Yen, Tzu-Kuei. "Chinese Workers and the First Transcontinental Railroad of the United States of America." PhD dissertation, St. John's University, 1977.

Yergin, Daniel. *The Prize: The Epic Quest for Oil, Money, and Power*. New York: Simon and Schuster, 1991.

Zagarri, Rosemary. *Revolutionary Backlash: Women and Politics in the Early American Republic*. Philadelphia: University of Pennsylvania Press, 2007.

———. *A Woman's Dilemma: Mercy Otis Warren and the American Revolution*. Wheeling, Ill.: Harlan Davidson, 1995.

Credits

Gallery No. 1

MOUNTAINS AND MONUMENTS

1.1 National Photo Company Collection, Library of Congress, Prints & Photographs Division, LC-F82-4820.

1.2 Harris & Ewing Collection, Library of Congress, Prints & Photographs Division, HEC 05419.

1.3 Harris & Ewing Collection, Library of Congress, Prints & Photographs Division, HEC 03415.

1.4 Harris & Ewing Collection, Library of Congress, Prints & Photographs Division, HEC 07072.

1.5 National Archives, Record Group 42, item 42-M-J-1, Records of the Office of Public Buildings and Public Parks of the National Capital.

1.6 Georgia Archives, Vanishing Georgia Collection, PCK 247-85.

1.7 Georgia Archives, Vanishing Georgia Collection, PCK 229-82.

1.8 Denver Public Library, Western History Collection, Louis Charles McClure, MCC-1992.

1.9 Cover of *Scientific American*, March 20, 1915, v. CXII, n. 12.

1.10 Denver Public Library, Western History Collection, George L. Beam, GB-8395.

1.11 Courtesy the National Park Service.

Gallery No. 2

ANIMAL FAMILIARS

2.1 Division of Rare and Manuscript Collections, Cornell University Library.

2.2 Matthew Hopkins, *The Discovery of Witches* (N.P.: Matthew Hopkins, 1647).

2.3 American Antiquarian Society, Charles Peirce Collection.

2.4 George Henry Preble, *Our Flag* (Albany, NY: J. Munsell, 1872).

2.5 Georgia Department of Archives and History.

2.6 Starke County Historical Society, Knox, Indiana.

2.7 Library of Congress, Prints and Photographs Division.

2.8 Library of Congress, Rare Books and Special Collections Division.

2.9 Massachusetts Historical Society.

2.10 Library of Congress, Manuscript Division, Herndon-Weik Collection of Lincolniana, Digital ID al0002.

2.11 U.S. Patent and Trademark Office.

HARD LABOR

2.12 Library of Congress, Prints & Photographs Division, Civil War Photographs, LC-B811-159.

2.13 Library of Congress, Prints & Photographs Division, Frank Leslie's Illustrated Newspaper, vol. 33, no. 836 (1871 Oct. 7), 61.

2.14 Center for Louisiana Studies, University of Louisiana at Lafayette, Harper's Monthly Magazine, 8 (March 1854): 447–463.

2.15 Picture History, Campaign Plain Dealer, October 6, 1860. Please confirm this image will work after cartoon is cropped.

BUTCHER'S BILL

2.16 Cornell University Division of Rare and Manuscript Collections, *Vanity Fair*, May 4, 1861.

2.17 Duke University, Rare Book, Manuscript and Special Collections Library, *Frank Leslie's Budget of Fun*, April 1, 1864.

2.18 Library of Congress, Prints & Photographs Division, Civil War Photographs, LC-B811-2367.

2.19 Documentary Drawings Collection, Library of Congress, Prints & Photographs Division, DRWG/US-Waud, no. 425.

2.20 Abraham Lincoln Presidential Library & Museum, *Frank Leslie's Illustrated Newspaper*, February 1, 1862, 173.

2.21 The Becker Collection, Boston, MA.

2.22 Library of Congress, Prints and Photographs Division.

Gallery No. 3

IRON HORSES

3.1 The Andrew J. Russell Collection, the Oakland Museum of California.

3.2 The Andrew J. Russell Collection, the Oakland Museum of California.

3.3   The Andrew J. Russell Collection, the Oakland Museum of California.
3.4   Stanford University Libraries, Department of Special Collections.
3.5   Central Pacific Railroad Photographic History Museum, © 2012 CPRR.org.
3.6   Lawrence & Houseworth albums. Gift of Florence V. Flinn. The Society of
       California Pioneers.
3.7   The Becker Collection, Boston, MA.
3.8   Stanford University Libraries, Department of Special Collections.
3.9   The Andrew J. Russell Collection, the Oakland Museum of California.

NATURE STUDY

3.10   Photo by William H. Smith, courtesy AIP Emilio Segrè Visual Archives.
3.11   Photo by Mrs. J. Robert Oppenheimer, courtesy AIP Emilio Segrè Visual
       Archives.
3.12   AIP Emilio Segrè Visual Archives, Segrè Collection.
3.13   Photograph by John P. Miller, courtesy AIP Emilio Segrè Visual Archives, Segrè
       Collection.
3.14   U.S. Department of Energy, National Nuclear Security Administration / Nevada
       Site Office.

NATURAL HAZARDS

3.15   Kansas State Historical Society.
3.16   Kansas State Historical Society.
3.17   Kansas State Historical Society.
3.18   Carl Iwasaki/Time & Life Pictures/Getty Images.

LIPIDS AND LIBERTY

3.19   From MAD Magazine No. 178 © E.C. Publications, Inc. Used with Permission.
3.20   Author's collection.
3.21   Farm Security Administration-Office of War Information Photograph
       Collection, Library of Congress, LC-USF34-100296-D.
3.22   National Archives and Records Administration, Records of the Environmental
       Protection Agency, 412-DA-13061.
3.23   Cartoon: Frank Boyle, Edinburgh Evening News.

Index

Page numbers in *italics* refer to illustrations.

A

Berlin, Ira, 86, 88

Bethe, Hans, 273, 296, 297, 302, 304, 309, 316

Bethe, Rose, 316

bicycling, 279, 370, 392–95, 401

Big Harry (enslaved laborer), 113

"big science," Manhattan Project as, 482n34

Bill of Rights, 96

Birch, William, 137

Bissell, Hezekiah, 256, 479n92

Black Giant oil field, 372–73, 376

Black Goose (locomotive engine), 252

Black Hills, 240, 241

Blackstone, William, 167

Bledsoe, Charles, 346–47

Bob (enslaved laborer), 136, 137

body, human: American, compared to European, 66; assembly lines and, 418–19; athletics, bodily proximity, and race relations, 343; atom bomb and, 312–13; Civil War and moving by legs and feet, 222–23; colonial beliefs about Indian bodies, 29–30; conservatism and, 425; dead bodies on Gettysburg battlefield, 220; as energy source, 362, 370, 393; environment, food linked with in Civil War, 223; executions, 54; gay and lesbian, 425; Great Awakening and, 404–5; King Cotton, slavery, and, 105, 118, 121–23, 131–32; Lincoln and, 166, 172, 178, 458n41; Lincoln Memorial and, 5; order vs. disorder and, 51; prostitution, 247, 335, 476n57; Puritan view of Quaker "quaking" as demonic, 37; Puritan witch crisis and, 24, 28, 38–42; Reconstruction and, 412–13; torture for witchcraft, 55; transcontinental railroad and control of, 253–54; women's bodies, 79. *See also* disease and illness; labor and laborers; muscle power; slavery

body politic: Lincoln on, 178, 180; Reconstruction and, 412

Bogue, Vincent, 169

Bohr, Niels, 273, 285, 286, 288–89, 292, 297, 304, 316, 481n17

Boime, Albert, 234

books and reading, 165–67, 170

Boorstin, Daniel, 436n21

Booth, John Wilkes, 195

Borritt, Gabor S., 457n27

Bottoms neighborhood, the, Topeka, 276, 324, 326–27, 333, 334–36, 356, 491n42, 492n51

Boudinot, Elias, 80

Boyd, T. A., 371–72

BP deepwater oil spill, 399–400

Bracy, Thomas, 39

Bradbury, David, 300

Bradbury, Norris, 294, 300, 311

Bradford, William, 30, 33, 68

bread riots in Confederacy, 208–9

breastfeeding and slaves, 123

breastworks at Gettysburg, 217

bridges and the transcontinental railroad, 249

Britain and the Seven Years' War, 68, 84, 97, 406

British colonialism. *See* American Revolution and natural law

Brode, Bernice, 298

Brode, Robert, 298

Brookover, Wilbur, 350

Brooks, Noah, 191

Brown, Cheryl, 354

Brown, James, 110

Brown, John, 110–11, 116, 120, 125, 129, 131–32

Brown, Kent, 212, 213

Brown, Leola, 341, 345, 346, 347, 354, 489n14

Brown, Linda, 277, 318–21, 324, 336–37, 345–46, 353–55, 357

Brown, Oliver, 327, 337, 347–49, 353–54

nitroglycerine, 248

Nixon, Richard, 378, 383–84

Norman, Ida, 335

Northern U.S.: transcontinental railroad route and, 234; vision for the West, 202. *See also* Civil War; Gettysburg, battle of

Northup, Anne, 104, 136

Northup, Henry B., 136–37

Northup, Solomon (Platt Epps): body vs. cotton and, 121; cotton harvest and, 116–17, 120; on cotton in bloom, 113; disease and, 132–34; dogs and, 130; enslavement of, 100–105; food and diet, 124, 126–27; rescue of, 135–38; on sugar plantation, 115; violence and, 109–10

Northwest Ordinance (1787), 92, 95

Norton, John, 37

Norton, Mary Beth, 440n96

NOW (National Organization for Women), 422

nuclear weapons. *See* Manhattan Project and the atom bomb

No. 119 (locomotive engine), 229, 230, 266, 471n10

O

Oakes, James, 461n103

Obama, Barack, 399–400

Occom, Rev. Samson, 87

octane, 372

Offurt, Denton, 168

Oglesvie, Martin, 329

Ohio Valley, 68, 69–70

oil. *See* energy, oil, and the 1973–1974 oil shock

Oklahoma City bombing (1995), 397

old age, 134

Olmsted, Frederick Law, 108, 109, 112–13, 120, 127, 133, 427, 451n52

OPEC (Organization of Petroleum Exporting Countries), 378, 395–96

Oppenheimer, Frank, 310, 314

Oppenheimer, Kitty, 298–99, 314

Oppenheimer, Robert, 272, 291; character of, 295–96; community and, 297–98; curiosity and, 286; doubters and, 304; family of, 298–99, 306; Hiroshima and Nagasaki and, 313–14; intellectual openness and, 302–3; Los Alamos site and, 290; on "organic necessity," 315–16; Perro Caliente ranch, 288; as poet, 289; religion and, 287–88, 307; testing and, 306, 308–10. *See also* Manhattan Project and the atom bomb

order and disorder: Jefferson's Monticello, natural law, and Declaration of Independence, 57–58, 61–62; Newtonian, 95, 406–7, 505n10; Puritans and, 27–28; scientific revolution and, 71

Oregon Bicycle Bill, 394, 401

organic economy and shift to mineral-based economy, 244–46

Organization of Petroleum Exporting Countries (OPEC), 378, 395–96

Orsi, Jared, 382

Orsi, Richard, 265, 470n10, 472n20

Otis, James, 74, 79, 81, 85

oxen, 246, 248, 252. *See also* livestock and draft animals

P

Pacific Railway Act, 184, 235, 257, 472n32

Paine, Thomas, 63, 67, 70, 74–75, 82, 86, 167

Pais, Abraham, 288

Paiutes, 260–61

Palevsky, Mary, 316

Palladio, Andrea, 58

Palmer, Fanny Frances, 258

passions, Lincoln on, 170–71

Patsey (enslaved laborer), 116–17, 135, 136, 137

5, 7–8; Lincoln's attitudes on, *177*;
nature as separate analytical category, 415–16, 506n32; Nazi racism, 315,
487n122; passing, 339. *See also* color
line, Topeka, and *Brown v. Board of
Education*
race conservationists, 328, 334, 414
Radio Emergency Associated Citizens
Team (REACT), 385
railroads: Civil War and, 222, 468n57; job
openings for blacks, 328–29; Santa Fe
Railway, 328–29, 337, 367; Southern
vs. Northern system, 204. *See also*
transcontinental railroad
"The Rail Splitter" cartoon, 150
Raynal, Abbé Guillaume-Thomas, 66
REACT (Radio Emergency Associated
Citizens Team), 385
Reagan, Ronald, 423
reason and natural law, 71
Rebel without a Cause (film), 375
Reconstruction, 191, 322, 410–13
Reed, Samuel, 230, 240
Reichbach, Norman, 358–60, 378, 379, 396
Reid, Brian Holden, 205, 463n2
religion: antinomianism, 35–36; British
safeguards of Catholic colonial subjects, 69–70; color line and, 353; energy
and, 280; Great Awakening, 403–5;
Manhattan Project and, 297–98,
306–7, 311; Oppenheimer and, 287–88;
Puritan witch crisis and, 26–27, 30;
Social Gospel, 333–34; Trinity, Christian, and Hindu concepts of, 306–7
reproduction. *See* pregnancy and
childbirth
republic: body politic, 178; Lady Liberty,
142, 145, 278, 280; Lincoln on Union,
182–83; Lincoln's organic, 151, 196;
Madison on Constitution and, 96;
of muscles and meat, 151; naturalistic
theory of, 94; political ecology of, 142,
143–47

Republican Party: Lincoln and, 175, 181;
Reconstruction and, 411; Revolution
of 1800 and Federalist thinking vs.,
408–10
residential segregation, 340
resources. *See* natural resources
Reunion (Guérin mural), 8
Revolution. *See* American Revolution
and natural law
"Revolution of 1800," 408–10
Richardson, Earl, 382
Rickert, George, 381
Ridley, Mr. (Topeka principal), 331, 332
rights. *See* American Revolution and
natural law; natural law and natural
rights
*The Rights of the British Colonists Asserted
and Proved* (Otis), 74
rivers: as Civil War transportation,
204–5; Lincoln, the Sangamon River,
and improvement, 167–69; Northern
blockade of Mississippi River, 206
rock: blasting, 251; bodies and, 252–53;
cutting, 238; moving, 248–49, 252
Rocky Mountains. *See* transcontinental
railroad
Roebling, Washington, 217
Roger, John, 48, 53
Rogers, Freddy, 339
Rolston, Holmes, 457n28
Roosevelt, Theodore, 370, 415
Rose, Harold, 495n90
Rosenzweig, Roy, 500n66
Rotblat, Joseph, 303
Rowlandson, Mary, 44
Royal Proclamation (1763), 69
rule of capture, 371
Russ, Charles, 382
Russell, Andrew, 230
Russen, Peter, 385
Rutherford, Ernest, 286
Rutledge, Ann, 192, 193

S

Sabbath, 118

Sackman, Douglas, x

Salem witch trials. *See* witchcraft crisis in colonial New England

salt shortage in Confederacy, 207

Sam's Sall (enslaved laborer), 112–13

A Sand County Almanac (Leopold), 415

Sandtown neighborhood, Topeka, 276, 325

Sangamon River (IL), 167–69

San Ildefonso Pueblo (NM), 298

Santa Fe Railway, 328–29, 337, 367

Sarah (enslaved laborer), 111–12

Sassacus, 32–33

Sassamon, John, 45

Satan: colonial witch crisis and, 26–27, 36–42, 48–49; Indians identified with, 48–49, 53; Pequot War and, 34

Saudi Arabia, 377, 397

Saunders, William, 196

Savage, Thomas, 43–44

Sawyer, Nathaniel, 329

Sawyer's Hill ski run (Los Alamos, NM), 273, 297

scarlet fever, 132

school segregation. *See* color line, Topeka, and *Brown v. Board of Education*

scientific revolution, 71

Scott, Berdyne, 335, 336, 340, 342

Scott, Charles, 347–48

Scott, Dred, 174, 177

Scott, Elisha, 329

Scott, Harriet, 174

Scott, John, 347–48

scurvy, 126, 208

Seaborg, Glenn, 302

Segrè, Elfriede, 273

Segrè, Emilio, 273, 296, 310

segregation in schools. *See* color line, Topeka, and *Brown v. Board of Education*

Sellars, Richard, 226

Seneca Falls Declaration of Sentiments, 83–84

sense of place, 355

"separate but equal" doctrine, 347, 348, 352

separation, episteme of, 506n32

separation and separatism, black, 320, 327–28

September 11, 2001, terrorist attacks, 397–98

Serber, Robert, 310–11, 314

Seven Years' War, 68, 84, 97, 406

Seward, William, 136

shamans, Pequot, 29

sheep. *See* livestock and draft animals

Sheldon, Charles, 333–34

Shepherd, Michael, 426

Sheridan, Philip, 184

Sherman, William, 184

Sherman Summit, 241

Shilts, Gary, 507n55

shoes and the Civil War, 224

Shoshone, 260–61

Shreve, Henry M., 457n36

Sierra Nevada. *See* transcontinental railroad

Simon, William, 390

skiing, atomic scientists and, 297

slavery: abductions into, 103–4, 212, 449n10; and animal domestication, 459n67; arguments for, 176–77; colonization plan, 187, 461n100; Declaration of Independence and, 92; development of labor system, 65; economics of, 90; emancipations and manumissions, 89, 92; Jefferson and, 62; justifications for, 90–91; Kansas-Nebraska Act and *Dred Scott* case, 173–74, 177, 181; legal support for, 92; Lincoln on western territories and, 173–82; Lincoln's views on, 162–63, 177–78, 185–91; Locke on, 84; natural

wood and the transcontinental railroad,
232, 243–44, 269
"wooing of the earth" (Dubos), 428
World War II: Germany's atomic
research, 290, 291, 303, 315, 487n122;
railroad jobs for blacks during, 337. *See
also* Manhattan Project and the atom
bomb
Worster, Donald, 461n103, 508n70

Y

yellow fever, 132–33
Yellowstone, 13, 367, 369
Yosemite, 13, 427
Young, Alice, 40
Young, Brigham, 261–62
Young, Thomas, 77

Weyerhaeuser Environmental Books

Iceland Imagined: Nature, Culture, and Storytelling in the North Atlantic
by Karen Oslund

A Storied Wilderness: Rewilding the Apostle Islands
by James W. Feldman

The Republic of Nature: An Environmental History of the United States
by Mark Fiege

The Promise of Wilderness: American Environmental Politics since 1964
by James Morton Turner

WEYERHAEUSER ENVIRONMENTAL CLASSICS

The Great Columbia Plain: A Historical Geography, 1805–1910
by D. W. Meinig

Mountain Gloom and Mountain Glory: The Development of the Aesthetics of the Infinite
by Marjorie Hope Nicolson

Tutira: The Story of a New Zealand Sheep Station
by Herbert Guthrie-Smith

A Symbol of Wilderness: Echo Park and the American Conservation Movement
by Mark Harvey

Man and Nature: Or, Physical Geography as Modified by Human Action
by George Perkins Marsh; edited and annotated by David Lowenthal

Conservation in the Progressive Era: Classic Texts
edited by David Stradling

DDT, Silent Spring, and the Rise of Environmentalism: Classic Texts
edited by Thomas R. Dunlap

The Environmental Moment, 1968–1972
by David Stradling

CYCLE OF FIRE BY STEPHEN J. PYNE

Fire: A Brief History

World Fire: The Culture of Fire on Earth

*Vestal Fire: An Environmental History, Told through Fire,
of Europe and Europe's Encounter with the World*

Fire in America: A Cultural History of Wildland and Rural Fire

Burning Bush: A Fire History of Australia

The Ice: A Journey to Antarctica

★ ★ ★